Reprinted 1984 from the 1864 edition.
Cover design © 1981 Time-Life Books Inc.
Library of Congress CIP data following page 517.

This volume is bound in leather.

BATTLE-FIELDS OF THE SOUTH,

FROM

BULL RUN TO FREDERICKSBURGH;

WITH SKETCHES OF CONFEDERATE COMMANDERS, AND GOSSIP OF
THE CAMPS.

BY

AN ENGLISH COMBATANT,

LIEUTENANT OF ARTILLERY ON THE FIELD STAFF.

WITH TWO MAPS.

New-York:
JOHN BRADBURN, No. 49 WALKER STREET.
SUCCESSOR TO M. DOOLADY.
—
1864.

CONTENTS.

---◆◆---

CHAPTER XVII.

CHAPTER XVIII.

CHAPTER XIX.

CHAPTER XX.

CHAPTER XXI.

CHAPTER XXII.

CHAPTER XXXVII.

CHAPTER XXXVIII.

CHAPTER XXXIX.

CHAPTER XL.

CHAPTER XLI.

INTRODUCTION.

ALTHOUGH the following narrative sufficiently explains itself, and is replete with evidence of the author's feeling, and of the point of view from which he has regarded the fratricidal strife still raging in America, it may be permitted him to remark in this place, that the impulse by which he was prompted in bearing arms for the Southern cause, was simply that inherent love of liberty which animates every English heart. With all to lose and naught to gain in opposing the tyranny of Federal rule, and with no legal or political tie to North or South, he could not, in manhood, stand idly by, and gaze upon the despotism which a blind and fanatical majority sought to thrust upon an unoffending and almost helpless minority.

Having travelled and resided long on the American continent, carefully studying national characteristics, he was not surprised by the inevitable disruption of the Union, nor at any time unaware of the causes tending to that result. Rather, his surprise has been that Southerners should so long have refrained from rising in arms against the accumulated insults and injuries which, for a long series of years, have been heaped upon them. They would have been unworthy of their origin, and must have shown themselves less than men, had they longer submitted to the degradation of being deprived of free speech and action amongst a people whose prosperity had been fostered by their industry, and whose history they had ennobled by heroic deeds.

Apart from all untruthful bias, although serving in a cause he enthusiastically espoused, the author has followed the fortunes of Southern armies in this narrative with an honest intention to present facts, uncolored, and exact in detail, so far as space would allow or his position and facilities enabled him to obtain them. Every statement he has made can be fully substantiated; he would esteem it unmanly, unsoldierly, and degrading, to speak untruly of these events.

The real source of Northern prosperity has been misunderstood; so, in the author's opinion, has the real character of the Yankee people. The nasal-toned, tobacco-chewing, and long-limbed gentleman of the present day inhabiting the New-England States, speaks the English language, it is true, in his own peculiar way, but Indian, Canadian, Irish, Dutch, French, and other bloods, course through his veins; and from his extraordinary peculiarities of habit and character displayed in this present war, it is extremely difficult to imagine which caste or shade predominates in him. He is a volatile, imaginative, superficial, theatrically-inclined individual, possessing uncommon self-confidence, and is very self-willed, arrogant, and boastful. His self-conceit is boundless: any one who disputes his ideas is a fool.

The peculiarities of Yankee character displayed during the present war are very amusing, but sometimes, it must be confessed, very offensive. When General Scott was in chief command at Washington, and promised to "disperse the rebels within thirty days," the Northern editors were lavish and servile in praise of "the great chief!" Columns upon columns of editorial flattery daily issued from their journals. A thousand anecdotes and incidents were narrated of him when a precocious child, and, if remembered rightly, it was said his first plaything was a cannon. McDowell, his talented lieutenant, came in also for his share of praise, although thousands asked : " Who is McDowell?" When the reports of the Washington Administration claimed a victory at Manassas, the whole nation vociferously chaunted the praises of Scott and McDowell; but when the truth leaked out the day following, not a newspaper in the whole country but vilified them both, calling the first a stupid, ignorant old blockhead, and the latter a traitor.

Butler had appeared upon the scene some short time before. Being from Massachusetts, (where none are found, of course, except men of extraordinary talents, genius, veracity, and bravery,) he was going forth from Fortress Monroe to massacre or "bag" the entire Confederate force at Little Bethel. The press was in ecstasies; a swarm of reporters repaired to head-quarters, and Butler could not sneeze but the fact was telegraphed North as something very ominous, and presaging no good to the rebels. Magruder and Hill whipped him completely in half an hour; and the press, as usual, poured out their vials of wrath, and he was treated to all the derision and vilification of an angry and disappointed populace.

McClellan next appeared in the arena, and the whole country was awe-struck at the supposed magnitude of his genius. None dared approach him save on tip-toe; dead silence prevailed wherever he went; reporters stretched their ears to catch the least word he uttered, which, after being highly ornamented and rendered very romantic, was blazoned forth to the North as the "last" good thing of the " Young Napoleon." All the world was supposed to be standing in breathless curiosity to know " what was coming next;" artists of various illustrated journals sharpened their pencils, and anxiously yearned to sketch the rapid succession of victories which were promised to be forthcoming; but time jogged along, and even Northern journalists began to grow weary of McClellan's inactivity. They had fully exhausted all their store of flattery and praise, and were now utterly fatigued with the task of fruitless and neverending laudation.

The " Young Napoleon " had been compared to Alexander, Cæsar, Hannibal, and Napoleon the Great; but nothing in the history or character of those famous leaders was considered fully adequate to the heaven-born qualities of George B. McClellan. His eyes, hair, mouth, teeth, voice, manner, and apparel, had all been described in carefully prepared leaders; and even his boots had something pertaining to their make and style indicative of the surpassing talents of the wearer.* His

---

* The *Washington Chronicle*, June twenty-second, furnishes us a case in point: "THE INFANT NAPOLEON.—An incident which occurred in the city of Philadelphia in the winter of 1826-7, is particularly worthy of record in our present crisis, inasmuch as it relates to the early history of one who fills a position commanding the attention and admiration of the world, and particularly of our own country. I will premise by saying I was in Philadelphia in the winter spoken of, attending medical lectures under a distinguished surgeon, then a professor in one of the institutions of the city. A son was born to our professor, and the event scarcely transpired before the father announced it to his delighted pupils. Scales were instantly brought from a neighboring grocer. Into one dish he placed the babe, into the other all the weights. The beam was raised, but the child moved not!

servant was idolized, and nothing could be too good for him; for it was through this important functionary that a gaping and delighted public were favored with the last and latest anecdotes illustrative of the great man, his master. Time went on, and the "Young Napoleon" suffered a series of defeats, not only fatal, but humiliating.* Although he attempted to conceal his dis-

The father, emptying his pockets, threw in his watch, coin, keys, knives, and lancets, but to no purpose — the little hero could not be moved! He conquered every thing! *And at last, while adding more and more weight, the cord supporting the beam gave way, and broke, rather than the giant infant would yield!* The father was Dr. McClellan, and the son — General McClellan! our young commander on the Potomac. The country will see a prophetic charm in this incident. Truly, he was weighed in the balance and not found wanting. May his present and future life stand the test as well! Surrounded as he is by traitors at home, while rampant rebellion is before him, I hear him amidst the jealousy and envy of cavillers quietly praying with Job: 'Let me be weighed in an even balance, that God may know my integrity!'" This beautiful incident of General McClellan's youth was *not* written subsequent to the Week's Campaign before Richmond, but at a time when he was the great idol of the North, and had much patronage within his gift.

* The following is the exceedingly modest address of McClellan after his disastrous defeat in the Seven Days' Campaign before Richmond, penned from his snug retreat at Harrison's Landing, within a hundred yards of numerous gunboats:

"*Head-quarters, Army of the Potomac,*
"*Harrison's Landing, July 4th.*

"Soldiers of the Army of the Potomac! Your achievements of the last ten days have illustrated the valor and endurance of the American soldier. Attacked by superior forces, and without hope of reenforcements, you have succeeded in changing your base by a flank movement, always regarded as the most hazardous of military expedients. You have saved all your material, all your trains, and all your guns, except a few lost in battle, taking in return guns and colors from the enemy (?). Upon your march you have been assailed day after day with desperate fury by men of the same race and nation, skilfully massed and led. Under every disadvantage of number, and necessarily of position also, you have in every conflict beaten back your foes with immense slaughter (!). Your conduct ranks you among the celebrated armies of history. No one will now question that each of you may always with pride say, 'I belong to the Army of the Potomac!' You have reached the new base, complete in organization, and unimpaired in spirit. The enemy may at any time attack you: we are prepared to meet them. I have personally established your lines. Let them come, and we will convert their repulse into a final defeat. Your Government is strengthening you with the resources of a great people. On this, our nation's birthday, we declare to our foes, who are rebels against the best intentions of mankind, that this army shall enter the capital of the so-called Confederacy, that our national Constitution shall prevail, and that the Union, which can alone insure internal peace and external prosperity to each State, 'must and shall be preserved,' cost what it may in time, treasure, and blood!   GEO. B. MCCLELLAN."

asters, the truth became known at last, and the long pent up expectation of the Northern press burst forth in a torrent of abuse. The English language being incapable of illustrating their feelings, new epithets were invented to denote their accu-

General Lee issued Order No. 75, after the Seven Days' Campaign before Richmond, which wonderfully contrasts with the above:

" *Richmond, July 9th.*

"On Thursday, June twenty-sixth, the powerful and thoroughly equipped army of the enemy were intrenched in the works, vast in extent and most formidable in character, within sight of our capital. To-day the remains of that confident and threatening host lie on the banks of the James River, thirty miles from Richmond, seeking to recover, under the protection of his gunboats, from the effects of disastrous defeats. The battle, beginning on the afternoon of June twenty-sixth, above Mechanicsville, continued until the night of July first, with only such intervals as were necessary to pursue and overtake the flying foe. His strong intrenchments and obstinate resistance were overcome, and our army swept resistlessly down the north side of the Chickahominy until it reached the rear of the enemy, and broke his communication with York River, capturing or causing the destruction of many valuable stores, and, by the decisive battle of Friday, forcing the enemy from his line of powerful fortifications on the south side of the Chickahominy, and driving him to a precipitate retreat. Our victorious army pursued as rapidly as the obstructions placed by the enemy in his rear would permit, three times overtaking his flying columns, and as often driving him with slaughter from the field, leaving his numerous dead and wounded in our hands in every conflict. The immediate fruits of our success are the relief of Richmond from a state of siege, the rout of the great army which has so long menaced its safety, many thousands of prisoners, including officers of high rank ; the capture or destruction of stores to the value of millions, and the acquisition of thousands of arms, and over fifty pieces of superior artillery. The service rendered to the country in this short but eventful period can scarcely be estimated, and the General commanding cannot adequately express his admiration of the courage, endurance, and soldierly conduct of the officers and men engaged. Those brilliant results have cost us many brave men, but while we mourn the loss of our gallant dead, let us not forget that they died in defence of their country's freedom, and have linked their memory with an event that will live forever in the hearts of a grateful people. Soldiers, your country will thank you for the heroic conduct worthy of men engaged in a cause so just and sacred, and deserving a nation's gratitude and praise.

"By order of General LEE,

" R. H. CHILTON, *Assistant Adjutant-General.*"

The following is the address of President Davis to the Army after the battles before Richmond : "I congratulate you on the series of brilliant victories which, under divine Providence, you have lately won, and as President of the Confederate States do heartily tender to you the thanks of our country, whose just cause you have so skilfully and heroically served. Ten days ago an invading army, vastly superior to you in numbers and in the material of war, closely beleaguered your capital, and vauntingly proclaimed its speedy conquest. You marched to attack the enemy in his intrenchments. With well-directed movements and death-dealing valor you

mulated contempt and scorn for the "Young Napoleon."* Yankee character delights in extremes: it is all adulation or all abuse.

Fremont, who once ran for President of the United States, had also experienced the changeful feeling of the Northern masses, and bore their strictures, we are told, with but little grace. When appointed to command the forces in Missouri, the newspapers, as usual, were literally crammed with sketches, anecdotes, and illustrations of the "great Pathfinder." Nothing too absurd could be said in his favor; all the river cities of Missouri were preparing grand receptions for him; Dutch lagerbier brewers were laying in large stocks to meet the forthcoming demand: for on Fremont's arrival, the land was expected to flow with milk and honey. Fremont was called "the coming man," "the great unknown," "the master mind;" in truth, he was extolled and looked upon as a demigod. St. Louis and the West ran riot with delight. Dutch cheese, Dutch beer, Dutch bands, Dutch every thing was the order of the day, and delightful guttural Dutch was the language of Fremont's embryo court, held with mock state in Choteau avenue. The "ragged" Confederates, however, put a sudden stop to the round

charged upon him in his strong position, drove him from field to field over a distance of thirty-five miles, and, despite his reenforcements, compelled him to seek shelter under cover of his gunboats, where he now lies cowering before the army so lately derided and threatened with entire subjugation. The fortitude with which you have borne toil and privation, the gallantry with which you have entered into each successive battle, must have been witnessed to be fully appreciated; but a grateful people will not fail to recognize you, and to bear you in loved remembrance. Well may it be said of you, that you have done enough for glory; but duty to a suffering country, and to the cause of constitutional liberty, claims from you yet further effort. Let it be your pride to relax in nothing which can promote your future efficiency, your one grand object being to drive the invader from your soil, and, carrying your standards beyond the outer boundaries of the Confederacy, to wring from an unscrupulous enemy the recognition of your birthright — community and independence! (Signed) JEFFERSON DAVIS."

* I have frequently heard distinguished Southern leaders speak of McClellan in the highest terms of compliment. His successful retreat through the Chickahominy swamp is considered by officers to be equal to the best deeds on military record.

It may not be generally known, but men of high position and great veracity have said in Richmond, that McClellan offered his services to the South when the war began, and that he asked to command a division. He was answered that, if his heart was in the cause let him join the ranks like Longstreet and others, and fight his way up to that position. There are documents which put this question beyond dispute, but I have not seen them.

of conviviality and expense in which he indulged. Disaster attended the Federal army in the West, and Fremont sank low in the opinion of even his former admirers. He was suddenly removed, and the Northern newspapers turned against him. What had become of John Pope, late Commander-in-Chief of the army of Virginia, was matter of speculation among all classes; but, from the fearful clamor raised throughout the North regarding his late series of brilliant defeats, it was considered possible that he had been sent on a reconnoitring expedition among those mountains where, as his despatches stated, he had driven poor Stonewall Jackson.* Rumor said that the

---

* Regarding this great chieftain (Pope, not Jackson,) his doings and his antecedents, it may not be improper to place upon record the following historical documents. He thus addressed the army of Virginia on assuming command :

"To the Officers and Soldiers of the Army of Virginia!—By special assignment of the President of the United States, I have assumed command of this army. I have spent two weeks in learning your whereabouts, your condition, and your wants, in preparing you for active operations, and in placing you in position from which you can act promptly and to the purpose. I have come to you from the West, where we have always seen the backs of our enemies—from an army whose business it has been to seek the adversary, and to beat him when found—whose policy has been attack, and not defence! In but one instance has the enemy been able to place our Western armies in a defensive attitude. I presume that I have been called here to pursue the same system, and to lead you against the enemy. It is my purpose to do so, and that speedily! I am sure you long for an opportunity to win the distinction you are so capable of achieving; that opportunity I shall endeavor to give you," etc.

A Northern authority, speaking of the depravity of Pope's troops in Virginia, writes:

"The new usage which has been instituted in regard to protection of rebel property, and the purpose of the Government to subsist the army as far as practicable upon the enemy's country, has produced a decided revolution in the feelings and practices of the soldiery, and one which seems to me to be regretted. Unless these innovations are guarded by far more stringent safeguards against irregular and unauthorized plundering, we shall have let loose upon the country, at the close of the war, a torrent of unbridled and unscrupulous robbers. Rapid strides towards villainy have been made during the last few weeks ; men who at home would have shuddered at the suggestion of touching another's property, now appropriate remorselessly whatever comes within their reach. Thieving, they imagine, has now become an authorized practice; and under the show of subsisting themselves, chickens, turkeys, hams, and corn, have become lawful plunder, with no discrimination as to the character or circumstances of the original owner. I blush when I state that on the march through a section of country, every spring-house is broken open, and butter, milk, eggs, and ham are engulfed before the place is reached by the main body ; and it does not seem to matter if such articles are the

Washington Cabinet had exiled him among the Indians of the North-West, where he might practise the art of war without sac-

only stock and store of the poor inhabitants. Calves and sheep, and, in fact, any thing and every thing serviceable for meat or drink, or apparel, are not safe a moment after the approach of our army; even things apparently useless are snatched up, because, it would seem, many men love to steal."

Regarding his attack upon Jackson's corps, and his repulse, he wrote:

"*Manassas Junction, August 28th,* 10 *P.M.*

"As soon as I discovered that a large force of the enemy were turning our right towards Manassas, and that the division I had ordered to take post there two days before had not yet arrived from Alexandria, I immediately broke up my camps at Warrenton Junction and Warrenton, and marched rapidly back in three columns.

"I directed M'Dowell, with his own and Sigel's corps, to march upon Gainesville by the Warrenton and Alexandria turnpike; Reno and one division of Heintzelman to march on Greenwich, and with Porter's corps and Hooker's division, I marched back to Manassas Junction.

"McDowell was ordered to interpose between the forces of the enemy which had passed down to Manassas through Gainesville, and his main body moving down from White Plains through Thoroughfare Gap. This was completely accomplished, *Longstreet, who had passed through the Gap, being driven back to the west side (! ! !)*

"The forces to Greenwich were designed to support McDowell in case he met too large a force of the enemy. The division of Hooker, marching towards Manassas, came upon the enemy near Kettle Run, on the afternoon of the twenty-seventh, and after a sharp action, routed them completely, killing and wounding three hundred, capturing camps, baggage, and many stand of arms (!)

"This morning (twenty-eighth) the command pushed rapidly to Manassas Junction, which Jackson had evacuated three hours before. He retreated by Centreville, and took the turnpike towards Warrenton. He was met six miles west of Centreville by McDowell and Sigel late this afternoon. A severe fight took place, which was terminated by darkness. The enemy was driven back at all points, and thus the affair rests.

"Heintzelman's corps will move on him at daylight from Centreville, and I do not see how the enemy is to escape without heavy loss. *We have captured one thousand prisoners, many arms, and one piece of artillery.*

"JOHN POPE, *Major-General.*"

Pope's reputation for truth is now so well known to friend and foe, and his despatches are so unique in every particular, that I refrain from any comments. Although "*Longstreet, who had passed through the Gap, had been driven back,*" Pope met both Jackson and Longstreet on the following day, and thus speaks of the result of the fighting on the twenty-ninth in the following "sensational" telegraphic despatch, penned on the morning of the thirtieth, which was read with uproarious delight by millions at the North, at the very moment, perhaps, when Lee was giving him his quietus:

"*Head-quarters, Groveton, August 30th.*

"We fought a terrific battle here yesterday with the combined forces of the enemy, which lasted with continuous fury from daylight until dark, by which time the enemy were driven from the field which we now occupy. Our troops are too much

rificing from five to ten thousand men at every exhibition of his genius. McDowell, Porter, and many old officers, who had

exhausted to push matters; but I shall do so in the course of the morning, as soon as Fitz-John Porter's corps comes up from Manassas. The enemy is still in front, but badly used. We have not less than eight thousand men killed and wounded; and from the appearance of the field, the enemy has lost two to our one. He stood strictly on the defensive, and every assault was made by ourselves. Our troops have behaved splendidly. The battle was fought on the identical battle-field of Bull Run, which greatly increased the enthusiasm of our men. The news has just reached me from the front, that the enemy is retreating towards the mountains. I at once pushed forward a reconnoitring party to ascertain this. We have made great captures, but I am not yet able to form an idea of their extent.

" JOHN POPE, *Major-General.*"

General Lee's despatch to President Davis regarding the Battle of Manassas throws light upon Pope's falsehoods:

" *Head-quarters, Groveton, Aug.* 30*th*, 10 *P.M.*

" The army achieved to-day, on the plains of Manassas, a signal victory over the combined forces of Generals McClellan and Pope. On the twenty-eighth and twenty-ninth each wing, under Jackson and Longstreet, repulsed with vigor attacks made upon them separately. We mourn the loss of our gallant dead in every conflict, yet our gratitude to Almighty God for His mercies rises higher each day. To Him, and to the valor of our troops, a nation's gratitude is due.

"(Signed) ROBERT E. LEE."

Pope had attained a place in history as a great falsifier long before assuming command of the Army of Virginia, as documents regarding his operations in the West fully demonstrate.

Respecting Beauregard's retreat from Corinth, General Halleck thus telegraphed to Washington, on the strength of Pope's reports:

" *Head-quarters, June* 4*th*, 1862.

" General Pope, with forty thousand men, is thirty miles south of Corinth, pushing the enemy hard. He already reports ten thousand prisoners and deserters from the enemy, and fifteen thousand stand of arms captured.

" Thousands of the enemy are throwing away their arms. A farmer says, that when Beauregard learned that Colonel Elliot had cut the railroad on his line of retreat he became frantic, and told his men to save themselves the best way they could.

" We have captured nine locomotives and a number of cars. One of the former is already repaired, and is running to-day. Several more will be in running order in two or three days. The result is all I could possibly desire.

"H. W. HALLECK, *Major-General Commanding.*"

General Beauregard's comments on the above, published in the *Mobile Register*, were to the following effect:

" *Head-quarters, Western Department, June* 17*th*.

" GENTLEMEN: My attention has just been called to the despatch of Major-General Halleck, commanding the enemy's forces, which, coming from such a source,

been accused of "treason" by this great and veracious Inca‧
pable, were said to be temporarily deprived of their commands,

is most remarkable in one respect—that it contains as many misrepresentations as
lines.

"General Pope did not 'push hard' upon me with forty thousand men thirty
miles from Corinth on the fourth inst., for my troops occupied a defensive line in
the rear of 'Twenty Mile Creek,' less than twenty-five miles from Corinth, until the
eighth inst., when the want of good water induced me to retire at my leisure to a
better position. Moreover, if General Pope had attempted, at any time during the
retreat from Corinth, to push hard upon me, I would have given him such a lesson
as would have checked his ardor; but he was careful to advance on after my troops
had retired from each successive position.

"The retreat was conducted with great order and precision, doing much credit
to the officers and men under my orders, and must be looked upon, in every respect, by the country as equivalent to a brilliant victory.

"General Pope must certainly have dreamed of taking ten thousand prisoners
and fifteen thousand stand of arms; for we positively never lost them. About one
or two hundred stragglers would probably cover all the prisoners he took, and
about five hundred damaged muskets is all the arms he got. These belonged to a
convalescent camp, four miles south of Corinth, evacuated during the night, and
were overlooked on account of the darkness. The actual number of prisoners
taken during the retreat was about equal on both sides, and they were but few.

"Major-General Halleck must be a very credulous man, indeed, to believe the
absurd story of 'that farmer.' He ought to know that the burning of two or more
cars on a railroad is not sufficient to make 'Beauregard frantic' and ridiculous,
especially when I expected every moment to hear of the capture of the marauding
party, whose departure from Farmington had been communicated to me the day
before, and I had given, in consequence, all necessary orders; but a part of my
forces passed Boonville an hour before the arrival of Colonel Elliot's command, and
the other part arrived just in time to drive it away and liberate the convalescents
captured; unfortunately, however, not in time to save four of the sick, who were
barbarously consumed in the station-house. Let Colonel Elliot's name descend to
infamy as the author of such a revolting deed. General Halleck did not capture
nine locomotives. It was only by the accidental destruction of a bridge, before
some trains had passed, that he got seven engines in a damaged condition, the cars
having been burned by my orders.

"It is, in fact, easy to see how little the enemy respect truth and justice when
speaking of their military operations, especially when, through inability or over-
confidence, they meet with deserved failure.

"If the result be all he desired, it can be said that Major-General Halleck is easily
satisfied; it remains to be seen whether his Government and people will be of the
like opinion.

"I attest that all we lost at Corinth and during the retreat would not amount to
one day's expense of his army.   G. T. BEAUREGARD."

To complete these documents, an able Northern writer thus speaks of Corinth
and its evacuation:

and enjoying whiskey-and-water among the anti-Administration party of New York. While the Yankee is extremely bitter towards unsuccessful

"The fortifications about Corinth are plain, ordinary intrenchments, constructed of earth and logs, not elaborate or expensive, hardly first-rate, about six miles in length. They are not superior to any of ours thrown up in a couple of days, and not equal in strength and science to those of our right wing. To speak the truth, they are precisely such as a great army, advancing, retreating, or remaining in the face of an equal foe, would throw up in a night. I was immensely disappointed in them. I have really got up in the morning, eaten my three meals, and gone to bed again, for the last month, in unutterable awe of these Gibralto-Sebastopolian fortifications of the enemy at Corinth. I walked round about them to-day, marking well their bulwarks, telling the towers thereof till my sides were sore with merriment and my lips sore with chagrin. With the single exception of the abattis of fallen trees, five hundred yards wide in front of them, there is nothing under heaven about the fortifications at Corinth — their situation, style, or strength — more than the most ordinary and temporary fortifications possess.

"I went all over the late tented field of the enemy—all over the fortifications—all over the town—talked with the frank druggist and the sturdy Irishman that had worked upon the railroad. And so do I write what I saw in grief, mortification, chagrin, and shame. I said yesterday: 'I'll write no more; others may; I can't. Patriotism will not let me write what I have seen and can swear to.' When I write such words as I am sometimes compelled to, if I write at all, I am afraid lest, in exposing military imbecility, I shall wound and damage our beautiful commonwealth that struggles so tremendously for existence and perpetuity.

"But I do religiously believe that it is best now for the commonwealth to hear and heed what is bitter, undisputed fact—the Confederate strategy since the Battle of Shiloh has been as successful as it has been superior. Taking the enemy's standpoint, and writing when and where I do, I cannot possibly imagine how it could have been more eminent for perfection and success. Taking our stand-point, the stand-point of the Union's hopes and Halleck's fame, I cannot possibly imagine how it could have been more mortifyingly disastrous. If the attack at Shiloh was a surprise to General Grant, the evacuation of Corinth was no less a surprise to General Halleck. If the one ruined Grant, the other has laid out in pallid death the military name and fame of Major-General Halleck.

"The druggist says he was two weeks getting away. But aside from such testimony, could the army of Beauregard be removed so cleanly, and completely, and noiselessly, during a night, or day and night, or two days and two nights? Did it require the tremendous concussion of the magazine explosion to get into our ears what we would not get into our eyes—the evacuation? Why, that was the final act of the mortifying drama. On Friday morning we went in. The prisoners that we captured amounted to about four hundred. Four hundred! Even the beggarly picket regiments and light artillery that fought us so boldly, got away. Those that we caught declare that they were kept in ignorance of the movements at Corinth, and were as much surprised at the evacuation as ourselves. Corinth has been searched in vain for a spiked or disabled gun. Shame on us, what a clean piece of evacuation it was!

men, and ungenerously visits upon them all manner of contumely and disgrace, he is equally unjust to those in subordinate commands who betray tokens of ability and success; particularly if they are so unfortunate as to entertain political opinions contrary to those of the Administration. It matters not what ability an officer may possess; if he is not politically identified with his masters, promotion is denied, and the press so effectually gagged that no word of commendation may escape it. Sigel,* Sturges, Grant, Buell, Rosecrans, and others,

"Never shall I forget the pertinacity with which that long lean line of Confederate pickets, backed, perchance, by some five thousand muskets and a few six-pounders, disputed every inch of our advance, while the vast, imposing host behind them—leaders, stores, cannon, commissaries, knapsacks, shoe strings, toothpicks, and all—quietly and leisurely flowed away from its intrenchments. I haven't seen the telegram that the Censor sent you. Surely it concluded with the stereotyped encouragement: 'Our cavalry in hot pursuit of the flying enemy.' At this writing there are no results from the 'pursuit.' I prophesied a fight at Corinth, and believed there would be down to the moment that I heard the magazines explode. Beauregard fooled me. I am not much ashamed at that. I am no strategist. I am no scout or spy, and employ none. It is my business to record the doings of the National rather than the Confederate army. General Beauregard fooled, hoodwinked, outwitted General Halleck. I *am* ashamed of that. I winced under it as much as if General Beauregard had spit in General Halleck's face—oh! more, of course! I am speaking the unvarnished, the unpalatable truth. My eyes are writing what they saw, my ears what they have heard, my conscience what it believes. And to say the galling fact, there is nothing here but chagrin and shame, disappointment and disapprobation over these empty intrenchments, this bootless, bloodless occupation of Corinth. Better for General Halleck that he had remained in St. Louis, or had never been born, than to have taken the field."

* Major-General Franz Sigel has proved himself an excellent soldier; and if he had been untrammelled by those in power, or given a distinct command away from Fremont and other incapables, he would have made a great name for himself long ere this. He was born in Baden in 1824, and graduated with much honor in the military college of Carlsruhe; and, in 1847, was considered one of the ablest artillerists in Europe. When the revolution broke out in Germany, he threw up his command and joined the insurgents. At one time he was in command of the insurgent army, and successfully retreated with thirty thousand, despite all the traps and snares laid for him by an army of eighty thousand. His generalship drew forth praise from some of the best soldiers in Europe. When the rebellion was crushed, Sigel emigrated to America, and settled in St. Louis, marrying the daughter of a gentleman in whose academy he taught. When the present war broke out, he received command of the Second Missouri Volunteers, and was soon appointed Brigadier. He served with distinction under Lyon, Fremont, and Curtis. He was removed from Missouri, and appointed to command the Twelfth Army Corps under Pope, in Virginia, and has greatly distinguished himself. Although

who have displayed traits of genius under adverse circumstances, have never been called to chief command, simply because
they were foreigners, or opposed to the dominant party in politics. Men of ability, without politicians to assist them, can
never expect to rise; and if it were known to-morrow that a
foreigner was in the ranks capable of guiding the destinies of
the nation, he might remain there in obscurity, and the continent be reduced to anarchy, ere Northern pride would succumb
to be led by any one who was not born on the soil.

The Yankee proper hates all foreigners, when any thing is to
be gained or given away. It is conceded, indeed, that Euro-
peans are serviceable as food for powder, and great pains are
taken to keep up a plentiful supply of this food by numerous
agents, who are busily engaged for this purpose in Europe.
But, although they cannot deny that the foreign element has
been the stepping-stone to all their past prosperity, and that it
has proved itself superior.to native blood upon every battle-
field, they will unblushingly protest on all occasions that "we
Americans" are the great rulers and master-minds, capable of
achieving any thing and every thing of which a mortal man
might dream. Poor unfortunate foreigners may sweat and toil,
and fight or bleed for them; but, were the war to cease to-morrow, hundreds would be shot down in the public streets, as
happened in Louisville and Baltimore: and for no other reason,
perhaps, save that they dare to think for themselves in the use
of the suffrage.

In the appointment and dismissal of their generals, the constant practice of the North has made them ridiculous alike to
Southerners and to all Europe. A man is called to command
because a political faction admires or thinks him capable;
though, probably, he has no notion of the duties of an officer.
Every new appointment serves to create a "sensation," and, for
a time, it appeases the clamor of the press. The newly-fledged
commander, however modest he may naturally be, finds himself
instantly transformed into a genius, and the eyes of the nation
are fixed upon him in ecstatic hope. Something in his eye be-

much sneered at by those in the Federal Army, and subjected on all occasions to
many slights and annoyances, Sigel is a much better General than many who have
been his superiors in command, and could do more with a division than half-a-
dozen such men as General Pope.

trays vast penetration, if not positive knowledge, of the future; his walk may be slow—he is a studious, long-headed man, and all will be well; his step may be quick and elastic—a sure sign of brilliancy and activity. If his speech is loud, he was born to command; if soft, he is dealing in mysteries. It matters not, indeed, what he is, or might have been, or what he has or has not done—he is a new man, and an untried one. He has many things in his gift, and is quickly flattered out of them by crowds of sycophants, who care not a jot who rules, amid the rack and ruin of the times, so that they themselves have secured something from the national plunder.

If the genius of the hour proves unsuccessful, he is immediately kicked from high places, and sinks into deeper obscurity than he had known before. No inquiries are instituted to ascertain how much he might have been to blame, and whether the disgrace has been caused by himself or his more culpable subordinates; it is sufficient that he has been unsuccessful. The Yankee demands success: it is the master passion of his life; if he cannot obtain a whole victory, he is willing to purchase half a one at any cost. Northern victories have been frequent on paper; but these, he is fully aware, are not sufficient to gratify European tastes, however much they may delight and comfort excitable and inflated Northerners.

The pride and self-love of the North are so extravagant, that the bare idea of defeat in any undertaking is hurtful and humiliating. They think themselves born to unprecedented renown; and it is a foregone conclusion, that no nation ever did, or ever can, approach them in those talents with which they suppose themselves to be transcendently endowed. In machinery of all classes, in ship and boat-building, in railways, telegraphs, cities, in energy and success, other nations of the world are supposed to be infinitely their inferiors. And, as to fighting on land or water! they firmly believe that one Yankee is worth any six "Britishers." In truth, the Yankee proper has hitherto thought, or been taught to believe, that the nations of Europe are seized with fear and trembling whenever an American stump-orator rises to speak.

Not long before the present war began, Yankee programmes of future operations in the Eastern and Western hemispheres were freely circulated and discussed; and the preposterous magnitude of them would have excited smiles of compassion in any but the inflated petty politicians of New-England. The whole country, from the Atlantic Ocean to the Pacific, was theirs; England was to be deprived of the Canadas, and American emissaries were already there laying plans for any expected or presupposed uprising of the people. England, of course, could do nothing in the matter. It was known that she was much averse to any American quarrel—in fact, feared it: and, should she dare to lift a hand in defence of her possessions, a fortnight would be all-sufficient to "clean out" the whole British empire, east and west. Ireland was to be made a republic, with Thomas Francis Meagher as president. England was also to be revolutionized, and Brown, Williams, or Jones, placed in the presidential chair. France was next on the list; Louis Napoleon was to be deposed, and the country partitioned. If Ledru Rollin or Louis Blanc were unwilling to take charge of affairs, the empire should be offered as a gift to their particular friend, the Emperor of Russia, as a token of commiseration for the injustice done him by the Western Powers. All the petty German kings and princes were to be sent to the right about; the Sultan was to be thrown into the Bosphorus, and his lands settled by Russian peasants or free negroes. Mexico was to be appropriated, and all Central America with it; Cuba, of course, was to be annexed; and many predicted that few months would elapse ere the Stars and Stripes should float over the walls of Moro Castle! The West-India, Bahama, and all other islands were to be appendages to the American Republic; and if no other use could be made of them, they were to be converted into coaling stations for the omnipotent Yankee navy, rather than that the detested banner of Old England should wave over any portion of territory in the Atlantic Ocean. From the Equator to the North Pole, and from the Canaries to the Sandwich Islands, no spot of earth was to be under any rule save the sway of the omnipotent Yankee; who, complacently picking his teeth on top of the Rocky Mountains, might at one view take in half the world, and call it his own.

This is scarcely an exaggeration of the wild dream of universal empire which haunted the brain of the excitable and self-sufficient Yankee. But the intoxicating idea was rudely disturbed; though not by any aggressive power desirous of forestalling Northern ambition by a similar career of conquest and domination.* When hostilities began, the Southerners were comparatively helpless for all purposes of war; their resources were inconsiderable, and but little of the material of war was at their command, save brave hearts and willing hands. Yet one short year had not elapsed ere this heroic people stood before the world resolute to defend their independence, armed with the spoils of victories in many a hard-fought battle-field.

---

* Even in this struggle, and toward the Border States, Southern leaders have shown no desire to act aggressively. The following was General Lee's address to the people of Maryland on entering their territory :

"Headquarters, Army of Northern Virginia,
"Near Frederick, Monday, Sept. 8th, 1862.
"To the People of Maryland.

"It is right that you should know the purpose that has brought the army under my command within the limits of your State, so far as that purpose concerns yourselves. The people of the Confederate States have long watched with the deepest sympathy the wrongs and outrages that have been inflicted upon the citizens of a commonwealth allied to the States of the South by the strongest social, political, and commercial ties, and reduced to the condition of a conquered province. Under the pretence of supporting the Constitution, but in violation of its most valuable provisions, your citizens have been arrested and imprisoned, upon no charge, and contrary to all the forms of law. A faithful and manly protest against this outrage, made by an illustrious Marylander, to whom, in better days, no citizen appealed for right in vain, was treated with contempt and scorn. The Government of your chief city has been usurped by armed strangers; your Legislature has been dissolved by the unlawful arrest of its members; freedom of speech and of the press has been suppressed; words have been declared offences by an arbitrary decree of the Federal Executive, and citizens ordered to be tried by military commissions for what they may dare to speak,

"Believing that the people of Maryland possess a spirit too lofty to submit to such a Government, the people of the South have long wished to aid you in throwing off this foreign yoke, to enable you again to enjoy the inalienable rights of freemen, and restore the independence and sovereignty of your State. In obedience to this wish, our army has come among you, and is prepared to assist you with the power of its arms in regaining the rights of which you have been so unjustly despoiled. This, citizens of Maryland, is our mission, so far as you are concerned. No restraint upon your free will is intended ; no intimidation will be allowed within the limits of this army, at least. Marylanders shall once more enjoy their ancient freedom of thought and speech. We know no enemies among you, and will protect all of you, in every opinion. It is for you to decide your destiny, freely and without constraint. This army will respect your choice, whatever it may be; and while the Southern people will rejoice to welcome you to your natural position among them, they will only welcome you when you come of your own free will.

"R. E. Lee, *General Commanding.*"

The valor and triumphs of the South by land and sea, under the most adverse circumstances, are recorded in these volumes. No people, no nation has struggled more manfully for freedom; and could England truly know the privations, sufferings, and patriotic self-sacrifice of the women and children in that far distant land, compassion would assume some material form to relieve the necessities of these descendants of her ancient and noble emigrants.

Yet the South is just as far from subjugation as when the strife began, despite the almost superhuman exertions of her enemies; and there is little doubt but that she will ere long claim recognition from the European Powers as an independent nation.

BATTLE-FIELDS OF THE SOUTH.

CHAPTER I.

First Acts of Secession — Measures of the Southern Leaders—Major Anderson and Fort Sumter — Southern Preparations for War—Drilling of Volunteers—Preparing to march — Patriotic Spirit of the South—Journey by Rail—Camp at Corinth—Regimental Officers—A Tragical Episode.

As an English resident in the then United States of America, I watched intently the progress of public affairs after the election of Abraham Lincoln to the Presidency, and the probable disruption of the time-honored Federation filled me with serious concern. The stirring political events that followed thick and fast were deeply impressed upon my mind as they occurred, and the most minute details of circumstances bearing upon the calamities that succeeded them are ineffaceable from my memory.

When the Southern leaders were called home by the States they severally represented in the United States Senate and House of Representatives, and those States had seceded from the Union, acts of confederation were immediately agreed upon; Montgomery (Alabama) being judiciously chosen as the temporary seat of Government. Several States had not as yet (April first) sundered from the North; yet no one doubted that they would all secede either unanimously, or by vast majorities, as they subsequently did.

The Southern leaders had for months past begged the parent Government to allow the seceding States to retire peaceably and without bloodshed; and commissioners had been sent to negotiate for the transfer of Government property hitherto mutually possessed. But the Government, instead of officially communi-

1

cating with the envoys, put them off with specious promises from day to day, until it became obvious that the North was manœuvring for *time*, in order to strengthen the coasts and harbors, and seize the most eligible strategical positions and thus by mere physical force resist, and if possible prevent secession. To have quietly allowed President Lincoln to reinforce the Southern garrisons and forts, would have been equivalent to submission; and aware, despite all asseverations to the contrary, that he *then* had on the way heavy reinforcements for Charleston harbor, Fort Sumter was instantly reduced, its colors hauled down, and the Confederate flag raised over its ruins.*

This decisive act was bitterly anathematized in the North,

* Major Robert Anderson, First Artillery, was commandant here. He is a native of Kentucky, and nearly sixty years of age. He entered the service as brevet second lieutenant Second Artillery, July first, 1825. On the evening of the day that South-Carolina formally seceded from the Union, (December twentieth, 1860,) a grand banquet was given in Charleston, at which Major Anderson assisted, and, apparently, very much enjoyed himself; so that a party of gentlemen accompanied him to the wharf, where a boat was in readiness to convey him to his head-quarters at Fort Moultrie; Fort Sumter, the strongest of all the forts, placed in the middle of the bay, not being tenanted. But the Major's inebriety was all assumed, for at midnight he spiked the guns, and conveyed all his men and stores to Fort Sumter; so that next morning, when it was thought the Confederate troops might take possession, the Union flag betrayed the fact that Anderson was already there. Our leaders were greatly incensed at the Major, but President Buchanan would not disapprove the act, and we had to bombard the fort.

Before hostilities commenced, however, the citizens of Charleston treated the Major and his little garrison with much considerate politeness, allowing them to procure fresh provisions from the city daily; and it was not until all negotiations had failed, and a large fleet had been sent by President Lincoln to the assistance of the fort, that it was bombarded and reduced by General Beauregard, after an expenditure of two thousand shot, during parts of two days. The Federal fleet outside the bar were witness to the whole transaction, but did not attempt to force a passage, even when a conflagration in the fort, the number of his dismounted guns, and the shattered walls induced the Major to surrender, April thirteenth, 1861. Anderson was allowed to march out with the honors of war, and to salute his flag. During this latter ceremony, one of his guns burst, killing four of his men—the first blood shed during the whole affair. When Major Anderson arrived among his friends in the North, he was greatly lionized, and cried up as a "martyr" by fanatics; and, on the plea of sickness, he used his leave to travel round the country, feasting and speech-making. He was promoted to the rank of Brigadier-General, and appointed to command the forces then gathering in Kentucky for the Western campaign; but he unexpectedly resigned, averring that the fatigues and hardships endured at Fort Sumter had ruined his constitution. In truth, he was not willing to jeopardize his easily acquired reputation, by commanding men in whom he had little confidence, and in a cause he thoroughly despised.

both from pulpit and press; but the clamor partook less of manly indignation than of hypocritical expostulation, and ill-concealed annoyance at the failure of the Government scheme.

Now arose the question—What were the prospects of success for the new Confederate Government? Their munitions of war were some hundred thousand stand of arms found in the State arsenals, and ammunition for twice as many. But for what purpose were these arms likely to be required? Not for vengeance, seeing that not one drop of blood had been spilt; and except the battered walls of Fort Sumter, no material damage had been effected. The danger clearly perceived was the intention of the North to force the Confederate States back into the Union, and to meet this a call was made for seventy-five thousand men, and heartily responded to.

The chief difficulty proved to be the proper equipment and command of the volunteers. The arms in the State arsenals were nothing more than common percussion muskets, and the cartridges proved almost useless, being filled with very old, common, large-grained blasting powder. Our ports were blockaded; the North had free communication with Europe; exchequer we had none; our opponents could raise millions at home or abroad; our leaders were few, of inferior rank and little reputation; our foes had one at their head fondly called by themselves "the greatest general of his age." Save Lee, Johnston, Beauregard, and Cooper, we had not one single officer of note; and the first-named was only a colonel of dragoons in the old United States service. It is true that several officers (among them Van Dorn, Longstreet, Ewell, and Evans) in the Indian countries, or on the Border, immediately threw up their commands, and joined the fortunes of their respective States; but little was expected of them, since they could only be regarded as men of theory, with but little experience in warfare. Common expectation, however, was most agreeably disappointed in these officers.

While General Scott and a host of officers were drilling and marshalling their men at Washington, the State of Virginia seceded. Her arsenals and naval works were, as a consequence, blown up or fired by the enemy, and evacuated; the only spoil that fell to our lot, at Norfolk and other places, being charred and broken hulls, empty dockyards, spiked cannon, and damaged ammunition. The seizure of Harper's Ferry secured to Virginia several thousand stand of arms; but beyond these, little fell to the Confederates; the Federal officers, before departure, having carefully planned and executed the destruction of all Government property, at the various factories and dépôts.

When it became evident, from the vast preparations of the enemy, that hostilities would very shortly commence, the Confederate capital was changed from Montgomery, (Ala.,) to Richmond, (Va.) The railroad junctions had to be protected, as within no great distance from our seat of Government were several lines of road leading to and through the heart of the Southern States to the very Gulf. Manassas station (on the Washington and Alexandria Railroad) was selected as commanding all approach from Washington in front, or on the flank, from Harper's Ferry, through the Shenandoah Valley. This accordingly became the grand rendezvous, and the troops that first arrived were camped there: some few were sent twenty-five miles to the front (Fairfax Court-house and station) to watch the enemy, while General Johnston proceeded down the Shenandoah Valley with all he could gather, to watch and oppose General Patterson, who was massing his troops on the Maryland bank of the Potomac, and threatening Harper's Ferry. General Pegram was in Western Virginia, watching the Federals in that direction, who, under General McClellan, were threatening to advance circuitously and take us in the rear. Such, in brief, might be said to be the state of things in the middle of April, 1861. I now proceed to a simple narration of facts, of which, for the most part, I was an eye-witness, throughout most of the engagements of the war.

And in the first place let me observe, that prior to the proclamation of April, 1861, in which President Lincoln warned us to "disperse to our homes in thirty days," there were many who fondly expected that common-sense would rule in the councils of the North, and that the Government would not force a war upon their "brethren" of the South. We were all mistaken; and when the proclamation was read on the bulletin boards of the telegraph offices in every town, crowds perused the document with roars of laughter, and derisive cheers for the great "rail-splitter" Abraham! Companies were formed upon the spot from among the wealthiest of the youth, and thousands of dollars were spent on their organization, drill, and equipment; indeed, had President Davis so desired, he could have had two hundred thousand volunteers within a month, for any term of service.

At the first whisper of war among these excited crowds, a hundred youths repaired to a lawyer's office, drew up a muster-roll, inscribed their names for twelve months' service, and began drilling in a concert-hall. Subscriptions for arms and accoutrements began to pour in, and an emissary was despatched Northward post-haste to get these requisites. Many among us having studied at military or semi-military colleges, the details of infantry drill were perfectly understood, so that squads were quickly placed under our care ; and in every vacant building-lot of the village might be seen some half-dozen or more going through the movements, at the command of striplings. Muskets, formerly used for holiday parades, were immediately appropriated ; and before a week had elapsed, two full companies were drilling thrice a day, and marched through the streets every evening to the sound of fife and drum. Banners of costly material were made by clubs of patriotic young ladies, and delivered to the companies with appropriate speeches ; the men on such occasions swearing that they would perish rather than desert the flag thus consecrated.

After a few days, one of these companies, originally intended for Pensacola, received marching orders, and in a brilliant uniform of rifle green, with red facings and gold lace, bade adieu to the little town of Yazoo, amid great rejoicing; and taking steamboat to Mobile, started on their twelve months' service, with light hearts and great shouting. Although the members of our company were individually rich, and the greater number of them well educated, we had much quarrelling regarding uniform and general outfit. Some desired costly attire, and the most expensive rifles ; but, upon consulting the State Executive upon the first point, we learned it was the desire of President Davis that all volunteers should be attired in grey flannels and light blue cotton pantaloons — such articles being inexpensive and more adapted for service. A note from the President to his old friend, our captain, concluded with these words : "The young gentlemen of your company must be thoroughly im-

pressed with the idea that their services will prove to be in
hardships and dangers — the commonest material, therefore,
will be the most durable; and as for arms, we must be content
with what we have : the enemy will come superabundantly provided with all things that money and ingenuity can devise ; we
must learn to supply ourselves from them."

Our officers were elected by acclamation from among the
more aged and influential, who insisted on taking up arms for
the country's defence. Several of these gentlemen already bore
the title of colonel, major, or captain ; but these were holiday
or honorary titles, in which nearly every old planter and merchant rejoiced : even the gentleman who made my boots flour-
ished in the style of " *Colonel* Smith." No great harm resulted
from this sort of ostentation in the previous circumstances of
the country, but had we selected younger and less influential
persons for such important positions at the present crisis, it
would have been much better for all.

To prevent us from prowling about the town, and to instil
discipline, it was decided to encamp in fields proffered for that
purpose. With an ample supply of tents and all things needful, we commenced camping, and the novelty was delightful.
From sunrise until sunset it was incessant drill. At evening
came parade ; and when all assembled on the greensward, and
scores of fair creatures visited the grounds, and strolled about
with brothers, sons, or sweethearts, we all thought it a fine thing
to be a soldier, to strut about, or dance quadrilles to the music
of a town band, made up of four German cabinet-makers. After
two weeks' incessant drill, guard-mounting, parades, etc., we
yearned for "active" service, and many began to murmur at
the monotony of daily routine. All wished to go forth and
fight the Yankees — not that the Northerners were deemed
worthy of that honor, but there was a strong desire to get to
" close quarters " with the enemy, and settle the question without further delay. There was not a youth but fancied himself
a match for any half-dozen New-Englanders ; and from morning
until night the surrounding woods resounded with the reports
of fire-arms.

Our men, however, did not really need such practice, for
every youth was accustomed to the woods and to hunting ;
each had killed his dozens of panthers, deer, or rattlesnakes ;

and with his own rifle could "bring down" any thing within a distance of four hundred yards. In fact, nine tenths of our company seemed born to arms, and were never so happy as when shooting. The country in which we lived had in early times been an unbroken swamp. Even after twenty years' settlement, we numbered but fourteen hundred voters in the county, (forty miles wide,) and at this moment the dense woods skirting the town, interspersed with a few cotton plantations, abound with reptiles of every description; and panthers, bears, deer, alligators, wolves, and wild cats frequent the byways. Still, though accustomed to fire-arms in the chase, we had never used muskets, and some practice was deemed necessary. A target five feet high and fifteen inches broad was erected, and opposite this, at a distance of one hundred and fifty yards, we took our stand.

"Now," said our captain, jocosely, "fancy the board is Old Abe, and, at the command 'ready,' let all cover it well." The allusion was received with a grin; and at the word "fire," a volley was admirably delivered, and ninety-five holes counted in the target out of a hundred who had shot. "Save your powder, boys," said the captain, with a smile: "you'll do." This would be marvellous if it were not accounted for by the fondness of the Southern youth for hunting and wood-ranging. As a proof of this, it is not uncommon for a party of youngsters to leave home without a word of warning, and with blanket and gun take to the woods for weeks at a time, depending solely on their rifle and knife for sport and food.

The Governor of the State having been requested to enrol us immediately in some regiment, made answer that he had but three regiments to fill, and had one hundred and fifty companies to pick from! In fact, he was perfectly bored with offers from every part of the State; and political reasons had, of course, some influence upon his selection. Under these circumstances the welcome telegram arrived, "Strike tents, and march for Corinth—the regiments will form there within two weeks." Great was our rejoicing to break up camps and start for the wars. Captains of other companies begged us to give up our call, and offered munificent compensation if we would let *their* companies report instead. Such offers were spurned with contempt. "Give up the chance of going to fight the Yankees?" No, indeed! We were "favored" individuals; and not all the

wealth of California could have bought us off in favor of others!
Poor fellows : how soon the tune changed ! glad would some
of these hot heads have been to return home, months subsequently.

For several days before leaving, parties and balls were of
frequent occurrence in camp and town, at the residences of
members': all vied with each other in passing the time agreeably ; and in our daily intercourse there was little or no distinction apparent between officers and privates. In fact, in
worldly matters, many of the privates were far superior to their
officers. The ambition of all was "to carry a musket in the
holy war" of independence ; and although our company of one
hundred men represented property in the aggregate worth not
less than twenty million dollars, I never saw any signs of in-
subordination, drunkenness, or foul language amongst them.
Having negro servants to do the cooking and camp offices, we had
passed our term of encampment very agreeably. Now that the
moment approached for departure, the busy note of preparation
was heard in all directions. With knapsacks well filled with
every thing needful by the hands of female friends, we formed
rank in marching order, revolvers and bowie-knives by our
sides, and, with muskets shouldered, listened to the remarks of
our captain, who, encircled by hundreds of our friends and
relatives, spoke in a fatherly manner to us of the duties we
should have to perform. If any were afraid to meet the enemy,
now was the time to say so, and retire ; for none were desired
of timid temperament, or who feared to fight for their country.
"Fight" was the word, he said : let none imagine that child's
play or a holiday excursion is before them ; for it was not so.
In a few weeks many of us would be numbered with the dead ;
and if any were afraid of death in their country's cause, let them
retire ; if any were of Northern birth or feelings, let them retire ;
or if any were physically incapable of enduring a soldier's duty
or fatigues, from infirmity, disease, or malformation, let *them*
retire also—and they should incur no blame. Yet no one
stirred—not a sound could be heard in the whole assembly
save occasional sobs from the fair spectators ; and, at the conclusion of the address, one loud yell* rent the air.

* The English "hurrah" is not heard in the Southern armies, but a yell not unlike that of the Indians when rushing to the charge.

Then the band struck up "Dixie's Land," and our colors waved in the wind, and amid cheers and tears from young and old, male and female, we gaily marched through town, towards the steamboat Hope; and, amid the cheers of the multitude, and waving of handkerchiefs, started for the rendezvous at Corinth. Though many tears were shed, and mothers clasped children to their bosoms for the last time; though fathers grasped the hands of sons, or bashful sweethearts and sisters wept copiously on our departure, not one word was whispered of probable "failure:" no sign of diffidence was betrayed by young or old, but the universal sentiment was: "Go, my son, never be shot in the back: be always in the front rank: fight as a Southerner, and, if need be, die like a patriot. Never ask 'quarter' from Northern hirelings. Be merciful in the hour of victory, and courageous under defeat: behave as men—as true sons of the South. If ever you act otherwise, never turn your face homewards again." Such was the language even of the fair ones we left behind; and that this was the idea of all seemed apparent, for at every place that the vessel passed in steaming down the river, crowds collected to greet us; and ladies literally burdened us with presents, trifles, fruit, and provisions: none were more enthusiastic for the cause than these same gentle ones. At every landing we chanced to stop, whether it were night or day, military companies were under arms to salute us, the "favored" ones, who had thus preceded them to the seat of war.

By railroad it was the same. The telegraph signalled our approach, and the newspapers having flatteringly noticed us as "one of the crack companies of the State," the stations were crowded with all sorts of people; tables with breakfasts, dinners, or suppers, were spread for our accommodation, and that of other companies on their way to Corinth; while young and old, whites and blacks, all seemed to vie in rendering our journey an unbroken ovation. Male and female schools would line the track and rend the air with shouts, or toss bouquets upon us by hundreds; planters would have wagon-loads of choice provisions for our accommodation. We picked up, at different stations, company after company likewise bound to Corinth, and our train gradually lengthened to fifty cars. Another and another train being filled, we at length formed three

long trains with six engines, puffing along at the rate of twenty
miles an hour. Such noises as the men made are indescribable.
Some of us were in passenger cars, but the greater number had
to put up with baggage cars having temporary seats; and for
want of sufficient ventilation, muskets were freely used in
knocking out the panels to admit air. Some passed days and
nights, riotously, on the roof, and beguiled the time with playing cards, or, having violins and banjos, with singing and
dancing, scarce heeding the many bridges that jeopardized their
heads, or the uneasy and dangerous rolling of overloaded and
ill-constructed cars.

Tired with this trip of one thousand miles—having travelled
this distance without leaving our own State—we were glad to
find ourselves at Corinth. This town owes its existence to the
intersection of two great lines of railroad, and except its two
thousand inhabitants, or thereabouts, and a few wooden stores,
contains nothing worthy of observation: its chief edifice is the
Tishomingo Hotel. The lines of railway that intersect here are
those of the Mississippi Central, and the Mobile and Ohio Railroads: the first was an unbroken line from New-Orleans, and
crossing the Mobile road at this place, ran to Grand Junction,
whence one branch went to Memphis, Tenn., and the other to
Huntsville, Chattanooga, and thence into Virginia; the second
ran direct from Mobile, passed the junction at this place, and
ran on to Columbus, Kentucky. In a military point of view,
the occupation of this point was of vital importance, as will
appear at once to any intelligent reader who glances at the map.

North of the town we found the fields and woods pictur-
esquely dotted with tents; we could see various regiments under
drill in the distance, and faintly heard the word of command
of field officers. On leaving the train, we took up the line of
march for our camping grounds; and ere sunset had pitched
tents, and our numerous mess-fires were surrounded with busy
and talkative groups. On the low grounds in the distance we
saw hundreds of camp-fires reddening the scene; and as the
moon rose over the woods, bayonets glancing in the moonlight
revealed sentinels keeping the regimental "bounds;" the hoarse
challenge of guards fell upon the ear; "patrols" and "relief
guards" went their rounds; and as the clear notes of bugles or
drums fell upon our unaccustomed ears at "tattoo," we all

began to feel that our liberty was suddenly circumscribed, and that we must make up our minds to be obedient, and observant of military discipline. One day was allowed for rest, and then commenced incessant daily drill in the manual exercise and company field movements.

As we formed but eight companies, several companies unattached, proffered themselves to our officers, to fill up the regimental quota. But the eight captains considered their respective commands very " select," as being composed of the *élite* of their localities, and so, much negotiation ensued. At last an ex-Governor of the State (an ex-U. S. Senator also) came forward with *his* " select" company, and, being well known, was instantly allotted the place of company I. Next day came another ex-U. S. Senator with *his* company—all representatives of " the first families," of course—and was unanimously assigned the place of company K. The companies being at last assembled, and all being proficient in company drill, there was great rivalry among us to see who should be considered " *the*" company of the regiment; but as field officers had not yet been elected, we were drilled as a regiment on successive days by different captains : and a pretty farce some of them made of it! We were put through all kinds of movements, and several of these extemporized colonels put us into figures that defied all extrication, and then, in despair, left the ground for the companies to " unbungle" themselves as best they could. Several, bolder than the rest, rashly promised to " form square" for us on the first convenient opportunity ; but after energetic endeavors, they ended by throwing all the companies into inextricable confusion, and left us all in high dudgeon at their bungling pretensions. At last a non-commissioned officer (a school-fellow of mine) got the boys together one evening, after dress-parade, and forming us into sections, formed square immediately : several captains taking note thereof, understood the manœuvre at once, and plumed themselves thereafter on their skill and experience. Generally speaking, our officers, with all their pretensions, were quite ignorant of tactics; yet, in truth, little should have been expected from them ; for they, like ourselves, were fresh from civil life, and knew infinitely more of law and of plantations than of life on the tented field.

After much canvassing, we elected field officers from the

regiment, and despite all electioneering and party spirit, selections were made from among the most deserving : our boys wisely preferring "talent and experience" to all other considerations of wealth and social position. There was much heart-burning, of course, among the non-elected, and several immensely wealthy gentlemen, who had travelled hundreds of miles to offer their services as "colonels," "lieutenant-colonels," and "majors," received not a single vote to gratify their vanity. To such the companies gave a blank refusal. "If you wish to serve with us, as you say, and to fight for the common cause, why not be sworn into the ranks, and prove your disinterestedness? We intend to vote for none who are not enrolled to serve with us ; and in our choice of superiors, we desire no other qualifications than 'ability and sobriety.' As to the champagne suppers eaten at your expense, gentlemen, they were no more than courtesies offered to each other, and returned. We are used to all that kind of thing at home. We should be happy to receive you into our ranks, and should you join, your 'talents,' no doubt, will soon remove every obstacle to quick promotion in the future." Such were the sentiments of our regiment, and generally of all others.

Although there were not less than six or seven regiments hard at drill when we arrived at Corinth, good order and sobriety seemed to prevail, and thus it continued for several weeks that we remained there. As might be expected, however, among thousands of hot-blooded Southern youths, rencontres *would* occasionally occur ; and as in the South pugilistic science is little resorted to, or understood, knives and pistols were used in emergencies, and several were killed, including two or three commissioned officers. Courts-martial were held, but investigations proving that these homicides were simply the results of legitimate quarrels, and not premeditated "killing," the offenders received only a reprimand.

One instance I may mention, to show the spirit of those about to fight for the freedom of their country. A commissioned (company) officer having donned his grey uniform and gilded shoulder-straps, began to strut about camp and assume "airs," eager to show his "little brief authority" on all occasions. This unfortunate fellow disgusted those who had elected him, and although the men were desirous of learning their duty thorough-

ly and expeditiously, he seized upon every opportunity to
"blackguard" his former associates. He was frequently told
how obnoxious his assuming manner was; but not heeding the
admonition, several threatened to take him out and "whale"
him. Laughing at these suppressed remarks, he dared to lift
his sword to slap one of the men when on parade: he was told
what the immediate consequence would be, but foolishly raised
the weapon again, and slapped one across the shoulders; when,
in an instant, the rifle was dropped, a bowie-knife flashed, and
the officer lay dead on the turf, stabbed five or six times in as
many seconds. The company did not stir, but looked on, and
applauded; the culprit quietly wiped his knife, resumed his
place in the ranks, and dress-parade proceeded as if nothing
had happened ! Courts-martial could not—or, at all events, *did
not*—attempt to exercise any jurisdiction in this, or similar
cases: they were reckoned affairs of self-defence, or "honor."

CHAPTER II.

APRIL having passed, and the intentions of General Scott not being as yet developed, it was conjectured that operations might commence simultaneously at different points. Troops were therefore sent to Union City, (Kentucky,) near Cairo, on the Mississippi, and to Columbus, (Kentucky,) on the same river; the latter place being the last station of the Mobile and Ohio Railroad, and of great importance in many ways. Troops were also hurriedly despatched to Western Virginia, but not in large bodies. Indeed, our infant Government seemed over-whelmed with care and anxiety to meet the storm that was rapidly approaching, and could scarcely attend to the wants of her little army. It is true the various State arsenals contained more arms than were necessary for the seventy-five thousand men called upon—thanks to the statesmanlike foresight of our leaders, and the coöperation of Governor Floyd, ex-Minister of War under Buchanan—yet their quality and effectiveness were very indifferent indeed, while the ammunition found at hand on the outbreak proved to have been made up of the very worst description of powder; so much so, that after the second discharge our muskets were so dirty as to become almost unserviceable.

The quartermaster's and commissary departments, also, were in great confusion, and the service far from efficient. Although the country abounded in corn-meal, bacon, flour, etc., it was evident our stores could not last for ever, as the two last-named articles were chiefly (and perhaps solely) to be found North. We were rich in cotton, sugar, tobacco, rice, hemp, etc., but these were not commissary stores, or absolute necessaries, and as we did not produce any other, and were not in any sense a *manu-*

facturing people, we found the whole North ridiculing us and our preparations for conquering our independence. Indeed, their common taunt was, "How can you live without us? Why, we will *starve* you into submission." At the outset, however, President Davis and his military advisers had foreseen, and provided for, many of our most needful supplies : with funds immediately furnished by private negotiation, they had bought up many millions of various rations in Northern markets, while merchants by the thousand quietly proceeded up the country and procured immense supplies of merchandise and wares, before the North had arrived at any distinct idea of our determination to be free, and of the certainty of warfare. The Israelites, as usual, far surpassed the Gentiles in shrewdness at this auspicious moment, and laid in stocks (procured on credit) which, in almost every instance, were retailed at rates from five hundred to one thousand per cent above ordinary prices ; cash being always exacted. Many of these gentry proved unscrupulous knaves during. the war ; for having husbanded their goods for one or two years, and converted them into coin, if they did not decamp from the Confederacy altogether, they found a thousand and one excuses for not bearing arms for the country that had enriched them, and in which perchance they had been born. This is true of Hollanders generally, and of Dutch Jews almost universally.

It becoming apparent that General Scott's main line of advance and attack would be from Washington towards the Confederate capital of Richmond, the majority of our forces were directed to a point mid-way between both places. From our camp ground we daily saw trains passing onwards to Richmond, the locomotives and cars being decked with flags and banners, while on the top of the cars bands of music might be seen, and crowds of soldiers shouting and yelling to us as they passed swiftly onward. The Washington artillery (four companies) from New-Orleans had gone the day before, and we almost envied them their trip to Richmond. We were much afraid the War Department would order us to Union City ; but one evening as we sat chatting round our camp fires, the agreeable order was given—" Strike tents ! pack up for Virginia, boys !"

Such rejoicing, such confusion, such hilarity, and obstreperous behavior as characterized our camps on the reception of this news, can scarcely be imagined. Some joined hands and capered round their camp-fires in an Indian war-dance ; pots were turned over, and immense bonfires made of straw and wood, while yells and howls rent the air, so that the drums and bugles at tattoo could be scarcely heard in the·unearthly din. Regiments on the hills, in. the woods, in the plain, and from every direction, caught up the shout, and for one full hour the whole scene far and wide was naught but noisy merriment and excitement. The ceremony of "roll-call" *that* night was certainly a ridiculous farce : the " orderly " was laughed at, and coughed at ; a general buzz and suppressed laughter ran along the whole company line, and the usual calls for "Smith John, Jones James," were received with derisive cheers, as if it were possible any one *could* be absent on so momentous and joyful an occasion.

Tents were soon struck, "four days' rations " were quickly cooked, and all the camp equipage expeditiously packed and carried down to the railroad station and properly guarded. Many journeys were necessary to transfer all our extra baggage to the dépôt, and from the alacrity of the men in proffering their services to carry things, and the cloudy, mystified appearance of those who had been detailed for that duty all the evening, our officers suspected that some strange barrel had been tapped by them in their frequent journeys to and fro. The incoherent answers of the men, and the long absence of the sergeant and his guard, caused a scout to be sent out, who reported that the sergeant and his squad were dancing in a bar-room, all of them in a blissful state of intoxication. A corporal's guard was sent to arrest them, but the tipsy sergeant challenged the corporal to play the violin, and in less than half an hour the fourth corporal and his guard were no better than their comrades, and commenced dancing like so many madmen. When discovered, the corporal was found seated upon an empty whisky·barrel, playing the fiddle, while all hands were industriously kicking their heels in a cotillion. They were of course marched back to camp under escort.

To prevent intoxication, the greatest precaution had been ta ken by our officers : no person was allowed to sell or give liquor to the men ; but as Southerners usually drink in excess compared with other people, every artifice was resorted to by the men to obtain it; as much as five dollars (£1) being freely given for a pint of liquor. But as all had to go to the well, and as guards were not over exact on an occasion like this, the men easily stole through the "lines," filled their canteens at some out-of-the-way "doggery,"* and before morning broke, nearly every man was amply provided for his journey.

With a full head of steam on, and with the Stars and Bars floating on the front of the engine, we gave one long and unearthly yell as we passed our old camping ground, and at the rate of twenty-five miles an hour, dashed along the road to Virginia in gallant style, the band playing "Dixie," and other tunes peculiar to the times. Four trains followed ours, keeping in sight all day ; and as we progressed farther on our journey, we overtook other trains, similarly freighted, and bound for the same destination.

At every town, the cars were received with much rejoicing; the ladies being foremost in the expression of their patriotism and fervor for the cause in which we were all embarked. Military companies were frequently drawn up at the dépôt; the men vexed beyond expression, because they had not, like us, received "marching orders." Collations were prepared for us on every hand, and if the train stopped but for a few minutes to replenish fuel or water, milk, buttermilk, boiled eggs, ham, bread, cooked vegetables, cakes, pastry, and a thousand etceteras, were lavishly bestowed upon us, while the old ladies would wave handkerchiefs, and shout : "God bless you, boys. Teach them how Southerners can fight; be men, and never give up." Such patriotism as the women displayed is certainly beyond all description; they seemed to give all heart and soul to the cause : where men would smile or look serious, mothers and daughters put on their best looks with their holiday attire, and while almost smothering us with bouquets, would cheer us onwards with words of hope and praise, and try to hide the eloquent tear-drops glistening in their eyes. The negroes, too, at the plough, in the cotton fields, or beside their cabin doors, rushed out, hat in hand, mounted the fence, and rolling their eyes in wonder or delight, would shout success to us on our journey.

We travelled to-day hundreds of miles through our own

---

* A low bar-room is so called.

2

State—to-morrow as great a distance through another—and yet there was always the same feeling displayed; there was no repining, but all rejoicing and hilarity: and, save through a district of a few miles in East-Tennessee, where the inhabitants are proverbially cold, hard-fisted, and of Abolition sentiments, through the influence of a few Northern office-holders, we never heard the slightest whisper of Union sentiment, but, on the contrary, the most intense Southern feeling. Although our men, in passing through the disaffected district, (East-Tennessee,) had frequent opportunities to wreak their vengeance on the persons or dwellings of a few Northern sympathizers, yet not a word or gesture was exhibited by the boys contrary to the behavior of gentlemen; and this, notwithstanding the incontestable evidence they possessed that some few miscreants had meditated our total destruction by obstructions on the rails, and attempts to fire bridges across the streams. At length, on arriving at Lynchburgh, (Virginia,) we thought our travels were at an end, for now we were on the sacred soil of the *first rebel* (!), the immortal Washington: but still our troubles and annoyances were far from ended. Many troops had arrived before us, and nearly every available spot in and around the city was occupied by forces from nearly every State in the Confederacy. After tedious and harassing marches to and fro, in search of camping grounds, we at last pitched tents outside of the amphitheatre of the Fair Grounds, and commenced to drill, as usual, three times a day. The guards were now so numerous and strict that it was next to an impossibility for any one to elude them, or obtain permission to visit the city, basking in the sunlight at the foot of the hill. The thought of "Lynchburgh tobacco" tempted many to make large investments for the campaign; but in this we committed grave mistakes, for we were compelled to carry every pound of freight we accumulated, and found from experience that tobacco of a far superior quality could be obtained thousands of miles away on the Gulf Coast.

After a few days' stay, we continued our march, and for the first time heard mention of "Manassas," and "Manassas Gap." Our quartermasters being inexperienced, we suffered many disappointments before we could leave: train after train started before us, and we had to bivouac around the railroad station as best we could for two nights, waiting for accommodation. At last we got started, and rapidly traversed one of the most beautiful regions in the world: hills and valleys, adorned with picturesque little villages, substantial and elegantly laid out towns, and colleges and schools without number. When night came on we travelled through a flat unbroken country. Seeing no houses for many miles, and supposing we were far from our journey's end, nearly all went to sleep, myself among the number. Feeling cold, I awoke, and looking out of the cattle-cars in which we were stowed, was astonished to learn we had arrived at Manassas station, thirty miles from Washington, and about eighty from Richmond.

I could scarcely believe that this was a great military dépôt, there being nothing within my range of vision to indicate that such was the fact. The station itself was a low, one-storied building, about seventy-five feet in length, with bales and boxes scattered about; a house of refreshment close by was uninviting, and except one or two small cottages scattered here and there, naught was to be seen. Two or three tents were standing close to the dépôt, with lights in them; a guard here and there walked his post noiselessly, and in the distance, on neighboring hills, a few smouldering camp-fires were discernible. Only a mound of newly turned earth, here and there, indicated that the spade and shovel had been at work in fortifying, while the muzzles of a few guns in the embrasures pointed up the track towards Washington. A trooper or two would occasionally go jingling past in the direction of a cottage a few hundred yards in advance; and from the lights in windows, and groups seated round camp-fires, in the orchard, I learned that the dwelling was General Beauregard's head-quarters.

CHAPTER III.

Arrival at Manassas—Appearance of Things by Night—Operations of our Army opposed to Patterson around Harper's Ferry — Forward Movements of the Enemy—Jackson opens the Ball—Colonel Maxey Gregg attacks the Northern Troops on the Railway at Vienna—Earthworks at Manassas—Strength of our Troops—Scouting Parties—Letter from a Friend, giving Details of the Action at Carthage.

OUR engineless train lay along the track, with others in the rear; no one was stirring; the stars shone out in the clear cold skies with unusual brilliancy. To amuse myself, I spoke to the nearest guard, and gleaned scraps of information regarding the topography of the country. "Do you see yonder chain of hills rising in the south-west, and running north? Well, that is a spur of the Blue Ridge; and where you now see the moon rising, and those flickering lights, *that* is the 'Gap,' through which the railroad runs from here to Strasburgh. From the latter place to Winchester, twelve miles, there is a break in the track. From Winchester, however, the road runs to Harper's Ferry, and there joins the Washington and Baltimore roads to the east, and with the Western Virginia and Ohio Railroads to the west. General Joe Johnston is at the Ferry with a small force guarding the passage; for if General Patterson and his forty thousand men' pour across from Maryland and Pennsylvania into the Shenandoah Valley, they can march on this place by the flank, while Scott moves down from Washington in our front. 'Tis fully sixty miles, however, from the Ferry here, and if we hadn't so many traitors and spies around at all points, night and day, our boys wouldn't be obliged to guard the 'Gap' yonder this cold night," (May first, 1861.)

The troops were nearly all from the far South, which accounted for their chilliness. Giving the guard a drink of brandy, we became friendly in a short time, and he continued: "Yonder black streak you see rising from the south south-west, running north, and turning off due east, is the timber around Bull Run; 'tis about three or four miles distant from here to any point, and the high grounds you observe rising abruptly beyond the stream — the table-land I mean, northward—and shelving to the east across the track, is Centreville. A small detachment and military telegraph post is stationed there watching the roads from the Upper Potomac and Leesburgh, coming in west, and keeping open communication with General Bonham, who holds Fairfax Court-House and the railroad station midway between Washington and this place. Trains run there night and day. See yonder!" said my companion, pointing towards Centreville. "They are working the telegraph! See them repeating the signals on yonder hill? Wait a minute, and you'll perceive the answer given from Beauregard's quarters."

In a few minutes, one of the men sitting around the large fire in front of the General's quarters, seized a long red fagot from the flames, and going to the north end of the house, began swaying it to the right and left, according to directions; now horizontally, again perpendicularly, and seemed to be cutting an imaginary circle at different angles. The signs were instantly repeated from post to post, and thus traversed fifteen miles within a very few minutes! "General Bonham's got his answer before now, I know," said the sentry; "I wonder what it is all about, though? There'll be hot work, shortly, or they wouldn't be working that machine so often at night." In a few moments I heard some distant voice shout out: "Third Relief. Turn out, Third Relief!" and after a little bustle, jingling of accoutrements, and a hurried calling of the roll, I saw bayonets glistening and advancing in the distance, to relieve my agreeable companion; so, giving him another drink of brandy, I bade him good night, and picked my way back again to our cattle-cars, to sleep as best I could for the rest of the night.

When morning came, we all thought that Beauregard and other generals would call and inspect or review us; but our vanity was not so flattered. We were marched some two miles past the station; our baggage was brought down by an engine and cars, and before we could well recover from a journey of thirteen hundred miles, we were unceremoniously marched into some large open fields parallel with the railroad, and about two miles from Bull Run. Camps being formed, drill was commenced and proceeded with incessantly. Little could be gleaned regarding Federal movements. General Joe Johnston had evacuated Harper's Ferry, we knew, and the act was much censured by non-military critics; as for the troops, they said nothing, but reposed implicit reliance in the wisdom and skill of our generals.

Patterson was massing his troops for a descent into the Shenandoah Valley, but at what point to expect his crossing no one could tell. Colonel Jackson (subsequently named "Stonewall" by way of distinction) was second in command under Johnston, and guarded the Upper Potomac with great vigilance. It was evident the Federals did not intend to force a passage at the Ferry, for we held the town and heights above it, and could defy all their attempts. It was soon apparent that they intended to cross higher up; so having no means or force to garrison the place, we destroyed the works, removed all *matériel*, and evacuated it; advancing higher up the river towards Martinsburgh, and for the most part lying in ambush. When their advance had crossed, Colonel Jackson's force (about three thousand) assailed them vigorously, took many prisoners, a few arms, and drove their main body back to the river. They had crossed, however, in such strength, that it was impossible to inflict any decided punishment with the few troops under his command; Colonel Jackson, therefore, retreated slowly and orderly towards Charlestown, (midway between Harper's Ferry and Winchester,) whither Johnston's main force had retired. While Johnston's and Patterson's forces were thus facing each other near Charlestown things were unchanged at Manassas. Reports, indeed, were circulated daily regarding the enemy's movements, but nothing of consequence transpired.

While seated by the tent-door one afternoon in June, I heard three distinct reports of light field-pieces from the direction of Washington, but did not attach any importance to the fact. Next day we learned that one of the Federal generals (Schlich by name) had been out on a reconnoissance, and met with a serious reception from a handful of Confederates. Schlich, or Schlick, had novel notions of warfare, and intended to carry on operations in a free-and-easy style : so embarking two or three Ohio regiments on a long train, with two field-pieces, he proceeded down the Orange and Alexandria road, with the engine in the rear. Colonel Maxey Gregg, with the First South-Carolina Volunteers, was guarding the road; and his scouts reporting the approach of the train, he prepared to give it a warm reception, and placed two field-pieces on a wooded eminence commanding a long curve in the road. Leisurely approaching, Schlick and other officers were enjoying themselves with champagne and cigars, unconscious of danger, when, as the train entered the curve mentioned, our guns opened with such destructive effect that seven cars were detached from the train, smashed to pieces, and nearly every occupant killed or wounded. The engine was instantly reversed, and disappeared in a few moments, leaving hundreds of killed and wounded behind. Unaware of their force or intentions, Colonel Gregg changed his position and retired towards General Bonham at Fairfax Court-House.

This incident was the origin of those wonderful stories manufactured at the North about "masked batteries," etc., and which served for a time to create hobgoblin notions regarding us, and to account for any reverse they might meet with at our hands.

As the month of June drew to a close, our preparations in and around Manassas began to assume a formidable appearance. Heavy guns were brought up, and earthworks began to rise in different directions around the station, but nowhere else ; woods were felled by the acre to give free range for artillery, and troops were placed in different directions, but with what design I could not imagine. The strength of our forces, and the number of guns, were not generally known. Quartermasters and commissaries seemed to be the oracles in such matters, and as they were supposed to be acquainted with the secrets of headquarters, the majority seemed to place implicit reliance in their statements. As might be expected, these important individuals were in great request, and answered the most simple interrogatories with great solemnity and caution. Our strength from such sources of information was put down at from seventy-five thousand to one hundred thousand; while the truth was, our whole army there assembled did not muster more than twenty thousand men, and twenty guns; Johnston having ten thousand men and twenty guns with him in the Shenandoah Valley.

Daily reports now began to possess interest. Pegram had been surprised and defeated by McClellan, at Rich Mountain in Western Virginia, (July twelfth,) and from reports of killed and wounded, it was very evident the Federals had no idea of amusing themselves by throwing snowballs at us. Scott began to push his outposts towards Fairfax Court-House, and sharp skirmishing was of daily occurrence; but with little damage to either side. We learned that our independent scouts around Alexandria caused much annoyance and loss by their unerring aim; and judging by the exploits of some few of those adventurous individuals who visited us in camp, I can not wonder that the Northern press was so bitter against them. They were well mounted and accoutred, and dead shots at five hundred yards. Most of them were gentlemen of means, who took delight in the work, and were as crafty as Indians in their movements.

In the beginning of July, scouting companies, mounted and foot, daily scoured the whole country, within and without our lines to the front; while lines of picket guards dotted Bull Run, and watched all the fords with such vigilance that several cows advancing to drink as usual, were mistaken for spies crawling among the bushes in the dark, and met an untimely fate. When one fired, some other feverish guard would follow suit from force of imagination, and within a few moments a succession of "poppings" could be heard along the whole picket line. This carelessness of the outposts caused us all much annoyance.

A company of Virginians held the railroad bridge over the Run, when about two A.M. their advance fired three shots in rapid succession. The nearest regiments beat to arms, and within two minutes drums were sounding in all directions, while the only words spoken were: "They are coming! It is a surprise! Old Scott is advancing over the hills with fifty thousand men!" Thump, thump, sounded the big drums, bugles called the "assembly," while the incessant rattle of small drums was alarming. "They are coming—fall in, boys, quick!" were the only words passed from one to another. "Fall in" we did, and in an immense hurry : some without boots, hats, or coats seized their arms, and the regiment was formed and drawn up ready for action within five minutes from the first alarm. Many were on the sick list, and had not been out to drill for days; yet out of two hundred who had thus shunned duty previously, not one was out of place in line of battle. Captains might be seen in their shirt-sleeves smoking cigars, men sat on the grass, expecting orders every minute, but after standing shivering in the cold morning air for an hour, all marched back to quarters, much disappointed and annoyed.

Alarms of this nature became frequent, and were often resorted to by our Colonel when desirous of ridding the doctor's list of a few score of those playing the "old soldier." For be it said, to the credit of our men, that, although many counterfeited sickness or ailments to escape drill, marching, or police duty, I knew none who would not turn out with alacrity whenever there was any prospect of a fight; some, indeed, who were really sick had to be forced out of the ranks, so anxious were all to do their duty, and render service in our common cause.

About this time I received the following letter from a friend in Missouri, descriptive of the battle of Carthage, and the uprising of the people in that State. It is inserted here as an authentic account of the incidents leading to the engagement, and of the rout of the Federal troops :

"Cowskin Prairie, McDonald Co., Missouri,
July 8, 1861.

"DEAR TOM': I suppose the heading of this letter will surprise you, for I·am no longer in my comfortable office in the good city of St. Louis, but one of Price's 'rebels,' camped in this out-of-the-way place, near the Indian nation. As you desire to know every thing regarding our movements, I will narrate things as they occurred since I last saw you.

"When the Border States found that a coercive policy was determined upon, Missouri was one of the first to oppose it. We had no arms, but were certain the sympathies of our people would sustain us. Lincoln's hirelings were stirring up the German element in different parts of the State, trusting by the distribution of arms in abundance, to overawe any expression of feeling in favor of our sister Southern States. Governor Claiborne Jackson, feeling that delays might prove dangerous, ordered (in May) the State Guard to go into encampments for their customary annual drill. Brigadier-General Frost pitched his camp in the outskirts of St. Louis, and called it "Camp Jackson;" a full regiment of the city companies assembled, and daily went through the customary exercises. The Abolition German element was opposed to this, and unknown to the majority of us, Captain Lyon led them in great numbers around our camps, and forced our men to deliver up their arms and disband. This was a piece of treachery we did not expect from Frost, our general, who we thought was favorable to sustaining State right principles. The cowardly Germans, however, were not content in thus humiliating us, but on some slight pretext, fired upon the assembled crowds, killing and wounding many; and getting drunk on lager beer, committed all manner of depredations in and around the city. The arsenals, and all the railroads, were in their possession, and as the city was watched from several points, citizens being arrested, arms seized, houses searched, etc., it was soon perceived that Lincoln and Lyon were determined to suppress, by force, any Southern feeling existing in the State, and to spare none that opposed them. As nine tenths of our State, to your own knowledge, was soundly Democratic and Southern, we awoke to find ourselves under the iron heel of tyranny.

"Determined that the State should not be manacled without a struggle, and fully informed that Lyon meditated seizing the capital at Jefferson City, Governor Jackson, in June, issued a call for fifty thousand volunteers, and transferred the archives to Boonville, about eighty miles above, on the Missouri River. Ex-Governor Sterling Price was named general in chief of these forces, *whenever they could be gathered*, and seven or eight brigadiers appointed to assist him, including Rains, Parsons, and others.* The call was immediately responded to by three or four hundred men, myself among the number; for I was tired of witnessing the tyrannical acts of Lyon, and his friends the Dutch Abolitionists. On arriving at Jefferson City, I found that all the State officers had gone to Boonville, with boat-loads of books, papers, and other property, and proceeding there I found that our collective force did not exceed seven hundred men, armed with such weapons as they could find, and attired in every variety of costume. Some had fine clothes and ' stove-pipes,'† some were ragged, if not totally destitute. Altogether, I felt discouraged, as you may suppose; for I knew that Lyon, at St. Louis, had thousands of men, well armed, well drilled, and uniformed; and, being in possession of the railroads, could throw a heavy force in our route whichever way we moved.

" The 'Southern Question' by this time seems to have aroused the rural population, and they swore that the Dutch in the river cities should not rule the State, even if supported by all the wealth and power of the Lincoln Government. We had not been at Boonville long, ere it was ascertained that Lyon and Blair contemplated a movement upon that place, in order to crush the rebels the instant they stirred. At this critical moment, Price being sick and unable to attend to business, Colonel Marmaduke took command of our force, if a body such as I have described deserves the name. But their strength consisted in the fact that a pure patriotism had caused them to take the field.

" It was soon ascertained that Lyon was approaching up the Missouri with several thousand men and half-a-dozen field-pieces. Colonel Marmaduke ‡ was fearful of the disparity in

---

* Brigadier-General Gabriel J. Rains is a North-Carolinian, and has greatly distinguished himself throughout the Missouri campaign. He is about fifty years of age; entered the U. S. service as brevet Second Lieutenant First Infantry, July first, 1827; Brevet Major, August twentieth, 1847, and held that rank in the Fourth Infantry when he joined Price in June, 1861. 'He was immediately appointed Brigadier General by Governor Jackson, and has been present in almost every fight.

† Dress hats are so termed.

‡ Colonel John S. Marmaduke is a Missourian: entered the service as brevet Second Lieutenant First Infantry, July first, 1857; was Second Lieutenant Seventh Infantry, August first, 1857; joined the Missourians at Boonville, with rank of Colonel, and on account of services is now Brigadier-General, acting in the same State.

force, and wished to retreat, but the men under Lieutenant-Colonel Brand were determined to 'fight.' When the enemy appeared, therefore, our handful of volunteers drew up in battle array and confronted them, and within two hours killed and wounded more than two hundred, our loss not amounting to a dozen. We then gave up the fight, and retired towards Cole Camp, where, it was said, a force of the enemy were stationed to intercept us; these were attacked during the night by Colonel Kane with a small body of rebels, and defeated, with a loss of more than two hundred men killed, one hundred taken, and five hundred stand of arms. This capture assisted in arming hundreds who were flocking to us on our line of march towards Warsaw, on the Osage River.

"Though pursued by Colonel Totten and a thousand cavalry, Governor Jackson safely reached Warsaw, where we rested, and began to look about us. Our case was desperate; we were but a few ill-armed men of all ages and all sizes, unaccustomed to military service, and less used to privations and sufferings. We had no tents, no commissary or quartermaster's stores, few wagons, and those of an inferior kind — in truth, we were a small band of patriots vastly in need of every thing but 'pluck.' As the enemy were making dispositions for our capture, and had full command of the railways, word was sent to General Price at Lexington to hurry along with his recruits, so as to form a junction with Jackson's small force, and, by common consent, both little wings met and joined in Cedar County, July third.

"Information was now received that Sigel had been despatched from St. Louis with over three thousand men by the south branch of the Pacific Railroad, and was actually in Carthage, not many miles distant in our front, while Lyon, Lane, and others were rapidly approaching on the flanks and rear! For a little army of not over three thousand badly equipped men, this was a sad situation, and all began to prepare for the worst; nevertheless, on the fifth of July, at two A.M., we boldly began our march towards Carthage. After a march of seven hours, word was brought by our scouts that Sigel was in front, with the number of troops first reported, and eight guns. Still we moved on, until between ten and eleven A.M. we came in full view of the enemy drawn up in three detachments, posted on a rising ground in the prairie, ready to dispute our passage. Although much tired with our long march, and although several hundreds in our command had no weapons of any description, we instantly prepared for the attack, and, pushing ahead, drove in the enemy's pickets. We had several old cannon, which had been pickèd up here and there on our route—pieces which had done no more than fire salutes on fourth of July celebrations and the like—but we were deficient in ammunition : these guns we were careful to place in commanding positions. Our small force of cavalry, after much discussion, was placed upon the wings, and hardly were these dispositions made, when Sigel's guns opened on us with great fury ; nor was it possible for our cavalry to attack them either in flank or rear, as intended, for their constant cannonade frightened the horses and made them quite unmanageable.

"After more than an hour of indecisive fighting and ' bushwhacking,' our officers, who were determined to bring the affair to a crisis, ordered a 'charge.' As soon as we began to advance at the ' double-quick,' the enemy broke and ran, crossing a broad creek in their rear, and destroying the bridge, leaving many score dead and wounded behind. They halted after a run of about two miles in the direction of Carthage, and many of us having crossed on logs and floating timber formed line, and followed in pursuit. We were badly circumstanced ; for the enemy had obtained a splendid position ; being concealed in the woods, their artillery could play upon us as we advanced through the open fields. Our cavalry, finding their horses of little value in such an irregular fight, dismounted and assisted us as infantry. Again closing up with the enemy, we fought them for about two hours, when they gave way, and made a running fight of more than four miles. We had thus driven them before us into Carthage, where they made a third stand on the edge of the town, and from behind houses or barns maintained a hot fire upon our advance. After some time, our numbers began to increase, and we determined to drive them from the town. Collecting all our strength, we again succeeded, by superior shooting, in driving them before us, and in our progress through the town captured many hundred stand of arms. Still following close after them, we chased them for several miles on the road to Rolla, and continued the pursuit until long after sunset! Their killed and wounded amounted to six hundred men, scattered up and down the road for a distance of twelve miles or more. The people of Carthage rendered us all the assistance in their power, furnished accommodations for our wounded, and provided us with refreshments, of which we were much in need.

"This victory caused great rejoicing, especially among the farmers, whose sons now came forward 'to help fight the Dutch,' and were anxious that other opportunities might soon offer for whipping the Abolitionists. For myself, I know not where all this is to end, or how we are ever to succeed in Missouri, where the river, the cities, and the railroads are held by the enemy. In other parts of the South our friends have railroads at their command, and manufactories of different kinds in their midst, to 'create' supplies; but here we have no commissary or quartermaster, no doctor, and but few arms, while the enemy have abundance of all things, and can collect any number of men from neighboring States to hurl against our little band of adventurers. Nevertheless, we shall prove tough subjects for Lincoln's minions to control, for we are hardened, and know the country so thoroughly, that not a ford or mountain pass but is well marked by scores of trappers and hunters in our ranks. We know that all the weight of the North and North-West will be thrown against us, but if their troops are to succeed they must be made of better metal than that we lately encountered at Carthage.

"The day after the battle, General McCulloch, of Texas, and General Pearce, of Arkansas, arrived to our aid with about two thousand men. It appeared that our forces and theirs were advancing to the same place, to prevent either little band being overpowered by a sudden dash of the enemy, who is said to have already an army of forty thousand men in the State. These are not Missourians, but a mixed crowd of Germans and others who have volunteered from every State, under German leaders. There are not five hundred Missourians arrayed against us, and St. Louis to-morrow, together with *all* the river cities, would carry any election in favor of the Southern cause, if uncontrolled by Federal bayonets. More of this soon.

"Yours,   POLK."

CHAPTER IV.

FOR several days I was unwell, and could not attend to duty, but being allowed to walk about at leisure, I frequently strolled down to the Junction, to watch the progress of our preparations. A large redoubt about half a mile long, and a quarter wide, had been erected since my previous visit; it was at least ten feet high, and as many wide on the top, with a large ditch in front. The batteries at the angles were semicircular, with embrasures for four thirty-two-pounders, the mouths of which looked like black bull-dogs, protecting the road. In the interior were other works of greater or less magnitude, connected by covered ways, all well provided with ammunition and bomb-proof magazines. There were several smaller batteries placed in front on elevations, and the works altogether seemed formidable enough to protect the dépôt and stores, should the enemy penetrate so far.

"But who are our generals?" thought I, walking about, and meditating; "our men are as brave as steel, but who are to lead them?" Our best officers are from the old army, yet none of them held higher rank than that of colonel. R. E. Lee was in the cavalry, and a lieutenant-colonel; Joseph E. Johnston was quartermaster-general, and ranked as lieutenant-colonel; Beauregard had been major of engineers; Evans, Longstreet, and others, did not rank higher than major of cavalry or infantry, and had seen but little service, except on the frontier among the Indians; Bragg was a retired captain of artillery; T. J. Jackson was professor of mathematics and of tactics in the University of Virginia; D. H. Hill was a lawyer; Polk, an Episcopal bishop in Louisiana, etc. This was all the talent we had, and much of it was only said to be "promising." General Lee was at Richmond, acting as Secretary of War; General Cooper was there also as adjutant-general; Bragg and Polk were in Tennessee, and Johnston in the Valley; Beauregard was alone at Manassas, having Evans, Ewell, Longstreet, and a few less known names, as subordinates in the approaching struggle.

Of Beauregard I knew little, but had heard much. He was continually moving about from place to place, his appearance and escort being so unostentatious that many met and passed without knowing him. It was his custom to walk in the garden of the cottage where his headquarters were established after meals, smoking; and it was there I first saw him. He is a small man, with a sallow complexion, a heavy black moustache, and closely cut hair. With the left hand in his trowsers pocket, a cigar in his mouth, a buttoned-up coat, and small cap, he is the exact type of a French engineer, and could not anywhere be mistaken for a civilian. He is jaunty in his gait, dashing in manner, and evidently takes delight in the circumstance of war. It must be confessed his modesty is equal to his merit— he is not imperious or overbearing, bears great respect for his brother officers of the old service, and is never seen to such advantage as when standing on an earthwork, and giving orders, or conversing with animated gesture.

It was now the fourteenth of July, and the enemy were advancing in four columns upon Fairfax Court-House. General Bonham's brigade of South-Carolinians held the post, and had fortified it. Having made every disposition for the fight, of which he was in anxious expectation, it was much to his chagrin and disappointment that he received orders to retreat when the enemy were but a few miles distant. With much cursing, the brigade hastily fell back to Centreville, and camped on the heights on the evening of the seventeenth, the enemy's fires being visible about a mile distant. On the same day our brigade received orders to move to the front, and we quietly bivouacked in the woods on the banks of the Bull Run to guard McLean's Ford. In this position we formed the right centre, and as our troops stood in excellent repute with the army, it was surmised that there was warm work in store for us—a supposition that was strongly confirmed when not less than seven guns of the Washington Corps were detailed for our support. From our position to Blackburn's Ford was half a mile, and there Longstreet was posted with a strong brigade. Ewell was to our right, lower down, and across the Run at Union Mills. While we stood in line of battle, scouts came in, reporting the enemy's approach *en masse*. In the afternoon an Alabama regiment came in, in good order, bringing all its baggage. They had skirmished with the enemy for several miles, taking advantage of every turn in the road, and firing from the woods with good effect. From their reports we learned that all the outposts had made good their retreat, and our skirmishers had done so much damage, that the enemy were extremely slow and cautious in their movements.

Towards nightfall four companies of our right wing crossed the ford and occupied a small valley which led to Centreville. Our pickets had not long been posted in the timber, when a cavalry scout came across the open, and reported the approach of a strong force. The men were all quietly placed and ready for business, when we distinctly saw several hundred Federals placed in the edge of the wood opposite, and could hear their conversation occasionally. One of our negroes, taking advantage of the darkness, went over to the enemy.

During the night the lieutenant-colonel, anxious for our safety, attempted to reach us. Thanks to the runaway, the enemy had inclosed us on three sides, the fourth being a range of hills, beyond which was the river. Determined to extricate us, the colonel swam the river, and before the morning dawned we had safely forded it, recrossed again lower down, and flanked the enemy. The sequel was exciting. Believing us to be surrounded, the Yankees moved cautiously towards the spot, and two battalions opened close volleys. Discovering their exact whereabouts by the flash, we all took accurate aim, and pouring volley after volley into them with great rapidity, scattered their force in all directions. Wet to the skin, but much elated, we were peremptorily commanded to retire across the Run by an orderly of the General's, who said our firing had

aroused every man in the division. As we approached McLean's
Ford through the woods, our outposts, horse and foot, were as
thick as flies, and such was the danger of being fired into, that
scouts had to be sent in advance to report our approach. The
ford was much deepened, and the river had risen. We crossed
as best we could on fallen trees; and as the moon rose, plainly
saw our horse pickets on the opposite hill, while the glare of
the enemy's camp fires around Centreville looked like thousands of stars flickering against the dark blue sky.

It was evident that the enemy were perfectly informed of the
topographical peculiarities of the region, for there seemed to be
little hesitation in their movements, but great knowledge of
available ground, and practicable roads. Their extended wings
and superior force led many to suppose that it was their real
intention to surround and cut us off from all escape. The men
laughed at such an idea, and, to use their own language, were
"spoiling for a fight." When the morning of the eighteenth
dawned, our regiments formed in line, and waited hour after
hour for the attack, which was now certain.

About noon, several shots in the direction of Blackburn's
Ford indicated that the advance was exchanging compliments
with our pickets. Shortly afterwards, I was sent on duty up
the Run, and, reaching an elevation, saw that the enemy had
crossed above Blackburn's Ford, and were shelling the woods
in all directions. Presently, several of our light batteries came
galloping on the ground, and an artillery duel immediately ensued, with fluctuating fortune; our volunteers, however, seemed
to have the advantage, for they worked their pieces with such
rapidity, that the Federal regulars retired, and allowed their
infantry to advance, which they did in fine style, and commenced to fan out in skirmishing order. Ours did the same,
and advanced. Presently the skirmishers on both side fell back,
and formed; then both sides advanced in line.

After some manoeuvring and firing, eight companies on our
side (they were the First Virginian Volunteers) deceived their
opponents by a well-executed *ruse*. Having first advanced
against the enemy, they suddenly turned and fled, at quick-time,
but in perfect line. With cheers, the Yankees pursued; but
when they were fairly drawn out into the open field, the major

in command gave the word, and the Virginians, facing about, fired a most destructive volley. Astonished, the Yankees stood aghast at their loss; and at the instant were charged by the Virginians, who threw themselves, with an Indian yell, upon the foe. Then the Federals threw away their arms and fled precipitately to the river bank: the artillery duel was resumed with great fury, shells bursting in all directions; and our infantry advanced on the enemy's flank, while distant musketry could be plainly heard like the pattering of rain. It was evident the enemy could not effect a permanent lodgment on the south bank; and, satisfied with the trial, they were retreating to Centreville, under cover of their numerous artillery. Advancing at a gallop across the open ground, our light batteries took up a position, and unlimbered with great celerity and coolness under fire, and so great was their precision of aim, that the enemy retired in haste. Our infantry pursued for some short distance across the river, while the artillery played until their shots fell into the Federal camps on the hill. Had a small force of cavalry been at hand, we might have inflicted serious loss and captured several pieces. As it was, the Federal enemy left many of their dead and wounded behind, together with several hundred stand of arms, and decamped in great confusion.

This auspicious opening of our campaign in Virginia spread great joy among the volunteers, and such was the enthusiasm it caused, that many regiments who, in ambush, had witnessed the fight, could scarcely be controlled by their officers: the Seventh Louisiana obliged their commanders to move forward into the open ground, to participate in the engagement, but they were too late, for the "game" had taken wing to their nest on the hills. It is strange to remark that the retreating foe shouted vociferously, and their bands struck up "Yankee Doodle" and other Northern airs, perhaps in joy for their safe retreat, it being impossible to imagine any other reason. At the critical moment, General Beauregard rode to the front, sent orders to Colonel Ferguson of his staff to pursue as far as practicable, and, galloping past our position, ascended a hill, whence he could view the Federal rout in detail. "Poor Tyler," said some one in the group, "his decapitation has come early;" and, true enough, his name has scarcely ever been whispered in the North since that fatal eighteenth day of July. In Northern reports, indeed, this affair is lightly spoken of as "a reconnoissance that was eminently successful in every way;" nevertheless, we positively know that that division was so roughly handled and dispirited that it was withdrawn to the rear, and did not fire a single shot in the great battle fought on the following Sunday. The escapes of Beauregard that afternoon were almost miraculous. Shells penetrated his head-quarters in a dozen places, bursting in the kitchen, and blowing the cooking apparatus about in all directions. The terrified black cooks struck work, and could not be prevailed upon to resume their labors till nightfall.

Expecting the attack to be resumed with great fury on the morrow, every preparation was made for it, strong picket guards being posted in all directions. It was while I was out on this duty, far away to the front, that news was brought of Patterson's retreat from the Shenandoah Valley into Maryland, his object being to effect a junction with the forces of General Scott around Washington in time for the great struggle. At the same time, telegrams informed us of Johnston's retreat to Winchester and Strasburgh; and he himself had arrived at Manassas on Friday night, (the nineteenth,) while Jackson, with one or two brigades, was on his way by railroad. The rest of Johnston's army, it was expected, would reach us before Sunday, and participate in the general engagement. This was excellent news, and Johnston's manœuvres raised him high in the opinion of the men.

During the night we picked up several stragglers from Scott's army, and learned from them that McDowell was in chief command, and had seventy-five thousand men. These prisoners did not wish to be sent far from Manassas, and for peculiar reasons. "Don't send us to Richmond," they said; "our army will be in Manassas before Sunday, and therefore we wish to save trouble. Lincoln and Scott both promise to be in Richmond within a week, and as the thing will be over so soon, we don't wish to be sent far off," etc. We could not help laughing at the simplicity of these would-be "conquerors," but allowed them to continue cherishing their fond expectations, resolved, however, to make breastworks of our bodies rather than allow these Northern hirelings to rule over us.

On Saturday morning, early, we were provisioned for three days, and every thing seemed to denote a forward movement on our part. Some sharp skirmishing occurred on our right, but towards nine A.M. we were withdrawn to the position occupied on Thursday. I did not, and do not, believe that an advance was seriously intended by Beauregard, although he is proverbially a dashing and spirited commander; for the enemy were in immense force on high ground, and superabundantly supplied with artillery. This partial advance was more probably a "feint," designed to make the enemy believe we intended to move forward, and thus engage their attention, and gain more time for our troops in the Valley, to join us. Up to Saturday noon, not more than five thousand had arrived, while, could we avert the impending attack until Sunday, it was thought all would have come up from that and other directions, making an aggregate of fifteen thousand additional to our strength. The idea, if correct, was commendable; yet, although Johnston had made every possible preparation for the transport of his force, unforeseen circumstances completely thwarted the design, and up to one P.M., none had arrived. The more observant were particularly silent — things did not exactly please them; yet these were the men to speak encouragingly to all, and plead unbounded confidence in the ability of our leaders.

To encourage the troops, a report was spread that all Johnston's force had safely arrived, together with several thousand additional from different quarters. All seemed pleased; and when tattoo sounded, a terrific howl rent the skies, commencing on our extreme right, and gradually extending away to the left. What it meant none could tell; the men seemed to shout and howl from an overflow of spirits, and from no other cause. Being on distant picket duty at the time, I could not help remarking the effect these Indian yells had on the Yankees. We had crept so close as to see them plainly moving about and hear their conversation. One of the pickets was very valorous in his speech; he was willing to stake any thing in the world that "the rebels would evacuate Manassas before morning! He only wished he came across half-a-dozen rebels! *He'd* show them what fighting stuff Union troops were made of—*he'd* show them what old Massachusetts could do!" etc. Determined to try the metal of this pugnacious individual, two of us crawled through the underbrush, Indian fashion, and waiting an opportunity, seized this bombastic New-Englander, without the shadow of resistance, and, having gagged and tied him, led him into our lines! From this trembling hero we learned that the greater part of McDowell's forces were on the move across country to Stone Bridge or the vicinity, and that the fight would certainly begin at dawn; heavy masses being sent round to turn our left, and get into Manassas by the flank. When we were relieved at midnight, we communicated our fragments of information to the officer of the guard, and returned across Bull Run to our regiment, bivouacked in a cedar grove, and refreshed ourselves.

But ere I attempt to give details of the important engagement of the morrow, I must be permitted, in a short digression, to speak of important movements that were taking place all night long within the Federal lines. Mr. Thornton, an English gentleman, possessed of a very large and handsome estate about a mile northward of Centreville, and, being of Southern sentiments, left his plantation on the approach of McDowell's forces, (on Wednesday night,) and fled with his friends across Sudley's Ford towards Manassas—a distance of some seven or more miles. Hearing that the Yankees invariably destroyed all property found deserted, he returned on Saturday through the woods to ascertain the fate of his house, barns, and stock. When within half a mile of his premises, he observed large columns of the enemy making a *détour* through the country, so as to flank Sudley Ford. That this was their intention he had no doubt, for it was far beyond our left wing, and the stream there only ankle-deep. He attempted to retreat at nightfall, but found that the ford was hemmed in by large masses of troops—far greater in number than he observed congregated round Stone Bridge, (our extreme left,) about two miles lower down the stream. Determined to advise our generals of these movements, he made several attempts to pass the lines, but failed and was fired at repeatedly. Penetrating the woods by cow-paths well known to him, (being an extensive stock-raiser,) he finally succeeded in crossing the Run, and set off post-haste for the nearest head-quarters. It was past two A.M. on Sunday when Mr. Thornton ushered himself into the presence of Colonel Nathan Evans, who commanded a brigade near Stone

Bridge. Evans listened to the narration, asked important questions, and, arriving at conclusions, maliciously showed his white teeth with a wicked grin, and, ordering coffee, dressed himself. Mounted men were immediately sent to Beauregard, yet no additional force arrived, and Evans was left to his own resources. Detaching a portion of his brigade, he immediately moved up towards Sudley Ford, and reenforced the Fourth Alabama Regiment and a Mississippi battalion he found stationed there.

CHAPTER V.

FROM various causes, I was destined to enjoy but little sleep, and was on the move nearly all night. The great lights around Centreville seemed to die out about midnight, but then arose a low murmuring noise, as if large bodies of men had thus early risen, and were marching through country west of the river. Soon afterwards, being sent to the outposts, my ear quickly detected heavy masses moving along the road towards Stone Bridge, and I could faintly hear the shouts of teamsters and artillery drivers whipping up their horses. The bumping of heavy wagons and artillery was distinctly audible, while now and then the command could be faintly heard in the still night—"Attention, battalion!—forward, march!" This continued passage of men along our front gave me very melancholy forebodings regarding the enemy's force, more especially as serious fears were entertained regarding the remainder of Johnston's command in the Shenandoah, for it was now nearly three A.M., and still no troops had arrived!

Could it be that the enemy had sent a heavy force, torn up the track, and seized the "Gap"? None could tell; few dared speak on the subject; but those who knew our weakness, and the necessity for the speedy arrival of reenforcements, whispered their fears of the deadly conflict that would be surely ushered in at dawn. Again and again cocks on neighboring farms carolled forth the hour. At last the first grey streaks of morning appeared in the sky, with the pure pale moon slowly descending below the distant woods. The waters of the river audibly rippled past — otherwise, not a sound was heard save the quick, sharp challenge, "Halt!—who goes there?"

By entering into conversation with a well-informed comrade, I ascertained the precise position and number of our forces. Ewell's brigade constituted our extreme right, and was across Bull Run, posted at Union Mills; D. R. Jones's brigade came next, being south of the river, at McLean's (or Wolf) Ford; Longstreet's brigade was at Blackburn's Ford; Bonham's brigade at Mitchell's Ford; Philip St. George Cocke's brigade was posted at Ball's Ford, three miles farther up stream ; while Colonel Nathan Evans, with two regiments, guarded Stone Bridge— making a distance of nine miles from the right to our extreme left. There were several other fords farther up, namely, the Red House Ford, and still higher, Sudley Ford, etc.; but Stone Bridge was generally considered our extreme left. The right of our line was much stronger than the left in position and numbers, even without considering the two reserve brigades of Holmes and Early, which were stationed with the former for emergencies.

At which of these points the meditated blow might fall none could foresee. Scott was said to be a crafty general, and there can be no doubt that he taxed his little genius rather heavily on this occasion to assist McDowell, who, as our prisoners assured us, held the chief command. I had scarcely returned to camp, about five A.M., when all were afoot and ready for moving. The sun had risen in more than usual splendor, and as I stood on a hill across McLean's Ford, gazing upon the distant landscape, the effect was beautiful. To our right and eastward, on the heights of Centreville, Porter's artillery was deliberately shelling Blackburn's and McLean's Fords, the smoke, in the most beautiful and fantastically formed volumes, curling away from the cannon's mouth. Westward, rose the dark outline of the Blue Ridge, which inclosed, as in an amphitheatre, the woods and hollows, the streams and open spaces of Manassas Plains. Smoke, ascending from the woods on both sides of the stream of Bull Run, eight miles away in the direction of Stone Bridge, told that the fight had commenced there, while the frequent reports of artillery proved that both sides were becoming angry, and replying sharply and vindictively to each other. Occasional sounds of musketry fire, fronting Blackburn's and Mitchell's Fords, indicated that Longstreet's and Bonham's brigades at the centre were engaged in heavy skirmishes, though the enemy seemed disinclined to attempt any serious assault upon those positions. As soon as the first guns disturbed the peace of this calm and beautiful Sabbath morning, Johnston and Beauregard had galloped forward, and taken up a position on a hill to the left and rear of Bonham at Mitchell's Ford, where a full view was obtained of the entire line of Bull Run. The enemy saw the group of officers, and shell fell thick in the vicinity. These demonstrations met with no response: our generals-in-chief were intently watching the development of McDowell's movements, and seemed undecided as to his real point of attack. They had not remained long searching the plain with their glasses, when an increasing volume of smoke four miles to the left revealed the fact that the Federals were in force at that point. This was presently confirmed by the arrival of orderlies, who reported that the fire was brisk at Stone Bridge; that we held our own there, but that a strong column under Colonel Hunter had successfully crossed higher up at Sudley Ford, driven Evans back, and was slowly progressing, at right angles to the river, towards the Red House.

Colonel Evans having been forewarned of this movement, as we have elsewhere shown, had posted about one thousand men and two light pieces near the intersection of the Warrenton Turnpike and Sudley Road. This handful of troops resisted the advance of Hunter, until they were compelled by superior numbers to retire across the Ford; and this being effected, they took up another position in the woods. The movement was misunderstood by the enemy, who, believing our force to be routed, halted at the Ford some little time to refresh themselves and fill their canteens. They then crossed in admirable order, and had advanced about a mile, when our two guns opened fire upon them, and blocked up the lane with dead. The enemy now hurried forward their artillery, and, soon overpowering ours, advanced again, meeting with a desperate resistance from Evans's heroes, whose precision of fire inflicted severe loss on the masses opposed to them.

While these events were progressing at Sudley Ford, other parts of the field began to develop more fully the enemy's plan of battle. The reader must picture to himself Wheat's immortal battalion (the Louisiana) and a few other troops still engaged with Tyler's (First) division of three brigades at Stone Bridge,* while Evans at Sudley Ford is slowly retiring before the four brigades of Hunter. Then Colonel Heintzelman, with the Second division, is seen moving towards Red House Ford between these two valiant leaders; and joining forces with Hunter, he proceeds—still at right angles with the river—to Stone Bridge, his object being to disperse the little force under Major Wheat, and allow Tyler's division to cross. Heintzelman was, in some degree, baffled and held in check. But arriving at and crossing the ford, he discovered one of our regiments (Fourth Alabama) drawn up to receive him. Recalling his skirmishers, Heintzelman cheered on the New-York "Fire Zouaves" (fifteen hundred strong) leading gallantly himself. Our Alabamians allow them to approach within fifty yards, when they deliver a volley from eight hundred Mississippi rifles, and scatter the Zouaves beyond all recall. They are reformed, harangued, reminded of their vows, their banners are shaken out, and cheers given for the Union—but "advance" they will not. The morale of these braves was destroyed : they were afterwards seen in companies, or small detachments, but never as a regiment.

Disgusted with their behavior, Heintzelman turned in his saddle, and observing the gallant appearance of the Fourteenth Brooklyn (New-York) Zouaves, placed himself at their head, and again advanced; but again the calm line of Alabamians

* General Thomas W. Sherman (brigadier of volunteers, in Tyler's division) is a fine, well-made man, six feet high, erect, moderately stout, precise in manner, but quick and voluble in discourse, fair complexion, and closely shaven. He was Captain First United States Artillery, and served during the Mexican war. His battery was well-known for its efficiency and drill, and was generally called "Sherman's battery." When he retired from the United States service he ranked as major. He lived in Louisiana for some time, and conducted a semi-military academy at Alexandria in that State, in which occupation he realized much money. When war seemed inevitable between the North and South, he gave up his academy, and offered his services to the Lincoln Government, to assist in killing the pupils who gave him bread. He was appointed Brigadier-General of volunteers, and made himself conspicuous at Manassas. In the old army he enjoyed great reputation as an artillerist, but now seems to have sunk into oblivion, or all talent has departed, for we never hear of him as distinguishing himself. His once famous battery, subsequent to his resignation, was commanded by Captain James B. Ricketts, of New-York, who greatly distinguished himself at Manassas, and quite eclipsed the fame of Sherman as an artillery officer.

delivered a fatal volley, and again the crack Federal troops broke and fled. A Massachusetts regiment was next brought up to clear the way, but this, and two other regiments which followed it, quailed before the murderous volleys of the "Fourth." The only regiment that *did* stand *two* volleys, was a Michigan, or Western regiment. Numbers, however, began to tell, and Bee, who commanded the Alabamians and Mississipians, slowly fell back. By this time, it will be seen, the enemy had three full divisions and many guns across the stream, and the conflict began to assume a sanguinary aspect. To oppose their advance we had two light guns and one regiment under Evans, Seventh and Eighth Georgia under Bartow, Fourth Alabama, Second, and two companies of the Eleventh Mississippi, and four guns of Imboden's battery under Bee—a total of six guns and five regiments against fifteen thousand (including "regulars" and "marines") and twenty pieces of rifled artillery. Such being the disparity of numbers, the fight was maintained with desperation on our side. The enemy's line, at right angles with the river, was increasing in length every moment; their design, so far as we could judge, was to cut us off from Manassas, and entirely surround our small but heroic band. To add to our misfortune two small brigades had been detached from the division in front of Stone Bridge, and, finding a fordable place, had crossed under Sherman and Keyes, and appeared forming to our right and rear, leaving sufficient force at the bridge to occupy our small force under Major Wheat.

On the left the fight up to this time had been desperate. The attack on Hunter's column at Sudley Ford was made by Evans with a full consciousness of the disparity of force, and he expected no more success than consisted in delaying the movements of the enemy; yet such was the ardor of his men and their precision of fire, that he accomplished wonders. They were so exhausted, however, with continually advancing to the attack, and were so much weakened in numbers, that at last the men for the most part were firing from the woods in skirmishing order, and, being excellent marksman, inflicted much loss. It was impossible at this time to concentrate them at any one point, for each was fighting in his own style— "bushwhacking," as it is called. Yet they did not flinch, but continued an incessant fusilade upon the enemy, who seemed to fear that the attack was from our main body. In that conviction, they moved but slowly down towards the Red House Ford, where Bee's Mississippians and Bartow's Alabamians were struggling against the craftiness and numbers of Colonel Heintzelman.

I have already recorded how five of their best regiments were successively beaten back by a single one of ours, or rather parts of two. Bee led his men admirably. Again and again he formed and reformed his little band, encouraging all with words of kindness and confidence. He frequently assailed overwhelming numbers to prevent them securing the passage of Stone Bridge, beyond which heavy divisions were waiting to cross. He was only relieved when Jackson's Brigade and Hampton's Legion were brought up; then joining with Evans, their combined forces formed a longer and better line, and repelled the enemy with more ease, although the strength and precision of the opposing artillery made fearful havoc.

It will be remembered that Major Wheat's Louisiana battalion were left sole defenders of the bridge itself. Although few in number, these heroic soldiers sustained every shock with unwavering courage, and on more than one occasion dropped their rifles, and rushed among the enemy with long bowie-knives. But when it was known that Hunter had crossed at Sudley Ford, and formed a junction with Heintzelman at Red House Ford, Sherman's and Keyes's brigades left the force at Stone Bridge, and crossed a few hundred yards higher up, as related above; and Wheat was sent to prevent their junction with the other forces on the same side. As the majority of Wheat's command were Louisiana Irish, they robbed the dead of their whisky, and were in high spirits when ordered to assail Sherman and Keyes. They could not attempt this alone, but, receiving reenforcements, wrought such havoc among the enemy that their progress was extremely slow and uncertain. The fighting was irregular. Now, the battalion would keep up a lively fire from the woods, creep through the brush, make a sudden charge, upset a cannon or two and retire. Again, they would maintain a deathlike silence until the foe were not more than fifty paces off; then delivering a withering volley, they would dash forward with unearthly yells, and as they drew their knives and rushed to close quarters, the Yankees screamed with horror.

It is only fair to state that the Federal Colonels Hunter, Heintzelman, and others, nobly did their duty, and handled their troops with great precision and judgment. Scott's idea of attracting our attention on the right, and at Stone Bridge, while columns were marching through the woods to cross at Sudley and Red House Fords, was an excellent one, and it was carried out to the letter by his scientific subordinates. Had not our small force made a terrible resistance, it was more than possible the day would have proved disastrous to us, for our line was scattered over a distance of more than eight miles up and down the river, and our weakest point had been selected for the assault.

The events I have attempted to describe occupied the time till midday. There could be no longer a doubt of the enemy's real plan; and our small force under Bee gradually fell back toward the Robinson House, against vast odds, suffering severely at every yard. Johnston and Beauregard furiously galloped to the left, to retrieve our failing fortunes. Hampton's Legion and Jackson's Virginia Brigade had already arrived to succor Bee, and were ordered to lie down behind a bit of rising ground, so as to form the centre of a new line when Bee retreated thus far. Riding up to Jackson, who, on a mound, sat his horse like a statue, viewing the whole scene, Bee said: "General, they are beating us back—we're obliged to give ground." "Well, then, sir," was the dry, calm reply, "we will give them the bayonet!" Riding hurriedly back to his men, Bee cheered them with encouraging words, saying: "Look at Jackson yonder, boys!— he is standing like a stonewall!"

Finding that the enemy still assailed our left with overwhelming numbers and fury, General Beauregard conceived the idea of a forward movement on the right, hoping that it might serve as a diversion. Ewell and Jones were ordered to move into position and attack. The latter general marched three miles, and took up his line within half a mile of the enemy; but the extreme right failed to fire, and after remaining three hours, Jones retired south of the Run. It has been said that Ewell never received these orders. Be this as it may, Ewell, Jones, and Longstreet remained idle with their magnificent commands, while the roar of battle to the left was increasing every moment. In the distance shot and shell were ploughing up the ground Towards Manassas the dark Federal line was approaching slowly, like an immense serpent moving through the fields, while the numerous artillery of the enemy belched forth grape and shell upon our weak and small line.

The situation was now exceedingly critical, but reenforcements were rapidly approaching from Bonham's and Longstreet's brigades on the right, together with several pieces of artillery and some cavalry. Seizing an opportune moment, General Beauregard led on one wing, while Johnston, grasping the colors of the Fourth Alabama, rode to the front; and with a wild yell our men advanced again, and quickly recovered lost ground, having to move forward under showers of shell and small shot that assailed them at every step. Brilliant as this charge was, the enemy, it was plain, were overpowering us by weight of numbers. They had seized a plateau on which stood two wooden houses (Widow Henry's, and the free negro Robin- son's) and had placed thereon Ricketts's and Griffin's celebrated batteries.

General Beauregard, determined to repossess himself of the position, formed his line for an assault, and his right rushed to the charge, while our centre, under Jackson, pierced theirs. The plateau was won, together with several guns, but the enemy some time afterwards threw forward a heavy force of infantry and dispossessed us again.

It was now about two P.M., and the battle still raged furiously on the left, though nothing, save skirmishing and an occasional discharge of ordnance, occurred on our right. The brigades of Holmes and Early were ordered up, and the first arrived opportunely at the moment when our generals were preparing for another advance: at the same time, additional pieces of artillery came galloping up, by their eagerness for action and cheerfulness inspiriting all with bright hopes for the future. At the word to charge, our men seemed to have received new life, and advanced with loud shouts to drive the enemy from the plateau. Our artillery replied admirably, but the enemy were more than a match for us, and inflicted much loss. Our infantry, however, nothing daunted by the forces massed on the hill, resolutely attacked them, and after a stubborn and sanguinary combat the plateau, with the enemy's guns and ammunition, was again in our possession.

Pursuing the foe through the fields, our men never seemed weary of slaughter, although their own ranks were perceptibly thinning. It was while driving the enemy through the " open " that Bee and Bartow, riding in advance of their commands, fell mortally wounded. The latter, with colors in hand, survived a few moments, and, smiling on his comrades, said : " They have killed me boys; but never give up the fight." The enemy were puzzled and astounded by the change which two hours had produced in the tide of fortune ; as for ourselves, though still inferior in numbers, we had now no doubt of success: our reenforcements were rapidly arriving from the right, steadily our advance was continued through fields and woods, over hundreds of dead—friends and foes.

Such was the state of the battle, when, from appearances in the distance, it became evident that the enemy were planning and arranging some great final stroke for our overthrow. But while they rallied their broken line, under shelter of fresh brigades, and prepared for the renewal of the struggle, signals from the hills warned General Beauregard to "look out for enemy's advance on the left." I must here remind the reader that the remainder of Johnston's army had been anxiously expected from the Shenandoah Valley during the whole of the previous night; and it was these troops—Kirby Smith's brigade—that had been mistaken for the enemy. As the train approached Manassas, Smith knew by the firing that a great struggle was in progress, and, having stopped the engine, he formed his men, and advanced through the fields. Every countenance was brightened by the intelligence of his arrival at this juncture. " Johnston's men have come at last !" was the remark from mouth to mouth, and that commander instantly made dispositions for an enlargement of our line. While this was going on, Early's brigade also came up from the right, (for though the message, as I have before stated, was sent at noon, it was not received until past two,) and was instantly sent to our extreme left, while Kirby Smith was ordered to assail the enemy's right and rear, which his advance through the fields enabled him to do easily. Other reenforcements were coming from Bonham, Cocke, and Longstreet, and as they arrived were placed in position for a general advance.

On the side of the enemy, Colonels Hunter, Heintzelman, Sherman, Burnside, Keyes, and others, saw the storm approaching, and made every effort to meet it. They had re-formed their line, and endeavored to outflank our left; but at the very moment when Major Elzey with Kirby Smith's brigade of seventeen hundred men and four guns, and Early's brigade, (Seventeenth Virginia, Seventh Louisiana, and Thirteenth Mississippi,) attacked them on the right flank and rear, Beauregard and Johnston, also, threw forward their whole line, and with loud shouts advanced to the attack; twenty pieces of cannon at the same time shook the earth with their deafening roar. Among other regiments the following formed this last grand charge, namely: Eleventh, Second, and Thirteenth Mississippi; Seventh and Eighth Georgia ; Seventh Louisiana; Sixth North-Carolina; Fourth Alabama ; Tenth, Seventeenth, Fourth, Fifth, Twenty-seventh, Forty-third, Eighteenth, and Twenty-eighth Virginia ; Stuart's Cavalry, and Hampton's Legion; Fourth, Second, and Eighth South-Carolina ; Third Tennessee ; First Maryland, etc.

When the order was given to advance, couriers were sent to our right, with instructions for Longstreet, Jones, and Ewell to make a strong demonstration towards Centreville. The roar of cannon and musketry on the left was terrible; clouds of smoke and dust hung over the entire plain ; high above the din of the strife might be heard one of the enemy's heavy pieces, a thirty-two-pounder, called "Long Tom." Simultaneously attacked on all sides, and with unexampled fury, the foe made a determined resistance on a rising ground in the vicinity of Chinn's House, and it looked like an island round which flames were gathering in all directions. Appalled by the unexpected change of fortune, the Federal commanders knew not what to do. It was now past three in the afternoon, yet no reenforcements were at hand, and their cannon were being captured at every turn. In vain they rallied their forces ; no sooner were they formed than our troops broke them again, until at last their line, thousands in number, sought safety in

4

sudden flight. The landscape was darkened by their fugitive masses flying in all directions, and pursued by the half-wild victors.

The pursuit was the business of Stuart's cavalry, aided by artillery, and the scene that ensued was awful and heartrending. Ten miles from Centreville Heights, these fugitive thousands rushed across Bull Run by the various fords, and horse, foot, artillery, wagons, and ambulances were entangled in inextricable confusion; the roads were blocked up, reenforcements arriving were seized with a panic, and every one rushed towards Centreville by the roads, through the woods and fields. To add to their horror, Jones's brigade on the right, without waiting for Ewell or Longstreet, attacked their reserves on Centreville, and turned what would have been an orderly retreat into a disastrous rout. Thousands rushing towards Centreville for safety, only arrived in time to learn that our troops were advancing on the village, and that Blenker's and other reserve corps, unable to withstand the pressure, were rushing towards Washington. For miles around clouds of smoke and dust obscured the landscape, while the rattle of musketry and the cheers of Jones's brigade, as they, rushing into the deserted camps, and seizing upon the artillery, only added additional fears to the horror-stricken multitude. Kemper's and Beckham's batteries, on our left, also pursued the enemy, and kept up such a destructive fire upon them, that at many points of the road, wagons, artillery, caissons, ambulances, and carriages were jammed in masses, and thus barricaded the roads. At these points the fugitives took to the fields and woods, throwing away their arms and accoutrements, and whatever might impede flight. Even the sick and wounded were dragged from ambulances, and their places taken by red-legged Zouaves; ambulance, wagon, and artillery horses had their traces cut, and were mounted by officers of every grade, from captains to generals and governors of States. Such a roar, confusion, and dust it is impossible to imagine. Every road leading from Manassas was crowded by the fugitives—soldiers in every style of costume, ladies, members of Congress, governors of States, editors, "special correspondents," "own correspondents," telegraph operators, surgeons, paymasters, parsons—all were running for dear life—hatless, bootless and ragged, dusty and powder-blackened. Behind them thundered our avenging cavalry and artillery; while the sharp rattle of musketry at the foot of Centreville Heights told where Jones and Longstreet hurled destruction on their flank.

CHAPTER VI.

The Pursuit—Immense Booty—Our Prisoners and their Behavior—A Ride over the Field of Action—Incidents of the Fight—Arrival of President Davis during the Action, and its Effect—Behavior of the New-York Fire Zouaves—The Victorious Army did not Advance upon Washington or Maryland—Relic-mongers on the Field of Battle—Personal Appearance of President Davis—Sketches of Evans and Longstreet.

THOUGH a general pursuit was ordered, it was found impossible to overtake the enemy, so precipitate had been their flight; and as we advanced, the signs of the dreadful combat of that day seemed to multiply at every step. The dead and dying are common to every battle-field; but here were broken cannon-wheels, deserted camps, overturned caissons, large supplies of commissary stores, files of prisoners, captured wagons, maimed and staggering animals, dead horses, cannons in the mud — innumerable proofs of the haste, confusion, and discomfiture of the enemy. Now small squads of cavalry dashed in advance, then scattering musketry could be heard faintly in the distance; now a line of Federal wagons were found blocked up in the road, the traces cut and horses gone; again we came up with squads of red and blue-legged Yankee Zouaves marching good-humoredly to the rear; now a captured battery jingled along in the same direction; and as for the procession of stores, tents, wagons, ambulances, and private carriages, they seemed endless in number and variety. Completely exhausted with our labors, the regiment countermarched and bivouacked in one of the deserted camps, where barrels of excellent fresh crackers, hogsheads of hams and bacon, boxes of cheese, raisins, white sugar, coffee, tea, macaroni, well-fitted mess-chests, blankets, mattresses, and whiskey in abundance, soon made us forgetful of our late privations.

Our men were frantic with the glory of the day and the opportune discovery of such plentiful supplies. The Yankees had been lavish of expense in preparing for the "trip to Richmond," and their accumulated luxuries had fallen into the hands of those who could appreciate them. We found large numbers of beeves slaughtered and ready for butchering in their camps, but all the animals had been stolen from neighboring farms on their march. In fact, the destruction of private property, generally, was so great, that farmers were raving—they had been despoiled of almost every thing, and nothing was paid for. Hedges and fences were all rendered unserviceable; stacks of hay and straw were carted off or burned, and the inhabitants had to flee to the woods to escape insult or violence. Not a horse or mule was left in the country for miles around; the fugitives had seized and driven them off to Washington—as many as three being often seen bestraddling one poor, jaded beast—so anxious were these invaders to escape us. Coats, hats, boots, muskets, and accoutrements lined all the roads, and every by-path leading northward; remnants of clothing hung on every bush; and over all dense clouds of dust arose, blinding and choking every one. As the last rays of the sun shone upon the neighboring hills, we could plainly discern, with the aid of glasses, the roads of retreat marked by dense lines of dust rolling over the dark green landscape in the distance.

The prisoners taken were more dead than alive—men so pale and exhausted I never saw. Their uniforms were in tatters; they were, for the most part, shoeless, hatless, and literally gasping for water. With hair dishevelled, powder-begrimed and dusty faces, bloodshot eyes, and unstrung nerves, they were more the objects of pity than derision. As night came on, bodies of troops were moving in all directions; cavalry jingled by with strings of prisoners, and such were their pitiful appeals for water in passing, that several of our negroes were constantly employed in drawing it for them. Many of the wells we found choked up with all kinds of rubbish—some being filled with ammunition boxes, offal, and earth. Standing on the heights of Centreville the entire plain was made visible by the large number of camp-fires and bivouacs; and over all arose the busy hum of voices. Everywhere lanterns and torches flickered in the gloom, while Manassas Junction seemed to be in a blaze from the multitude of lights and fires. Every

house in Centreville was converted into an hospital—long lines
of wounded were carried in mournful procession, while in retired spots fatigue-parties were opening trenches for the dead.
But all were thoroughly exhausted; few were tempted by
pleasure or curiosity to move, and about nine P.M. our men
were sound asleep in their tents or around their watch-fires,
and the sentinels themselves stood as stationary as statues.

The incessant rumbling of batteries, wagons, and ambulances
broke my slumbers, while ever and anon I started up half in
fear: I was fighting the battle over in my dreams, and in this
state of semi-consciousness experienced far more danger and
adventure than I had done in the actual engagement. Aroused
by the crowing of cocks at twilight, I refreshed myself with a
bath in Bull Run, and found all kinds of clothing floating past,
torn, muddy, and bloody. · Then, having received orders to
proceed to Manassas, I procured a good mount, and chose the
most circuitous route, by Stone Bridge and Sudley Ford. My
course was for some distance parallel with the river, through
scenes of carnage and destruction indescribable. Near the
bridge crossing Cub Run there were not less than a dozen
wagons overturned; wounded men were sheltering themselves
under trees from the heavy rain; tents were torn and flapping
in the wind on every hand, and the mud was almost impassable. Approaching Stone Bridge, my sight was pained by corn-
fields trodden down; meadows trampled to mud; farm-houses
riddled by shot and shell, and orchards destroyed forever;
chimneys and gables, stone fences and walls, were crumbling
in ruins, while the dead, and sometimes the dying, lay in heaps
as they had fallen.

Having crossed Stone Bridge, I perceived that the face of the
whole country in front was disfigured, if not destroyed; and
here numerous mounds of newly-turned earth bespoke the
labors of fatigue-parties. The scene was too melancholy. Re-
crossing, I proceeded up the stream, and passed the large and
beautiful fields over which the Federals had marched in their
flank movement and line of retreat. As much as possible, this
movement had been concealed from us by marching through
the woods; but as I approached Sudley Ford, the proofs that
great bodies of men had passed here were multiplied. ₁The
Ford was not more than knee-deep; and as I crossed, every

step convinced me that the combat had begun in earnest the moment it was attempted by the enemy. The old Stone Church and all the neighboring houses were perforated with shot, and the ground was thickly covered with branches of trees cut by shot and shell. All the houses, barns, and out-houses, and also the church here, were used as hospitals, not less than five hundred of the enemy being under the treatment of their own and our surgeons.

Hastening towards Manassas, I came upon the fields where the enemy's flanking column had been routed on the previous afternoon. The ground was excessively heavy from the fall of rain, and I did not examine it minutely; in fact, the sight of the wounded — of headless and limbless trunks, and all the sad aspects of war — was too revolting, and I passed hurriedly by without numbering or examining the large pits newly opened for the reception of the dead. This was the spot (about two miles from Manassas) which the closing scenes of the day had rendered forever memorable, some additional particulars of which may here be given.

From a distance, on the day of battle, I had observed the gradual lengthening of a large black line from Sudley Ford towards Manassas, but until the afternoon could not comprehend it. This, however, was the brigaded force of the enemy preparing for the final struggle; and about three P.M., not fewer than twenty-five of our pieces opened fire upon it. Our scattered infantry, at the same time, were re-formed and reenforced, but so steady was the progress made by the enemy, that Beauregard had thought it prudent to call up Colonel Jackson with the reserves to protect the retreat that seemed inevitable. Colonel Evans had not proceeded many yards on this errand when he was recalled, our general having been warned by the field telegraph that troops were approaching on the left. Whether they were friends or foes could not be determined, till an orderly, dashing forward, resolved all doubts. " Colonel Terry," said Beauregard, his face lighting up, " ride forward and order General Kirby Smith to hurry up his brigade, and strike them on the flank and rear."

This important episode in the events of the day occurred in front of the enemy. At the same moment, Manassas station was the scene of a transaction not less memorable for its bearing upon the final issue of the struggle. The Richmond train, which had started at seven A.M., but from various accidents did not arrive sooner, was drawn into the station, and from it President Davis instantly alighted, and, mounting his horse, galloped towards the scene of action. The first person he met was his own brother, Colonel Joe Davis. "Return, brother," said the latter, "the day is lost — they have outflanked us, and will be here in less than half an hour." "If that be true," the President replied, "our right place is on the field with the boys." Rapidly galloping towards the line of fire, he discovered Kirby Smith's brigade advancing at the "double-quick," in obedience to the order just received from Beauregard, and the President being recognized, a wild, enthusiastic yell burst from the men as they furiously dashed on the Yankee flank, and instantly broke it! The scene of confusion that then ensued was truly appalling. Believing that the whole of Johnston's army was in the rear, the right wing of the enemy broke and fled in inextricable confusion, crossing the Run at different points, and infusing a panic into whole brigades and divisions, as already related.

To return to my remembrances of the field after the battle. Manassas Junction, when I reached the spot, resembled a vast fair. Hundreds of persons were moving about from enclosure to enclosure, viewing the parti-colored prisoners, who were temporarily confined in sheds. In one place were several hundreds of muscular fellows in red trowsers and caps, blue jackets and white gaiters; these were the famous Fire Zouaves of New-York, about whom so much had been said and written by the whole North. Their behavior was scandalous, and outraged all decency; it being incredible that troops who had behaved so cowardly before an inferior force, should still be so full of bombast as to insult the very men who had voluntarily deprived themselves of food and blankets to feed and warm them. But let this pass. In all directions were prisoners of every grade, of every corps, and every imaginable style of uniform. Around the dépôt were piled immense stores of flour, rice, sugar, coffee, clothing, medicines, ammunition, and, conspicuous above all, thirty pieces of cannon. Other pieces were in our hands, but had not yet been brought in. The rain pouring in torrents, rendered walking impracticable; so, having fulfilled the orders intrusted to me, and satisfied my curiosity, I remounted, and crossing the fields south of the Run, rejoined my regiment, now snugly encamped in the Yankee tents beyond Centreville.

It would be difficult to imagine any thing more dreary than the face of the country over which I had journeyed. The rain was pouring in torrents, thunder rolled and crashed in every direction, and stately trees were struck down by the lightning. Conveyances were sunk in mud up to the axles; horsemen picked their way as best they could; the whole army was wet, dreary, drowsy, dirty, and mud-locked. It was physically impossible for troops to advance in such weather, and not all the ingenuity of man could have moved an army over such a country. But even had this been possible, the army was totally unfit to move. We had gained an important victory by accident, but our troops required far more experience than they then possessed to commence siege operations and beleaguer the capital of a numerous and opulent people. Small as our army was, it was deficient in every thing but courage: the quartermaster's, commissary, and other departments were in the hands of inexperienced civilians; the cavalry was totally inadequate to our necessities; the artillery weak and unorganized, imperfectly supplied with matériel of the worst description, and indifferently disciplined. It was impossible it could be otherwise in an army so hurriedly formed as ours had been; and hence, having a fair knowledge of the facts, I cannot but fully concur in the majority vote of the council of war which decided against an advance on Washington. Besides military, there were doubtless cogent political reasons for this decision; but though partially informed, it is not my province to speak of them here.

Leaving the direction of affairs to those responsible for them, and with unbounded confidence in their ability, our men betook themselves to gayety on a small scale, or occupied their leisure hours in writing home; the daily mail occasionally weighing not less than one ton. Strangers poured into Manassas daily to see the "sights," and carry off "relics." Uniforms, arms, buttons, caps, and even skulls were seized with avidity, and where Bartow, Bee, Fisher, and other heroes had fallen, the woods were stripped of every branch that could be converted into a walking-stick or cane. The vitiated tastes and vulgar curiosity of these people were disgusting. Hundreds of non-combatants daily trudged through the mud from field to field, examining localities with intense curiosity and loquacious patriotism. Even when, during warm weather, the effluvia from graves and unburied matter was unbearable, these relic-mongers might be seen, hovering over the fields like carrion crows, carrying off all kinds of trifles, including twenty-four pound shot and shell ; any imaginable article, heavy or light, that could, with any show of reason, be called a " relic."

During the week, when the weather had cleared and the scorching July sun blazed again as of old, by common consent we all took to the woods, and encamped there. As for " Jeff. Davis," it appears that when the rout of the enemy was complete, he had ridden without escort along the lines ; but his features and figure were so well known that he was quickly discovered, and loud yells of delight rang out from our whole army. Taking advantage of the fall of evening, he " dropped in " upon our officers, (many of whom were fellow-townsmen, or ex-members of the U. S. branches of Legislature,) to have a quiet chat. As I had never seen a live President, my curiosity was on the *qui vive*, and when his presence was whispered to me, I found him sitting at our colonel's tent-door, with a circle of captains and lieutenants, conversing very quietly on State affairs, but with no more animation or sign of pleasure than if a victorious army was not around, or a beaten one flying from, him. In citizen attire, with beaver hat, and smoking a cigar, he listened to all that was said, assented or dissented with a nod of the head, and some time afterwards, mounting his grey mare ambled off to Manassas, as unostentatiously as if he were the least person in the Confederacy. Since then I have seen the President frequently on different fields of battle, and have observed little change in his habitually modest and thoughtful demeanor, although on many occasions his proud and victorious troops, unconscious of his presence, were rending the skies with their shouts or charging the enemy with unexampled fury.

The brigadier under whom we had hitherto served pleased the men so little that it was deemed advisable to appoint in his stead Colonel Nathan Evans, whose generalship and gallantry at Stone Bridge and Sudley Ford had won for him universal esteem. We had been informed that our command was under marching orders, and parade was just over when three horsemen galloped into camp, and saluted the colonel. These were none other than Evans, Longstreet, and Ewell—names that are now forever hallowed in the hearts and history of our gallant army. From their style of riding and peculiar seat in the saddle, I at first sight took them for dragoons, and was not mistaken. Evans was very restless, and his horse reared and chafed, and plunged to the right and left all the time he staid with us. He is about forty years of age, with a head of the cast of Tom Moore's; slightly bald; small restless black eyes; heavy black moustaches; and when he smiles, displays incomparable teeth; but has a quick, cunning, and snappish look, although his manner is polished and polite. His countenance looks like one who dissipates occasionally; he is of medium stature, angular in his movements, never happy but when in the saddle—a perfect soldier in every thing, and "swears like a trooper."

Longstreet is a powerfully-built man, somewhat bald, about five feet ten inches high, with sandy hair and whiskers—the latter allowed to grow untrimmed. He possesses a fine bluish-gray eye, of great depth, penetration, and calculation; seldom speaks unnecessarily, seems absorbed in thought, and very quiet in manner. Ewell I did not see distinctly; he was continually moving about, prying into our camp arrangements, and looking towards Manassas with his glass. All three were dressed as citizens, with heavy black felt hats on, and except pistols in their holsters, were unarmed and unattended. These officers have since acquired immortal fame. I myself have been witness to their achievements, of which more anon.

CHAPTER VII.

Battle of Oak Hill in Missouri — The Confederates under Price and McCulloch are surprised, but prove victorious — Death of the Federal General Lyon, and Pro. motion of General Fremont — Misunderstanding between Southern Generals— Cruel Devastation of the Country by Federal Troops — Character of Fremont— Siege and Capture of Lexington by Price—Immense Booty.

THE scene of action now shifts to Missouri, and, as before, I am able to give authentic details of the events that took place in that State, having received the following letter descriptive of the battles of "Oak Hill" and "Lexington:"

"DEAR TOM: My last letter informed you that, after the action of Carthage, the small commands of Price, McCulloch, and Pearce were on their way to Cowskin Prairie, in order to recruit and organize. We had not remained in this wilderness of a place many days when information was brought that Lyon and Sturgis had suddenly ceased their pursuit, bewildered by the unexpected discomfiture of Sigel at Carthage. After a halt, Lyon, Sigel, and others formed a junction at Springfield, where they numbered some twelve or fifteen thousand men, well armed, disciplined, and counting among them a heavy force of U. S. regulars of all arms. In the mean time we our-selves were receiving reenforcements, and in a few days could count upwards of nine thousand, under the command of General Price; of these, however, thousands had no arms whatever, and had to depend entirely on chance for their future supply.

" Not only were we deficient in weapons, but when the march on Springfield commenced our commissary and quartermaster's departments, but recently organized, proved very indifferent, and it was seldom the men drew full rations. They made up for all deficiencies, however, by laying violent hands on every thing that came within reach, appropriating large quantities of green corn, and eating it. They also extensively patronized the various corn-cribs on their several routes, and, shelling the corn, pounded it between rocks until reduced to powder, and then made bread. Hogs were plentiful, as also beef cattle; and farmers, being friendly to our cause, willingly sold all things for Confederate paper, so that it much relieved the commissariat, and eased the line of march. Ben McCulloch, with his small column, led the way; Pearce of Arkansas followed; and last came the hero and patriot, Sterling Price, with his ragged, half-fed, and ill-armed band of Missourians.

"After many days of toilsome travel, we approached a point thirty miles south of Springfield, where it was reported Lyon and Sigel were encamped on hills beside the road. We halted until the next morning, and then, cautiously advancing, found that the enemy had decamped and gone in the direction of Springfield. Their strength we could not ascertain with precision, but they were said to number at least ten thousand men, well armed, well drilled, and counting thousands of "regulars" among them. They also had a strong force of cavalry, and some twenty pieces of artillery—Totten's battery being considered one of the best in the old Federal army. Our effective force amounted to about five thousand ill-armed, badly drilled men, and some six thousand horsemen, who were, for politeness' sake, called cavalry; but they had not a particle of discipline among them; they had been drilled to serve on foot, and were armed with every imaginable weapon; their horses, too, were little better than skeletons.

"Finding that the enemy had fallen back the day previous before our advance-guard, we hurried forward in pursuit; but after a march of some twenty miles, the men were completely broken down from fatigue and the want of proper supplies. On the tenth of August we camped at Wilson's Creek, about ten miles south of Springfield, and the whole country was scoured for provisions. Whatever the fields produced was instantly appropriated, and many of us thanked Providence for the abundance of green corn. Ben McCulloch had halted his advance on the right of the road, assisted by Pearce, while Price was on the left of it; and thoughtless of danger—in fact, never dreaming of Lyon being in the vicinity at all—threw out no pickets; or if any *were* in advance, they were few indeed. In the evening little was thought of but amusement:

most of the boys were dancing and kicking up their heels until a late hour, as lively as if the enemy were a thousand miles away. But hardly had the sun risen, when the sharp report of firearms on our right and rear awoke every one, and the word passed from mouth to mouth: 'They are here! fall in, fall in! we are surprised! quick! quick! we are surrounded! fall in! fall in!' McCulloch *was* surprised, as none will venture to deny, and before his line was formed, loud drumming in Price's command convinced him that we were all alike in a precarious condition. Sigel, in fact, was attacking our right and rear with great vigor, and his shot and shell were bouncing into our camps and throwing every thing into confusion.

"When our men had recovered from their excitement and formed line, it was found that Sigel had already advanced some distance, while Lyon, hearing that Sigel was fairly engaged, pushed the centre and left with great energy. Totten's battery was admirably posted on an eminence, and ploughed up the ground in our front. Yet there old Price, our gallant commander, rode up and down the line, with white hair streaming in the wind, cheering, forming, and encouraging his ragged musketeers, who, by their incessant discharges and their accurate aim, stopped Lyon's advance, and equalized the fight in the centre and left, while McCulloch was stemming the storm on the right and rear. Observing the destructive effect of the fire of Sigel's guns, McCulloch determined to make a bold dash, and, if possible, silence them. Collecting a few Louisianians, he rushed to the right and rear, and found one of our batteries already engaged in that quarter. Some confusion was caused by the accuracy of our fire, taking advantage of which, McCulloch dashed forward with his companies, and before the enemy could recover from their astonishment, five guns fell into our hands, and other forces instantly following up the movement, our irregular horse dashed in upon them with a terrific yell, discharging their shot-guns, rifles, and revolvers, at short distance, captured their sixth and last piece, and began cutting and slashing about them with the wildest fury. Sigel was totally routed! His infantry, opposed to ours, were not better than Dutchmen usually are; and their flight was expedited by artillery, which hammered away at them, dropping shell into every little group, and clearing our whole front in that direction.

"But while the battle progressed in our favor on the right, Lyon was pushing Price with great vigor in the centre and left. Our men stood manfully to their guns against the accurate and deadly fire of the Federal 'regulars,' but their loss was considerable, for the enemy occupied a hill, and every advance upon them was opposed by discharges from their whole force. At length, owing to the success of our right, Price was reenforced both with men and artillery; perceiving which, it was obvious to Lyon that nothing short of desperate courage could turn the tide now setting against him. Rallying his forces in a gallant manner, he rode to their front, and waving a handkerchief, cheered them on, making himself a conspicuous mark for our musketeers. He had been wounded in the leg early in the day, but rode to the rear, had it dressed, and laughingly observed that 'all was going on well,' and 'he'd turn up trumps before night.' As our men advanced up the hill against the masses of infantry launched against them, Lyon (whom I recognized, on the field, having frequently seen him in St. Louis) was riding hastily from point to point, cheering and leading his men; but when we reached the top of the hill he was not to be seen, and I concluded he must have fallen by one of the many muskets that were pointed at him.

"On reaching the brow of the hill, we found the enemy strongly posted, and apparently determined to make a stout resistance. We cheered, and made a rush for the guns, but masses of their infantry came forward and protected the retreat; and it was not until our whole force was collected and hurled at this point, that they finally gave way, and left the field in great confusion. Having secured the field, the wildest excitement and howling ensued; our cavalry were sent forward to follow them up, but little was effected. We captured many prisoners and arms, besides ammunition and stores. We pursued the enemy several miles, and then returning to camp, made ourselves comfortable on the good things which had fallen to our lot. The body of poor Lyon was found among the dead, and was decently coffined and sent to Springfield for interment. It was discovered that two small buckshot had penetrated, one above, and another below, the left nipple: death must have been almost instantaneous.*

"In this action, we captured six cannon, many wagons, a quantity of stores, and five or six hundred stand of arms. Our loss was estimated at two hundred and fifty killed, and one thousand wounded and missing; of these Price claims to have lost one hundred and fifty killed, and five hundred wounded. The loss of the Federals in killed, wounded, and prisoners, was about two thousand. Of the battle-field I can say little, except that our safety was due to the impetuosity and valor of our men, as both Sigel and Lyon crept upon us during night, and took up commanding positions, from which the latter was driven with much difficulty, and not until after an obstinate and bloody fight. We ought to thank God that things turned out so favorably for us, as the most sanguine could never have anticipated such a complete overthrow of the enemy.

"When our troops had fully rested themselves, and the various departments were reduced to a better system of daily routine, it was the desire of Price to move on with the whole army towards the Upper Missouri, seize the enemy's stores, supply the unarmed with weapons, and, if need be, procure them upon the battle-field, ere the foe could recover from his late defeat, and mature fresh plans. As one reason, I ought to mention that information was constantly reaching us that Fremont, the new Federal Commander-in-Chief, was actively en-

---

* Major-General Nathaniel Lyon was a Connecticut Yankee of the abolition type; not more than forty-five years of age, small in stature, wiry, active, with dark hair and complexion, small black eyes; fond of military pomp, but an excellent, though restless, and ambitious officer. He entered the United States army as Second Lieutenant, July first, 1841; was made Captain by brevet, August twentieth, 1847; and arrived in St. Louis in April, 1861, having been sent from his post far in the South-West to stand a court-martial on the charge of peculation. His great activity in aiding the suppression of Southern feeling in St. Louis endeared him to the abolitionists; he seized the arsenal, erected defences round the city, disarmed the Camp Jackson Southern sympathizers, and rapidly rose from the rank of captain to that of Major-General in two months. His cruelty to all suspected of Southern sentiment, and in the administration of affairs, will long be remembered by all who had the misfortune to live under his brief and arbitrary rule. But his bravery was undoubted, and had his troops imitated his reckless daring, events might have proved very unfavorable to us in Missouri. His body was interred by us in a metallic coffin at Springfield, but subsequently given to his friends, who removed it north to Connecticut, where it now reposes beneath a costly monument.

gag*d in forming a large army in St. Louis, and, having unlimited funds and supplies, was likely to take the field in great
strength.   The desire of Price, however, did not meet with the
approval of General McCulloch, who wished to fall back on
the frontier of Arkansas, and allow the enemy to weary themselves in huntiug for him.   Price was patriotic enough to waive
every personal consideration, but in this case his judgment was
against concession, and as the State had not then 'formally'
seceded, he held no commission under the Confederate seal, and
was not bound to obey McCulloch.   Accordingly, finding there
was no prospect of arriving at unanimity, either in sentiment
or action, he pushed forward alone towards the Missouri, and
was everywhere hailed as the chief and father of all.   You never
saw such patriotism as was displayed on every hand; and
although, at best, we were a poor undrilled body of adventurers living upon the public, and trusting to heaven for supplies, our regiments and brigades were animated with a burning
enthusiasm for action, and an unbounded confidence in our
leader, which were enough to carry us through any enterprise.

"Everywhere, as we proceeded, signs were multiplied of the
wanton waste and recklessness of the Dutch dastards and Northern fanatics in the pay of Fremont.   He was the most ultra
abolitionist who could be found, and Frank Blair pointed him
out as 'of the right stripe'—the 'coming man'—'one who
would put the war upon a proper footing! seize and confiscate
the property of all who dared oppose the ruling system of
Northern Government,' etc.   Truly the barbarities of our enemies are beyond all description.   All law—save military law—
is suspended, banks robbed of specie, wealthy men '·compelled'
to contribute largely for the wholesale destruction of friends
and relatives, to say nothing of their political rights; prisons
full in every city where their rule is paramount; *Habeas Corpus*
laughed at, dwellings seized, property confiscated, negroes sold
and carried away, farms destroyed, cattle driven off, barns,
houses, burned before their owners' eyes, while mothers, wives,
sisters, or daughters, are insulted and disgraced, and oftentimes
murdered.   All this is true.   God forbid I should exaggerate;
and were I willing to do so, things are so bad they could *not* be
painted worse, with all the coloring in the world.   Our whole

5

march to this place has presented harrowing sights—wid6ws, wives, children, and the aged, standing houseless by the wayside, their homes in flames and ruins, 'because the rebels are coming, and it is a military necessity!'

"You will not ask if they are Missourians who have done these things; you know the character of our fellow-countrymen too well. These destroyers are the valiant German and Dutch heroes of Sigel, runaways from battle-fields, who show their paltry spite to helpless little ones, whose fathers and brothers are fighting for freedom of thought, word, and action. Heaven forbid that the name of Missourians should be placed on such a record! Yet there *are* ambitious leaders among them, who riot in devastation, and care not who perish, so they may rule. A German republic or empire is their dream, and already their general is assuming all the trumpery and airs of foreign courts — already he travels in state, has a German bodyguard, tricked out in what appears to be the cast-off finery of a third-class theatrical wardrobe. When he travels on the river, an entire steamboat is not more than sufficient to accommodate the majesty of Fremont; guards pace before his door night and day; servants in gay livery hand around catawba on silver waiters; grooms and orderlies flit about like poor imitations of the same class of servants in German cities, while the ruling language of the court is *very* low Dutch, redolent of lager-beer and schnapps! But to return to the true object of this hurried letter.

"From those constantly arriving in camp, it was ascertained beyond a doubt that Fremont was strongly fortifying all important cities on the Missouri River, to serve as a safe base of operations, whence supplies could be easily transported into the interior by wagon-trains or boats. Lexington, held by Colonel Mulligan and a heavy force, was known to be strongly fortified, and being on high ground, it commanded all approaches from the interior, while the river was kept open for the transit of any number of troops from St. Louis. Price determined to march forward and attack it, but was informed that large bands of outlaws from Kansas, under General Jim Lane and others, were devastating the whole country on his left flank, and threatened to get in his rear. Suddenly diverging from his proper route, Price sent Rains and Parsons up in that direction, with a small force of determined men; and so secretly was the expedition conducted, that they unexpectedly came upon Lane at a creek called Drywood, and after a confused fight of some hours, drove the enemy from the field, pushed forward to their headquarters at Fort Scott, and captured it, with every thing intact. Joining the column under Price again, our army of five thousand effectives and five guns pushed forward towards Lexington, and arrived in the vicinity on the thirteenth of September.

"Our 'irregular' horse (for I can call them nothing else) did good service in scouring the country for supplies, and keeping the enemy within the lines of the town, and although frequently invited to combat, the noble Yankees remained quietly within their chain of breastworks, and refused every offer. By the eighteenth, our ammunition-wagons and artillery had arrived, and the infantry being sufficiently rested, Price broke up his encampment at the Fair Grounds, several miles from town, and advanced against the city. The Fair Grounds, I may tell you, would have proved an admirable position for us had the enemy ventured to attack; indeed, it was surmised that, upon hearing of our appearance at Lexington, Fremont would have collected his available force in St. Louis, and coming up in boats, re-enforced Mulligan, and chased us out of the country.

"Our General was aware of the strength of the city, and made his dispositions accordingly. He knew there were several steamboats under the bluff, and that the enemy's supply of water depended entirely upon the river. An assault was out of the question, as the college buildings and other strong edifices had been converted into forts, and mounted with guns which swept every approach. Our men knew, however, that there were immense supplies of all kinds in the place, including cannon, horses, wagons, ambulances, thousands of small-arms, important state documents, and much specie, which had been robbed from banks throughout the country; and as some thought the officers were too slow and careful in approaching through the outskirts, they resolved to charge the enemy's line of intrenchments placed higher up in town. They made the trial, and suffered considerably, and were then satisfied that cautious measures were the best. Rains's force moved forward, and without much opposition occupied a good position north-north-east of the breastworks, and with two batteries maintained an effective and destructive fire upon them, from which there was no escape; Parsons moved up south-south-west, and was also favorably posted; each of these brigades having supports·within call, should the enemy sally down from the hill, and attempt to dislodge them from their hastily-constructed field-works. A heavy body of sharpshooters, thrown out in front, were ready to harass and cut off the gunners, and all such as might appear in sight carrying water from the river or the wells. By these operations gradual approach was made upon the foe, who lost every hour from the deadly accuracy of our skirmishers, and made several attempts to dislodge them, without success.

"While these events were transpiring at Lexington, Price received word (September eighteenth) that General D. R. Atcheson (formerly President of the United States Senate) and Colonel Saunders were coming down the north bank of the river to support him. Having reached a point twenty-five miles above the city, two thousand of this force crossed with Saunders, Atcheson being left in charge of the remainder. General Jim Lane, however, was also approaching in the same direction with a heavy force of his Kansas 'Jayhawkers' to re-enforce Mulligan in Lexington, and, finding Atcheson with so small a force, vigorously attacked him. The Missourians knew these 'Jayhawkers' of old, in many a border fight, and, taking to the woods, they maintained such a murderous fire that Lane was soon routed, with a loss of more than two hundred, while Atcheson lost but ten! The Missourians then effected a junction with Price, and instilled new ardor into the whole army.

"Lane was defeated, but now it was known that Sturgis was approaching, also, on the north bank, his object being to cross over and assist Mulligan, with over fifteen hundred cavalry. To accomplish this, he depended upon the ferry-boats for transportation; but these boats, lying snugly under the bluff, Price determined to capture, at whatever cost, particularly as a large steamboat also lying there was reported to contain considerable quantities of stores. Directing Colonel Rives to this point, that officer carefully approached from the west, along the river's edge, partly within view of the fortifications, and effected the important capture in gallant style, removing the vessels beyond reach of destruction. Mulligan saw the manœuvre when too late, but opened a vigorous fire upon the party, and as many men fell, on account of the enemy's possession of a house on top of the bluff, several companies were detailed to attack it. Although advancing under a deadly fire from musketry and artillery, the Missourians took the house in gallant style, but not without loss ; nor were they allowed to hold it with impunity. As this house was within one hundred and fifty yards of his main works, and could be made to command them, Mulligan collected a strong force, sallied forth, and retook it, slaughtering its captors without mercy : not one man was spared. Still the enemy were not allowed to retain possession ; our forces, having attacked and carried the high grounds to the north, so pounded the house from this position that it was soon vacated as untenable.

"Thus we were gaining ground on all sides, and the enemy's position becoming more and more circumscribed every hour ; while our artillery, moving upon conquered positions, blazed away right and left, sweeping every thing before them. Mulligan's position, however, was still a strong one, and he could have held out for a long time, but, being completely cut off from water, his men were failing in strength every hour. Hearing that Sturgis was fast approaching the north ferry landing, Price got up steam on his captured boats, and transported a strong force over to that side, under Parsons, who managed the enterprise so warily, that Sturgis barely escaped capture; his whole command retreated in the wildest disorder, leaving hundreds of tents, camp equipage, and large stores behind, untouched.

"Since the first opening skirmishes on the thirteenth, we had gradually worked our way through the town ; but real business, as I have said, commenced on the eighteenth, and this with great success on every hand. It now being the twentieth, over fifty hours of incessant fire had been maintained on both sides, the loss of the enemy being very considerable. Seeing his boats captured, and that Lane and Sturgis, instead of fighting their way to him, had 'skedaddled' in all directions, Mulligan showed evident signs of yielding, and it must be remembered that he found it impossible to obtain water for his men, who were on constant duty night and day. At the same time, fearful of Fremont's or some other officer's arrival to raise the siege, our men redoubled their efforts, and maintained a heavy fire from every point, the result of which was that Mulligan hoisted a white flag on his works towards four P.M. on the twentieth. Firing then ceased, and loud, deafening yells from all points of the compass informed me that the brave Mulligan had unconditionally surrendered.

"When the Federals stacked arms, and marched out, we found that we had captured four thousand effectives, rank and file, half a dozen colonels, one hundred and twenty commissioned officers, several stands of colors and brass bands, two mortars, five rifled guns, over four thousand stand of arms, scores of sabres, lots of cavalry and wagon harness, eight hundred horses, numerous wagons, mules ambulances, and medical outfits; immense supplies of every description; much clothing, shoes, tents, ammunition, and camp utensils, together with about one million dollars stolen from various banks, which we instantly returned. Mulligan's sword was politely returned to him by Price with a 'neat speech,' and all the prisoners being paroled, were immediately sent North on their way rejoicing. Such jubilation was visible in every camp as I will not attempt to describe, although, from your description of Manassas, I suppose one scene is very much like another in this respect. My left arm was wounded in the assault on the bluff, and has caused me much suffering; but to keep my promise I have partly written and partly dictated this scrawl, so that you may form some idea of our doings. The mails between us are few and far between, but I look for a letter from you every day. Love to all your boys and any old friends, for I suppose you meet old schoolmates every day in various regiments. I do not know how long Price will remain here, but, judging from reports and Fremont's uneasiness in St. Louis, suspect Price will be again moving, heaven only knows where, in a few days. Yours always, POLK."

CHAPTER VIII.

WITHIN a short time it was definitely settled that we should move up the country to Leesburgh—a stone's throw from the Potomac and Maryland. What our ultimate destination might be, none knew or cared. Any thing to get away from Manassas and Centreville, any place where we could have a change of scene, and find butter, eggs, and poultry procurable for money, all such articles having been consumed where we then were, or so few remaining that fabulous prices were asked for them. A couple of chickens could not be had for less than five dollars, (£1;) milk was one dollar per gallon; butter, fifty cents per pound; whiskey hardly attainable at ten dollars (£2) per gallon, and other things in proportion. When it was known, therefore, that we had orders for Leesburgh, Loudon County—the most fertile and richest county in Virginia—we were envied by every corps in the army, and were generally looked upon as the advance guard of some important movement.

Taking up the line of march, we passed northwards through the most picturesque and delightful farming country the eye perhaps ever beheld. All was decidedly English in aspect, and the people remarkably so. The lands were highly cultivated; the cattle fat and of superior stock; the farm-houses, out-houses, and negro quarters were all substantially and neatly built; they were also scrupulously clean, and marked by an air of comfort and contentment superior to any thing I had seen farther south. Mountains and valleys, hills and dales, fine springs and majestic woods

came into view at every turn of the road, while overloaded barns
and corn-cribs, neat school-houses, and rustic churches by the
wayside, cosy villages, and strong, masculine, rosy-cheeked inhabitants, contrasted favorably with the tumble-down appearance,
sallow, fever-and-aguish aspect of the immensely wealthy, but
careless and fast-living Cotton States. The habits, dress, look,
language, and all things reminded me much of England; but
nothing more so than the buxom, rosy-faced, and white-aproned
mothers and daughters who lined the wayside, and brought out
of their store to entertain the weary soldiery as they toiled up
the hills of this beautiful region.

Our reception by the inhabitants was enthusiastic and cheering. It had been rumored that Loudon County was a den of
traitors to the patriotic cause, but such cordial behavior was a
more than sufficient contradiction of the calumny. This county, situated in the north-eastern corner of the State, was mountainous and rolling in its physical character. The Potomac ran
on two sides, north and east, separating it from Maryland,
while in the north-west we could see the mountains which sep-
arated us from the Shenandoah Valley. Harper's Ferry lay
under the northern extremity of the Loudon Heights, the Potomac washed its foot, while on the opposite bank towered perpendicularly the heights of Maryland, commanding the Ferry,
by its only lines of approach from Loudon County or the Shenandoah Valley. The distance by the river (unnavigable here)
from Leesburgh to the Ferry was about forty miles; the land
route was about thirty-five miles, with two or three very small
towns in the valleys—among them Lovettsville, on the south
bank, and but four miles from the Ferry. A body of the enemy were reported to be in possession of this last-mentioned
place, and General Evans grinned good-humoredly in reply to
inquiries, and promised to "shake them out of it one of these
fine mornings!" The whole aspect of the country from Leesburgh to the river, north and east, and far in Maryland, was
unbroken rolling land, but to the north stood a cluster of three
isolated hills, the tallest and most conspicuous of which was
called the "Sugar Loaf."

The Federals occupied the last-mentioned eminence on our
approach, and from it they obtained a full view of all that

transpired on our side of the river, with the advantage of being but fifteen miles distant from their forces at Harper's .Ferry, and the same from Poolesville, where General Stone commanded a large force. Their pickets lined the whole river from the Ferry to Washington, so that it was impossible for troops to approach the Potomac without being discovered, when the fact was instantly telegraphed from post to post to McClellan, who was now chief in command. To deceive the enemy, however, Evans had divided his force into small parties, with an over-allowance of tents; and as white canvas-covered wagons were continually seen moving about over the hills, and as our various camps were wide-spread and plentifully supplied with fuel, it was thought by their journals that Johnston was in chief command of our troops, and had not less than from thirty to forty thousand men.

The truth is, that Johnston and Beauregard were manœuvring around Fairfax Court-House with the main army, while Centreville and Manassas were being impregnably fortified; the total force with which ,we made so great a show numbering only some three thousand infantry, with four light field-pieces, and a squadron of cavalry. Evans, however, moved us about continually; now we marched opposite the Sugar Loaf, our tents still standing in the old camp-ground near 'Leesburgh; next day would find us in some other direction; so that at last the enemy were completely deceived as to our number or position, and were ever on the *qui vive*. So complete was the illusion, that our scouts daily informed us of counter-movements by the enemy, who, with whole brigades and divisions, were continually marching ᵥfrom place to place to prevent our supposed attempts at crossing! The Federal commander Stone was an old schoolfellow with Evans at West-Point, and smart messages, it is said, were frequently passed between the rival commanders across the river. Picket-firing was constantly maintained between the guards on opposite banks of the stream, with more animosity, however, than decided effect.

The enemy was still on our side of the Potomac at Lovettsville, and it was determined first to entice them into the interior, and then surround them, if possible. Scouts came in daily, correctly informing us of the position, number, and depredations of the enemy, but we were sorry to learn that the inhabitants of the surrounding country patronized them. The people of Lovettsville and Waterford were chiefly Pennsylvania Quakers, who had of late years settled there, and although their creed forbade warfare, they fought amazingly well with the tongue in favor of Unionism, and had on several occasions betrayed our men to the enemy. General Evans had warned them against harboring the foe, but they replied by concocting a plan to destroy all our cavalry in the neighborhood. An old broad-brimmed proprietor of an antiquated hotel invited the captain of cavalry to halt and refresh his men. The soldier willingly did so, but while engaged at dinner, the premises were surrounded by several hostile squadrons. Our men mounted and fought their way out as best they could, but lost half their number in killed and missing.

Exasperated at the perfidy of these fanatics, Evans summoned his brigade, and leaving camps standing, to deceive the telegraph at the Sugar Loaf, sallied forth towards Lovettsville long before day. When the sun rose over Maryland, we had just halted on a lofty hill and lay in the woods. The scenery on either hand was enrapturing. East of us lay the wide expanse of Maryland and Loudon, bathed in gold; the Potomac, winding to the sea, was covered with a dense white vapor that sparkled like molten silver; clouds capped the Sugar Loaf; while to the west rose dark lines of mist-covered hills and mountains, with snow-white villages dotting the undulating landscape. The column pushed rapidly forward; but ere midday large black clouds gathered on the mountains, and a tremendous rain poured into the valley. At "secure arms," our boys trudged along manfully through mud and water, and as we approached our destination, horsemen were seen hovering in the advance, and rapidly disappearing. With our cavalry to the front, we moved forward at a quick pace, and, halting within a mile of the town, unexpectedly came upon a large body of horse, who were instantly charged by our troopers. A desperate encounter ensued; the enemy gave way, a running fight took place; friend and foe simultaneously charging through the town in the greatest confusion. The enemy were at last driven into the river in sight of their whole force drawn up on the opposite bank. Next morning, finding the place deserted, and the enemy being dislodged, we took our departure, without damaging the village, although both officers and men were sufficiently incensed to have burned the miserable place to the ground.

Excursions of this nature were now of weekly occurrence, but we were not made acquainted with the reasons for them. Only we knew that Evans seemed to delight in keeping his men moving, and his only answer to the remonstrances of sundry fat old officers, who did not much relish marching and countermarching, retreating and advancing, was to swear roundly, and threaten to kick them out of his office. It cannot be denied that our position was a critical one, and required great caution. The enemy at length became aware that we did not meditate crossing, and massed their troops at different points to dislodge us, if possible, from the fertile region of which we had possessed ourselves. Banks at Harper's Ferry, Geary at the Sugar Loaf and Point of Rocks, Stone at Poolesville and Edwards's Ferry, were encompassing us north and east; McCall was at Drainsville, sixteen miles farther east on the south bank, and could cut off our retreat across Goose Greek to the south by a bold and dashing movement; Centreville and Manassas were thirty miles distant, and from the state of the country it was impossible to bring up supplies or receive reenforcements; yet Evans was told "to hold the place at all hazards;" and such instructions to a "fighting" general were likely to be fulfilled to the letter.

The possession of Leesburgh was, in truth, of paramount importance to us. It was populous and wealthy, and, withal, situated in a county more fruitful in supplies than any other in the State. The people of Leesburgh had been somewhat disaffected to our cause, but that had all passed, and now none were more enthusiastic for independence. The rail and other roads from Washington to Winchester ran through the town, and should it fall, a large area of fruitful country, with the accumulated crops, both in Loudon and the Shenandoah Valley, would fall into Northern hands—a consummation devoutly wished by the Federals, as Maryland was incapable of supplying their wants. They had, moreover, to pay for what they got from their "friends;" whereas by being quartered among the rebels, that inconvenience would be spared them, and a vast expense saved.

Our service under these circumstances was exceedingly irksome. With a river front of over forty miles to guard against a superior force and a multitude of spies, the utmost vigilance and self-denial were indispensable. Our videttes, who were young and inexperienced, occasioned much annoyance and unnecessary marching, and such was our habitual life of excitement that we could not call a single hour our own. Night and day reports would come in of some imaginary "advance" or "crossing," and whether it were night or day, fair or foul, we marched to the threatened point, to find our suspicions groundless. At last, Evans vowed in his wrath to hang the first man that brought in false alarms, and the officer commanding likewise, for permitting it. After this informal order, we were much relieved, and enjoyed our leisure hours as best we could in town or country. For once, however, the cavalry were correct in their reports, as I will proceed to show.

Some of Geary's men at Point of Rocks were in the habit of crossing the river in large boats, and despoiling the country; besides committing all manner of outrages upon unoffending women and children, whose fathers or brothers were in the Southern army, and not unfrequently burned down their houses. A company of foot was sent up to watch for these marauders, and lay *perdu* in the woods for more than a week without success. At last two large scows were seen approaching, containing more than a hundred individuals, some few being renegades, but most of them New-England soldiers, and all well armed. Two other scows, similarly freighted, were descried crossing at a point higher up the river.

Both landing-places were in full view of our men, who waited until the greater number of the Federal soldiers had departed on their shameful errand, when the guards at the boats were surrounded, and of course they had no alternative but to surrender at discretion. The prisoners were secured in the woods, and we awaited the return of the marauders. After a few hours, one of the parties approached in a body, well laden, and observing military order against a surprise. Unconsciously, they advanced within our ambuscade, when our captain stepped forward, and demanded a surrender. He was answered with a volley, but before they could reload, every man of them was weltering in his blood, dead or wounded.

The second boat's party, who were approaching by the same track, heard the firing, and rushed towards the landing-place; our heroes fell back some few paces, and awaited their approach. Having to pass the spot where their companions lay, they halted and gazed with horror on the destruction before them. But at the same moment our commander called upon them to surrender, and they did so. The dead and wounded were then placed in a scow, and two men, paroled, conveyed them across.

On counting over our spoil it was found that we had captured in this little affair one hundred and fifty fine English rifles, sixty revolvers, six swords, and over one hundred prisoners, besides having killed or wounded seventy-five others. We procured wagons for the plunder of the Yankees, as well as for the arms and accoutrements, and marched our prisoners to town—the civilian renegades in front. Not a man in our party was scratched in this encounter, but it tended to embitter the feeling between the respective pickets on the river-bank, and the firing became incessant. Indeed, the Yankees brought down whole regiments to oppose our guards, and maintained an incessant fusilade from sunrise till dark. Not only so, but field-pieces were brought to bear upon every tent or hut within range; and several poor farmers and laborers were unhoused. When our artillery answered, they invariably retired, and at last mounted some heavy pieces on a rising ground behind Edwards's Ferry, and incessantly shelled, in the vain hope of destroying Leesburgh, which they had not manhood enough to attempt to take. But their firing was mere waste of ammunition. Their numerous shell, from some unknown cause, though thrown from rifled cannon of the very best quality, always fell short a mile. The distance was not more than two miles and a half.

CHAPTER IX.

IT now appeared, from the presence of large bodies of the enemy at all the fords of the river, and the activity they displayed in fortifying every available site, that McClellan was determined to raise an impregnable barrier against our attempts upon Maryland. From Washington to Harper's Ferry the riverbank seemed to be one vast line of mud forts and field-works, well armed and guarded, while the continual ascent of smoke from inland camps made us aware that large bodies of troops were waiting orders. Although possessed of fine sites for counter-fortifications, General Evans never essayed to build, and save one small field-work that crowned a rising ground midway between Edwards's Ferry and Leesburgh, and our own invaluable bodies, we had nothing to withstand the enemy's approach. " Don't talk to me of earthworks," Evans would petulantly exclaim ; " I have more fortifications now than I can well arm ; besides, these Mississippians don't want to commence digging; they want to *fight*, not to build. As long as I have such a brigade in command, I can safely defy all that old Stone can do. In fact, if I had but two or three more regiments, I would cross over and whip the rascals out of Maryland."

As October advanced, it became apparent that the enemy were resolved to try once more the fortune of war. McClellan's force was powerful, highly disciplined, and finely appointed; and the clamors of the press seemed to indicate that public opinion would precipitate hostilities. A general of the ranting, raving type of Abolitionism (N. P. Banks, of Massachusetts) commanded Harper's Ferry and the whole line of the Upper Potomac, and it was confidently expected that he would succeed in breaking "the backbone of rebellion." On our side, to watch and profit by the false moves of this New-Englander, General Turner Ashby and his cavalry were stationed at Charlestown, in the Shenandoah Valley, and kept continually hovering between that point and Harper's Ferry, intercepting supplies, capturing foraging parties, and making frequent dashes into the enemy's line, and even occasionally crossing into Maryland, burning railroad bridges, and destroying the Washington and Ohio Canal—one of the chief sources of Federal supplies. At the same time Evans's force was distributed along the river, and our light battery was continually moving from point to point, shelling the enemy's camps. Occasionally they would take up a favorable position, wait for the military train at Point of Rocks, and destroy a locomotive or two; but their favorite practice was firing at canal-boats as they approached Washington with supplies. Confederate forces had rendered the Lower Potomac unnavigable by numerous batteries armed with Armstrong and Whitworth guns, and we endeavored to imitate the example by stopping all traffic on the north banks of the Upper Potomac. These incessant demonstrations and the raids of Ashby's cavalry so incensed the Federal troops that they swore eternal enmity against every Secessionist.

Being out on picket, we enjoyed ourselves amazingly among the farmers, who willingly furnished all things needful, and as our camps were near the little town of Waterford, many pleasant hours were spent there among the pretty Quakeresses and widows — the latter being numerous and handsome. With their little town of one street screened by surrounding hills, the inhabitants seemed perfectly happy and contented: they possessed a fine mill, two woollen cloth factories, several tanneries; had a large meeting-house, two small chapels, a newspaper, and excellent grazing land all around them. In general aspect, Waterford looked much like an English village, only that the inhabitants were prouder in step, wore better clothes, and had rosy, well-cut features that plainly indicated the best of "blood." A large number of the men had decamped into Maryland; but the women, Heaven bless them! were as true as steel, and behaved like heroines on all occasions.

From deserters and intercepted travellers we gleaned particles of information occasionally, which left little doubt that recent acts of boldness were but forerunners of mischief, and every day witnessed greater vigilance and caution on the part of officers. The more distant detachments were called in, and, save a picket guard, under special instructions, our whole force fell back some ten miles to Goose Creek, at which point all flanking forces from Drainsville must of necessity make their first appearance. This was a ruse designed to bewilder the enemy, who were accurately informed of all our movements by spies among the townspeople of Leesburgh. As for our men, what this habitual retreating and advancing might mean, none could tell—it sufficed that Evans ordered it, and the men obeyed cheerfully, although frequently compelled to march in drenching rains and impassable mud. In order to be posi-tively informed of the enemy's movements and intentions, several Marylanders in our command volunteered to cross the river, dodge the pickets, and push into the interior as far as Baltimore, sixty miles distant. The most remarkable of these daring fellows, Elijah White, was a rich Maryland planter, who possessed several fine plantations around Pooles-ville, but had forsaken all and joined a cavalry company in Loudon County. His knowledge of localities was so perfect that he was the acknowledged authority in all matters regarding the topography of the country from Alexandria to Harper's Ferry. He frequently swam the Potomac at different points, and knew more fords in it than any octogenarian within a hundred miles. The enemy set all kinds of traps to catch him, but his magnificent grey mare had such speed and endurance that he passed like a phantom from place to place. He was singularly reserved in manner, although gay and buoyant; and there can hardly be a doubt that the master passion furnished a chief motive for his frequent wild adven-tures. Be that as it may, his services were invaluable in time of necessity, and his daring greatly relieved the anxiety of Evans, for whose discomfiture the enemy were continually manœuvring.

We had pitched tents one evening, after a long march in the cold winds, and were lying down for a smoke on a bundle of hay by the camp-fire, when I heard the jingling of spurs and harness, and looking up, saw White on his grey wearily ambling by. The invitation to take a cup of *bonâ fide* coffee was eagerly accepted by my old acquaintance; and his mare having been well provided for by the black boy, White was so charmed with the savor of sundry beefsteaks broiling on the coals, that he consented to take up his quarters with us for the night. With a circle of some twenty officers and privates, we made a pleasant party round the immense fire of blazing oak logs. Some were engaged with cards; others were writing letters; a fiddle was not far distant, with a laughing crowd of dancers going through a cotillion; many were cooking, eating, and sleeping, and picket-guards were going out on duty. "What's the news, White?" asked one. "How's all the girls in Maryland?" chimed in another. "How much is whiskey worth over there, Lige?" questioned a third; and so on.

"I'm mighty tired, boys," said the trooper, smoking and reclining, "but we had a first-rate time of it. We fooled the Feds., as usual, and had a jolly old spree in Baltimore; danced with the girls, had lots of tip-top whiskey and cigars, and brought back letters for the fellows; went wherever we darned please; seized two of McClellan's orderlies with despatches—found them in bed a little way back—and brought them over safely, papers and all. We had some difficulty in crossing at the old place; so while some of our videttes were fussing about and attracting attention, four of us, in Yankee costume, swam our horses, and soon reaching a friendly house, changed clothes, and put off again, for we could hear the Yanks galloping about furiously in all directions. Our boys took to the timber, and never left it until within thirty miles of old Baltimore.

"Talk of Maryland being sound on the Union question— 'tis all bosh! I've lived there for fifteen years, and should know something about it, and I'm positive that ninety-nine out of every hundred are true Southerners, if they only had a fair chance to express themselves. The truth is, boys, Maryland waited too long, and lost her opportunity to declare for secession. She was waiting till Virginia had gone out; but when that took place her State was crowded with Federal hirelings, and having neither arms nor organization, was obliged to submit to brute force.

6

"Freedom of speech, indeed! or freedom of the press!—it is all nonsense; none dare speak openly, and should the newspaper editors even hint at Yankee tyranny, Fort McHenry is assigned them, without judge or jury. As for habeas corpus!—that is a thing of the past. While I was in the city, the members of the Legislature and Senate arrived, and every one of them who was in the least suspected of Southern feeling was waited upon, either when he landed from the car, or at his hotel, and, without the slightest explanation, conducted to the dungeons of Fort McHenry in the bay! There are fortifications of immense strength overlooking the city, and every gun in every battery is shotted, *and pointed at the city!* As the tyrants confess with a laugh, 'all these works were raised, *not* to protect your city, but to destroy and lay it in one indistinguishable heap of ashes should the slightest indication of a revolt betray itself!'

"And they claim that Marylanders are loyal, and have brotherly love for them! Yes, as much love as the lamb bears the wolf. A lady cannot walk the streets in a dress of her own choice without its being noticed and commented on by hundreds of blue-coated soldiers or spies; and should she wear any colors indicative of Southern sentiment, is immediately arrested and insulted. As for taking 'the oath of allegiance,' so-called, thousands have done so from sheer necessity; but they do not, and will not, consider themselves bound to be faithful to those who have proved unfaithful to every compact and every instrument bequeathed by our fathers. And they are right. What can the thousands of Maryland do? Is not the State overrun by all the villains and spies the North can control or hire? Were they to rise, like raving, unarmed fools, it could only be to be mercilessly butchered by trained bands of hirelings—the offscourings of the earth! Far better as it is, to play the hypocrite with hypocrites! but the day will come when the true sentiments of Maryland and Kentucky will be fully known; and when their fate is inseparably linked to ours, we shall be prone to pity and commiserate, rather than revile them for their helplessness."

"Well, Lige, no one disputes all that. We know that old Maryland is 'sound' enough, and has two or three full regiments at Manassas; but take a drink out of Tom's canteen — prime old rye, too — and go on with your trip," said one who was yawning, and wanted something exciting to keep him awake.

" Well, boys," continued Lige, refilling his pipe, " one of my trips is much like another. As we approached Baltimore I told the boys we had better separate, and meet as strangers at one of the hotels. We did so, and as the guard was not over-vigilant around or in town, I got along very well, and met several friends, taking good care to avoid any I suspected. Having stabled the mare at an out-of-the-way place, I called on an old friend, and was surprised to find him giving a party to some dozen Federals. He laughed, and introduced me as a friend from New-York, and, before long, we passed the bottle freely, and got along swimmingly. I bore out my character as a New-Yorker admirably, and spoke splendidly about the ' Union, one, and forever,' the ' Old Flag,' and a hundred other bygone catch-lines; and was put down by the Yankees as ' a regular brick.' I did not drink much, but danced with the girls, condoled with them on the trials and privations of the times, and procured a large amount of information, dropped, in scraps, from the half-intoxicated Federals, relative to the number and disposition óf troops on the Upper and Lower Potomac. That night I slept at my friend's house.

" According to promise, I called on one of the Federals next morning, and as he was officer of the day, we walked arm-in-arm over the fortifications, every thing being explained to me, and by well-put questions I extracted all the information possible, and by comparing statements, arrived at pretty accurate facts and figures. From W —— I obtained the ' sign ' and ' countersign,' by which regularly initiated Southerners might detect each other, and by this means spent several days very agreeably in the city. I was surprised, however, to find so many belonging to the organization, for I could not be in any assembly long ere signs were exchanged, and I have not unfrequently heard staunch members of the club speaking very loudly in favor of union in presence of the Yankees, when at the same moment signs to the contrary were passed between us. They manage this thing well in Baltimore, and have plenty of funds to assist our needy sympathizers who come under their notice. Constant correspondence is maintained with Richmond, and twice a week despatches are sent there by means which the Yankee authorities can never discover."

"How about the ladies, old friend ?"

"Well, you may laugh, but of all the Marylanders, the women are the most ardent and open in the expression of feeling. When officers ask them to play or sing, they usually comply by performing the most rebellious kinds of music, in the most modest and artless manner, causing the visitors to sit uneasy in their seats, and look very serio-comic. Not that such things can always be done with impunity ; for I know some, and have heard of other instances, where our female friends have been put into jail for speaking or singing seditious sentiments, or for causing excitement by wearing party colors. As for the Baltimore theatres, they are controlled by the Federal authority, and are nightly crowded by soldiers, who sit hour after hour applauding clap-trap pieces, in which Union soldiers accomplish miracles of heroism ; or, if they die, it is with the Stars and Stripes wrapped around them, and with a great flourish of trumpets."

A burst of derisive laughter gave the trooper, who was growing eloquent with his subject, time to take breath, when he continued:

"It strikes me, boys, that the Yankee proper may be truthfully termed a theatrical and imaginative being, and be wrought upon by ' effect ' more than the French, even, whom they endeavor to ape in matters of taste. From childhood they are supplied with a multitude of books of equivocal taste and morality ; their historians are partial ; their swarms of novelists are persons of fervid imaginations, reared in all the forms of atheism, millerism, free-love, and spiritualism ; most decidedly are unreal in all things, save what pertains to the almighty dollar ; but in *that* they are enthusiastic cheats, and worship the golden calf with more devotion than the Jews. Their theatres everywhere, as well as Baltimore, are the public expounders of prejudice and bad taste. Until of late all battle-pieces had for subject the wars with Great Britain, and we know that one Yankee was always considered equal to a dozen Britishers, and on the stage, like Samson, they slew their thousands with loud applause, and ended with a large expenditure of 'blue fire,' a waving of banners, and the stereotyped finale of 'Hail Columbia' or 'Yankee Doodle.' This theatrical taste was well developed at Manassas. Orators first addressed the troops, music took up the theme, and with waving banners they marched to battle, and, with few exceptions, 'bolted' at the first fire. There was plenty of shouting, indeed, when out of danger; but though their best regiments cheered till nearly hoarse—though the 'old flag' was shaken out to the winds, and 'Yankee Doodle' broke upon their ear in brilliant variations — nothing could induce their red-legged desperadoes to advance a second time to encounter our 'ragged rebels.' History has not been just to the North, whose merchants have become princes on the products of the South, and whose books have been volumes of lies."

"That is all very good, White," broke in a fat old captain; "but go on with the narrative; 'taps' will sound presently, and I must be off to my guard."

"When our party had sufficiently enjoyed themselves, and effected the purposes intended, we met and devised plans for the return. From the information of a trusty friend, it was deemed advisable to be extremely cautious, as every thing on the Upper Potomac indicated movements of importance, and the different fords were doubly guarded. General Baker, Lincoln's right-hand man, had been in secret conference with the authorities for several days, and in private circles bragged of what *he* was going to do. *He* was not going into winter quarters until the vile 'ragged rebels' were driven from his front, and he did so on secession soil, and at rebel expense, etc. Knowing that General Baker was acting in conjunction with Stone, at Poolesville, there could be little reason to doubt after this from what quarter the blow was likely to fall upon us, so we hastened back again as speedily as possible.

"The nearer we approached the river, the more difficult it was to proceed. The Yankees had so many men lying along the main roads, that it was almost impossible to travel. We picketed our horses in the woods when near Poolesville, and held a council of war. I proposed to procure the countersign by stratagem, if possible, and go into Poolesville. The rest of the party vehemently dissented from such an adventure, but promised to stay at the house of a friend till my return. Having resumed my Federal uniform, I proceeded cautiously along the road, and at length came within view of picket-guards round a fire, at the fork of the road, which compelled me to halt. Hitching the grey. in the woods, I now proceeded on foot, and crept among the brushwood until within thirty paces of the nearest guard. There I lay for an hour or more, until some one approached, and I faintly heard the countersign of 'Bunker Hill' given, and being satisfied, cautiously returned, mounted the mare, and galloped along the road, roaring the *Star-Spangled Banner.*

"'Halt!' shouted the picket, as I unceremoniously approached. 'Who comes there?' 'A friend with the countersign,' I answered, hiccuping, and pretended to reel in the saddle. 'Advance, friend, and give the countersign,' replied the Yankee with a laugh, for, thinking me an officer returning from a jollification, he scarcely noticed the countersign. Passing along I could not help lingering near my old plantations; regiments of New-Englanders were camped upon them, my woods, fences, and barns were all destroyed, and they had converted the dwellings into guard-houses, where dozens of Dutch and Irish were howling in intoxication. Possessed of the countersign, I found no difficulty in passing from place to place, and enjoyed myself until midnight with a lot of officers who were bent on a drinking bout. And now comes the most important part of my story.

"One of these men had brought important despatches from McClellan, and was to return before sunrise. 'But,' said he, 'if they think I'm going to travel thirty miles again to-night, Stone is much mistaken. I shall just go out of town, and put up at P——'s for the night; what say you, Smidt?' said he to another aide. 'You are not going on with your papers to Banks to night, eh? They'll keep, man, they an't important, so let's make a, night of it, and put in an excuse of lame horses!' Both agreed to the plan, and about an hour afterwards proceeded on their way together. I knew P——'s plantation very well, and resolved that both their persons and papers should visit *this* side of the river, and immediately started for my party, with a view to the accomplishment of my project.

"Having watched in which room these worthies were domiciled, we lay in wait some time, and then, resolved to commence action by separating them, I rode up to the house, and inquired 'if Captain Smidt was there; I had been told he was, and had been sent by General Stone to call him immediately.' Smidt soon made his appearance, cursing and swearing in everry dialect of Dutch and English. 'Some cot dem tyful hat watched him, sure, unt he was a gone schicken, else how old Shstone know him not gone?' While I condoled with Smidt, he was seized and secured without a show of resistance. We then waited a short time until P—— was about to blow out the candle, when I knocked again. He was in a terrible temper, and having shoved the candlestick close to my face to see who it was, almost staggered with astonishment. Seeing that he recognized me, I presented a revolver at his head, and placing a finger on my lip, passed in, leaving a companion to stand guard over him, while I went up stairs.

"I knocked at the door of Smidt's room: his companion answered me, and I entered. He was surprised, but glad to see me. My remark, that 'I had heard him state his intention to stay at P——'s all night, when in the tavern, and thought I'd follow suit, intending to go on and join my regiment in the morning,' was quite satisfactory. After smoking and partaking of some brandy I had with me, we talked for a long time on the subject of arms and accoutrements. He had a magnificent pair of Colt's navy revolvers, and it was my ambition to effect his capture without bloodshed. I handed over for inspection an Adams's self-cocker, (unloaded,) and he pushed across the table his loaded weapons. I fingered them coolly for several minutes, and with apparent thoughtlessness cocked them both. Then suddenly presented them at his head, informed him who I was, and commanded him to dress immediately and follow me; 'resistance is useless,' I remarked: 'the house is surrounded.' Deadly pale and almost paralyzed, the aide dressed and was conducted to his horse. We started off without a whisper, and soon arrived at the spot where Smidt was guarded by my companions.

During my absence the boys had gagged him, to stop his

eternal prattle; and when he recognized his companion handcuffed, I thought his hair would stand on end with astonishment! With our prisoners in the centre, we briskly trotted
along the bright moonlit road, and ere long caught a distant
view of our camp-fires in Old Virginia. The river, we knew,
was well guarded, at nearly all points; hence, for the sake of
caution, we stole through the woods and formed our plans. It
was resolved that two of our party should advance boldly to
the river, give the countersign, and inform the picket that they
had volunteered to cross into Virginia to reconnoitre. This
news would spread up and down the bank, and the mounted
men especially would feel anxious to converse with their comrades and attend little to their posts for a while. The ruse
answered admirably; and when I saw one particular spot deserted, our party issued from the wood and swam their horses
across.. No resistance was offered by our prisoners; we had
explained to them the importance of silence and obedience,
and our revolvers were always pointed to enforce submission.
Scarcely had we crossed when, in the distance, we saw two
squadrons of the enemy dashing along the bank. 'Twas lucky
we had used all expedition, as some darkies at P——'s must
have informed on us. As I stood in a thicket listening to their
angry conversation, I could not help laughing heartily at their
annoyance, and they must have heard it; for I heard one say,
' That's him; I know his voice, major!.' 'That you, White?'
'Yes, that's me; how are you, major? Fine night, isn't it? I
shall give you another call shortly?' I could scarcely get out
of the way before a perfect shower of shot was dropping all
around me. I cantered to town; and here I am."

At the conclusion of White's story, we made some hot
punch, as best we.could, and wrapping coats and blankets
around us, lay beside the expiring camp-fire, and were soon
fast asleep.

CHAPTER X.

Position at Manassas—Ashby at Harper's Ferry—His Preparations for Attack—
Our Artillery co-operate—Incidents of the Fight—General McCall leaves
Drainsville, and threatens our Retreat—Our alarming Position—To Goose
Creek and back again.

DURING the month of October there was no change in affairs
at Manassas or Centreville. At the latter place, fortifications
had been erected under the superintendence of Generals Gustavus Smith and Beauregard, and were generally considered to
be impregnable. Our pickets were at Fairfax Court-House, but
the Yankees were in winter quarters to the front, and could
not be coaxed to advance. Active movements were on foot,
however, at Harper's Ferry, and General Banks had pushed his
outposts several miles up the Valley. Ashby, with his cavalry,
whose daring raids I have mentioned, grew bolder every day,
and solicited reenforcements. These were not granted him, the
authorities perhaps judging it prudent not to fight, although
the gallant trooper swore roundly that he would do so.

Collecting every available man, he made a vow to drive the
foe from their intrenchments into Maryland; and for this purpose procured two or three light field guns, and an old twenty-
four pound smooth-bore; the latter he ingeniously contrived to
mount on the axles of a wagon. With his regiment of cavalry,
and several hundred militia, Ashby gradually approached Harper's Ferry, and sent a courier to Evans, asking him to co-óper-
ate. Our commander had no orders to leave Loudon County,
and it would have been certain destruction to detach any considerable portion of his command, although he ardently admired
Ashby's bravery, and yearned to assist him. Knowing him to
be weak in artillery, Evans gave permission for two of our
pieces to march to his assistance, ascend the Loudon Heights,
and annoy the enemy's rear when marching out to attack

Ashby, to destroy the mills, storehouses, bridges, etc., around the Ferry as far as practicable, but by no means to leave the heights and descend into the valley. Four companies of our regiment accompanied the guns and started towards Harper's Ferry at three A M., October thirteenth, 1861, and camped within two miles of the place at sundown

At four A.M. next morning, we cautiously took up the line of march, and when within a mile of the Ferry abruptly left the main road and approached the Loudon Heights. We could distinctly see the tall bold rocks at Harper's Ferry, encircled by mists and clouds; and as we journeyed quietly through the forest and ascended the steep wood-covered mountains, the sun rose, revealing the Potomac swiftly flowing through the natural flood-gates I have elsewhere described, with here and there a white dwelling of the town sleeping in the quiet morning air, at the base of the gigantic rocks which overhang the Ferry. With excessive labor we pulled the pieces up the face of the hill, and had them in an ambushed position overlooking the town long before the enemy had sounded *reveille*.

The camps of the foe in Maryland and about Harper's Ferry were distinctly seen; various trenches, forts, and earthworks looking towards Charlestown, were counted and examined with glasses; the whole panorama of the Shenandoah Valley lay several hundred feet below us, while on every road leading to and from the Ferry we saw numerous picket-fires and videttes. There was no sign of Ashby or his command : but when the mists of morning cleared away, and the distant woods towards Charlestown were visible, small faint columns of smoke indicated where his forces lay along the Bolivar road. At the base of the hill on which we were, the Shenandoah ran on its course to the Potomac, a mile northward at the foot of the town, so that on the north and east two different rivers ran winding through the landscape, while beyond the first-named stream in the valley lay the picturesque village of Bolivar, where the commandant of the post, chiefs of arms, factories, and merchants delighted to dwell in the peculation times of the old Government. The chief buildings were now converted into barracks and storehouses, establishments that Ashby had long beheld with a jealous and covetous eye.

About seven A.M., I observed several horsemen dash from the distant woods and approach Bolivar in great haste. The drums began to beat very wildly. Shortly afterwards clouds of dust indicated Ashby's approach. At eight A.M. to a minute he halted on the Bolivar road and fired a shot at the infantry barracks : this was a signal to us; we hoisted a red flag, and two shots answered that all was right. The enemy were not long in assembling, and could be seen swarming into their field-works and rifle-pits. Skirmishers were sent out by both parties, and little puffs of smoke and faint reports told that they were hotly engaged. Banks did not seem inclined to leave his fortifications, yet to draw Ashby forward sent out two regiments as decoys ; they were saluted with round shot and shell, and, quickly turning, fled to the woods south-west of Bolivar, where again volleys saluted them, and a squadron of cavalry dashing forward on their flank cut down many and dispersed the rest in wild confusion.

Ashby now advanced several hundred yards nearer, and the foe brought forward field-pieces and fresh regiments to oppose him. While this was progressing our artillerists had taken accurate range of the chief storehouse, mills, and other buildings, and began to shell them. This unexpected assault seemed to discomfit the enemy within the town and suburbs, and although they endeavored to save their stores, most of them were fired, and the buildings destroyed. Had they ascended the Maryland Heights (not more than half a mile across the Potomac) our position would have proved untenable, for they were much higher than those of Loudon, on which we were posted. Failing this, our cannonade was maintained with great vigor ; and when fresh parties of the enemy began to cross from Maryland in flats, a few shell were directed towards them with decided effect. At length the Federals advance in line of battle ; and Ashby, having sent his militia to meet them, the latter, at the first fire, broke and fled. The Yankees seeing this, gave a tremendous cheer, and ran forward with the bayonet, but in broken lines ; and as they advanced towards the woods, a regiment of cavalry, who were concealed ready for the opportunity, dashed in amongst them, and in a few moments were pistoling the foe and slashing them awkwardly with their sabres. But the cavalry attack was made in great confusion, and most of the enemy effected their escape by running into a large fortified house used for barracks in Bolivar. Ashby observed this place, and stealing along the road with his twenty-four-pounder on wagon-axles, directed a few well-aimed shells at it, broke the walls, blew off the roof, and the refugees were glad to make for their nearest lines.

This unsatisfactory style of fighting was maintained with fluctuating success until noon, when a courier swam the Shenandoah, ascended the mountains, and begged our colonel to bring his force into the valley, and assail the enemy on the right, while he pushed the centre. Against this, it will be remembered he had received the strictest orders; and although the men crowded round him, and begged to be led against the enemy, the colonel was compelled to refuse. The cannonade was then renewed with great fury by either party, and many shell came screaming over the heights on which we stood, but did no harm. Ashby, seeing that he was greatly outnumbered, and that the enemy were endeavoring to surround him, used his field-pieces with such destructive effect as to hold them in check while he drew off his small force to a better position. The militia by this time had become accustomed to the fight, and, gallantly advancing, repulsed the enemy; while Ashby, conspicuous on a white horse, led on the cavalry, and made several brilliant charges. Having effected his main object, namely, the destruction of the mills, storehouses, and bridges of Harper's Ferry, he retired towards Charlestown, with several hundred stand of arms, some prisoners, much ammunition, and quantities of stores, which had been seized by his troopers at unprotected points while the fight was raging. As he retired behind the woods, scouts came in and reported the enemy endeavoring to cut off our retreat; but by expedition and coolness we soon descended the mountains, and reaching the main road, occupied the point crossing a hill, and placed our pieces in position, ready for a determined stand. The enemy perceived that we had taken up a strong position, and over-estimating our force, retired without firing a shot.

While bivouacked that night, a courier came dashing towards us, and brought the stirring news that McCall, with a heavy force, was marching from Drainsville to cut off Evans at Lees-burgh. The latter, therefore, had hastily retreated to Goose Creek, ten miles nearer Centreville, and we were ordered to follow in his track, and if the enemy had really entered the town, a courier would inform us of it on the road, and give time to branch off towards Winchester, to get under the protection of Ashby. This indeed was startling news. The men had travelled much, and were excessively weary. The colonel decided not to call them up for a few hours, but give them rest. Towards twilight all were quietly awakened and informed of the state of things; the men good-humoredly arriving at the conclusion that we had better "up stakes and dust" out of the neighborhood in "a mighty big hurry." Our wagons were sent out of the way by a road leading south-east, with directions to halt at a certain point for further orders. We marched through Hillsborough like shadows—all were in bed and not a dog barked—and continued at a great pace towards Leesburgh. Towards evening we halted on a large hill overlooking the town, and received orders to keep to the woods and proceed on to our brigade at Goose Creek. The rain fell in torrents, and the roads were awful, as all roads in Virginia are at this season. When within a mile of the creek, a courier brought orders to halt for the night, and proceed to Leesburgh at break of day. With much swearing and grumbling at Evans's idea of strategy, the order was obeyed, and shoeless, foot-sore, and dirty, we pitched tents on our old camping-ground, one of the companies being detailed to hold the mudwork on the hill, towards Edwards's Ferry, called by the dignified term of "Fort Evans," though it had no guns, and was not pierced for any. This company, together with the other three, detailed men to picket at the river as usual, and were instructed to wait until further orders.

CHAPTER XI.

WHILE our brigade was away from Leesburgh, and pickets
were no longer at the river, many negroes crossed the stream,
and informed the Yankees of our whereabouts. Several Unionists, also, had conferred with their friends, and every acre of the
vicinity had been accurately mapped out by their engineers.
We had long suspected old farmer Trunnell of treachery—his
only son had joined the Northern army, and was a brigade commissary in it. It was to his knowledge of localities that the
Yankees chiefly trusted when placing their batteries, and he
had often been seen directing artillerists in their efforts to shell
the town. His father was extremely wealthy, and had an extensive plantation near the river, adjacent to Ball's Bluff. He
had large dealings with our army, and was paid thousands of
dollars for supplies. His negroes frequently ran away to Maryland, but invariably returned after a few days' absence; a circumstance which rendered it highly probable that the old man
corresponded with his son. He himself and his whole household were peculiarly insulting to our soldiers, and I myself
have frequently seen signal lights at his house answered from
the hills in Maryland. Yet he lived undisturbed in his home-
stead, and was neither insulted nor annoyéd by any one.

Our return to Leesburgh caused some speculation, but the
answer to all inquiries was, that " we were to hold the place

until the enemy appeared, and then retire." Unlooked for by any, the remainder of our brigade marched into town late on Saturday evening, and pitched tents in the accustomed place. Having had but little rest during the past week, I congratulated myself on the prospect of a long nap now that our whole force was come to relieve us; but it fell to my lot to be ordered on guard, and we made ourselves as comfortable as possible round a camp-fire, little dreaming of the stirring events in which we were about to act a principal part.

One company of the Thirteenth Mississippi had been detailed to picket the river on our left from Carter's Ferry to the head of Harrison's Island; one of the Seventeenth picketed to Edwards's Ferry on our right; horse pickets were on duty still lower down the river, watching the ferry, where Goose Creek flows into the Potomac; another company of horse were watching Goose Creek bridge and the Drainsville road on our right flank and rear; a company of horse were also on our extreme left up the river, and one of the Eighteenth Mississippi occupied Fort Evans midway between the river and town. This was our disposition on Saturday night, October twentieth. Our active lieutenant-colonel had gone out to examine the posts along the river, but had not visited the woods around Ball's Bluff. It was a wild desolate place, and the guards disliked duty in the neighborhood. The Bluff so called was about thirty feet above the level of the river, and not more than one hundred yards from Harrison's Island, the level of which was some twenty-five feet lower than the Bluff. The island, however, was fringed with timber, and could conceal thousands of men. Little notice had been taken of this cheerless looking place, and few guards of either party were seen in its vicinity, although the island was in undisputed possession of the enemy. It was at this point that the enemy's spies and engineers had crossed a few days previously, and seeing only a few tents on the outskirts of Leesburgh, had reported that three companies held the town.

About three A.M., Sunday morning, our lieutenant-colonel rode into camp hastily, and in a few minutes every man was under arms; tents disappeared without noise, and we were drawn up in line of battle. We knew not what to surmise, unless another retreat was contemplated—perhaps to Goose

Creek, through mud, two or three feet deep, as usual! The doubt was soon resolved. Evans and his staff were seen approaching through a dense mist, and our men being formed in columns of division at half distance, the old gentleman addressed us almost in the following words: "Gentlemen, the enemy are approaching by the Drainsville road, sixteen thousand strong, with twenty pieces of artillery! They want to cut off our retreat! We must *fight!*—you need not expect any reenforcements, for none can arrive in time if they were sent. I am going to lead you out to meet them, and if you obey orders we shall give the Yankee rascals a sound thrashing! You have met them before, so have I—we both know of what they are made. I shall be as economical of human life as possible, and shall not sacrifice one man unnecessarily. Gentlemen, I fully rely upon you, and have unbounded confidence in your courage and patriotism! Gentlemen, good-morning." Before the General rode off, some few essayed to cheer, but the prevalent feeling was despondent. None cared so much about a fight on equal terms—if any thing, they would willingly have accepted a challenge from any *two* regiments the enemy could produce; but, much as we all admired our commander's pluck, it appeared hazardous for a brigade of two thousand seven hundred men, with four guns, to meet in mortal strife not less than sixteen thousand of the enemy, with twenty pieces of artillery!

The die was cast, however; all the baggage had moved many miles to the rear, and we marched across Goose Creek bridge and along the Drainsville road to meet the enemy under General McCall. As the sun had not yet risen we approached the mouth of Goose Creek, crossed it, and passed near the guns of the enemy commanding these points without being observed; had they perceived us defiling from the woods along the road, a finer target for their rifled pieces could not have been desired. We proceeded towards Drainsville some two miles and halted, just as the sun rose; and, as our haversacks were empty, smoked our pipes with great gusto in lieu of breakfast. A courier came down the road and informed Evans that the enemy were six miles away, but had not stirred since six P.M. the previous evening. We marched back to await their approach, and bivouacked in the woods. Presently two of our mounted troopers came up with a Federal courier, who had been captured proceeding on his way with despatches from McCall to Stone. His papers betrayed little, yet sufficient to reveal that it was designed to draw us from Leesburgh along the Drainsville road, while Stone crossed and occupied the town. Evans was the very last man to be deceived by such a transparent trick, and as we marched back across the creek and halted in the woods along the Edwards's Ferry road, he drily observed, showing his teeth, as usual: "They won't come that way, boys; but,,had they done so, we would have given them what they never yet had—a d——d good whaling!"

As we lay in the woods all Sunday, the church bells were sweetly ringing, and nature seemed to sleep in the glorious sunshine of the Indian summer—all around us wore an unnatural calm, and every man as he quietly sat or slumbered beneath the leafy shade seemed lost in reverie. We had nothing to eat, our wagons and stores were far away towards Manassas, and every half-hour reports would come in that the enemy seemed very busy at the river, while the glittering of long lines of bayonets could be plainly seen moving to and fro. As if from intuition all the cottagers left their humble dwellings and farms, and hurried away to town, while the soldiery, half famished, despoiled the gardens, and feasted on raw vegetables, or stole a few ears of corn from the barns, eating it raw. The stillness was oppressive, and all complained of thirst; a few unslung their knapsacks and hurriedly wrote letters home, sending them by couriers passing to town.

As the sun began to decline, the enemy's batteries at Edwards's Ferry furiously shelled in every direction, aiming particularly at Fort Evans, the red earthworks of which could be plainly discerned dotting the green hill, and overlooking a bend in the road near the town. Shell were screaming over our heads through the air in great numbers, even when darkness covered the scene; and bursting in all directions, they presented a rather pretty pyrotechnic display—the white circles of luminous smoke seeming to hang with great sensitiveness and delicacy in the air.

When all was quiet again reports came in that the enemy were bringing up many boats from various creeks below, and shortly afterward a courier arrived post haste and reported that seven hundred men had landed at the Old Ferry at the foot of our road. Three right companies of the Eighteenth Mississippi were sent down there—one went into the timber round the Ferry House, with orders when the enemy advanced to fire and fall back; the second was to act similarly, and the third to protect the retreat and entice the enemy on. They had returned, however; and soon afterward their tattoo was sounded, and we could plainly hear the men answering roll-call. We were ordered away lower down stream to the mouth of Goose Creek—the enemy had been at both places trying their boats. We picketed all night, nearly frozen to death, had nothing to eat, wore light summer clothes, and had no blankets or fires.

Why these three companies were detached so far from the main body I could not tell; we were immediately under the guns of Edwards's Ferry, and were not informed how to retreat. When the sun rose next morning, (October twenty-first,) we anxiously awaited orders of recall; but receiving none, the captains determined to fall back. Seeking the banks of the creek, we followed a hog-path by the water's edge up-hill, and were particularly fortunate in not tumbling over the precipitous banks. We kept to the woods, and had not crossed the hill five minutes when the heavy guns at Edwards's Ferry began to shell furiously, many of their missiles falling in close proximity to our halting-place. Within ten minutes more we heard the music of fife and drum, and, looking over the hill, saw a strong force of the enemy issuing from the lane where we had picketed all night, with cavalry in front, and guns. Their infantry followed in martial array, and turned up the stream toward Edwards's Ferry. Their appearance was martial and imposing. "At last," thought we, "now comes the tug of war!"

Not being more than a mile distant in the plain, our companies enjoyed a fine panoramic view of every thing passing. When the enemy had formed line of battle, and artillery was placed in the road, a squadron of cavalry were sent out to reconnoitre. They galloped gaily toward Leesburgh, and passed a company of the Eighteenth ensconced in the woods. The gay-looking horsemen had not proceeded far, when they suddenly came upon the Eighteenth, drawn up across the road behind some timber, and, receiving a withering volley, turned and fled, having to run the gauntlet of the company, who, from their covert, fired heavy loads of buck-shot into them as they passed. From our position on a hill to the right, we clearly saw the discomfiture of the cavalry; their officer commanded them to move forward a second time, but they were so discouraged that no persuasion could induce them to stir.

Fresh troops now began to pour across the river from the mouth of Goose Creek, and from Edwards's Ferry, until at last there were many regiments drawn up in line of battle, well supplied with artillery. The position of the Eighteenth being known, the enemy began to work their batteries with great vigor, firing twenty-four-pound spherical case-shot, and shelling the woods in all directions. The Eighteenth then fell back towards town, and formed line to the left, with the Seventeenth to the right of the road, and at the foot of a hill on which the artillery was placed in Fort Evans—the first regiment having its left on a bank of the Potomac, while the right of the second regiment lay on Goose Creek, In the rear were the Thirteenth Mississippi and the Eighth Virginia, and still farther beyond was a masked battery in the woods designed to sweep the road, should we be forced back. Skirmishers were sent out to our front, but no enemy appeared; scouts reported them ten thousand strong, with twelve pieces drawn up at the Ferry, but there were no indications of an advance. They still kept shelling the woods vigorously, and their percussion shell fell very close to us, as we lay waiting an attack, smoking, laughing, and eating raw cabbages to assuage hunger.

To our left and rear, however, about two miles up the stream, things began to assume a lively aspect. One company of the Thirteenth, on picket there, had been surprised and driven in by a regiment which had unexpectedly marched out from the woods around Ball's Bluff. The company fought well, and, once getting the enemy on broken ground, began to deal destruction among them with a rapid and accurate fire. The captain was in his shirt-sleeves, and the men not much better attired. "Halt and surrender!" roared the Federal commander, galloping towards our men, as they were falling back; "don't fire, we are friends!" Our men, however, had jumped into a field, and each man, taking refuge behind a sheaf of corn, kept

on "popping" away with great rapidity and precision. The
Yankee colonel ordered his men "forward," but they did not
stir, and seemed inclined to fall back for protection to the
woods. Then our bare-headed captain of the Thirteenth ordered his men to reserve their fire, and advance at the charge!
Strange to tell, these eighty brave boys, with a yell, boldly
advanced at a run towards the beautiful line of the enemy, suddenly halted, delivered a murderous volley, and then charged.
The enemy did not stand, but retired to the woods, and kept
up a desultory fire from their covert. A cavalry company
hearing the musketry, when far up the river, advanced, dismounted, and used their Maynard rifles with fine effect, and
drove the enemy still farther into the woods.

The Federals, however, were pouring across at Ball's Bluff
in great force, and two companies of the Eighteenth being
ordered there to sustain the pickets, the battle commenced in
earnest. At one time the enemy were driven in, but, being
shortly afterwards reenforced, they drove our men completely
out of the timber into the open ground. When they essayed
to advance still farther, however, our gallant boys reserved
their own, but drew the fire of the enemy, and when within
seventy yards blazed away with awful precision, and with a
yell charged them through the woods, loading and firing rapidly as they advanced.

It was now midday, and still our brigade, with few deduc-
tions, remained idly on the Edwards's Ferry road, and had done
nothing, except eat raw vegetables. The sudden falling back
of our small force at Ball's Bluff, about one P.M., told plainly
that the foe were in great force, and soon afterwards their
cannon began to roar. The Eighth Virginia (four hundred
strong) were ordered to proceed to the spot, and drive in the
enemy. Their arrival greatly relieved the wearied pickets, and
the firing became lively, but it was plain that the enemy outnumbered us at all points, and we heard their long volleys
with great anxiety and impatience. It was not known at what
point the enemy meant to make their most vigorous attack.
Our great strength had been reserved for the defence of Fort
Evans, and, finding the enemy were not inclined to advance,
Evans determined to do so. Our orders were to attack the

enemy, and "make the business short." "Forward, boys," said our General; "if they won't come to *us*, we must go to *them*, and in less than an hour we'll make them wish they had never been born."

The Eighteenth led, and following came the Seventeenth and Thirteenth, with four howitzers. As we reached the highest point in the road, we saw the enemy drawn up in beautif l order, in columns of companies, with many pieces of artillery and some cavalry; above them, on the other side of the river, were three batteries placed on a hill, and all ready for action! Several brigades had not crossed, and we could plainly see them with arms stacked! As we silently moved forward, an Adjutant galloped to the front, and the column halted. The enemy plainly saw our whole force, but reserved their fire. "They have nearly surrounded us at the Bluff," he said, "and the Eighteenth is to countermarch to their relief!" So the Seventeenth and Thirteenth countermarched to their old position, and after pulling down the fences, we began our race of two miles to turn the tide of battle. As we left the road a strange sight was presented, and which caused many a hearty laugh. Some hundred or more of our regiment who were sick, had escaped from the hospitals, knocked over the doctors and parsons who tried to prevent them, and marched out to participate in the fight, and now fell into rank with great good humor! As many more had left the hospitals in the morning contrary to orders, and not knowing the whereabouts of their respective regiments, had directed their steps to the line of fire, and fought manfully. As we ran towards the scene of battle, the roar of the enemy's musketry and cannon was deafening.

"Lige" White, who had been very active all day, rode up to us and confirmed the statement that our small force was nearly surrounded: he knew every inch of the ground perfectly, and piloted us into a position immediately in front of the enemy's centre. The enemy did not expect us in that direction, and a lull in the firing immediately ensued. Our fatigued comrades seemed with one accord to leave the battle entirely to us; and we did not disappoint their flattering expectations. Advancing through the woods in good order, we at last came in sight of a large open field where the centre of the Yankee semicircular line of battle was supported by four howitzers. Knocking down the fences, we jumped into the open and re-formed, as coolly as if on parade. The four right companies instantly dashed up a rising ground to the right, and dispossessed the foe of a patch of woods that commanded their centre. Though vigorously assailed with shot and shell, our right companies fired so quickly, and with such murderous accuracy, that the guns were soon deserted; but the fire of the enemy's infantry at the same time was so well sustained that had, we not been wise enough to load and fire on all-fours, not a man of us would have escaped. We had the advantage of a full view of every movement made by the enemy, and all their advances were chastised with such heavy loss that they contented themselves with the cover of the timber on the Bluffs and could not be induced to advance.

Such a roar of musketry, for the numbers engaged, I never heard. Many fell on our side. The four right companies had over one hundred killed or disabled; but though two thousand men—some of the very best in the Federal army, and under Baker—were opposed to them and kept up a semicircle of fire, our men held on like bloodhounds, and neither threats, commands, nor entreaties of officers could induce them to fall back and re-form the regiment. The men would *not* do it; the enemy were before them; they would advance, if ordered, but no falling back for any thing. In fact, these four companies were fighting the battle alone, and the enemy were losing scores every moment. Our men had bought large quantities of buckshot, and reserved them for "close quarters," as they termed it, and were now using them with terrible effect. Besides the ordinary musket cartridge, they put in from eight to sixteen buckshot, and kept up the fire with so much effect that the enemy's front and all around the guns were strewn with the dead and wounded in hundreds.

General Baker having been killed shortly after our fierce onset, Colonel Coggswell now commanded the enemy, and thought to make good his retreat by a flank movement to Edwards's Ferry. While he deliberated, the Seventeenth came in on our left flank, and the rest of our regiment assailed him on the right. For some time the battle raged with great fury, and it seemed to us there was no end to the stream of fresh troops relieving the enemy. But Colonel Coggswell had succeeded to the command in a luckless hour. Endeavoring to move by the left flank, in order to effect a junction with Stone at the Ferry, he was intercepted by our lieutenant-colonel, who advanced against him with six companies, and having surrendered, we had the satisfaction to see eight hundred prisoners, with the chief in command, marched to the rear.

The fighting still continued in the centre, as if the troops were unaware of Coggswell's surrender, but as it was not our object to shed blood unnecessarily, we all ceased firing for a few moments. Our company was detached from the regiment, and rested on the right of the Virginians, who lay in the woods. We were soon ordered to advance across the open ground at the double-quick, to join the regiment drawn up in the woods at the edge of the river, and as we did so, up rose the enemy on the Bluff, and poured a heavy volley into us; but we dropped in time, rose up instantly, rushed on, discharged our pieces in their faces, and drove them over the Bluff on to the bayonets of their friends, thirty feet below. Such slaughter, such havoc and mangling of living men, it has never been my lot to witness in any battle. Our men were wrought up to fury, and fought like fiends; no unfair advantages were sought, nor did any act contrary to the rules of war; but, greatly outnumbered at all points, they eagerly seized upon every opportunity to inflict chastisement, and from their masterly use of the musket, killed and wounded twice as many as their own number actually engaged.

The centre of the enemy was now completely broken, and the remnant driven over the Bluff into the river; the guns were ours, and dragged off; the right was captured to a man; and the left had disappeared under the high banks of the river, and dispersed in small parties, endeavoring to cross. As we lay in line of battle, expecting a fresh attack, I plainly saw the wrecks of three large flats, on which hundreds had perished. They had been used for bringing over reenforcements, and returning with wounded, but such was the consternation among the troops, that large numbers rushed on board, trampling upon the wounded, until they all sank together amid frightful screams. Colonels and captains had deserted their commands, and throwing off their clothing, escaped by swimming; at one time the river seemed covered with heads, and when, being ordered back, refusing to return, nearly all were shot by our men. On the island we saw several regiments drawn up, but the rout and destruction of their comrades appalled them: they would not advance, and, to prevent loss from our accurate fire, they were led off from the island into Maryland. Several houses on the island had been converted into hospitals, and the hundreds of suffering beings who lay around the field presented a harrowing sight.

The sun had now set, the battle was over, and various companies of men were detailed to bear off the wounded, bury the dead, secure arms and prisoners, and hold the field. Our right was still threatened, and every available man marched to support the Thirteenth, who held Fort Evans. The enemy, indeed, had not advanced an inch, but there was no certainty regarding their movements.

At night I went to the Bluff to look after the wounded. The sight was an awful one; the groans in every direction fearful to hear. Burial-parties were busy with spades, and many a noble boy might be seen consigned to his last resting-place. Crowds of carriages and conveyances were on the ground, bearing off the wounded, while the hospitals in town were thronged by ladies, young and old, lending their tender aid in all manner of offices. Indeed, while the battle was progressing, crowds of women gathered on a neighboring hill, and wept and bewailed, while many a good sturdy fellow kept in-doors, ready to shout for either party, and did not stir out till victory had saluted our banners.

The Yankees who had hid themselves along the bank of the river were loth to come forth, but after much persuasion, they voluntarily came forward in a body, threw down their arms, and marched to town very good-humoredly, and, after being refreshed, were sent towards Manassas that same night. The quantities of arms we found along the banks surprised me — all being of English manufacture, having on the plates, "Hall, London;" "Bond, London;" "London Tower," etc. The stream at the crossing appeared to be literally choked with broken boats, dead bodies, and arms — not less than one hundred dead being piled up under the Bluffs in dozens, and scores in other places, and the sand all gory. The woods around the Bluffs were all cut down or splintered by shot, the trunks of the larger trees looking as if millions of rats had been gnawing them. The number of arms captured was near two thousand, four howitzers, much clothing, a few stores and ammunition, eight hundred prisoners, twenty officers, two colonels, one or two stand of colors. The killed and wounded were about two thousand, not including the three large boat-loads that sank, or numbers that fell on the island from stray shot, and from our fire late in the evening. Our loss was not more than from two to three hundred killed, wounded, and missing.

It surprised me at the time, and is still sufficiently remarkable to be worthy of note, that General Evans was not upon or even near the field until the last shot had been fired. Then, however, he came galloping upon the ground, and highly complimented us, saying that he had been anxiously watching us, at the same time observing the enemy's movements along the Edwards's Ferry road. If the truth must be told, he directed our movements from his office in town, two miles away — or between that point and Fort Evans — and was swearing lustily all the afternoon ; yet, although he fondly expected the enemy to approach the fort, they did not do so; hence every disposition was made at Ball's Bluff by Colonel Burt, of the Eighteenth, who fell while cheering on the four right companies in their headlong massacre of the enemy. Another remarkable fact: when the Yankees had safely reached the shores of Maryland, they began to cheer like madmen, but for what, will ever remain a mystery. One of the boys dryly remarked, that "the darned fools cheered because they got back safely!" Others said, "they cheered because they felt so mighty big over another victory!" Both were probably near the truth !

Our whole force now lay in the woods round Fort Evans, anxiously looking for the morrow, for all expected the enemy to advance, and endeavor to retrieve their fallen fortunes. Morning came, and scouts reported them strongly fortified, with large reserves, about to cross. We waited until noon, and although the rain poured in torrents, Evans was anxious to entice them forward. The Thirteenth was ordered to open the fight, and draw the enemy out; for this purpose the right wing of the regiment was used, to counterfeit weakness, the left being held in reserve. The Yankees accepted battle, and a large regiment advanced to the attack; the right of the Thirteenth seeing this, were maddened, (because not called in at the Bluff,) and assailed the New-Englanders with such fury that they broke and ran, the Thirteenth chasing them through ploughed fields, over their breast-works, and past their guns. The guns would have been brought in, but being so far from all support, the men fell back without them. It was in vain that all kinds of expedients were used to entice the enemy on, for, although our small force was too much exhausted and insufficient to attack, we all desired the enemy to advance and try their fortunes. The rain fell in torrents all day, and at midnight three guns and loud cheers were heard from the other bank of the river; the enemy, twelve thousand strong, with twelve pieces, had successfully recrossed the river, and were cheering in consequence!

Fearful that other forces would move down from Drainsville, and cut off his communication, Evans once more fell back to Goose Creek, where a South-Carolina regiment, a Louisiana regiment, and four guns of the Washington Artillery, reenforced us. Here we anxiously awaited battle from McCall, or any one else who dared to approach. Our reenforcements were eager for the strife, and could a hundred thousand dollars have purchased a battle, they would willingly have subscribed that amount. The Louisianians in particular were fretful for a fight; they had marched from Centreville in a very short time, and in order not to delay, kicked over their barrels of flour, and journeyed with empty haversacks. This regiment was entirely composed of Creoles and Irish—a splendid lot of men, and highly disciplined by Colonel Kelly. They have since greatly distinguished themselves in "Stonewall" Jackson's division, having turned the tide in many battles.

CHAPTER XII.

Effects of the Battle of Leesburgh, or Ball's Bluff, on Public Opinion in the Country, North and South—The Yankees claim a Victory as usual—General Stone arrested and sent to Fort Warren—Remarkable Incidents of the War—A Fraternal Rencontre—The Negroes with either Army—Humorous Incidents—Evans is sent to defend his Native State, South-Carolina—General D. D. Hill assumes Command—Fortifications are erected—We prepare for Winter Quarters.

For two or three weeks previous to the battle of Leesburgh, the Northern papers overflowed with joyful expectations regarding the movements then in preparation. The Administration organ at Washington predicted that "in a few days the rebels would suddenly drop out of Leesburgh;" others said, "We shall begin to make history next week;" "let all prepare for a succession of Union victories that shall eclipse all the doings of the Old World!" It may well be supposed that enough had occurred to disenchant them of these bombastic ideas; but no, the Federal generals, to cover up their defeat by misrepresentation, acknowledged having met with reverses at Ball's Bluff, but triumphantly rejoined: "We have captured Harrison's Island, and hold it against all efforts of the rebels!" The fact is, they had always held undisputed possession of the island; yet the mainland was so much higher as to command it, and had our artillery been present in the battle, not twenty men of their whole force could have escaped.

When at length the story was truthfully told by the New-York *Times* and *Tribune*, the whole North was thrown into consternation and mourning over "the massacre," as they termed it, and began reviling each other for urging McClellan to advance at all against Richmond. Massachusetts was particularly affected by the direful news, for two of its "pet" regiments (the Fifteenth and Twenty-third) had suffered fearfully, and many young men of the first families had fallen, including the promising son of the poet, Oliver Wendell

Holmes, most of the men having been enrolled in Boston and Worcester. New-York also felt very much humbled on account of the decimation of the Forty-fourth, one of its crack regiments, which boasted of more professional pugilists and blackguards than any other from that State, except the red-legged Fire Zouaves. Pennsylvania was in mourning for the rout of the First California Regiment, (fifteen companies strong,) which had been raised by Baker in Philadelphia, and which was petted and feasted, and paraded at Washington by Lincoln himself, and called the "Invincibles." Other States had each its special reason for mourning, and so, from one reason or another, the entire press howled over the disaster for a full month.

In the South, however, our success was not regarded with proportionate admiration; the people expected the "boys" to do well, and when their victory was recorded, it only excited smiles and modest comment. As far as our brigade was concerned, scarcely a man spoke of it, save to show how much more might have been gained by the presence of artillery, or if the preliminary movements in which they had been engaged during the previous week had been less fatiguing. General Evans, indeed, was much lauded in the newspapers, biographical sketches appearing from different pens, tending to prove that the General was an extraordinary soldier; the men, however, could not help believing that his plans were faulty, and that had it not been for the ferocity of the troops, the affair would have ended very differently. Be that as it may, the South-Carolinians claimed the battle as theirs, since Evans was of that State; while the gallant Mississippians thought all the honor belonged to them, as they had done all the fighting; and in truth, the Virginians did very little. Poor Stone, the Federal commander, was bullied unmercifully by the Northern press, and being in Washington on business, where he dined with McClellan, he was on the following morning arrested and sent to Fort Warren, without a word of explanation.

Among the numerous incidents that fell under my notice illustrative of the sometimes tragical, sometimes laughable, occurrences of civil war, the following may be mentioned as properly pertaining to the battle of Leesburgh. Two young men, brothers, acquaintances of mine in Kentucky, had always differed in politics, and when the war broke out, Howard, the younger, sought the Southern army, and Alfred that of the North. They shook hands at parting, and said it was probable they should meet again on some field or other. Alfred obtained a captain's commission; Howard, with many fellow-statesmen, shouldered a musket in our regiment. When the battle was over, Howard was searching for the bodies of friends who had fallen by his side, and stumbled over something. "Halloa!" said the object, in a hoarse voice, "who are you?" "I'm a Southerner," replied Howard; "you are one of the enemy, if I'm not mistaken, and know, of course, that the field is ours." "Well, yes, I have some faint recollection of a fight; but all I remember is much smoke, a great noise of musketry, and of some active fellow in a white cap knocking me down with a musket, and then I fell asleep." When they advanced to one of the camp-fires, Howard recognized his brother Alfred, and he himself was the man who had knocked him down with the butt of his musket in the confusion of the battle!

By the next incident I shall relate we were much amused. One of our best soldiers was a rough Scotchman named Black, who had relatives in the South, and, desiring to get to them, joined the Northern army, with the intention of deserting at the first opportunity. When on picket guard at the river, he pretended to bathe, and, being a good swimmer, manfully struck out for the Virginia shore. When midway, he turned and shouted: "Good-by, boys; I'm bound for Dixie!" "Come back, or we'll shoot!" answered the guard. "Shoot, and be d—d, you white-livered nigger-thieves," shouted Black, and in the midst of a shower of Minié balls, he safely landed among us. He willingly entered our service, and proved an admirable soldier. During the battle he performed many feats of daring, and at night formed one of a corporal's guard who escorted a full company of Federals off the ground. As Black was laughing and joking, the captain of the Federals remarked to him: "I ought to know that voice!—is that you, Black?" "That's me!" jocosely replied the Scotchman. "I hope you're well, captain, you and all the boys! I couldn't stay with you, you see; it wasn't because I feared to fight, but I like to fight in the right cause always." It is needless to say Black was escorting his old company, officers and all.

At the commencement of the action our men perceived
among the enemy several negroes, who seemed to take great
care of themselves, and could not be induced to leave the trees
behind which they fought. Many of us took a "pop" at the
darkies, but always missed. When the fact became known to
our colored boys, who always persisted in going to battle with
us, they dropped the wounded they were carrying off, and immediately formed plans for capturing "de black 'Bolition
teeves." It was very amusing to see their display of generalship. "Go back to the rear, boys," said the officers, "this is
no place for you!" But the darkies would *not* go back, and
lurking behind their masters picked off the enemy's officers at
a rapid rate. At last the regiment made a sudden charge,
when, to our surprise, we found that not less than half a dozen
black fellows had preceded us, and were each bringing out a
prisoner of the same color, abusing them roundly, and kicking
them unmercifully. "You black rascal you!—does you mean
to fight agin white folks, you ugly niggers, you? Suppose
you tinks yourself no 'small taters' wid dat blue jacket on and
dem striped pants. You'll oblige dis Missippi darkey by pulling dem off right smart, if yer doesn't want dat head o' yourn
broke." "You are a mighty smart nigger, you is!" said one.
of our cooks to his captive; "comin' down Souf to whip de
whites! You couldn't stay 't home and let us fight de Yanks,
but *you* must come along too, eh! You took putty good care
o' yourself, you did, behind dat old oak! I was a lookin' at
yer; and if you hadn't dodged so much, you was a gone chick-
en long ago, you ugly ole Abe Lincolnite, you!"

Some of our servants were fortunate enough to pick up many
valuables, including diamond-pins, watches, rings, and money,
and as at Manassas, they selected the finest Federal uniforms
they could discover, in which they dressed themselves, and
then promenaded round town with their sweethearts. I discovered my servant one morning making coffee, completely
dressed in the grandest style, from boots to the gilded shoulder.
straps, of some unfortunate Federal officer. In their conversation, they seemed to look upon the Yankees with contempt,
and especially because they didn't fight to suit them. "Talk
of dem Yanks comin' down to whip us! Dey must be sick!
Why, massa can whale a dozen of 'em 'fore coffee is hot, fair

fight. Dem Nordon darkies is no 'count, and yet dey puts on all de airs in the worle. If eber I ketch any of dem darkies comin' in *my* way, or foolin' wid me, dis chile is goin' to make *somebody* holler, sure!"

General Evans had received command of all the forces in South-Carolina; and as that State was threatened with invasion, he now hurried forward to perfect arrangements; his successor in our command was General D. H. Hill, (brother-in-law to "Stonewall" Jackson,) and a very superior officer. General Griffith (cousin of the President) commanded the brigade. From the moment of his arrival, Hill was continually in the saddle, and, nearly always alone, soon made himself master of every acre in Loudon County. I shall have to speak of this officer again. He had already achieved fame at Little Bethel as colonel of the Carolina Volunteers, and greatly emulated Jackson in all his doings. Having selected fine sites near the river, he commenced fortifying with great vigor, much to the annoyance of the enemy, who had meditated crossing the ice during heavy winter, and surprising us before reenforcements could march up from Centreville. The mud-work at Fort Evans was also enlarged, covered, made bomb-proof, and pierced for six thirty-two pounders; long lines of rifle-pits were dug during night close to the river and elsewhere; a hill was fortified to the south, commanding Fort Evans; and another, more important still, north of the town, which commanded every approach. Figuratively, our fortifications were lions without teeth; for guns could not be spared at Manassas; and the roads were in such bad order that it required twenty-four oxen to draw one thirty-two-pounder a distance of twenty-five miles, and taking not less than three days to do it. Hill worked hard, however, and placed six heavy pieces in position, and astonished the enemy by shelling them out of their battery behind Edwards's Ferry.

In the mean time it had become apparent to all that some grand move was planning in Maryland; for heavy masses of troops were continually seen moving from point to point. Our cavalry force was therefore increased, and guarded the Upper Potomac; and now all being prepared as far as our means permitted, we committed the event to fortune, and in November received the joyful order to go into winter quarters.

CHAPTER XIII.

FOR the next two weeks scarcely any sound was heard but that of axe-men engaged in felling trees; and within a very short time we were all well housed in log-huts, covered with layers of straw and mud. The fire-places being large, admitted "sticks" of wood four feet long; and sometimes ten logs of this length constituted a fire. Some bought stoves to cook on, and built additional dwellings for their servants; but within the fortnight all were comfortably provided for. Our commanders occupied some princely residences owned by Union men in Maryland, who had been large lottery-dealers, and possessed of immense wealth. The various regiments were placed on the east side of the forts, ready to occupy them within five minutes' notice.

Amusements of all kinds were soon introduced, but chiefly cock-fighting, as in summer. Men were sent out in all directions to buy up game fowl; and shortly there rose up a young generation of "trainers," versed in every point of the game, and of undisputed authority in the settlement of a quarrel. These, for the most part, were gentlemen from the Emerald Isle, not a few of whom were in every regiment in the service. In the matches, regiment fought against regiment, and company against company, for stakes varying from five dollars to two thousand dollars a side; and such was the mania for "roosters" that the camps sounded like a poultry show, or a mammoth farmyard. "Snow-balling" was also a favorite pastime with the Southerners, and, together with skating and sledging, much delighted them; the majority had never seen snow or ice, except when the latter was used with "sherry-cobblers," "whisky-skins," "cocktails," etc.

I was loth to leave the brigade; but service called me to Richmond. So, having partaken of all the enjoyments of "singing clubs," "negro minstrels," "debating clubs," and the like, I departed for Manassas by a quartermaster's wagon, and soon arrived at Centreville. The outposts and guards at the latter place were extremely vigilant—annoyingly so, I thought; and for the slightest irregularity in our "passes" and papers, would have sent us back to Leesburgh. Fortifications of immense strength and extent arose on every hand, and were all well mounted. Though I could not comprehend the half of what fell under my notice, I felt strongly impressed that no army in the world could capture the place by an assault in front or flank. For miles these earthworks could be seen stretching through the country; and I counted not less than five hundred heavy pieces, without numbering them all.

The troops were comfortably quartered in well-built frame-houses, placed in lines of streets, with parade-grounds in front; sinks, gutters, and other sanitary arrangements seemed complete. The care and forethought displayed by our generals for the comfort, health, and convenience of the men surprised and delighted me: large bakeries, wash-houses, infirmaries, black-smiths' shops, numerous sutlers' establishments, (where no liquors were sold,) chapels, parade and drill-grounds, head-quarters, chiefs of departments, immense stables, warehouses and State dépôts—even a railroad connecting the place with Centreville to facilitate communication and send supplies.

The only drawback here—and this was sufficient to mar the whole—was the incredible quantity and tenacity of the mud. Locomotion in rainy or damp weather baffles all description; and to say that I have seen whole wagon-trains fast in the road, with mud up to the axles, would afford but a faint idea of the reality. If timber had been plentiful, the roads might have been "corduroyed," according to the Yankee plan, namely, of piling logs across the road, filling the interstices with small limbs, and covering with mud; but timber was not to be procured for such a purpose; what little there might be was economically served out for fuel.

8

On arriving at Richmond a wonderful contrast to the well-disciplined order of Manassas presented itself. The Government offices were quiet and business-like, but no other part of the capital was so. The hotels were crowded to excess, as they always are; and great numbers of officers in expensive uniforms strutted about on " sick leave," many of whom had never been in the army at all, and after running up bills with all classes of tradesmen, would suddenly depart for parts unknown. The marvel was, that people could be so deceived, for it is no exaggeration to say that every third man was dignified with shoulder-straps, and collectively they far outnumbered all the officers at Manassas! In theatres, bar-rooms, and shops, on horseback or on foot, all wore the insignia of office. Not one was to be found of less rank than captain, and as for colonels—their name was legion! I was measured by a youth for a pair of boots, and bought some dry-goods of another, one morning; in the evening I saw both of them playing at billiards at the " Spottswood," dressed out in bran-new uniforms, with insignia belonging to the rank of major! This was sufficient explanation; and it did not at all surprise me afterwards to hear that nearly all the thousand and one gambling hells were kept by captains, majors, and colonels. General Winder, the provost-marshal, subsequently made it a punishable offence for any to assume uniforms except soldiers. The change was sudden and ludicrous in effect.

The floating population of Richmond was made up of the strangest elements. Some came to see friends, others with wonderful inventions or suggestions for Government. Not a few were impressed with an idea that the Cabinet needed their advice and counsel; but the majority of these strangers came with the modest determination to offer their services at large salaries, pretending that if they were not accepted for this or that office, some State or other would feel humbled, perhaps secede from the Confederacy, and I know not what. It was laughable indeed to hear the self-sacrificing Solons holding forth in bar-rooms or in private. Their ideas of all things military were decidedly rich, and would have astonished poor Johnston or Beauregard, who were put down as mere school-boys beside them. General Washington Dobbs, who had been engaged all his life in the leather business somewhere in Georgia, had come up to proffer his valuable services as briga- dier; but being unsuccessful, his patriotism and indignation electrified the whole private family where he boarded. Colonel Madison Warren, some poor relation of the English blacking- maker, had lived in some out-of-the-way swamp in the Caro- linas; he came to Richmond to have a private talk with the President, to let him know what *he* thought about General McClellan and old Scott. Not getting an audience, he offered himself for the vacancy of quartermaster-general, and not being accepted, was sure that Jefferson Davis was a despot, and that the Southern Confederacy was fast going to the devil.

Smith had a self-loading, self-priming field-piece, that would fire a hundred times a minute, and never miss. Each gun would only weigh twenty tons, and cost ten thousand dollars. He had asked a commission to make a thousand of them only, was willing to give Government the patent right gratis; and they would not listen to him! How *could* the South succeed when neglecting such men as Smith? Jones was another type of a numerous class of patriots. Tracts were necessary food for the soldiers. He (Jones) "only" wanted the Government to start a large Bible and Tract house, give him the control of it, and he would guarantee to print as many as were needed, and sell them as cheaply as any body else, considering the high price of every thing. Jones, like a thousand others, did not succeed with any of the departments, and after being jammed and pushed about in the various lobbies and staircases for a whole month, arrived at the conclusion that the Confederate Government was not "sound" on the Bible question, and, therefore, ought not to be trusted in this enlightened and gos- pel-preaching age!

When the high price of every necessary is considered, it appears strange that the city should be so crowded. Boarding averaged from two dollars to five dollars per day at the hotels, and not less than ten dollars per week in any family. Boots were thirty-five dollars per pair; a suit of clothes (civil) one hun- dred and seventy-five dollars; military, two hundred dollars, or more; whiskey (very inferior) five dollars per quart; other liquors and wines in proportion; smoking tobacco, one dollar and fifty cents per pound; socks, one dollar per pair; shoes, eighteen dollars to twenty-five dollars; hair-cutting and shaving, one dollar; bath, fifty cents; cigars (inferior) four for one dollar, etc. The city, however, knew no interruption to the stream of its floating population, and balls, parties, and theatres, made a merry world of it; and Frenchmen say, it was Paris in miniature. Four in the afternoon was grand promenade hour; and, in fine weather, the small park and principal streets were crowded. Military and naval officers would sun themselves on balconies, or stretch their limbs elegantly at hotel-doors. Here it was that I first saw Commodore Lynch (late U. S. N.) of "Dead Sea" notoriety in literature, and Commodore Hollins, the "hero" (?) of Greytown.

The first-named was a small, quiet, Jewish-looking man of about fifty; thin, sallow complexion, and curly black hair, small black eyes, and very meek in appearance; wearing a cloak, like a man of economical habits and limited means. No one would take him for the "Tartar" which he undoubtedly is, when aroused; he is indefatigable in all that pertains to naval affairs. Hollins is about five feet six inches, broad-shouldered and stout, grey hair, whiskers, and moustaches, full face, a fine forehead, a lively blue eye, slow and solemn in deportment and conversation. He always seems to be walking on the quarter-deck, with his eye on the shrouds. No one would take him to be a person of much energy, ashore, but every movement betrayed that his proper station was that of commander of a seventy-four. He wore a plain dark grey suit and cap trimmed with a gold band, on which was prominent the anchor and cables—in such a costume he looked more like an old major of foot than any thing else.

Hollins's son and myself were soon fast friends; and through him I became acquainted with many persons, who have since become distinguished in the war. Roger Pryor, a Virginian and brigadier, was formerly Congressman from Virginia, and distinguished himself in the halls of legislation more by his combativeness than eloquence; more than once he challenged the Northerners who were disrespectful in their language towards the South. He is a young man, rather thin and tall, with a feminine face, delicate moustaches, and long black hair. He is veritably one of the "fire-eaters," and with a brigade of

Mississippians once under his command, and lately of Louisianians, he has made his name famous. Major-General Magruder is about forty years of age, thick-set, voluptuous in appearance, very dressy and dandified, "showy" in his style and bearing, and nearly always mounted. He was an artillery officer in Mexico, under Scott, and gained an enviable name for efficiency in that branch, as also in engineering. He looks like a man too much given to dissipation, and is incapable of planning a battle, although very vigorous in fighting one. If appointed to fortify a place, there is no man on the continent that could do it better. He commanded the small Confederate force that defeated Butler in the engagement at Little Bethel, and was ably assisted by Colonel D. H. Hill, now a General, commanding at Leesburgh. When the war commenced, Magruder was registered on the U. S. army roll, "Captain company I, First Artillery." I saw dozens of other generals, since known to fame, and conversed with many, but defer speaking of them until their names occur as prominent actors on the stage of events.

CHAPTER XIV.

The Battle of Belmont, on the Mississippi, described in a Letter from a Friend— The Forces of General Pillow surprised by Grant—The Southern Troops narrowly escape a Defeat—Reenforcements from General Polk and Columbus—Arrival of Polk on the Field—The Federal Troops defeated and Spoils taken— Characters of General Pillow and General Polk compared—Misrepresentations of the Northern Press.

I HAD only just returned to my regiment at Leesburgh when I received a letter from a Kentucky friend, serving under General Polk, at Columbus, descriptive of the engagement at Belmont, which had been fought some time before at the village of that name in Missouri:

"*Columbus, Ky., Nov. 10th*, 1861.

"DEAR TOM: You will, ere this reaches you, have heard more than one account of the late fight at Belmont; but this will satisfy you that I am all right, and ready to have another 'shake' with the Great Anaconda, so much talked of in the North. In my former letter, I fully informed you of the stupendous works raised here by General Gustavus Smith, and of our having occupied Belmont opposite, so as to command both banks of the stream. But the enemy appeared to know as well as we did that our force on the west bank was not very formidable, nor our works of a very threatening character, and so determined to surprise General Pillow some fine morning.

"In pursuance of his amiable purpose, Grant collected a fleet of large river steamboats, and embarking at night, steamed down the river unobserved. Within a few miles of Columbus and Belmont, the river makes a sudden bend, and behind this bend Grant disembarked his forces, and began to advance towards Belmont, through the woods. When morning broke, the action commenced; the first intimation of the enemy's presence being a succession of rapid volleys. The troops were soon under arms, but the sudden surprise precluded all idea of a regular line or plan of battle. We at Columbus had heard the rapid fire for more than an hour, but knew not its cause. The word was passed to our brigade to 'fall in;' and before we could conjecture the meaning of all this, General Polk rode up, and informed us, very briefly, that Pillow had been attacked by an overwhelming force under Grant, and that we were going to the rescue.

"In a short time we were steaming across—not to Belmont, but towards the Yankee landing-place up the river, keeping as close in shore as possible to avoid notice; for had the enemy boldly advanced down the river, and engaged the boats, disregarding our batteries, nothing in the world could have saved us. We had not proceeded far, when their guns on the battlefield were turned against us, but without effect, and we were soon landed in the timber on the enemy's flank and rear. Advancing out of the woods into the 'open,' we were received with volleys of musketry and grape; but the aim was too high or many would have suffered. When we arrived at close quarters, we discovered the enemy rapidly falling back from their main attack, and seeking to regain their boats. Thus invited, we attacked them vigorously with the bayonet, and for a full hour chased them through woods and fields, making every shot tell among the retreating crowd. We captured several pieces of cannon, and drove them to their boats. The scene at the landing was awful. The miserable wretches were rushing on board in great confusion, while our men kept up a continual shower of lead amongst them. We made several attempts to capture some of the boats, but did not succeed.

"Although not on the field when the fight opened, I fully understand the true position of affairs, and must say that the fight was a desperate one. When the enemy were reported landing troops a few miles above, the garrison in Belmont consisted of only two regiments. Pillow, with four regiments, immediately crossed and assumed command. He had scarcely done so, when Grant's advance opened fire, and the fight soon became fierce and obstinate. The enemy, who knew our weakness, would have succeeded in surrounding our left only for the destructive fire of a battery placed there, and the rapidity with which troops in support maintained their deadly volleys. This wing was severely taxed, as was also the right; but despite all their efforts, the enemy could not force them, though assisted by powerful artillery.

"Having failed in his attack on the wings, Grant knew there was little time to spare, and repeatedly hurled his strongest force at our centre, which occupied open ground. The firing here was incessant, and we gradually gave way. Pillow then ordered a charge, and the first line of the enemy was driven in confusion upon their reserves. But our ammunition now began to fail, and word came that the wings could not maintain their position if the centre gave in, as there was every reason to fear it would do. Again a charge was ordered, which proved no less successful than the first. It was now found that our only battery had not a cartridge remaining, and most of the troops were similarly circumstanced; there was no alternative but to fall back until reenforcements should arrive from Columbus.

"Taking up a strong position on the river-bank, Pillow arranged his lines for the final assault of the enemy; it being supposed, as they had full possession of our camps, and were firing them, that Grant would hurry forward his columns, and give us no time to re-form. As fortune would have it, three regiments arrived at this critical moment to reenforce us, and it was determined to move them up the river-bank and get in the enemy's rear. The enemy had seen our boats crossing, and played on them with a heavy battery; but the guns at Columbus replied, and in a few moments the enemy's pieces were silenced. Finding that Polk himself was crossing, and landing troops far up the river on his line of retreat, Grant immediately began to fall back, but had not proceeded far when he encountered Louisianians, Mississippians, Tennesseeans, and others formed on his flanks, subjecting him to loss every moment, while the guns at Columbus continued rapidly firing across the river, and from the high position of the works, were made to tell with deadly effect. Under these circumstances resistance was hopeless, and Grant reluctantly ordered a retreat, but while conducting it was subjected to a terrific cross-fire from our troops, while Polk in person was pushing their rear vigorously, capturing prisoners and arms every yard of the road. The confusion, noise, and excitement were terrible, the enemy rapidly retreating to their boats, and our advance columns pouring deadly volleys into them; thus almost miraculously changing a defeat into a glorious triumph for our arms.

"The number of dead and dying that blocked up the landing-place was very great, and it seemed a matter of wonder to me how so many men could have successfully embarked and made their escape in so short a time. Had our officers been active, and brought down some field-pieces in time, we might have disabled the boats, and caused awful havoc among their densely packed numbers. We captured several hundred prisoners, several thousand stand of arms, and a few cannon, but, as the enemy simply came with their arms, and did not even carry a blanket to impede their activity in this enterprise, little else of value.

"General Pillow has to thank his stars that Polk so quickly came to his succor, or, instead of being hailed as victors, we might all have been snugly provided for in some New-England fort or penitentiary. Yet his vanity is not less conspicuous now than it was in Mexico, and he is eternally carping at "the bishop," as he terms Polk, who, nevertheless, is a capable and laborious commander, accessible at all times by high and low, a thorough disciplinarian, and fine engineer. If he chose to leave the army in former times and enter the Episcopal Church, and become a learned bishop among his brethren, it surely does not detract from his repute as a gentleman, a Christian, and a scholar, to say that he resigned his charge in answer to the especial call of the Executive, who demanded the service of all talented men in behalf of the common cause. Polk was a good bishop; he is now an excellent and accomplished Major-General, and possesses the entire confidence, love, and respect of all who know or serve under him. Pillow is annoyed, however, because he himself was not placed in chief command at Columbus—a position for which he is totally unfitted, as subsequent events will fully demonstrate.

"But to return to the battle. This, as you know, is the first time I have ever been under fire, and I confess I felt very uncomfortable. We were convinced that our boys had been having the worst of it all the morning, or our haste would not have been so pressing. We had scarcely landed when one of Pillow's orderlies rode up and begged us for God's sake 'to hurry up,' as the boys were hard pressed, and had been fighting a

long time against odds, and were only recovering from the confusion in which they had been thrown. As we marched out
into open ground we gave loud yells, and commenced firing.
Many of our men falling every moment, the thought continually occurred to me that my turn would come next, yet inspired
by the example of our officers, we rushed to close quarters,
determined to bring matters to a conclusion. But enough; I
shall not attempt to describe further this battle-field to you, but
conclude, humbly thanking God for the victory.

"I have to-day received late Northern papers; it is unnecessary to say that Belmont is put down as 'Another National
Victory,' etc., in very large capitals, with 'full accounts of the
Rebel loss.' To believe these scribbling fools, 'the back-bone
of the rebellion' is well-nigh broken; yet, between ourselves,
I think the job will prove too big, and break their hearts and
pockets over it first. . . .   Yours, as ever,   * * * "

CHAPTER XV.

Winter Quarters continued—Scant Rations supplied to the Troops—High Prices of
Provisions and Clothing resulting from the Blockade—Sufferings of the Poor—
Refugees from Kentucky—True State of Public Feeling there—Letter from a
Friend, containing an Account of the Opening of the Campaign in Kentucky and
Tennessee—Battle of Mill Spring, January first, 1862—General Zollicoffer and
most of his Staff killed—Surrender of Fort Donelson, February ninth—Strange
Conduct of General Floyd.

THE monotony of camp life was felt severely during the
winter, notwithstanding the resources I have mentioned in a
previous chapter. General Hill was a strict disciplinarian, and
would permit none to be out in town after nightfall, unless furnished with a pass countersigned by the Provost-Marshal. So
strictly was this rule enforced that I have known a whole squad
of officers arrested and put under guard, including two full-
blown Colonels and sundry Majors, simply for going to and fro
unarmed with the necessary "countersign."

With books and writing materials, many of us made the
winter evenings pass off very agreeably, while others had become proficient in vocal and instrumental music; so that if we
could only smuggle a gallon of apple-brandy into camp, a roaring fire of logs, pleasant punch, and entertaining society made
our cabins very enjoyable.

The usual discomforts of a deficient commissariat we had of
course to endure: a variety of rations were allowed which were
never forthcoming. Coffee, sugar, rice, vegetables, and beans,
we never had, save for two or three weeks during the first year
of service; we knew, however, that Government did the best
it could, and therefore, as patriots, did not murmur, but bought
what we could. Coffee, as Southerners, we could *not* do without; hence, if on picket, we exchanged tobacco for it with the
Yankees, but otherwise used parched barley as a substitute, as
the whole South was cheerfully doing. Bacon or beef, with·
baker's bread, or flour, were the only rations we had regularly:

any luxurious addition to this simple fare we had to purchase, and this at the most preposterously high price. For example: even in this, an agricultural country, turkeys sold for four dollars and five dollars each; two chickens, ditto; wretched liquors at twenty dollars and thirty dollars per gallon, and seldom to be had even at that; common coarse homespun jeans, five dollars per yard; common Manchester prints, one dollar per yard; common white cotton shirts, five dollars each; linen, ten dollars; cotton socks, one dollar per pair; boots, common, and clumsily made, twenty dollars to thirty-five dollars per pair; common felt hat, ten dollars; coffee, three dollars per pound; tea, five dollars; brown sugar, fifty cents per pound; white, seventy-five cents; flour, twelve dollars to fifteen dollars per barrel; bath, seventy-five cents; hair-cutting, seventy-five cents; shaving, twenty-five cents; washing, three dollars per dozen; the most common writing-paper, twenty dollars to twenty-five dollars per ream; printing paper was not to be had at any price—many suspended publishing, others printed a sheet not much larger than quarto; horse's feed per day, two dollars; boarding, from fifty dollars to one hundred dollars per month— one dollar per single meal. These items may suggest to the thoughtful what great trials and privations the poor had to endure in consequence of the war!

With regard to wearing apparel, when money and cloth were exhausted, friends at home would send on our cast-off clothes, in big bales, together with whatever the numerous "soldier-serving societies" could furnish; so that, all in all, although we looked like a regiment of dilapidated dandies, we were warmly clad, and laughed good-humoredly at each other's grotesque peculiarities of costume. I have more than once caught our good old major darning his socks, and espied the spruce, good-looking adjutant cobbling up his parade boots! The ladies, Heaven bless them! were ever at work, night and day, in our behalf—their flannel petticoats have been made into undershirts; their white skirts converted into lint; and I have known the blankets snatched from their beds and sent to the soldier, shivering on the snow-covered hills or plains of Virginia.

During the winter we received several excellent recruits from

Kentucky, who had successfully run the "blockade," and joined our fortunes. I personally knew them when in college, and was much interested in the intelligence they brought concerning the affairs of that State. The revolutionary party had formed a Provisional Government and passed acts of secession; still Governor Magoffin filled the chair, to which he had been elected before the war, and his term was not expired. When hostilities commenced, no one doubted which cause had the sympathies of the people of Kentucky, but by artifice men were admitted to her councils, who, under the name of "neutrals," played fast and loose with the populace, until Lincoln perfected his plans for their enthrallment. It was argued by these leading men, that Kentucky was, and always *had* been, a true Southern State, and would so remain, but in this quarrel of "extremes" she would preserve a strict and "armed neutrality!" — an idea that could only have found favor with a people who had been taught from childhood to believe in State Rights, and who scoffed at the idea "that any man could be found who should *dare* to interfere with the sanctity of the Constitution."

When the plans of the Northern Government were matured, the people of Kentucky had not to wait long to find the man "who should *dare*," etc., for the Secretary of State coolly took upon himself the direction of their State affairs, elected whom he pleased, and imprisoned whom he desired. When compelled to supply her quota for the war, the Lincolnites officered the men, monopolized every contract, dictated laws to the State, and, in short, ruled with a rod of iron. No one was permitted to pass from city to city without having sworn allegiance; schools were invaded, and Southern children held as hostages for the behavior of their parents! property was confiscated, men were thrown into loathsome dungeons on mere suspicion, negroes were taught to despise, mock, whip, and murder their late masters, while mothers, daughters, or sisters were insulted, violated, and murdered. Such were the results brought about by the treachery or cowardice of those whom the people elected in good faith to expound their views, and among the betrayers of the parent State must be numbered one of her own most gifted and trusted sons. As long as history lasts will his name be handed down with curses and maledictions.

My knowledge of the campaign in Kentucky and Tennessee

is derived solely from friends who participated in it; among other letters received by me, I present the following from a young artillery officer, who had good opportunities for knowing the facts of which he speaks :

"*Bowling Green, Green River, Ky., Jan. 20th, 1862.*

"DEAR. TOM: If there is one class of persons more likely than another to bring disaster upon our sacred cause, it will be those half-witted editors who imagine that every thing is wrong which they do not themselves comprehend. Before I came to Bowling Green I must confess that their articles had some influence upon me; and *I,* among the rest, could not 'see why Sidney Johnston did not muster his forces, advance farther into Kentucky, capture Louisville, push across the Ohio, sack Cincinnati, and carry the war into Africa,' etc. But since my arrival here, my thoughts have materially changed, and my wonder *now* is, how the commander has courage enough to stay where he is, and how he has managed to deceive the enemy as to his real strength. We were led to believe that there were at least one hundred thousand men here, and that the fortifications were frowning terrifically with cannon. All this, my friend, is pure fiction. We have not more than twenty-five thousand men, all told, and I think cannot count more than fifty light field-pieces. It is true, we have some few dozen heavy siege-guns, but by no means enough to frighten an enemy seriously bent on mischief. The position of Bowling Green is an admirably selected one, with Green River along our front, and railway communication to Nashville and the whole South. Had we simply to contend with an enemy advancing from Louisville, and attacking in front, we should have nothing to fear; but, as you are aware, our flanks and rear are threatened by an immense force, and, although they have made no demonstrations in those quarters, I cannot believe their generals to be so blind as to be unaware of their advantages by the Cumberland and Tennessee rivers. Grant, who is now at Cairo, longs for an opportunity to retrieve his disgrace at Belmont, and while he has full command of the rivers, there is nothing to prevent him from advancing with his gun-boats and transports upon Nashville. True, the rivers are low at present, and it may be a question whether his vessels can ascend them, even at a flood — this remains to be seen. The only warlike obstructions to his progress would be Forts Henry and Donelson. If, when Buell advances in concert, we do not 'get out of the way in a hurry,' the Anaconda may give this little army a hug not pleasing to our prospects."

The subjoined is part of a letter from the same friend, at a later date, descriptive of engagements in which he participated:

"*Murfreesboro, Tenn., Feb. 20th,* 1862.

"FRIEND TOM: I am 'hit' at last, and must tell you all about it. When writing to you last from Bowling Green, I had apprehensions that all was not going on well with us, and stories were circulated round head-quarters regarding 'immense forces' 'somewhere;' by which there was reason to conclude we should be compelled to relinquish our hold of Kentucky, and possibly cross the Tennessee! We were not long left in suspense. Buell dared not attack us in front, but waited for Grant to ascend the Cumberland in our rear. Our right flank was threatened also by a large Federal force under Thomas at Somerset, which was advancing against Crittenden's small force at Beech Grove.

"Zollicoffer, being but second in command to Crittenden at Beech Grove, had but little influence in the management. Our troops had been almost in a starving condition for some time, and had but scant rations for several months. Crittenden was fully informed of the Federal advance at Columbia and Somerset, but did little to prepare for the attack. In fact, it is said that he was incapable of commanding, from social failings, and did not heed the many warnings of friends, who foresaw that the enemy were bent on surrounding him. On learning that Thomas was at Mill Spring, Crittenden set out to meet him, thinking it possible to drive him from his fortified camps. On the morning of the nineteenth of January, (Sunday,) Zollicoffer's advance exchanged shots with the enemy, and the battle opened with great fury. Zollicoffer's brigade pushed ahead, and drove the Federals some distance through the woods, and were endeavoring to force their way to the summit of a hill which fully commanded the whole field. The Federals fought desperately for this position, but scarcely any thing could withstand the dashing onset of our troops. Misinformed as to their true position and number, Zollicoffer was rapidly advancing up-hill, but unexpectedly rode up to an Indiana regiment, mistaking it for one of his own. Not being able to retreat, he determined to sell his life dearly, so rode forward with his staff, and began pistolling right and left at the officers, but soon fell, mortally wounded, and with him most of his staff. The fall of this commander greatly confused the troops; but finding himself overpowered, and determined to make a bold push for victory, Crittenden himself rode to the front, and endeavored to gain the hill: after three hours' fighting, he was obliged to retreat to Beech Grove and push onwards to the Cumberland, leaving many dead, wounded, some prisoners, stores, a few pieces of cannon, and other things behind him.*

"When this news was brought to Bowling Green, it explained why Johnston had been so careful in transporting all supplies and ordnance to the rear for more than two weeks. None doubted that a retreat was inevitable: the enemy had shown their strength on our right, and driven in Crittenden, while Grant was preparing to ascend the Cumberland. The fortifications were dismantled and blown up. General Buckner watched Green River and our whole front; the sick and baggage had been sent away many days before; and while Buckner was engaging the enemy along the river-bank, our whole force departed.

"Floyd, as you will remember, had been under Lee in Western Virginia, among the mountains, but as that campaign, from paucity of numbers on our part, had been productive of more expense than profit, he was ordered to cross the mountains and report to Johnston at Bowling Green. His force was a small one, but well seasoned; so that, upon Grant appearing in the Cumberland, he was ordered to Fort Donelson, and was chief in command by seniority. Buckner's force was also ordered there, and

* General George B. Crittenden is a Kentuckian, about fifty-five years of age. He entered the United States service as brevet Second Lieutenant, Fourth Infantry, July first, 1832; resigned April thirtieth, 1833, was appointed Captain of Mounted Rifles, May twenty-seventh, 1846, and served with much distinction in the Mexican war, and was appointed Lieutenant-Colonel Mounted Rifles, December thirtieth, 1856. He is generally considered to be an excellent and reliable officer when free from the influence of drink and gay company. It is said that, previous to his appointment as commander at Beech Grove, he had rendered himself unfit for service by intemperance, and there are many who protest that he was greatly under the influence of liquor during the battle of Mill Spring. This vice is too prevalent among talented men of the South.

myself with it, but our total strength did not amount to more than fifteen thousand men, and we had but little artillery. Very soon Grant steamed up the river, and having captured Fort Henry without difficulty, approached Donelson to find it prepared for a fierce resistance. His fleet of steamboats came up within a few miles of us and landed immense masses of troops, while light-draught iron-clad gunboats opened on us fiercely, both night and day. When the Federal troops came within view, it was determined to march out and give them battle. In the mean time, the fort, indeed, kept up a lively fire from three tiers of guns upon the boats, doing considerable damage, and keeping off their steady advance. The lower tier, or 'water battery,' as it was termed, was served splendidly, and sank several vessels, killing commanders of note, and wounding Commodore Foote, chief of the flotilla. •If I am not mistaken, we engaged twenty gunboats, and sank or crippled five.

"When it was determined to give battle in the open ground, our men were jubilant, and, though fully aware of the disparity of numbers, resolved to sell their lives as dearly as possible. Floyd, Buckner, and Pillow were in chief command: nothing could withstand the impetuosity of our men; they heroically drove the enemy before them at all points with the bayonet. Still, all this heroism was useless; fresh divisions of the enemy arrived hourly, and each day saw their lines around us growing stronger. As often as they approached our outer works they were repelled with great slaughter; yet other regiments would follow, and our men, completely exhausted from want of rest and food, and numbed by the intense cold — fires were prohibited within the works, though snow and rain constantly fell—were completely unstrung and incapable of further action. A council of war being held, it was determined to march out and invite battle, rather than die like rats in a hole. Accordingly, for the third time we marched out against the enemy; but we found them fortified, and loth to meet us in the open, although far away from our guns and under the protection of their own. Never did men fight more gloriously than ours: when I heard their yells ringing in my ears as they advanced at the 'charge,' I almost felt tears rolling down my cheek, as, wounded in the arm, I retired within the fort, incapable of further exertion. This day was the most glorious of all! Well might the enemy retire to the woods when they saw the boys advancing with deafening shouts and levelled bayonets. All, from the highest to the lowest, performed their part with exemplary valor, and I may safely predict that the defence of Donelson against such fearful odds will be one of the brightest pages in our future history.

"At the close of the third day—after this last attack—a grand council of war was held; what its purport was I know not, but in the stillness of the night Forrest's cavalry took their departure by the only point of egress remaining, and, soon afterwards, Floyd's command followed them. Thinking the movement was general, I procured a horse, and arrived at Nashville. General Pillow also made his escape with a few of his troops, leaving the brave Kentuckian Buckner to do the best he could with his small command. In explanation of this strange proceeding on the part of our chief, I hear it whispered that Floyd was afraid of falling into the hands of the Federals, having, when Secretary of War under Buchanan, surreptitiously supplied the South with more than the fair proportion of national arms, without which the war could not have been begun. This may be all true enough, but can never exculpate him for deserting his post at such a trying moment.

"As might have been expected, Buckner was appalled at his situation, and after the departure of Pillow, he surrendered the fort and the remaining troops to General Grant, who spoke in complimentary terms of 'the splendid but useless resistance of the rebels.' The number of prisoners was about six thousand; and whatever else fell into the hands of the enemy was of very little value, as most of the guns were spiked or broken, and with regard to stores, we had none, the men, with but few exceptions, not having tasted food for three days. This affair has thrown great gloom over the country, and of course is the subject of Hallelujah Choruses North! Our people are waking up, however, and begin to understand it requires numbers, as well as 'pluck,' to beat back the invader; and I have no doubt, when properly considered, the fall of Donelson will be an invaluable lesson to us.   Yours ever,   * * * "

CHAPTER XVI.

Battle of "Elk Horn," Missouri, March seventh, 1862—Incidents and Sketches of the War in that State — Colonel Fremont superseded in the Command of the Federals—General Van Dorn—Our Guerrilla Horse—Breach of Parole by Northern Troops—McCulloch and McIntosh killed—Our Forces retire—The Loss on either side.

"*Elk River, McDonald Co., Mo., March 14th*, 1862.

"DEAR TOM: Your last was received and perused with much pleasure, and here am I on the confines of Missouri, within a few hours' travel of Arkansas and the Cherokee Indian territory, endeavoring to pen a few lines to satisfy your ardent curiosity. You have, doubtless, had reports of our previous manœuvres since I wrote from Lexington in September, and ere this reaches you in the far East, a thousand newspapers will have related very curious tales regarding our recent battle with the combined forces of Curtis and Sturgis* at Elk Horn, a few miles from here. Still, such details as I may be able to supply will not be unacceptable to you.

"The fall of Lexington was an unexpected and heavy blow to the Union party throughout the whole North. Fremont was so exasperated that he instantly began to muster every available man, intending to surround and capture us. Lane had been reenforced, and was advancing from the west; Sturgis was moving from the north; while Fremont, with a heavy command, began to advance from the east, thinking to cut off all retreat by the south. Our victory, however, had aroused a spirit of resistance throughout the length and breadth of the State, and volunteers flocked to Lexington by thousands. A few days after Mulligan's surrender, Price had not less than twenty-five thousand men around him, but lacked arms, provisions, wagons, tents, and ammunition; and besides these, from ten thousand to

---

* Brigadier-General Samuel D. Sturgis, U. S. A., ranked as captain, Company E, First Cavalry, in 1860. He was stationed near St. Louis when the troubles commenced, and rose rapidly.

fifteen thousand more were gathered at different points north of
the river, endeavoring to form a junction with us, and, like the
rest, unarmed. Price had been promised a heavy wagon train
of ammunition and provision from the south-west, and McCulloch was to have sent an escort for it, but after many trying delays, it was known that the train was not on its way, and thousands of recruits were obliged to disperse to their homes again,
hoping that ere long things would be more favorable for taking
the field.

" With almost superhuman exertions, Price managed to keep
around him some fifteen thousand men, and as the foe were closing in upon him from different directions, started the baggage
and provisions southward, together with most of the infantry ;
at the same time ordering the cavalry to make demonstrations
calculated to deceive Lane, Sturgis, and Fremont. The cavalry
acted their part·so well that the different columns of the enemy
thought themselves threatened, and halted, while Price's main
army had stolen several long marches upon them, and were
making rapidly towards the south-west. At Springfield we
learned that a different plan of campaign had been decided upon
by the Confederate generals, and that Hardee's forces were withdrawn from the south-east. Pushing on towards Neosha, Price
formed a junction there with McCulloch, and the Missouri Legislature, in full session, unanimously passed the Ordinance of
Secession, amid salvos of artillery, and with the rapturous approval of representatives from every county in the State.

" As the combined forces of the enemy were still approaching in great numbers, and evidently bent on mischief, Price and
McCulloch fell back to a strong position at Pineville, (McDonald county,) and awaited Fremont's approach. The main body
of the Federals were at Springfield, but had an advance division much nearer the Confederate leaders Our boys were particularly anxious for Fremont's advance, for as his main body
was composed of Dutch and Germans, they looked forward
with pleasure to the task of thrashing them. Imagine then, if
you can, our astonishment to find, from prisoners, that Fremont
had been thrust from the command by Lincoln, and that his
whole army, in a state of mutiny, was running a race towards
Rolla and St. Louis!

"Here was news indeed! Lincoln 'did not approve Fremont's emancipation proclamation and confiscating programme; the North were fighting,' he said, 'to preserve the Constitution intact, etc., and that we should be treated in this war as wayward brethren, whose rights were guaranteed on return to duty.' Fremont's heavy expenditure was another objection to him, especially as Frank Blair and other pets of the Administration had so little influence with him, and he had forestalled Lincoln himself in the favor of the abolitionists. Political aspirants thought, too, he was endeavoring to supplant them in the good graces of those who should live to vote in 1864, and his enemies even imagined that he was endeavoring to follow in the footprints of the Napoleons, and make himself Emperor of all the Dutch, most of whom had flocked around him like geese from all parts of the Union. This last accusation was certainly groundless, if for no other reason simply because Fremont lacked the nerve to attempt any *coup* so dazzling. Place the fact in whatever light we please, Fremont received peremptory orders to resign, and the messenger had the greatest difficulty in gaining admittance to his tent; the whole camp being in a terrible uproar, and all discipline abandoned! Halleck, the Veracious, is appointed in his stead, but how long would you insure *his* head?

"On learning that the troops of Fremont had retreated, Price immediately prepared for the pursuit. He followed them several days, capturing many prisoners and large quantities of stores, and at last halted his weary column at Springfield — that city of changing masters! It seemed unwise to proceed farther; the enemy had halted at Rolla, or a little beyond, vastly superior in force, and were making preparations for another advance.

"While recruiting and drilling his men, Price watched for the first movements of the foe, and early in January they began to advance. Price had taken up a strong position and fortified it, expecting that McCulloch would move forward to his assistance, but that commander did not stir, nor make the slightest diversion in his favor; so that, finding the enemy closing in upon him rapidly, he withdrew from Springfield, and was obliged to cut his way through towards Boston Mountain, where McCulloch was reported to be. After hard fighting and infinite toil, this was successfully accomplished, and all were agreeably surprised to find General Van Dorn there — the newly-appointed general-in chief of the Trans-Mississippi Department. This appointment had been wisely made by President Davis, for there was evidently little unanimity of feeling existing among commanders, but less querulousness, perhaps, on the part of Price, than of many others. 'Old Stirling' had begun the war without any means whatever, yet had captured ten thousand stand of arms, fifty cannon, hundreds of tents, together with many other things needful to an active army. No other generals in the department could show half as many proofs of their prowess, though all had done well.

" Our sufferings during the campaign had been extreme, but setting the inconveniences aside, had tended to harden us and make our limbs as tough as steel. Continually marching through non-inhabited districts, we had to depend upon Providence for supplies. Over mountains, through 'gaps,' across rivers and creeks, our progress was toilsome and weary; but few doctors meddled with any one, and not more than a hundred names could be found upon the sick-list at any time during our frequent and rapid journeyings. Our cavalry led a hard life, and must have been made of brass to support the trials incident to their daily duty. Among the mountains a party of these 'irregular' horse would watch all the roads, conceal their fires, and hang around the enemy with a pertinacious determination that no man should stir without their knowledge, and at the least opportunity making a dash at the foe, capturing and destroying as they went, living as best they might, and doing whatever they pleased, generally. As scouts, these men were invaluable — they were here, there, and everywhere — it was impossible to follow in their track. Their dress was of skins or any thing that came to hand, and so long as grass was found for their hardy, wiry Indian horses, the riders cared little for food, dress, leisure, or relief from duty.

"The enemy vowed vengeance against these hardy fellows, and sought to train their own horsemen to the wild, half-Indian kind of life practised by ours. But just imagine obese Dutchmen rivalling the swiftness, daring, and endurance of our wiry frontiersmen! They were posted on mountains and in the 'passes,' to guard fords, bridges, and roads, as ours did, but their loss was continual, and the mysterious disappearance of stores, horses, wagons, and men unaccountable; so at length they were withdrawn, and the experiment abandoned as an expensive and fruitless one. Entirely masters of the roads, and every route by land or water, our horse seldom troubled Price for supplies of any kind, save ammunition, but frequently drove into camp large numbers of beeves, hogs, fodder, corn, and whatever could be purloined from the enemy. Flank, front, or rear, the Federals hardly dared to move except in large bodies; guerrillas lay in every bush, and many an enemy was found lying dead at his post, without a trace of those who did it. These Partisans were remorseless; they expected little mercy if captured, and spared few found in arms against us. Some of our men falling into the hands of the enemy were hung on the spot; but this only heightened the animosity on either side; and when Federal soldiers were found dangling from trees by the roadside, the enemy thought it expedient to recognize our Partisan Rangers as 'legitimate' soldiers. After this our scouts usually paroled their prisoners.

"But of what avail is the parole with men who seem to have no honorable instincts, and scoff at an oath when voluntarily given? Look at the conduct of Mulligan's men—upwards of four thousand we paroled at Lexington! Nine tenths of them were from Illinois and Ohio, and had not been home more than a week, when it was argued, 'No faith should be kept with rebels;' and these men were instantly enrolled into new regiments and sent forth to fight again in some other quarter! This is incontrovertible; and the same perfidy has been enacted in regard to *all* those paroled in various directions, whether the men can be prevailed upon to re-enlist or not. These are stubborn, ugly facts, and no wonder, I say, that Partisans for a time forgot the usages of war, and retaliated with signal vengeance. But to my story once again.

"Scouts informed us that the enemy were strongly posted on rising ground at a place called Sugar Creek, about sixty miles distant, having a force of some twenty-five thousand men, under Curtis and Sturgis. It was also reported that they did not intend to advance until the arrival of heavy reenforcements, which were rapidly moving up. Although not twenty thousand strong, Van Dorn resolved to attack them, and sending word to Albert Pike to hurry forward with his brigade of Indians, moved out of camp on the fourth of March, with Price and McCulloch's forces, his intention being to surround the enemy's advance, some eight thousand strong, under Sigel, at Benconville.

"That excellent officer, however, was not to be so caught; he was far superior to Van Dorn in generalship, and successfully slipped through his fingers, fighting as he went towards the main body at the creek. This retreat of Sigel was admirably conducted, and though he could not successfully withstand our advance, he fought manfully and scientifically, losing many men, some prisoners, and stores. He effected a junction with Sturgis and Curtis, however, and on the seventh both armies were in full view of each other. Early in the morning, Van Dorn had made every disposition for attack, and the advance began. The enemy were strongly posted on high ground, as usual, their front being covered with a heavy body of skirmishers and artillery, but they gave way as we advanced in like order upon them, and fell back upon the main body. Price's forces constituted our left and centre, while McCulloch was on the right.

"To prevent the junction of reenforcements, known to be on the way, Van Dorn's attack was made from the north and west, his columns almost surrounding the foe. The fight was long and obstinate. Every commander handled his men in an admirable manner; and though the superior metal of our men forced the enemy before them, they constantly re-formed under a superior fire of artillery, and renewed the conflict as fiercely as ever. For *once* we had met good fighters. Our antagonists were nearly all Western men, and their fire was rapid and accurate. We could not bring all our artillery into play, and this proved a great disadvantage; besides which, it was soon perceived that Van Dorn's idea of 'surrounding' the enemy was a bad one; for they were equal to us in number, and in much better position. We boldly pushed forward, however, up hill, under a murderous fire; and when we gained the level, found our work a little easier, so that we captured some hundreds of prisoners, several cannon, one or two standards, many wagons, and some stores, and every thing promised a complete rout of the enemy. They repeatedly fell back, but re-formed and continued the fight, Price on the left and centre, hurling his Missourians upon them with irresistible fury, so that their line became shaken, and required but a little additional effort to break it in two.

"Perceiving this, Van Dorn ordered McCulloch to repress his ardor, but keep up the enemy's attention on our right, while he threw forward the whole of the centre and left, so as to completely sweep the field. But McCulloch and his second in command were both killed, and there were none to direct the progress of the troops, who felt they were now pushing on to victory; the various colonels, in fact, did not stop to inquire who had succeeded to the command, but each was doing his best in his own way. The enemy were before them, and they neither knew nor cared for any thing more : of strategy, they were almost, if not quite, ignorant; the men were in disorder, but still fought on, regiment mixed with regiment. Thinking that his orders would be obeyed, and not knowing that McCulloch and McIntosh were among the slain, Van Dorn pushed forward his centre and left as best he could, and after much hard fighting, drove the enemy from their position, inflicting much loss. It was now far past noon.

"Curtis and Sturgis, perceiving the confusion on our right, rallied their commands, and presented a formidable front, the skilful Sigel covering the retreat in a slow and masterly manner, so that, though we had thoroughly beaten them, they were retiring in excellent order to other positions some miles to the rear; and success was not so decided as it would have been had the various commands been under better discipline. Cheering on our men, Price' and the other commanders re-formed their regiments and began the pursuit in earnest; but it was a continual running fight for the distance of two miles; and the men were so intoxicated with success that discipline seemed forgotten, and thousands fought without orders, 'pitching in' wherever the enemy seemed in force, or inclined to continue the engagement. At last, worn out with fatigue, we all halted, and Van Dorn, taking up his quarters at Elk Horn Tavern, commenced burying the dead, and providing for the wounded, who covered a space of over three miles.

"The camps of the enemy had fallen into our hands, with many prisoners, stores, cannon, etc.; and the men were so excited with their success that it was impossible to form them into line for exigencies. Van Dorn indeed surmised that reenforcements had reached the enemy in great number, and felt himself too weak to accept another engagement on the morrow, should the enemy force one upon him; he therefore ordered the sick far to the rear, and, destroying so much of the booty as could not be transported, began to prepare for a retreat. Officers did all in their power to gather and re-form their commands during the night; but it was a work of impossibility, as, completely broken down by long marches over hills and mountains, together with many hours of hard fighting, hundreds lay in the bushes completely exhausted, and weak as children. Coupled with this, our supplies were exhausted, our artillery had but a few rounds of cartridge remaining, and our ammunition wagons were miles in the rear. Under the circumstances, Van Dorn wisely decided upon falling back, and refusing another engagement, should the enemy, from reenforcements, have the hardihood to move forward and try the fortunes of war a second time.

"Early in the morning, scouts informed us that the enemy, having been largely reenforced, were advancing upon us, but Van Dorn had made every disposition for falling back to a strong position some seven miles to the rear, at which point our supplies of ammunition had halted. Covering this movement with a well-displayed disposition of force, the enemy were received with great valor, and their advance checked. Sharp fighting ensued, but they made feeble efforts to move forward, seeming to be highly delighted that we were falling back, and desirous of nothing more agreeable. In truth, their movements seemed to be nothing more than a feint in force to cover their own retreat! Most of our forces had retired, however, and the idea did not seem to be countenanced by our commander, who withdrew quietly, and halted six miles to the rear, bringing away between three and four hundred prisoners, seven cannon, stores, wagons, and other booty. It was impossible for us to have withstood the enemy a second time, had they been seriously inclined for battle, for all our ammunition was expended, and the artillery, for the most part, had fired their last shell to cover our retreat. The enemy did not follow, however, but, after resting on the old battle-field a few hours, turned their columns eastward, and were in full flight!" [This is incorrect. My friend was too far from the field after the first day's engagement to know the exact truth. The Federals occupied the field after the second day's fight, and remained there until Van Dorn had retreated many miles from it. The truth of history requires this correction.]

"What their loss may have been during the skirmishing of the sixth and the battle of the seventh of March, cannot be ascertained; but, from the large number of dead and wounded, I think that three thousand would not cover it, irrespective of prisoners and sick that fell into our hands. Our loss was heavy, but nothing near that of the enemy. Price* thinks that one thousand will cover all.

"I expect that Halleck the Veracious will issue a grand account of this Federal victory for the amusement of the North.

* This gallant officer received a severe wound in the right arm during the action, but could not be prevailed upon to retire. When the war broke out between the United States and Mexico, Sterling Price resigned his seat in Congress, and led a regiment into New-Mexico, capturing Santa Fé, and routing the Mexicans in several engagements. Although not a military man by education, he evinced great talent and an uncommon idea of strategy, having frequently out-manœuvred several generals sent against him. His services were of such note that no history of that war fails to bestow upon him the praise his many brilliant achievements deserve. He was Governor of Missouri in 1853, and filled the chair with remarkable ability, having successfully saved the State from the Republican sophistry of Senator Benton, when that demagogue canvassed it in favor of Fremont, his son-in-law. In person General Price is very farmer-like. No one would suppose his predilections to be martial. He is more than fifty years of age, about five feet ten inches in height, strongly made, thick-set, and inclined to obesity. He has a large, round face, of a ruddy complexion, short-cut grey hair, small and restless grey eyes. In his movements he is slow; in manners extremely social and unpretending, a plain, out-spoken man, true as steel, and an unflinching patriot. There were great objections raised against his commanding a large force; for the few thousands under him were indifferently drilled, and he was considered too lax a disciplinarian to accomplish much against the well-educated officers sent against him. Whatever may have been achieved was due more to the indomitable energy and reckless bravery of his men, than to any great display of consummate generalship. Greatly beloved as he is by the masses, I think Government acted wisely in placing others over him; for there is always danger to be feared from the movements of uneducated, though oftentimes successful, talent.

"This is a terribly wild, barren country for a campaign. The boys seem to enjoy good health, however; but it would be of much greater advantage to the cause did proper disciplinarians come among us, for although brave and hardy enough for any enterprise, we lack educated officers; and without them, little of importance can be effected against a numerous, well-appointed, and highly disciplined enemy. The late battle proved all this; and although we whipped the Yankees by sheer audacity, 'rough and ready' fighting, with any weapons that may be at hand, can not maintain a contest successfully with an army ever increasing in number, and supplied with the most costly arms in the world, and with every comfort and improvement provided which science has invented or money can procure.   Yours,   POLK."

CHAPTER XVII.

"DEAR MAJOR: When our regiment received marching orders at Manassas in December, and were ordered up the Valley with old Jackson, you were among the first to congratulate me upon 'active service,' and all that kind of thing, but believe me I would willingly have gone back to winter quarters again after a week's trial, for Jackson is the greatest marcher in the world. When we moved up here, our first orders were for a march to Charlestown; next day we moved back to Winchester, in a few days again back to Charlestown, and thence from one place to another, until at last I began to imagine we were commanded by some peripatetic philosophical madman, whose forte was pedestrianism. With little or no baggage, we are a roving, hungry, hardy lot of fellows, and are not patronized at all by parsons or doctors; the latter have a perfect sinecure amongst us.

" 'Stonewall' may be a very fine old gentleman, and an honest, good-tempered, industrious man, but I should admire him much more in a state of rest than continually seeing him moving in the front. And such a dry old stick, too! As for uniform, he has none—his wardrobe isn't worth a dollar, and his horse is quite in keeping, being a poor lean animal of little spirit or activity. And don't he keep his aides moving about! Thirty miles' ride at night through the mud is nothing of a job; and if they don't come up to time, I'd as soon face the devil, for Jackson takes no excuses when duty is on hand. He is about thirty-five years old, of medium height, strongly built, solemn and thoughtful, speaks but little, and always in a calm, decided tone ; and from what he says there is no appeal, for he seems to know every hole and corner of this Valley as if he made it, or, at least, as if it had been designed for his own use. He knows all the distances, all the roads, even to cow-paths through the woods, and goat-tracks along the hills. He sits his horse very awkwardly, although, generally speaking, all Virginians are fine horsemen,* and has a fashion of holding his head very high, and chin up, as if searching for something skywards; yet although you can never see his eyes for the cap-peak drawn down over them, nothing escapes *his* observation.

"His movements are sudden and unaccountable; his staff don't pretend to keep up with him, and, consequently, he is frequently seen alone, poking about in all sorts of holes and corners, at all times of night and day. I have frequently seen him approach in the dead of night and enter into conversation with sentinels, and ride off through the darkness without saying, 'God bless you,' or any thing civil to the officers. The consequence is, that the officers are scared, and the men love him. He was a student at West-Point, but never remarkable for any brilliancy. What service he has seen was in Mexico, where he served as lieutenant of artillery. At one of the battles there his captain was about to withdraw the guns, because of the loss suffered by the battery, and also because the range was too great. This did not suit our hero; he advanced *his* piece several hundred yards, and 'shortened the distance,' dismounted his opponent's guns, and remained master of the position.

* General Jackson was never known to put his horse out of a trot, except when desirous of escaping the cheering of his men, on which occasions he would raise his cap, discovering a high, bald forehead, and force his old "sorrel" into a gallop. This old "sorrel" war-horse is well known throughout the army; with head down, it seldom attempts more than a trot, but stands fire well, and that may be the reason why the General prefers and always rides him. Many gentlemen, imagining that the hero would appear to better advantage on a blood animal, have presented several to him, but they are seldom used. When our army entered Maryland, in September, 1862, in order to get in the rear of General Miles at Harper's Ferry, and secure the fourteen thousand men under his command, Jackson's corps was stationed east of Frederick, and an influential citizen, in token of admiration, gave the Commander a very valuable horse, that he might appear to advantage. Jackson mounted in the public street, and was immediately thrown into the mud! The old "sorrel" was again brought forth, and the General ambled off, very good humoredly, never essaying to mount "fine" horses again.

"After the Mexican war he left the army, and was professor of mathematics and tactics in the University of Virginia, but was generally looked upon by the students as an old fogy of little talent, and over-gifted with piety. It is my opinion, Major, that Jackson will assuredly make his mark in this war, for his untiring industry and eternal watchfulness *must* tell upon a numerous enemy unacquainted with the country, and incommoded by large baggage-trains. Jackson evidently intends to supply himself at Federal expense, and as he is a true fire-eater and an invincible believer in our 'manifest destiny,' poor Banks will find him a disagreeable opponent to confront in the mountain passes or at the many fords. The Virginians have an idea that he is veritably 'the coming man,' and from the numbers joining him, it looks as if he meant mischief. But to form an accurate idea of the doings of this man, it is necessary to state in proper order the various affairs in which he has been engaged since last I saw you.

"Before Jackson was sent to the Valley in the beginning of December, 1861, General Ashby, with his own regiment and other cavalry detachments, making a total of some twelve hundred horse, assisted by a few companies of foot, (militia,) was watching the river-front from Harper's Ferry to Romney, and very little could transpire of which he was not fully informed. At this time the enemy were strongly posted at Romney and Bath southwards, and Banks, with his whole army being north of the Potomac, it was evident that some great movement was in contemplation, which prudence demanded should be watched by a strong force. Accordingly Jackson was sent to Winchester with his old brigade, three thousand strong, and one battery of four pieces. He had not been in chief command many days ere his restless spirit began to appear, and he seemed bent on mischief—if he could not beat the enemy, he was determined to annoy them.

"As Washington was blockaded on the Lower Potomac by our batteries at Cockpit Point and other places, they still received large supplies by the Baltimore and Ohio Canal, which runs parallel with the Potomac from Washington, and branches off on the Upper Potomac to Wheeling. If the 'dams' could be destroyed up the river, Jackson conceived that it would sorely perplex the enemy to supply their large army around

Washington. Accordingly the General marched his force to the Potomac, and amid the cold and snows of this region had his men waist-deep in the river, endeavoring to tear down 'Dam No. 5.' Although much labor was expended night and day for several days, we did not accomplish our object, but lost somewhat from the continual fire of the enemy. We desisted from the undertaking for a week, and as the enemy had retired from the river-bank, we returned again, and after many efforts effectually destroyed the 'dam,' so that the canal was unnavigable, and remained so a long time. The amount of fatigue our men endured over this work, laboring as they constantly did in the water above waist-deep, and in the intense cold, can never be sufficiently appreciated. I feel certain that hundreds of them will be ruined for life by rheumatism and the like.

"When this was accomplished, Jackson was desirous of surprising the Federal force stationed at Bath, and, though inferior to them in number and equipment, was resolved to capture or crush them. Without much time for preparation, and allowing none to know whither he was bound, Jackson gathered his little force of twenty-two hundred men, and amid the snow, sleet, rain, and ice of the first days of January, 1862, began his march. No one can tell the horrors of this march We had to travel over fifty miles of the roughest country in the world, and were obliged to take unfrequented roads to keep the movement secret. Over hills our few wagons toiled along; ice was on the ground, and neither man nor beast could maintain a footing. Sometimes, indeed, horsemen, infantry, wagons and all, would slip over an embankment. Men were bootless, hatless, and ragged; horses could scarcely stir; no tents were carried, and all had to sleep out upon the snow as best they could; for being within a few miles of the enemy's posts, we were not allowed to kindle fires.

"It is no exaggeration to say that I have frequently fallen asleep, and, on awakening, found a foot of snow all over me! We soon discovered that the snow kept us warm, and when the 'halt' sounded, it became customary with our men to make a sort of arbor with sticks, which was covered and packed close with snow on three sides; creeping underneath this and leaving their heads only uncovered, they were comfortable for the night! This was a decided novelty; but, believe me, Jackson was cursed by every one for this mad adventure, and looked upon as a maniac for dragging his command about through a bleak, cold region without supplies, and losing men and horses every mile—man and beast tumbling down on the ice, and dislocating limbs at every rod. Nor did we accomplish the object for which we started. Ashby's cavalry arrived at the appointed time, and took up a position on the outskirts of Bath to take the enemy in the rear, but it was impossible for infantry and artillery to get up in time; so taking advantage of our slow travelling, the enemy retreated to the Potomac, (not more than one and a half mile distant,) and got safe across before we arrived. The cavalry, it is true, did some independent fighting, and skirmished with the enemy in gallant style; but though killing, wounding, and capturing a few, not a thousand such adventures would compensate for the loss sustained by this hurried and painful march. This was about the fourth of January.

"Having rested two or three days in Bath, and lived upon the Federal stores found there, Jackson made daily demonstrations at the river, picket firing and displaying his force, collecting boats, chopping down timber, and the like, till the enemy imagined that his command was the advance of a large force about to cross into Maryland. Shields was then in command of the Upper Potomac, but had the largest part of his force in Romney, a town south of the Potomac,.across the Alleghany, in Western Virginia. He felt certain that we were bent on crossing, and, though forty miles above, transferred his whole command to the north bank to dispute our supposed passage. As soon as Jackson was informed of this, he marched up the south bank to Romney, surprised and captured many of the enemy, and destroyed what he could not carry away of Shields's immense stores!

"Did you ever hear of such a manœuvre in your life? It was a lucky hit for us, and we supplied ourselves with wagon-loads of goods of every description, including wines, brandies, cigars, and a thousand other things. We forgot much of our annoyance with Jackson in this trip, and all began to think 'he had method in his madness,' and was 'a pretty good sort of old gentleman enough, but a little too much inclined to "double quick" movements.' As might have been expected, Shields was particularly annoyed to find himself imposed upon by the small force under Jackson, and, keenly feeling the loss of his stores and small garrison at Romney, was moving heaven and earth to catch 'Stonewall' in some trap. Jackson was too much of a fox for him, however, and when it became apparent that Banks and Shields were preparing to send heavy forces across into Virginia, Stonewall collected his brave little corps from different points of the river, and had every thing in readiness for retiring down the Valley, whenever circumstances should demand it.

"You may be sure that, under such an active marauder as our leader, our wagon train was well supplied with all things needful, thanks to the superabundance of the enemy; and that when we finally bade farewell to the river towns on our return trip, our baggage was much more considerable than when we had arrived there. In truth, most of our infantry and cavalry had amply supplied themselves with all things needful; for among Shields's supplies at Romney, we captured hundreds of rifles, pistols, swords, much cavalry and wagon harness, many horses, and, together with what we picked up here and there in our many inroads within the enemy's lines, made up a respectable amount of booty.   ASHTON."

"*McGackeysville,* *March 26th,* 1862.

"P. S.—Before this arrives, you will have learned that Jackson has had a fight with Banks and Shields, at a place called Kearnstown, in which affair I received a shot in my arm. I am doing well, thanks to a strong constitution and the unceasing kindness of the Virginian ladies, who act towards us like mothers or sisters. When last I put pen to paper, I did not seriously imagine that old 'Stonewall' intended moving in such fearful weather; but when it was known the General's servant had packed up, I knew we were all bound for a tramp somewhere. 'Whenever I misses massa a little while in de day, I allers knows he's prayin' a spell; whenever he's out all night, I knows we's goin' to move next day; but when he stays out and comes back to have a long spell of prayin', I knows dare's goin' to be a fought somewhar, mighty quick, and dis chile packs up de walibles and gets out ob de way like a sensible colored pusson!' This colored thermometer was 'packin' up de walibles'—pots and pans; so there was nothing to be done but ' grin and bear it.'

" Sure enough we *had* a long trip: our leader marched us nearly blind; but as he was always in front himself, cheering on the men, all bore it patiently. As we drew near a place called Kearnstown, it was ascertained that Banks and his second in command, Shields, were in strong force in and around Winchester, and great circumspection was necessary to entice a part of their commands after us, so as to whip them in detail. Shields came after us, all primed and cocked for a fight, and we ' tolled ' him to Kearnstown, where the first shots were exchanged. We had not many troops, (not more than twenty-two hundred,) while our opponents must have had ten thousand. For some time it proved to be an artillery fight, in which our pieces stood up nobly to their work, against heavy odds, and suffered considerable loss. Shields was unable to discover our line of battle or our real force, but had to feel his way; and as his regiments approached the woods in which we lay, our boys poured in rapid volleys, and could scarcely be restrained from abandoning their covert to charge. Observing their increase of force at different points, we frequently changed ground, and presented a different line of fire, so that they seemed puzzled to make out our intentions or movements.

" About three in the afternoon, on the twenty-third of March, it became evident that Shields was advancing upon us with all his force; and we obtained information from a prisoner that Banks, considering the Valley cleared of Jackson, had gone to Washington, leaving Shields in command. Finding that the enemy was rapidly approaching, Jackson disposed his little force of twenty-two hundred as best he could, on the right and left of the road, Brigadier Garnett commanding the left, Jackson the centre, and Ashby, with his cavalry, the right. Heavy skirmishing was maintained on both sides until about five P.M., when a full brigade of the enemy were observed by Ashby endeavoring to get in on our right and rear, while the fire continually increased in volume in the centre and left. Well knowing that our little force would be totally surrounded if this flank movement should be permitted, Ashby determined to put a bold face upon matters, and attack them. Observing their advance, covered by a cloud of skirmishers, approaching through open grassy fields, he gathered around him several companies, and dashing out from the woods, killed or captured nearly every one of the sharp-shooters; then riding up to the Federal column, his men discharged their pieces, and galloped back to the woods in a shower of shot from the enemy, which being aimed too high, did but kill three of our men, and wound half a dozen more. Determined to clear their front, the Federal cavalry now rode forward at a swinging gallop, but had not proceeded far, when Ashby again advanced, sabre in hand, and his men were soon among the enemy, cutting and shooting right and left, and driving them, in great confusion, across the open ground. So obvious was their rout that the infantry of the enemy opened to let their discomfited horsemen through to the rear.

"While Ashby's gallant little band was thus checking the enemy on the right, and effectually retarding the Federal flank movement, the fight was raging with great fury on the left and centre. Garnett and Jackson found themselves overpowered by numbers, but determined to keep up the fight at all hazards until darkness should come on, through which they might securely retreat down the Valley. Garnett begged for ammunition, but the wagons had long been started on the march, for fear of capture, and he had to rely on the bayonet. This was called into requisition several times, but could not resist the many heavy regiments continually sent to the front. Observing a long stone fence running across a very large open field, which the enemy were endeavoring to reach, Garnett determined to seize it as a natural breastwork and hold the enemy in check. Shields ordered his men to move forward at the 'double quick' and seize the position, but had not fairly started on the run before the Twenty-fourth Virginia (Irish) ran rapidly forward, and arrived at the fence first, so that when the enemy approached they were received with a deadly volley at ten paces, which killed two thirds of them: the rest retreated to their former position in the woods, from whence they maintained an ineffectual fire until dark.

"Despite the heroism of our men, we had suffered so severely, that some time after seven P.M., Jackson withdrew from the field, with a loss of some five hundred killed and wounded, nearly three hundred prisoners, and two pieces of artillery. Jackson evidently did not anticipate meeting with such a heavy force of the enemy; for they were reported as retreating from Winchester; but this proved untrue, for they were, as the battle proved, posted in considerable number, and during the fight had the better position of the two, much cavalry, and powerful artillery. Garnett has been censured, and some say by Jackson, and was threatened with a court-martial for not maintaining his ground on the left; but any commander would have acted similarly under the circumstances, for he was entirely out of ammunition, and completely overpowered by artillery; so that he had no alternative but to fall back or be annihilated. His artillery had been captured by numerous cavalry; yet he inflicted more loss upon the enemy than he himself suffered, and withdrew his small force from the field, as coolly as if on parade.*

"We withdrew rapidly southward, but the enemy did not pursue until next morning, by which time we had got far on our journey. Having rested at Strasburgh, we rapidly pushed across the mountain towards Harrisonburgh; Ashby's cavalry and the enemy's being continually engaged to our rear in fierce skirmishing, in which the latter suffered considerably. After many hardships and fast travelling, we reached this place on the twenty-sixth, the enemy's advance having halted at Harrisonburgh. Jackson is much censured for this fight, and although he acted according to orders, is cursed by every one. We lost no baggage, nor any persons of prominence, but the enemy had

---

* Brigadier-General Richard Garnett, who commanded the left, has been accused as the cause of our defeat on this occasion. Jackson commanded him to hold his position at any sacrifice, but being entirely out of ammunition, he did not do so. It was ascertained during the engagement that Shields had already prepared to evacuate Winchester, and that all his baggage had passed through that same morning— he was only fighting, in truth, to secure a safe retreat. Garnett, of course, was unaware of this, or he would have obeyed, and Winchester been ours; for when our forces retired, the enemy were amazed, and, instead of retreating themselves, followed us up very closely and spiritedly. General Garnett is a Virginian; entered the old service as Second Lieutenant of infantry, July first, 184; was captain Sixth Infantry, May ninth, 1855; and resigned, to enter the Confederate service. He is reputed a very able officer, and has seen much service in Western Virginia, under Lee, and subsequently in every fight in the Valley under Jackson.

several officers killed. Shields himself was desperately wounded in the arm by a shell. There seems to be the fulfilment of
his own apostrophe to heaven, in this man Shields. He was a
very successful and dashing general of volunteers in Mexico,
commanded the New-York Volunteers there, and at one time
led on the Palmetto (South-Carolina) Regiment in a storming
party, in which he was successful. Several years subsequently,
at a banquet in Charleston, (South-Carolina,) he had greatly
eulogized the South-Carolinians for their gallantry and heroism,
and in token of admiration for Southern valor, wished that his
right arm might be palsied or shattered, rather than draw a
sabre against the sons of the sunny South.

                                                  " ASHTON."

CHAPTER XVIII.

Fall of "Island No. 10," April fifth — Battle of Shiloh, April sixth — Capture of Guns — General Albert Sidney Johnston killed — The Battle resumed at Daybreak—The Enemy are reenforced by Buell—The Confederate Army retreats— Great Loss—False Reports of the Federal Generals.

"*Corinth, Miss., April 10th*, 1862.

"DEAR TOM: In exchange for your last entertaining epistle, I send the following hurried scrawl. It would seem that the army of the West bids fair to rival that of Virginia. As you are doubtless aware, we have fought another great battle, in fact, *two*, which I consider are without parallel on this continent, and approach more closely to European conflicts than any thing which either you or I have participated in as yet. To give a plain statement of things, let me begin at the beginning and go through in proper order.

"After the disastrous affair of Fort Donelson, Johnston reformed his army, and remained some short time at Murfreesboro, but subsequently fell back to Corinth to defend the Memphis and Charleston Railroad. Beauregard came on from Virginia and inspected Columbus. It was deemed inadvisable to defend that place; the works were blown up, and all the cannon and stores transferred to Island No. 10, which it was thought might be converted into a little Gibraltar, and successfully beat back the enemy's flotillas on the Mississippi. The command was given to General Mackall; Beauregard was installed second in command at Corinth.* What few troops we had were being

---

* Beauregard had strongly fortified this island, and it successfully withstood a fifteen days'. bombardment from a heavy fleet: Being called to superintend operations at a distant point on the mainland, in Mississippi, the command was given to Major-General Mackall, on the third of April, and, two days later, it was captured by the combined land and naval forces of the North, under command of General Pope and Commodore Foote. A large canal, twelve miles long, was dug across a peninsula formed by the winding of the river round the mainland, and thus the island was taken in the rear. The loss to us was a painful one, and quite unlooked·

daily augmented by fresh arrivals from Pensacola, New-Orleans, and Columbus, so that in a few weeks we had quite a respectable army of about forty thousand men.

"It was known that Buell's force, numbering forty thousand strong, were hurrying on from Kentucky to join Grant, who, with eighty thousand men, was about to cross the Tennessee, and drive us by degrees into the Gulf of Mexico, or elsewhere. He had already crossed the river, and was camped at a place rejoicing in some dozen houses, and having Shiloh for its name. Johnston gathered every man he could, and marched out to give battle. We camped within five miles of Shiloh on Saturday night, April fifth, and could plainly see the long line of camp-fires. Our cavalry had been closer for many days before our arrival, and were noticed by the enemy, but not molested. Early next morning, (Sunday,) and long before dawn, our line of battle was quietly formed, and as we had no camp-fires our presence was not known. Marching in three grand divisions, commanded respectively by Hardee,* Polk, and Bragg, we approached nearer to the enemy's camps, deployed columns, and commenced the attack.

"When about two miles distant from Shiloh, the enemy had

---

for—we expected an engagement there, but its capture was neatly accomplished without it. The enemy captured Mackall himself, two brigadiers, six colonels, six thousand stand of arms, five thousand rank and file, one hundred pieces of siege artillery, thirty pieces of field artillery, fifty-six thousand solid shot, six steam transports, two gunboats, one floating battery, etc., etc. Did not Beauregard know of the canal being dug before he left? Many think so.

* Major-General William J. Hardee was brevet Lieutenant-Colonel Second Cavalry, in the old service, and for a long time commandant of cadets and instructor in artillery, cavalry, and infantry tactics, at West-Point, New-York. His famous work on *Tactics* is the approved text-book, both North and South, and has proved of incalculable benefit to us; for when war commenced, it was our only resource for instruction, and is now in the hands of every one. It was compiled at the desire of, and approved by, President Davis, when Minister of War under President Pierce, being made up of adaptations from the French and English manuals. General Hardee was for a long time on the Southern coast, superintending fortifications, but was appointed to organize and command a brigade in South-Eastern Missouri. After the battle of Lexington, (September, 1861,) he was withdrawn from that State, and sent to reenforce the command of Sidney Johnston, in Tennessee. At Shiloh our line of battle marched in three divisions, Hardee commanding the first; and by his rapid, skilful movements, contributing much to the rout of Grant and his large army at that place. He has proved himself an excellent leader and fierce fighter, but is said not to possess much genius for "planning" a campaign.

seen us, and a general alarm was raised, with some appearance of confusion on one part of their line, though Grant had been informed of our vicinity the night before. As we advanced, daylight began to appear, clouds of sharp-shooters fanned out in our front, and innumerable little puffs of smoke dotted the dark green landscape over which our lines were rapidly moving. Presently long curls of smoke from the wooded hillocks to our front were answered by screaming shells and loud reports, and artillery bugles were sounding up and down our line. We galloped to the front, and opened a brisk fire, while to the extreme right and left we could faintly hear pattering volleys of musketry. The sun now rose in true Southern brilliancy, and shortly became intensely warm. At all events, it so seemed to us of the artillery, for we pulled off coats and jackets, strapped them on to caissons, and rolling up our sleeves, began to 'roll into' the Yankees with great gusto. Such a noise you never heard, and I am deaf even now; but feeling determined to pay off old Grant for our scrape at Donelson, our onset was fierce and dashing, and the continual command was: 'Forward, boys, forward!' Sometimes we moved up a few hundred yards, unlimbered, and worked away awhile, then moved forward again, until at last we found ourselves blazing away among the tents of a Yankee division, having to withstand the fire of not less than twelve pieces, with only three out of our four guns, the other having been upset by a stray shell and rendered unserviceable. Our ammunition, too, was nearly exhausted, and as supplies were far to the rear, and our infantry were now rushing through the camp, we stopped firing, and retired to a patch of woods while the guns cooled.

"About this time our brigadier passed by, and said hastily: 'Hold on a while, boys, we are hard at it in front, and will find some better guns for you in a few moments.' In half an hour the musketry fire somewhat subsided, and orders came to unhitch teams, and select a set of guns from some twenty that had been captured. We did so, and claimed for our use four splendid brass fellows—two six-pound rifles, and two twelve-pound howitzers. Having found lots of ammunition, we were ordered in again, and went forward at a gallop, the newly-found horses being much superior to our old mules, and powerful in harness. Thus re-equipped on the battle-field, we turned the enemy's guns upon them. It was now nearly eleven o'clock. Reports from different parts of the field represented Hardee and Polk as having driven the enemy pell-mell before them, capturing camp after camp, and immense supplies of all kinds. The continual change of scene—from the fields to the woods, and from camp to camp—and the incessant fighting, so confused the sense of time, that I could not believe it to be more than seven A.M. The heat, however, began to be very oppressive, and as we gradually became short-handed, officers dismounted and served the guns with right good-will.

"We were no longer able to range over the field as before; our progress was checked. The enemy had collected in great force towards our front, and had several powerful batteries in full play against our further advance. Had we not been reen-forced in time, our little battery would have been snuffed out; but Bragg, under whose care the artillery had been placed, sent ample succour, and the duel between us became hot and deter-mined. I had noticed our infantry cautiously moving up through the woods on their flank, and orders came to cease firing. The enemy saw the danger and moved up their in-fantry. Suddenly, up sprang several of our regiments, and, with their customary yell, ran across the open ground and up the slope, without firing. Though dozens of them were knocked over by artillery every moment, they pressed forward, their colonels and colors in front, until, as they drew near the ene-my's infantry, volley upon volley of musketry met them with a savage greeting; yet they gallantly carried the position.

"The artillery fight lasted full half an hour, reenforcements went up rapidly, until at last the guns were silenced, a wild yell rent the air, and immediately the order came: 'Artillery to the front.' We moved forward with all possible speed, and passed the scene of the fierce engagement I have described' and found not less than twelve guns deserted, as many more having been drawn off during the fight. The loss in infantry seemed large. The enemy had received an awful lesson, but fought to the last. Our opponents at this point were Western men, fellows of true grit, who fought like heroes, disputing every inch of ground with great determination and valor. We came to a place where Kentuckians and Mississippians had encountered some Dutch regiments from Missouri and Ohio — it was like a slaughter-house, and but few of our men were visible among the killed.

"The fight was not over, however, by any means, as incessant musketry on our flanks fully proved. It seemed, from the line of fire, that our wings were outflanking the enemy, or that they had been fighting too fast for us in the centre. After a little breathing-time, we commenced the onward movement a third time — deserted camps being to the right, left, and on every side of us. The temptation of so much plunder led scores of our young troops to halt, on some excuse or other; and the result was, that hundreds were lost to their respective regiments, and hung behind for purposes of spoil. I was sorry to see this, and remonstrated with many; but their excuses were so natural and plausible that little could be said; the majority had not been from home more than a month, and having beaten the enemy in their immediate front, thought the game was all over for that day. Many were footsore; others famished; and not a few perfectly exhausted. But now the enemy had re-formed their line again, and had scarcely got into position, before their artillery opened on us with great fury. Their first shot killed several horses and smashed up an empty caisson. We changed position somewhat, and got within better range of our friends, whose horses and caissons were behind an old farm-house. We hammered away at the house and blew the roof off, knocked in the walls, and got a sight of the caissons. We did not much care about the guns, for they were firing very rapidly and wildly.

"After a little manœuvring, we pointed fairly at the caissons, and were about to fire. 'Hold on!' shouted our captain; 'point at the guns until ordered — there is a little game on foot.' The 'game' aforesaid was concocted by our captain and the colonel of our supports. The infantry were to creep up on all-fours, while we maintained a furious fire, and being concealed by the smoke, should wait until all our shot was concentrated on the caissons, when the infantry were to make a sudden rush, and secure the guns. The plan succeeded admirably: we suddenly opened fire upon the caissons, and blew most of them up; but before the guns could be removed, the infantry were upon them, and desperately engaged with opposing regiments. The guns were ours, and proved to be of beautiful bronze, very elegant and costly.

" The line of the enemy was temporarily broken, but fresh troops came pouring in, and ultimately forced us to retire ; yet in strengthening one part of their line, they weakened another, and, by a vigorous push, our infantry and artillery made a wide gap lower down to our left, and rushed through it like a torrent. The fighting now became very confused; different sections of the enemy's line wavered and broke, and were crowded into a very small space by large masses in their rear, which seemed undecided which way to go, or what to do. Of course our generals did not give them much time to consider, but poured in upon them, and drove them in confused masses towards the river. The fight was desperately maintained by the Western men, who fought like panthers; but it was of no avail; our admirable plan of battle was still maintained by the quickness and coolness of our several chiefs, among whom I would especially mention General (Bishop) Polk and old Bragg. The latter, of course, was ever with his beloved artillery, and seemed as cool as a cucumber, among thirty pieces blazing away like furies. Polk, however, had achieved a great success in capturing that arch-braggadocio Prentiss and his whole brigade— the same bombastic hero who, when in command at Cairo, ' was going to play thunder ' with us, as the boys termed it. But while all were in high spirits at our evident success, and at the prospect of soon driving the enemy into the Tennessee, couriers looking pale and sad passed by, reporting that Johnston had been killed while personally leading an attack on a powerful battery.* This news wrought us all up to madness, and

---

* Major-General Albert Sidney Johnston was a Kentuckian, and about sixty years of age; tall, commanding, and grave. He was a graduate of West-Point in 1820, and appointed lieutenant of Sixth Infantry. He served in the Black Hawk (Indian) war, and left the army. He migrated to Texas, and was soon appointed Commander-in-Chief of the State forces; commanded a regiment of Texans in the Mexican war, and was appointed major and paymaster of the United States army; soon after promoted to Colonel of Second United States Cavalry ; and, in 1857, was sent as Commander-in-Chief of United States forces against the Mormons. He was in California when the South seceded ; and although Lincoln's spies dogged his footsteps, he managed to escape, and by passing rapidly through the South-western

without waiting for a word of command, all pushed forward and assailed the enemy with irresistible fury, driving them down to the edge of the river in utter confusion and disorder.

"It was now about four o'clock, and Buell was reported as rapidly advancing to Grant's relief, but was yet several miles from the river's edge. From some cause I could never ascertain, a halt was sounded, and when the remnants of the enemy's divisions had stacked arms on the river's edge, preparatory to their surrender, no one stirred to finish the business by a *coup de main*. It was evidently 'drown or surrender' with them, and they had prepared for the latter, until seeing our inactivity, their gunboats opened furiously, and, save a short cannonade, all subsided into quietness along our lines.

"Night came on, and great confusion reigned among us. Thousands were out in quest of plunder ; hundreds had escorted prisoners and wounded ; scores were intoxicated with'wines and liquors found ; yet still the gunboats continued their bombardment ; and Buell's* forces arriving in haste, crossed the river and formed line of battle for the morrow. It could not be denied that we had gained a great victory—thousands of prisoners were in our hands, including many officers of all ranks ; we had captured eighty pieces of cannon, enormous quantities of ammunition, and stores of every sort ; many hundreds of tents, camp equipage, hundreds of horses and wagons,

Territories in disguise, arrived safely at Richmond, and was appointed Commander-in-Chief of the West. President Davis, in answer to those who said Johnston was "too slow," remarked : "If *he* is not a general, there is not *one* among us !" *Such* praise, from *such* a man, speaks volumes for Johnston's true merit. He was of Scotch descent, and very much beloved in military circles. His early death was a great blow to the South. It is much to be regretted that our Southern generals persist in rushing to the front, for their example is not required to stimulate the men : rather, our soldiers require to be held in check.

* Major-General Don Carlos Buell is from the State of Ohio, and, previous to this present war, was Captain, Assistant Adjutant-General at Washington. He served during the Mexican campaign, and with distinction, having been twice breveted for gallantry. He was always looked upon as a quiet, methodical, and "safe" officer ; and when McClellan selected leaders from the "regular" service for the volunteers on General Scott's retirement, Captain Buell was appointed Brigadier-General in Kentucky, and soon after rose to the rank of Major-General. His deportment is gentle and soldierly ; he thoroughly understands his business, and despises that coarse vulgarity so common among Federal leaders of the present day.

much clothing, and eatables of every possible description, many standards, and, in fact, wagon-loads of every thing pertaining to the camps and commissariat of a superabundantly supplied enemy. But where were our men? With the exception of a few thousands of well-disciplined troops under Bragg and others, our whole army was scattered abroad, as will generally be the case with young and raw troops, if not kept firmly in hand. Yet our outposts brought word hourly that large masses of the enemy were moving across our whole front, and it could not be doubted that ere the sun again rose, the whole of Buell's and Grant's forces combined would be hurled upon us.

"Although Beauregard had committed a great mistake in not pushing the enemy to conclusions the day before, he exerted himself untiringly for the morrow. Stragglers were gathered, positions taken, and the greatest exertions made to secure the invaluable spoil of the battle-field. Every spare horse and wagon in the service was employed in the work, and property worth many millions was conveyed to the rear during night. The artillery were sorely taxed; their horses were occasionally used in transporting supplies during the night, and could scarcely get an hour's rest. Couriers and orderlies were dashing to and fro, inquiring for this or that General, who could not be found; despatch-bearers were looking for Beauregard and other chiefs; thousands of wounded were groaning around us; large fires were consuming every thing that could not be transported; and so it continued till midnight. Wearied beyond all expression, I lay down on bundles of straw, with my feet to the fire, and soon was fast asleep.

"I know not how long I had slept, but it seemed that in my dreams I heard constant picket-firing, mingled with which were hurried voices and the clanking of chains. Arousing myself, I found that our battery was about to move off, and that another battle was inevitable. It was not yet twilight, but our men were moving to and fro, and all seemed inspired with new life and confidence. Everywhere large fires indicated the destruction of Federal property, which plainly showed that Beauregard did not consider himself strong enough to hold the ground any longer.

"At dawn picket-firing increased rapidly; and in an hour

after sunrise we fired our first shot. The shattered regiments and brigades collected by Grant gave ground before our men, and every one thought that victory would crown our efforts a second time; but after we had wasted our newly acquired strength on the dispirited battalions of Grant, Buell poured in his fresh troops, and the fight became terrible again. In some places we drove them by unexampled feats of valor, but sheer exhaustion was hourly telling upon both man and beast. Until noon we retained the ground heroically, but it became evident every moment that numbers and strength would ultimately prevail, so that although we had gained every thing up to this hour, a retreat was ordered.

"Beauregard had prepared all the roads for this movement: there was no hurry or confusion, but every thing was conducted as if in review. We slowly fell back, leaving little of consequence behind, General Breckinridge and his Kentuckians bringing up the rear. We thus in an orderly manner fell back about two miles, and obtaining a favorable position for our small force, re-formed line of battle, and waited several hours. The enemy did not stir; they seemed content to hold the field and not pursue, and did not move five hundred yards from their original position of the morning. General John Pope, of Kentucky, was intrusted with the duty of following us up, but acted very cautiously and fearfully, contenting himself with capturing two or three hundred exhausted and footsore Tennesseans, who lay down by the roadside. From personal observation and conversation with those who should know, I think that our total loss would approximate to about six or seven thousand killed, wounded, and missing: the enemy confess to twice that total among themselves. We lost but little equipage and no guns; but, as I have said, have dozens of fine pieces as trophies, and an awful amount of baggage.

"Yours always,   *   *   * ''

" N. B.—I see that Pope claims to have captured *not less* than ten thousand prisoners, and other prizes in proportion! So says his despatch to Halleck. Truly these Federal Generals are a voracious and veracious race of knaves. Beauregard says he had not more than twenty thousand men in line in the fight on

Monday, and I *know* that Johnston could not muster twice that number when the fight opened on Sunday! Pope adds in his despatch to the good folks at Washington: 'As yet I have seen nothing but the "backs" of the rebels!' If he lives long enough, I pledge my existence he will see more in our faces than he'll find time to stay and admire. Write soon.

"Yours, again,   *   *   *"

CHAPTER XIX.

Movements in Virginia, and opening of the Campaign, April, 1862—Troops begin to move on the Upper Potomac in March—McClellan prepares to flank Manassas by marching heavy Masses up the Shenandoah Valley, and crossing the Mountains at Snickersville—A general Retreat is ordered by Johnston—He retires to Culpeper Court-House, and makes his Line behind the Rappahannock—Ruse of the Enemy, and Design upon Yorktown—The Approach to Richmond in that Direction is not so easy as conjectured by McClellan—Our "Lines" at Yorktown—McClellan's Progress is stopped there—Balloon Reconnoissance of the Enemy—Artillery Assaults on our Works—Great Distress amongst our Troops—Outpost Adventures—Ambitious Generals—Attack on Dam No. One—Frightful Destruction of Life—Horrible Neglect of the Wounded by the Federals—A Texan in search of a Pair of Boots.

OUR batteries along the Potomac below Washington had been so active during winter as to completely blockade the capital, causing much distress and privation among its inhabitants, so that the army itself could not be regularly supplied, and hundreds of horses were dying for want of forage. The only railroad that communicated with Washington was overworked night and day: the Washington and Ohio Canal was broken up, and an immense number of vessels were detained in the Lower Potomac, unable or afraid to run the gauntlet of our batteries scattered up and down the stream. It was in vain that the United States gunboats would sometimes cannonade at long range, and attempt to silence us: when their convoys arrived abreast of some patch of wood, an unknown battery would suddenly open, and sink them with apparent ease. For many weeks no vessels could pass; and down in Hampton Roads a perfect forest of masts was gathered, waiting opportunities to ascend.

Thus, instead of besieging the rebels in Richmond, as had been so often promised; instead of "driving us to the wall," "breaking the backbone of rebellion," or "the terrific Anaconda hugging us to death," etc., all which had been promised

11

a thousand times, McClellan's Grand Army was in uncomfortable winter quarters, and could not be furnished with regular rations, because the rebels had cut off supplies from the river. It was plain, however, that public opinion would force McClellan into action long before the proper time; for until May the roads in Virginia are impassable. Towards the beginning of March heavy masses of troops were reported moving up towards Harper's Ferry, and almost simultaneously our batteries on the Lower Potomac became wonderfully silent. The Federals claimed a "great success" over them; but the truth was all guns were quietly removed and the batteries abandoned long before the gunboats gave their final shellings. A "great move" was evidently preparing by both parties, but few could guess its object. Banks and others at Harper's Ferry were in great force, and were beginning to move up the Shenandoah slowly and cautiously. General ("Stonewall") Jackson had been detached from Manassas before Christmas, with about three thousand men, which, together with those already in the valley, might make a total of ten thousand, but certainly not more. He was ably seconded by Generals Ewell and Ashby, and no three men in the Confederacy knew the country better. Although their force was small, and that of the enemy large, they unexpectedly appeared and disappeared like phantoms before Banks and Shields, acting like "Jack-o'-lanterns" to draw them on to destruction.

Our position on the Upper Potomac at Leesburgh was also threatened at not less than four points, namely, westward, from Lovettsville and Harper's Ferry; northward, from Point of Rocks; eastward, from Edwards's Ferry; and our rear from Drainsville. It was thought by some that our movement would be directly westward into the Shenandoah, to Jackson, distant thirty miles; but a heavy force of the enemy was between that point and our present position, and were tightening the lines around us every day. An advance column had sought the Blue Ridge, and were passing south-westward, evidently intending to flank and get in the rear of Johnston by passing through the mountain "gap" at Snickersville. This, of course, Johnston wisely foresaw, and during winter had been quietly transporting his immense stores towards the Rappahannock, removing every cannon that could be spared, and filling the empty embrasures with hollow logs, painted black, which even at a few yards' distance much resembled thirty-two and sixty-four pounders.

To diminish the number of his troops during the heaviest part of the winter, Johnston had granted thirty days' furlough to all of the twelve months' volunteers who should enlist for the war. Although the entire army accepted these terms and re-enlisted, only a few thousands were permitted to depart at a time. But although this movement was known to McClellan, he did *not* know that for every man going home on furlough, a regiment travelled on the same train towards Culpeper Court-House and our lines on the Rappahannock River. In fact, McClellan was quietly maturing plans for the surprise and capture of Centreville and Manassas, when Johnston suddenly gave orders for a general retreat, and all our army began to move rapidly southward.

This retreat was certainly one of the finest things of the war and the brilliancy of its design and execution presaged a glorious summer campaign. Se perfectly were all things arranged and so quietly performed, that all stores, baggage, sick, *matériel*, and guns were removed far to the rear before any of us could realize the possibility of retreat; and it was not until our brigade, after several days' march over hills and impassable roads, came upon the main army defiling southward through Fauquier County, that we discovered the movement to be a general and not a partial one. All were in the finest spirits, and the line of march was so perfect and orderly that not a hundred stragglers were seen at any time, and the continual tramp of columns was as regular as if on parade. This great retreat was undoubtedly a master feat of the originator; but the exact schedule of movements, routes, time of junction, transportation, and a thousand other important points were calculated and fulfilled with so much nicety that it fills me with impartial admiration for Lee and Johnston, together with many talented subordinates. Each army corps, in breaking up quarters for the march, effectually destroyed every thing that could not find transportation, so that when the enemy advanced they found naught but smoking ruins and shattered breastworks.

With regard to our brigade, Hill had so arranged it, that as we marched out at three A.M., (March fourth,) immense fires burst out in the valley and on the hills from Harper's Ferry to within a few miles of Drainsville, effectually destroying immense stacks of wheat, straw, hay, clover, etc., so that when our force arrived on a neighboring hill, the scene was like a grand illumination, for many miles. The Yankees in Maryland and from Sugar-Loaf Observatory could not understand it at all, and their telegraph lights and rockets were working in all directions. It is true enough that much property was thus destroyed which did not belong to us; but we had previously offered to purchase these large crops; the owners knew we were about to depart, and would not receive Confederate scrip. Besides, they were well-known Unionists, and although not one of them had ever been molested or insulted, to my positive knowledge, we were *obliged* to destroy all such stores, or they would have fallen into the hands of the enemy. It seemed to be the desire of our generals, as far as practicable, to render the enemy's advance as irksome as possible—to make the once fair fields a barren waste. It did not require much to do this, for all the farmers had fled southward with movables and valuables, and had left their fields untouched since previous harvest. They "did not know who might be the ruling powers when crops grew," and hence did not sow.

When our whole army had crossed the Rappahannock, it was drawn up in line, and waited a week for the enemy, hoping to entice them into an engagement; but McClellan refused the challenge, and moved down the stream near the seaboard. To contract our left, all fell back across the Rapidan, and increased the strength of the right against all flanking manœuvres. Large fleets of transports were gathered at the mouth of the Rappahannock, but few knew their object or destination. Lee, however, who was now commander-in-chief, closely watched the Federal movements, and perceived that while making a show of force along the Lower Rappahannock, they would certainly not attack; their object being to transport their force with great celerity to the Yorktown Peninsula, thinking to surprise Magruder at Yorktown, and quietly seize Richmond before any troops could be marched to oppose them. This undoubtedly was

McClellan's design; but he proved a novice compared to Lee; for twelve months before, this accomplished soldier had read McClellan's plans so effectually, that when the enemy marched up the Peninsula, their progress was suddenly arrested by a long line of powerful fortifications belting the country, from York River to James River, and completely stopping further invasion. 'Tis true, that McClellan's force was well handled, and for the most part lay before Yorktown before our troops were there in strength to oppose them. For ten days, indeed, Magruder displayed his ten thousand men and few guns to such advantage that both McClellan and Burnside believed that Lee and Johnston were there before them. The whole army, however, arrived within a few days, and the breastworks frowned with *réal* cannon.

But while both armies are resting along their extensive lines, let me say a few words regarding General Lee and the various fortifications on this peninsula from Yorktown to Richmond.

When the war broke out, Robert E. Lee was a lieutenant-colonel of cavalry in the United States army, but was generally considered to be the first engineer in the service. He had greatly distinguished himself in Mexico, and shared with Beauregard the highest honors of that campaign. It was Scott's practice never to patronize subordinate talent, although all his renown was achieved by it; so that while he continually thrust himself upon popular favor, and obtained the highest rank possible in the service, he never spoke a word in favor of those to whom he was undoubtedly indebted for his greatness. For all that Scott and the War Office cared, Lee might have lived and died a lieutenant-colonel, while others infinitely inferior to him were promoted for political reasons.

Virginia having seceded from the Union, Lee tendered his services to his native State. His patrimony was situated on Arlington Heights, overlooking Washington, and he knew every inch of the ground and all its capabilities. He had indeed occupied it with a small force, but was ordered to fall back to Fairfax Court-House by the Minister of War. He was the only man capable of filling the seat of Minister of War, and, upon going to Richmond, was installed in that office, and fulfilled its Herculean duties with great talent and despatch. The line of the Rapidan and Rappahannock rivers was selected by him as our point of defence; while Beauregard preferred Manassas and Bull Run—much inferior situations, although "accidental" victory crowned our efforts and immortalized the latter place. The defeat of Pegram in Western Virginia by McClellan and Rosecrans, at Rich Mountain, occurred before Manassas, as I have mentioned in another place.

A few weeks after the Yankee rout at Manassas, Lee was sent to Western Virginia, with only a few raw recruits, under Wise and Floyd, to contend against the numerous and well-provided thousands who flocked to the Federal standard from Ohio and other adjacent States, having canal and railroad communication beyond all their necessities. What Lee needed in men he made up by skilful manœuvres, and by well fortifying different mountain passes and important hills. It was said, because he did not fight, that "he was afraid," that "he was one of the old school," etc. The truth is, he did not dare to fight, except on very advantageous terms, which Rosecrans was too much of an officer to grant. There was no excuse for the *latter* not offering or seeking battle, for his force was large and super-abundantly supplied. Lee, however, completely foiled him on every occasion; and thus the time passed, until the fall of heavy snows completely blocked up the roads, and rendered all that mountainous region an inhospitable waste.

As Charleston (South-Carolina) was threatened, Lee left the care of his troops to Floyd, and took command there, putting the coasts and harbors in complete defence, and rendering his work almost impregnable. The extensive works, however, which he had planned for the defence of Richmond and its vicinity, occupied much of his time, and when our winter quarters broke up the army were, for the most part, gratified by the announcement that he had been selected by Government for the post of commander in-chief. Those who knew the true merits of this modest, retiring, but skilful officer, foretold great things of him; nor were the most sanguine expectations disappointed, as subsequent events fully demonstrated. "System" seemed to be suddenly infused into all ranks, and volunteers gradually cooled down into quiet, business-like, stoical regulars. There was less "fuss" and more regularity; so that within a few weeks it was evident some mind was at work which could attend alike to great and little matters. Not that our army was absolutely without order previously, but there now seemed to be more of intellect displayed in the movements, and results were effected with less noise and bluster than formerly.

Of the fortifications at Yorktown and elsewhere on the peninsula, it is desirable to say a few words, otherwise it will be impossible to understand the movements that occurred there. The occupation of Hampton Roads by large fleets, and the menacing appearance of Fortress Monroe, with its immense number of troops and munitions of war, rendered it necessary for some force to watch the peninsula. This duty was assigned to General Magruder, who often ventured to the vicinity of Newport News, (the most southern point of the peninsula,) and greatly annoyed General Butler, who then commanded the fortress. Butler was tempted to open the campaign of 1861 before Scott, by marching upon Magruder in the hope of overwhelming him. Having made his preparations, he found the Confederates posted at the village of Little Bethel, and was soundly thrashed by a much inferior force in less than sixty minutes. Magruder remained master of the peninsula, and scoured the country between Yorktown and Newport News until the close of the year. His pickets were numerous and vigilant, and captured several hundred negroes who had run away from their masters and sought the Yankee lines.

Following the example of Butler, Magruder set the "contrabands" to work on his chain of fortifications, extending from Yorktown (on the York River) south-westwardly along the banks of the shallow Warwick to Mulberry Point, on the James River — a distance of about nine miles. The distance from Yorktown to the head-waters of the Little Warwick was about five miles; the land was low, flat, and marshy, unprofitable alike to friend or foe; but on the point where the chain of redoubts came to the springs of the Warwick, the western banks of that stream were much higher than the eastern, and the land was partly wooded, partly broken into fields. The Warwick itself was not more than one hundred feet wide at any point, and shallow; and as it was generally dry in summer, Magruder had made a series of dams, which held the waters and converted it into a succession of small lakes. Not only was the river "dammed," but also the marshy, swampy land which extended from Yorktown to its head. Thus, our position on the right was a "water-front," and on the left also, for the most part; here, however, as the water was derived from the snows and rains of winter, the depth was generally not more than three feet.

The character of these various works was admirable, and exactly suited to the topography of the immediate district. Yorktown itself, our left, was of immense strength, as was also Mulberry Point, the extremity of our right wing; Lee's Mills was considered the centre of the line. As the enemy would be necessarily obliged to cross or cut the various dams in approaching to attack, these points were protected by batteries of various calibres, enfilading and otherwise. It would be impossible to attempt detailed descriptions of them, for whatever of skill we possessed in science and engineering was there displayed in elaborated earthworks; and sheer madness alone could induce the Federals to attempt the line by assault. McClellan saw at a glance the work before him, and prepared to approach by parallels, and shell us out at discretion, while the majority of his troops were elsewhere employed. It was conjectured that his true plan would be to arrest our attention by vigorous bombardments and a display of force in front, while he strongly reenforced McDowell at Fredericksburgh, in order to move on Richmond from the north; fleets of gunboats and transports at the same time passing the extremities of our wings on York and James rivers, to throw strong forces on our flanks and rear. This was all seen by every intelligent soldier in the army, and the general expression was: "These immense works are a monument of Magruder's skill and industry, but are of no avail, for the enemy can ascend the rivers on either hand, and then we are emphatically cooped up, to be destroyed at leisure."

Lee and Johnston saw that our position was untenable, but determined to hold it until Huger, at Norfolk, should have dismantled his many fortifications, destroyed the naval establishments, and evacuated the seaboard. This was a military necessity. We had no navy, and could not expect to contend with a first-class naval power in arms against us. Norfolk had supplied us with many cannon and stores of all kinds; but while our ports were blockaded, it was sheer madness to incur vast expense in keeping open naval establishments and depots when all our small craft were blocked up in harbors. This·should have been done at first. Ours was a defensive war even upon land; it could not be otherwise on water. It is true that our infant navy achieved great glory in its encounter with the United States vessels, and the names of the Merrimac, Manassas, Arkansas, Sumter, and Nashville can never be forgotten; and it is doubtful whether any navy in the world did so much with such indifferent resources.

While Huger was preparing to evacuate Norfolk, most of our troops were retracing their steps up the peninsula towards Richmond, and not one brigade was unnecessarily detained at Yorktown. General D. H. Hill commanded Yorktown and the left wing; Magruder the right; Longstreet the centre; while Johnston was chief over all. Many episodes and incidents worthy of remembrance daily occurred between the advanced posts of both armies, which served to keep up a bitter feeling between us. McClellan made daily reconnoissances with his large balloon, which remained up occasionally many hours: his apparatus and balloon, however, were always two or three miles from the front. Nevertheless, our rifled guns frequently made rather close shots, and compelled the aëronauts to descend. In some instances our shots cut their gearing.

Determined to discover with certainty how many guns were in position, and how many embrasures masked, they occasionatly moved down to the front and opened a fierce cannonade with field-pieces, and a few rifled twenty-four-pounders. Such tricks were unsuccessful: the most of our guns were parked in the rear and covered, so that at a distance none could tell what they were. A few moments would have sufficed to bring them down to the batteries, but this we never found necessary. About one hundred guns were always ready night and day, frowning through embrasures, with caissons well protected; and in some places we had a few twenty-four, thirty-two, and sixty-four-pounders ready for the assailants. We never found occasion to use them.

Whenever the enemy approached with this design, and opened

fire upon us, the regiments would spring to their arms behind the breastworks and allow the artillery to amuse themselves. While we were sitting down, the enemy's shell fell thick and fast over our heads, and filled the woods in our rear with volumes of sulphurous smoke. Not one man of ours was lost during these frequent visitations, but the enemy sometimes suffered very severely. On one occasion, not less than a dozen twelve-pound howitzers opened on our six-gun battery—our pieces were silent, and not a soul stirred. Two corporals begged permission to have a shot each; directing two twelve-pound rifles at the Yankees, fully a mile and a half distant, their reports were immediately followed by the explosion of several caissons, killing the commandant and thirty men, twenty horses and upsetting four pieces! Our boys could not restrain their pleasure, and jumping on the breastworks for more than a mile, waved their hats and howled as Mississippians and Louisianians only *can* howl—a yell with a true Indian ring in it! The remaining pieces of the Yankee battery continued firing with great wildness, rapidity, and fury; still the boys remained on the breastworks, laughing and yelling, and though commanded to come down when shell were chipping the earth near their feet, nothing could induce them to budge until a battery lower down opened on the enemy, and smashed them up with one discharge!

Such experiments were too costly to be repeated, so that any one portion of our lines was seldom visited more than once. The enemy contented themselves with erecting mortar batteries of great strength, so as to effectually shell us out if possible, when the bombardment regularly opened. McClellan's position was certainly an unenviable one, but such was his popularity with the men, that they performed immense labors with axe and spade at his bidding, and seldom grumbled. With a very large army (one hundred and seventy-five thousand men) encamped in low, swampy lands, sickness and disease was very great. As no roads, except a few ordinary ones, existed from Yorktown to any point of his lines, flanks, or rear, it was necessary to fell the forests and make them. Regiments were thus engaged for weeks cutting avenues of communication, while thousands plied the axe and covered the dirt with layers of logs, the interstices of which were then filled with branches, and all covered with a thick coating of tenacious, marly soil. In dry weather, and for the use of light teams, these "corduroyed" roads might well serve; but as this was the month of April, the logs sank lower and lower, so that heavy wagons, and teams dragging siege-pieces and mortars, moved but slowly, and the various routes were blocked up by division quartermasters and commissaries endeavoring to transport necessary provision to the front. Such was the scarcity at one time, that every wagon in the service was insufficient to supply the daily necessities of his army, and McClellan's siege operations were delayed. Many deserters came over to us and begged for food.

But, alas! if such was the state of McClellan's forces, what was the condition of our own? Flour and bad bacon, indeed, were for the most part, regularly served out in half rations; but as for tea, coffee, sugar, molasses, rice, baker's bread, or crackers, fresh meat, salt, or clothing—these were things unknown to us for many months; the only thing of which we had a superabundance was *cartridges!* Sugar, rice, and molasses *should* have been forthcoming; but then we knew that our few railroads in the South were overworked, night and day, in transporting troops and *matériel*, and such was the press of Government business that no civilian, except on army affairs, could ever obtain a "permit" to travel twenty miles on the various railroads. The men fully understood the difficulties of our situation, and never uttered a word of complaint. They fried the abominable bacon for its fat, which they mixed with their flour, and this, with water, was the chief food of all for many weeks.

Such was our poverty, indeed, that many negro servants, hitherto faithful to the fortunes of their masters, deserted during the darkness of night, and reported us as ragged, starving, footsore, and spiritless. Except in the latter respect, their reports were but too true. In lieu of coffee or tea, we gathered holly-leaves or sassafras-roots, to boil down into tea, and felt thankful for this barbarous decoction, although much debility and sickness resulted from using it. All this was so well known to the enemy, that their pickets would taunt ours in coarse language that stirred up our men occasionally to deeds of rashness, such as a surprise of the enemy's outposts *about*

dinner-time! The well-fed- rice- cracker- fresh meat- sago- ham-
bean- pork- molasses- sugar-eating, and tea- coffee- and whisky-
drinking Yankees, in fine warm clothes, would often shout to
us: "How do git along, you sassafras-drinking sons of ——?"
"Oh! you mouldy, ragged —— rebels! what's the price of soap
in Dixie?" Taunts might serve their purpose very well when
out of danger behind trees, but as soon as any of us "fell in,"
and marched out to give appropriate answers, these gentlemen
in blue would invariably "skedaddle!"

I have known instances, indeed, of soldiers from the Gulf
States having, unknown to the officers, sallied out beyond our
extreme outposts during the night, penetrated the enemy's
lines, and brought back provisions in abundance, often having
slung over their arms from two to four rifles, the property of
Federal sentinels who opposed them. I repeat, I have known
several instances of this kind where parties of six would go
out on such expeditions, and, from experience in Indian warfare, would scatter in the timber, prowl about the enemy's encampments, and return unscratched, with a heavy load of eatables—the chief weight being of coffee and sugar. One or two
particular instances I consider worthy of especial mention.

One day while on duty near Dam No. 1, we observed within
the enemy's lines a flock of sheep grazing, the distance from
us being about two miles. We had been joking on the subject
and remarking what fine soup they would make for our hungry
men, when I observed a tall ragged Texan intently eyeing them.
Lifting his two-feet-and-a-half diameter straw hat from his head,
he began to scratch as if in profound meditation. It was towards evening, and he was returning from twenty-four hours'
picketing in the front. "What's the matter?" I inquired.
"Nothin'," he replied; "but I was just a-thinking I should
like to have some mutton for supper!—*our* folks get nothin' but
cartridges to eat." Tired as he was, he answered company roll-
call, and shortly afterwards passed me, stealing cautiously towards the enemy, hiding behind fallen timber, and having
crossed the dam, disappeared.

After a while I heard several shots fired in the direction of
the sheep, but, of course, took little notice of it, for firing was
continual from morning till night. As "tattoo" was sounding

I was about to repair to my own post, when some unaccountable object seemed to be crossing the dam. One of the guards challenged—" Hold on, boys," was the reply ; " wait a minute—I've got him all right;" and before I could recover from astonishment, my friend of the large straw hat appeared clambering up the face of the breastwork, heavily laden with something, and, on close inspection, I found he carried a large sheep and a fat lamb on his back, the legs tied round his neck, a bundle swung around his middle, four rifles hung from his shoulders, and his own trusty Enfield grasped firmly in the right hand, cocked and loaded. " But where did you get the rifles?" I inquired. " Oh ! well, the darned fools wouldn't let me get the mutton peaceable, so I had to shoot four of 'em !" This instance is but one of a class, for which I can vouch from personal knowledge.

The enemy had been taught that we were a pusillanimous race, effeminate, lazy, unacclimated, and physically inferior to themselves. Our mode of life at home — the abundance of money, dependence upon slave labor, and inaptitude for every thing save cotton, rice, and sugar-raising—might give countenance to such ideas; and it is equally true that habitual slothfulness had thrown every species of manufacture into their hands. But history should have taught them that the South was ever foremost in fight, and that while Northern troops had never fought South during the Revolution of 1776, Southern armies had traversed all the North, and had left their bones on every battle-field. The same is equally true of the war of 1812, and of the expedition into Mexico, for the impartial student will be surprised at the numbers lost by us compared with the North in those transactions, and at the number of times the Cotton States have shown in the front, in every movement of danger. All this, however, was not considered. When McClellan took command of the enemy in August, 1861, his words were: " There shall be no more defeats, no more retreats; our progress will henceforth be unchecked and glorious." The press also had been continually chanting anthems over their own superiority and our wretchedness; every picket fight had been magnified into " a great success," " complete victory," etc., all printed in alarmingly large capitals, until at last every drummer in McClellan's army considered himself a hero.

Surprised to find us more than a match for them in the everyday encounters at the lines, and annoyed to find that their newspapers sometimes told awkward truths by "accident," different ambitious generals sought to distinguish themselves at their respective posts, and to do something of which to boast. On one occasion it was designed to march a heavy force into the woods near Lee's Mills, and surprise four of our companies picketed there. Our outposts quietly gave the signal of approach, and as a full brigade turned into a lane in line with our battery, some half dozen second shell were fired very rapidly, and split up the column, cutting the commander and horse completely in two—the fire of our four companies in extended order did the rest, and the New-Englanders broke and fled in great confusion, leaving many dead and wounded behind. They had to retreat within view of our lower batteries, which, as they passed their front, shelled the woods and broke them a second time.

On another occasion, some of our pickets advanced farther than necessary, and captured several field-officers. Expecting retaliation, strict watch was maintained, and on the Sabbath a full regiment appeared to take vengeance on our pickets, but none were seen. The Yankees had not proceeded far, when up rose four companies, and having delivered a slaughtering cross-fire, charged with a terrible yell. The enemy broke, and we were never troubled with them afterwards at that point.

Our outposts, however, could not keep quiet, and every chance that was presented was improved to slaughter the enemy, for they held them in profound contempt. The enemy devised a new plan for picketing. They owned a great many dogs, and when on outpost duty, Mr. Yankee would quietly light his pipe and play cards, while the dogs rambled through the woods, and gave the alarm of any approach! The faithfulness of their dogs saved them on many occasions from loss, for the animals would howl and retire from any one unless dressed in blue. As woodsmen, the enemy were complete novices compared to us; but this was as might be expected. There were Maryland regiments, however, in their service who were equal to us, but these were not trusted—McClellan thought, and wisely, that with the first opportunity they would "skedaddle" to the rebels!

Our various batteries commanding the dams seemed to give the enemy much uneasiness and annoyance. They erected heavy counter-batteries, but still could not show in force at any point without suffering loss, and so determined to try the experiment of taking one of these defences. Towards Yorktown, the various dams were successively numbered 1, 2, 3, etc., until their approach to Lee's Mills, where the river became sufficiently deep to obviate the erection of more. "Dam No. 1" was consequently situated on land that held but little water, the causeway being about twelve feet broad. The battery which protected it was triangular in form, containing three guns, with a long embankment or rifle-pit connected with it on either side, but situated in very low land. The position of the enemy was much higher, with rising hillocks up and down the face of the swamp, which were, of course, converted into earthworks, and mounted not less than twenty-two guns, commanded by their accomplished artillerist Ayers, (I follow Yankee authorities.) It was impossible for us to use our guns with much effect, since they were always assailed by enfilade.

To obviate this, we were constructing a powerful battery in the rear of the first, the work being chiefly performed by the troops on picket there. While this work was in progress, a North-Carolina regiment was stretched along the right rifle-pit, and four companies of a Louisiana regiment occupied the left. Yankee sharpshooters, posted in trees, had discovered that the three-gun battery was oftentimes comparatively deserted about noon-time, and as the causeway, or dam, was broad, it would not be very difficult to cross the comparatively dry swamp, under cover of their guns, seize the place, break our chain of defences, and throw over large bodies of troops. Accordingly they gathered a large force silently in the woods, and at the hour of noon made a rush across the causeway, our pickets fighting desperately as they retreated, instead of falling back upon the rifle-pits without delay, after once firing their pieces, conformably to order. As a consequence, the enemy were half-way across the dam and swamp before any alarm was given.

When the assault was known, the North-Carolinians in the right rifle-pit seized their arms, and having fired one volley with destructive effect, unaccountably retired. The Yankees, once in possession of the battery and right rifle-pit, were much in the situation of the man who gained an elephant in a raffle, not knowing what to do with it! Swarming over the works, they fought and overcame the few guards who resisted them, and received heavy reenforcements as fast as possible. The four companies of Louisianians who had gallantly held their pit, were joined by the remainder of the regiment, and rushing into the battery commenced the work of slaughter silently, but with terrible vigor. Having entered the works in two wings, the unfortunate Yankees were thus surrounded, and the first cross-fire delivered by the Louisianians cut them down by scores: many more were destroyed with the sabre-bayonet when our men closed in upon them. Those who attempted to jump out of the breastwork were shot down by our Georgians, who now occupied the right pit. Reenforcements crossing the dam were obstructed by the dead, the wounded, and those seeking to return, so that scores fell right and left into the swamp, and were half buried in mud and water. The saddest part is yet to tell. Smith, who commanded the Yankee brigade, seeing his men overcome and slaughtered in the battery, ordered Ayers's twenty-two guns to open fire, in order to cover the retreat, but in doing this, their shells killed as many of their own men as of ours. The Louisianians in the battery and the Georgians in the rifle-pits continued the work of destruction, and of the few that escaped, many sank into the swamp, and could not extricate themselves from the mud.

This affair lasted about half an hour; the enemy numbered near two thousand, while our force did not exceed half that number. The scene of carnage was frightful; several hundreds of the enemy might be seen lying in all directions in the battery, many along the causeway, and more to the right and left of it in the swamp. Our loss was unaccountably small, and never did Louisianians use the bayonet with greater good will, for they had met for the first time "real" Yankees, (Vermont,) who had done more lying and boasting than those of any State in the North—always excepting the arch-hypocrites and negro-worshippers of Massachusetts. Proud as were our men of this affair, all regretted one thing, namely, that the gentlemen in blue had not proved to be Massachusetts men. There was not a regiment in the service but would have willingly marched fifty miles for a fair fight with double the number of them.

Smith, the Federal Commander, kept up the cannonade till long after sundown, but with more destruction to his own wounded than to us; for as we screened ourselves during the fire, it did not cause us the loss of a man. This conduct, if nothing more were added, affords ample justification for the assertions of the enemy that their commander was completely intoxicated during the whole affair, and incapable of conducting it. During the night we endeavored to extricate the wounded from the swamp, but our men were repeatedly fired upon; and even when a flag of truce was sent across next day, begging, in the name of mercy, that we might be permitted to look after *their* wounded, whose groans and cries were heartrending, this inhuman commander refused to receive it, and our men, being fired upon a second time, retired, and allowed the poor wretches to die from loss of blood or hunger. For two days and nights this barbarous conduct was kept up, and the enemy were allowed to lie festering in the sun, nor was any thing done for them until their own regiments (Third, Fourth, and Sixth Vermont) were withdrawn from the scene. This was done, doubtless, to screen the "real" loss from their own troops. During the night, however, many of our men ventured across the dam, and brought in some of their own dead, and buried many of the enemy's slain, to stay the increasing stench that arose from putrefaction. We also dragged out of the swamp some who had sunk to the armpits in mud and water, but who had sustained themselves by clinging to stumps and roots.

Although my thoughts were far from cheerful when standing in the battery and gazing on this awful scene of slaughter, I could not but smile at the indifference of a tall, hard-fisted, and very ragged Texan, who was cautiously "hunting up a pair of boots and pants." He was warned not to show his head above the parapet, for the Yankee shapshooters, armed with rifles of a long range, with telescopic "sights," were "thick as blackberries" in the woods to the front, and were excellent shots.

12

"Darn the blue-skins, any how; who's scared of the blue-bellies? (that is, Eastern men.) Let all the Yankees go to ——, for all *I* care. Let 'em shoot, and be d—d! I'm bound to have a pair of boots, any how!" And so saying, he passed over the parapet, down its face, and returned with the body of an enemy, which he had fished out of the water. He first pulled off the boots, which proved to be an excellent pair; then proceeding to rifle the pockets, he found sixty dollars in gold. He was much astonished and delighted at these discoveries; but when he examined the haversack and found it well stored with capital rations, including a canteen full of fine rye whisky, he was electrified with sudden joy, dropped boots, haversack, and money upon the ground, and half-emptied the canteen at a draught. Setting down the can, he smacked his lips, and thus soliloquized: "Well! poor devil, he's gone, like a mighty big sight of 'em; but *he* was a gentleman, and deserved better luck. If he'd been a Massachusetts Yankee, I wouldn't a cared a darn! but these fellows are the right kind. They come along with good boots and pants, lots to eat, money in their pockets, and are no mean judges of whisky. These are the kind of fellows I like to fight!"

It was not from a brutal feeling that our men rifled the dead, but sheer necessity; and although they stripped them of any thing needed, the bodies were invariably interred with decency, and *not* mutilated, as the Northern press delighted to asseverate on all occasions. Hardened as we were, men would joke under any circumstances — some would even smoke during action; and it was not uncommon to hear one remark, when burying the enemy: "Well, Lincoln, old Scott, and McClellan promised 'em farms each in Virginia when all was over—old Virginny is large enough to accommodate 'em all with lots, seven by two!" But this I wish to repeat—there was no brutality displayed on any occasion that came under my notice on any field on which I was present. It is true the prisoners were unmercifully joked occasionally, but I have always seen the wounded treated with the utmost care; and it became a usual expression in the hospitals, when all did not progress well with patients: "If I was only a Yankee, the darned doctors would do more for me than now." The dead, on all practicable occasions, were decently

buried; and in many cases I have known putrid carcases handled and coffined by our men, and even a board placed at the
head of the grave, as at Leesburgh, with the words: "Here
lies a Yankee; Co. H, Fifteenth Massachusetts." I am em-
phatic about this subject, for many infamous misrepresentations
have been widely circulated regarding us by the Northern
press.

CHAPTER XX.

Fall of New-Orleans, April twenty-fourth—Preparations of Commodore Hollins for the Defence—Bombardment of the Forts—Naval Engagements—Destruction of Cotton — Evacuation of the City—Possession taken by Commodore Farragut—Arrival of General Butler—His brutal Attacks upon the Ladies of New-Orleans—Examples from his General Orders.

"Baton Rouge, April —, 1862.

"DEAR FRIEND : Our beautiful city has fallen, and the detested flag of our enemy floats over the Mint!

" The story of our disgrace is a long and painful one to me, but remembering your kindness in fully informing us of the progress of events in Virginia, it is but right I return the compliment; though my narrative may be wanting in many particulars which history, at some distant future, can alone be expected to unfold.

" When the bombardment of Fort Sumter proved that the South was determined to rid her soil of the enemy, troops were also sent to Pensacola, seized Fort McRea, Barrancas, and Warrenton, and laid siege to the enemy's fortifications (Fort Pickens) on Santa Rosa Island. Our forces there began to increase very rapidly, and, under the command of General Bragg, were wrought up to a fine spirit of discipline and efficiency. Except the night surprise of the enemy on Santa Rosa, nothing of moment transpired, the respective forces being content to fortify their positions and otherwise remain inactive. Commodore Hollins, who was cruising in the Gulf when we declared independence, brought his sloop-of-war to New-Orleans, surrendered her to the Confederate authorities, and accepted service under our banner. It was natural to surmise that New-Orleans would soon be blockaded and attacked by the enemy's fleet; to meet which contingency, General Anderson was put in command of our land forces, and Hollins of the naval department.

"The latter began to prepare for the enemy by the construction of fire-rafts, and of various impediments for the bar of the river, and other shallow places, besides superintending the construction of some rude iron-clad floating rams and batteries, the principal of which was a vessel called the Manassas. With his small flotilla, Hollins could not pretend to accomplish very much, but he resolved to attack the Federal blockading vessels at the mouth of the river, the destruction of which, it was hoped, would enable us to obtain supplies from Europe before the Federal navy should be reenforced. In this design he was so far successful that he sank one sloop-of-war and disabled several others; but as the ram Manassas proved unmanageable, and had injured her machinery, Hollins withdrew and returned to the city, well satisfied with his achievements. In the mean time Lovell had succeeded Anderson in the military command; numerous volunteers had joined our forces, and even the colored men, free and slave, formed battalions for the defence of the city. Fortifications and breastworks innumerable were thrown up, to prevent all approach by the lakes of the Mississippi. These works were important, and, as you know something of the topography of the country, I enumerate them, but am not positive as to the number of guns placed in each.

"Fort Jackson was on the west, or right bank of the river, nearly opposite Fort St. Philip, and twenty-five miles from the 'Passes' leading into the Gulf. It was a very strong, casemated fort, intended for over one hundred guns, and will conveniently accommodate five hundred men. Much labor had been expended on this fort, and it was thought to be impregnable, but adverse circumstances destroyed all our hopes regarding it. Fort St. Philip was on the east or left bank of the river, nearly opposite Fort Jackson, seventy miles below the city, and, being a heavy casemated fort, was intended for over one hundred guns. It was bombarded by the English in 1812; it had accommodated four hundred men. Fort Livingstone was situated on Grand Terre Island, at the mouth of Barrataria Bay, and was destined for twenty or more guns. Fort Pike was a casemate fortification, placed at the Rigolettes, or North Pass, between Lake Borgne and Lake Pontchartrain, commanding the entrance to the lake, and the main channel to the gulf in that direction. The amount of its armament I could never learn; Fort Macomb guarded the South Pass, between Lakes Borgue and Pontchartrain, and had a dozen or more guns. Fort Dupré was a small fort commanding Bayou Dupré into Lake Borgue. Proctor's Tower was another small work on Lake Borgue; and Battery Bienvenue at the entrance of Bayou Bienvenue into Lake Borgue. Besides these latter small batteries, mounting a few guns, were the Chalmette Batteries, above Fort Jackson, and much nearer the city.*

"From the enthusiasm of our population, and the alacrity with which they mustered under arms, it was considered impossible for the enemy to successfully 'run' the forts on the river and effect a landing, for a long chain of breastworks stretched away in different parts of the city suburbs, and at one time we had not fewer than twenty-four thousand men under arms, including three thousand free negroes, who volunteered to defend them. Notwithstanding all this apparent enthusiasm, there were undoubtedly many traitors going to and fro in our midst; and much information was carried to the enemy by runaways, and by fishermen who were allowed free passes to transact their business on the river. Some fifteen or twenty thousand bales of cotton were in warehouses or on the landing ready for shipment, in case the enemy should leave the mouth of the river, together with much tobacco owned by foreign merchants. Our planters persisted in sending cotton down the river, and this acted as a temptation to the enemy to attempt the capture of the city.

"Society at New-Orleans showed little sensitiveness to the great struggle in which we were engaged. Festivity was the order of the day; balls, parties, theatres, operas, and the like, continued as if we were not in the midst of a furious war, with our beloved sons, brothers, and relatives bleeding and dying on distant battle-fields. We felt too secure. We considered it impossible for any force to capture the place. 'Jackson, with a handful of men, and a few cotton-bales, had defeated Packenham in 1812,' many said; and as we considered the enemy much inferior to the British in all re-

---

* All these positions, guarding the approaches to New-Orleans from the Gulf, are distinctly shown on the ordinary maps.

spects, and our present defences vastly superior to those of former times, all were confident of victory in case of attack. None doubted the loyalty of our people, our generals, or the Government. Shipwrights were busy in preparing new rams and floating batteries; foundries and steam-hammers were in full blast, night and day, preparing boilers, machinery, and iron plates; and several mammoth rams and iron floating batteries were promised at an early day by the contractors—two Northern men. So much delay, however, occurred in fitting and finishing them, that when the enemy approached we had none of these vessels to assist in the defence. Worse than all, our generals at Corinth were continually calling upon Lovell for troops; so that our original twenty-four thousand rapidly dwindled down to a very low figure. Northern papers boasted that their fleets and forces could annihilate our city at any time; Butler was reported to have said, 'he held the keys of New-Orleans;' but all such talk was considered pure Yankee twaddle, and none ever dreamed he had foundation for such boastings.

"Depending entirely upon our river batteries, we anxiously awaited the enemy's approach; but they seemed tardy in their movements, and cruised about the Gulf with evident indecision, so that every one began to smile and say : 'They would think twice before attempting a rehearsal of the scenes of 1812!' I do not remember what force the enemy had in gunboats, at the mouth of the river, but the fact soon became known that Commodore Farragut was in command, and that he made light of our fortifications. As it was considered unadvisable to attempt a defence of the 'passes,' the works at those points had been dismantled some time before, and the guns carried to the city. We had sunk barriers (sunken vessels, etc.) in the river about a mile below Forts Jackson and Philip, and it was thought they would effectually stop the enemy's progress; but the swiftness of the current carried many away, and before others could be placed there, the enemy slowly steamed up the stream in strong force, on the sixteenth of April, and prepared to attack the forts.

"In the city these threatening appearances were but little heeded—we considered ourselves impregnable; Farragut's boats

were treated with contempt, and even the terrific bombardment
was looked upon as a fine spectacle. Duncan, in Fort Jackson,
kept all fully informed of the progress of events below; thousands flocked down the river, and on the Levees viewed the
bombardment with evident pleasure, for it was soon ascertained
that the enemy's fire was inaccurate, and that few, if any, of
their eleven-inch shell ever touched the forts. At night the
greatest vigilance was maintained to inform commanders of
the enemy's movements. On the twenty-third the terrific bombardment had continued a whole week; they had thrown over
twenty-five thousand shells; and Duncan reported that two of
his guns in Fort Jackson were dismounted; half a dozen killed
and wounded was the total loss, and the works were as sound
as ever.

"The evening of the twenty-third closed as others had done
for the past seven days; our defences were thought to be impassable, and strong hopes were entertained that Farragut
would soon give up the conflict as fruitless and abortive. Towards three A.M. on the morning of the twenty-fourth, the enemy were descried creeping up the river in full force, and as
they steamed abreast of the forts were received with deafening
roars from our artillery. The conflict then became furious; the
enemy fought admirably, however, and passed the forts, Farragut leading in the Hartford; but had not proceeded far when
they encountered our small fleet of seventeen vessels of different kinds. Except the old Manassas and the Louisiana, the
rest of our vessels were vulnerable, so that the destruction, confusion, and noise were terrible. The Louisiana was unmanageable, and could only use two of her nine guns; so when it was
perceived that nothing could prevent the enemy from breaking
our line, she was run ashore, and blown up, although the enemy's broadsides had not injured her in the least. The Governor Moore, another of our boats, acted nobly among the enemy's twelve heavy sloops of war and gunboats, and fired her
last cartridge at point-blank range, but was also run ashore and
blown up to prevent capture.

"The action was in full progress when news reached the city
that Farragut's fleets had passed the forts and had successfully
engaged our ships. The scene of confusion that ensued in

town defies all description. People were amazed, and could scarcely realize the awful fact, and ran hither and thither in speechless astonishment. Very soon the flames seen issuing from shipyards in Algiers and other places, cônvinced them that the news was authentic, and that Government officers were then busily engaged destroying every thing that was likely to be of value to the enemy. The unfinished Mississippi and other vessels were scuttled or fired, ammunition destroyed, and shot sunk in the river. The people, on their part, proceeded to the various cotton-presses, rolled out thousands of bales, and applied the torch; countless cotton ships were also sunk or fired, steamboats by the dozen similarly destroyed. As the roar of cannon drew nearer, the heat of the sun, and conflagrations in every direction, made the atmosphere oppressively hot, while dense columns of smoke darkened the air. The scene was one of terrible grandeur, the effect of which was much heightened by the tolling of alarm bells in the city.

"Banks, and all who had any thing to save, were busy sending away their valuables; and their having done so in good time prevented several millions of specie from falling into the hands of the enemy. Long lines of army wagons, carriages, pedestrians, and horsemen, left the town by every avenue; the wildest consternation and dejection seemed to have seized all; the revulsion of feeling was awful. Having narrowly escaped capture in the naval engagement, Lovell rode rapidly by the Levee road, and arrived in town about two P.M. Crowds gathered round him while he related the chief features of the engagement below, bearing testimony to the heroism of our little navy of indifferent vessels, and seeming heart-broken at the unexpected calamity which had befallen us. He considered it advisable for his few soldiers to retire without the limits of the city to avert a bombardment, and this idea was fully indorsed by the City Council. Accordingly, late in the day, his whole force of not more than two thousand effective men departed by rail some fifteen miles above the city, with orders to keep within easy call in case of emergency. It now became a difficult task for the City Council to preserve order, as many, under the guise of patriotism, were laying violent hands on the property of others. Sad faces and angry gesticulation met one at every turn; people seemed paralyzed, and could not comprehend the extent of the great and humiliating visitation. The thing was incredible!

"At Fort Jackson and Fort Philip our loss had been trifling—not a hundred men in all. Their guns were untouched; ammunition plentiful; the walls intact! yet Farragut had passed them, under an annihilating shower of rifled shot, and was still approaching, carrying all before him, shelling right and left wherever there seemed to be the least appearance of opposition. He was within a few miles of the city—the smoke from his vessels could be plainly seen curling over the woods in the bends of the river, and he must soon arrive. Whatever was to be accomplished must be done quickly; no time was to be lost in idle recrimination or empty rage; moments were precious, and the watchword of all was *work!* Large stores of tobacco were now burned on every hand, save where a foreign flag floated to protect it. Sugar, molasses, and rice, in thousands of hogsheads, were thrown into the river or scattered through the streets and gutters. Men seemed wrought into a frenzy of desperation, and broke, or burned, or sank every thing that might prove of use to the enemy, so that within a few hours subsequent to Lovell's official information the whole city presented an indescribable scene of confusion, and property worth many millions was destroyed in an incredibly short space of time. This scene of uproar and confusion continued throughout the day and all night, while now and then heavy guns could be heard down the river, as if the enemy were cautiously approaching and firing at every object that seemed suspicious. Crowds of the poor were enjoying a rich harvest by this wholesale destruction of property, and scores of them could be seen with baskets, and bags, and drays, carrying off to their homes whatever of sugar, molasses, rice, bacon, etc., fell in their way. A low murmuring noise filled the air—it was the conversation of assembled thousands. Many were unanimous for destroying the city, rather than permit it to fall into the hands of the enemy; but the opinion prevailed that, owing to the great numbers of poor, the place was entirely at the mercy of the foe, and nothing should be done to tempt a bombardment.

"On the morning of the twenty-fifth, Farragut's advance was

observed steaming up towards the city. When abreast of the Chalmette batteries, on both sides of the city, he was saluted with volleys from the earthworks, but, being uninjured, ran past and cast anchor at intervals before the city, with ports open and every preparation made for a bombardment. Farragut then opened communication with the Mayor, and demanded the surrender of the town, together with Lovell's forces; but the latter were now far away, and Mayor Monroe commenced a spirited correspondence with the Commodore. He admitted they had no force with which to oppose the enemy; yet as they came uninvited, and as the people disclaimed all relationship with the Northern Government, it was impossible to make a formal surrender of the place. If the Admiral desired the removal of objectionable flags floating over the City Hall, he must do it by his own force; for not a man, woman, or child, of any color, could be found in their midst who would lay a traitor's hand upon the flag of their adoption.

"In the mean time, the destruction of property continued on every hand; and at length Farragut was so exasperated, that he swore he would reduce the place to ashes unless the State flag was removed from the principal buildings. Still, so long as Forts St. Philip, Jackson, and the Chalmette batteries remained intact, it was thought that something might be done to save the city, and in this hope the correspondence was protracted. But evil tidings were in store for us! While Farragut and Mayor Monroe were exchanging angry letters of great length, the sad news reached us that Forts St. Philip and Jackson had surrendered to the enemy on account of a mutiny among their garrisons. When Duncan heard it, he used every means in his power to persuade his men to return to their duty, and even threatened to turn his guns upon them. He was in earnest, and a desperate man; but, on examining his guns, he found many spiked, several dismounted, and not less than three hundred men clamoring around him for a surrender. The situation of the heroic Duncan was pitiable. He begged, besought his men to stand to their arms, vowed that the forts were impregnable, and that he could blow up all Butler's transports * in a

* Butler's land forces were on Ship Island and Mississippi City. Had he attempted to march overland upon New-Orleans, the "Levees" would have been cut and his men drowned in the swamps.

trice, if they only resolved to stand by him to the last; for it was an eternal shame to give up the works, provisioned as they were, and scarcely touched by the enemy. All the eloquence in the world, however, could not affect these soulless traitors; and as poor Duncan, ragged, dusty, powder-blackened, and exhausted, narrated the circumstance of his fall, he wept like a child, while crowds around him remained mute with astonishment, and hung their heads as men doomed to humiliation and shame.

"Farragut, being informed of all these things, was in a hurry to expedite the full and formal surrender of the city before the arrival of Butler, who was now known to be on his way. The correspondence between the Commodore and the Mayor had lasted from the twenty-fourth to the twenty-eighth, and on the last-named day Farragut vowed to bombard the city if the State flag was not hauled down, giving forty-eight hours' formal notice for the removal of women and children. He did not put this threat into execution, however, but reiterated his demand on Monday, the thirtieth, without effect. On Tuesday morning, he sent on shore a party of two hundred marines, with two brass howitzers, who marched through the streets, and, forming before the City Hall, the objectionable State banner—the sign of all State rights—was torn down, and the Stars and Stripes, an emblem of tyrannical oppression, raised instead. The ceremony was witnessed by a silent crowd of many thousands, but it went off quietly; the force returning to their ships without a word of reproach or the least sign of resistance.

"But the detested flag had not long remained on the dome, when some young men ascended and tore it down, and dragged it through the streets in triumph. Then Farragut moved his vessels closer to the city, and again threatened to bombard it, but again abstained from doing so. Many of the citizens fired upon the vessels, but did no harm. Yet, the first man that advanced to meet Farragut on his landing, and welcome the return of Federal authority to the city, had scarcely taken the Commodore's hand, ere a shot from the crowd sent him to eternity! The enemy, however, were careful not to move about in detached parties; for there were bands of desperate men who had vowed to slay all who came in their way, so that they remained on board, and did not attempt to stir through the city until the arrival of Butler's force, which landed on the first of May.*

* The rule of General Butler in New-Orleans has been forever rendered odious and detestable by his many acts of cruelty, despotism, and indecency. Nor shall I add more than say, that he has rendered himself contemptible to friends and foes throughout the civilized world. His General Orders are a mass of cruelty and folly—an eternal monument of his debased and indefensible character; and in his persecution of women, he has shown his unmanly disposition and temper, beyond all former example. I subjoin a few specimens of his General Orders:

" Headq-uarters, Department of the Gulf,
New-Orleans, 1862.

" General Orders, No. 150.

"Mrs. Phillips, wife of Philip Phillips, having been once imprisoned for her traitorous proclivities and acts at Washington, and released by the Government, and having been found training her children to spit upon officers of the United States, for which act of one of those children both her husband and herself apologized and were forgiven, is now found on the balcony of her house, during the passage of the funeral procession of Lieutenant De Kay, laughing and mocking at his remains; and upon being inquired of by the Commanding General if this fact were so, contemptuously replies : 'I was in good spirits that day.'

" It is, therefore, ordered that she be not ' regarded and treated as a common woman,' of whom no officer or soldier is bound to take notice, but as an uncommon, bad, and dangerous woman; stirring up strife and inciting to riot.

" And that, therefore, she be confined at Ship Island, in the State of Mississippi, within proper limits there till further orders, and that she be allowed one female servant and no more, if she so chooses. That one of the houses for hospital purposes be assigned her as quarters, and a soldier's ration each day be served out to her, with the means of cooking the same, and that no verbal or written communication be allowed with her, except through this office, and that she be kept in close confinement until removed to Ship Island.

"By command of Major-General BUTLER.
"R. S. DAVIS,
" Captain and Acting Assistant Adjutant-General."

The truth of the case is as follows: Mrs. Phillips (wife of Philip Phillips, formerly United States Senator from Alabama) was standing on her balcony ; and when the *cortége* passed, many children in the next house—who had a dancing party—ran to the balcony, and all began to laugh. She was treated barbarously on Ship Island, and went deranged ; but Butler laughed at her sufferings, and would not mitigate the punishment, saying that " all women were strumpets who laughed at Federal soldiers." He wished it to be believed that he was fearless, yet he wore armor under his clothes, slept on board ship, and was never for a moment without an armed guard, whether in or out of his house, while several pistols, ready cocked and capped, lay beside him, and sentinels walked within five paces of him. He had a large sign placed in his office in the St. Charles's Hotel, with the inscription : *"A she adder bites worse than a male adder."*

"This is the simple narration of our fall and lasting disgrace. No blame can attach to Lovell or to other officers in command— all did their duty ; but none expected that Farragut would ever

"Special Order, No. 151.

"Fidel Keller has been found· exhibiting a human skeleton in his window, in a public place, in this city, labelled ' Chickahominy,' in large letters, meaning and intending that the bones should be taken by the populace to be the bones of a United States soldier slain in that battle, in order to bring the authority of the United States and our army into contempt, and for that purpose had stated to the passers-by that the bones were those of a Yankee soldier, whereas, in truth and fact, they were the bones purchased some weeks before of a Mexican consul, to whom they were pledged by a medical student.

"It is, therefore, ordered that for this desecration of the dead, he be confined at Ship Island for two years at hard labor, and that he be allowed to communicate with no person on the Island, except Mrs. Phillips, who has been sent there for a like offence.

"Any written message may be sent to him through these head-quarters.

"Upon this order being read to him, the said Keller requested that so much of it as associated him with ' that woman' might be recalled, which request was, therefore, reduced to writing by him, as follows:

"'New-Orleans, June 30th, 1862.

"'Mr. Keller desires that a part of the sentence which refers to the communication with Mrs. Phillips be stricken out, as he does not wish to have communication with Mrs. Phillips.'   (Signed)   F. KELLER.

"'Witness : D. WATERS.'

"Said request seeming to the Commanding General to be reasonable, so much of said orders is revoked, and the remainder will be executed.—By order of Major-General Butler.   R. S. DAVIS,
" Captain and Acting Assistant Adjutant-General."

The truth is, that Mr. Keller was informed by the soldiers that the Mrs. Phillips on the Island was a prostitute ; and as he knew there was an infamous character of the same name, he declined all communication with her. Having discovered his mistake, and found that she was Mrs. Senator Phillips, he wrote frequently to Butler to recall his protest, and be allowed to see the afflicted lady. The request was refused, and his punishment increased.

" Head-quarters. Department of the Gulf,
" New-Orleans, June 30th, 1862.
" Special Order, No. 152.

" John W. Andrews exhibited a cross, the emblem of the suffering of our blessed Saviour, fashioned for personal ornament, which he said was made from the bones of a Yankee soldier, and having shown this, too, without rebuke, in the Louisiana Club, which claims to be composed of chivalric gentlemen :

"It is, therefore, ordered that for this desecration of the dead, he be confined at hard labor for two years on the fortifications at Ship Island, and that he be al-

dream of running the batteries below; and none could imagine that the enemy could find entrance into the forts and corrupt the men. Had Government shown less confidence in the land defences, and hurried on the construction of a powerful fleet of iron-clads, Farragut's passage of the forts would have involved him in certain destruction, History may reveal on whose heads should rest the blame and shame. There has been vile treason among us, but who the traitors are few can tell; yet it is preposterous to suppose that Government would have neglected any thing for our defence and safety had not overweening confidence of those in command led them to report daily that 'the city was impregnable, and fit for a defence of any length.' Our

lowed no verbal or written communication to or with any one except through these head-quarters.—By order of Major-General Butler.

"R. S. DAVIS,
"*Captain and Assistant Adjutant-General.*"

A lady friend, who has known Butler for years, writes as follows:

"I have known Butler by sight and reputation some fifteen years, and so was not at all surprised by his order No. 28, nor would any woman be who has lived so long in the city of which he is a resident. It seemed to me quite natural that he should seek to place as many ladies as possible in a position in which he would feel most at home with them. If there be feminine spite in the insinuation, it is a pity his character is not likely to contradict it. You know how unscrupulous he has always been as a politician; but perhaps you don't know that in his legal prac tice he is as coarse and brutal as he is able. One day he was cross-examining a witness with his usual insolence, when somebody ventured to hint that even General Butler might condescend to treat an eminent professor of Harvard College with a little respect. 'Pooh,' said bully Ben, 'how long is it since we hanged one of those fellows?'"

Considering the character of the infamous order issued by Butler with reference to the ladies of New-Orleans, the following will be thought a well-designed act of retributive justice. Preparations were making for a dress parade, and a number of officers had congregated in front of the St. Charles, Butler's head-quarters. A handsome carriage was driven in front of the hotel, accompanied by servants in livery, with every sign of wealth and taste in the owner of the equipage. The occupant, dressed in the latest fashion and sparkling with jewelry, drew from her pocket her gold card-case, and taking therefrom her card, sent it up to Butler's rooms. The next day himself and lady called at the residence indicated on the card—a fine mansion in a fashionable part of the city—where a couple of hours were agreeably spent in conversation, followed by the introduction of wine and cake, when the highly delighted visitors took their departure. Picayune Butler did not appreciate the fact that he had been made the victim of a successful "sell," until he learned shortly afterwards that he had been paying his respects to the proprietress of one of the most celebrated *bagnios* in the State, who is at this time "*considered a woman of the town, plying her vocation as such.*"

pride and vanity are sorely punished, our routes to Texas and the Gulf completely broken up, and ere long you will find the Father of Waters swept by innumerable gunboats, totally severing us from all communication with States west of the river. Excuse haste; I am dejected and weary, shamed, mortified, humiliated. I scarcely know what to think or say, but am confident if Providence has punished our once gay city by turning it over to the enemy, it will return to us again, purified from all that has long festered in our midst, and brought upon our country this unspeakable calamity.

"Yours, etc.,   EVANS."

CHAPTER XXI.

An army so suddenly gathered as ours, will always abound in incompetent officers. The privilege of volunteers to elect their own officers may seem at first like an excellent provision for the selection of the most competent, but experience has proved that this privilege, uncontrolled by some competent authority, is the parent of many abuses, and countenances great incapacity. The question with the men is, *not* "who is the best soldier," or "the most experienced among us," but "whom do we like best?" Hence the most wealthy are usually selected for offices of importance and trust, although experience almost invariably proves that the greatest amount of talent is found in the modest and unpretending.

We had not been in service long ere this was apparent to all, and though many officers were nothing but an incumbrance, pride and love of power would not permit them to resign the gilded stars or shoulder-straps of office. Murmurs and complaints indeed were not wanting against some in every corps who had been elevated by momentary popularity, nor did this discontent arise from that unhappy habit of murmuring so prevalent among newly raised troops. What the capacity of our Generals might be, none dared to inquire—it was enough that the Administration, or General-in-Chief, had selected and intrusted them with commands, and the men were far too patriotic to question their discretion and choice. But in regard to regimental officers the men were not so delicate; they were criticised unmercifully, and their deficiencies magnified tenfold.

In regard to the medical staff, Government had unconsciously, perhaps, yet grievously erred. How so great a multitude of incompetents could have cajoled the Medical Board is to me a

13

profound mystery. In every regiment there were not less than a dozen doctors, from whom, for the most part, our men had as much to fear as from their Northern enemies. Our company boasted of six who put M.D. to their names by virtue of diplomas from some far-distant college or other; but if shaken all together, their medical knowledge would not have sufficed 'to prescribe with safety a dose of simples! This is truth; and were I to lengthen the subject by adverting to the terrible loss arising from malpractice in, or profound ignorance of, the fundamentals of surgery, as evidenced on the plains of Manassas, I might sorrowfully exclaim with the celebrated Dr. Stone of New-Orleans: " Our army has suffered infinitely more from surgical ignorance than from shot or steel of the enemy." Such fearful havoc I could never have imagined, as occurred from medical incompetency. Dead were being daily buried in scores; hundreds, if not thousands, were lost to our little army before and after Manassas, from the blind stupidity and culpable pride of medical pretenders. But how could we expect otherwise? The young delighted in this fine field of practice, and became expert at the expense of the living; their elders (I cannot say betters) would lounge about and discourse pompously of every thing but their profession, while the hospital stores gave abundant opportunities for indulging in their favorite habits of intoxication. Time certainly improved this state of things, as it afforded the younger opportunities of improvement, but at what an expense of life and limb was their professional education completed!

Another class who patriotically rushed to Richmond and obtained salaries to which they were unaccustomed, was a race of long-jawed, loud-mouthed ranters, termed for courtesy's sake ministers of the Gospel. With profound respect for a class "called of heaven" for the administration of holy offices, I may be allowed to observe that, taken as a whole, these long-bodied individuals who were saddled on our regiments simply considered themselves "called" to receive one hundred and twenty dollars per month, with the rank of captain, and the privilege of eating good dinners wherever chance or Providence provided—to be terribly valiant in words, and offensively loquacious upon every topic of life, save men's salvation. Where they all came from, none knew or cared to know, especially as but little was seen or heard of them, save when some fortunate "mess" had turkey or chickens, and *then*, of course, the minister was sure to put in his appearance, and fuss about until invited to dine. Most of these gentlemen were particularly condescending in their small talk, could wink at "trifles" after a few weeks' residence, and sometimes betrayed alarming proficiency in handling cards at a social game of poker.

The sermons preached to us were decidedly original. On one occasion I was almost petrified to hear one of the most popular of these camp-preachers confess before an audience of a thousand intelligent beings that "it has never yet been positively known whether Christ came down from heaven to save the body or the soul of a man!" I also remember having heard such words of wisdom from the lips of some of these worthies as the following: "It is certain that God is infinite, and therefore He requires some infinite habitation—therefore space is infinite, and was possibly prior to God." Another quietly remarked to his hearers: "Man cannot fulfil the law—all you have to do is to believe, trust to God for and in all things, and as to the rest you may do as you please." Again, another said: "If I disagree with my brother upon points of religion, it is not much matter; he may believe in universal salvation; another denies that Christ was God; one believes in infant baptism, and another does not; but all these little things are not of much consequence, my brethren; all are trying to get to heaven as best they can, and all no doubt will finally reach there—*at least, we hope so!*"

It is hardly necessary to say that little or no good was effected in the army by these "gospel ministers," (as they termed themselves;) their conduct was not as correct as it might be; and they seemed so eaten up with indolence that they were usually considered as bores and drones. They were seldom or never found administering to the sick or dying; service was offered occasionally; but in time of battle or in the hour of anguish at the hospital, they were looked for in vain. Little, however, could be expected from such a class of men. The majority had received "calls" to retire from blacksmithing or wood-chopping to preach the Gospel, and as they enjoyed but little celebrity or remuneration at home, they patriotically offered their services to Government, and were assigned duty among us. The proof of their "divine vocation" is seen in their subsequent conduct, for when Government, in its calmer moments, reduced their salaries, these spiritual heroes for the most part resigned, alleging as reasons that eighty dollars per month and rations was insufficient *remuneration* (!)

Nevertheless, truth compels me to add, by way of exception to this general condemnation, that many good and true men were to be found, who, by their upright conduct, self-denial, and zeal, counterbalanced much of the evil here adverted to. Among others who were distinguished for their correct deportment, persevering industry, unaffected piety, restless activity, and sound moral instruction, I would mention the Episcopalians and Roman Catholic priests. The latter, especially, were remarkably zealous; their services were conducted every morning in tents set apart for the purpose; and on Sunday large crowds of the more Southern soldiery were regular in their attendance and devout in their behavior; and I have not unfrequently seen General Beauregard and other officers kneeling with scores of privates at the Holy Communion Table. Such an instance occurred on the morning of Manassas, and I could not help remarking it, as I rode past in the twilight on that eventful occasion.

The Jesuits were perfect soldiers in their demeanor; ever at the head of a column in the advance, ever the last in a retreat; and on the battle-field a black cassock, in a bending posture, would always betray the disciple of Loyola, ministering to the wounded or dying. No hospital could be found wherein was not a pale-faced, meek, and untiring man of this order. Soldierly in their education and bearing, they are ready for any thing—to preach, prescribe for the sick, or offer a wise suggestion on military or social affairs. It is to the foresight and judgment of one of them that Beauregard and Johnston escaped death or capture at Manassas, for had they not met one of these missionaries during the heat of the conflict, and heeded his modest advice, one or other of these calamities must have inevitably ensued.

CHAPTER XXII.

Things at Yorktown Lines continued—We evacuate Yorktown Lines—Battle of Williamsburgh, May fifth—It is claimed, as usual, by the Federals as a "Brilliant Victory"—Facts of the Matter—We offer the Enemy Battle twice before entering our Lines around Richmond, etc.

EVERY day saw our troops gradually leaving the lines, and the labor imposed upon us who remained was excessive and exhausting. We had in truth been doing "double duty" in the front ever since our arrival; but the brigade having "unfortunately" won good repute in the army, we endured the natural consequences, and were worked almost to death. It seems strange that generals should thus treat all troops of any celebrity; but such I noticed was almost invariably the case, while prim and spruce brigades, which had done nothing but eat rations and parade were always found snugly encamped to the rear, luxuriating in idleness. Our position might be considered very "honorable," and officers might pompously speak of "posts of honor," and such like, but many like myself would have been infinitely more contented with less of the "honor" and a greater allowance of rations, in a position somewhat more distant than the one occupied ever since our arrival. Sleeping without blankets on wet clay, or upon a bed of fence-rails, often indeed sleeping upon the fence itself, balancing and roosting on rails like game-cocks, was not very poetical or easy, although the general might strut about and talk largely of "reputation," "imperishable glory," and the like; and being awakened twice or thrice each night by stray bullets whistling around breastworks, was not quite so desirable as some ambitious youths "at home" might imagine! I had seen much service, it is true; but the climax seemed attained among the muddy, watery, slippery roads and breastworks of Yorktown lines. I know not what style of picture artists may draw of us in forthcoming times, but suppose men of genius will paint in glorious colors, in which all the pomp and circumstance of war will be duly portrayed, with bands and banners, fine cloth and gold lace; but should any disciple of the beautiful and true require "a living model," he can dress his subject at the nearest rag-shop, and I promise it will be pronounced "truthful and lifelike" by any who fought in 1861 and 1862. Except our arms and accoutrements, all things else were worthless. Garments were perforated in all manner of places; some had shoes; but few rejoiced in more than one suit of under clothes, which had never seen soap for months—for soap we had none. A little longer stay at Yorktown lines, and I might have exclaimed with Falstaff: "There is but half a shirt in my whole company."

When nearly all the troops had left, we of the honorable rear-guard received notice to pack up and prepare for departure. Having nothing to pack, it was with great facility that we formed in line and marched out of the breastworks about nine P.M., Saturday, May third. A strong picket-guard was left in front "to keep up appearances;" but the enemy were as well aware as ourselves of our every movement, having made frequent ascents with their large balloon to satisfy themselves on this point. The works were left intact, but, save a few unwieldy columbiads, all ordnance had been carried off many days previously. Our men made "dummies," and put them in the embrasures, besides stuffing old clothes to represent sentinels. These latter had placards on their backs highly complimentary of course to the "incoming" Yankees: but without noise, and in perfect order, we sallied forth towards Williamsburgh. The artillerists at Yorktown had applied slow matches to their large pieces, so that during the whole night the heavens were illuminated by discharges, the immense shells bursting in all directions among the Yankee advance posts.*

* A good story is told about Congressmen, a number of whom proceeded to Yorktown to see the sights after the evacuation. A Michigan colonel was in command of the guard. Citizens were prohibited admittance. Several came up and asked the corporal for permission to pass, on the plea that they were Congressmen. The corporal stated the case to the colonel.

"They are Congressmen, are they?" asked the colonel.

"So they say."

When we had travelled some fifteen miles, a "halt" was sounded, for a few moments' rest; but I was so fatigued that I fell sound asleep, and did not wake till long after sunrise, by which time our troops had all passed, except a few stragglers, who hurried on in great haste, bringing the agreeable news that the Yankee cavalry in great force were close at our heels! I immediately took to the woods for safety, and reached Williamsburgh about noon. Expecting the enemy to pursue, our brigade was in battle array; but up to two P.M. none had appeared; so the line of march was resumed, and we halted in the streets of Williamsburgh, before Johnston's headquarters. The Warwick and Yorktown roads converge a short distance east of this little town, the whole eastern part of it being cleared like a lawn, and exactly suitable for a fight. Several earthworks fully commanded all this open space and the east portion of the town, having been erected by Magruder to protect his late winter-quarters. A few pieces of artillery were pointed eastward along the roads, when suddenly the enemy appeared, and, under cover of the woods, commenced shelling our redoubts.

It was evident a fight must come off at this place, so several brigades were countermarched through Williamsburgh, and took up positions in a strip of wood on the edge of the town. The artillery were exchanging shots very briskly, and the greatest confusion was manifested by the inhabitants. The "pattering" of musketry now became audible, but it was generally supposed that the fight would be postponed until the morrow, (Monday.) The enemy's cavalry, however, were particularly active in charging upon a few stragglers who endeavored to break across the open ground, when several squadrons of ours attacked them sword in hand, upon which they broke, re-formed on a rising ground, and as our men galloped towards them a second time, they discharged their revolvers and disappeared. We captured many, and the advance of infantry in line across the open ground drove them through the woods for two miles. At sunset all was over: our outposts were fully

"Well, let them pass, and go where they please," said the colonel. "Let them tramp on the torpedoes, go into the magazines, and where there is any prospect of their being blown to the dévil, for *that is the quickest way to end the war.*"—*Northern Paper.*

two miles east of the town in the woods, and maintained their ground. General Longstreet was intrusted with defending the rear of the army, and made every disposition to entice the foe into open ground, so that he might soundly thrash them on the morrow. The retreat of the main army continued as if nothing had happened; and as our flank was threatened 'by a force which had been hurried with great despatch up the York River, Hood's Texan brigade was "double quicked" to West-Point to oppose the movement.

While our brigade bivouacked west of the town waiting for orders, I could not help laughing at the wo-begone features of some of our men, who, supposed to be sick, were sent to King's Mill Landing on the James, for shipment to Richmond; but the Yankee cavalry unexpectedly appearing, dispersed them like chaff. Several days before our departure from Yorktown, the doctors had informed us that all incapable of marching to Richmond (seventy-five miles) should give their arms to the ordnance sergeants, and proceed to King's Mill Landing, (seven miles,) where steamboats would be ready for their conveyance. As no fight was deemed possible, many "played possum," or "old soldier," and pretended to be terribly affected by rheumatism. But the steamboats had all gone, and to the astonishment of our "sick," the Federal cavalry appeared on a neighboring hill, when all these limping, rheumatically-affected gentlemen threw away their walking-sticks and clubs, and made a rush towards Williamsburgh. While laughing and chatting round the camp-fire, near the roadside, a cavalry friend of mine rode up spattered with mud, "Tom, letter for you—can't stop—warm work to-morrow!" and galloped off through the mud at a fearful rate.

Our conversation had been prolonged far into the night, and as great activity was being displayed by Longstreet, prudence suggested the necessity of obtaining some little rest. It was not thought that a general engagement would ensue on the morrow, but it was imagined that the enemy would move heaven and earth to snatch some sort of victory from our rear-guard, in order to magnify it abroad. When the stars paled, our men were awakened and fell into line without drums or bugles. Outposts in the woods below Williamsburgh were strengthened, and ordered to fall back in good order should the enemy attack in force. The foe, under Generals Heintzelman, Hooker, and Kearny, were not long in approaching: long lines of blue coats were reported coming up the roads, with strong bodies of skirmishers on the flanks. The "popping" of pickets and outposts soon changed into the distant "pattering" volleys of men in line; artillery began to roar, and the battle of Williamsburgh was fairly opened.

Our advance now began to fall back as directed, and were endeavoring to entice the enemy into open ground. It seemed to be the wish of Longstreet to have "a fair fight and no favor." For this purpose our troops were drawn up in the long open "green" previously described, several breastworks were in the rear, and heavy supports behind them. Finding our men rapidly giving ground, the enemy left the woods, where they had been fighting under cover, and boldly came forth on the green, in beautiful order, to attack several earthworks in which were no cannon. They advanced with cheers, and waving banners; but when they had half surrounded those places, and were within seventy paces, up rose our men in the works, and poured volleys into their faces. They broke in utter confusion, sought the woods, and were mown down by grape-shot from guns to the right and left. Similar experiments were tried by the enemy during the morning, but always with disastrous consequences. One redoubt was assailed not less than three times by different brigades, and successfully repulsed by a single regiment of South-Carolinians, under Jenkins. They actually entered one mud work which had been held by North-Carolinians, but while in momentary possession a regiment of Louisianians swarmed over the parapets and killed all within it. Cannonading was incessant along the line, which, as could be observed by the smoke, was beautifully kept.

Every trick that could be imagined was resorted to by Longstreet to entice Heintzelman into open ground; but that officer remembered Manassas and knew perfectly well the mettle of our regiments. In vain brigade after brigade dashed across the "open," jumped the fences, and attacked the foe in the woods, and then fell back to invite them on; but it could not be accomplished. About noon it seemed as if Longstreet was desirous of retreating—the enemy perceived it and ventured into the open ground. As quick as thought they were attacked with great fury, and our defence was changed into an attack! Artillery seemed to have acquired new life; galloping into the open, they unlimbered and commenced a fearful duel at short range! Gun after gun was abandoned by the enemy, while artillerymen unemployed would dash with spare horses under fire, and secure the trophies. Infantry in all directions were shouting and entering the woods in front, and every one seemed to wear a pleased and laughing countenance. "If they *won't* advance to Richmond, we'll make them advance to Yorktown," was the common expression.

From the line of fire it would seem that Heintzelman *was* inclined to return, for our musketry and artillery were advanced a mile in the woods. But rain had fallen the previous night and rendered our progress irksome and slow, for the roads were of light sand, or deep tenacious mud. Wherever we moved the woods were strewn with dead bodies, and arms plentiful. Those of our men who possessed only old muskets or inferior weapons exchanged them for better while advancing, so that the enemy had not thrown them away many minutes ere they were being handled by superior artists, and with deadly effect: The wounded, if at all able, would invariably pick up a good rifle on their way to the rear; so that spare ordnance wagons were continually moving off with valuable spoil.

After driving the enemy about a mile through the timber, and with considerable slaughter, Longstreet halted his veteran division, and re-formed. He then endeavored to entice Heintzelman into an advance, but, failing in this, he "let loose" his men once again, and the Federals were driven still farther back at all points. The enemy were approaching their supports, while we were leaving ours behind us. This would not answer; so that having conquered fully two miles of ground, and driven the enemy from our front, we began to retire, carrying off whatever was likely to prove useful. I myself counted six field-pieces, and several thousand stand of arms, and (though not said in vanity, but for sake of example) among several hundred prisoners were five troopers of the "Fifth United States Dragoons," whom I had captured without trouble. At nightfall the field was scoured in search of arms, and many prisoners were taken, who, lying on their faces during close action, pretended to be dead, but willingly came forward and seemed anxious to be paroled, but *not* exchanged. Having done as much as possible for our dead and wounded, and thrown strong picket-guards along our front, our men were allowed several hours for rest; and about two A.M. next morning the line of retreat was continued, and all the forces marched away as undisturbed as if the enemy were a thousand miles distant. As we never had any "spare" transportation in the most prosperous times, (and of course very little in presence of an enemy who could well supply us,) many of our wounded were left behind in Williamsburgh, and scores of dead left unburied. This, of course, was a "military necessity." Longstreet was far in the rear with his corps, and had to hurry on to the main army. No enemy pursued, however, and it was not until Tuesday evening, (May sixth,) sixteen hours after we had left, that the enemy entered Williamsburgh in force.

This affair was heralded by McClellan as a "complete victory;" and the newspapers quoted McClellan's despatch, in large capitals: "The enemy are running! I will drive them to the wall!" Large editions, expressly for European circulation, spoke of the rebellion as "nigh broken up," and described our troops as "ragged, hungry, footsore, and dispirited—all they want now is one more twist of the Anaconda's coil," etc. I will not deny that two or three hundred Dutch, Jews, and unnaturalized foreigners were captured by the enemy's cavalry, and that some few of them, tired of war, took the oath of allegiance, and went North; but this was blazoned abroad with great exaggeration, and the silly multitude of Abolitionists piously believed what newspaper penny-a-liners wrote, and thought the backbone of rebellion *was* broken. Facts are stubborn things, and truth stranger than fiction; but if driving our enemy fully two miles over the battle-field by an inferior force, capturing their cannon, together with thousands of arms, and hundreds of prisoners, killing and wounding an aggregate of four thousand or more, sleeping on the battle-field, and retiring at leisure with great booty — if all these things, by any conceivable logic, can be twisted into a "Complete Federal Victory," "Grand Smash-up of the Rebels," etc., as claimed by the official despatches and newspapers of the

North, I should very much like to see what a Federal *defeat* is like. They have lied, however, so often and so unblushingly, that we can but laugh at their overweening vanity and unscrupulous falsehoods ; words are thrown away on the subject. From prisoners we ascertained that Heintzelman, Sumner, Hooker, Kearny, and other divisional commanders, had directed the Federals, from which it was easy to infer that their force numbered forty thousand strong. Longstreet commanded on our side, and I *know* did not handle more than twenty-five thousand men. The character of the fighting at the onset was brilliant and dashing on both sides, and the enemy displayed more spirit for a few hours than I had ever seen before on battle-fields; but when they had fairly met our men once or twice, they evinced little desire of marching into open ground. The several charges made by them on our rifle-pits were well conceived and gallantly attempted, but our fire was so steady and unerring, the rush of our men so determined, that, despite all their teaching and splendid appearance, they invariably broke before our "ragged rebels."

Several incidents which came under my notice are illustrative of events that were happening along our whole line. We captured several of "Sickles's Brigade" — an organization of New-York "bullies" and "roughs;" and the position of which corps was ascertained to be on the edge of timber to our front, where they had erected a barrier by piling branches against the fence-rails, behind and through which they maintained a galling fire, but would not advance into the open. The Nineteenth Mississippi were in front of this place, and learning that the immortal Dan Sickles and his "pets" were opposite, formed ranks, (seven hundred strong,) rushed across the "green," and with deafening yells assaulted the place, clambered over the fence, delivered their fire at ten paces, and drove this brigade several hundred yards before them into the woods, capturing many prisoners. Superior officers were displeased at the affair — the regiment was recalled, and assumed its old position without a word. The gallant colonel of this regiment (Colonel Lomax) was shot during the day; his negro servant recovered the body in the Yankee lines, and carried it on his back several miles, conveyed it to Richmond to the bereaved wife, and kept the promise he had made her — namely, *never to let his master's body fall into the hands of the enemy.*

Though I disapprove of eulogizing particular regiments, except for special reasons, there are several corps which have been mentioned in terms of praise by the enemy, and if I add a few words regarding them, it is but to show the general spirit of the army, and what other regiments would have done if similarly circumstanced. Some of the South-Carolinians, under Colonel Jenkins, were ordered to hold a redoubt, in which, I believe, no cannon were mounted; it was a little in advance of the general line and an especial mark for the enemy's shells. The men did not expose themselves, but lay close under the walls, and except that the colonel appeared on horseback, standing on one of the platforms, no one would have supposed that it was held by more than a corporal's guard. Guns from a neighboring battery replied to the enemy, and for half an hour the Carolinians seemed to be lost in a little island, around which an angry ocean raged in vain.

The enemy ceased their fire, and troops approaching to attack the redoubt, rushed across the intervening space, and then surrounding the work in horse-shoe form, approached still nearer. Those who knew the character of Jenkins were well aware that he was but quietly awaiting the proper moment. It came when the foe were not more than seventy paces distant, when, in a moment, up rose the Carolinians in the redoubt, a simultaneous report was heard, and hundreds of the enemy fell in all directions. They re-formed rapidly, and advanced a few steps nearer, when another volley, heavier than the first, circled the parapet with smoke, and the enemy fled in great disorder. A cheer rose from the redoubt, artillery opened with deafening sounds, and the Carolinians, as before, crouched under the walls. Three several attempts were made to take the work, but each signally failed, the last being most disastrous, for Jenkins, seeing a fine opportunity to charge, withdrew part of his regiment behind the work, and when the volley was given, a "charge" was ordered, and the Yankees retired confusedly to the cover of the woods, and made no more efforts to take the position. Had they possessed themselves of the place it could not have served them, for our guns in regular line would have massacred them in it.

Another small redoubt was held by North-Carolinians; the enemy stealthily approached and took it by escalade, our men suffering considerably in retiring. A Louisiana regiment was in the rear, and saw the whole affair. Without waiting for orders, they rushed across the open ground, dashed headlong into the redoubt, and all who escaped over the parapet were shot down or bayoneted by two companies who remained outside for that purpose. In this, as in all other instances I have witnessed of the Louisianians, their recklessness and daring have always astonished me, yet, considering their material, half Creole, half Irish, none need be astonished to find them nonpareils, when fighting for their homes and liberty against a negro-worshipping mixture of Dutch and Yankee. In this, as in all other fights witnessed by me, the cavalry had very little to do—the Yankee horse were always in the rear collecting stragglers, and forcing men to keep their lines. The day before had witnessed slight cavalry skirmishes, resulting in our favor, but nothing of the kind had transpired on Monday—it was entirely an affair of infantry and artillery.

The artillery, it cannot be denied, behaved nobly, and, it must be confessed, effectually "snuffed out" the enemy more than once during the day. I cannot account for the fact, yet in all truth it *is* fact. When no one opposes them, the drill and accuracy of the enemy are very fine, but I have ever remarked that when ours meet them at close quarters, they work their guns very rapidly, but fire extremely wild. When Mowry's and Couts's field batteries were sustaining a duello against great odds, and had disabled several of the enemy's pieces, fresh ones were ever at hand to replace them, and keep up the fire. Once during the day Couts had silenced four guns, and some of the Richmond Howitzers, unemployed, seeing him overworked, volunteered to dash in under fire, and bring the guns off. Unhitching the horses from their howitzers, they galloped into the smoke, and within a few yards of the foe brought off four magnificent rifled pieces, which they very gallantly presented to the chivalrous Couts upon the field, and in view of both armies. Obtaining permission to open fire on the enemy, the howitzers, under McCarthy, drove their guns up to within a hundred yards of the enemy, and worked them with such effect, that they were driven from their position in the woods within half an hour. The whole face of the timber in McCarthy's front was literally blown to pieces, and when we subsequently advanced in that direction, our path was impeded by dismounted cannons, caissons, numbers of dead horses, and scores of infantry.

The morning after Williamsburgh, I, with others, was detailed to escort a batch of prisoners to Richmond, and in hurrying on I overtook troops marching to West-Point, the head of the York River; rumors being rife that Franklin and other Federal generals were disembarking a large force there to assail us on the flank. The main army, however, had travelled with such celerity, that they were beyond the line of West-Point, so that the Texans in that vicinity actually constituted part of our rear-guard; Longstreet, as usual, farther to the rear with his victorious and veteran force, being not far distant in case of emergency. The idea of this flank movement did credit to the genius of McClellan, but its performance was a miserable failure. Franklin's forces at that point far outnumbered ours, for Hood's Texan brigade was the chief corps to oppose him. After disembarking, Franklin lingered and loitered near his transports and gunboats, until Hood beat about to find his whereabouts. Without proper knowledge of the topography of the country, Franklin put his troops in motion, and had not progressed many miles ere he discovered Hood advantageously posted in line of battle, and without giving time to deploy, the Texans were upon him, decimating his ranks with unerring aim. The fight was wild and confused—Franklin hurriedly fell back before an inferior force, and did not halt until under the guns of his flotilla. Hood had punished him severely in a two hours' fight, and sensibly fell back to the main army at his leisure. This affair was claimed as "a decided success" by the Federals, but *facts* speak for themselves.

CHAPTER XXIII.

Military Transactions in May—Our Army continues to fall back upon Richmond—I am despatched to the City with Prisoners—Hospitality of the Virginian Farmers—News received *en route*—Evacuation of Norfolk—Destruction of the Merrimac—The Defences of Richmond—Treatment of Prisoners—Our Army forms Line of Battle North of the Chickahominy—Position of McClellan—I receive a Staff Appointment—Table Talk, etc.

As before remarked, I was ordered to conduct a batch of prisoners to Richmond, and to spare them unnecessary pain in running the gauntlet of our army camped along the roads, it was deemed best to proceed by the James River. At night we sought the shelter of the farm-houses on our route, and met with a truly hospitable reception. Every thing that could be possibly provided for our comfort was lavishly displayed, and I was agreeably impressed with the neatness and comfort exhibited in their dwellings. Courtly, high-toned, and refined, the style of these old Virginians impressed me much with what I could remember of the hale and hearty squires of England, whom they very much resembled in manner and means. My prisoners seemed delighted with their treatment, and many professed their willingness to take the oath of allegiance, and remain South, as some of them subsequently did, and, entering our ranks, made excellent soldiers. Throughout our progress across this beautiful section of country, I never heard an offensive word whispered regarding my charge, and although we sometimes remained all night in houses of those whose sons had already died in the war, except a few words of natural complaint, I never heard or saw any thing that would indicate the existence of that revengeful feeling which the Northern papers were continually asserting against us. My own feeling, now the battle was over, was to treat them as I would have wished to be treated, had our positions been reversed, and, although it necessitated an outlay I could ill spare, there was nothing I could purchase for their comfort that I failed to do. Had fortune thrown in my way such men as Seward, Lincoln, Blair, Sumner, or Hale, I should have been tempted to use some of the handcuffs out of the wagon-loads which old Scott had sent to Manassas for very different individuals. In such a case it would have been a good joke; but in the present instance, a cruel one.

When we hailed a steamboat above Berkeley, I learned the following facts. Huger, I was informed, had not made a successful evacuation of Norfolk, and much valuable property had fallen into the enemy's hands. This arose from an act of treachery on the part of a Government employé. When Huger received orders to evacuate, he immediately made every possible arrangement for that purpose. Immense stores were conveyed away, and most of the troops had left, when the captain of a small steamboat hitherto in our employ (a Northerner by birth) thought to make capital by going over to the enemy a few miles distant at Fortress Monroe. The enemy immediately commenced shelling our works at Sewell's Point, and, receiving no response, determined upon landing troops. Several vessels had already escaped up James River, from Norfolk, and others were sunk; but it became a matter of dispute as to what should be done with the Merrimac, which, a short time before, had become famous by sinking the Cumberland and other vessels under the guns of Fortress Monroe. It was alleged that her draught of water was too great for James River; pilots disputed the possibility of steering her safely over the "bars," if lightened; but while this indecision reigned in council, the enemy's guns were heard at Sewell's Point; the Merrimac was hastily coaled, and slowly steamed down to frighten the enemy off. It was thought that a night engagement might ensue, but as it was positively stated that she would not answer helm, she ended her brief but glorious career by being blown up shortly after midnight, and within a mile of the enemy!* The Fede-

* It appears from an authentic account of the event that the officers of the Virginia had no orders for her destruction; but after the evacuation of Norfolk they held a council on board, and determined to carry her into James River, if possible, which could be done, the pilot said, on eighteen feet draught. The ship was then drawing twenty-two feet, but all hands were set to work lightening her by throwing overboard coal, ballast, etc. By midnight she was lightened to eighteen feet; but

14

rals were so quick in their movements that our "burning parties" had scarcely made their escape from the various ship-yards ere Norfolk was again in the hands of the Yankees. Huger conducted his retreat with great order, and was far out of harm's way.

In our progress up the James we hailed and conversed with the Patrick Henry and other war vessels, which were steaming about City Point, (fifteen miles from Richmond,) in anticipation of the enemy's approach, and assisted a gunboat in towing up the iron-clad Virginia No. 2, which required completion. This was the first time I had seen any specimen of our infant navy, and must confess the splendid appearance, quickness, cleanliness, neatness, and obedience of the seamen were in favorable contrast with the sleepy, lackadaisical dandyism of the officers—many of whom were mere lads. That they all had "pluck" and "dash" in superabundance, their quick eye and

it was then found that her wooden hull, below the plating, was exposed, and that the westerly wind prevailing had so lowered the water in James River, that with eighteen feet draught she could not be taken up far beyond Newport News. Thus daylight would find her under the guns of the iron-clads Galena and Monitor, which could easily capture or destroy her by firing into her below the armor. Another council was held, and it was resolved to destroy the great ship. Her decks and roof were saturated with oil, her crew of three hundred and fifty men were disembarked in small boats, trains of powder were laid from each port-hole to different parts of the vessel, and these were lighted at a given signal. Simultaneously the ship was on fire in many parts, and after burning several hours the flames reached the magazine about four o'clock in the morning, when the Virginia was blown up with an explosion heard thirty-two miles distant.

In a despatch sent to the *New-York Times*, from Fortress Monroe, under date of the fourteenth, we read :

"At four o'clock this morning a bright light was observed from Fortress Monroe in the direction of Craney Island. Precisely at half-past four o'clock an explosion took place which made the earth and water tremble for miles around. In the midst of the bright flame which shot up in the distance, the timbers and iron of a steamer could be seen flying through the air. No doubt was entertained that the Merrimac had ceased to exist

"From men found on the island we ascertained that the Merrimac lay buried on Saturday at a point nearly a mile from the head of the island. During the night she had been brought back and brought ashore. Her entire officers and crew were landed on the island, and a slow match was then applied to her magazine. She was torn to fragments by the time her crew got out of reach of her. Negroes state that the officers and crew of the Merrimac passed through the adjoining county on the mainland about eight o'clock in the morning, to the number of two hundred. They said they were on their way to Suffolk on the line of the river leading from Craney Island to Norfolk."

recent services well betokened; but there was a "something" in their affectation, their manner of walking, and their use of the telescope which impressed me with a strong idea that the greater part were "novices," and owed their gold bands and white gloves more to political and family influence than "service" or sound qualification. The men were truly magnificent specimens of bone and muscle—mostly foreign-born, from the merchant navy; and, dressed as they all were in the neat blue uniforms captured at Norfolk, reminded me much of what I had seen in the British navy in American waters—bronzed and rosy fellows, active as cats, and fit to fight a frigate at any odds.

While at City Point I was informed that General Magruder was alarmingly unwell at one of the many beautiful residences near this point; but it was whispered confidentially: "Oh! he's not very sick! he's been on a spree because Johnston would not fight at Yorktown! It is only the effect of too much Bourbon and chagrin!" This was probably the truth. This accomplished but "nervous" officer very much desired to fight and immortalize his name at Yorktown, behind the lines he had so scientifically planned and perfected in secrecy; but Lee and Johnston could penetrate more deeply into the enemy's plans there than the fighting engineer deemed worthy of consideration; and to engage a superior force, with our flanks unprotected and assailable at any hour by powerful and resistless fleets, would have been an act of madness. As it was, we could not retreat without a severe fight, and had reason to consider ourselves extremely fortunate in escaping as we did. The true line of defence, as foreseen by the astute Lee a year before, was nearer Richmond; and it had been magnificently mapped and fortified by that officer, without noise or puff, even when the majority of the unthinking were loth to consider him any thing more than a quiet, inoffensive officer, possessing more of religion than strategy. For my own part, though smiled at by the would-be wiseheads, I heartily rejoiced to hear of Lee's appointment as Commander-in-Chief; nor were my opinions of him hastily formed, or doomed to disappointment, as results will amply prove.

In approaching Richmond, my eye was actively engaged in

scanning the landscape and river-banks for batteries to resist the coming enemy, but none were visible, nor indeed were any in progress. A few earthworks below City Point had been successively abandoned, and those which had the hardihood to oppose the Federal gunboats were destroyed by the first broadside. Nearer the city, I observed an immense raft concealed under the banks and trees, which was said to be amply sufficient to blockade the river. It was not closed, but could be within an hour's notice. We had passed several bluffs, which, if properly fortified, could effectually stop the enemy in the narrow windings of the river, but as yet no works were erected, and no cannon mounted. This I considered gross negligence or incapacity in Secretary Mallory, who had charge of naval affairs. Some charged the Administration with imbecility; others shook their heads, as if the final hour were rapidly approaching; while a few, I thought, betrayed more pleasure than pain in the anxiety and the feverish excitement of the majority.

Of President Davis I knew something, but nothing in his character was like the picture angrily drawn of him by the unthinking. He could *not* attend to every thing; after appointments were made, the most he could do was to *suggest* on matters pertaining to the duties or requirements of those in the various chairs of office. It would not only be presumption, but gross ignorance, to suppose that *he* did this, or ordered that. His own duties were more than any dozen men, except himself, could have pretended to perform; still, although laboring night and day, planning, counselling, providing, receiving visitors, writing, speaking, he was blamed for every thing that went amiss. He bore it all, however, without murmuring. The press might abuse him, office-seekers annoy him, petty councillors bore him, mistakes and bickerings of his Cabinet vex him; State, political, social, or religious deputations pester him with demands, petitions, and a thousand other daily annoyances; yet the poor, pale, hard-working President bore it all with philosophic equanimity. Putting on his blue flannel overcoat, he would mount his chestnut mare, smoke a cigar, and take a quiet ride, unattended, through the streets in the afternoon, as calmly and unostentatiously as if he were merely Mr J. Davis, proprietor of a two-hundred-acre farm, with a round dozen of bouncing babies. Heigho! who would envy the poor President? If a negro were worked a twentieth as much, his master would be imprisoned or fined for inhuman treatment!

After delivering my prisoners at Libby's Tobacco Warehouse—the chief of many such establishments in the city—I endeavored to obtain accommodation at the " Spottswood " and other hotels, but found it an impossibility, every house being crowded to excess. I must confess, too, my personal appearance was any thing but prepossessing, and when I pushed my way through a crowd of dandily attired officers and civilians, I was gazed upon as something of a phenomenon; for *my* part I looked upon them with contempt, for although dressed in all the colors of the different arms of the service, from Generals down to Captains, their unblemished linen and gold braid told me plainly they were for the most part impostors, boring the various departments for commissions, or for some kind of employment, and disporting their figures on the sunny side of Capitol Square. In vain I offered any price for a bed, and even proposed giving five dollars for the privilege of sleeping on the floor of the reception-room. All that I have said of Richmond in a previous chapter—of the fabulous prices obtained for necessaries, the scenes of perpetual gaiety, the uninterrupted waste of money, and the imposition everywhere practised—might be here repeated; but enough. The one redeeming feature of the city may, however, be mentioned. I never saw the least symptoms of intoxication in the streets, owing to the discipline of martial law, and the almost impossibility of obtaining liquors.

The prisoners, as I have said, were confined in tobacco-warehouses fitted up for their use, near the river, which served admirably for temporary prisons. Being very large, four stories high, and of great capacity, they were capable of accommodating several hundreds of men each, and being well guarded, it was almost impossible for a prisoner to effect his escape. The food allotted to those in durance was that usually allowed to soldiers, but in greater quantity and variety than ever fell to our lot in camp. Every convenience was allowed them, and, except room for out-of-door exercise, I saw nothing in the arrangements that merited the denunciations of the Northern press about our barbarous treatment of prisoners in our terrible tobacco-warehouses. Considering all things, they seemed to enjoy themselves very much; they were permitted every facility for purchasing things not allowed by our regulations for diet; ministers and others frequently visited them — particularly Catholic priests—and books, clothing, and money were often bestowed upon them. On the other hand, the men, generally speaking, behaved themselves as became their situation; though occasionally some ill-bred fellow among them would excite to sedition, and the culprit being discovered, he was removed, and punished. Several, I know, were shot for attempting to escape; and on one or two occasions men particularly vulgar to ladies in passing, after having been duly warned, and on a repetition of the offence, were shot at and wounded by the guards. Hundreds were sent south, in various directions, to make room for fresh arrivals, and from the preparations of Government for additional prisons and hospitals, it became very evident that stirring events were expected at no distant day.

Hospitals were numerous, the chief being Chimborazo on the east, and Camp Winder west of the city, each capable of accommodating several thousands. Their situation was the best to be had, and Government had done all in its power to render them comfortable and commodious. They looked like large forts at a distance, with their whitened walls and banners; but on close inspection proved to be long rows of wooden buildings, marked off into divisions, streets, and wards: on inspection I found an abundance of all things provided that the medical department could possibly furnish; though some kinds of medicines were very scarce, particularly quinine, of which very little could be obtained, even at twenty dollars per ounce. The doctors, however, appeared to me to be very indifferent, and lacking of much kindness and capacity; they were seldom in their offices, often promenading with ladies, and were great consumers of whatever wines and liquors Government intended for the sick. This may account for the pressure of business among coffin-contractors and grave-diggers, and for the stream of hearses continually running to and from the cemeteries. I saw but few clergymen in the hospitals, but was deeply impressed with the piety, self-devotion, and unceasing attentions of those good angels called "Sisters of Charity," who were ever in motion, night and day, in ministering to the sick. They had an especial hospital of their own on the Brooke turnpike road, called "St. Joseph's;" and it was a perfect paradise of cleanliness and comfort.

From information I could gather round the War Office, it appears that Johnston had remained in line of battle more than a week several miles north of the Chickahominy, in the vain hope that McClellan would attack. The Federals, however, remained at a respectful distance, and seemed as disinclined for combat in open ground, with a river in our rear, as they were when we invited them in March, with the Rapidan in our front. Slowly advancing towards Richmond, McClellan took up the pursuit, and sharp skirmishing occurred as we crossed the Chickahominy at Mechanicsville bridge, five miles from Richmond. It surprised me much to hear that our whole army was so near the city, and it surprised me still more to learn that I was transferred from my regiment to an officer's position on the staff. My future duties would be light, pay increased, forage allowed, with daily opportunities of passing and repassing to town. I felt ashamed to leave my old regiment, with which I had served so long, for I thought it looked unpatriotic to leave the gallant foot to go prancing at the heels of a chief of artillery. My company did not object. I could benefit them considerably in many ways, and, promising to be with them in the hour of battle, I mounted my unruly mare, drew all arrears from the paymaster, and invited several of my old superior officers to a supper in town, in order to finish my career in the infantry with due honor and solemnity.

We were in high spirits during our little supper, and much was said regarding the merits and qualifications of various generals and heads of departments, which would have startled the gentlemen mentioned could they have heard it. But when were soldiers in want of topics for conversation? Captain Smithers and Major Jones, at one end of the table, were professionally discussing the results of the war, and were very declamatory in style; Lieutenant Jenkins was narrating some romantic adventure among the pretty Quakeresses of Loudon County, and had two listeners; Lieutenant-Colonel Dobbs was explaining "formations" and "changes of front" to Captain

Johnstone, who, Scotchman-like, was disputing the authority
'of Dobbs's version of "Hardee;" while Lieutenant Moore
entertained half a dozen round the fire with his reminiscences
of the Emerald Isle.

Said Major Jones, emptying his glass: "Smithers, I entirely disagree with you. The campaign wasn't worth a cent
till Lee took the helm, and I believe that Davis himself endeavored to map out operations before that. See what miserable failures Roanoke and Donelson were. Who was com-
mander-in chief before Lee? Nobody that I know; and the
fact of sending men to be cooped up, surrounded, and destroyed on that island, speaks volumes for the stupidity and
incapacity of somebody. I don't mean to say that a stouter
resistance might not have been made by a better general than
Wise. Wise has proved himself a first-rate orator, writer, and
politician — is greatly beloved in Virginia — but all these
things go to show that it requires something more than popularity to make a general. Fort Donelson, also, was left to
be erected by the State of Tennessee, and see what a miserable
waste of money it was. Fort Henry was evacuated even by
the Federals on account of the flow of water into it; and although Donelson was something better, far more eligible sites
could have been selected, and the Government grant of half
a million put to a better use. Look at New-Orleans, also!
Lovell, a man without reputation, was left in supreme com
mand of that all-important place; the batteries below it were
insufficient against iron-clads; the construction of new gunboats was given to Northerners resident there, and although
their inactivity and incapacity were known to the authorities,
they were allowed to shilly-shally until the enemy came, and
passed by the forts unscratched — our ships were burned,
Lovell evacuated the city, and it fell. Don't tell me, Smithers; every one knows there has been gross mismanagement
in several cases; until Lee came in there was no visible
head at work, and those that were at work, the fathers of
these blunders, had better keep themselves invisible still."

"Don't say any thing more, Major," said Johnstone, with
a strong accent; "I have a great respect for 'Hardee,' for
he is a good kind of Scotchman, from Glasgow, as my friend
M'Gregor informs me, but there is no doubt about it that

Beauregard was badly whipped at Manassas by that old Stirling man, McDowell. I knew some of the McDowells in Scotland, and good people they were. Beauregard is a good officer, and all he wants is a little Scotch blood in him to make a first-rate strategist. But we all know that had old Mac followed us up vigorously after passing Sudley Ford, we should never have been here now, I'm thinking, drinking bad whisky, at four o'clock o' the morning. Why, man, our right wing was never engaged at all. Longstreet, Jones, and Ewell hardly fired a shot all day; and there was the left overlapped by the Yankees at three in the afternoon, and when we *did* drive them back, and got them into a panic, Beauregard hadn't more than two regiments at their heels. Old Evans, at Leesburgh, did the thing handsomely; he killed more than the number of his own men actually engaged; made prisoners of twice as many, and drowned the rest. I hear he came from Fife before entering the Northern army. Yes, dear old Scotland has given a good many men in this war—there's McClellan from Argyle, and Scott from Dumfries, and —— "

Johnstone might have gone on claiming Southern celebrities for natives of Scotia, but Moore, becoming indignant, swore roundly that Beauregard was from Limerick, and Lee from Cork, so that those of us who had not gone beyond a dozen glasses, were obliged to take care of those who had, and to conduct them to chambers, where they might dream over the question of Homer and Garibaldi being Irish or Scotch, without fear of using empty bottles for weapons.

Having seen some, who required it, comfortably provided for the night, Dobbs and myself retired to the same room; while smoking, the conversation turned on Jackson, whose movements in the Valley began to excite interest about this time. The Major had seen him at Manassas, and spoke of him dispassionately. He had not achieved much greatness in that conflict, but received a name there which will be as imperishable as history.

" I received letters a few days ago from Ashton," said my friend, " who is now with Jackson in the Valley ; you knew Ashton very well. Amuse yourself while I take a nap, for 'tis nearly dawn, and I must be out in camp early."

CHAPTER XXIV.

AT this period the Conscript law came into operation, and there was much grumbling among such as fell under its provisions. Those who had been in the army at all, for however short a period, were not averse to remaining in the ranks; for they knew absolute necessity alone had compelled Congress to pass such a law, and if liberty was to be gained, it must be by great sacrifices of individual convenience and pleasure. Lincoln had called out seventy-five thousand men at the commencement of the war, and having received every additional man the States offered, he had now an army of not less than seven hundred thousand in the field. There was little opposition made in our several States to the call of the President; some thought, indeed, the act was an unconstitutional one; yet the men were rapidly supplied, and discussion deferred until times of peace. Accordingly, when Johnston had fallen back to his line of defence around Richmond, we found many new regiments awaiting to join us.

The exactions of this law, however, were very oppressive to many, and seemingly despotic; hundreds who had volunteered for and served one year, had not been resident in the South more than a few months when the war broke out; so that to put such men on an equality with those born on the soil who had not served at all, seemed like the shadow of absolutism. There was much murmuring, therefore; and many, rather than serve for an indefinite period as the price of citizenship, abandoned the cause, and sought protection from the consuls of their several countries.

The character of the conscripts, who entered willingly on the service, was excellent, and they bore the jokes of the volunteers with a good grace. Physically, they were the flower of the nation, tall, well-made, sinewy fellows, who considered their knapsacks no greater weight than a pair of gloves. We all expected them to behave well in action, nor were we disappointed. Their shooting was splendid. Many of them would have entered the army before, but had been in regiments which were refused service at the beginning of the war; some did not know how much they were needed; and others again, though brave and ripe enough for a fight at any time, had formed such disagreeable notions of camp life from letters and journals, that they felt a decided repugnance to entering the ranks until compelled. Taken altogether, the morale of our troops, though always good, at this period was excellent. As they took up the lines assigned them, naught but good humor and hilarity was visible, for they well knew that Johnston *could not* fall back farther, and that the conflict must soon come. This they desired, and were aching to pay back with interest the taunts and insults of the over-fed and bombastic Yankees of the Yorktown lines.

A part of Huger's division from Norfolk had arrived through Petersburgh and the south side of the James; rapid progress was made with defensive works and obstructions to prevent gunboats ascending the river; earthworks of magnitude arose on every side around Richmond; and the speedy appearance of Yankee encampments north of the Chickahominy gave eloquent indications that things were coming to a crisis. The earthworks had been designed by Lee more than ten months ere our army reached their position. They were constructed in different shapes, to suit the conformation of the ground; they swept all the roads, crowned every hillock, and mounds of red earth could be seen in striking contrast with the rich green aspect of the landscape. Redoubts, rifle-pits, casemate batteries, horn works, and enfilading batteries were visible in great number, in and out of the woods, in all directions; some were mounted with heavy siege pieces, of various calibre, but the majority were intended for field guns. Heavy ordnance was scarce, and home-made cannon often proved worthless and brittle, in many instances killing those who put them to the "proof."

It was reported that the enemy's gunboats and iron-clads were approaching up the river, and had contemptuously "snuffed out" several mud batteries that had the temerity to fire. The Monitor, Galena, and other iron-clads, were actually at City Point, fifteen miles from Richmond, and feverish excitement possessed all, save the calm, cold, smiling gentlemen of the War Office. Many large boxes from the various departments stood on the sidewalks ominously labelled "Lynchburgh," and I could not help smiling to see how the features of bystanders lengthened while gazing upon them. "Well," said they, "I suppose Johnston is going to give up Richmond like every thing else, and will continue to 'fall back' until we are all swimming in the Gulf of Mexico." There was not the slightest trepidation observable in the Government offices; all things went on as usual, and President Davis took his evening ride as placidly as ever. It was seen, however, that the enemy could never come up the river to Richmond, for heavy works had been hastily erected and mounted at Drury's Bluff. The immense raft was considered impregnable; the crew of the late Merrimac manned several large rifled pieces, the banks and woods swarmed with sharpshooters, while several excellent rifled field batteries were ready, with the supports, to the rear.

At length, when the enemy's gunboats came within easy range, the sailors at the land batteries on the south side, and the guns of the Washington Artillery corps on the north bank, poured such a stream of shot and shell into them as to present an unbroken sheet of flame from the woods. At the same time care was taken that our firing should be accurate. No sooner had the gunboats opened the shutters of their ports, than every gun was directed at the vulnerable point, and a shower of small shot poured in, so that the gunboats were soon rendered useless, and "backed out" to greater range.* Dozens of our shell, we could perceive, exploded among their gunners below deck, and

---

* A late Northern paper says: "The armor of the Galena, which was pierced by the projectiles of the rebel batteries below Richmond, was three inches thick. The Monitor, has thus far stood the fire with her five-inch plates, but as guns of enormous calibre and projectiles of great momentum are in vogue, it is safe to increase the thickness of the armor.

such was the destruction that none of the crews ventured to appear above board. Their firing, however, was hotly maintained, but, as our position was on a bluff, their shell passed overhead, and did but trifling damage. This lasted for several hours, when the discomfiture of the foe was so complete, that all their gunboats and iron-clads withdrew in disgust, and never troubled us again. From Northern accounts we learned that not less twenty gunners were killed in one iron-clad alone, and several boats so much shattered internally, that they were quietly taken down to Fortress Monroe for repairs, and members of the press were forbidden to visit or inspect them. It was admitted that our shore batteries had fully repulsed them, and this acknowledgment from men accustomed to the falsification of facts speaks volumes for our success.

Notwithstanding the efforts of Government to prepare for the approaching conflict, the ominous look of large packing-boxes on the pavements, and the removal of iron safes, led thousands to believe the army would evacuate Richmond, and perhaps give up Virginia also, as untenable. Many conveyed property to the interior, and there existed a feverish excitement among the little merchants. Jews and Germans were converting every thing into cash at ruinous rates of discount, sometimes paying four hundred dollars in paper for one hundred dollars in cash; while others of their brethren changed goods into tobacco, which they stowed away in cellars, preparatory to McClellan's arrival; though very secretly accomplished, the thing was known, and no notice taken of it by our authorities. The idea of giving up Richmond was heart-breaking, but so doubtful were appearances that it was not until Governor Letcher, in an audience with President Davis, had been positively assured that "Virginia should not be given up, but defended until the streets of Richmond ran with blood," that any certainty was felt regarding ministerial measures. When the Governor rehearsed the substance of his interview with the President to the assembled Legislature, a popular outburst of feeling ensued: all swore to reduce the place to ashes rather than surrender, and the faces of all were flushed with patriotic pride as they armed themselves for the coming conflict. The enemy, indeed, had vigorously pushed their advance to the neighborhood of the capital, and on the right of their line were but four miles distant from it.

To understand the posture of affairs at this time it is necessary to form an intelligible idea of the locality and of the positions occupied by the rival armies. Richmond is situated at what may be considered the head of the Yorktown peninsula. On the south side the peninsula is washed by the James River; on the north, by the York River, to within seventy miles of the capital. The York River is continued by its tributary the Pamunkey River, which approaches within a few miles of the capital. At the foot of the peninsula, where the James flows into Chesapeake Bay, are Newport News and Hampton Roads. So much for the general geography of the Richmond peninsula, as shown on ordinary maps.

The approaching battle-fields may be represented by an imaginary square, the sides of which indicate the four quarters. At the bottom or south will be Richmond, and the rear of our army; the upper side, or north, will represent the rear of McClellan's forces. We must now suppose that a river rises in the south-west, and runs easterly, but in the centre of the diagram flows rapidly north-eastwardly—this is the Chickahominy, cutting the imaginary equator diagonally; and the equator itself is the common front of both armies. It will thus be seen that McClellan's right rested north, and his left south of the stream, the communication being maintained with both wings by several bridges, his centre resting on both sides of the stream at Bottom's Bridge.

From Richmond there are five roads which cut the Chickahominy at right angles, in the following order, from west to east: the Brook (or Hanover Court-house) Turnpike; the Mechanicsville Turnpike, (the village of Mechanicsville being on the north side of the river, and the headquarters of Fitz-John Porter, commanding the Federal right wing;) the Nine Mile Road; York River Railroad; the Williamsburgh Road; the Charles City Road; and the Darbytown Road. From the curve of the river across our front, our left and the enemy's right rested *on* the stream, but at the Charles City Road (our right and the enemy's left) were far from the stream, it being many miles to their rear.

The whole front, a distance of about seven miles, was

strongly defended by field-works of all kinds, to suit the ground. Between our left and the enemy's right, the ground dipped, the head of the stream being in the centre, but friend and foe had high ground which còmmanded Mechanicsville Bridge; the pickets of either army being within a hundred yards of the bridge. This bottom land on our left being partly well timbered by the swampy nature of the ground, was the scene of daily skirmishing, and from the superior position of their guns, and their closer proximity to the bridge, it was indisputably in the enemy's possession, and was well defended by elaborate works. The distance of the enemy's right was not more than four miles from Richmond; that of their left about seven miles.

McClellan did not attempt to push his left and centre across the Chickahominy until more than a week after the tents and flags of his right were seen around Mechanicsville; in fact, the weather was unsuitable, and the proposed line of formation was in an unhealthy swamp of woods and fields. The circumstances left McClellan no choice. Between Richmond and the Chickahominy there is an insensible fall of the land, and we had already occupied the relatively higher position, where the lands were better cultivated and drier, and less encumbered with timber. Our line being thus formed, McClellan had no alternative but to camp his forces in counter line, although he must have seen that his hospitals would soon be crowded, from chills, fevers, ague, and rheumatism among his troops.

Having taken up his position, McClellan began to fortify various points, and particularly the continuations of the five roads mentioned which passed through his lines. Thousands of men were daily employed in throwing up earthworks, building new or repairing old roads, felling timber to uncover our front, and locate his divisions, so that for a few days scarcely a shot was exchanged by pickets, save on our left, and *there* Fitz-John Porter's sharpshooters and our own were blazing away night and day. As it was for some time considered probable that the enemy would attempt to force the James, our right was extended two miles towards it; but after the repulse at Drury's Bluff, there seemed to be no further indications of any new attempt, and Longstreet removed his division, and camped in regular line across the Charles City road.

Our effective force, including Huger's arrival from Norfolk, was about eighty thousand; it could not have been much more, for the strength of the several divisions was not near their maximum; and our army, as well as McClellan's, was terribly weakened by sickness and ailments of various kinds; in our case arising from insufficient clothing, poor flour, and bad bacon, owing to the poverty of our commissariat. McClellan confesses to have lost thirty thousand men, from all causes, since his operations began on the peninsula (March) up to the middle of May. This appears incredible, but we have his own words to vouch for the fact. Our loss from all causes was great, but not a tenth of this number. The transports of the enemy brought immense supplies of every kind up to the head of the York River, (West-Point,) and dépôts were numerous up the Pamunkey, being easily supplied thence to the army by excellent roads, and the York River railroad, which Johnston, in retreat, wisely or unwisely, left intact. The Northern merchantmen also ascended the James River, steamed up the Chickahominy, and made immense deposits of all things along its banks, conveniently in the rear. Guns and munitions were thus abundantly provided, and ere many weeks McClellan's army was snugly provided for in their lines before Richmond.

Our generals, as usual, were calculating upon the capture of this booty, before many suns had set. In fact, it has been suggested, and I believe it to be true, that Johnston's only reason for leaving the York River Railroad untouched in his retreat, was to invite the enemy to make immense deposits at the dépôts in West-Point, and along the Pamunkey, in order eventually that himself and Jackson, by combined movements, should capture all, and replenish our exhausted stores. Be this as it may, it is certain that inconceivable quantities of baggage and *matériel* accumulated in the rear, and so confident were Northern merchants of McClellan's success, that *they* also gathered immense stores in the rear, so as to be able to open sales in Richmond simultaneously with its occupation! Ridiculous as this may seem, the most incontestable facts prove it to be true.

Both armies had now been nearly a month in position, and did nothing from day to day but skirmish, and waste ammunition in fruitless cannonades. Our men were camped in the woods and fields adjacent to the roads; picket-guards, strong bodies of skirmishers with supports, presented an unbroken front to the enemy, but they did not seem inclined to take the initiative. Whole brigades were in line in open fields, night and day, within a mile of the enemy, inviting an attack, yet the foe never came from the woods, but contented himself with throwing up formidable redoubts, and creeping towards Richmond inch by inch. It was evidently McClellan's wish to avoid a field fight, his idea being either to starve us out, or gradually get near enough to shell Richmond at discretion. Every inducement was held out by Johnston to draw the enemy from their works and woods into the open space before us, but his endeavors were unavailing.

At length it became known to our commanders that McClellan designed moving his left and centre nearer to us, and it was determined to attack him before his heavy masses could be brought up in proper order. Several reconnoissances were made to test the truth of the information we had received, and it was also confirmed by the daily reports of our pickets. In due time all doubt was removed. General Casey drove in our pickets, and camped on the Williamsburgh road, within a mile of us; the left centre and centre of the enemy down the railway and Nine Mile Road were at the same time thrown forward, and every appearance indicated that they meant to precipitate an action. In this attitude of expectation I must leave the two armies for a short time, in order to follow the fortunes of Jackson in the Shenandoah Valley.

15

CHAPTER XXV.

Occurrences in the Shenandoah Valley—Battles of "Front Royal," May twenty-third—Capture of Winchester and Thousands of Prisoners by Jackson—Rout of Banks's Corps—Immense Booty.

ASHTON'S letter from the Valley* read as follows:

" Our retreat after the battle of Kearnstown was very rapid and fatiguing ; Jackson forced his men along the Valley Pike all night, for we were but few in number, and Shields's force very large. Without much rest, we pushed through Strasburgh, and took the road towards Charlottesville, and had thus got a start of over twenty miles ere the enemy's cavalry came in sight. Ashby, as usual, was in the rear, and nobly beat back the foe, and saved us from annihilation ; every rise in the road was disputed by him, until at last the Federals seemed weary of fighting, and contented themselves with hovering in the rear.

" At Harrisonburgh the enemy gave up the pursuit, but we continued our route, ten miles farther, to McGackeysville, having travelled the whole distance of seventy miles without halting for more than a few hours. At McGackeysville we found that Ewell, with a force of ten thousand men, had crossed the Blue Ridge, and formed a junction with Jackson. This surprised us, it having been thought that his division was with Johnston ; it appeared, however, that he had been hovering around Fredericksburgh, on the Rappahannock, watching a division of McDowell, who held the nucleus of a force† destined to march on Richmond from the west, while McClellan made his attack on the east. Knowing that McDowell dared not move alone, and that Shields threatened, to annihilate

---

* See end of Chapter Twenty-third, page 217.

† This force, in addition to his own division, was to consist of the troops of Banks and Shields, from the Shenandoah Valley, and those of Milroy, Blenker, and Fremont from Western Virginia.

Jackson, Ewell had wisely crossed the Ridge and hastened to our assistance.

"It was now hoped by all, that Shields would leave the Valley, push on through Harrisonburgh, and attack us at Mc-Gackeysville; but, after some days, it was ascertained that he remained enjoying the fruits of the battle of Kearnstown, and was waiting until Milroy and Blenker should clear Western Virginia, and arrive on a line with him, when they would all join McDowell at Fredericksburgh. Jackson was not many days at McGackeysville, when a courier from the Georgian, Colonel Johnson, arrived, and informed him that Blenker and Milroy, with their Dutch division, were advancing eastward in Western Virginia, and that his small force of fifteen hundred men was falling back before them.

"When this news was received, Jackson, finding his original command fully rested, left Ewell's force of ten thousand at McGackeysville, and sallied out during the night, none knew whither. Keeping to the mountains until he arrived at Port Republic, he struck the Valley Pike there, proceeded on, by night and day, towards Staunton, and then, without entering the town, shaped his course north-west through the mountains. After a fatiguing march of seventy miles in three days, through valleys, over mountains, and along frightfully muddy roads, he arrived at nine A.M., May tenth, in sight of Colonel Johnson's little force, which was drawn up in a narrow valley, at a village called McDowell, with the heavy brigades of Milroy and Blenker in line of battle before him. This valley was not more than two hundred yards wide, having steep mountains on either hand, that on our left being called Bull Pasture Mountain. Jackson's men having been allowed a rest of two hours, he and Johnson immediately prepared for battle, and skirmishing began in all directions.

Milroy and Blenker seemed confident of success, and handled their troops admirably; they had several pieces of artillery, we had none. At two P.M. the fight commenced in earnest, and Jackson immediately pushed his men forward to bring matters to a crisis. Observing that they suffered from our incessant and accurate musketry-fire, and that their commands would not stand close work, Milroy and Blenker marched their men by the right flank up, and on, to Bull Pasture

Mountain, leaving their artillery strongly posted on the mountain to our right, thinking to gain an elevated position, and destroy us. Their artillery was a great annoyance, but we soon followed the plan of our enemy—marched up the mountain by the left flank, and when arrived at the top, fighting as we went, found it to be an admirable place for an engagement, being perfectly flat. The contest was here renewed with great fury, and we drove the enemy a considerable distance, until night put an end to hostilities, and the enemy slunk off in the darkness. Arrangements were made in expectation of the engagement being renewed in the morning, but when our pickets, finding no opposition, moved forward a considerable distance, it was discovered that the foe had left their dead and wounded, together with a quantity of stores, and had hastily decamped.

"Every arrangement was instantly made for pursuit, and ere midnight our cavalry scouts came in and reported that large fires were seen burning in the direction of Franklin, and that in the hurry and confusion of defeat, and a forced march, immense supplies lay along the road, and that quantities were burning in all directions. We buried our own dead — about one hundred in number — and that of the enemy — some three hundred — and at daylight commenced the pursuit. The distance to Franklin was forty miles, and the road one of the roughest that mortal was ever doomed to travel; but so rapid were the movements of the enemy, that, although we travelled the forty miles in less than twenty hours, they had reached Franklin before us, and were drawn up in a strong position, occupying the right and left of a road that ran between two mountains, Franklin being in their rear. Jackson thought it probable we might be able to flank them, and sent out a force of cavalry to reconnoitre, who reported that not a single road or cow-path was discovered by which we could get round the enemy. They had artillery on the hills, and every movement we made was clearly seen by them, so that it was deemed unadvisable to attack with our small force, strongly posted as they were, and inaccessible except in front, through the gorge.

"Learning that his success at McDowell had so frightened Milroy and Blenker that they had called upon Fremont, who was a few marches behind, Jackson determined to deceive them and fall back. After remaining at Franklin part of two days, he ordered his cavalry to be unusually active, and make incessant demonstrations in all quarters; if necessary, they were to fall back on McDowell, leaving the enemy to infer that strong forces were near at hand; Jackson, in the mean while, refreshed his own and Johnston's men, and began to retreat through McDowell more swiftly than he had advanced. Marching at a rapid rate, he reached the Valley Pike at Mount Crawford, eighteen miles from Staunton, and learned that Banks's force had fallen back from Harrisonsburgh to Strasburgh. Moving at a fast rate down the Valley Pike, Jackson proceeded onwards to Newmarket, and was there joined by Ewell's force of ten thousand, which had been awaiting us at Swift Run Gap. Our whole force now amounted to about fourteen thousand men. After a little rest, we all proceeded across the Shenandoah Mountains, and camped near Lurah, in Page Valley, about twelve miles from Front Royal — the rear of Banks's army in the Valley.

"This requires some explanation. When Shields found Jackson strongly posted at McGackeysville, he declined to advance against him, as I have already mentioned, and withdrawing his forces from between Woodstock and Harrisonburgh, he regained the Valley, determined to push on towards McDowell at Fredericksburgh, and commence the 'on to Richmond' movement from the west. Banks also had the same destination, having his force scattered up and down the Valley, the rear being at Front Royal. Blenker and Milroy were similarly bound through Western Virginia, but their defeat had diverted Fremont from his proper route, who immediately went to their assistance. Thinking, therefore, that Jackson was busily engaged in that distant quarter, and not likely to trouble them in the Valley again, Banks and Shields were quietly making their way towards Fredericksburgh, unconscious of danger, when, on the morning of May twenty-second, Jackson and Ewell, with fourteen thousand men, were meditating an attack on their rear.

"To make all sure, Ewell was detached with ten thousand men to seize Winchester, the enemy's grand dépôt, before they could turn and flee, and—as Banks would be obliged to pass through that town—to man the fortifications, and keep him to the southward, while Jackson should strike his column on the flanks, and seize the baggage. With this object Ewell started northwards, and we southwards, towards Front Royal. Although we had been camped within twelve miles of the latter place several days, our movements and position had been kept so secret that the Federal commandant knew nothing of our presence until the attack was actually made on the morning of the twenty-third of May. The Louisianians, as skirmishers, having encircled the place, Jackson, in battle array, marched up to the village, and after some little fighting captured the First Federal Maryland Regiment, seven hundred strong, under command of Colonel Kenly, and immediately seized the town, together with immense stores. During the afternoon our cavalry attacked the enemy at Buckton station on the railroad, and after smart skirmishing, captured several hundred prisoners, and such quantities of stores that they had to be destroyed. Judge of Banks's astonishment when informed of this! Never dreaming of such a trick, he had established extensive dépôts up and 'down the valley — that at Winchester being worth millions of dollars. He had but one way to retreat—by the Valley Pike—and that was held by us; with Ewell marching rapidly towards Winchester to seize the fortifications, and get still farther in his rear.

"We had accomplished much at Front Royal and Buckton station, and, expecting that Banks would not attempt to move for several days, were meditating proper methods of attack along their line of retreat, for Banks had a very large army, and could not well be assailed in regular form by our small force; but judge of our surprise when, next morning, (twenty-fourth,) word was brought that Banks's whole command was racing up the Pike towards Winchester at an awful rate, and in the wildest excitement. Such marching you never saw—cavalry and infantry and baggage-wagons were dashing along at headlong speed in hot haste to reach Winchester, the roads being strewn for miles with every imaginable article known to campaigning. Our cavalry and infantry attacked them at all points, and in every conceivable way; but this army of twenty thousand men pushed along, running and fighting as they went, jumping over fences, leaving wagons, cannon, and thousands of prisoners in our hands. Cavalry were incessantly charging the foe or driving batches of prisoners to the rear. Now the enemy's infantry would halt, and make a show of fighting, but our men gave a yell and a volley, our cavalry plunged into their broken ranks, and they were ruthlessly cut down. In truth, we had been marched and overworked too much to take full advantage of the glorious opportunity now presented; but all did the best they could. The retreat of the enemy was so rapid that it was impossible for infantry to keep up with them, and most of the duty devolved on cavalry. They seized hundreds of fresh cavalry horses, remounted, and were again after the enemy at full gallop, capturing scores of prisoners every mile, and yet the pursuit continued all day.

"At the village of Middleton a New-Jersey regiment of horse turned to fight, but our cavalry rode against them so furiously that the enemy were instantly unhorsed, fifty of them being killed, one hundred wounded, and two hundred and fifty captured; so that from wagons, baggage, dead, wounded, and prisoners, the roads were almost impassable. Wagons by the dozen were driven from the road, and the traces having been cut, the teams might be seen running wildly about in all directions. The scene was that of Manassas over again. Every field was crowded with fugitives who waited to be captured, while scores of ambulances were filled with footsore or wounded .Federals, and driven to the rear, the men seeming speechless from astonishment. Colonels, Majors, Captains, rank and file, were marched indiscriminately to the rear, while on dashed our wearied cavalry, pistolling and cutting down the still retreating enemy. So it continued all day long on the twenty-fourth, until, perfectly broken down with the labor, we camped at Newtown, a few miles from Winchester.

"Ewell had not been able to get into Winchester before Banks arrived; and as the place was strongly fortified, Jackson deferred all attack until the twenty-fifth, by which time it was hoped our exhausted infantry would arrive. For miles along the road towards and beyond Winchester, large and innumerable fires told that the enemy were destroying their supplies, and already on their retreat towards the Potomac. Such a sight I could never have conceived. The whole country seemed on fire, yet every approach towards Winchester was still as death, which led many to suppose we should have a hard fight before gaining the town on the morrow.

"We had between two and three hundred wagons in our possession untouched, and supplies of every description beyond calculation, so that our wearied and famished soldiery enjoyed themselves hugely, and did not care a straw what the morrow might bring forth. We had beaten Banks—that was an all-sufficing fact; and Jackson, who had been cursed for his long marches and incessant fighting, was now idolized, and every one saw into and loudly applauded his rapid movements and his unexampled success. Standing on a hill near our camps, the sight on the night of the twenty-fourth was awfully grand; whichever way the eye might turn, fires illuminated the dark and distant landscape, and it seemed that the destruction and loss to the enemy were incalculable. Their immense amount of supplies and baggage is explained by the fact that this part of the Valley had been used as the grand dépôt, not only for Banks himself, but for supplying the commands of Shields, Fremont, Milroy, Blenker, and others, besides the accumulated stores destined for McDowell. Such a race, riot, confusion, loss in men and *matériel* as Banks suffered on that eventful day are totally beyond my power to describe.

"Early on the morning of the twenty-fifth, Jackson began to move on Winchester. Dense columns of smoke issuing from the town made it evident that the enemy were busily engaged in burning stores; but as Jackson did not relish this idea, he pushed forward, and, meeting with a feeble resistance, we rushed into the town, driving the foe through every street; even women and children assisting us by throwing brick-bats, or whatever they conveniently could, from the windows. The fight was neither long nor sanguinary; the Federals were more scared than hurt, yet our cavalry commenced a hot pursuit, and hung within a few yards of their rear, fighting and chasing them in the same style as the day before. By our opportune arrival, much property was saved of incalculable value, including several hundred boxes of new arms of various sorts, for all branches of the service, besides a vast supply of medicines, a few cannon, and countless articles of value.

"It was about noon ere the pursuit commenced in force; and

as our men were now well clothed, and provided with an abundance of all the necessaries and many of the luxuries of life, all were gay and anxious to push forward, and, if possible, drive the enemy into the Potomac. Hurrying forward towards Charleston, we found that Banks had shaped his course towards Williamsport, and ere he had crossed over to that town, our advance was well up with him; while the number of dead, wounded, and prisoners along the road showed what havoc Ashby had made among the foe with his cavalry. Hats, caps, muskets, boots, wagons, dead, wounded, prisoners, burning stores, sabres, pistols, etc., lined every yard of the road, while hundreds of fatigued and famished Yankees concealed themselves in every wood, making their way towards the Potomac as best they could, footsore, unarmed, ragged, and totally demoralized. Had our men been marched less, and fully recruited from their terrible mountain fights and journeys, it would have been impossible for Banks to have drawn off a single regiment; but, as we were far more fatigued than they, the punishment inflicted and the vigor of our pursuit were not half as effective as they might have been. Never giving up, however, Ashby still hung on their rear, and unmercifully thrashed them whenever they turned to fight. At last, totally prostrated from fatigue, and helpless as children, we reached the vicinity of Williamsport, on the evening of the twenty-sixth, and found that all who remained of the enemy had effected a passage across the river at different points, and were safe in Maryland.

"The bare idea of our excessive labor during the pursuit on the twenty-fourth, twenty-fifth, and twenty-sixth, is enough to terrify me, for the whole route travelled was more than fifty miles, and every furlong of it witnessed an encounter of some sort; so that when we found the foe had escaped, most of us felt infinite relief. The complete details of our success can never be known, but, speaking roughly, we had captured thousands of prisoners, killed and wounded hundreds more, seized miles of baggage-wagons, immense stores of every imaginable description, together with many cannons, thousands of small arms, ammunition by hundreds of tons, clothing, medicines, public documents of value, thousands of shoes, and had burned millions' worth of property for want of transportation. Throughout the whole route from Strasburgh to Williamsport, in every lane and every field, booty still lay where the enemy had left it, and for many days after our arrival on the Potomac, cavalry had little else to do but sally forth, and pick up small parties of prisoners endeavoring to make their way to the river. All description of this memorable defeat of the enemy under Banks must fall short of the reality. Such sights I never expected to behold in the whole course of my existence. The confusion, rout, noise, destruction, incessant discharge of arms, the utter prostration and consternation of the enemy, were appalling, and although I know nothing of this kind will ever be heard North, and that the Federal leaders will speak lightly of the facts,* God

* The following Northern items regarding these events will not be uninteresting, as illustrative of their feeling and "exaggeration of truth," namely:

" *Washington, May 26th.*—We have passed a very exciting day in Washington. The intelligence received last evening to the effect that General Banks had fallen back from Strasburgh to Winchester, was understood to indicate rather a precautionary measure on his part, than the result of any immediate movement of the enemy. The tidings of this morning, announcing the occupation of Winchester by Jackson, and the withdrawal of Banks, after an engagement of six hours, in the direction of Martinsburgh and Harper's Ferry, placed matters in a new light, and aroused serious apprehensions, not only for the safety of his little command, but for the Baltimore and Ohio Railroad, the city of Baltimore, and even the Capital. Later in the day the reports of the rioting in Baltimore and of the rout of the entire force of Banks, by the quick march and overwhelming numbers of Jackson, intensified the excitement. The secessionist sympathizers, too greatly elated to conceal their joy, openly expressed their belief that the host of Jeff. Davis will overrun Maryland and the District within twenty-four hours.

One Truth about the War told by a Yankee.—Wilson, says a Northern journal, one of the Senators from Massachusetts in the Yankee Congress, confessed or charged the other day, in a speech from his desk, that there was an organized system of lying practised in the management of the war. This is probably the first truth that Wilson himself has ever told about the war. It is notorious that old Scott justifies lying as a necessary part of the science of war. To such a mind, treason to his native State, his hereditary sovereign, presented no difficulty. It is probable that he first introduced the system of lying as a part of the strategy of war, and, indeed, as the means of beginning it, for he was at Washington for some months before the close of Buchanan's administration. The first lie that we remember, bearing directly on the beginning of hostilities, was the pledge made by Buchanan to the South-Carolina delegation in Congress, that the military status of Charleston harbor should not be changed. The pledge was violated on the night of the twenty-sixth December, 1860, by Major Anderson removing his forces from Fort Moultrie to Fort Sumter, and attempting to destroy the defences of the former. The second important lie in the initiation of hostilities was the assembling of troops in force at Washington on the pretext that an attack would be made on the Capi-

forbid that any army of ours should be so broken up and so totally demoralized as was that of the vain-glorious and arrant

tal, and the inauguration of Lincoln would not otherwise be permitted. The third was, the assurance that due notice would be given to the authorities of Charleston, if it were determined to reenforce or provision Fort Sumter. The notice was not given until the fleet despatched for the purpose was presumed to be at the mouth of Charleston harbor. But we have no idea of going further with the narrative. The lying of the Yankee Government, Generals, newspapers, and people about the war, is an Augean stable into which we will neither take our readers nor go ourselves.

NORTHERN ACCOUNT OF "FRONT ROYAL" AND "WINCHESTER."—The following extract from the correspondence of the *New-York World* admits the defeat of the Federals, and tries to palliate it by exaggerating the superiority of the Confederates in numbers:

"William H. Mapes, commanding pioneer corps, arrived and reported to Colonel Kenley, who gave orders immediately where they should be stationed, and they continued with the remainder of the little force, doing noble service, and holding in check successfully not less than six times their number. Seeing the danger of their position, the commander of the brigade gave the order to retreat, which they did in excellent order, across the Shenandoah. Mapes was then ordered to burn the bridge, which was accordingly fired, by placing upon it piles of fence-rails, but was not destroyed. The rebels came on so closely and hotly that we were driven away, and did not succeed in the attempt. They soon arrived, and crossed the bridge on the north branch of the Shenandoah, which they succeeded in firing and destroying, but not, however, in detaining the rebels, who, cavalry and infantry, plunged in and forded it, and were soon upon the other side.

"Soon was received the unwelcome news that the enemy had surrounded them, flanking them with superior numbers right and left.

"Our men, undaunted, dashed upon them with such vigor as to effect their escape, and cut their way out from the coils of the rebels thrown around them, not, however, without being again surrounded and so effectually beset on every side, behind and before, with the most insurmountable superiority, both in the numbers and freshness of the rebel troops, that they were completely destroyed or captured, together with their noble Colonel and other field-officers.

"The severity of the fight beggars all attempt at description."

(The enemy tried to effect their retreat through Winchester, and the same writer gives a graphic account of the disasters attending that retreat, and the still greater slaughter at Winchester.)

"Presently General Williams, who had not left Strasburgh, came riding rapidly with his staff to the head of the column, and the soldiers raised a hearty cheer as he passed, which continued up the column as he advanced up the front. General Banks soon followed, and was greeted with similar manifestations of pleasure and confidence in their commander.

"We followed closely, and the road was filled with wagons, some broken down, others with the mules cut suddenly away, and all deserted by their drivers, who had taken fright on the appearance of a few of the enemy's cavalry, and fled in a Bull Run stampede.

Abolitionist, General N. P. Banks. How many millions of dollars they have lost in this retreat of three days will never be known, and perhaps can not be calculated; but this I do know, that we are now wallowing in the luxuries of life, and Jackson has sufficient stores to last an indefinite time, should we successfully transport them out of the Valley. Excuse haste, and believe me yours, ASHTON."

"The infantry were kept somewhat in the rear until the General and his body-guard had advanced, to ascertain the position of the enemy, and the space between was filled with the baggage-wagons, which were being repossessed by their timorous guardians, under the inspiring influence of wagon-master's whip, who, enraged at the cowardly rout, was driving them back with unmerciful lashes to their deserted charges. Men were now seen flocking back, and the baggage-train was again supplied with teamsters. . . . . .

"The other end of our column encountered the force which was to have been sent to attack our rear. First the Zouaves d'Afrique, body-guard of General Banks, had been stationed in the rear, to burn the bridge across Meadow Creek, three miles from Strasburgh, after all had passed except the cavalry, under General Hatch, who was yet to come up and ford the river. While they were besmearing the bridge with tar, unexpecting any danger, the enemy charged down upon them from the mountain on the left, cutting them up in the most unmerciful manner, and capturing all of them except five. . . . . .

"Presently there was a commotion, a sobbing among the women, and a running to and fro, which brought me to my feet in time to find our forces were started on a retreat; and, as I saw flames rising from the burning buildings not far off, and heavy volumes of smoke roll upward from them, I began to realize that we were to abandon Winchester. The enemy were in the other end of the town, as the rattle and echo of the musketry up the streets and between the houses most plainly indicated. All the streets were in commotion. Cavalry were rushing away in disorder, and infantry, frightened by the rapidity of their mounted companions, were in consternation. All were trying to escape faster than their neighbors, dreading most of all to be the last.

"Presently the enemy's cannon boomed in the rear, and a small cloud of smoke in the sky, suddenly appearing, and then dissolving, showed where the shell had exploded. Some shells fell among our men, and the panic was quite general for a short time. Guns, knapsacks, cartridge-boxes, bayonets, and bayonet-cases, lay scattered upon the ground in great confusion, thrown away by the panic-stricken soldiers. . . . . .

"Colonel Gordon and staff are safe; also General Williams and staff. While retreating through Winchester, women from the houses opened fire of pistols upon our soldiers, and killed a great many of them."

My reader will not fail to observe from the above, that General Banks's body-guard is composed of negroes, and that the women of Winchester killed "a great many" of the Yankees.

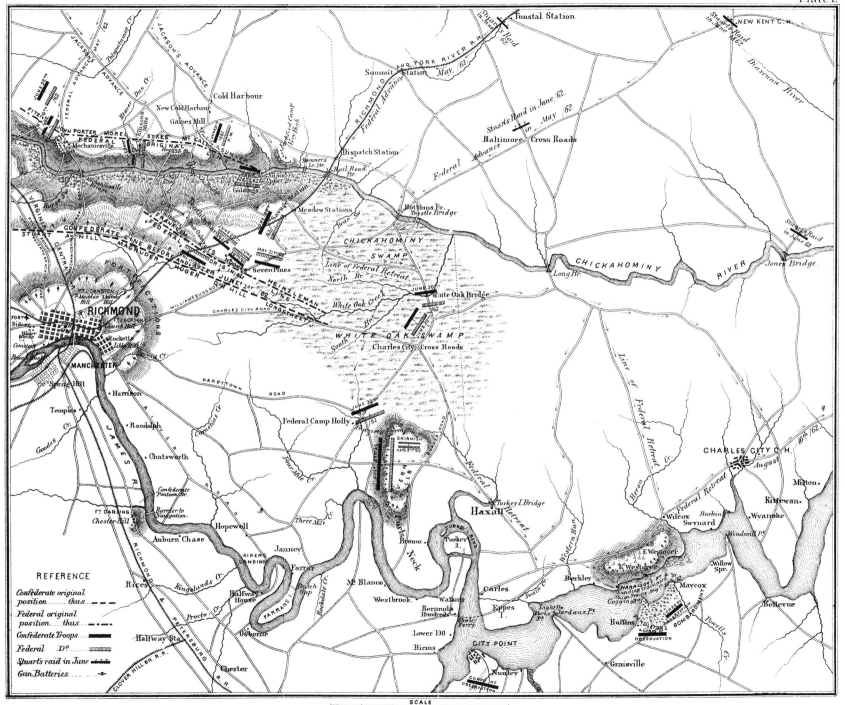

SKETCH MAP ILLUSTRATIVE OF THE BATTLES OF SEVEN PINES, FAIR OAKS AND THE "WEEKS CAMPAIGN" BEFORE RICHMOND &c.

Plate I.

REFERENCE

Confederate original position .... thus ─ ─
Federal original position .... thus ┄┄┄
Confederate Troops .... ▬▬▬
Federal Do .... ▤▤▤
Stuart's raid in June .... ┼─┼─
Gun Batteries .... ┼

SCALE

0 1 2 3   6 Miles.

CHAPTER XXVI.

Battle of the Chickahominy, or "Seven Pines"—The Plan of Battle—Annihilation of the Enemy's Left—Loss of either Army—General Johnston wounded.

ON Friday, the thirtieth of May, our camps presented nothing unusual, nor were any movements in progress that indicated the early commencement of hostilities. During the night, a thunderstorm of unusual violence shook the heavens, and rain fell so heavily that the whole face of the country was deluged with water. The men in camp were exposed to all the violence of the storm, and the roads were rendered impassable, with mud three feet deep. The enemy were even worse off than ourselves, as the bottom lands at the head of the Chickahominy were flooded, and the stream itself much swollen. Active operations on their right were impossible.

Early in the morning (Saturday, May thirty-first) it was whispered that Johnston intended attacking their left; but in answer to the inquiry, "In such weather?" it was answered that the bridges were washed away, rendering it impossible for McClellan to send over any of his right and centre to the assistance of his left, and that a large force would be thrown against his left, effectually crushing it before reenforced. Huger's division, it was understood, was to move down the Charles City road, (our extreme right,) and thus outflank and turn the enemy's left, while Longstreet pushed our right down the Williamsburgh road, (two miles from Huger,) and Whiting advanced his division near, and down the railroad, (our right centre,) thus hotly engaging the enemy at three points. As I have already said, it was impossible for McClellan's right and right centre to be engaged, the bridges having been washed away by the floods.

I was informed of the intended movement at six A.M., was soon in the saddle and away, since the opening fire was to come from Huger at eight o'clock. The affair was not known to any in town, but as I saw heavy columns of troops moving towards the Charles City road, I spurred along through the mud, and soon came up with the infantry advance of Longstreet toiling through the mire on the Williamsburgh road. Regiments and brigades occupied woods on each side the road, ready for orders to move, but hour after hour passed, and no gun from Huger told of his whereabouts. The heavens were surcharged with clouds, rain-drops fell thickly, and from the unusual silence of pickets to the front, I supposed the action had been postponed. I saw Longstreet and others were mortified at Huger's slowness; President Davis, and members of his Cabinet, seemed perplexed, and rode from point to point, anxiously expecting to hear Huger's guns open; but when, near noon, it was ascertained he was not yet in position, Longstreet determined to open the action and fight it alone. Our whole front was occupied with thick woods on marshy ground, the water in many places being two feet deep. I cast my eye to the rear, and saw brigades forming battle line in the woods : a courier dashed up the road, and soon after the chain of pickets began to "pop" rapidly in the front, a large body of sharpshooters dashed across the open in skirmishing order, entered the timber to the right and left of the road, and ere many minutes were rapidly firing in the front.

Now began the slow advance of our regiments through the woods in support, and a few pieces of artillery were endeavoring to push up to the front through the frightful depth of mud. Horses were lashed and goaded, but all to no purpose; artillerymen were up to their middle in mire, tugging at long ropes, but their progress was very slow indeed; for the gullies, holes, pools, and rocks, threatened to capsize them at every turn. The enemy were reported in strong force at Barker's Farm, a large open tract about a mile distant, and well protected by a series of well-mounted redoubts and field-works.

As soon as our pickets had advanced and begun to skirmish, they were met by several regiments to the left of the road, but immediately a finely drilled regiment of North-Carolinians (the "Fourth") advanced up the road at "double-quick," took the enemy in flank, delivered a volley, and dispersed them. This cleared the way, and our regiments were slowly advancing through the woods, up to their middle in mud and water, having to brush off occasionally a cloud of skirmishers that disputed their passage. Casey, who commanded the Federals at Barker's Farm, was heavily reenforced by several brigades, and seemed inclined not to dispute our advance very vigorously until we emerged from the woods into the open farm, and in front of his earthworks and batteries. His pieces then opened fire with shell, but not one of ours could be brought to the front to reply, so that shot and canister were tearing through the woods, and inflicting considerable loss upon us.

The North-Carolinians, having dispersed the first body of the enemy, marched into the woods on the left of the road, and advanced on Barker's Farm comparatively covered; Mississippians and others having worked their way through the swamp, did the same to the right. No attempt was made by our troops to advance far along the road, for hostile batteries swept its entire length through the farm. When our advance, therefore, had arrived at the edge of the woods, the open space in front was seen covered with troops, several batteries at the same time blazing away and rendering all advance impracticable. General D. H. Hill commanded on the right, and Brigadier-General Anderson the left of the road; but until their whole force could come up, they ordered their men to lie down for a short time, and allow the shell and grape-shot to pass harmlessly over them. Hill was impatient to begin, but, as the line was not formed, he obeyed the advice of his men, and dismounted, but, instead of going to the rear, he quietly leaned upon his horse's neck, and criticised the enemy's fire.

As the various brigades moved into line, driving all before them, our line of fire seemed to be more than a mile in extent, though Huger and Whiting, on the right and left, had not yet used a cartridge. The enemy now began to move forward his infantry, mistaking our inaction for indecision, but was severely punished; for as our men received orders they moved forward in solid line, presenting an unbroken sheet of musketry fire. As there were no earthworks to the right and left of our advance, it was determined to flank and attack their centre.

One of our batteries now opportunely appeared in the open, and beginning to work vigorously, drew upon it the fire of the enemy. Taking advantage of this, several of our regiments

crept through the low brushwood in front of the redoubt, and
at a given signal from the flanking parties, made a rush for the
guns, cleared them, and, entering pell-mell into the earthwork,
bayoneted all who opposed them. The guns, both inside and
outside the work, were all captured.

Rapidly re-forming, though under fire of new works which
opened in all directions, we once more advanced, and this we
did again and again on various points, until about 3 P.M., when
the battle raged with great fury. Additional pieces were arriving to assist us, but their progress was very slow on account of
the roads, which were beyond all description boggy, and broken
by immense mud-puddles, half drowning the unfortunate cannoniers, and upsetting caissons and ambulances. It was impossible,
of course, to go through the woods, and as Casey's first line of
defence was broken, troops and ammunition wagons were all
moving to and fro along this one miserable narrow road in the
greatest confusion. The enemy's position and camps, to my
great surprise, I found comparatively dry, the water having
drained off. Pleased with the firm, level ground, our mud-cov-
ered men of the Lynchburgh battery now lashed their horses
into a gallop, and dashed off through Casey's camps to the front
with a wild cheer.

The line formed by our men now advancing through and past
the camps to attack fresh positions, which vomited shell and
grape upon us, was truly magnificent. I recognized Anderson,
with Louisianians, North-Carolinians, etc.; Jenkins with his
South-Carolinians; Wilcox and Pryor, with Mississippians and
Alabamians. Floridans, Mississippians, and Georgians had
opened the fight, and, after resting, were advancing again; so
that when their unearthly yells rang from wing to wing, the
enemy stopped firing for a moment, and suddenly reopened
again with terrific fury. Their vigorous onslaught told plainly
that Casey had brought up Sedgwick, Palmer, and other divisions, and was calculating much upon the impassability of abattis
that covered the front of his batteries and earthworks. Busy as I
was, dashing about from point to point, it was impossible to learn
what regiments were yelling so much in this place, or keeping
up such incessant musketry fire in that; all that I could perceive
was, that their masses of infantry, though brought into-action
with much ability, precision, and neatness, never pretended to

offer us much resistance, but gradually fell back, or broke into confusion after a few volleys, when our men yelled and charged· Their resistance, however, was much stouter than at first, and they did not seem to place so much reliance on their earthworks, which now successively fell into our hands, with scores of dead lying in and around them in all directions.

It was now about four o'clock, and Longstreet's corps, under D. H. Hill, had driven the enemy a mile through their camps, capturing prisoners, stores, cannon, flags, redoubts, and whole camps of tents still standing. Still the fight continued with great fury. In fact, the attack down the Williamsburgh road had been so vigorously pushed that we were far in advance of our general line, and our attack seemed to be triangular, Whiting and Huger having attempted nothing right or left. It was apparent also that we had progressed too far, and the enemy pushed forward a large force, against which our exhausted men could not successfully contend. Determined to hold the ground until re-enforced, our troops occupied several of the enemy's field-works, turned the captured guns upon them, and by murderous discharges of musketry succeeded in checking their advance. By this time it was nearly dark, and General Johnston determined to move up Whiting on the left, in order to draw off some portion of the enemy's force. This movement relieved the pressure on Longstreet and Hill, who, reenforced and rested, advanced again, and drove the enemy entirely off Barker's Farm and the surrounding openings into the woods.

Whiting's attack now absorbed their whole attention. As we had advanced too far from our general line, they thought to attack Longstreet on the left flank and rear; but this was anticipated, and retiring with loss, they paid undivided attention to Whiting, who was advancing through the woods parallel with and not far from the railroad. It was much too late for this attack to have been begun, and the approach of darkness made any important result impossible. Cannonading, however, went on fiercely, and it was deemed possible that a large battery in the woods might fall into our hands; but the space all around it had been cleared of timber, and the ground was so swampy that the work seemed to be placed on a small island. The Tennesseeans moved forward and drove back the infantry; our artillery progressed slowly up a miry lane, and were compelled to fight

16

at every turn. Johnston and his staff rode to the front, and while ordering an attack, a battery opened from a thicket, and a piece of shell wounded him severely in the groin: the shock stunned him, he fell from his horse, broke two of his ribs, and was conveyed from the field with little hope of recovery.

The Tennesseeans charged through the woods, dispersing the infantry, and advancing to the battery through water up to their middle, took it, but had to retire for want of support. By this time it had become so dark that it was impossible to proceed farther; the flash of artillery was incessant; shells screamed through the air in luminous flight, and, bursting, made a beautiful pyrotechnic display; but it was impossible for our infantry to feel their way in the gloom. The enemy's musketry flashed in the darkness like sheets of flame; but their fire, except in so far as it served to protect the flanks of their batteries, was a mere waste of ammunition. Keyes commanded the Federals at this point, and had prepared his line with great precision and care;* but had Whiting commenced earlier, there can be no doubt he would have driven them on a line with Longstreet's advance down the Williamsburgh road. As it was, the latter officer, with Hill as coadjutor, had made a fearful gap in the left wing of the enemy, but without producing any decisive result. We had gained a battle, but nothing more.

As I rode down through the enemy's camps, gazing at the destruction on every side, I met Franks, one of Longstreet's aids, looking as blue as indigo. " What's the matter, Franks? Not satisfied with the day's work?" I inquired. " Satisfied, be hanged !" he replied. " I saw bld Jeff, (Davis,) Mallory, Longstreet, Whiting, and all of them, a little while ago, looking as mad as thunder. Just to think that Huger's slowness has spoiled every thing ! There he has been on our right all day and hasn't fired a shot, although he had positive orders to open the fight at eight o'clock this morning. It is true that Longstreet and Hill fought magnificently, as they always do, and

---

* General Erastus D. Keyes, United States army, is from the State of Maine; entered the service as brevet Second Lieutenant Third Artillery, July first, 1832; and in 1861 was Major First Artillery, commission dating October twelfth, 1858. He has risen rapidly during the war, and is about forty-five years of age. His division behaved well at "Seven Pines," and although General Whiting assailed it furiously, was so well placed and protected by batteries that all our efforts were of little avail.

have gained a brilliant victory; but had Huger obeyed orders, we should have demolished the enemy; as it is, their left is routed and demoralized, and we have gained nothing more substantial than a brilliant battle, when it was intended to have embraced an attack at three points, and all along the line, if the enemy accepted it. Johnston is wounded, you know, but is awfully mad about the miscarriage of his plans; the doctors say he will recover. Just to think that our best generals *will* poke themselves in the front—Sydney Johnston was lost in that way, and I have seen both Longstreet and Hill foolishly riding in front of the enemy not less than a dozen times to-day. Hill must be a shadow or an immortal, for he exposed himself often enough to get his quietus a dozen times to-day." My friend rode away towards Richmond, and I to the captured camp.

Teams were already hauling away cannon, stores, tents, and other booty; ambulances by the dozen were slowly moving off to the rear; while stretcher-bearers, in long, solemn procession, conveyed away the wounded men to temporary field-hospitals. Lamps flitted about in all directions, camp-fires were burning, and men cooking supper from the abundance of all things found in tents and commissary stores. General Casey's effects were all seized, including his wardrobe and private papers. His mess-table stood, as it had been left ready for dinner; the plates and cups untouched; beds, bedding, camp furniture, desks, clothing, arms, provisions, stationery, and all things in abundance were found, including a hundred barrels of whisky, which had already been tapped, and half emptied by our weary men. Prisoners were coming in every minute; dead and wounded lined the roads, or lay scattered through the fields and woods, and, as night advanced, their moaning was distressing to hear. Every thing of use or value was soon conveyed to the rear, and long before morning little remained on Barker's farm, save the wounded, the dying, and the dead, piles of old clothes, and general rubbish unfit to be conveyed away. Our own wounded were rapidly conveyed to Richmond by ambulances, private carriages, and the railroad-trains, which ran all night without interruption.

As morning approached, every thing was prepared for the reception of the enemy, should they advance; but General

Pryor and others, who held the battle-field, were ordered to fall back to our original position, should they attack in force. Several who deserted the enemy under cover of the darkness, informed us that Heintzelman, Sumner, and others had arrived; the former being second in command to McClellan, who was also present, and intended to "push" us. When morning broke, the pickets opened in a lively manner upon each other, and the attack began. Pryor's troops were of such excellent metal that they refused to fall back, and it was not until after they had thrashed twice their own number, and were in danger of being flanked, that they quietly fell back across the farm. The enemy did not follow; and Pryor's men sullenly occupied their old ground, south of the battle-field; none but a strong picket-guard being left to hold the place. Next morning (Monday) the enemy occupied Casey's camp-ground again, but betrayed no inclination to accept our invitations to advance nearer Richmond.

While this was progressing on Sunday, down the Williams- burgh road, the enemy endeavored to dislodge Whiting's ad- vance, near the railroad, from the ground captured the evening before. A lively fight was the consequence, during which our forces withdrew to their original lines, whither the enemy dared not follow. This latter skirmish was productive of little good, and we lost several promising regimental officers, including the brave Lomax, Colonel of the Third Alabama Volunteers—a man whose brilliant promise was worth a hundred such com- bats. If Huger had been tardy in his movements down the Charles City road on Saturday, he was stirring and lively enough on Whiting's left in this fight, and must have marched his men unmercifully through the mud. He looked hale and hearty, and laughed good-humoredly as his advance moved into the woods, preparatory to the engagement. His attack, how- ever, was countermanded, and the whole line assumed its original position, to lie idly on their arms for another month.

Our army seemed little affected by this victory; it did not cause any confusion or laxity whatever, and except for about half a mile square, in the vicinity of the Williamsburgh road, there was little to disturb the peace and quiet of our lines in the sunshine of Sunday morning. Except for the ambulances and carriages, conveying away the wounded to Richmond, there was little to indicate the slaughter of twelve thousand Federals the day before. Our own actual loss was not more than a third of that number, incredible as it may seem.* There was much inquiry among the soldiers at other parts of the line regarding the particulars of the engagement, but the victory was looked

* General Johnston says, in his report: "We took ten pieces of cannon, six thousand stand of arms, one garrison flag, four stand of regimental colors, a large number of tents, besides much camp equipage and stores. Our loss was four thousand two hundred and eighty-two killed, wounded and missing; that of the enemy is stated by their journals to have been ten thousand, although, no doubt, that figure is far below the truth."

In the following address, the President, from his own personal observation and his past career, has shown himself to be a judge of good fighting, for none have fought more bravely than himself. Such testimony and such praise will appeal gratefully to the feelings and pride of our army, and will excite still more that affectionate gratitude for them which animates our whole land. For no halting testimony and no niggard praise does the President pay our heroes: "Nothing could exceed the prowess with which you closed upon the enemy, when a sheet of fire was blazing in your faces!" Noble men! The President says, he can neither ask nor desire any thing better:

"*Executive Office*, June 2d, 1862.

"To the Army of Richmond.

"I render to you my grateful acknowledgments for the gallantry and good conduct you displayed in the battles of the thirty-first of May, and with pride and pleasure recognize the steadiness and intrepidity with which you attacked the enemy in position, captured his advance intrenchments, several batteries of artillery and many standards, and everywhere drove him from the open field.

"At a part of your operations it was my fortune to be present. On no other occasion have I witnessed more of calmness and good order than you exhibited while advancing into the very jaws of death, and nothing could surpass the prowess with which you closed upon the enemy when a sheet of fire was blazing in your faces!

"In the struggle in which you are on the eve of engaging, I ask, and can desire, but a continuance of the same conduct which now attracts the admiration and pride of the loved ones you have left at home.

"You are fighting for all that is dearest to men; and though opposed to a foe who disregards many of the usages of civilized war, your humanity to the wounded and the prisoners was the fit and crowning glory to your valor.

"Defenders of a just cause, may God have you in his keeping.

"Jefferson Davis."

"The General will cause the above to be read to the troops under his command."

The following, printed in extremely large type, appeared, by General Butler's orders, in his organ, the *New-Orleans Delta*, June twelfth, 1862: "On May thirty-first, Richmond was evacuated, and General McClellan took possession of the city! General Banks had driven Stonewall Jackson headlong to the foot of General McDowell, who before this had probably kicked him over the border. So end the drama!—it is enough " (!) Comment is unnecessary.

upon as a matter of course. Notwithstanding the vigilance of guards, many persons from Richmond rode out to see the field, but invariably brought something for the wounded, and took one or more to town in their conveyances; oftentimes providing for them in their homes, tending them with paternal care, and paying private surgeons to treat them rather than allow them to be roughly handled in the Government hospitals. Too much praise cannot be bestowed on the noble-hearted Virginians, male and (particularly) female, who were ever ready with open arms to succor the poor, ragged, bleeding Southern boy, fresh from the field of victory; for had many of us been sons rather than strangers to them, their care, comforts, watchfulness, and Christian charity could not have been greater. The loving care and kindness bestowed on our unprepossessing, ragged soldiery can never be effaced from the memory of any who saw it on this and numerous other trying occasions.

CHAPTER XXVII.

Further Details of the Chickahominy Battle—Longstreet succeeds to the Command—General Lee the acknowledged Chief—Skirmish at Fair Oaks, an Episode—Gossip of Officers—Scenes and Incidents of the Battle—Our Negro Servants—The Louisiana Zouaves—Brigadier-General Jenkins and the South-Carolinians—Care of our Wounded in Richmond—Hospital Scenes.

DURING the week it was confidently expected the enemy would marshal their forces, and make a rush upon us in retaliation for the thrashing we had given them; and to be prepared for such emergency, our Generals held their troops well together, and the utmost circumspection seemed to guide all plans and dispositions of force. Owing to the frightful gash Johnston had received, the command devolved on Longstreet, or seemed to do so by common consent, for though Gustavus Smith and others, perhaps, ranked before him, their energies were taxed in offices that became them more than "field" operations. Lee was now seen on horseback more frequently, and scarcely a day passed without my meeting him ambling along the roads, and in all kinds of out-of-the-way places. Though naturally quiet, thoughtful, and polite, the responsibility resting on him rendered his deportment even more so than usual, and had a stranger met him, his manner was so quiet and placid, his dress so humble, and his gait so slow and unofficial, that he would never have recognized in him one whose genius and resources commanded the unbounded confidence and hopes of the nation.* Brigadiers, with couriers and orderlies at their heels dashing to and fro, would have presented a much more impressive idea of importance and dignity, than the meek, gray, haired gentleman who passed us a few minutes before, without uniform, or blazing stars on his shoulder-straps, or distinctive color.

* It was evident that Longstreet was chief in the field only until Lee should vacate his rooms in the War Office, and permanently assume command.

Alarms were frequent during the week, both night and day, and the Texans under Hood, down the railroad, and Wright's Louisianians and Georgians, down the Williamsburgh road, were continually popping at the enemy. These skirmishes were not of an important character, but since McClellan and the Northern press have manufactured out of them "a brilliant victory," which they term "Fair Oaks," it is necessary to give the reader some idea of an affair our men never termed more than a skirmish.

Some few days after the battle of "Chickahominy" or "Seven Pines," the enemy in possession of the old battle-ground vacated by us gave it to "Sickles's" notorious brigade to hold, and to signalize their occupation they attempted to drive in our pickets. The First Louisiana were then in front, and learning that the New-York "roughs" were in the vicinity, and occupied a small copse to the right of the road, and south of Barker's Farm, a plan was formed to advance, and drive them away. Without consulting General Wright, eight companies of this regiment assailed Sickles's men, and though the enemy were superior in number, they drove them out of the thicket with much loss. Enraged at their rough treatment, Sickles's warriors, being reenforced, advanced again, but were a second time repulsed. It was an unimportant affair, and as the ground was not necessary to us, the Louisianians retired to their former position, and nothing was said or thought about the matter. Several of their pickets were subsequently captured, who informed us that Sickles's "roughs" and Meagher's "Irish brigade" swore to be revenged.

Several days after, a North-Carolina regiment, not three days from home, which never drew trigger, were sent out on picket, and occupied the left of the road near Sickles's brigade; the Louisianians were on the right, in their old picket-grounds, and a Georgia regiment still farther to the right. General Wright's orders were to hold their positions, and, if attacked, reenforcements should be forthcoming. Sickles's men seemed to invite a combat, and the gallant Louisianians, nothing loth, advanced, drove in their outposts, occupied the thicket, and were advancing into the open ground after them, when three full brigades stood in view. The Louisianians, scorning to retire, were assailed with great fury, while flanking regiments moved on the right and left of the thicket, and waited for their retreat. Finding themselves overpowered, the Louisianians fell back through the wood, were followed up, and had to sustain a three-sided fire. Having secured themselves behind a fence, they continued the fight, expecting the arrival of reenforcements every minute. The North-Carolinians on the left, though perfectly raw, sustained an unequal musketry fire for three hours, and gave not an inch of ground. The same may be said of the Georgians on the right.

Seeing that our men were not reenforced, the enemy endeavored to get farther on our right, flank, and rear, by marching two regiments through the woods. But a Georgia regiment, (the Fourth,) hearing the continual fire, marched on our right through the woods to succor their brigade companions— the Louisianians—and, having a strong affection for them, were maddened to think they had been played such a trick and overpowered. This flanking party had not progressed far ere they unexpectedly came upon the Yankees quietly taking ground on our right and rear. A volley was instantly given, and a charge ordered. The enemy were amazed ; they were on our ground, and we on theirs; the fight was of but a few moments' duration, for the Federals fled, but, not knowing our exact position in the woods, came across several small parties, who slew them as they ran. The Georgians were fearfully excited on this occasion, and, disobeying all orders, rushed after the enemy, and often transfixed them to the earth. This affair was very short, but the carnage great, and occurring accidentally, aggravated the rage of the Georgians to an uncontrollable degree. This charge seemed to settle the. affair. Sickles, Meagher, and others, were disappointed, and retired very early to their original position, ours being exactly the same as in the morning. I should hardly have mentioned this affair in connection with "Seven Pines," fought but a few days before, but as the Northern press required some new "sensation" to counteract the effects of Casey's annihilation, McClellan accommodated them with a flaming and false account of this skirmish if I mistake not, he called it "the Battle of Fair Oaks," but the occurrence was really as here described, for I was on the ground and witnessed it from first to last.

I had been to Richmond, and was returning to camp, but,

passing down the Niñe Mile Road, stopped at an old wooden church, which had been converted into quarters by one of the Generals. While lighting a cigar at a fire before the door, I observed a black boy very busy with soup and chicken, and the odor was very agreeable and enticing. "Whose boy are you?" I inquired of the negro, as he handed me a live coal. "Why, Lor bress you, 'Massa Tom! doesn't you know dis darkey? Massa Frank is here, and all of them!" But before I could be gone, Frank came clanking along with his heavy spurs, and insisted on my dismounting. "Recollect we've got chickens, and the devil knows what all, for supper, so tumble down and join us; you can't better yourself much, these times!"

Without more ado, I hitched the mare to a tree, and entered the old church, which I found converted into a quartermaster's office, with a party of officers and privates engaged in cards. The pulpit was gone, the windows broken, the shutters converted into tables, and carpets used as make-shifts for blankets and bedding. Soap-boxes were our seats, an empty hogshead was turned on end and served as table, and an excellent supper was soon smoking before us. "I know you can't 'go' rye-coffee, Tom," said Frank, but, giving me a sly wink, introduced me to a bottle containing rye-whiskey. Pipes were lit, and cards resumed, but, preferring the open air, several of us sat on the doorsteps, or lolled on the grass round the fire, and were soon busy discussing the "Chickahominy" fight, or "Battle of Seven Pines," as the Yankees term it.

"How came it to be called 'Seven Pines?'" asked some one.

"From Federal accounts," said a grey-haired paymaster; "it seems there were discovered seven pine trees standing apart in an open field near Casey's head-quarters, and his encampment was called so after them. 'Tis a pretty name enough, but I think, as we defeated them so utterly, they should have left naming the field to us. It would have looked more modest. Johnston calls it the 'Battle of Chickahominy,' from the river that runs across our front and to their rear. It was up this river that the celebrated Captain John Smith sailed when captured by Indians in early days. These banks were the hunting-grounds of pretty Pocahontas who saved his life. The story would read better had Smith married the poor lass."

"Well," said another, "the locality is forever famous, but I see that McClellan, as usual, claims it as a 'victory.'"

"You were not foolish enough to suppose he would commence telling the truth at *this* stage of proceedings? It is true he is the best man they have, but when the North, displeased with Scott's defeat, were beating about for a successor, had not McClellan fed the national vanity by sending flaming 'sensation' despatches about his defeat of Pegram at Rich Mountain, Western Virginia, they would never have given him a thought; for it must be confessed politicians do not seek out and reward true merit, while any dependents remain unprovided for. McClellan has attained his present flattering position by falsehood, and will seek to maintain it in the same manner. Falsehood is their settled plan of action. You remember the column of lies that appeared after Manassas, Leesburgh, etc.

"They have the most fertile imaginations of any race on the globe, and could battles be fought on paper, and with woodcuts, instead of powder and sabre-cuts, the *Herald*, *Times*, *Tribune*, together with Harper's and Leslie's illustrated papers, would settle the business in gallant style. Their illustrations are certainly the most extraordinary productions of the age; it suits the multitude, 'pays' well, no doubt, and that is all any of them care for—they would squeeze a dollar until the eagle howled."

"I think the prisoners we took," said the major, "could give a version of 'Seven Pines' rather different from that published by McClellan. When Stone failed, and Baker fell at Leesburgh, McClellan was indignant at the idea that *he* was said to have ordered their unfortunate advance. Baker was dead and could not speak; Stone, who *could* speak, was immediately incarcerated in Fort Warren. If the commander-in-chief did not order that movement, who *did?* Casey is accused of imbecility and cowardice because he has suffered a defeat, and is now moved to the rear. But this system of falsehood and hypocrisy cannot last long, although I believe if the enemy were 'whipped out of their boots' they would still shout 'victory, victory,' as loudly as ever.

"There is no doubt that poor old Casey was sadly out-generalled and beaten by Johnston, but had not our attack been delayed on the right and left, we should have driven them all into the river. Did you hear that we captured Casey's private papers, public documents, etc.? It is so. A young man in the Twelfth Mississippi seized them and gave them to Whiting. Though the capture was important, and effected at great peril, the youth has never been complimented."

"Speaking of that regiment," said another, "I saw great bravery in one of their cooks. The darkies, as usual, *would not* remain in camp, but marched ·out with the rest, and fought behind their masters. When General Rhodes had pushed the enemy through their camps, capturing breastworks as he went, a ball struck him in the arm, and he became faint from loss of blood. As it seemed a critical moment, he refused to leave the field, but still cheered on his men as if nothing had happened. 'Archie,' a black boy, volunteered to go for water and bandages, and, mounting a horse, plunged along across the line of fire, and soon returned. The general was much relieved, and remounted. The enemy were now bringing forward their reserves, and as no reenforcements appeared to our rear, it seemed that, weary though all were, we should be compelled to 'stick it out.' Falling back into one of the redoubts, Rhodes turned the captured guns on their late owners, but his men were failing fast from fatigue and want of ammunition. Although the enemy maintained a fierce triangular fire, he defied all efforts to dislodge him, and was lost in volumes of smoke. 'Archie,' perceiving that his company was short of cartridge, volunteered to run the gauntlet and make his way to the rear. The distance was fully a mile, but this brave boy ran rapidly along, filled half-a-dozen haversacks, and brought back several well-filled cartridge-boxes found on the way. He had scarcely re-entered the redoubt when a fierce clatter of musketry told the advance of our supports, and the day was ours. The darkies, generally, behaved like trumps, but this case came under my own observation. Ben, there, smoking and grinning among the pots, had a hand in it, and has a full suit of regimentals, somewhere, taken out of their tents! But if you ever let all the soup boil way again, sir," said the major, smiling, "and run off to the fight, somebody's head will feel sore, Ben!"

Ben chuckled, and said he "didn't care for de Yanks, nohow; dey was no 'count anyways, 'cept make a big noise; couldn't hit a squirrel in a year, he didn't believe." The sound of a fiddle and darkies dancing to the rear of the church led Ben away, and the conversation continued.

The appearance of the prisoners was very dejected, and little information could be extracted from 'any of them. I saw one tall, hard-fisted Alabamian carrying a stand of captured colors, and conducting some dozen Pennsylvanians from the field, including the standard-bearer. The latter seemed contented with his fate, and joked good-humoredly about the fortunes of the battle. "He wouldn't have surrendered," he said, "but found himself surrounded by three regiments, and gave up instantly to the first man that appeared." The Alabamian denied this stoutly but jocularly; observing, in a whisper: "I found him sitting upon the colors behind a tree. Although I was alone, he made no resistance, but marched very quietly to the rear, anticipations of our tobacco-warehouses having no terrors for him."

"During the fight," said one, "I was much amused at the coolness of St. Paul's Louisiana Zouaves. They stood in line with North and South-Carolinians, but were very restive, because ordered to lie down in the brushwood and wait for orders. Their red breeches were a conspicuous mark for the enemy, but they lay so low, and kept up such a lively fire, that the enemy would not advance. 'Well, boys,' said General Anderson, riding up, 'the enemy are before us, and in strong force!' 'Did you say, "Charge them," general?' asked Goodwin, their commander. 'Yes, boys,' replied Anderson, 'remember Butler and New-Orleans, and drive them into h—ll!' No sooner said than done. This handful of determined men crept through the chapparal, until within fifty yards of the foe, and although exposed to a cross-fire, suddenly rose, rushed with a yell upon the Pennsylvanians, delivered their fire at fifteen paces, and routed them with the bayonet. This affair was witnessed by the whole left, but none comprehended why so few should have attacked so many. The charge was a brilliant but mad one, and the Zouaves suffered loss, for the enemy, discovering the smallness of their number, instantly re-formed, and poured in upon them a destructive fire. Our line instantly moved up, however, and the advance was again resumed. I afterwards saw some of these Zouaves conducting many prisoners to the rear, dozens being bandaged about the head and arms.

"These Louisianians seem to be great epicures, for scarcely one came off the field without having a well-filled haversack, and a canteen of liquor. Where or how they got these things is a mystery, yet I couldn't help noticing that many of the enemy were so affected by liquor as to be scarcely able to walk. I heard one of the Zouaves, sitting by the roadside, bathing his leg in a mud-puddle, swear he had shot four men that day, and would not grant quarter at all: their cry was, 'Orleans and Butler the Beast!' They gave no quarter, and expected none. One Louisianian, while drinking at a spring, was shot at; the Yankee missed fire, and then approached to surrender. 'I do not understand you,' said the Creole, in French, and despatched the unfortunate Dutchman with the bayonet. This sort of thing occurred several times during the day; the Louisianians were so exasperated at the thought that their homes were possessed by the enemy, that they all seemed to be blind with passion and revenge. Longstreet personally presented a fine battle-flag to this battalion a few days since, in highly complimentary terms."

"The South-Carolinians deserve praise," remarked some one, "and I am glad that Jenkins displayed himself to advantage on that occasion. He acted as brigadier, and I do not see why the Secretary of War does not make him a general. He is highly educated in military matters, and far surpasses many of those political generals who are incessantly blundering among us.*

* Brigadier-General Jenkins is said to be a Northern by birth, and was First Lieutenant First Artillery in the old service. He left the army, and was principal of a flourishing military academy near Charleston (South-Carolina) when the war broke out. He then raised a company, and was elected Colonel of the Fifth Regiment from that State. He afterwards recruited a regiment fifteen hundred strong, called the "First Palmetto Sharpshooters." His conduct during the whole war in Virginia has marked him as a very superior officer. He greatly distinguished himself at "Williamsburgh," (May, 1862,) and commanded a brigade at "Seven Pines," where his generalship was loudly praised even by Northern journals. He is comparatively young, and can do more with raw troops, or recruits, than any officer I have seen in the field, rapidly bringing them up to a high state of efficiency. He has been wounded several times; but as long as 'tis possible to sit in the saddle, so long will he lead, and his fine voice can be heard far and wide. As a disciplinarian, he has few equals; and even when cannon are roaring in front, he gallops

The Northern papers are loud in their praise of the steady manner in which his troops advanced against all difficulties, and marched over heavy abattis up to and into their batteries. It was a grand sight, indeed, to witness that memorable advance. Nothing could stop them; our ranks were shattered by shell and grape, yet the gap was instantly closed up, and through swamp, over timber, across fields, through camps, our progress was steady and uninterrupted; officers in front, and men cheering and yelling like an army of demons. It is said that D. H. Hill lost many men, while waiting for his division to form, but soon made the enemy repay him with interest; for as his Alabamians, Louisianians, Mississippians, and Virginians rushed from the woods across the open, in splendid order, they carried position after position rapidly, and forced the fighting at a killing pace.

"Do you know I think our artillery acted indifferently. The truth is, we could not bring up pieces on account of the roads. Carter's battery did good execution; the Lynchburgh battery also. They drew their pieces by hand through the woods and along those boggy roads, and opened fire at twenty yards. I saw our guns not more than fifty yards distant from those of the enemy on several occasions; and when the fight was over the pieces stood almost muzzle to muzzle. We captured over a dozen very fine pieces. I myself counted twelve, and superb brass pieces they are—called 'Napoleon' guns, I believe."

"What should you say the general loss was?"

"As far as I can ascertain," said the major, "our killed and wounded would number about four thousand—not over that—besides a few dozen prisoners taken. General Hatton was killed on Saturday evening on the left. You must recollect that on Saturday morning down the railroad our men were surprised, and that, together with a few prisoners, Brigadier-General Pettigrew fell into their hands. The enemy confess their killed, wounded, and missing at nearly twelve thousand men, besides several standards and cannon. How many prisoners were taken I could not say, but I myself counted several hundred on their way to Richmond."

about, sharply reminding the men to "dress up! dress up there!" Should he live, South-Carolina may rejoice in the possession of such an officer.

Although the number of our wounded was not considerable, Government endeavored to provide comfortably for them; and for this purpose stores and warehouses, in various parts of the city, were fitted up, and surgeons, public and private, detailed to superintend them. There were several "committees for the wounded" in operation among the better class of citizens, and every thing that private means could do was devoted to the needy. From sunrise until sunset the bed-sides of our poor fellows were never deserted by kind friends, and I have known frequent instances where ladies attended, night after night, for weeks, fanning, washing, and feeding them; reading or writing for them, etc., so that the poor boys were oftentimes even bored by their many attentions and unceasing care. Scores were taken from military hospitals into private families, and tended for months, free of charge, and treated more affectionately than they might have been even at home. First-class surgeons gave their advice and attention gratuitously, and I know several medical men of standing who neglected lucrative practice to assist our men. Some took them home, and cared for them there; others instituted private hospitals for their proper treatment; and I remember instances where individuals have been comfortably provided with homes and proper scientific treatment for many months, not being allowed to depart until fully recovered from wounds or ailments. Frequently during the battle of "Seven Pines," I saw hundreds of citizens drive their vehicles near the battle-grounds, and convey away the wounded; to see a muddy, ragged, bandaged soldier lolling in a fine silk-trimmed carriage was no uncommon sight.

In fact, so great was the anxiety of citizens to carry off the wounded, that one of their omnibuses, approaching too near the enemy's lines, on Sunday morning, was captured by an ambuscading party, and carried off in great triumph as a rebel trophy. This omnibus was but one of many furnished by hotels for this humane purpose, and several were capsized in the mud, and rendered useless for all future service. The poor fellows seemed perfectly contented with their treatment, and lay in bed smoking cigars or drinking "brandy toddy," as happy as lords. In fact, many of them rather liked the change, and would not exchange their honorable scars for any amount. Cigars, brandy, fine food, and raiment, were such a contrast to rags, constant duty, hard fare, and incessant marching.

Some who came out of camp to visit these invalids would look round with almost a jealous eye upon the many comforts provided for them. Ragged, sunburnt, and ill-fed as they were, many could but jocularly smile, and good-humoredly wish some friendly bullet had thrown *them* into such comfortable quarters. When the wounded in turn visited their comrades in camp, their appearance was so much improved, they looked so bright and cheerful, and had so many stories to tell about pleasures and pastimes, that our doctors caught many feigning sickness, in order to be sent to hospitals in town.

The theatres were a great temptation, and as convalescents were permitted to attend them, with properly signed "passes," these places were nightly crowded with military audiences, scores having arms in slings or bandaged heads. Such pieces, such music, such yelling and laughter were never heard before; the poor Germans in the orchestra were tired to death with repeats of "Dixie," "My Maryland," and the "Marseillaise" — tunes which the audience accompanied with vocal efforts of their own, or embellished with a running accom. paniment of stamps and howling. "Blood-and-thunder" productions were greatly in vogue, and those pieces wherein most of the characters were killed, rose decidedly in the ascendant. "A tip-top fight" was what the boys delighted in, and an unlucky hero would never fall without an accompanying yell of "Bring on your ambulance!" Had these men had free access to liquor, its effect would have been disastrous; but this was successfully prohibited, thanks to the vigilance of the Provost-Marshal, General Winder.*

---

* Brigadier-General John H. Winder is a native of Maryland, and about sixty years of age. He entered the service as Brevet Second Lieutenant of Artillery, July first, 1820; resigned August, 1823; appointed Second Lieutenant First Artillery, April second, 1827; Captain First Artillery, October seventh, 1842; Brevet Lieutenant-Colonel First Artillery, September fourteenth, 1847, and commanded at Barrancas Barracks, (opposite Fort Pickens,) Florida, when the war began. He has been acting as Provost-Marshal-General at Richmond during the war, and renders essential service in that department; in truth, no half-dozen men could fulfil the labors of this eagle-eyed and indefatigable old man.

17

The greatest amount of affection seemed to be lavished upon privates; officers, for the most part, were treated coldly by the masses, and allowed to shift for themselves as best they could, for it was considered far more honorable to carry a musket than to loiter round Richmond in expensive gold-corded caps and coats. Volumes might be written upon the great kindness shown to our troops by the ladies of Virginia: although the women of Winchester, Leesburgh, Charlottesville, and other places, did much for the common cause, their noble-hearted and open-handed sisters of Richmond far surpassed them all. Nothing that human nature *could* do was left undone; and although much of this kindness and care were thrown away upon rude, uncouth objects, their humanity, patience, and unceasing solicitude are beyond all praise.

But what shall I say of the army doctors and nurses? *There was a great improvement!* On the field, they endeavored to do their duty; but surgeons of Virginia regiments evinced more care and anxiety than any others, and seemed to be far more skilful and expeditious. The field hospitals presented an awful sight. I entered one, but never desire to see another. It was an old dilapidated house, with scarcely any thing standing except the brick chimney. The sufferers lay inside and outside on straw, but such was the flow of blood, that all their garments, bedding, straw, and every thing around was of a bright red color. In one corner I saw a large pile of arms and legs; many already dead were lying on the grass, with blankets thrown over them, while not far distant, in the woods, a party were engaged in digging long trenches for sepulture. These things were passing under the eyes of all, and those just brought in from the field were spectators of operations going on, hearing moans and groans incessantly. Sickening as such sights were, our men bore up under it wonderfully well, and did not wince at all when called upon to take their place upon the unhinged door which served as an operating-table. Yet, how could all this be otherwise? Such is the reality of war, and those who paint it in glowing colors, with all the pomp and circumstance of triumph, should never fail to add a few words

of truth against encouraging the sacrifice of life for the sake
of ambition and unsubstantial causes. Had it not been for
the great love evinced for us by the good people of Richmond, hundreds of wounded would never have answered
roll-call again; and but for their paternal care, coupled with
the extraordinary exertions of Government, the increasing
warm weather would have added greatly to our bills of
mortality.

CHAPTER XXVIII.

DURING dinner on one occasion the subject of "imagination" came up, and I was very much amused with the views of all parties upon its "power and effects." There were several city and army doctors present, who, considering the subject to be an entirely professional one, would have monopolized all our attention ; but several broke in with their individual experience, and leaving others to decide what is, and what is not, imagination, told some very amusing and occasionally tragical stories regarding its "power and its effects."

"When the fight at Manassas had terminated," said Adjutant Flint, " being then in the ranks, I was detailed as one of a ' burying party,' and was out all night and most of the following day. As our regiment had been engaged near Centreville, I was hunting along the slopes for any poor fellow who required assistance, when my attention was called to moans in the bushes near by. I called some comrades, and began to seek for the sufferer. We found him leaning against a tree, near which a shell had exploded—his countenance was ghastly pale, and he rolled his eyes apparently in great torture. ' What's the matter, Lieutenant ?' I asked ; but he groaned and fell on his face. ' What can we do for you ?' inquired another. ' Oh ! leave me to my fate, boys,' was the sorrowful and faint reply. ' I'm dying every minute, and can't last long—I'm bleeding internally, and my blood is flowing fast ! Farewell to my own sunny South ; good-by, boys, and if any body shall ever visit Holly Springs, tell 'em that Shanks died like a patriot for his country, and shot four Yankees before he fell ! Give my love to the Colonel and all the rest of the boys, and when you write don't fail to give my last dying regards to Miss Sally Smith, if any on ye know her, and say I was faithful to the last.'

"Affected beyond all words by the poor lieutenant's simplici-ty and sufferings, we determined to carry him to the nearest am-bulance, and ask a doctor to look to his wound. We placed him in a blanket, and in solemn procession had proceeded about half a mile, when he positively refused to go farther. 'Let me down gently, boys, I can't stand shaking—there isn't much blood in me now, nohow, and I feel I'm passing away from this vale of tears and wicked world every minute, and can't last long.' A doctor was passing at the time, with sleeves rolled up, looking more like a gentlemanly butcher than any thing else; and in whispers we spoke of the condition of poor Shanks, who was now groaning more piteously than ever. 'I think he's bleeding internally, doc,' said I, 'for I don't see any blood, al-though his momentary contortions are awful to look at—if he wasn't suffering so much I should be tempted to laugh.' 'Where are you hit, lieutenant?' inquired the surgeon tenderly. Oh! don't touch me, doc, pray don't—I'm mortally wounded under the left shoulder-blade, the ball has ranged downwards, and I'm bleeding internally.'

"In a trice Shanks's coat was cut in all directions, but yet there was no wound visible, until, to stop his lamentable groans the surgeon asked again: 'Where *are* you hit—don't groan ever-lastingly, Shanks, but place your hand upon the wound, and let's see what can be done for you.' The place indicated was as sound as any part of his body, and after searching in vain for half an hour, and cutting the clothes off his back in search of blood, the doctor gave Shanks a slap on the seat of honor, laughing as he said: 'Get up, Shanks, and don't make a fool of yourself any longer; you are as sound as a trout, man—your wound is all imaginary.' We all began to laugh heartily, and were about to take signal vengeance on him for making us carry him half a mile through the mud and bushes, when Shanks jumped up as lively as ever and threatened to whip any man who should dare laugh at him—a threat that would have been fulfilled to the letter. I was sorry for the poor fellow, but learned that a shell had burst within a few feet of him, and feeling certain that he was wounded by a fragment, he suffered all the symptoms of a wounded and dying man; in proof of his sincer-ity, poor Shanks had lain out in the rain all night, and when we found him, he looked the most lamentable object for a first lieutenant that can possibly be imagined. The story got wind in some mysterious manner, and Shanks always had an engagement on hand to 'whip somebody,' until at Gains's Mill he fell mortally wounded; he was the last line captain left in his regiment, all his confreres having dropped in less than an hour."

" This war has caused many of us to rise," said Captain Todd, reflectingly ; " but how long any of us will remain in the land of the living it is difficult to say. At Bull Run I was orderly of my company, and felt greater pleasure in carrying a musket than wielding a sword as at present. The enemy were swarming across Blackburn's Ford in great force, and we, as skirmishers, received them with a brisk and deadly fire until ordered to fall back. Our captain had fallen within a few feet of me, with his face to the enemy, and for a long time we fought around him like tigers, and finally carried off the body. I felt sensible that a shot had grazed my side, and was very faint. To fall then was to be thrown into the enemy's hands so mustering all possible strength, I managed to get back to the regiment, which was re-forming some little distance in the rear, preparatory to at- tacking the enemy in line. The excitement and bustle of the moment drove all other thoughts from my mind—we fell in, ad- vanced, delivered our fire, and repelled the enemy very hand- somely ; but while reloading, I thought of my wound, and felt a sharp pang in my side, which, together with drops trickling down, made me certain I was seriously hurt; the musket fell from my hands, and I fainted.

" I had not lain many moments when the noise awoke me to consciousness, and I tore open my jacket, pulled off my shirt and reduced it to rags. I applied the bandages to my side, and felt relieved, although I was so sickened with the sights around me that I forebore to look at my own hurt. Removing one bandage and replacing another I saw no blood, and to my as- tonishment discovered I was uninjured. Had any one discover- ed me at the moment I should have died from mere shame, for I could have sworn my hurt was a serious one. The truth is, a shot must have passed very close, for my jacket was cut ; but the drops I felt trickling down were nothing but perspira- tion, and the sudden pang naught but a sudden rush of cold air upon my exposed person. I could never have imagined the possibility of my being so deceived by imagination, but yet such is the candid fact. During the day I heard several complaining of dislocated shoulder-blades, broken ribs, etc.; but these generally were imaginary hurts arising from the concussion of shot or shell. At Drainsville I saw one young man lying under a tree, and his left arm seemed lifeless; he said it was hanging by a few shreds to the shoulder, but he had not looked at it. Upon examination I saw that a shell must have passed very close, for the flesh was puffed up considerably; yet beyond this the doctors said there was no injury. The concussion had caused the swelling. I have frequently seen men fall from this cause, and remain senseless for a long time; and several in our regiment have become hopelessly deaf in the same way. My hat has been blown off twice by the rush of air, and I have more than once felt my cheeks tingle, and grow hot from the closeness of shots."

"But this is all one-sided," said Lieutenant Small. "I have known imagination to work as powerfully with members of the profession as upon their patients. When the wounded were being brought into the churches of Leesburgh, friend and foe were accommodated alike with whatever we had, and the ladies were working like angels in various offices of mercy and kindness. Outside one of the churches a tent was raised for the reception of the dead. I sought for a poor friend of mine among the many bodies, and found two Yankees, thrown in among the others. They were sighing, and I immediately pulled them out, placed a body under their heads for a pillow, and examined their hurts. One had received a shot in the left eye; being a common round musket-ball, it had passed round the skull, and come out at the left ear. In the second case, the ball had passed in a direction exactly the opposite of this. They were not dead, and I felt annoyed that they were thrown aside to die, while many of their comrades were comfortably provided for in churches and schools.

" The doctors were busy and treated me like a Union sympathizer, and to my appeals on behalf of suffering humanity, swore roundly that they had something more important to attend to, particularly as the two Yankess were pronounced by all the faculty as 'hopeless cases.' My appeals to the ladies were answered by instant kindness. They proceeded to the 'dead tent,' and told me these sufferers had been there all day, and were considered dead. I procured some excellent whiskey for them, their faces were washed, more spirit was administered at proper intervals, food was given, and to the astonishment of all the doctors these two fellows were walking about the streets of Leesburgh in less than three days, comfortably smoking their pipes, or fighting their battles over again round the fire of the mess-rooms. I know, too, an instance of a young man who came off the field of Manassas, with a cloth tied over the top of his head, and was begging all to pour cold water on it, for a shell had passed so close as to scalp him. Upon examination he proved to be unhurt, but the concussion was so great as to cause all the feeling of being scalped, nor could he be convinced of the contrary until after looking in the glass, when he exclaimed, with great naïveté : 'Well, I'm mighty glad the har is thar, but if I didn't think I war scalped by that ar shell, you can just shoot me, that's all; for them whizzing, screechy things make my head ache and knees to tremble just to think on 'em! So I an't scalped, doc, eh? Well, if I didn't think I was, I be darned! particular as my head feels half off even now, and I can't hold my neck straight to save my life.' "

" I had a patient at Warrenton," said another, " who caused me much annoyance and vexation. The wound was in his thigh, but he persisted in saying that the ball had not been extracted, though any one could see from the character of the wound that the shot had passed out. For several days I tried to convice him that he was progressing favorably, but as soon as my back was turned he represented my cruelty to him in such fearful colors that the brigade surgeon came and had angry words with me. I explained matters, and upon examination he apologized, laughingly, and said he would perform the operation himself. My former patient, on learning that the brigade surgeon was about to work upon him, seemed in ecstasies, and would not allow me to go near him again, saying to himself: 'I have found one among the crowd who understands my case, and that darned ball will come out at last.' At dressing-time, the brigade surgeon appeared before my thick-headed patient, made a terrible display of his instruments, and asked Number Five 'if he was ready?' The parade of knives and lancets did not move a muscle of Number Five; rather he seemed pleased, and the mock operation proceeded. His thigh was properly dressed, and after several flourishes of the probe, a ball was shown to the patient, who seemed much rejoiced, and smoked his pipe with greater pleasure than ever. His health began to improve daily, and he was soon convalescent, but all the kindness in the world could not make him like me as at first, and although it was explained to him subsequently that the operation was only a 'sham,' he persisted in thinking the brigade surgeon a fine fellow and myself a fool."

The conversation soon changed to other matters.

"I beg leave to differ with you, Captain, upon that point," said one. " I cannot believe that the universal sentiment of the Charleston Convention *was* in favor of Stephen A. Douglas: there were many there who even knew more of the true char- acter of the man than *I* did, and were fully aware that a person of his unsatisfactory standing could never be the standard-bear- er of the South, and bring about that reconciliation which was long necessary between the North and ourselves. The idea of secession was not a new or strange one. All who have studied the current of adverse views for the past few years are as fully aware as myself of the fact that the leading men of all sections saw the inevitable result which the fanaticism and power of the North would bring about; and it was the object of the South to prove how much the North loved us by seconding our proper candidate, John C. Breckinridge. It was the proof that we needed, and finding the North resolved to crush out all our hope of justice or a fair hearing in the councils of the nation, it was determined to make a bold push for freedom, and forever separate from those who, from the mere accident of possessing power and numerical strength, were determined to out-vote all our propositions, right or wrong; to carry the high hand of power over us, and force us into a state of uncomplaining ac- quiescence; and to quietly become, once and forever, the hum- ble producers of those staples, the handling and exportation of which were annually enriching them and impoverishing our- selves. The natural excellences of our coast for harbors and arsenals were never looked into; lighthouses, breakwaters, and repairs were never considered; we had no right to suppose that dockyards and the like should be placed South, for these things might eventually increase our prosperity, and that *must* not be!

"Then, again, territories were crowded by Northern immigration, so that the political balance should always remain with them; railroads could not be constructed South to the Pacific — better routes were always found North, and when private enterprise was excited to compete, Government appropriations were always made to Northern speculators. Even the routes of our commonest products were always directed Northward for exportation and trade, and for many years there seemed to be a settled plan with Northerners to favor all that pertained to themselves, and ignore our commonest rights and interests. The results are, that the tide of emigration has always been guided North. The army and navy establishments were always located there; Government works and improvements were to be found there only; private enterprises of a national character were always well patronized and protected there; and, although not a manufacturing people, whatever spirit of emulation or competition was exhibited among us, it never met with favor. In all things their maxims were apparent: 'We are more numerous, and will rule as it suits ourselves — *our* interests must be always attended to — we know nothing of the rights, privileges, or customs of those who did most to gain our independence; all we know and remember is — *ourselves!*'

"These are not *my* ideas alone, but the sentiments of the whole South. Were not Douglas, Buchanan, Pierce, Dickinson, and infamous Butler, supposed friends of the South, fully aware of all these grievances, and did they attempt to ameliorate our condition, or seek to obtain for us common justice, or even an impartial hearing? Ambitious as they were for favor, the North was always courted, as being the most populous, and whatever praise they seemed to bestow upon us was qualified in such a manner as to be construed in *any* way. Douglas, of whom much has been said, was *not* a truthful or reliable man, for it is on record that in his campaign against Lincoln for the Senatorship in Illinois, his speeches were adapted to suit communities; so that what pleased those of Chicago — namely, a mild sort of abolitionism — was changed into ultra-Southernism in the lower counties of the same State. Much of the same hypocritical style was adopted by his opponent Lincoln, who, had he expressed the sentiments in Massachusetts, openly' avowed in Southern Illinois, would have been mobbed and hooted through the public streets. This is not hearsay, but *positive knowledge* orally obtained during their canvass of the State."

"It seems providential," remarked another, "that the disruption of the Union *has* taken place, and especially at this time, for the North was gaining ground too rapidly, and insensibly reducing us to servitude. A longer delay would only have added greater odds against us, as the election of Lincoln fully proved that no respect was paid to the feelings or interests of the South. We had forewarned the North, moreover, of the consequences — we had solemnly done so — it remained with them, therefore, to prove their *disinterested* love of the Union by electing one that should have satisfied both parties. When a contract is made by several for their individual and united good, it betrays bad faith in any to attempt imperialism or despotism, because time and fortuitous circumstances may have enriched them, individually, at a greater rate than others. The old compact was made for the *good* of the several States making it, nor were local institutions objected to, in the days when Southern troops marched through Massachusetts, and New-Englanders remained at home."

"There is a decided difference in blood, climate, and predilections," said a third. "It is said we are come from a common stock; but certainly the hot blood and high-toned spirit of the South cannot be one with the icy, fanatical, psalm-singing Puritanism of Massachusetts. Is it not rather traceable to the courtly, plumed, and belted cavaliers of Maryland and Virginia — men whose lineage is traceable through heraldic honors, who carried swords by right of birth — and not those whose history, either in their old or their new home, could not be brought to light without causing them to blush? The North, in short, has supplied a field of enterprise in which but little capital was necessary, and hence it has become the common receptacle of all races and classes of men, while few have journeyed South, where comparatively large means were necessary to start them in competition with the residents. Some, like birds of passage, have come to enrich themselves, but not to settle as permanent residents in a country whose productions, climate, manners, and resources were totally unlike all to which they had been formerly accustomed. 'It cannot be denied by any who have lived in the South, and studied its character, that we have intermixed less with in-comers than those of the North."

"I agree with those views in the main," said one, "yet I cannot but think that much blame is due to us for our habitual carelessness and apathy in things pertaining to our rights and necessities. We have looked upon human nature incorrectly, and attributed to it more honesty and honor than it possesses, and now we feel surprised to find the world other than we expected. We might have seen long ago, that, with a great influx of abolition feeling and atheism into the country, it was time to prepare for the 'irrepressible conflict;' instead of which, by remaining inactive, we allowed the deluge to burst upon us before the ark was ready. From the year 1832, when South-Carolina first seceded, and Jackson forced her back into the Union, until the present hour, it was clear to all that a disruption was inevitable, and ti behooved us to prepare for it as quietly as South-Carolina did, and not waste our energies in useless congressional debates, which could never wring one particle of justice from the absolutism of the jaundiced-eyed majority."

"'Tis true that our leaders did not exert themselves discreetly," said another, "or the same results could have been obtained with less cost. Except among a few, there was no system of united action; and those few, from paucity of means and insufficient influence, maintained profound secrecy and gave no inkling of ulterior objects. Calhoun and others spoke sententiously, and their hints contained volumes of meaning to the student; but the majority had such implicit confidence in the honesty and integrity of the North that any thing to the contrary would have been construed into downright treason, because too apathetic in watching the current of events and the 'manifest destiny' of our cause."

"That is correct," said another, "but it must be confessed that our statesmen have been more energetic and watchful since the time of Calhoun than before, and it is mainly owing to President Davis that our country has risen at all. Since his *début* in public life, Jeff has applied himself to the study of past history, and of men and measures. No one understands the wants and aspirations of the South better than himself, and from early manhood he has kept his own counsel and been patiently planning affairs as we see him now. In Congress he was ever willing to undertake any office or responsibility that might enlighten him regarding our peculiarities and resources; and his West-Point education gave him an assurance of his powers, which displayed themselves brilliantly and conspicuously in the campaign of Mexico. Indeed, our highest officers were jealous of his talent, and, viewing him as a dashing and ambitious Southerner, threw every conceivable obstacle in his way to prevent him from superseding them.

"When Jefferson Davis undertook the office of Secretary of War under Pierce, he was in a position for which he was preeminently qualified, and made himself perfect master of all that pertained to that office. There was not a fort or barracks throughout the length and breadth of the country which was not familiar to him, and at the same time he fixed his eye attentively on all the rising talent of the army, and made a note of those students at the various military and naval colleges who had distinguished themselves, and might leave the seclusion of private life under the pressure of times to come. There was scarcely one officer that came within his knowledge, whose qualifications, antecedents, sentiments, and ambition were not duly chronicled and remembered, so that when hostilities *did* eventually break out between us, Davis had but little difficulty in making judicious selections from whatever talent patriotically joined our ranks and cause.

"The knowledge that he acquired as Minister of War has proved of incalculable advantage to us, for he knows exactly what the North can and cannot accomplish, and fully understands all its resources beforehand. Whatever information he lacks is periodically transmitted through proper channels, so that he seems gifted with double sight, and astonishes the Cabinet at Washington by his accurate information of their designs and plans. Coming, as he did, in daily contact with such men as Scott, Lee, McClellan, Beauregard, Heintzelman, and a host of other talented officers, he could not be far from understanding the aspirations and particular qualifications of each: in fact, President Davis was the first to exclaim, from his thorough knowledge of the man, 'McClellan is the best officer they could select; but they will not keep him long!' a remark which seemed prophetic. Nor can we forget the part which Davis and his friends instigated Floyd, Cobb, and others to play when Cabinet Ministers to Buchanan—it may seem disreputable, but I don't think so, for self-preservation is the first law of nature. When it became evident that North and South could no longer live amicably together, and that dissolution was inevitable, Floyd, as Minister of War, prepared for the crisis by quietly sending the South her fair proportion of arms. The transaction was a secret one, but yet was commented upon by watchful men at the North. It was said, however, that we might soon be engaged with Spain or some other power, and that the South was the best location for them. Cobb, in the Treasury, did many things to embarrass the North, and facilitated all movements as best he could for our welfare and uprising. His financial abilities, or talents of any sort, were not much; but silence and discretion were all that was required of him."

Another remarked: "I cannot but admire the patriotism and alacrity with which army and navy officers joined the fortunes of their respective States; though they knew well that the declaration of independence was merely an 'experiment,' and that every chance was against us, for we had neither army, navy, nor resources of any kind. Many of these men were fast rising to eminence in the old service, and would have been comfortably provided for upon retirement. Much of their property was situated North, and all the expectations of years were at stake; but, old or young, they immediately surrendered every thing and offered their services to us, although for a long time our cause seemed one of Herculean labor, and devoid of prospective success.

"Lee, for instance, was considered one of the finest engineers in the service, and was second only to Scott in the estimation and love of the people. Albert Sydney Johnston stood perhaps higher as an active commander, but few, if any, surpassed him in a thorough knowledge of his profession, or greater ability in council. His property and effects were in Northern hands; he was offered chief command in the field; but he abandoned all, and, bereft of every thing, offered himself to his native State. Johnston, Beauregard, Van Dorn, Evans, Longstreet, Ewell, and a host of others, made similar sacrifices, and for a long time were without any settled rank or command. They had to fight their way up, and have successfully done so. The same may be said of the navy. Lynch, Tatnall, Ingraham, Hollins, and others, followed their illustrious example. Maury—the world-renowed Maury—had all to lose and nothing to gain by joining our cause; but he did so, and refusing the offers and hospitalities of kings and princes, busied himself, industriously, in any department where his services might be of value. Hollins, indeed, brought his ship with him, and was cursed for it from east to west by the North. We cannot expect to do much with our navy at present, but we have talent enough in the forthcoming times of peace to found a navy which shall eclipse the achievements of our army, if cruel necessity occasion its services to be called for. There are many still in the army and navy of the North who rightfully belong to us—some refused to believe in our ultimate success, and thought a bird in the hand was worth two in the bush; others resigned, but could not get South; some were accused of sympathy and imprisoned; while others quietly settled down into business, and now await the adjustment of affairs, to come and live among us."

"Yes, yes," said one, emphatically; "I expect there will not be scores only, but thousands expressing excellent Southern sentiments 'when the war is over,' and asserting their sympathies were always with us. There will *then* be thousands of Jews and Dutch willing to swear the same until black in the face; but if I am not mistaken, our people understand *that* question as well as Government, and will take more than usual care to protect themselves against the hordes which have been the chief movers and instigators of all the isms, usurpation, and despotism of the North. There are hundreds of democrats in New-York and other States, particularly in the West, who now sincerely regret that avarice and love of power prompted them to 'use' the fanatical masses to lift them into power, and habitually support measures which they knew were tyrannical and unjust. The people have already considered every phase of that subject, and will act discreetly in the future."

CHAPTER XXIX.

Talk about Slavery — Comparison of the Slave System with the Free-Labor System of Europe—Comfortable Condition of Negroes on the Plantations—Their Indifference and even Dislike to Freedom — Insincerity of the Northern Fanatics—Their Treatment of Free Negroes—-Crucial Tests of the Doctrine that all Men are born Free and Equal—The Question considered on religious and social Grounds—Attachment of Negroes to their Masters—Anecdotes.

"WELL, Tom, I have just received a letter from home, which informs me there is scarcely a white person in our whole parish!" said Frank, one evening after supper. "What if the darkeys should grow discontented and rise?"

"If there had been any such possibility," one replied, "the Yankee Government would soon have seized upon it for our destruction or chastisement. There is no likelihood of such an event, however. I know districts in Mississippi where there are not more than one or two old white men to a slave population of from three to five thousand. In fact, all our plantations are conducted by the negroes themselves, in the absence of overseers or masters. I have offered large salaries for overseers for my places, but they never stay long—they are all off to the wars. My wife informs me that all things are progressing quietly and favorably as ever—my mulatto boy Bob superintends the Upper, and Black Jim the Lower Place, and have raised excellent crops in my absence. Talk to *me* of our darkeys rising to massacre the whites! Why, I wager my life that all the inducements in the world could not draw off *my* servants from me. Most have grown up from childhood with me, and lived as I have done; and when one of these rabid Abolitionists counts the cost of keeping servants, he would be loth to expend as much upon white labor. Just look at Nick out there, round the camp-fire, kicking up his heels in a dance! that boy costs me much more — yes, double what I should have to pay for cook hire in Europe; and more than that, when he gets old,

18

no matter how much money he may have by him, I am compelled by law to provide for all his wants.

"Think you that the Major's boy would buy his freedom, although to my knowledge he has two thousand dollars in gold, hid away in an old stocking? You know as well as I do that all our boys are making money—some as much as twenty dollars per week — by washing, cooking, selling things, and the like, but reason with them about buying their freedom, at ever so low a figure, and they grin, jingle the dimes in their greasy pockets, and tell you: 'Massa libs better dan I kin, and when dis chile gets ole, Massa must take care ob him.' And sure enough we *must*. They argue, and to the point it seems to me, thus: 'I am Master's boy, and must do what he tells me. No matter what the price of things may be, I must be well fed and clothed, and my health carefully attended to by his own physician, or some other, even should he have to pay ten dollars for a visit. He gives me from one to two dollars every week for spending-money: I live in the house with him, grow up with him, attend him in all his sports: my wife lives with me, and he takes care of both, in sickness or health, in youth or age. If I do not act properly, he sells me, but few negroes are sold who mind their business.'

"Count up the cost, in times of peace, and tell me whether this, and my other boys, do not cost me more than two and a half or three dollars per week, the average wages of two thirds the laborers in Europe? And more than this, I cannot tell one of my boys, 'I don't need your services,' when grown old—the law forbids it, if even I were so inclined. But who would be inclined to part with a boy, even like grumbling Nick yonder, who played with him when a child, whose mother rocked him in the cradle, and whose father taught him the first use of a gun, how to swim, how to catch and ride a horse, and a thousand other things? There may be, and no doubt are, many who feel differently, but speaking for myself, I could *not* part with my negroes, even if assured that the capital invested in them would return me five times as much in ordinary commerce. They receive three suits of clothes every year, and shoes as often as they need; their holidays are fixed by law; in wet weather they are kept within doors; they have good, comfortable cabins, plenty of fuel, and little garden-patches to cultivate for themselves; as for their hen-roosts, they.are better stocked than my own. If I want eggs or garden-stuff, I buy from them, while Nick yonder, and several other of my boys, have full license to cut all the timber they desire into cord-wood, and sell it to steamboats for their own pocket-money. Three of these fellows have sold four hundred dollars' worth of cord-wood to the boats in one year; many other boys also, and none of the masters ever get a cent for the timber. In fact, I have frequently acted as clerk for them when in the field, and sold hundreds of cords to steamboats—the money being handed over to the black rascals, who trot off to the first show and spend it. I tell you, Tom, you cannot induce one of *my* boys to leave me, at any price. My motto is: 'If my servants are discontented with all I do for them, let them run off if they choose.'· They always come back again, I notice, and behave better than before."

"It would seem," said one, "that the Federals are greatly mistaken in their estimate of the negro. But if they *are* equal to the whites, why do not Northern fanatics give their fair daughters in marriage to them? They talk much of the equality of the races, but tell me, are Hottentots socially your equals? Would you be bothered with them as gratuitous servants? I think not. Lincoln, the high-priest of Northern anti-slavery fanatics, has publicly declared to a deputation of colored folks, that they are 'unfit to pretend' to equality, and that the best he could advise them was 'to go to Africa, their original land, or some other place, and raise settlements for themselves!' Arguments may be multiplied, but the same conclusion is arrived at, namely, that they are an 'inferior' race, and unfitted to cope with the whites. Northern fanatics groan, and say we should instruct them and elevate them. Why do not *they* do so? Is not Sambo *their* servant as well as *mine*? And are his colored servants paid, and fed, and clothed, and provided for in old age as mine are—as mine are *obliged* to be by law? No! When Sambo the waiter loses his robust appearance and solemnity of behavior, or Nancy, the cook, grows feeble over pots and pans in the kitchen, they are 'discharged'—no further responsibility rests with the employer, who has drawn from them all the wear and tear of years. Not so with us. We *must* take care of them—their misdemeanors are visited upon *us*, and disgrace those who own them.

"As for going to church, there are no objections—there *can* be none; and, believe me, my darkeys go more frequently than *I* do, and have tri-weekly meetings among themselves. This is encouraged; for the more pious a negro is, the better servant he becomes in every sense of the word. If he chooses to leave me, and pay for his hire, he can follow any business that pleases him best. I have now two boys who have so hired themselves from me at five dollars per week, who in barbering or blacksmithing make thrice that sum, and have large savings in the bank. Think you I could 'prevail' upon either of them to buy their freedom at one thousand dollars or fifteen hundred dollars each? Why, they would laugh at the proposition. They know well that as long as they do their duty, I have nothing to say, but protect them against every one; but if they get 'their back up,' as we say, put on airs, or disobey, I thrash them as I would my own son."

"In running off our negroes," said another, "the Federals are much in the situation of a man who bought an elephant at a sale because it was cheap! they do not know what to do with Sambo. They make him work incessantly at breastworks and feed him indifferently; but, as yet, we have done all the ditching ourselves, and Nick yonder laughs when we return to camp wet and hungry. Of the two, he is by far the better off. Do you know that these boys charge ten cents per piece for washing clothes, and without soap? By Jupiter, they are making money, and I have serious thoughts of entering that business myself. But jokes aside, old Alick, who was offered his free papers for a three hundred dollar bill, has made fifteen hundred dollars this past year, and now does business with a horse and cart, charging his master five prices for every thing, the old rogue!

"What the Federals will do with the darkeys is difficult to say. When peace is declared they will nearly all return home; some of them have already escaped from the tender mercies of the Yankee, and are in 'Dixie' once again, fully determined to travel away no more. You know Pete? Well, when I was in

Canada, the little fool took up a notion that he must be 'free,'
and accordingly ran off. I did not trouble myself about him,
but hired a white boy to wait on me, and found it much more
inexpensive. When I was about to return South again, up turns
the rogue Pete, and with tears in his eyes begged me to take
him home! he had spent all his money, and found it difficult
to live as a 'free' man. I know several wealthy darkeys in
Louisiana—much richer by far than I am—who own plantations and make splendid crops of sugar and cotton. In fact,
the free boys of New-Orleans raised a battalion fifteen hundred strong, and offered themselves for service to Davis,
but were refused! Their flag had for motto: 'We never surrender.' Think you one could prevail upon any of *those* fellows to leave home? Freedom, however, does them no good—
they have all the vices, but few virtues of the white, and are
rather a nuisance to communities than otherwise. The free
State of Illinois forbids negroes of any stamp to reside there,
under heavy penalties. State Legislatures have enacted laws
forbidding free darkies to remain in many of the cotton States,
for their habits are injurious to the morals of those in servitude.
But how do they evade it? Why, rather than leave, and live
in free States, ninety-nine out of every hundred bind themselves to masters again for form's sake, and thus remain with
us."

"If the negro is really so unhappy as Northern orators pro-
claim, why do our servants go to battle with us?—how comes
it that officers *cannot* keep them from the front? You know as
well as I, that Dave behaved gallantly at Manassas, and received his free papers from the State of Mississippi—passed in
full legislative style—his price being paid to the owner by the
State treasurer; but what did Dave do? He still keeps to his
old master as before, and tells him to burn his papers if he
chooses, 'he's as free as he wants to be, while old massa libs!'
What induces these servants to fight for us? I ask again.
Who induced those two boys to leave their pots and pans, and
shoulder a musket the other day, and get shot? Not their
owners, certainly. What keeps our darkeys so quiet and industrious at home, now that we are away, tempted as they are by
Lincoln's emissaries? Surely one old white man cannot sub-

due three thousand blacks if they are discontented! Why, there are thousands of plantations in the South at this moment with no white person to look after them, save our wives or grandmothers! Do you find darkeys shouldering muskets and going forth to fight for Lincoln? In all my observations I never knew of but three negroes who were found in arms for Lincoln, and they were in the Fifteenth Massachusetts, and pretended to be dead when our black boys found them on the battle-field.* Do you think Nick out there considers a Northern darkey his equal? Tell him so!—you could not insult him more grossly than to insinuate such a thing!"

"There cannot be a doubt," said another, "that blacks have occasionally been treated very barbarously by owners, but it is against all logic to suppose that any one, let him be ever so brutally inclined, would wilfully cut, maim, or habitually illtreat, that or those which were to him a source of profit or income. It is the interest of a master to protect and well treat those that augment his riches, and to sustain, improve, and cultivate their physical powers, that they may continue to do so, even if State laws, heavy fines, or confiscation of property did not *enforce* it. This may account for the greater longevity of blacks over the whites.

"In our whole army there must be at least thirty thousand colored servants who do nothing but cook and wash—nine tenths of the ditching falls to *our* share—yet in all these thousands I have yet to hear of more than one hundred who have run away from their owners! This is true, although they are continually moving about with 'passes' at all hours, and ten times more frequently than masters: what greater opportunities could be presented for escape? They are roaming in and out of the lines at all times, tramping over every acre of country daily, and I have not heard of more than six instances of runaways in our whole brigade, which has a cooking and washing corps of negroes at least one hundred and fifty strong! Bostick lost one in a singular manner. The boy was sick, and his kind, brave old master gave Joe a 'pass' to go to his mistress in Georgia—a thousand miles away—together with fifty dollars

* This was written before the negro regiments were raised under General Banks at New-Orleans.

for his expenses, and fifty dollars pocket-money—all in gold. Joe went safely as far as Knoxville, when some of Parson Brownlow's disciples persuaded him to leave the cars, and stay in East-Tennessee as a 'free' man! That same night some of these Abolitionists waylaid the 'free' man Joe, their recognized colored 'brother,' robbed him, and then beat his skull in pieces! Bostick, the 'slaveholder'—that term which horrifies Northern free-thinkers—paid the best detectives he could procure, to find—heavily fee'd the ablest counsel to prosecute, if found—and finally offered a reward of five thousand dollars for the arrest of the murderers of his slave-boy Joe! Another boy ran away from our regiment, and crossed over to the enemy; he found how things were, and returned across the river to 'Dixie' again, under a shower of bullets. These are not solitary instances. Examples as much to the point as these might be cited by all."

"Major Walton, Chief of the Washington (New-Orleans) Artillery Corps, had a boy who ran away," said another, "and the rogue informed the enemy how things stood at Centreville during the winter months of 1861 and 1862. His description of our batteries was pretty accurate as to name and number, but when he attempted to describe their positions and bearings, his head was at fault. I know an instance of a boy who ran from the Eighteenth Mississippi, just before Manassas, July, 1861. He was recaptured during the engagement; for the Yankees putting him in the front, together with other runaways, made him very uneasy, so he slipped into our lines again, but was seized by two colored men, who observed the manœuvre, and was handed over to his master. His owner refused to see him, and the general wish of our servants was, that he should be hung or shot for a traitor! He was given over to them, and met a death at their hands more violent than any white person's anger could have suggested. Incidents of this kind, however, illustrative of the colored people's loyalty to the South, are too numerous and tedious for enumeration.

"Northern fanatics use the opening clause of the old Declaration of Independence, and say, 'All men are free and equal.' They pervert the true meaning of what Jefferson wrote, but if they believe it, in its widest sense, as they preach, why do not opulent Abolitionists equally divide their riches with negroes who brush boots? Jefferson was a scholar, a gentleman, and a Virginian, and could not mean it to apply in a social sense, or otherwise his own, and every other Southern State, would have seceded at that early day. It is from a wrong, fanatical construction put upon these words that Abolitionism has grown so rampant in the North, and been converted into an instrument for securing place and favor, and therewith the emoluments of office. If 'all men are free and equal' in the sense they pretend, the Hottentot, Aztec, Digger Indian, Cannibal, and Bar· barian are our brothers, and should eat, drink, intermarry, and share riches with us.

"True, in a spiritual sense, 'all men *are* free and equal;' each has a soul of immortal price to save, and the servant may rise higher than his master in spirituality—which many undoubtedly do. Against this we have nothing to say. But even here we see there is some kind of 'inequality,' or all men would be born under the Christian dispensation, and not require the labors of missionaries. One soul is equal to another before its Creator only in so far as each fulfils the law prescribed for it, but in every other sense the idea is a profound absurdity.

"Test the assertion that all are born equal in a social sense by a practical illustration. Does the black butler North marry his employer's daughter? Such an idea would turn the head of Lincoln himself! Or fancy a Northern cotton-spinner telling the poor boys and girls who work over seventy hours in the week for some three or four dollars of wages, that 'all men are born free and equal!' Would he not be amazed to find his poor emaciated employés demanding an equal partition of his profits? The difference of Capital and Labor is well understood by Yankees when it affects themselves; but although they eat sugar, rice, molasses, and grow rich from the produce of slave-labor, without the slightest qualm of conscience, they treat the negro, when amongst them, as absolutely below the relationship of consanguinity and social rights — yet insist that *we* are barbarians for treating them *more* humanely, because not admitting their chimerical absurdities regarding the abstract questions of human freedom. We are all slaves in some degree. Sovereign to sovereign, and man to man—it is in courts as it is on plantations; place holds its head above place, power above power, merit above demerit. There are inferior and superior animals; there are angels, archangels, cherubim and seraphim, all of God's ordaining; but while all harmonize in the grand conceptions of an all-powerful, all-wise Creator, talent and merit can always break the bonds of class, or of sphere, and ascend higher and higher forever!

"Did you ever remark our servants on a march? They make me laugh. Soon as the word 'march' is whispered abroad, these fellows bundle up their traps, and get them into the wagons, by some sort of sleight of hand, for I know that my baggage, with 'little tricks' added, far outweighs the authorized sixty pounds — a captain's allowance. After safely stowing away all they can, the cooks shoulder some large bundle of curiosities of their own, and with a saucepan, skillet, or frying-pan, all march some fifty yards in front of the band, whistling and singing, forming in regular or irregular files, commanded by some big black rogue who, with a stick and a loud voice, enforces discipline, among his heavy-heeled corps. And thus they proceed far ahead, monopolizing all attention as we pass through towns and villages, grinning and singing as they go, and frequently dressed up in the full regimentals of some unfortunate Yankee or other. They scour the country far and wide for chickens, milk, butter, eggs, and bread, for which they pay little or nothing; always stoutly swearing they have expended all 'massa' gave them, and unblushingly asking for more. Why, sir, I am positive Nick and our other boys beg or steal half they pretend to purchase; and yet do not fail to charge us, the 'cruel masters,' five times the ordinary value of the articles. Such is the wastefulness of these fellows, that our pay of one hundred and thirty dollars per month does not begin to furnish the table as they would have it even for their own eating. The other day I gave Andy ten dollars for market money, and the wretch brought me back two antiquated hens, and a pound of fresh butter, 'without a cent to spare,' as he solemnly swore! There is no such thing as making one joint serve twice—it doesn't suit them; and if you preach economy, the villains grumble without end, and think you are stingy, or, what is worse, whisper that 'Massa's gettin' like de Yankees, now he's up Norf!' "

"There's Benton yonder, singing a song among the pots," said another; "for two months he regularly went over the fields to Dr. Edward's, and asked for milk and butter 'for the sick,' and on returning to camp sold the former at one dollar fifty cents per gallon, and the butter at one dollar per pound! His master was enraged when informed of it, and made his hide tingle, for he is well treated and has enough to spend. Besides, these fellows not only cook for us, but hire themselves out to different messes, and what with charging the poor boys ten cents each for washing a pair of socks or a handkerchief, bartering, buying whiskey at five dollars per gallon, and retailing it at fifty cents each drink of one eighth pint, they are making lots of money, and frequently loan it out at heavy interest.

"I received a letter a few days ago which informed me that the darkeys of Vicksburgh gave a ball, and realizing one thousand dollars, handed it over 'for de boys in Varginny!'—for *us* their 'inhuman masters,' as Northern cant will have it. Not only in Mississippi, but the colored folks of every town in the South have given balls, parties, and fairs, for our benefit, and sent thousands of dollars, clothes, blankets, shoes, etc., for 'young massa and de boys.' In truth, our servants feel as much pride in this holy war as we do, and are ever ready, as we have frequently seen, to prove in battle ' dat de Soufern colored man can whip a Norfern nigger and de Yankee to back him!'"

"Until the present," said Frank, "I never thought our boys possessed half so much spirit as they do. Fight! why, you might as well endeavor to keep ducks from water as to attempt to hold in the cooks of our company, when firing or fighting is on hand. In fact, an order has been frequently issued to keep darkeys to the rear in time of battle, but although I lectured my boy about it, I was surprised to find him behind me at Manassas, rifle in hand, shouting out: 'Go in, massa! give it to 'em, boys! now you've got 'em, and give 'em h—ll!'"

"There was a very old, gray-haired cook in an Alabama regiment," Jenkins remarked, "who *would* follow his young master to the war, and had the reputation of a saint among the colored boys of the brigade; and as he could read the Bible, and was given to preaching, he invariably assembled the darkeys on Sunday afternoon, and held meetings in the woods. He used to lecture them unmercifully, but could not keep them from singing and dancing after 'tattoo.' Uncle Pompey, as he was called, was an excellent servant, and an admirable cook, and went on from day to day singing hymns among his pots round the camp-fire, until the battle of 'Seven Pines' opened, when the regiment moved up to the front, and was soon engaged.

"Uncle Pompey, contrary to orders, persisted in going also, but was met by another darkey, who asked: 'Whar's *you* gwine, uncle Pomp? You isn't gwine up dar to have all de har scorched off yer head, is you?' Uncle Pompey still persisted in advancing, and shouldering a rifle, soon overtook his regiment. 'De Lor' hab marcy on us all, boys! here dey comes agin! take car, massa, and hole your rifle square, as I showed you in de swamp! Dar it is,' he exclaimed, as the Yankees fired an over-shot, 'just as I taught! can't shoot worth a bad five-cent piece! Now's de time, boys!' and as the Alabamians returned a withering volley and closed up with the enemy, charging them furiously, Uncle Pompey forgot all about his church, his ministry, and sanctity, and while firing and dodging, as best he could, was heard to shout out: 'Pitch in, white folks — uncle Pomp's behind yer. Send all de Yankees to de 'ternal flames, whar dere's weeping and gnashing of — sail in Alabamy; stick 'em wid de bayonet, and send all de blue ornary cusses to de state ob eternal fire and brimstone! Push 'em hard, boys! — push 'em hard; and when dey's gone, may de Lor' hab marcy on de last one on 'em, and send dem to h—ll farder nor a pigin kin fly in a month! Stick de d—d sons of ——! don't spar none on 'em, for de good Lor' neber made such as dem, no how you kin fix it; for it am said in de two-eyed chapter of de one-eyed John, somewhar in Collusions, dat —— Hurray, boys! dat's you, sure — now you've got 'em; give 'em goss! show 'em a taste of ole Alabamy!' etc. The person who saw Uncle Pompey," added Jenkins, "was wounded, and sat behind a tree, but said, although his hurt was extremely painful, the eloquence, rage, and impetuosity of Pomp, as he loaded and fired rapidly, was so ludicrous, being an incoherent jumble of oaths, snatches of Scripture, and prayers, that the tears ran down his cheeks, and he burst out into a roar of laughter."*

"Their devotion to dead or wounded masters," said another, "has been exhibited on so many trying occasions, that allusion to it may be unnecessary; but I have seen examples of it, which · were never exhibited by brothers or relations. They would search for whole nights and days for a wounded master, and pull off their own coats to keep him warm, tear up their shirts for bandages, and in lieu of a stretcher, carry him to hospital on their backs! Nor did danger terrify them. Directly the fact was known that 'Massa' had fallen, the hunt for him immediately commenced, whether the action was over or not; and I have seen several instances where the poor boys have been wounded while dragging their masters out of action. At present, little notice is taken of these things, for matters of greater importance attract attention, but it cannot be that acts of such self-sacrifice and devotion will escape notice in times to come. Although more bother, expense, and anxiety than they are worth, I am sure that old associations are so strong, we would not part with our negro servants for any price. In sickness they are ever watchful for our safety, as in the hour of danger; and many a score of boys have I seen weeping by the road-side, when it was known master had fallen.

"The stories our boys send home about the war are vastly amusing. Some of the young soldiers frequently write for them; a few nights ago, while I was reading, Sergeant Smith,

---

* Among the incidents of battle near Richmond, the following amusing scene is said to have occurred near the Mechanicsville road. The Eighth and Ninth Georgia were ordered out to repel the enemy, when, upon the men falling in, one of the Ninth stepped from the ranks and told the captain, "he wasn't able to face the music." "You are scared," said the captain; "lay down your gun and accoutrements, and retire, sir." The chicken-hearted gentleman did so, when shortly afterwards there stepped forward a good-looking darkey, named Westley, well known in camp, who asked permission to put on the deserted accoutrements, and shoulder his gun. The request being granted, Westley followed the company into action, and though the shells and Minié balls of the enemy were falling thick and fast about him, Westley never wavered, but brought down a Yankee at every fire. Such a deed is worthy of remembrance, and should inspire our soldiery with tenfold energy and courage, if possible, for if servants will do this, what may not be accomplished by the master?

in the next tent to me, was good-naturedly writing an epistle to the wife of Yellow Jim, who stood by, dictating what to say. 'Tell her, Massa Smif, ef yer please, dat I'se gettin' on blazing, dat de Yanks is scared an' won't fight. Tell her I'se gwine to save all my money, an' will bring home lots of tings from de battle-fiel. Tell her I'se got a big shell what fell among de dishes todder day, and dat when it busted, it knocked de turkey an' soup higher dan a kite — which it did: but *dis* chile wasn't on hand about dat time, for he heern it screechin' an' comin' along, an' he just lay low behin' a big oak, four feet thick! but you needna tell her dat, Massa Smif, kase she mought tink I was one ob dem skary darkies, which ebery body knows is a lie; for I woughpt big black Bill todder ebenin' in less nor no time, Massa Smif, an' made dat black nigger's head bigger dan de soup-kettle — ask all de boys ef I didn't! And tell her, Massa Smif, ef *you* please, dat de kernal and all de big boys sez I'm de best cook on de place, 'cept *your* nigger, Massa Smif. And tell her I'se been totin' about a whul lot o' tings for her, an' has a Yankee gineral's clothes, which I'se gwine to ware de fust time I sees her; and say I sends 'spects to ole massa and all de folks up to de house, an' dat young massa hasn't woughpt me neary once since I'se been in ole Virginny, and says he's goin' to give me my 'papers' when de war is over, if I wants to. You needn't tell her, Massa Smif, dat de guard put me in de Calaboose for getting tight, for young massa's been in dere twice for the same ting. Any body gets tight once in a while,' etc."

CHAPTER XXX.

" *Charlottesville, June 20th,* 1862.

"DEAR FRIEND: In my last I informed you that before
Jackson left Page Valley to attack Banks's rear in the Shenandoah, Shields had already left, and gone eastwards across the
Blue Ridge, towards Fredericksburgh; also, that Fremont was
across the Alleghanies, with Milroy and Blenker, too distant
to afford Banks any support, so that we were enabled to attack
him with impunity. You will remember that Banks, after his
route, crossed the Potomac, and that our army remained in possession of the immense booty we had taken. I will now relate
the events that followed.

"Jackson was now anxiously watching the movements of
Shields and Fremont, who from the east and west might cross
the mountains, re-enter the valley, and cut off his retreat. We
had not lain idle more than a week, when it became known that
both those commanders had turned the heads of their respective
columns towards Strasburgh, *fifty miles to our rear,* and were
rapidly marching to that point, thinking that, should they
reach there in time, we might be compelled to accept battle
from their joint forces (thirty thousand) or surrender at discretion. Thus menaced, it was obviously necessary for Jackson to
hurry on his movements, and he did so with more than usual
expedition. Having destroyed all the baggage that could not
be transported, he turned his column towards Strasburgh, and
commenced a backward movement in the last days of May.
The roads were in fair condition, and marching very rapidly,
we drew near the town on the third day. Little rest was allowed, and all pushed forward with remarkable celerity.

"As we approached Strasburgh, our advance cavalry were

opposed by the enemy on the Pike, and were positively informed that Shields and Fremont were already there. These commanders, however, had not formed a junction, but were in sight of each other—the first-named on the east, and the latter on the west side of the Shenandoah River, which at this point is not very wide. So long as they had not joined their forces Jackson cared but little, feeling confident of soundly thrashing either of them; indeed, he would not have hesitated to attack both had they stopped his march. We had destroyed all the bridges in our route, and as Fremont could not well attack us on the flank, and Shields was doomed to be a spectator for want of bridges to cross, Jackson boldly marched forward, drove in Fremont's Dutch cavalry, took up a position between two mountains, and offered battle to Fremont, or to both, should they choose to join forces for that purpose. Fremont was mortified to find Jackson so strongly posted, and as he could not be flanked, and his troops were unreliable for a desperate attack in front, he deferred all movements for a few hours, hoping that in the mean time Shields could devise means for crossing.

"Those few hours' delay were ruinous to both Federal commanders, for during the night Jackson decamped, and in the morning Shields and Fremont looked in vain for him. The weather now proved unfavorable for fast marching, and rain began to pour in torrents, rendering the roads impassable. Still, onward pushed our army down the Pike, as hard as mortals could go; for there was no doubt our successes and escapes had greatly exasperated the enemy, and, numerous as they were, and perfectly fresh, they would leave nothing undone to overtake and punish us, *if they could.* Dashing along the muddy roads as best we might, Ashby and his cavalry in the rear skirmishing and bridge-burning, we endeavored to reach Mount Jackson, that point being considered a place of safety. It was surmised by some that Shields might push through Page Valley and appear in front, while Fremont followed up the rear; and this he might have done, had he been daring enough to attempt it. Still marching as fast as possible, our wearied force at last reached the vicinity of a small village called Edinburgh, and, crossing the Shenandoah, burned the bridge. We were now not far from Mount Jackson; but the army was so fatigued with its long march over a muddy, rough, and hilly country, that a 'halt' was absolutely necessary. Fremont's pursuit was completely checked by the destruction of the bridge; and, as a further precaution, while the infantry were resting several miles beyond, Ashby's cavalry watched the banks.

"The Federals were greatly disappointed to find the bridge gone, but manfully began to rebuild it. This was a work of several days—a respite gratefully improved by our exhausted men; but it becoming known that the enemy had again crossed, and were in pursuit, our main army took up the line of march towards Harrisonburgh, while Ashby, as usual, was in the rear with his cavalry. The enemy were far superior to us in horse—they were more numerous, and their animals in excellent condition, so that it required great exertions on the part of Ashby to check their determined onslaughts. Every rise in the road was seized by our men, and held as long as practicable; each patch of timber concealed some of our horsemen; so that although the enemy evinced more ardor and courage than ever witnessed before, our frequent ambuscades cost them dearly. From early morning until evening, all along the route, cavalry skirmishing was incessant, so that Ashby's regiment of one thousand men was completely broken down with fatigue.

"As we neared Harrisonburgh, evening was fast approaching, and the column turned towards 'Brown's Gap.' The enemy seemed to understand the importance of this movement, and pushed our rear-guard more fiercely than ever. Our cavalry had charged the enemy, and driven their horsemen upon the infantry; but a full brigade came galloping forward, and we retired. The brigade of Ashby now came up, and, with loud shouts, attacked the Yankees and completely routed them, killing and wounding many, capturing several; among the latter their brigadier-general, a fine, soldierly, and handsome Englishman, named Wyndham. This officer loudly cursed his command in unmeasured terms for cowardice, swearing roundly that he would never serve with them again; for although he had been urging them forward the whole day, and personally leading, he could make nothing of them.

"Finding that the enemy's infantry were near at hand, Ashby

sent information to Ewell, who soon countermarched three
regiments, and made dispositions for attack. The enemy deployed their men right and left of the road, and advancing
through the woods some distance without opposition, commenced cheering lustily. Several open fields intervened, and
their 'Bucktail Rifles' (Pennsylvania Reserve Corps) came forward in fine style; but as they approached a strip of woods, on
each side the road, our infantry rose up, and delivered a volley
full in their faces, and charged upon them. They broke and
ran, and while doing so, out rushed Ashby's cavalry, and overtaking them in open ground, cut and thrust without mercy,
driving them in confusion upon their reserves. It was now so
dark that, afraid of further ambuscades, the enemy halted, and
we continued our retreat.

"I have now a sad event to relate. While Ashby was leading the First Maryland infantry in a successful charge, an enemy concealed in the bushes, and favored by darkness, took
deliberate aim and mortally wounded him. Judge of the universal grief when this was known. Ashby, the chivalric cavalry leader, loved by all, to close his immortal career by the
shot of an unseen enemy! Alas! my friend, this was a sad
blow to us, and to our cause, for he was the ablest and most
dashing officer in the service—gentle and kind, brave to rashness, idolized by all ranks, and feared by all enemies.* The

---

* A friend of mine published the following regarding the last day of Ashby's
life : "It was a busy one. Scarcely had he ordered his baggage train to proceed
before the enemy opened fire upon his camp. With but two companies of his old
cavalry he prepared to meet them ; seeing this, they immediately withdrew. The
command was then moved slowly through Harrisonburgh, and drawn up three hundred yards from the opposite end. Soon a regiment of 'blue coats' came charging
it through town, around the bend, in full sight of Ashby's men, who stood as if
fixed to the ground. When within a short distance the enemy's horse began to
slacken their speed, only giving us time to render the salute due them. Soon their
ranks were broken, and in confusion they fled through the streets.

"Never before had I heard our noble general utter such a shout. It was not one
caused by victory over a brave foe after a hard contested fight, but only seemed
designed to shame an ignominious band for running before they were hurt. We
had begun to entertain a high opinion of this body of cavalry. In one instance it
flanked and charged upon a battery, which was left without a support—a most
daring feat for them. (Here General Ashby stood by the guns, fired every load
from his three pistols, and brought every thing away safely.) Soon we were moving
along the road to Port Republic, the enemy pressing closely. Ashby's eagle eye

19

rest of our march was a melancholy one. We had beaten back the enemy, it is true ; but not a thousand such successful combats could compensate for the untimely death of our beloved and gentle Ashby ; meek as a child in peace, fierce as a tiger in battle, night and day in the saddle, ever restless and watchful, always in advance when danger threatened. To see him ride to the front in the crisis of battle, and, waving his sword, shout out, 'Follow *me!*' was a sight which none will forget

was upon them, as watching for an excuse to give them battle. An excuse, and even the necessity for a fight, soon became evident.

"The road was very bad, the train moved slowly, and the main body of the enemy's cavalry was only a mile from its rear. They gave us no time to prepare to meet them. Ashby had but begun to form his men, before three regiments, with colors flying and bands playing, emerged from a wood three quarters of a mile distant. Bearing to our right, they charged, presenting a beautiful sight. Ashby could contain himself no longer. Gently drawing his sabre, and waving it around his head, his clear-sounding voice rang out his only command : 'Follow me.' The dash was simultaneous. Fences were cleared which at any other time would have been thought impossible. The enemy came to a halt. It was but for a moment. As they heard the strange whizz of the sabre around their heads, they broke and ran. The work of slaughter commenced. At every step Ashby, followed closely by his men, cut them down, or sent them to the rear. For two miles and a half the chase continued, and became more bloody at every step. Never before did our General or his men use their sabres so unsparingly. None but those who have witnessed a similar scene can imagine the spectacle. Enraged by deeds too horrible to mention, led by a general whose presence exerted a mystic influence over every heart, the bravery of the men knew no limit, and seldom was a summons to surrender heard. The scattered fragments of the three regiments hid themselves behind their column of infantry three miles beyond the point of attack ; and the pursuit ended not until this infantry opened fire. Here Ashby drew up his men, and remained beneath their fire, and waited for reenforcements from Jackson. We took forty-four prisoners—among them the colonel commanding the brigade of cavalry. The infantry having arrived, Generals Ashby, Ewell, and Stewart (of Maryland) led them to the fight. Here Ashby's gallantry could not have been excelled. Having led the First Maryland regiment in a charge, which sent the enemy flying from that quarter, he sought the Fifty-eighth Virginia, and still between the two fires he ordered the charge. His horse fell dead ; he arose, beckoned to the men, and whilst in the very act, a ball entered low in his left side, came out near the right breast, and shattered his right wrist. Falling mortally wounded, not even a groan or a sigh was uttered by the dying hero. He was brave whilst living, braver still in death. The men were not discouraged, but pressed on, and soon the victory was ours. Night closed the fighting. The noble Ashby fell between six and seven in the evening. The news went like a flash through our lines. Every heart was wounded. The aged, the young, and hard-hearted wept. Nature made deeper the gloom ; and soon the darkness of the night made still darker the regions of the mind. He now sleeps in the University Burying-Ground, near Charlottesville."

who witnessed it. Gentle, good, kind, Christian, heroic soldier, a host in himself—may he rest his honored head in peace, and posterity honor his name for his countless acts of daring and chivalry!

"Having retreated during the night, we· halted two miles from the village of Port Republic, and watched a further development of the enemy's plans. Shields's division was on the east, and Fremont's on the west side of the Shenandoah River, nearly parallel, and it seemed the latter was desirous of attacking Jackson while Shields should cross the bridge at Port Republic and get in the rear: the commanders were in sight of each other, and not more than two miles apart. But if they imagined that Jackson would be so silly as to leave the bridge unguarded on his right flank and rear, they were egregiously mistaken; our commander having made it his first object to secure and cover the bridge with artillery, but so concealed that only a few infantry were visible to the enemy. Next morning (June seventh) Fremont slowly advanced, and cavalry skirmishing was incessant all day, but with little effect on either side. The Federal commander wished to draw out Jackson from the bridge, and a fine position he had taken; but that crafty leader laughed at him and remained where he was, so that if the enemy were determined to fight, an advance was the only course left open to them.

"The advantage gained by fast marching is here apparent, for had we been less active, Shields would have advanced up the east bank of the river, and, having secured the bridge at Port Republic, would have crossed over, and got in front. It was fortunate, therefore, that Jackson had been able to out-race them, and arrive first. On the evening of the seventh, after cavalry had ceased skirmishing for the day, I ascended a hill, and had a fine view of Fremont's and Shields's commands. They were then abreast of each other, on different sides of the river, but made no disposition for uniting, nor had any bridges been begun for that purpose, while we hugged the west bank in close proximity to the bridge, and waited for Fremont, whose advance had already begun. During the night of the seventh, scouts came in and informed us that Fremont had marched two miles towards us, and was drawn up in line of battle at a place called Cross Keys. It was not a village; there were no more than half a dozen houses scattered around, and all that gave it a name was a rude country church and cemetery.

"On the morning of the eighth, we were already prepared for them, but nothing more than heavy artillery fire took place, and many imagined that nothing of importance would transpire. In the afternoon, however, infantry skirmishing brought on a fierce engagement, and for a time the fight was hot and heavy. We had not more than seven thousand engaged, and they about ten thousand; and, although we rapidly gained ground, they manœuvred so well that we accomplished little. Artillery fire was fierce on both sides, and several houses were quickly destroyed by our joint efforts, for, being finely placed, each was afraid of the other occupying them. During the engagement in a little valley, it was discovered that Shields's cavalry advance was endeavoring to surprise and capture the bridge, and had already driven away our infantry; but when the head of their column appeared intent on crossing, several guns opened on them with grape and canister, killing and maiming dozens at every discharge. Finding it impossible to force a passage, Shields withdrew two miles down the river, and left Fremont to fight his own battle.

"As night approached, events were progressing favorably for us; we had driven the enemy from the field, and had pursued them more than a mile, capturing many prisoners, and small arms; but as another and a fiercer battle was in store, Jackson halted, hurriedly buried his dead, and secured his prisoners, and finding that Fremont had fallen back to Harrisonburgh, a distance of three miles, determined to attack Shields on the other side of the river. His entire force having crossed about midnight, and his baggage-train being safe on its way towards Charlottesville, Jackson destroyed the bridge, and prepared his men for the battle of Port Republic, which was to take place early in the morning, drawing up his lines as close as possible to the enemy. As the sun rose I observed that Shields's force was admirably posted between two hills, his wings being much higher than the centre, with artillery on the hill-sides to strengthen them. They occupied, in fact, the corner of a valley; and it seemed impossible to flank them, mountains being on their left, and the river on the right. Their guns also were all admirably disposed, and had full command of every approach, so that when heavy skirmishing opened at eight A.M., it seemed evident to many that although we were of equal force, except in artillery, it would prove a tough and sanguinary experiment before the enemy could be dislodged from their stronghold; add to this, they held the road for retreat, and could destroy every man of us, should we endeavor to follow them between the mountains.

"Nothing daunted, and assured that Fremont was unwilling, were he able, to cross and join commands, Jackson opened the fight with great vigor, being determined to close his brilliant Valley campaign with a signal victory over his old enemy. Afraid to move forward from the mountains, Tyler (for Shields was absent) seemed content to stay where he was, and would not meet us in open ground, so that we suffered somewhat in approaching him. Several attempts were made to turn his flanks, and capture the guns, without success, yet in every instance where they advanced, our troops immediately rushed to the attack with loud yells, and drove the enemy back with slaughter. Again and again, we used every possible stratagem to draw them, and when all failed, we pushed up in front, determined to bring the affair to a finish.

"While pushing them severely in front and attracting attention by the vigor of our attack, a small force was sent along the mountain-side on their flank, which suddenly charging down their rear, filled the wing with consternation; at the same time a body of chosen troops, bent on death or glory, rushed up hill on the opposite wing, and after a sharp and sanguinary encounter, seized the guns. The effect of these daring and successful movements was electrical. Finding both wings broken and showers of small shot assailing the centre, the enemy rallied and endeavored to dispossess us, but in a struggle of infantry against infantry the result ceased to be doubtful. As soon as the enemy appeared in line, to renew the combat on the wings, our men there raised a terrific yell, and advancing at the "double-quick," dodged the enemy's volley, and rushing into them with the bayonet, drove them in confusion on the centre, which Jackson was now assailing with every disposable man, shot and shell flying over us, and dealing destruction on the enemy.

Tyler perceived that all was over, that his troops were thoroughly beaten, and could not be rallied, and now fought desperately to keep open the road for retreat. The destruction was immense, for crowded as they were, every shot told with marked effect, and such was the panic that seized them, hundreds scattered over the hills, while in the distance our cavalry might be seen in every direction charging on the hill-sides far above the battle-field. The battle had raged from eight A.M. until past noon, and the field presented a harrowing sight as we pushed forward in pursuit. Five or six pieces of artillery, thousands of small arms, dozens of wagons filled with stores, many ambulances, twelve wagon-loads of ammunition, hundreds of prisoners, several standards, tents, camp equipage, horses, pistols, sabres—all were scattered about as we rushed forward in the chase, and such was the ardor of our men, that their vengeance seemed insatiable, while an enemy remained in sight.

"But the most singular incident of the day was Fremont's behavior. Hearing that we had crossed to the east side of the river, and were thrashing Shields's command, he formed his division and marched from Harrisonburgh towards the scene, and finding the bridge gone, began shelling across in all directions; this he continued doing for several hours, so that many who were burying the enemy's dead were killed or maimed. White flags were displayed, but this heroic gentleman would not respect our labors, but continued firing without intermission long after the fight had closed! How very valiant this was!*

"When night closed in we found that our killed and wounded amounted to three hundred, and that of the enemy to one thousand, not counting the fight of Cross Keys, where our loss was three hundred, and that of Fremont five hundred.

"Thus ended Jackson's memorable campaign in the Valley, a

---

* General Patterson, in a recent speech at Philadelphia, gave Fremont's character in brief. He declared that he was "a statesman without a speech, a soldier without a battle, and a millionaire with 'nary red.'" He could only abbreviate the description by calling him an unmitigated humbug. His staff usually comprised nearly sixty officers.

chapter in history which is without parallel, but though the majority think that these movements were all his own, it may not be so. He was constantly in receipt of orders from Lee, and he faithfully obeyed them. No man in the army is half so obedient as old 'Stonewall,' or so determined to be obeyed; the result is, that no army has shown greater endurance, marched farther, fought more frequently, suffered less, or done half the work that has fallen to our lot. Our men seem to know intuitively the designs of their commanders, and they second them without a murmur. Where we are marching to now, I cannot form the least idea, but as we move eastward, it is whispered that we go to Charlottesville to recruit, and after being heavily reenforced, may re-enter the Valley again, and perhaps push for Maryland. All at present is profound mystery, but I am sincerely rejoiced at the prospect of some little rest.

"A messenger starts to-night across country for Richmond, and I hurriedly close to send by him. Yours, ASHTON."

CHAPTER XXXI.

FROM the preparations in progress it was apparent that operations would soon recommence on a scale far surpassing any thing hitherto attempted. Longstreet and Hill on our right, on the Charles City road, made frequent reconnoissances towards the interior and the river to ascertain the enemy's strength and position on their left wing. McClellan never opposed these movements, and was possibly unconscious of them, for they were chiefly made at night, or in unpropitious weather, when our Generals would frequently sally forth on a march of ten miles, and return almost without the knowledge of the main body of the army.

By these movements Lee had satisfied himself of McClellan's true position on our right, and felt convinced he possessed but few and unimportant dépôts on the James River, or the Chickahominy; but had established communication with the York River to his right and rear, as being safer to navigate, some considerable distance nearer to his head-quarters, and affording greater facility of transportation by the York River railroad, which ran through the centre of his lines. The Brook Church, or Hanover Court-House turnpike, (leading from Richmond to Hanover Court-House, the White House on the Pamunkey River, and West-Point on the York River,) was McClellan's right, situated in a fine, open, undulating country, highly cultivated and picturesque. This turnpike was the extreme left of our lines, and chiefly held by cavalry, and a few pieces of artillery, placed in several fine redoubts sweeping all approach.

To ascertain the enemy's position, resources, and force through this line of country, seemed to be an absorbing thought with General Lee, and although the army was not up to the standard he desired, and unfit for immediate offensive operations, he felt desirous of ascertaining beyond all doubt what McClellan had done in seizing upon the natural positions of the country, establishing dépôts, obstructing old or forming new roads, etc. Unknown to any, Brigadier-General J. E. B. Stuart received orders and prepared a small force to make an incursion upon McClellan's rear, and inform himself as far as practicable upon all the points mentioned. Selecting parts of the First Virginia Cavalry, (Colonel Fitz-Hugh Lee, son of our chief,) Ninth Virginia Cavalry, (Colonel Fitz-Hugh Lee, nephew of our chief,) four pieces of Stuart's Flying Artillery, and four companies of the Jeff Davis Mounted Legion, all proceeded down the Branch turnpike, on Wednesday evening, and bivouacked in the woods. From scouts, out several days before, it was ascertained that the enemy had a strong force of cavalry quartered on the proposed route, and that a fight would be inevitable. Rising with the sun, Stuart, with his fourteen hundred men, dashed along the roads, and as the enemy's pickets were unable to tell what the immense cloud of dust meant which they descried in the distant landscape, our force actually rode through one of their cavalry encampments before the alarm was given. The enemy were for the most part absent at the time, and sustained but little loss save the total destruction of their stores, the capture of their spare horses, and a few prisoners. These latter, being mounted, were placed in charge of the rear-guard, and the excursion proceeded.

The delay at this camp had given the enemy warning, and when Stuart progressed some miles farther, several squadrons of United States dragoons were observed drawn up on a slope ready to receive him. A halt was sounded, two squadrons were sent forward, who dashed upon the enemy at full gallop. The Federals remained long enough to discharge their revolvers, and not attempting to charge down-hill, broke and fled precipitously. Their officers were the last to retire, and seemed disgusted with the poltroons they commanded. A few accoutrements, pistols, and horses, were found here and in a neighboring camp, and Stuart and his men dashed forward on his equestrian excursion, as gaily as ever.

They had proceeded but a few miles when a strong body of the enemy was discovered admirably posted, with skirmishers thrown out in front. Our advance, consisting of one squadron, went ahead, drove in the outposts, and rode in full view of the enemy, five squadrons strong, and attempted to draw them out. The Federal commander, not observing our whole force screened in woods a mile distant, sallied forth to exterminate our advance. The latter, however, returned up the hill, and over it, and when half-way down were joined by another squadron; both advanced again, and met the enemy advancing up on the other side. Latane gave the word, and our horsemen, spurring their steeds into a maddening gallop, charged among the enemy, and were sabring and pistolling right and left before they fully recovered from their astonishment. The conflict was hand to hand, and conspicuous in our foremost ranks were an English-man and a Prussian, (captains of dragoons,) who had volunteer-ed on Stuart's staff. The fight lasted about ten minutes, and ended in the flight of the Federals, who dispersed in all directions, and took no heed of their trumpets sounding the "rally."

As our men pushed forward down into the level plain they were again attacked by a fresh body of horse; but a third squadron coming to our assistance made the combat more equal, and finally routed them with loss. We captured many prisoners, a lot of fine horses, sabres, trumpets, and pistols, together with their well-provisioned camps found a half-mile further on, with all things as their owners had left them; among other articles, lots of superior saddles and harness were immediately appropriated; other things were burned.

Having refreshed his men, and remounted many, Stuart continued his career; everywhere he was cheered on by the country people, who, informed of events by the frightened Yankees, lined the roadside, waving their hats and handkerchiefs in high glee. "I told 'em you'd come along one of these fine mornings!" said a fine old gentleman, standing at his door with two daughters, and shaking with laughter. "Take care of my son Harry, General, and drive all the skunks into the river!" "Hurry on, boys, hurry on; the varmint an't more nor a mile ahead—we're all Union (!) down here, you know!—one of their camps is just over the hill, and has lots of horses. Darn 'em! Go in, boys, give 'em h—ll!" "Hold on, colonel," said a fine young girl with a gun in her hand, "I've got four of the rascals in the house; they thought to hide until you passed, but seeing our boys coming I made them deliver up their weapons, and stood guard till you arrived!"* Sure enough the Federals were there, but were soon accommodated with horses, and being placed in charge of the rear-guard, on went the column again; clouds of dust rising on every hand, and artillery jingling along the roads. Negroes on fences, negroes on door-steps and wood-piles, others at the plough or spade—all rushed forward, yelling and clapping hands like madmen. "Pile in on 'em, Massa Jeb; we an't no Yankees down dese diggins—fotch it to 'em, white folks, and make 'em clar out ob ole Virginny; we want none ob 'em among dese chickens." Such were their acclamations as we passed on in our circuit of the country.

As the whole rear of McClellan's army was by this time fully alarmed by fugitives flying in all directions, it would have been madness in Stuart to have followed the usual roads in its vicinity; accordingly he pushed towards the routes of their dépôts on the Pamunkey, near the White House, and intercepted large wagon-trains approaching, laden with stores of every description, and destroyed them. The horses and mules were intrusted to the rear-guard, and so proceedings continued: wagon-trains being seized on all the roads leading to dépôts and headquarters, and burned; their guards and drivers accommodated with spare horses, and sent to our rear. On approaching villages, all United States property was burned; among the prisoners seized, several army surgeons, captains, quartermasters, commissaries, and other officers, were obliged to mount mules and follow us, much to their astonishment and chagrin.

Approaching Tunstall's station on the York River railroad, the command was divided, to scour all the roads, with orders to meet at a designated rendezvous. Several schooners espied at anchor on the Pamunkey were seized and burned, together with their valuable cargoes of clothing and stores, but several

---

* The young lady mentioned, whose name I now forget, is a distant relation of the immortal Washington.

others slipped cables and escaped. Some half-dozen wagon-yards, with scores of vehicles of all kinds, were fired, and the teamsters added to our list of prisoners. Plans were laid for capturing the afternoon military train then due at Tunstall's: soon the locomotive was heard approaching, and time not suffic ing to tear up any portion of the track, troopers lined the sides of the road, and were ordered to take deadly aim at the engineer. Some of our men commenced firing when the engine was fully a hundred yards distant; but the driver turned on extra steam, and rushing past the station, shoved off several logs placed on the rails. Many of the passengers, to escape the hail-storm of shot, jumped off the train and were crippled. Some few ran to the woods, but were picked up by our men, together with many who ran from the station on our first approach. All were taken, but the train escaped, although many on it were killed or wounded; the cars being for the most part uncovered, or freight-trucks. The gallant fellow who drove the engine was also killed by an accurate shot; his bravery and foresight deserved a better fate.

Continuing their raid in all directions, the detached parties destroyed United States property to the amount of several million dollars, always securing whatever arms, horses, or prisoners fell in their way; until, wearied with labor, they made for the appointed rendezvous, which was not far from New Kent Court-House, at a small village where several main roads joined. The first party that arrived found that the place con-tained several finely furnished sutlers' stores, and dépôts of goods deposited thus far in the rear of the army, to be convey-ed up to the front as circumstances demanded. They were, in fact, central or wholesale establishments, to furnish regimental sutlers, stocked with every thing that could be required, having tasteful bar-rooms attached, in which were sold champagne, and all sorts of expensive wines and liquors. Our fatigued and dusty men hitched their horses and entered, without ceremony, but were so unprepossessing and unpresentable, that all present rose, including several field-officers who had trotted to the rear "to spend the day" convivially. "Brandy, gentlemen ?" inquired the fat proprietor urbanely—"certainly!" and, present-ing decanters, our men began to imbibe freely. "Might I inquire to what cavalry you belong, gentlemen?" asked the proprietor, acutely surveying their dusty figures from head to foot. "We?" answered one, laying violent hands on a box of Havannas, and emptying the decanter, "oh! we are Maryland cavalry, just arrived; a new regiment raised in Baltimore, just returned on a scouting party after the rebel Stuart!" "Stuart, eh? You don't mean to say that he is in our lines; do you? Well, let him come, that's all, and although I'm not in the army I'll show him a thing or two; just see if I don't!" And as his eye glanced over a fine case of revolvers exposed for sale, he seemed as valiant as Ajax. The rest of the company were dressed too finely to shake hands with our dusty fellows, so smoked and talked apart in dignified reserve. Hearing the approach of a squadron, our troopers went to the door, and the landlord prepared bottles and glasses for his expected visitors. "Are those coming some of your party, gentlemen?" "Yes," was the reply, "and as 'tis no use of fooling any more, we are Stuart's cavalry."

All present were struck dumb with astonishment, but were soon disarmed and made prisoners. As there were four or five large establishments of this kind in the neighborhood, the command paid attention to all, providing themselves with shoes, clothes, new weapons, and literally "ate out" the establishments, until not a box of sardines or can of oysters or preserves remained on the premises. Such a feast our men had not enjoyed for many months; all took whatever articles were needed and destroyed the rest. Fruits, preserves, sardines, oysters, bread, fine biscuit, crackers, champagne, brandy, whiskey, and ale, were consumed with great glee, but none of our men forgot their perilous situation: all remained sober.

About twelve P.M. on Friday night, we prepared for the start home, and as it was out of the question to pass by the same route, on the right of McClellan's lines, Stuart determined to make the grand tour, and find his way out by the left. The whole army was aroused, and cavalry patrolled all the roads, but none knew the country so well as Stuart, who pushed forward by unfrequented lanes and paths, and safely arrived on the banks of the Chickahominy. No bridges being near, Stuart swam his horse across, and all followed save the artillery. An old farmer had witnessed the crossing, and showed the way to a broken bridge a little way up the stream. This was quickly repaired with logs and underbrush, and just as the first dawn of morning topped the trees, the whole command was safely on the south bank.

Our troopers proceeded very cautiously, for they were still in the enemy's lines, and at the most difficult stage of the journey. The main body followed a by-path through the woods, leading to the Williamsburgh road, but scouts were sent out ahead and on the flanks. "Who goes there?" and a shot was the almost instant challenge. Our scouts rapidly fell back to the main body, as directed, and as the Yankee mounted outposts pursued, they speedily found themselves in the midst ot us, and were secured. This occurred on several occasions, but, by good fortune and daring, the whole command reached the Williamsburgh road, and, utterly exhausted, halted on the outskirts of our lines, the enemy being within a mile, and in full force, in pursuit. Excitement had strung both man and beast, since their start on Wednesday night; but now that all were safely through the adventure, and passed through Longstreet's division (the right) on their way to camp, on the Brooke Church turnpike, (the left,) their appearance was most jaded, care-worn, and dusty, having been more than sixty hours in the saddle, almost without drawing rein!

The fruits of this excursion were several hundred head of horses and mules, more than a hundred prisoners, a perfect knowledge of McClellan's position, force, and resources, and the destruction of property to the value of several millions. The enemy were signally defeated on several occasions, in combats with an inferior force. We killed and wounded many, remounted all that required it, furnished the command with fine weapons, saddles, harness, and clothes, humiliated McClellan, and lost but one man — brave Captain Latane, who commanded in the last combat. Singular as it may seem, our chief officers in this excursion had fought against the very companies and squadrons commanded by them when in the United States service; and among the first prisoners captured was the trumpeter of Colonel Lee's old company of dragoons. Many of the prisoners took the affair good-humoredly, mounted on mules as they were, but several doctors were apostrophizing Jupiter and all the gods about the cruelty of placing them on saddleless animals with sharp vertebræ, and swearing roundly against riding sixty miles without rest or food! But grumbling availed them nothing; ride they *must*, and the chapfallen, wretched appearance of these sons of Galen was ludicrous in the extreme, and their horsemanship wonderful, under the circumstances.

The appearance of our gallant troopers was certainly very unprepossessing. The men were dusty, dirty, and looked more like negroes than whites. Their horses could scarcely move, for in addition to the long gallop, their riders had overweighted them by loading their saddle-bows with strings of shoes, bundles of blankets, and new weapons of various kinds: not unfrequently the horse and entire outfit were Federal property. Several of the men were scarred or cut, but manfully sat their saddles, and marched along through our lines as gayly as possible, saying "they would not have missed the trip for any thing." Such an adventure was worthy of remembrance, and those who participated had some right to feel proud. As for McClellan, there can be no doubt that he felt deeply mortified, but he resorted to his old practice of telling half the truth; and in his despatches to Washington, spoke of it as a trivial affair, and scarcely worthy of mention. In retaliation, the Federal cavalry made frequent incursions into counties within the limits of their own lines, though never attempting to cross ours, and spoke of such exploits as something wonderful. Had they crossed our line, and committed half the havoc acknowledged to have been done within their own, their achievements might have been worthy of mention, but they knew too well the character of our men to attempt any such adventure.

General Stuart was formerly a Second Lieutenant in United States dragoons, but, upon the secession of Virginia, offered his sword to his native State, and raised a company of cavalry. He was soon afterwards elected colonel, and acted as brigadier. He was always found on hazardous duty, and won the confidence of all. His forte was cavalry; of infantry he knew little, and, perhaps, cared less; nevertheless, he frequently commanded regiments on foraging excursions during the winter months, at Manassas, and kept the cavalry well supplied from his inroads to the vicinity of Drainsville, and other places near Washington, under the eye and care of Federal commanders, who laid plans to punish him for his audacity.

On one occasion he started from Manassas with several regiments of infantry, a small force of cavalry, four pieces of artillery, (Couts's battery,) and over a hundred wagons. The spies of the enemy had informed them of his departure during the night; rockets were seen ascending at various points, and when morning broke, the enemy were discovered in great force near Drainsville. Stuart's wagons rapidly retreated, and the fight was opened by infantry. The combat lasted some time; but, owing to incapacity or want of foresight, Stuart found himself outflanked, and subjected to ambuscades at every point. The wagons were now far to the rear, and our small brigade began to give ground before a superior force. Couts's battery had contended for more than an hour with thirty pieces placed on a rise, with caissons and horses screened by farm-houses. Having lost nearly all his animals in this unequal conflict, Couts fell back, his men drawing off the pieces by hand, many of the cannoniers pulling ropes with one hand and carrying a shell in the other, so as to be able to stop occasionally and fire. Kentuckians, South-Carolinians, Georgians, and Virginians disputed the ground inch by inch, and inflicted much loss by their accurate fire. Yankee officers begged their men to charge upon our retreating regiments, and often appeared in front to show the way; yet the Federals could not be induced to move, but allowed our whole force to retire in good order. One of their flanking parties, however, advancing down the railroad, was assailed with great fury, and suffered loss; so, although Stuart halted some two miles distant, and invited another attack, the enemy would not pursue, but rested where they had fought. Next day reenforcements were sent up, when we advanced again, and endeavored to draw on an engagement; but the Federals remained close within their lines, and allowed us to forage without the shadow of resistance.

Stuart has been much censured for his conduct in this "surprise," and has seldom figured since in command of infantry. As a cavalry officer he stood second to Ashby only in Virginia, and, from his thorough knowledge of the country, was of incalculable service on all occasions. It was at Williamsburgh I first saw him. Commanding the cavalry rear-guard on that occasion, he was obliged to fall back before superior numbers, and rode up to Johnston's headquarters in the village to report, just as the enemy appeared advancing on the redoubts from the Yorktown and Warwick Court-house roads. He appeared much fatigued and overworked, and would have served admirably for a picture of Dick Turpin when chased by officers on the road to York. His horse was a splendid black, with heavy reins and bit, cavalry-saddle, and holsters; foam stood in a lather upon him, and he was mud-splashed from head to hoof. Stuart himself wore no insignia of command: a common black felt hat, turned down in front and up behind; a heavy black overcoat, tightly buttoned; elegant riding-boots covering the thigh; a handsome sabre, carelessly slung by his side, and a heavy pair of Mexican spurs, that jingled and rattled on the pavements, were all I could see of this splendid horseman and dashing leader. Thickset, full-faced, close-cut hair, and ruddy complexion, he looked more like Ainsworth's "gentleman of the road" than a young, daring cavalry chief of thirty summers. He leaned in his saddle and communicated with General Johnston, and as both smiled, I could hear that his party had been chased by "old Emory" of the Fifth U. S. Dragoons, whose light artillery could now be heard blazing away south of the town.

As Johnston stands conversing with General Griffiths of the Mississippi Brigade, we have a full view of that well-known officer. He is uncovered, and his small compact head is finely developed. His hair is grey, and cut close; his deep-set grey eyes are full of meaning; his features calm as those of a Jesuit; his complexion is ruddy; he wears military whiskers, and no moustaches; his uniform is of a grey color with facings of light orange, and stars on the throat. In manner he is decided and unequivocating; short, sharp, and dry in conversation; decision of character is plainly seen in the close-set lips: altogether, he is a spruce, neat, compact little man. Although there are no signs of extraordinary intellect, or marks of a man "truly great," his quiet smile and twinkling eye betray a person of disciplined tastes and habits, possessed of much craftiness and cunning. I saw little of him around Manassas, but at Yorktown lines he was continually on the move, riding one of the finest chestnut mares the eye ever beheld; a small, active, wiry,

20

fine-blooded, and swift animal, much like the owner. His so-licitude was sleepless, and though visiting the principal redoubts and points daily, I have known him to gallop into our battery near midnight, not five minutes after the alarm gun fired, and though the distance ridden was over a mile.

This distinguished man is a whole-souled patriot, brave to a fault, and, did he consider his services would aid our cause more by shouldering a musket than marshalling large forces, he is one who would willingly enter the ranks. I have seen him under many various circumstances, but always observed in him the smart, active, quick-sighted officer, scrupulously at-tired in unform when on duty, but in plain citizen dress when not. Soon as his wound, received at "Seven Pines," permitted, he retired to his farm for a few weeks, and although I travelled in the same car, he was dressed so unprepossessingly, that I did not notice him until he arrived home, when a large crowd of farmers, children, and old women gathered round him at the station to welcome back their "old neighbor, General Joe John-ston," in an unceremonious manner which bespoke volumes of mutual good feeling and fellowship. At the opening of the re-bellion he was Lieutenant-Colonel First U. S. Dragoons, and act-ing Quartermaster-General at Washington, but immediately join-ed the fortunes of his native State, (Virginia,) and has since risen very high in the estimation of the South. ·

CHAPTER XXXII.

IN some previous chapters I have endeavored to picture the condition of our army and the feeling of our men, reproducing, as nearly as possible, such conversations among comrades as it was but natural should occur. It is true, I cannot pretend to graphic skill, or scenic effect, in the report of those gossips; but they are faithful in substance, and they offer me the readiest means of placing much on record that would otherwise run into tedious detail. As I must once more resume the conversational method, I can only hope that faults of style will be overlooked, and the intention only regarded.

"If by accident any European were to visit our lines, what a poor opinion he might form of the true merit of our soldiers! Accustomed to see fine bodies of men, splendidly drilled, and tastefully uniformed, he would be inclined to look upon us as a parcel of ragged, ill-lfed, slovenly-looking, mud-colored militia, unfit for service, and doomed to discomfiture at the first volley from an enemy. Even the Federal army, though uniformly attired in blue, and smart in appearance, would hardly appear more effective in his eyes, when compared with the brilliancy and neatness of European regiments. It is true that no people who are fighting for their independence can be expected to make the same military display as the old-established standing armies of Europe; yet it is much to be regretted that, through the poverty of Government, we have to depend for clothes upon the industry and charity of our friends at home. A braver army than ours, or one more creditable in its physique, never existed; and were we but well dressed, our European friends would have little cause to smile. 'Results,' however, are all that is necessary; and so that we beat the enemy, and ultimately triumph, we can very well forego the pomp and circumstance of war. In peaceful times, I have no doubt that our 'regulars' will present a fine and imposing appearance, for Southerners have good taste in attire, and means will not be lacking to put our military establishment on a sound and magnificent footing. What think you, Major?"

"I agree with you. It matters little how we are dressed at present; there are no ladies at our parades, or I might be tempted to make an outlay in fine cloth and gold lace; but as our fancy manœuvres and field-days are usually with the enemy, I am content to appear in any dress that is fit for wear and tear. So that my weapons and my horse are all right, I care little for the rest. Yet there is one thing I do regret, namely, that our regiments are without 'bands' to cheer them on the march, and dispel the depressing monotony of the camps. True, bands are allowed by the 'regulations,' and much money has been expended in procuring instruments; yet those of our boys who have musical talent refuse to enter the band, from false pride, considering it dishonorable to exchange the musket for a musical instrument, as if they desired to shun the battle-field. They will contribute readily enough; we have now not less than twenty-five hundred dollars in hand to procure instruments, but, except the leader, a Frenchman, and two German volunteers, we have not a man to play them!"

"That is true, old friend, and in those regiments which *have* succeeded in getting up bands, the performance is so wretched for a few months that their dismal noises are an intolerable nuisance. Yet it cannot be avoided; we lack cultivated talent, and many 'who volunteer to do the blowing,' as the boys say, have seldom seen, and certainly never before touched, a bugle or cornet. There are the customary drums and fifes, and the 'regulation' tunes for 'reveille'—'Roast Beef,' 'Tattoo,' and every necessary call; but in walking through camps at any of those times, we hear all kinds of drumming; and as for rival fifers!—they seem to be in an intense screeching agony, whenever called upon, and know no tune except 'Dixie,' or the doleful and eternal 'My Maryland.' It is absolutely necessary, Captain, that something should be done; all our commands are now given by word of mouth, even in drilling. Such a sys-tem is exhausting to commanders, and it causes indecision and confusion in the ranks, from the failure of the voice; while in battle it is impossible to be heard at all. Fancy every officer bawling out the word of command, and oftentimes the wrong one, in some abominable falsetto amid the din of arms and the tramp of hurrying feet. In our cavalry and artillery corps the trumpet is used, and with splendid effect. Why cannot our infantry be commanded with the bugle?

"Under innumerable circumstances music is necessary to the soldier, and has a beneficial effect. How inspiriting it is to hear a good band strike up a cheerful tune on a long march, how stragglers jump to their places, how quickly the file is dressed, and how easy the step becomes, no matter how weary or how long the march may be! It seems to me we look like a regiment of geese marching through town, without the strains of music to mark the time. If Jenkins were here he would smile and say : 'These things are different in Europe.' They are so, and they will be different here in time. The old armies have their light and heavy infantry and cavalry, their rifles, and every branch of the service well represented, each having its particular part to play in skirmish or battle; but owing to our hurry in forming the Southern army, and the continual succession of stirring events, we have but three classes—artil-lery, infantry, and cavalry—without further distinctions; and one regiment is considered as 'heavy' as another if it musters only five hundred men. The enemy have splendid bands, for there are German, Dutch, Italians, and French in their ranks by tens of thousands. Not so with us. The ruling foreign element with us is Irish, and, although Irishmen are passion-ately fond of music, they still cling to the musket, and make music of their own in the hour of battle. I wish we had a hundred thousand of them; they make the best soldiers in the world."

"We *have* some good bands in the service, Major, though I confess but few of them. The Louisiana bands are occasionally good, and that of the First Virginia Foot is one among a thousand. But, as you observe, it is to be regretted our boys will not volunteer to play, instead of lavishly throwing their money away on those who have no talent for it. The want of uniformity in our 'calls' is notorious; what one regiment beats for 'tattoo' its next neighbor will furiously drum for 'reveille.' All the men know is that drums are beating for 'something,' and they turn out with alacrity to ascertain what that something is. But this is not in form, and though commanders look upon the matter lightly, it may be the occasion of much mischief. Take a case in point: At the battle of 'Oak Hill,' in Missouri, the camps and commands of Price and McCulloch were some distance apart, and the Missourians, it is said, were so much accustomed to beating drums at all times, that when they were suddenly attacked by Lyon, McCulloch took no notice of the call, until Sigel opened fire upon his pickets, when he ascertained that for *once* the Missouri drummers meant something by their thumpings. I do not say that such a thing would happen with us, for as volunteers we are the best drilled in 'essentials' of any troops in the world, and are ever on the alert, more frequently moving in search of the enemy than being sought. But although uniforms, fine bands, pipeclay, and all the rest are desirable things enough, we must, for the present, be content to do without them. To speak of other things more essential to our success and existence as a nation, what think you of our weapons? Are *they* all you could desire? What say you, Robins, of the artillery?"

"You have called an incompetent authority for judgment upon such an important point, for as I am not an educated officer, I know but little of the science of gunnery, and less of casting guns. As a volunteer I am not a bad shot, but that is another thing. I know this, however, that if the various battle-fields had not supplied us with new weapons, we should have been badly off at the present time. Our supply of good guns, when the war opened, was very inadequate; and although we have upon our side the best engineers and artillerists of the old service, we have never yet succeeded in making pieces equal to those brought into the field by the enemy. In fact, it is dangerous to use guns of our own manufacture, for, to my knowledge, many have exploded upon the first trial in the field, and others have been so inaccurate they were worse than useless. We succeeded in procuring some good ones from England, by vessels which ran the blockade; and the fact that our Government has not purchased European guns of any other manufacture, speaks well for British superiority in this respect.

"We have captured hundreds of excellent guns from the enemy, of all which the 'Parrott' is my favorite, being much lighter, more durable, stronger at the breech, of longer range, and safer to handle. The 'Parrott' gun, you know, was invented by a Georgian, and patented before the war began; the enemy have extensively patronized the weapon. But of all guns, I most admire Whitworth's English breech-loading pieces. We had several of them during our blockade of the Lower Potomac in the winter months of 1861 and 1862, at Cockpit Point, and other places, and their accuracy was amazing, while the unnecessary, unsightly, dangerous, and detestable ramrod business was entirely discarded, and the rapidity of fire greatly increased. It requires no great amount of scientific knowledge to see that the rammer and ramrod are totally behind the age, and should be discouraged and disused. All that is required of a good gun can be realized by breech-loading, and, from experience, I can do more with such a weapon than any other. It occupies less room in working, and saves the men from unnecessary exposure and loss. In England, I know, the invention of Armstrong is patronized; they may have potent reasons for the preference, but our men prefer Whitworth's weapon."*

"I agree with you entirely, Robins," said the Major, "in regard to the ramrod; I think it should be abolished. Half the men you see walking about town with arms in slings have been hit while loading, for the enemy fire high, and had we breech-loading muskets in our battles, few would have been struck at all. There are other important reasons besides this for objecting to the ramrod. In a rifle, accuracy entirely depends upon the cartridge properly 'chambering,' as with artillery. It is difficult to load a rifle perfectly tight at any time, and especially in the heat of action, for the best of rifles 'lead' so, that it is a matter of impossibility to ram home the charge; but if we had

---

* This was written long before Whitworth was patronized by the English Government.

breech-loaders, the weapon might 'lead' at the bore, but a fresh cartridge introduced at the breech would clean it. Try both methods, and you will perceive that rapidity and accuracy are gained by using the breech to load, for if you lose your ramrod in the confusion or excitement, how much is your weapon worth? The 'thumb' should be the only ramrod—you do not lose that often, and whether the weapon be 'dirty' or 'leaded,' your charge is sufficiently 'home' for every purpose; besides, much closer fitting cartridges can be used, without the process of greasing or ramming, for the thumb does the last, and a fresh bullet the former. During one of our battles, I saw a youth fix his ramrod to a tree, and endeavor to push the cartridge 'home' in that way, for the musket was so 'dirty' from use, that it was impossible to ram the load. Here was a situation for the boy to be in—ramrod bent, and the musket useless!"

"Since the enemy have supplied us with arms," said another, "we have had a good variety of weapons among us—the EnglishEnfield rifle, by various makers; the old Harper's Ferry musket; the Harper's Ferry Minié musket; the new and old Springfield musket, rifled and smooth bore; and last of all, that heavy, unhandy, clumsily-made thing called the German or Belgian rifle, which carries a ball equal to that of a young six-pounder. The Belgians or Germans, who use this weapon, must be hard, large-fisted fellows, used to playing with a pair of fifty-sixes; for it is certainly the most ungainly rifle mortal ever used; being furnished with a heavy oak stock, and trappings of iron and brass, sufficient to decorate a howitzer. Those I have seen apparently come from some part of Austria, judging by the name-plate. The Mississippi rifle is also too heavy, and carries a large ball; though good for its time, it is now superseded by lighter and more accurate weapons."

"Take a seat, Adjutant," said Robins, as Lieutenant Nixon entered the tent. "We have been speaking of the different kinds of weapons, and by general consent it seems breech-loaders are preferred; what think you?"

"I am a better judge of pens than rifles, perhaps, but many old wiseheads still seem to prefer the smooth-bore musket—

brown Bess, as it is called—and consider it more destructive than any."

"Yes," said the Major, "their reasons are peculiar; I have frequently heard them. They tell you that at short range, with buckshot, you can kill more than with the rifle. But how often do we get within that short range? If we mutually advanced until within a hundred yards, and then blazed away until one or the other were exterminated, I should decide for a smooth-bore musket, and a sufficiency of buckshot. But suppose the enemy occupied a skirt of woods, and not coming out, we were ordered, as usual, to advance over a thousand yards of open field, and *force* them out—must your men be exposed to their fire, for that distance, until you arrived within a hundred yards, the maximum effective distance of the ordinary musket? The foe would pour several volleys before you could return them, if you ran ever so fast. What condition would your line be in for the onset, after being thinned by their shot, when you halted to re-form, fire, or charge? Surely the case is a plain one. You would have lost many men, the remainder would be sorely fatigued, and their nerves shaken, so that when they *did* fire, half the volley would be thrown away; and there you stand before an untouched regiment fit to annihilate you, if they have the pluck to move forward."

" 'Their rifle fire at a thousand or five hundred yards would not be effective,' you say? True, with such shots as the New-Englanders; but if they were Western men opposing you, your regiment would be sadly deceived, for they shoot as well as our best. But suppose they failed to hit a single man for a few hundred yards, would young troops unhesitatingly advance under such a threatening fire? Scores would drop from trepidation; for they are usually more frightened than hurt. Give these same boys good breech-loading rifles, without fears of the all-important ramrod before their mind, and they can advance, firing volley for volley, and loading as they walk or run—a feat impossible, if the ramrod is to be drawn and returned in a hurry. With a good breech-loading rifle that cleans itself, as I have explained, if troubled with dirt or lead, a well-made tape cap, and sword-bayonet, our boys would prove invincible."

"Well," said the Adjutant, "European nations who fight more frequently than we, on a grander and more scientific scale, still retain the ramrod and percussion-cap; it must be conceded that as the subject vitally interests them, there must be powerful reasons for adhering to that system, though personally I agree with what you say, and know that you do not insist upon the tape cap, but a nipple suitable to both. As for the sword-bayonet, we have never yet used it except in a few unimportant combats. It is far preferable, however, to the old bayonet, and would prove a valuable side-arm in close encounters, where the rifle or musket is useless. In every way, it is a valuable improvement, and put to a variety of useful purposes by the men, when the old bayonet would not be of more utility than a stick."

"The Maynard rifle," said a cavalry man, "is the favorite with us, and proves a destructive weapon when one becomes accustomed to handling it, mounted, or in a skirmish. It is light, simple in structure, and can be used with both caps; the only objection is, that you have to be careful in preserving the empty brass tubes, or you will not be able to make new cartridges. I wear a belt round me, which holds fifty, each in its hole, handy for use, but I object to the brass tubes, for, if lost, it is difficult to replace them in active service."

"I consider that the 'Maynard' was never intended for the army—for that, among other reasons, it is admirably fitted for hunting, and was, perhaps, invented for that purpose; though light and of easy carriage, too much care is requisite in preparing the cartridge for ordinary vidette service. Did you ever see any of those globe or telescopic-sighted rifles, exclusively used by Berdan's battalions of sharpshooters in the Federal army? They are a very accurate weapon, but expensive, I am told; yet the Federals have not done much mischief with them. The men are trained to climb trees, lie on their back, crawl rapidly through the grass, have grass-green pantaloons to prevent detection, etc.; but with all the usual systematic boasting regarding them, our Texans and others are more than a match for them. We have picked off a greater number of them than we have ourselves lost by their wonderful shooting; but as our men do not waste much time in skirmishing, but hasten to 'close quarters,' I have not heard much of them for some time, although a few months since nothing was talked of, North, but the extraordinary achievements of 'Berdan's Sharpshooters.' To believe their reports, nearly every general in our army has fallen under their ' unerring aim.' The best sharpshooters with us are to be found among the Missourians, Texans, Arkansans, Mississippians, and Alabamians—men accustomed to woods and swamps and to Indian warfare."

" Speaking of losses," said one, " we have suffered fearfully from disease, but not so much in proportion as the Federal army, judging from their frequent statements. Our men seem to stand campaigning much better than theirs. It was said by the Northern journals that winter would cause more loss to us than a dozen battles, for it was thought we could not stand cold, hail, frost, sleet, and freezing weather; but I think the health of our troops was much better during that period than in summer. Men with strong wills can do or suffer any thing. We erected comfortable cabins in two days, and having timber all around us, kept up roaring fires of logs.   During the summer and fall, however, our hospital-lists were heavy with chills, fevers, rheumatism, and the like, but now we are thoroughly acclimated, and the hills, snows, cold winds, and mud of Virginia are as bearable and pleasant to the boys as their own sunny South, near the waters of the Gulf.   Here is Dr. Wilson, smoking at his ease.   What have *you* to say regarding this matter, Doctor?   No long, barbarous, four-footed professional terms, if you please !"

The fine old doctor appealed to remarked, that: "In plain English, the commissary department has not done its duty. When our youth were called to the field, they were unaccustomed to hardships or privations — being for the most part well-educated, comfortably circumstanced, and never subjected to any labor at home harder than a week's hunting.   They were lavish in their expenditure, had superabundance of clothing, and servants to attend them.   All this was reversed in camp.   Money, for a time, was plentiful, but supplies could not be obtained round the country, for our troops swarmed like locusts over every thing eatable; nor could their wants be supplied from home, for all transportation was so much occupied with troops and munitions, that after the first month's service, sugar, coffee, molasses, and rice—things we thought *impossible* to do without — were seldom given in rations, although

abundant enough far South. Our boys, again, were careless;
eating any thing or every thing that came in their way;
and as the digesting organs are not made exactly of steel, or
copper, such abuses brought on very natural consequences.
Again, their clothing, though light and sufficient for Southern
use, was not durable enough to withstand the change of climate, and the variable weather of a hilly country, in comparatively Northern latitudes; besides which, they were reprehen-
sively careless, moving about in all weathers, and unceremoniously squatting down in dry or damp places. Much of all
this was occasioned by the continual movements of our generals, and as the men seldom troubled that abortion called a
'knapsack,' but simply marched with arms, accoutrements, and
rations, every medical man in the army foresaw that hundreds
would be sacrificed.

"Young men of refined habits, inhabitants of cities, have
made the best of soldiers; while, strange as it may seem, those
bred in the country, and accustomed to woods and fields, have
frequented the hospitals far more than any others. This can
only be accounted for by the thoughtfulness, neatness, and scru-
pulous cleanliness of the one, compared with the carelessness
and thoughtlessness of the other. But the chief cause of all our
sickness has arisen from the lack of good, well-cooked food, regularly changed and diversified. What kind of bread can you
expect boys to make, who have never seen the process, and are
not furnished with proper ingredients or utensils for rendering
it wholesome? For several months it was the common practice in the army to make up the flour into 'slapjacks' or 'frit-
ters,' which were nothing more than a thin mixture of flour
and water fried in a sea of bacon-grease! I know regiments
which have been in the service sixteen months, and three
fourths of the time have had naught for rations but flour and
very poor fat bacon. I do not complain of Government, for I
know the heart of the President bleeds, and he would willingly enter the ranks, rather than fill the position he does,
while thousands of office-seekers and petty malcontents are
growling around and vilifying him, as if he were something
worse than a common thief; but I *do* say, that our poverty

and carelessness in the commissary and quartermaster's departments, have much to do with these disasters.*

"When we were appointed to our several posts, what did these much-abused doctors find? Hundreds of sick, lying on the bare ground; no hospitals, but simple tents to withstand the weather; and oftentimes not a grain of medicine of any kind on hand, nearer than Richmond! And how stood matters in the capital? All in confusion, and short of supplies. In the hurry of the first months, hundreds of so-called 'doctors' thronged the city in quest of preferment, and to my own knowledge — either from incapacity or carelessness — the heads of the Medical Department appointed scores of·men who could scarcely write their own names, or tell the difference between salts and strychnine — impostors who brought disgrace upon an honorable profession, and were unfitted to administer poison to a dog!"

"Yes, the doctor is right," said another; "things are gradually improving, but the price of our experience has been awful; though nothing like the mortality among the enemy from similar causes — if _that_ is any consolation. McClellan acknowledges to· have lost nearly fifty thousand men during his stay on the peninsula, chiefly from sickness! Johnston always managed to keep him in some kind of swamp or mudhole, and when a certain person complained of his inactivity before 'Seven Pines,' he answered: 'I _am_ fighting, sir, every day! Is it nothing that I compel the enemy to inhabit the swamps, like frogs, and lessen their strength every hour, without firing a shot?' That was all very well, but I am con-

---

* There are many honorable exceptions to the carelessness and incapacity of which the doctor complains, and all must join in eulogizing the Herculean labors of Assistant Quartermaster-General William L. Cabell. This officer, by unceasing labor, night and day, has brought up his department to a high state of efficiency. His despatch of business is marvellous — he seems to understand, intuitively, the wants, shortcomings, and capacity of every one with whom he has business. He found his department in a chaotic state; but by constant and untiring labor, he has done much to place our army on a comfortable footing, while, by prudence and forethought, he has prevented unnecessary expenditure, and greatly facilitated the designs and movements of our generals. He is a Virginian, about thirty-five years of age; entered the old service as Brevet Second Lieutenant of Infantry, July first, 1850; was Captain Seventh Infantry, March third, 1855; and appointed Captain Assistant Quartermaster, March eighth, 1858. This gentleman's labors are beyond all praise.

vinced if Lee had not taken the helm when he did, we might
have been 'falling back' towards the Gulf.

"I see there is some difference of opinion on this point, and
therefore keep to the doctor's chain of thought. There is no
doubt that good bread and pure water are the two essentials
of a soldier's welfare. He may exist for a long time, and do
excellent work without any thing more, but these he *must* have.
Beauregard managed things very indifferently at Corinth, in
those respects; there was a superabundant supply of excellent
water a few score feet below the surface, but yet few wells were
dug; men scooped up sufficient water from the surface, or from a
few indifferent springs, but the quality was wretched, as all
water usually is in the South. Much sickness was the consequence. Halleck, on the other hand, had not been in Corinth
more than three days before he bored for water, and had many
fine artesian and other wells in operation, which would have
more than sufficed for three times the number of men in both
armies. Virginia is the only place where fine water is abundant in the South, yet at Yorktown and other places the quality
and supply were inferior. The same may be said of Manassas.
Although Bull Run ran there, the men had an aversion to using
that stream, except for washing purposes. How strange our
generals never thought of digging wells!"

"The bread question," said the doctor, "is an all-important
one; old troops become expert bakers in time, but young ones
only spoil the flour, and ruin their digestion. In truth, flour
should not be distributed at all; 'cracker bread' is what is required, and it takes up no greater amount of transportation
than flour. By giving the men good hard bread, it relieves
them of many duties; for oftentimes flour is served out when
there are no utensils in which to make it. I have frequently
seen men receive their ration of flour after a hard day's march,
when the baggage-wagons with the pots and pans were far ahead.
I have often pitied our boys when, under these circumstances,
the poor fellows have had to bake their flour in the ashes, or toast
the dough on a stick — any thing, in fact, to satisfy hunger!
The British troops in the Crimea were sadly perplexed about
cooking, and hundreds died from the improper preparation of
food. Soyer endeavored to teach them better, but they never

succeeded so well as their French neighbors. We excel both in that respect, and although not 'a nation of cooks, have done wonderfully well.

"Our generals *did* endeavor to erect large bakeries to supply the army, but they were too small, at Manassas and elsewhere. Those that *could* bake *would* not—'they enlisted to shoulder a musket,' they said, and could not be prevailed upon to try their hands at bread-making, though hundreds were professional bakers, and excellent workmen. The scarcity of salt, soda, and other articles has sorely tried our men in preparing bread; and even if they succeeded in purchasing these and other necessaries, there was no transportation allowed for such articles. One wagon was the maximum allowed to each company; and if the roads proved heavy, the order came, 'lighten the wagons,' and every article but tents and such like was pitched into the roads; pots and pans were among the first to be sacrificed. Generals and others, however, always found room for *their* traps, and men did not fail to notice and grumble at it. For why should a colonel be allowed to carry his stove, desk, bedstead, and trunk, when room can scarcely be found or allowed for a private's coffee-pot or frying-pan? The rank and file are socially superior, in a majority of cases, to those who command them; and with all deference to the present company, I think our officers have not shown sufficient interest or solicitude for the comfort and well-being of their men."

"In many instances, that is true," said one, "but as to myself, there has been so much grumbling and growling about the subject of 'baggage' with quartermasters and others, that I have thrown all mine away. I have my sword, a blanket, haversack, canteen, and a change of under-clothing thrust in a light knapsack, and let every thing else go; for our wagons are always far off—you never *can* find what you put in them—and as we are continually moving about and fighting, I find my load sufficiently heavy without adding to it. Hundreds of officers do the same, I find; and, except the brigade is stationary, never think of increasing our bulk of baggage. When ordered to march, I am at the head of my company, heavily laden as any; the boy makes a fire when the 'halt' is sounded, and throwing myself down on my blanket, I share rations with some 'mess' or other, and am ready to move or fight at a moment's warning. As for thinking of toilet and appearance, a full supply of pots and pans for cooking, etc., in times like these, it is all nonsense. Our wagons are scarcely sufficient to carry tents, ammunition, and flour. We are lightly armed, lightly fed, march rapidly, fight frequently, and so that we beat the enemy, and get barely enough to sustain life, we ought to be contented. Such an army as ours can never be whipped—generals and privates are all lean animals, little else but bone and muscle, reduced to a proper fighting weight, and all the better for not being encumbered with the baggage of a Xerxes!"

CHAPTER XXXIII.

June twenty-sixth—Commencement of the Week's Campaign before Richmond—
Battles of "Mechanicsville," "Beaver Dam Creek," and "Ellison's Mills"—
Terrific Battle Scene—Preparations for a further Advance.

THE reader may picture to himself a party of officers belonging to the "ragged rebels" seated together at my window, comparing notes, and speculating on the probabilities of speedy hostilities. "McClellan seems to think he has not sufficient troops, and asks for more. He makes the startling admission that he has lost not less than fifty thousand men since his arrival on the peninsula in March! I cannot comprehend how this can be, unless sickness has decimated his ranks. As he owns to have had one hundred and eighty-five thousand at that period, he must have one hundred and thirty-five thousand men now, unless the scattered remains of Banks's, Fremont's, Milroy's, and Shields's corps have been gathered and sent to him. There cannot be a doubt, however, that he has drawn largely upon McDowell, who has been hovering around Fredericksburgh for the past two months. As there is water communication between him and McClellan, I should not be surprised to find, when the next battle comes off, that McDowell is either with him, or has largely reenforced him. Conjecture as we may, this continual line of ice-wagons passing under our windows all day, shows that the hospitals are being prepared for emergencies."

"Orders have already been issued to 'clear the hospitals,' I learn," said another, "and that I regard as one of the best of signs. Our commissariat, also, has been unusually active during the past week in delivering extra supplies, and every man is furnished with sixty extra rounds of ammunition. All the field-forges and blacksmiths' shops, in and out of the army, have been busy night and day for the past week, and hundreds of horses have passed through the hands of the farriers. All

21

these things mean something; but more remarkable than all is the fact that *Jackson, instead of returning to the Valley, as the enemy expected, has turned the head of his column towards Hanover Court-House, on the enemy's right and rear!*"

"This explains, then," said one, "why Lee sent him such heavy reenforcements. After his brilliant series of victories over the Federals, he fell back, as usual, to recuperate, and the Yankees, expecting his speedy reappearance among them, detached several corps to watch for and overwhelm him if he advanced. Thus, the force of Milroy, Shields, Banks, Fremont, and McDowell, which were primarily intended to advance from the west upon Richmond, and coöperate with McClellan on the east in reducing our capital, are scattered up and down the Valley, strategically, to watch and capture the redoubtable 'Stonewall,' while the Texan and two other brigades are sent round to reenforce him at Charlottesville. But instead of running into the snare prepared for him, Jackson knows his opponents are beyond supporting distance of McClellan, so is ordered to advance rapidly on their right and rear, while we coöperate by an attack in front. *This* is evidently the plan, and, if properly executed, will redound to the glory of Lee, who framed it. McClellan, however, is fully aware of this movement, and although he cannot prevent the impending 'crash,' he is energetically preparing to meet it. Fitz-John Porter, you know, commands the right, McClellan the centre, and Heintzelman the left."

"Heintzelman is a crafty old fellow," said another, "and is not to be caught with chaff. Do you know I have seen large volumes of smoke ascending along their whole line? I knew it indicated destruction of stores, and heard General Almsted say as much on Sunday, (June twentieth.) 'Old Heintzelman,' said he, 'is a wily old major; see those large bodies of smoke ascending on their left—they have been frequent for the past few days, and Mac is preparing for the worst.'"

"But I have seen no peculiar disposition of force in *our* lines for an aggressive movement, if one is contemplated."

"There is no particle of doubt that it *is* contemplated, but Lee will not weaken any point of his lines until the decisive moment, for McClellan might attack on a weak side. When Jackson is in position, you will see Lee's divisions move as if by magic!"

"He has changed all our brigades entirely within the past week, and commanders now have different troops; what does all that mean?"

"I do not know," said another, "that my reasons are correct, but I think Lee has simply acquiesced in the long-expressed desire which State regiments have had of being brigaded to‹ gether, so that if successful or otherwise, they have only them‐ selves to thank or blame. This plan of brigading excites great emulation, and State pride will carry the boys through difficul‐ ties they might not attempt if joined with other troops. What‐ ever the reasons, the thing is done, as far as practicable, and the commands so changed and divided that I scarcely know *what* regiments are commanded by this or that general, al‐ though up to the present time I was well informed."

In short, however we might speculate, it was generally known that a grand action was inevitable, for Jackson's move‐ ments from Gordonsville were rapid, and fully known to half the people of Richmond. On Wednesday, June, twenty-fifth, it was rumored that he had reached Hanover Court-House, fifteen miles to the right and rear of the enemy, and the general anx‐ iety was oppressive. Rockets at night were continually as‐ cending on our left, which Jackson answered, and his last or‐ ders were to move next day in the rear of Mechanicsville. Longstreet's and D. H. Hill's divisions suddenly marched from the Williamsburgh road on Wednesday, and bivouacked on the Mechanicsville road, Huger and others being left to hold the right against any attack. General Ambrose Hill's division was on the Meadow Bridge road, to the left of Longstreet, and General Branch's brigade occupied the extreme left on the Brook Church (or Hanover Court-House) road.

On the north bank of the river, at Brook Church Bridge, the enemy had collected in force, to dispute the advance of Branch, but on learning that Jackson was in their rear, they offered but a feeble resistance. Branch's brigade, therefore, crossed over rapidly about three P.M., and pursued the enemy down the stream, and passed the Meadow Bridge, where General Ambrose Hill was crossing. Thus far events had kept Jackson on our extreme left, endeavoring to get farther in the enemy's rear; Branch's brigade was the centre, and Ambrose Hill's division the right of our forces, which had crossed. In this order they fought and pursued the enemy vigorously, capturing many field-works and some cannon. The fight from Meadow Bridge was obstinately maintained, the rattle of musketry and booming of field and siege-pieces being well-nigh deafening. The day being fine, a splendid view was obtained from Longstreet's position, on the south bank, of the progress of the battle on the north side. The advance of our men through the green fields could be plainly seen, in face of the volleys of musketry incessantly poured in upon them from every wood and thicket. Porter's field-pieces were admirably worked, and occupied every position of value; the movements of his infantry were executed without confusion.

From this position the enemy were seen to be gradually falling back, making it evident that Jackson was advancing too close upon their rear, although as yet he had not fired a shot; while the confusion, clouds of dust, roar of ordnance, and excitement of couriers round Porter's head-quarters at Mechanicsville, told how vigorously Branch was pushing forward our centre, and driving the enemy out of the earthworks they had erected at various points. Hugging the north bank, Ambrose Hill maintained an unbroken line, and from the appearance of smoke rising closer and closer to Mechanicsville, it was evident that he was rapidly gaining ground, and felt certain of storming the village before sunset. Branch was still some distance behind; yet Hill, with his fourteen thousand men, determined to push on, and drive off the enemy that held the bridge, so as to open and clear the way for Longstreet and D. H. Hill. After much hard fighting this was accomplished, and the latter Generals pushed forward across Mechanicsville Bridge with their divisions, and soon formed line at right angles with the river. Meanwhile Ambrose Hill had re-formed his troops, and commenced an attack upon Mechanicsville itself, which brought on a terrific fight.

This place had been admirably fortified by Fitz-John Porter, who, as an engineer and artillerist, had bestowed much care and labor upon the works. Its strength was such that if Jackson had not been hovering in the rear of the enemy, it is probable that Hill would have felt himself too weak to attempt its capture. Artillery on both sides now opened with a terrific roar, and, as evening fell, the flash of guns and long lines of musketry fire could be seen in bright relief against the blue and cloudless sky. After a deafening cannonade of half-an-hour, and while showers of shell were screaming through the air, and lighting up the face of friend and foe when they burst, loud yells from the distant woods assured us our men were advancing to the assault. For a moment a deathlike silence reigned over all; and then again, our approach being seen, the enemy's artillery opened with extraordinary rapidity, until it seemed as if every tree in the forest was cracking and shivering to pieces. Barns, houses, and stacks of hay and straw were in a blaze. By their light our men were plainly visible rushing across the open spaces through infernal showers of grape, and swarming into the breastworks. The explosion of caissons was frequent, and the constant pattering of musketry within the village showed our men were there also. In a little while the Federal guns were silent, a loud noise of many voices was heard, and then a long, wild, piercing yell, as of ten thousand demons, and the place was ours.* Presently the enemy's artillery might be seen flashing from mounds and hillocks lower down the stream, rapidly throwing shell into the village; but suddenly ours flash from out the darkness not far from them, and the duel continues with much fierceness as Hill is reorganizing for another advance.

While this was progressing at the village, General Ripley's brigade moved still farther to the left and front to attack the intrenched position of the enemy at Ellison's Mills, but owing to the darkness and the strength of the place, had to retire with loss. This mill was situated on ground higher than the country immediately surrounding it, and the water which worked it ran through a swamp, debarring all assault in front. The road ran beside this swamp, and up a rise situated between the Federal camps on the right and their field-works to the left of the mill. Their artillery swept all approach through the fields and by

---

* Pickett's brigade, of Ambrose Hill's division, always distinguished itself. Brigadier-General Pickett is a Virginian, but was appointed to West-Point as a cadet from Illinois. He entered the old service as Brevet Second Lieutenant Eighth Infantry, July first, 1846; was breveted Captain, September thirteenth, 1847, for meritorious services; and gazetted Captain Ninth Infantry, March third, 1855. He joined his mother State when it seceded, and has proved an excellent officer.

the road. All timber was carefully cleared away, and the only possible method in which the position could be attacked was by crossing the creek and swamp higher up, and getting in the rear. In the excitement and darkness, Ripley advanced his line through the open fields, and had reached the road and swamp in front, when suddenly the enemy opened with grape; at seventy yards, and mowed down whole files of our men. The word to "charge" ran from wing to wing, and our men running down the bank to the road· beneath, were stopped by the impassable swamp and abattis; to the right, up the rising road, cannon also blazed in their faces, and well-posted infantry poured in showers of small shot. Our loss at this point numbered several hundreds, and was an unnecessary sacrifice of human life. Retreat was the only alternative, and under cover of the darkness, it was effected with little additional loss. From Ellison's Mills and Beaver Dam Creek, (the latter two miles down the Chickahominy,) the enemy maintained an incessant cannonade until late in the night, and the luminous flight of shells made a beautiful and comparatively harmless pyrotechnic display, which was witnessed with pleasure by thousands.

When Ambrose Hill had captured Mechanicsville, Branch's brigade arrived upon the scene, and dispositions were instantly made for renewing the conflict early next morning. Ellison's Mills on our left, in front, and Beaver Dam Creek on the right, in front, were considerable obstacles to an advance. These positions were equidistant and within range of each other: they completely commanded the roads, and all approach to them was guarded by artillery, which threw twenty-four pound shells into every thicket and bush to our front. Ambulances, carriages, and litters were busy in collecting and conveying the wounded to Richmond; prisoners were collected, spoil secured, and various divisions put in proper order and position for Friday's operations. The tramp of men was incessant; artillery and ammunition wagons toiled along; stragglers were brought in; captured cannon and stores sent to the rear, and from Brook Church turnpike to Mechanicsville, a distance of several miles, lights were flitting in fields and woods, searching for the wounded, or burying the dead. The enemy had suffered more severely than ourselves, though protected by frequent field works and rifle-pits, which had to be carried with the bayonet. The character of Porter's troops, however, was not the best, for had they fought as ours did, the number of those lost on either side would have been reversed.

As we anticipated, McClellan had been heavily reenforced after the battle of "Seven Pines." Among the first prisoners I encountered were the "Bucktail Rifles" and "Pennsylvania Reserve Corps," which formed part of General McCall's division, hurriedly sent from McDowell's army round Fredericksburgh! McCall, then twelve thousand strong, together with parts of Fremont's and Shields's Valley troops, had reached McClellan, and had augmented his force by at least twenty thousand men. We were evidently outnumbered, but this news came too late. The prisoners, numerous as they were, spoke confidently of McClellan's success, and seemed to pity us for daring to attack him. They did not know where he intended to make his "big fight," but as heavy forces were posted at Gaines's Mills, (his centre on both banks,) it was possible our overthrow would be consummated there. I never saw such impudent and bombastic fellows as these Pennsylvanians were—always excepting New-England troops. Although they had been soundly thrashed by Jackson in the Valley, and by Lee at this place, they spoke of "strategic movements," "change of base," etc., as solemnly as donkeys.

About midnight, our preparations being completed, Brigadiers Featherstone and Pryor moved up towards Beaver Dam Creek on the right, and Brigadier Maxy Gregg, towards Ellison's Mills, on the left, Jackson being still to the enemy's rear, and converging towards the Chickahominy, in the direction of Coal Harbor, near Gaines's Mills. Featherstone's Mississippians, in advance, hugged the river, and halted on a wooded slope near the stream, within five hundred yards of the position of Beaver Dam Creek. The movement was effected silently, and in the dim light I could plainly see the work before us. A farm-house was situated about half a mile from the river, on high ground which sloped towards the bank. A creek ran in front of the dwellings, and at right angles to Featherstone and the river. No bridges were discovered on which to cross and get in the rear, where rose majestic woods filled with troops. The "rise" was crowned with strong breastworks, commanding all approaches, and rifle-pits on the flanks covered the creek. Pryor, and his Louisianians, occupied higher grounds to the left of this position, screened by woods, while the entire front was open fields.

Featherstone, who commanded, had been to consult with superior officers, and returning about four A.M., (Friday, June twenty-seventh,) found the enemy had discovered his covert, and were vigorously shelling it. His men jumped to their arms, and advanced in the twilight—when from the mound to the left in front, from the banks of the creek on the flanks, and from the elevated rifle-pits to the rear, came rapidly and more rapidly the flash of artillery and musketry. The disparity of numbers and position would have appalled any troops but those selected to storm the place. Skirmishers advanced to the front, and, occupying bushes on the edge of the creek, maintained a brisk and deadly fire, and in a short time cleared the opposite bank, while the main body advanced with loud shouts to the attack. Volunteers from both brigades constructed temporary bridges on which to cross, but the passage was obstinately disputed and many were killed.

Once across, the infantry fight became animated, while three companies of artillery poured showers of shell into the enemy's works, and silenced several guns. Pryor, on the left, was slow in his advance; but Featherstone, riding over, soon urged them into rapid motion, and as our right had pushed some distance ahead towards the left rear of the Federal position, the Louisianians assailed the right with terrific yells, and finding a passage across the creek, were soon on a line with our right. The enemy's infantry, though numerous, seemed disinclined to venture on open ground, so while our wings held theirs in check, an assault in front was determined upon. For this, however, Pryor deemed our force insufficient; and having sent for reenforcements unknown to Featherstone, Brigadier Wilcox came on the scene with his Alabamians. The chief command would now have devolved on Wilcox, but he waived his right, and our artillery opened at shorter range with a terrific noise; suddenly the cannonade ceased, and up sprung our centre, rushed across the creek, up the "rise," over the dry ditch, and in a few moments were swarming over the parapet, shooting and bayoneting the troops defending it.

The sight at this moment was awfully grand. Men standing on the parapet were fighting in every conceivable attitude, and as the sun brilliantly rose over the tree-tops, illumining the scene, the semicircular line of fight, with its streams of fire, bursting of caissons, shouts, yells, and charging on the right and left — the centre occupied by the strong redoubt, crowds of combatants rushing in and out, with a sea of heads swaying to and fro round our banner floating on the wall—all was soul-stirring, sublime, and horrible. The fight on and around the hill, supports advancing from the woods, the volley and rush of our men to prevent it—the occasional discharge of cannon in the works—men clambering up and tumbling from parapets—the yells, shrieks, and shouts of friend and foe in that central position, clouded with vapor, and its floating banner—all spoke of a terrible attack and a desperate resistance. One wild yell!—out poured the enemy; and as they rushed across the open ground to their brethren in the woods, there came Southerners through the opening in pursuit — reeling, bleeding, shouting, powder-blackened, and fainting, madly firing random shots, and sinking from fatigue. Quickly the line was formed in rear of the works; all joined in the final charge; cannon belched forth grape and canister into the woods, tearing down limbs and trees; then one ringing shout passed along the line; "double-quick" was the order given, and drawing the enemy's fire, our men replied at fifty yards, yelled, charged into the timber, and scattered them like chaff before the wind. All was over!—the foe hastily retreated through the wood, where our cavalry could not follow. Cannon, small arms, prisoners, and stores, were the trophies of victory; Wilcox took up the advance, while, wearied with several hours' severe fighting and loss, the other two brigades rested round the well-contested redoubt.

In the midst of all this din, loud reports from the left, and stray shell screaming over head, told that Gregg's South-Carolinian brigade was similarly engaged at Ellison's Mills. Profiting by Ripley's discomfiture the previous evening, Gregg determined to cross the swamp some distance higher up, while engaging the enemy's attention in front. At the moment, therefore, that the engagement opened on his right—fully convinced he had naught to fear from any force sent from Beaver Dam Creek to operate on his right flank—he crossed the greater part of his command a mile above the battery, and screened them in the timber; then posting a cloud of skirmishers in front of the guns to draw their fire and annoy the enemy's supports, the word was given. Our artillery opened fird, and at the same instant our infantry rushed in from the rear and seized the work; others, ascending the rising road, poured into the Federal camp, and subjected the enemy to a destructive two-sided fire, while shells poured thick and fast on their line of retreat. Gregg displayed his usual judgment in this brilliant affair, and his success doubtless expedited matters at Beaver Dam Creek.

It was now past eight A.M., and since both routes were open, troops began to move in strong columns, shouting and yelling vigorously as they passed the positions, and saw guns, prisoners, and stores strewn on every side, with fatigued, dusty, and ragged brigades resting in the shade. " Time " was evidently an object with General Lee; he knew McClellan had endeavored to force Porter into an energetic resistance thus far, so as to gain time to protect his centre on the north bank, situated in the neighborhood of Gaines's Mills, near the river. Cavalry scouts were, therefore, rapidly pushed ahead, and infantry followed, batteries being at hand to withstand any sudden exhibition of force, and open the fight, should the enemy feel desirous of trying the fortunes of war in any of the very large open farms intervening between us and Gaines's property. Ellison's Mills and Beaver Dam Creek were, in fact, the impediments thrown out to obstruct our advance; and, though brilliantly fought actions, were simply considered as preliminary to others of greater importance within a few hours' march.

The advance, therefore, was prosecuted with vigor, and it was scarcely nine A.M. ere the several divisions were rapidly approaching the enemy. General Ambrose Hill was in the centre, bearing towards Coal Harbor; Generals Longstreet and A. P. Hill proceeded along the edge of the Chickahominy on the right, while Jackson was still far to the left, threatening the enemy's right rear as he gradually converged towards the river. In this order the three columns proceeded through the country towards Gaines's Mills, but were frequently halted and formed in line to invite a combat with the enemy in fair open ground. They would not accept our frequent challenges, however, but slowly retired through the woods, feeling confident in the strength of their position at the mill. Arriving at Hogan's plantation, one and a half miles west of the mill, General Lee took up temporary quarters there, while the columns of Ambrose Hill and Longstreet halted in the open to await the arrival of Jackson's right at New Coal Harbor.

Unacquainted as I was with the country, I had several narrow escapes from horse pickets stationed on roads that ran through dense woods; more than once I ran the gauntlet of their pistol-shots; until, being by no means inclined to offer my life a sacrifice to motives of curiosity, I returned to our advance lines scattered through the timber, and hitched my horse among scores of others round Hogan's house. Here Lee, Longstreet, and a crowd of dignitaries were gathered in council upon the doorsteps and grassy sward, and as I had never before seen so many of our generals together, I amused myself by making such observations as I could; solacing myself with a smoke, and in the mean time studying an interesting chapter in physiognomy.

CHAPTER XXXIV.

The Week's Campaign before Richmond, continued — Battle of Gaines's Mill — Sketches of the Generals previous to the Battle—Position of Jackson—Advance of Wilcox, Featherstone, and Pryor—The Centre under Ambrose Hill — The Texan Brigade brought into Action—McClellan's Infantry Charge—Defeat of his Right Wing and Centre—The Field of Battle—Capture of Guns and Booty— Death of Major Wheat—Confederates in Striped Pantaloons.

HOGAN's residence, Lee's temporary quarters, was not far from the river, and I could distinctly see our batteries and troops at Garnett's farm (Magruder's quarters) on the south bank, and in a direct line across. It was now about one P.M., and as we had full possession of both banks thus far, several couriers rode over to Magruder, and one of his heavy batteries immediately opened upon the woods on the north bank, about a mile to our immediate front, in order to clear the way for our further advance. Our skirmishers were far ahead, popping away in the timber, and in addition to this evidence, the occasional discharge of field-pieces told we were gradually working towards Gaines's Miils. The enemy had abandoned a fine field-work in Hogan's orchard, and several other important structures still closer to the river. This house was badly shattered by our shot and shell, and seemed to be very shaky; in the upper rooms we saw large stains of blood, near where a shell had entered; we were told by prisoners that McClellan had used the place occasionally in his journeys along the lines, and that on one occasion, while all were in bed, a shell came whizzing across, and cleared its way completely through the walls, killing one aid-de-camp and severely wounding another! Be this as it may, *some* were killed at this spot during our frequent artillery duels; the out-houses bore every appearance of having been used for hospitals, while numerous mounds of earth spoke of sepulture.

The whole yard and orchard were now occupied by general

officers, aids, couriers, and prisoners. Lee sat in the south portico absorbed in thought. He was neatly dressed in a dark blue uniform, buttoned to the throat; his fine calm open countenance and grey hair would have tempted an artist to sketch him in this thoughtful attitude. Longstreet sat in an old garden-chair, at the foot of the steps, under shady trees, busily engaged in disposing of a lunch of sandwiches. With his feet thrown against a tree, he presented a true type of the hardy campaigner; his once grey uniform had changed to brown, and many a button was missing; his riding-boots were dusty and worn, but his pistols and sabre had a bright polish by his side, while his charger stood near, anxiously looking at him, as if expecting a morsel of bread and meat. Though the day was warm, the General's coat was buttoned up as well as it could be, and as he ate and conversed freely with those around him, it was evident that his sandy beard, moustaches, and half-bald head, had latterly had but distant dealings with a barber. He is a little above medium height, thick-set, inclined to obesity, and has a small inquiring blue eye; though thoughtful and slow of motion, he is remarkably industrious. He was a major in the United States army, and being absent in the South-West when the rebellion opened, he hurried on to the scene of action, and has greatly distinguished himself. He appears to be about thirty-five or forty years of age, and is now Major-General C. S. A. Of his frequent successes, much is said in the course of this narrative.

Maxy Gregg sits his horse in the shade, conversing with a few about the affair at Ellison's Mills, and seems a very modest, quiet gentleman, of about fifty. His hair is grey; he has full whiskers and moustaches and a ruddy complexion; in person, he is thick-set, of medium height, and is jocular in his manner. His uniform looked the worse for wear; even the three stars upon his throat being dingy and ragged, while his common black felt hat would not bring half a dollar at any place in times of peace. But he is well mounted and armed, and keeps an eye on General Lee, by whom he expects to be called at any moment. He is a famous lawyer of South-Carolina, and when the United States were at war with Mexico, President Polk offered him the majorship of the first additional regiment of regulars which was then being raised. He served during that campaign, but achieved no distinction until the affair at Vienna, when he successfully smashed up a Dutch General's reconnoissance on the railroad, as narrated in another place. Gregg is called! he leans his head through a window and converses with Lee, but trots away as if dissatisfied. "There goes Gregg," some one remarks, "looking as black as thunder because not appointed to the advance."

Wilcox, Pryor, and Featherstone are also present, conversing freely and gaily, as if about to start upon some pleasant "pic-nic." The latter is a long-bodied, eagle-faced, quiet man of thirty-five years, without moustaches or whiskers, with a prominent Roman nose and compressed lips; he leans forward uneasily in his saddle, and with his downcast eyes appears very thoughtful; but he is a desperate, unflinching man when once aroused. He seems to take little notice of complimentary remarks regarding the action at Beaver Dam Creek in the morning, but is absorbed and anxious for the work assigned him. He is a thorough soldier, and when commanding the Seventeenth Mississippi, drilled his battalion thrice a day through all the heat of summer, apparently enjoying the exercise more than any. At Leesburgh he led his regiment in the last charge, and drove many of the enemy into the river. He is a lawyer and politician of note in Mississippi, very careless of dress, and very blunt in his manner.

Having received orders, Wilcox, Featherstone, and Pryor ride off at a gallop, and some prophesy that the advance will soon begin. Besides these and other generals, there are a few civilians present, chiefly land-owners in the neighborhood, who have come to see the havoc perpetrated by General Sykes's regulars, who were encamped around here. A courier comes galloping forward, delivers his papers to Lee, who soon after mounts, and with Longstreet and staffs, proceeds to New Coal Harbor, where it is said Jackson's right wing has already arrived. Magruder's guns have stopped their cannonade, and the advance begins, through the woods towards Gaines's Mills.

Jackson was in position at New Coal Harbor on the left, and Ambrose Hill in the centre; it now devolved on Longstreet and D. H. Hill to move forward and get into position on our right. With skirmishers thrown out in the woods, Longstreet moved cautiously forward, and drove in the enemy's outposts as he proceeded. Halting in the woods, west of Gaines's House, Pryor's column was sent forward about three P.M. to clear the woods and river-bank, south of Gaines's House, of a force stationed there to annoy us. After this was accomplished, and the enemy driven across a creek eastward, and at right angles with the river, (running here east and west,) part of Longstreet's force left the woods and halted around Gaines's House, beyond range of the enemy, on rising ground to the north.

To facilitate a full conception of this heavy and obstinate battle, let the following suffice in lieu of maps.

The reader is requested to imagine a large field, more than a mile square. The north-eastern and north-western quarters will represent high flat lands, with the Federal force occupying the north-eastern quarter, backed by woods. A creek, which runs from the north to the Chickahominy, forms the southern boundary of this supposed square. The Federal cannon command the north-eastern quarter, which is flat and level, as also the south-eastern and south-western quarters, which are considerably lower. In the south-western corner stands Gaines's House and Mills, by which we approach on a road that ascends north-eastwardly to the centre of the field, runs through McClellan's position, and terminates in the north-eastern corner. A road also comes into the field at the north-western corner, and it was at this point (New Coal Harbor) that Jackson arrived. A line drawn due east and west will represent a broad brook running eastward into the creek to the rear of the Federals; but the only wood in this square field borders this brook from the centre point running due west, being a steep and timbered ascent on to the plateau of the north-western corner. In a word, it might be said the north-eastern and north-western quarters are much higher than the south-eastern and south-western quarters; the latter much lower, and all ascent to the north-western quarter debarred by a broad brook, with timbered land abruptly rising at the back. With cannon on the north-eastern corner, where the enemy stood in line of battle, they swept the other three quarters; but to prevent the passage of the brook and woods, the common boundary of the north and south-western quarters, a strong breastwork overlooked the brook in the woods, while through the timber and up the hill rose many rifle-pits, and above all some dozen pieces of artillery, placed on the edge of this belt of timber, covering the breastworks, rifle-pits, etc., and sweeping all approach from Gaines's Mills in the south-western quarter. This brook and wooded hill was also the front of the north-western quarter, so that all approach to the enemy was over such difficulties, while several field-works were erected on the line due north and east to prevent all flanking movements in that direction.

McClellan's position was admirably chosen and well fortified. To defend it he had brought over many troops from the south bank (his south centre) by bridges not more than a mile distant, protected from all attack by a strongly fortified camp and hill in the south-eastern corner of the field, its foot being washed by the creek before mentioned, which empties here into the Chickahominy. When Longstreet's and D. H. Hill's division, therefore, debouched from the woods near the Mills in the south-western quarter, the glitter of bayonets made the Federals plainly visible in battle array on the high grounds of the north-eastern quarter. A few shell were thrown at the head of our column, but without doing hurt, and not a shot was fired from the belt of timber crowning the ascent from the centre, west and north-western boundaries of the plateau. The enemy wished us to suppose that the passage to the north-western quarter would be undisputed, and that all they desired was a fair, open fight, when we reached the plateau.

It was now four P.M., and Ambrose Hill having opened the fight to the left, Pryor, Wilcox, and Featherstone moved through the woods to the west. Having got sufficiently under the hill to prevent loss from shell thrown from the north-eastern quarter, each commander gathered his troops well together, gave the word, "File right, double-quick!" and under a storm of lead from the hill, ran eastward, parallel with the brook, gave the word, "By the left flank—double quick!" and in less than three minutes, Wilcox on the right, Featherstone in the centre, and Pryor on the left, were rushing along the open towards the brook. Here, having descended the "dip," they jumped into the brook, and tumbling or clambering over logs and brushwood, found themselves confronted by a heavy force of the enemy who were posted behind a long breastwork, and in rifle-pits on higher ground to the rear. The manner of our approach was the best that could be devised, for had these brigades marched in the fields, instead of creeping through the woods and hollows, to the west of this "rise," few would have survived the hailstorm which awaited them. By cautiously approaching at right angles with the brook, until near it, giving the word, "File right—double-quick," until each had got into position in line, and then, "By the left flank—double quick!" it brought the brigades directly under the rising ground, protected from the fire of the north-eastern quarter; and by rapidly moving, they got so near the brook, that cannon on the rise to the rear could not be depressed sufficiently to hit, without killing their own men, who were now hand to hand with ours at the brook, and obstinately defending their line of breastworks.

In such a position, and on such broken ground, officers saw it would be impossible to ride, and as many horses had been shot in the morning at Beaver Dam Creek, Wilcox, Featherstone, Pryor, and other officers, left their steeds in the woods, where they had been quietly drawn up since two P.M.; and when orders came to advance, they buttoned up their coats, pressed down their hats, drew their swords, and dashed forward on foot, giving the word of command in tones which were audible amid the roar of musketry. Though many fell in the rush while "filing right" from the woods, and "by the left flank" across the open, down the "dip" to the brook, none faltered; ranks closed up as soon as broken, and each brigade seemed emulous of the others in keeping a straight and unbroken front, as if executing "double-quick" movements in a divisional drill,

There was much confusion at the brook, which had been deepened and made still more difficult by every impediment that could be devised. But, once across, our men scaled the wooden and earthen line of wall that overlooked it, and were soon desperately engaged with masses of infantry, who retired up the hill and kept up a deafening roar of musketry against our farther advance. The situation was critical, but while our skirmishers "fanned out" in front, and from behind every tree

22

fired into whole regiments before them, lines were re-formed, and cheers told of our continual progress. The enemy's skirmishers, concealed in bushes, disputed the ground inch by inch, while an unbroken line behind them on higher ground fired upon us, over the heads of their sharpshooters. In fact, there were "three tiers" of combatants opposed to our advance—first a dense body of skirmishers; next, a few yards to the rear, and on higher ground, an unbroken line of battle; and thirdly, still farther behind, and on the edge of the unwooded plateau, a line of cannon, which depressed as much as possible, fairly shaved our heads, blew off our caps, and broke our bayonet-points! "Warm work, this!" one of the generals remarked, as he ran in our rear towards the right, with a regiment to meet a flanking force entering the woods from the north-eastern plateau— "warm work, colonel, but push them hard, sir, for every thing depends on us." This admonition was not necessary to stir up our men, for they knew that fewer would fall from rushing to "close quarters" than by advancing slowly, and firing from "long taw."

Accordingly, the word rang out from wing to wing, "Forward, march!" and, with indescribable yells, the advance began. The woods were soon completely filled with smoke, so much so that the position of the enemy could only be ascertained by the sudden flashes of light across our front. Standing erect, our men would reply with a deliberate volley, at fifty yards; rush forward, crouch and load, while the return volley swept over our heads, and cart-loads of leaves and branches cut by the storm well-nigh buried us. Our men in return aimed up hill, but sufficiently low, at the line of legs just visible under the smoke; and such was the precision of fire, that as we steadily advanced, we had to stride over bodies which lay just as they had fallen, in regular line, but seldom with the faces turned towards us. The destructiveness of our fire far surpassed any thing I have ever witnessed; but owing to the Indian or Zouave style of fighting instinctively adopted by our men, namely, of standing erect, taking deliberate aim, and firing; instantly bending low, or crawling several yards to the front; rapidly loading, waiting for a "return;" and judging of distance by the line of legs visible under the dense vapor, which did not fall within two feet of the ground—our casualties were unaccountably few, and those were of men mostly shot in the hand or arm, owing to the overshooting of the enemy.

So far I have described the progress of the battle under Wilcox, Featherstone, and Pryor, the result being that the enemy are gradually falling back through the woods to the plateau in the north-eastern and north-western corners of the field. But at the same time Ambrose Hill was vigorously pushing the centre of the enemy's line, and some of Jackson's forces had come into action on the left, from New Coal Harbor, by the road approaching the field in the north-western corner. Being driven from the woods and up the hill on to thé plateau by our right and centre, the enemy fell back, and immediately threw forward a heavy force of artillery, which swept the open fields and tore down the edge of the captured woods in which our forces were resting and re-forming.

Fatigued and torn as we were, work more desperate was yet in store for us. In the north-eastern corner of the field heavy masses of infantry stood in admirable order about half a mile distant. It was easy to see from the array of shining bayo-nets, the waving banners, and the perfect circle of artillery flame rapidly shelling north and south-west, that before we could advance through their still standing camps many thou-sands would inevitably fall. Ambrose Hill attempted to move forward in the centre, but his division, thoroughly exhausted by hard marching and constant fighting, was unequal to the task, and was withdrawn in favor of Whiting's division of Texans, Alabamians, and Mississipians. The troops of the two latter States had succored Pryor on the left, and had been actively engaged since the combat opened, but the Texan Bri-gade was held in reserve, and as this was the first "great fight" in which they had participated in Virginia, a desperate part was assigned them to act.

While dispositions were being made for the final struggle, the sun sank upon the scene, and perhaps mistaking the cause of our inactivity, McClellan moved up heavy masses of in-fantry to drive us from the woods. Their advance was beau-tiful, and as they came on in unbroken line, with colors wav-ing and men cheering, a thrill of admiration was felt by all. When within a hundred yards, our men, who lay close to the ground in the edge of the timber, received the volley, and rose to their feet at a "ready!" The Federal commanders then sprang to the front, and led on their men to the "charge!" They advanced a few yards in unbroken line — a few paces nearer their line began to waver, and swayed from wing to wing like a curving wave, and ere they recovered from their apparent indecision, our whole line delivered an accurate and deadly volley. Then high above the roll of musketry might be heard the yell of our men, as dashing headlong through their own smoke, they fell upon the disorganized masses of the enemy, bayoneting, pistolling, and knifing, in the wildest manner — driving them in the utmost confusion through their camps, seizing many guns, and approaching within a few yards of the cannon hastily thrown forward to cover the fugitive masses.

As yet not a single piece of our artillery had been brought into action, and as the lands were flat and open, their guns opened upon us with redoubled fury; the right of their lines was still held by powerful earthworks, and our right exposed to a flank movement. This was attempted by the enemy, but Ambrose Hill, in withdrawing from the centre, had marched by our rear, and lay in wait, under cover of the conquered strip of woods, so that when their forces appeared on our right, Hill rose up to meet them. They were apparently astonished, and while engaged in re-forming their lines, and bringing forward fresh forces, their right was assailed with great fury by our left, and at the same time Jackson's main force, assured of our victory, was rapidly marching through the country to their right and rear.

The absence of artillery sorely perplexed us, and particularly on our left, where the Federal cannon were sweeping all approach with canister and grape, playing north and southwest. Several regiments had been thrown forward to capture these pieces, but having proceeded some distance, were exhausted and baffled by the enemy changing position and gradually retiring. Occasionally rising to their feet, our thinned and bleeding regiments staggered forward a short distance farther, and suffering severely, again fell on their faces, and picked off scores of cannoniers, completely unmanning several guns. When charged by cavalry, our men, without forming square, closed up their broken files, and received the enemy with such unerring aim that they never essayed to gallop down upon us again. Their infantry next appeared, but, without waiting for them, our men rushed forward and fired, which caused them to retreat in unmanageable confusion. Again and again their artillery opened fire, and it was evident they were gradually preparing to retreat. Suddenly their movements were accelerated. A wild shout arose to the rear! — on came the Texan Brigade, at a run, the officers in front, charging among their redoubts and guns; soon their right was broken, and while desperately engaged against great odds, the whole line closed up, and a hand-to-hand conflict ensued at all points! Clouds of dust, woods smoking on every hand, long lines of musketry fire, the deafening roar of artillery, and piercing yells, arose on every hand, while the dark, dense mass of the enemy slowly retired through their camps, across the creek and through the woods in the north-eastern corner of the field; the bursting of caissons, and the explosion of ammunition wagons, lighting up the scene on every hand.

But while Whiting, Hood,* Archer,† Pryor, Wilcox, Featherstone, Ambrose Hill, and others, were hurling their commands at the stubborn enemy, and rapidly capturing guns, munitions, and prisoners at every turn, the distant roar of cannon several miles away to our front, breaks upon the ear. News is soon brought that Jackson in person is breaking the enemy's line of retreat towards their fortified camps on the north bank of the Chickahominy, and that he has already captured several thousand prisoners, including cannon, wagons, and officers of all ranks.

---

* General John B. Hood is from Tennessee, and was for some time in the old army, but resigned, and followed the legal profession in his native State. When hostilities commenced he was among the first to take the field, and was appointed Colonel of the Fourth Texan Infantry, and subsequently placed in command of the Texan Brigade, which consisted of the First, Fourth, and Fifth Texas, Eighteenth Georgia, and Hampton's Legion. He led the brigade on foot in the famous charge of the batteries, and rendered his name forever famous. He is a splendid-looking, dignified man of about forty-five years, possessing a melodious and powerful voice, and has the look of a dashing officer, and is much beloved. He now ranks as Major-General.

† Brigadier-General James J. Archer was appointed by the United States Captain of Volunteers, April ninth, 1847, and these being disbanded, was promoted Captain Ninth Infantry, March third, 1855. He is from Maryland, a good officer and commands a fine brigade.

Thus at eight P.M., Friday, June twenty-seventh, the Battle of Gaines's Mill was over, and the victory was ours! Couriers and generals and regiments moving to and fro, told that the enemy were to be hard pushed, and in anticipation of fresh hostilities on the morrow, nothing was to be left undone which might annihilate the right wing and centre, which had been opposed to us. It was obvious, indeed, from the roar of musketry to our front, and southward across the creek, that we were driving the enemy closely towards their fortified hills and camps on the banks of the Chickahominy, yet McClellan might even make a second attempt to maintain possession of the north bank, under cover of his numerous fortifications, which were still untouched. These could be seen, not more than a mile distant, with camp-fires burning; while rockets ascending in the star-lit sky, were communicating with Heintzelman and the left wing before Richmond on the south bank.

The field was rich in booty. I myself counted fifteen magnificent brass and bronze field-pieces, pointed south-west and north-west, with caissons and horses and dozens of cannoniers, exactly as they were left by the vanquished owners. Camps, clothing, thousands of prisoners, and immense quantities of small arms, banners, drums, and other appurtenances of war, were gathered in a few hours, while most of the troops lay fast asleep where they had halted, many using a dead Federal for a pillow! The destruction was awful; and if many guns fell into our hands, heaps of blue-jackets round them told that they had been heroically defended. Many horses were shot; and the enemy, finding themselves unable to carry off the pieces, had deliberately cut the throats of the uninjured animals to prevent them falling into our hands. In fact, several artillery-men were caught in this inhuman act, and bayoneted upon the spot. The ground round the cannon was dyed purple. Judging from the placid countenances of many, I thought they were only sleeping; but on closer inspection invariably discovered a small hole in the side of the head, made by the unerring bullet of our sharpshooters!

Two old farm-houses—one in the north-eastern and another in the north-western quarter—had been converted into field-hospitals, and when I passed, the large yards were covered with Yankees, many of their own surgeons attending them. Our loss seemed to be in wounded, but theirs in dead! Though we had much the worse position, and no cannon to assist, the numbers of their dead, particularly in the woods, surpassed all I could have believed. The timber was literally crowded with blue-jackets, and regiments which had won those positions could scarcely find sufficient ground on which to bivouac, without trampling upon the poor creatures strewn in all directions. The groans of the wounded were heartrending, yet our men lit fires, and cooked their suppers as unconcerned as if naught had happened, while not ten paces from them they could not step without treading upon some dead or wounded enemy. Generals, colonels, and regiments were scattered through the timber, all engaged in boiling water or cooking bacon on pronged sticks, while ambulances and carriages were slowly moving to and fro all night, carrying off the wounded and bumping against some inanimate carcass in the darkness. "Hospital-corps," litter-bearers, and others, were everywhere busy, while now and then a sufferer would pass in a bloodstained blanket, carried by six companions in solemn procession, a seventh leading the way through the woods with burning brands or lanterns. Ammunition wagons were busily engaged in distributing cartridge for the morrow, while artillerymen were cleaning the captured guns, and the movements of couriers delivering orders, the tramp of troops and the rumble of artillery, bespoke active operations in the morning. Spades were everywhere in request for interring the dead; comrades, pipe in mouth, consigned their relations to the humble grave without tears or words, while a few, more thoughtful, lingered by the camp-fires and talked of the incidents of battle.

Among the many who perished on this occasion, none was more regretted than Major Robert Wheat, who had gloriously fallen while charging at the head of his Louisiana Battalion. All regretted the death of this valiant soldier, and many a stout heart was wrung with anguish when it was whispered: "Poor Wheat is gone!" "Bury me on the battle-field, boys!" said he, expiring beneath a majestic oak, surrounded by his weather-beaten Spartan heroes—"the field is ours, as usual, my boys—bury me on the battle-field!" He was interred beneath the lonely, wide-spreading oak, where he had fallen, and as his face in death was lit by torches, generals and privates flocked to see the manly form of one whose voice and sabre had led in so many dangerous encounters, and who died without thanks from those who should have delighted to acknowledge his merit by promotion.

Colonels gone; captains, lieutenants, and scores of privates gone; captains commanding regiments, and sergeants companies! Such was the state of things at Gaines's Mills, but none had faltered. Files were ploughed down by grape-shot and shell, yet brigadiers and colonels on foot in front waved their caps and swords—the only word heard above the din of battle was "Forward!" and amid hailstorms of lead the men "closed up" without a word, and annihilated the enemy's ranks with murderous volleys at short distances, closing with the foe, and scattering them in all directions. Regiments thus engaged suffered severely as a matter of course, yet it was impossible to estimate our loss at more than a third or fourth that of the enemy.

While roaming over the field, gazing on the heaps of slain, I counted not less than ten Federal standard-bearers who had been laid in a small ditch in one of their camps. I knew them to be such by the leathern belts used for carrying the colors, and could not but remark that several were shot in the head and body by numerous balls, as if an entire volley had been fired at them. They were fine, well-developed, muscular fellows, and lay in death with closed hands as if the colors had been torn from them. The branch-covered huts scattered all round were filled with dead, and our men were quietly reposing in the rudely-made bunks, while the proprietors, doubtless, in many cases, were stretched in death but a few feet distant.

As soon as the camps had fallen into our hands, and the enemy had retreated, our men laid violent hands on whatever food or clothing they discovered. They were so thoughtless in this respect that I saw many of them attired in suits of Yankee clothing, so that it was oftentimes difficult to distinguish between them and our prisoners. I could not blame the poor fellows for securing clothing of some kind; the greater number of them were ragged and dirty, and wearing-apparel could not be obtained at any price in Richmond. It was grotesque to see a tall, well-developed Southerner attired in clothes much too small, but the men themselves were delighted with the change, and strutted about with gold-corded shoulder-straps and striped pantaloons, often not sufficiently long to cover the ankle. I forebore making unpleasant remarks about the danger of wearing such clothes: several of our men were shot in consequence; venturing beyond the lines, they were mistaken for enemies, and before explanations could be offered, were laid lifeless.

CHAPTER XXXV.

AT break of day I was sent to the capital, and had to pass over the greater part of the battle-field. Turning with a sickening sensation from the sight of bloodshed and the hundreds of inanimate bodies which lay on every hand, I galloped off towards Gaines's House, and felt much relieved with the refreshing air. The lofty Federal camp beyond the creek, on the edge of the Chickahominy, in the south-eastern quarter of the field, was still standing, and so many tents crowned the hill that it seemed as if it were still occupied; but this fact was being ascertained by six pieces of our artillery, which were rapidly shelling it, without eliciting a reply. Leaving the field, and plunging into the woods, I rode at a rapid rate towards Hogan's House, overtaking and meeting ambulances, private carriages, omnibuses, and other vehicles, all engaged in errands of mercy. I could have turned to the left and crossed the Chickahominy near Hogan's House, which would have taken me to Magruder's quarters at Garnett's Farm, seven miles from Richmond; but as my orders led me on the north bank to Mechanicsville, and thence to town, I had excellent opportunities for viewing the route taken by our army.

The quarters of Gèneral Sykes had been in a house near Hogan's, and among other things, a friend handed me several Northern illustrated papers brimful of "Federal victories" extravagantly sketched. The large open fields around were the camping and drill grounds of Porter's large force of "regular" infantry and artillery. The retreat had been conducted with much order, and comparatively few stores fell into our hands;

the enemy having burned them beforehand, together with many wagons, the ashes of which were still smoking. Passing on to-wards Beaver Dam Creek, deserted encampments were visible in the woods on either side of the road, among which I strolled for some time, observing that they contained many valuable medicines, which, together with other useful things, were under guard.

Beaver Dam Creek and Ellison's Mills were totally deserted, and except for a few wounded men limping about, a stranger would not have recognized these places as the scenes of the terri-ble struggle in the twilight of Friday morning. The hot sun pre-sently made us aware that there were bodies in the woods not yet buried, and, although parties were at work here and there, it was several days ere all the putrefying matter was covered. The neighboring houses were badly shattered by shot and shell, and in many instances nothing remained but a solitary and shaky chimney of brickwork. Mechanicsville was converted into one vast hospital; many citizens, old and young, satisfied their cu-riosity by lounging about the breastworks, or idly gazing on the crowds of prisoners passing on their way to Richmond. As I trotted over the wooden bridge which had been held by my old regiment, imagination began to picture the straits to which McClellan had been reduced by the generalship of that modest and unassuming professor of the Christian religion—Robert E. Lee!

Maintaining his front unbroken, and parallel with theirs on the Chickahominy until Jackson should appear at Hanover Court-House, threatening their right and rear, Lee rapidly masses his troops on our left wing. Branch at the same time crosses the stream at Brook Church Bridge, drives the foe past Meadow Bridge, where Ambrose Hill instantly crosses, joins forces and uncovers the front of Mechanicsville Bridge, where Longstreet and D. H. Hill cross and join forces. Marching by three routes, Mechanicsville, Ellison's Mills, and Beaver Dam Creek successively fall, and the enemy is vigorously pushed to Gaines's Mills, where Jackson joins us and completely routs their entire right wing, and pierces their centre *from the rear !* Driv-en across the river, McClellan's right and right centre are dou-bled up in the low swampy lands, behind his left centre and left. But now that he has his whole force on the south bank, and has lost all communication with his dépôts on the York River, will he, in desperation, taking advantage of the presence of our heavy forces on the north bank, concentrate and hurl his entire strength against our right, and endeavor to seize Richmond before we can recross to repel the attack? This would be a bold stroke, but it would take more time to prepare for such a movement than Lee will grant, and even if he did essay such a feat, our defences and force are sufficient to hold him in check until our left could cross and take him in the rear. He is thoroughly aware of our style of fighting by this time, and would not hazard his existence in such an enterprise, and will undoubtedly retreat towards the James River.

Such was the current of my thoughts·when the clattering of hoofs behind induced me to turn, and I saw it was an old friend attached to Stuart's cavalry, who had participated in all the adventures of his dashing chief. His news interested me.

As soon as Ambrose Hill had taken Mechanicsville, and Jackson's advance through the country had cut off the Federal communication with their dépôts on the Pamunkey and the head of York River, Stuart had been ordered to advance rapidly and secure whatever was possible ere the enemy had time to destroy it. On Thursday, therefore, he moved down the Branch turnpike, and proceeded towards the Pamunkey, where his presence was least expected or desirable, as large quantities of all kinds of stores were piled ready for burning. As Porter was not then defeated, the order had not arrived for their destruction, so that Stuart captured scores of horses, wagons, ambulances, and immense supplies of every kind, besides several hundred prisoners. My informant, who was there, expressed great surprise at the extensive dépôts captured, and stated that vast quantities of ammunition, many weapons, and several cannon fell into our hands. Having properly secured all these invaluables, Stuart destroyed half a dozen schooners, having first seized the cargoes; several others slipped cables and escaped. Proceeding through the country, every Federal establishment was visited, large or small, and every thing of value appropriated. At the head of York River much United States property was taken, and wagon-loads destroyed for want of transportation; but among the most singular discoveries made, was that of great quantities of dry goods and gro-

ceries, held by private individuals, who were waiting for
McClellan's triumphal entry into Richmond to transport their
stocks, and philanthropically open business to feed the hungry
and clothe the naked rebels! It was difficult to convince the
owners of such valuables that McClellan was beaten, for they
laughed at such an idea and thought us all mad; but when
marched to town, and accommodated with lodgings in our tobacco-warehouses, in company with hundreds of men in uniform, their astonishment was amazing. Yet such was the implicit reliance of the North in McClellan's promises of "pushing us to the wall," possessing Richmond "in six days," and
daily editions of "victories," etc., printed in the *Herald*, *Times*,
and *Tribune*, that many large houses sent confidential agents
to Richmond to effect sales a few days *before* the time assigned
for his entry into our capital, so that they might secure the
cream of the market in sales or barter. That such was really
the case, is proved by the fact that several of these agents
made their way from Washington *viâ* Gordonsville and Lynchburgh, and were nearly choked with vexation when arrested
in Richmond, and compelled to see hundreds of Federal prisoners pass the windows of rooms in which they and other
"commercial travellers" were confined!

Expecting to hear our guns open every moment, I felt uneasy in town, and was desirous of getting out to camp again as
soon as possible. The people of Richmond, however, seemed
perfectly easy in their minds, and carried on their usual avoca-
tions with the utmost unconcern. Many stores in the principal
streets were converted into comfortable hospitals, while crowds
stood round the doors reading the list of inmates, parents hoping
to find the names of their sons, and other relatives or friends
anxious to be informed of the fate of those dear to them.
These lists were of great service, for the sufferers were deposited in whichever infirmary was nearest, there being no such
thing as State or regimental hospitals. Business of all kinds
was brisk; wagons, carts, carriages, and ambulances were passing and repassing in long lines through every thoroughfare,
while grey-haired gentlemen "buttoned-holed" each other at
street-corners, or gathered round any horseman who seemed to
have lately arrived from the field. Cavalry-men galloping towards the War Office always awakened interest, and I saw

several couriers encircled by a crowd of idle questioners, and so pestered with inquiries that they could not dismount to breakfast for a full half-hour. Squads of prisoners, under mounted escort, were passing to and fro; in front of tobacco-warehouses, just opened for their reception, long lines of prisoners stood in single file, having their names registered before entry, while the rooms and windows of all the stories were crowded with men from every branch of the service.

Hitching my horse to a lamp-post, I went into a restaurant and called for a few eggs and a small steak; for which, together with a cup of warm "rye" coffee, I was charged five dollars only! Mounting again, I lit a cigar, cursed all extortioners and usurers, and was soon on my way down the Nine Mile Road, determining to reach Gaines's Mills by passing the Chickahominy near Magruder's quarters at Garnett's Farm. When I arrived—about ten A.M.—Magruder was about to make an attack on the enemy's left centre, not more than a mile distant, and standing on one of the breastworks I could plainly see their immense line of fortifications, from which they kept up a continual discharge of shells. The Seventh and Eighth Georgia had been sent down to attack this mammoth battery, which swept both sides of the railroad; they had driven in the outposts, and under a murderous fire, jumped into the battery; but other places to the rear opened upon them, rendering it impossible to stay there, so that they were withdrawn with considerable loss. What Magruder meant in attacking this stronghold with such a small force, unsupported,, none could imagine. It was now certain that the enemy were all on the south bank, and in greater force at this point (their left centre) than anywhere else; hence, to make any impression at all, required heavy forces. If this was merely a diversion, the thing is explained, but Magruder evidently did not look upon it in that light, for surrounded as he was by his own and Governor Letcher's staff, he rode about in a great fume, swearing and cursing like one half-tipsy. Nothing more was attempted during Saturday at this important point, and, except skirmishing among the pickets, all was quiet along our right, held by McLaws, Huger, and others.

As the day advanced, it became known that McClellan had withdrawn all his forces from the north bank, and that their camps had fallen into our hands.   To prevent any attempts to force our right, Longstreet and the Hills recrossed their divisions from Gaines's Mills, and began to march to the rear of Magruder and Huger's forces, taking up the line of march on the Charles City and Darbytown roads in the direction of James River, so as to come up with the enemy in that quarter and bring on an engagement.   Early on Sunday morning it was ascertained they were in strong force to our right, on a plain of pines at a place called Frazier's Farm, about eighteen miles from Richmond, (three miles from James River and their gunboats,) occupying a line with a six miles' front, in a swampy, thickly timbered, and irregular country.   To ascertain their true whereabouts, Lee sent the First North-Carolina Cavalry to reconnoitre, who plunged into their camps at break of day, and galloping to and fro in all directions, lost many men.   Early on Sunday morning, also, Mississippi and Louisiana pickets at Magruder's and Huger's front were attacked in force, but instead of giving ground, drove the enemy down the roads and through the woods, into and past their breastworks, and found them to be deserted.   Far from profiting by this discovery, and commencing the pursuit, these generals allowed the foe to pass across their front, instead of piercing his line of retreat by advancing down the Nine Mile road, the railroad, and the Williamsburgh road, which would have cut these forces of the enemy into so many fragments.   Thus, strong forces were allowed to pass unmolested from the left to the right of the enemy, which were halted at Frazier's Farm and Malvern Hill, and caused much trouble and unnecessary destruction of life afterwards.

On Sunday afternoon, however, (twelve hours after the vacation of the enemy's breastworks had been announced by pickets,) Magruder began to move down the road in pursuit, and met with little resistance.   Long lines of casemated batteries arose on every hand, all approach being protected by rifle-pits, felled timber, and other obstructions, so that it seemed McClellan had been fearful of surprise, and, instead of the " on to Richmond " movement, had prepared for a siege!   Large supplies of ammunition and commissary stores were discovered on every hand, and from the number of overcoats, knapsacks, and other articles lying around, it was evident they had "ske-daddled" in a great hurry. In one place I saw four tiers of barrels, fifty yards square, in a blaze, scores of barrels being all strewn round, containing ground coffee, sugar, rice, molasses, salt, tea, crackers, flour, meal, etc., the heads of the barrels being broken and their contents lying on the ground. A little hut used as a post-office and news-dépôt contained papers, letters, United States mail-bags, account-books, stationery, and similar things, but everywhere the torch had been applied, so that as our troops advanced in line of battle they marched over red smouldering ashes.*

While our troops were thus cautiously advancing through the deserted camps, a strange phenomenon came into sight on the line of railroad from Richmond. Mr. Pearce (Government ship-builer) had constructed an iron-clad one-gun battery on the framework of a freight-truck; the front and sides being cased with thick iron plates, having timber inside eighteen inches thick, the sides and front slanting towards the top, which was open. A thirty-two pound rifle had its mouth through an embrasure in front, a well-protected locomotive shoving it forward, the driver being protected by a surrounding wall of cotton-bales! Its motion was slow, for the battery weighed some sixty tons, and several shaky wooden bridges had to be crossed. Having arrived at a point where the Nine Mile Road crosses the railroad, General Griffith, of the Mississippi Brigade, was speaking to the engineer, when the enemy fired a shell at it, a fragment of which struck Griffith, and he shortly afterwards expired beneath a tree. The "Railroad Merrimac" instantly advanced, and was soon engaged in dispersing the flying enemy, its large shells exploding right and left in the woods with loud detonations.

Large columns of white sulphurous smoke now rose up into the sky, their beautiful spiral forms and broad-capped tops look-ing like mammoth pillars of ivory rising from the dark and distant line of timber. The enemy were destroying ammuni-tion ; but to prevent further waste of such valuables, the "Merri-mac" ran along towards "Savage Station," and routed several

* Major Bloomfield, of Magruder's staff, found an immense Federal flag in these camps, which McClellan had received from New-England ladies, to whom he pro-mised that many days should not elapse ere it floated in triumph over the captured capital at Richmond !

batteries drawn up to oppose its progress. The destruction caused by this single gun was very great; for, having arrived within full view of the enemy's retreat, their long lines of wagons and glitter of bayonets presented conspicuous marks for the gunners, who fired constantly on every side, inflicting much loss.

When our infantry arrived at "Savage Station," we found the enemy's rear-guard drawn up to receive us, consisting of Casey's and Sickles's men. Our troops hailed their presence with loud cheers, and commenced the attack with great fury, but the enemy seemed disinclined to prolong the contest to any length, so decamped in great haste, leaving much baggage and valuables behind, including a whole service of silver with the crest and name of "Dan Sickles" engraved thereon. Passing over the disputed ground, our men continued the pursuit until far in the night, when they changed their route towards Frazier's Farm, on the south, while Huger continued to advance towards it from the north side.

When the enemy had left their camps on the north side, however, and the Hills, together with Longstreet, had recrossed to reenforce our right, Jackson was left to pursue them on to the south side, and if possible get in their rear, so as to place them between two fires. He endeavored to cross, but the enemy held the bridge with much gallantry. Jackson, however, occupied their attention with a vigorous cannonade, while he constructed bridges higher up stream, and thus crossed his force within a few hours, on Sunday afternoon. Thus Jackson was advancing towards the enemy's right flank; Huger in their rear; Longstreet, Magruder, and the Hills on their left flank, while General Holmes was hastily endeavoring to make a long circuit round the latter, and cut off McClellan from James River. The whole country occupied and traversed by these moving armies was a mixture of swamp and sand-hills, broken up into numerous brooks, intersected by few roads, and those of such a wretched description that four men could not pass abreast in many places; and being thickly timbered, our advance was slow and tedious—artillery and wagons being far to the rear.

Where the enemy had secreted themselves in this densely

23

timbered and swampy country, none could tell; whether they had sought any of the James River landings, or pushed for the mouth of the Chickahominy, was a matter of speculation, for there were no indications of their whereabouts when we resumed the pursuit on Monday morning, (June thirtieth.) It reminded me of hunting a fox among furze-bushes; but the misery of it was, all were obliged to advance slowly, for McClellan was still superior to us in force, and it was possible that over-haste might bring us suddenly upon him, drawn up in battle array, before we could arrange our scattered forces for defence.* Such tedious, slow, fatiguing marching I never

---

* A leading journal remarked on this subject : " Those who have not understood the delay in bringing the retreating McClellan to decisive battle, would need no further explanation than a simple view of the scene of operations. The country is level and covered with almost unbroken forests, filled with dense undergrowth, and interspersed with swamps. There are but few places where one can see a hundred yards around him. McClellan had therefore admirable opportunities for concealment. It must be borne in mind, also, that his army is very strong and well appointed ; and under the pressure now upon them, his men are exhibiting more than their ordinary courage. McClellan is doubtless fighting with his best troops and bravest generals, and is exerting the utmost energy, under the most powerful of motives. Under these circumstances it is necessary to be very circumspect, lest our pursuit leads us into a murderous ambuscade, for which such a country affords many opportunities. We have to hunt McClellan on each morning, after his night's retreats, as men hunt tigers in their lair and the jungle.

" Hence it is, that for several days past, the morning has been consumed in reconnoitring after the fugitive McClellan, and finding out his new position ; and the battle that should ensue has been delayed till evening. Morning returns to find McClellan gone again, when a fresh hunt takes place.

" But the danger that McClellan may receive such supports as might extricate him from his present dilemma, creates a great desire to see him at once brought to extremity. Already there are rumors that reenforcements have arrived in James River. We doubt much, however, whether effectual help can be brought in time to save him. Our latest Northern papers (June twenty-seventh) state that Fremont's, McDowell's, and Banks's command are to be consolidated under General Pope, and sent to reenforce McClellan. A division of McDowell's troops under General McCall is stated, on the same authority, to have already joined McClellan at that date ; and this was doubtless true, for McCall has arrived.

" Our generals fully share the universal desire to put final victory beyond the reach of contingency, by securing it at once, and have put forth their utmost diligence to accomplish this result. Those who murmur at the delay do but murmur at the wilderness of the Chickahominy and its bogs and swamps. If the deferring of our hopes shall, however, result in the accomplishment of our grand object by the simple blockade of McClellan, we shall have occasion to rejoice that it has occurred. Every additional day multiplies the terror of McClellan's condition, and puts him more and more in our power."

before witnessed, over flints and rocks or heavy sand: our columns creeping along through the timber, now halting, then advancing, and halting again—first forming line of battle, and then resuming the march, under a scorching sun, along dusty roads, with clouds of sand getting into the eyes and mouths of the men, who were not allowed to leave the ranks even to get a canteen of water. Sometimes couriers dashed past to the rear, saying, "We've found 'em!"—advanced artillery would throw a few shell; a short silence; and the slow, snail-like motion of our columns would recommence.

It was said the enemy were in force at Frazier's farm—Huger aproached in the rear of this place, and we in front, so that if the fox was found, dispositions seemed perfected for running him down. Fortune, however, is variable, and we had wearily marched far towards evening, ere we received any tidings of the ubiquitous McClellan, retreating through the forests by narrow by-paths. It was now generally considered he had made good his escape, and that all our toil was in vain; for even had we overtaken him, many thought it a dangerous undertaking to attack his masses with one or two exhausted divisions, as it was certain he would open the fight with his extreme left—troops that had marched but little and were entirely fresh, under the immediate command of Heintzelman and McCall.

CHAPTER XXXVI.

Pursuit of McClellan continued—Battle of Frazier's Farm, June thirtieth—Terrific Fighting—Total Rout of the Enemy—Capture of Major-General McCall—Precarious Position of General Hill—His Genius and Daring—Gossip with a Contraband.

It was now about half-past five P.M., and the sun was fast sinking behind the woods, when Ambrose Hill's advance column halted; cannonading was plainly heard on our left, in front, from the supposed route of Huger, and couriers brought word that the Federals were disputing his passage across a creek. To our front the roads ascended, with a few fields on either hand, and among the timber on the high ground I saw small spiral columns of light-blue smoke ascending, which assured us that troops of some kind were there. Shortly afterwards a few musket-shots were heard in that direction, and some of the cavalry came galloping down towards us with the news that the enemy occupied the open high lands constituting "Frazier's Farm," five miles north-east of Darbytown, on the Newmarket road. The place was represented as good for defence; the woods right and left of it swarmed with skirmishers; the ascending grade of the road was swept by cannon, while all attempts to flank their left would meet with broadsides from the gunboats at Curl's Neck, in the James River, two and a half miles distant.

Nothing daunted, Hill sent word to the rear for our artillery to hurry forward, and immediately commenced his advance. Throwing our regiments to the right and left of the road, in skirmishing order, a lively fire soon ensued, the enemy gradually giving ground before us. This system was pursued by them until we had traversed half a mile, when we came upon their first line of infantry, and fighting commenced in earnest. Sixteen guns now began to belch forth shell, canister, and grape upon us with a stunning roar, and the only battery we had upon the ground could not be brought into position to reply. Yet never wavering or halting, our various regiments pressed forward under an incessant storm of lead. To add to our horrors, the gunboats of the enemy now threw immense shells at us, which tore off the tops of the trees, and so entangled our feet with the *débris* that it was like advancing over felled timber. Such monster shells I never saw. At the same time, long iron bolts, continually tearing through the timber, looked like small lamp-posts.

Still, "onward" was the word, and heroically did our wearied men rush forward to contend with the fresh and untouched divisions of the enemy. Now driven back, fresh troops poured in to take their place, and our men continually found themselves opposed to several "reliefs," ere any other of our regiments came up. But once hand-to-hand with infantry, and out of the way of cannon, our fellows advanced manfully to the contest, and soon smashed up their first line of defence. Drawing artillery from our front into the middle of their camps, so as to sweep the rising ground, a second line confronted us, and the fighting was even more terrible than before. Volleys upon volleys streamed across our front, and in such quick succession, that it seemed impossible for any human being to live under it. Our firing was quick but irregular; and the men, as usual, proved such adepts with the rifle, that officers were tumbled over every moment.

Footing having been secured on the high ground, the struggle was more equal, and the whole scene was observable at a glance. We were in the timber, on the edge of the field, whereon Frazier's house stands—woods to our left, right, and front, whence the enemy in strong force poured incessant volleys upon any who dared approach their guns, now in full play in the open fields. When our line was re-formed, however, and the wings began to press forward, Featherstone, Pryor, and Wilcox pushed the centre vigorously, and the first-named, making a rush for the guns, seized them, but had to fall back under the fire of a heavy force, and suffered much. Wilcox and Pryor performed prodigies of valor with their exhausted brigades, yet McCall's resources seemed to have no limit, for as soon as one regiment was vanquished another was pushed forward in its place, so that it required great efforts to drive them back. Featherstone and Fields made another dash at their batteries, but were so shattered they could not hold them. At last, after resting some time, these two commanders rushed at them again, and secured the guns beyond all hope of redemption, for our whole line advanced simultaneously with loud yells, and drove the enemy handsomely from the field about half-past eight P.M., after one of the most stoutly contested battles through which we had as yet passed.

Pushing our column forward again, we followed up the enemy's retreat, and did not halt until they were driven more than a mile; but although frequently assailing us in the darkness, it was only for a few moments, for our troops invariably charged upon them, but seldom firing. While our advance was pushing forward, and the enemy's gunboats lit up the heavens with vivid flashes, and shell and iron bolts whizzed and screamed through the air, tearing down the trees like things of pasteboard, a singular incident occurred in the captured camps round Frazier's house. Some Virginia and other troops were leaning on the guns, and conversing about the battle, when a party of horsemen rode up, the chief of whom said: "Who guard these guns?" "We do," was the answer. "That's right, boys," was the pleasant reply; "don't let them fall into the hands of the enemy; heavy reenforcements will arrive shortly. What brigade are you?" inquired the speaker, for it was so dark nothing could be distinguished. "Forty-seventh Virginia!" was the quick reply. Two of the horsemen turned to flee; but our men detecting the mistake they had made, fired and killed them; the third person, whom they arrested, proved to be no other than Major-General James McCall, United States Army, one of those who had commanded in the engagement.

Though late in the night, the enemy determined to make another effort for the recovery of the guns and battle-field, so that while our column moved ahead, unmindful of further danger, a flash of light broke upon their path, revealing the enemy again drawn up in battle array, supported by fresh artillery. Fatigued as we were, from marching over twenty miles, and fighting for several hours, this apparition of the enemy again appearing to our front, with fresh troops, seemed to dishearten all, for it was now ten P.M., and dark as Erebus. Fighting in the woods is unpleasant at any time, stumbling over fallen timber and stumps; but to find an enemy excellently posted on well-known ground at ten o'clock on a moonless night, with swampy timber on either hand, and a solitary, dusty road to retreat by, and no artillery in support, was sufficient to appall the best of troops; much more so a body of men who had travelled more than twenty miles on a hot and dusty road, without refreshment, and had but just been relieved from a four hours' contest.

Surprised but not discouraged, our men rapidly formed, under a storm of shot, and taking aim at the stream of fire before them, stubbornly contested the ground inch by inch, and sullenly fell back in admirable order, fighting as they went. Thinking to annihilate our small band of heroes, and recapture all that had been lost, this fresh corps of the enemy now advanced with loud cheers; but our fire was so accurate and well-timed that they soon slackened their pace, and moved forward more cautiously. The position of General Hill was precarious in the extreme. His division was badly shattered by the previous fight, and he was fully a mile from the battle-field, and obliged to accept another engagement. Holding his ground, he sent for reenforcements; none were within several miles of the spot. Remembering the heroes of Wilcox and other generals who had fought with such fury a few hours before, but were now resting in the rear, he dashed off, and, finding them re-forming, hurriedly explained how matters stood; his appeal was answered with deafening yells. Running forward at the "double-quick," these Spartans began to yell more loudly the nearer they approached the scene of conflict; when it was found that the cheering of the Yankees had subsided, and that they were in full retreat again, for, thinking our unearthly noises proceeded from a fresh division advancing to the attack, they were loth to engage them; slinking off in the darkness, they did not fire another shot.

It was fortunate for Hill that the enemy *did* retire; for although he had handsomely whipped them in the first engagement, and bravely held his ground against their fresh divisions in this last encounter, it was not possible he could have successfully withstood them with his few torn and wearied brigades, had they been sufficiently courageous to push their temporary advantage. With his men under arms, therefore, and excellently posted, he remained in position nearly an hour, expecting other demonstrations in his front; but all was still, until the distant tramp and shouts of Magruder's division agreeably broke upon the ear, as they gaily marched upon the scene, and relieved him of all further anxiety. Gathering the remnants of his gallant division, almost decimated by continual hard-fought engagements, Hill retired to the rear to recruit and re-form, while Magruder's men bivouacked in the enemy's camps, among guns, prisoners, and spoil; their hearts pained by the heart-rending cries of the wounded and dying. The scene upon this, as upon all battle-fields, was truly painful and horrible. The engagement had been obstinately contested, and was a bloody one; for placed as the enemy were upon rising ground, well protected by artillery, every inch had been stoutly contested, and was marked by prostrate bodies of friend and foe.

When the engagement commenced it was not expected that Hill would be left to maintain the contest alone. It was thought that Huger* would have fallen upon the enemy's rear; but, as usual, that commander was behind time, and Hill, as a consequence, was almost annihilated. It was said that Huger would have arrived in time to assist in the sanguinary contest, but on the way found the enemy had destroyed the bridge over a

---

* Major-General Benjamin Huger appears to be near sixty years of age. He is of medium height, thick-set, and stout; full face, ruddy complexion, with grey hair, heavy grey moustaches, grey eye, slow of speech and motion, evidently slow of thought, and sits his horse uneasily. Like most of our generals, his uniform is much worn, and far from imposing, so that few would take him for a major-general. He is brave to a fault, but that does not compensate for the want of a quick, penetrating intellect, and rapidity of movement. When the Norfolk Navy Yard (Virginia) was destroyed and evacuated by the Federals, April twentieth, 1861, he was appointed commander of that post, and elaborately fortified it with hundreds of guns found there, bidding defiance to all the vast armaments fitting out at Fortress Monroe. He evacuated the place in April, 1862, according to orders, and served, as we have shown, at "Seven Pines," and during the "week's campaign" before Richmond. The army has spoken bitterly of his "slowness," and he was removed from active operations, and appointed Chief of Ordnance. He entered the old service at an early age, and when hostilities commenced was Brevet Colonel, Chief of Ordnance, being stationed at the extensive arsenal of Pikesville, in Maryland. He has a son in our army, who has greatly distinguished himself as captain of artillery.

creek, and hotly disputed his passage with many guns. An artillery duel ensued, in which we vanquished them. Our cavalry rode over to secure the pieces, but were met by a strong force of infantry and obliged to return. Hearing the firing at Frazier's, the Federal commander retreated, after delaying Huger more than five hours, and joined forces with McCall against the heroic Hill.

Had not Hill's division been made of steel, rather than flesh and blood, they could not have withstood the many hardships of these trying days, for after fighting desperately at Mechanicsville on Thursday, they marched to Gaines's Mills and fought five hours on Friday; rested part of Saturday; travelled a circuitous route and a terrible road of forty miles on Sunday and Monday, achieving another brilliant victory, unassisted, against great odds! Hill, however, is a general of genius, and had it not been for the scientific handling of his men, few would have slept uninjured on the torn and bloody field on Monday night· All were prostrated with fatigue, and lay on the ground without fires, or covering, or food, too weary to think of any thing but rest.

To show the character of the fighting for the past few days, I will merely state that when Featherstone's and other brigades went into action on Friday morning, each mustered an aggregate of from two to three thousand men, but when returns were made late on Monday night, they could not muster more than from five hundred to one thousand fit for duty! Colonels, majors, and captains without number were absent on the rolls— a few killed, the majority wounded, and several sick! Such mortality could not be long sustained; yet though we suffered considerably under the many disadvantages of ground, insufficient force, and the absence of artillery, I must again affirm, from a close inspection of the field, that the enemy's loss doubled ours, not including the hundreds of prisoners, thousands of small arms, and many cannon captured. Singular as this may seem, such is the fact, attested by all who were eye-witnesses of this and other engagements, and if there is one cause more than another to which it is attributable, it was undoubtedly owing to the visible protection of a just and protecting God!

On either side of the road, through the thickly growing forests of sedged pines, lamps and lights were flitting through the night, where dead and wounded lay in scores. Most of the fighting had taken place in the timber, and deep marks in the light sandy soil, with bodies of friends and foes scattered in profusion, told where regiment had met regiment in the shade, and rushed together in the deadly shock of battle. Standing near Frazier's house and looking towards Richmond, the land gradually falls, but at this spot more abruptly; so that the enemy drawn up in battle array on the open farm, screened from sight by timber on all sides, had an unbroken view of our approach, and could tear us with their heavy batteries, no matter how we might mnaœuvre, while from the river came mammoth shell and iron bolts from their gunboats, snapping the trees as if they were matches. This selection of ground again shows the genius of McClellan; but it also fully demonstrates to all, that though superior in numbers, transportation, and *matériel*, he declined meeting us openly with any thing like equal numbers. The whole army had long desired a fair fight in open ground—*we* had frequently proffered it, though of inferior force—but this long-desired equality we never enjoyed; had we done so, all would have willingly placed their hopes and expectations on a single battle, fully convinced that we could vanquish them in less than an hour. On the contrary, this vaunted army, on which so much care and treasure had been lavished—this General McClellan, who was "pushing us to the wall," and gaining new "victories" every day!—rears breastworks on every hand to protect his army against "a few miserable rebels," who assail him in his strongholds, destroy his right wing in two days, rout his centre on another, and close up with his rear-guard in the very face of his gunboats! Still they shout with stentorian lungs, "On to Richmond!" "Victory! victory!" "Another great battle! another big smash-up of the rebels!" etc.

Truly this battle was more than an ordinary one, all things considered, and will prove the never-fading honor of Hill, if the impetuous spirit of that gallant soldier does not meet with an untimely fate. He was everywhere among the men, leading and cheering them on in his quiet and determined manner. He saw the overwhelming numbers with which they had to contend, but calmly planning his designs, he was fiery in the execution of them, giving counsel, as if in private life, but mounting his horse and dashing to the front whenever his battalions began to swerve before the masses of the enemy. Discovering their weakest point, he assailed it with fury, and ordering up the whole line, led them into the conquered camps, hat in hand, and never rested a moment until the enemy were driven a mile beyond! Nor was he contented then, for knowing the value of time, he pushed his advance far ahead, and so punished the enemy that they recalled a whole army corps to arrest his ardent progress.

Returned from viewing as much of the field as was possible in the darkness, I observed a light in Frazier's house, from which also there was smoke ascending. Feeling somewhat cold, I entered, and, as I expected, found it occupied by many of the wounded. Before the fire sat a middle-aged negro wrapped in a blanket and shivering.

"What's amiss, uncle?" I inquired, taking a coal and lighting my pipe.

"De Lor bress you, massa!—de chills, de chills, sar!"

Supposing a little liquor would not hurt him, I gave him a drink, as also to the wounded, as far as it went.

"Were you here, uncle, during the fight?" I asked, taking a stool.

"No, sar!—dis chile was in de woods! de best place, I tink, when dem ar bullets come a whistlin' and singin' roun' yer head. Was I scart, eh? I tink I *was* scart—it was worse nor half a dozen scarts to dis darkie. Well, you see, massa, it was dis way. When ole massa hert de Lincumbites was comin' roun' dese diggins, 'Pete,' says he, 'I'se gwine to Richmon', an' I wants you ter see to things, an' mine de Lincumbites don't run off with any thing; dey won't hurt you,' says he, 'but if dey only catches *me*, I'm a gone chicken!' Well, massa, one ebenin', while I eat supper, up comes a whole lot of Lincumbites, and says dey, 'Where's de master, nigger?' 'In Richmon',' says I, an' went on eatin'; but a big fellow says to me, 'Hi, nigger, you're wanted out here,' an' I went out. 'How many chickens has yer got?' says one. 'Who's dem turkeys 'long to?' says another. 'If yer don't bring me out some milk I'll burst yer head,' says some one in de crowd. 'Pull dat bed out here,' says some one. 'Tuch him up wid de bayonet,' cried another, an' 'kase I couldn't begin to speak to 'em all, somebody kicks me on the shin, and I runs in de house. One of de men wid traps on shoulders next comes, and makes 'em kind o' quiet, but I finds out dey hab taken my supper, and de bed, an' de chairs, and didn't leave me my ole pipe!

"Ef dis is de Union folks, tinks I, dey won't suit dis darkie, sure! so after dey stole all de chickens, and de turkeys, and cabbage and taters, I tought it was about time for dis chile to leave. So I packs up two or tree things in a yaller handkercher, and puts out. 'Halt, dar!' says a big feller wid a gun. 'Where's you gwine, darkie?' 'I'm gwine to Richmon',' says I, 'to massa, to get somethin' to eat.' 'Oh! yer tick-head nigger,' says he, 'doesn't yer know we'se de Grate Liberation army ob de Norf, an' come to set all de niggers free?' 'I'se a free colored pussun, any how,' says I, 'an' kin go anywhere I'se a mind,' says I; an' was goin' to pass him, when he hits me wid de gun, and two soldyers seizes me by the scruff ob de neck, an' hauls me up before de kernel.

"'Where did you find this colored feller?' says he, smoking a cigar, big like, and frowing out his legs. 'Where did you cotch de conterbran'?' says another, drinkin' whiskey. 'I guess dese unfortunate peoples don't know de blessin' of de Union, an' de ole flag!' 'I'se a free man, sar,' says I. 'Hole yer tongue,' says he, getting kind o' red; 'if dese people don't know de blessin' ob liberty, an' don't 'preciate us, dey must be taught, dat's all! Is dar no diggin' to be done, captin?' says he to another one lyin' on a bed. 'I guess so,' says he, 'dare's nofing like it.' 'Take him off to de guard house, sargent,' says he, and kase I said, 'I'se free,' de sargent begins an' kicks de clof out ob my pants. An' dare dey hab me, massa, more nor a week, diggin' ebery day, an' feedin' me an' lots of other darkies on black beans an' pork massa's hogs won't eat. But when I hear de firin' goin' on—'now's de time for dis chile,' says I, and I gets out ob de way rite smart for an ole darky. Fust I gets to de right, but de bullets fly so mighty thick I runs off somewhar else; den one ob dem big screechin' things comes along, an' I begins to say my prayers mighty fast; den while I lay b'hind a tree, our folks comes up, makin' big noise, an' I lays bery close to the groun'; but which way I go, it seems as if *some* darned bullet was chuckin' in to me, so I gets mighty scart, an' runs clar into de swamp, and dar I stays until jist now, when I crawls home agin' shiverin' in ebery joint! Nobody talk to me, massa, of de Norf. I knows how it is—dey only wants to work de life out ob de colored folks, an' den dey gives 'em deir 'free papers,' to let 'em starve when dere's no more bressworks to dig. Dey can't fool dis chile—*he* knows more nor he wishes to know about deir Grate Norfern Libratin' Union army; but ef all de darkies are done to as dey did to dis pussun, de darkies better stay wid ole massa, an' lib as he like, and have doctors to look at 'em, and hab dimes to spen'. Lor' hab mercy on us, massa, but dere's many dead folks lying aroun' ole massa's place. De Yanks used to talk big ebery day 'fore yer come along, and dey was going to do debble an' all, but I guess dey knows as much about ole Virginny *now* as I did *before* dey trabbled from the Norf to give de Suvern boys a shake! Big fools, an't dey, to tink dey're good as us, whose born on de ole place, and grow up wid white folks' children? Why, dey an't half as good as some darkies, if dey *is* white folks and talks big!"

CHAPTER XXXVII.

WEARIED beyond all expression by the continual marching and fighting of the past week, I procured a bundle of hay and a few handfuls of corn for my jaded horse, and throwing myself down on a heap of straw beneath the pines, sought some little rest. The continual movement of troops, however, through the night, passing and repassing by a single road within a few feet of me, disturbed my slumber, and half asleep or awake, I heard all kinds of voices and noises around me. Huger's division had at last arrived somewhere in the neighborhood. Jackson's, Longstreet's, and other divisions were distributed in every direction through the neighboring woods, and it was difficult to ascertain in what order; for, having left my horse for five minutes to drink a cup of "rye coffee," kindly proffered by an aide, I was nearly an hour in finding again the much coveted bed of straw. First, I found myself among Magruder's men; next, I turned down the road a few yards, and found myself in Whiting's division, and, strange as it may seem, I had hunted among nearly all the divisions of the army ere I found my voracious horse, which had eaten up all my bedding.

Unstrapping a blanket, I threw myself among leaves and branches upon the sand, and did every thing I could imagine to court sleep; but just as my eyes closed, some one would shove me and inquire: "Where is Lee's head-quarters?" "Is this Longstreet's division?" and so on. At other times, I suddenly awoke and found some one mounting my horse in mistake for his own; then, again, loud reports of musketry in front awoke all, and brought us suddenly to our feet. At length, in despair, I rode down to a brook, watered my horse, washed my face, and stood, with bridle in hand, dozing against a tree until morning broke.

More asleep than awake, duties called me in various directions, and the universal bustle indicated that a general engagement was anticipated. Infantry were busy cleaning arms, field officers stood aloof in groups, conversing; generals and staffs moved to and fro, while couriers were everywhere inquiring for Jackson, Longstreet, Hill, Magruder, and all the generals in the army. None could tell where these officers were. A few moments before, such an one was seen passing up the road, another down, but where they were at any particular time the best informed could not pretend to tell. In and out of the woods, they were moving incessantly. "Where *is* old Jackson, I wonder?" petulantly inquired a dusty courier, with his horse in a foam; "I wish to heaven these generals would have some fixed spot where they might be found; but the devil of it is, old Jackson is *always* moving about. I think he even walks in his sleep, or never sleeps at all, for here have I been hunting him for the past hour." Every body in the group laughed, except one seedy, oldish-looking officer, intently listening to the picket-firing in front, whom nobody thought to be more than some old major or other. " Here is Jackson, young man," said the officer, turning quietly, without a muscle moving. " Return to your post, sir," said he; "this paper requires no answer." And he put it in his pocket, and trotted off as unconcerned as if nothing had happened. " Who would have thought *that* was he?" we all exclaimed. "Oh! 'tis just like him," said one; "I have known him to dismount and help artillery out of the mud for half an hour at a time, and ride off again without being discovered. He is always poking about in out-of-the-way places: not unfrequently he rides unattended to distant outposts at night, and converses with the pickets about the movements of the enemy, and without more ceremony than you just now saw exhibited. It is his continual industry and sleeplessness that have routed Banks, Shields, and others in the Valley. He is continually moving himself, and expects all under him to be animated by the same solicitude and watchfulness."

It was now past seven A.M., and our advanced guard had been on the move some time, but without discovering the slightest clue to the whereabouts of McClellan and his army. It was conjectured that he had been travelling all night through the swamp to reach his gunboats at the river, but in which direction none could imagine. Our troops occupied all the main avenues of his retreat, yet no signs were visible of the route pursued by him. There was but one road left open to him, and that was merely a wagon-track through dense timber, where it was considered improbable any of his forces would pass, although it was far nearer to the river. With troops on three sides of him, it was thought he might make a desperate stand, once again, and endeavor to turn the fortune of war. He was *somewhere* in this irregular, marshy, swampy, and densely-timbered country, but at what precise point none could imagine.

We had captured many laggards of his army, but they were unable to give the slightest intimation of his route. All they knew was, that his rear was heavily guarded by artillery and cavalry, the latter having orders to shoot any who broke ranks and lagged behind. The teams had gone far ahead, escorted by horsemen, and many drivers had been shot on the spot for unruly behavior. Thousands of the army were ragged, torn, and wounded; but were encouraged by McClellan, who said "he had the rebels, now, just where he wanted them, and should be able to take Richmond much more speedily than before." *They* did not believe him, nor did any of the army; the immense crowds of dead and wounded, and their hasty retreat, told too plainly that they were badly whipped, and had better make for their gunboats as speedily as possible. A few hours before the battle of Frazier's Farm, McClellan, they informed us, had addressed the troops there with visible emotion; he besought his men to cheer up, and not be discouraged—begged all, in the name of God, not to disgrace themselves again, but fight manfully for the Union and the old flag! He was confident of whipping us—he had all things "cut and dried" for our destruction at Frazier's, and was going to attack us with fresh troops, and annihilate our first division before others came up. His position was much higher than ours; the artil-

lery excellently placed, etc.; and he passionately begged the
men to stand to their arms, for he intended to destroy us, and
push on to Richmond. These prisoners told a doleful tale of
affairs since the fight opened at the Branch turnpike on Thursday afternoon. The rank and file knew nothing of Jackson's
approach in the direction of Hanover Court-House; but thé
officers knew: and when asked what the immense destruction
of stores meant along the line, they answered ambiguously,
spoke of a probable "change of base," "clearing of the rear," and
of a speedy "march to Richmond." When Porter's right wing
was driven out of Mechanicsville, Ellison's Mills, and Beaver
Dam Creek, McClellan laughed, and said he was only "drawing
the rebels on to destruction" at Gaines's Mills; and when the
whole of the right and part of the centre were driven thence,
he said that now the rebels were fairly caught in his toils, he
had gotten us all on the north bank, and was going to hurl his
strength at our right, feeble as it was, and capture Richmond in
one day, before we had time to re-cross and oppose him.

This was all believed by the multitude, who relied implicitly
on his word, until the heavy wagon-trains of Porter and other
generals began moving towards the James River on Friday
night, Saturday, and Sunday, and the torch was applied to
their stores. When, added to this, our advance moved down
the railroad, and routed their chosen rear-guard at "Savage
Station" and other places, then the men began to think
McClellan was fooling them, and that "on to Richmond" was
a hoax! The consequence of this conviction spreading among
the troops may be imagined. There were heavy forces stationed at Frazier's to retard our advance, and McCall, Heintzelman,
and others, thinking them sufficient, McClellan and the rest
pushed forward into the swamp; but when these generals were
defeated, McClellan, fearful for the safety of the remainder, detached a whole corps at nine P.M. to arrest our further advance.
Their troops, these prisoners informed us, had been on the
move night and day since Thursday: the entire army was demoralized, and only kept under subjection by large forces of
artillery and cavalry hovering in the rear. The cavalry were
of no use they said, only to intimidate the infantry, and were
always stationed in the rear during a fight, to cut and shoot any

24

who lagged behind or broke into disorder, allowing no one to pass from the field unless wounded!

Here was a sad picture! Cavalry employed to force their infantry to the front! That this is true, is verified by scores, and I myself have seen their cavalry cut and thrust among them when routed, disordered, and unwilling to advance, particularly when our picket-posts were skirmishing in the vicinity of Munson's Hill and Arlington, during the month of September, 1861.

Foot-sore, jaded, ragged, and oftentimes wounded, long files of prisoners passed us during the morning, feeling heartily glad to have fallen into our hands. Many sat by the roadside, chatting intelligently of the course of events; one and all agreed that it was now impossible to surround McClellan, for he was near his transports, and had a large flotilla of gunboats, with ports open and ready to bombard our army, should we approach too near. Had we but possessed gunboats on the river, we might have achieved wonders; but destitute of this arm, we could only follow as far as practicable, and do our best. From an officer among the prisoners, I heard an incident related, which may be considered worthy of remembrance.

In April, 1861, when General Scott made a great fuss in the papers about the peril of Washington, among the first to volunteer their services was the celebrated "Seventh Regiment" of New-York City—a corps that was the pet of the whole country, being, perhaps, better drilled than any other volunteer regiment in the world. They mustered about eight hundred bayonets; had four or five fancy suits; the best of arms; the best blood of New-York was enrolled in their rank and file—in short, the men of this regiment were dandies and "exclusives." They had a pretty drum corps of forty drummers, and a splendid mixed band of seventy silver and reed instruments; and when they thought proper to parade, the whole city was on tiptoe with curiosity. Upon their arrival at Washington, and during the entire journey, artists of illustrated sheets were ever on the spot ready with pencil in hand to sketch the most insignificant event. When at the capital, these carpet knights refused to cross the Potomac for active service, and soon returned to New-York with flying banners, as if returning from conquest. Then came the time when Banks's army, routed by Jackson at Front Royal, rushed in disordered masses to Washington, and again the cry was raised of "the Capitol in danger," and the "gallant Seventh" volunteered to go to its defence a second time. This time they found a master in McClellan, who unceremoniously marched them to his lines in front of Richmond! In a few days the "week's campaign" opened, and the first fight in which they participated was at Frazier's Farm, where they left hundreds of bodies and knapsacks behind them! I had seen scores of our men with knapsacks, on which was painted "Fifteenth Massachusetts," "Twelfth New-York," "Twentieth Rhode Island," "Seventh New-York," etc., but it never occurred to me that this was the "Seventh New-York" whose fine appearance in Broadway and in Washington, on festal occasions, was the everlasting theme of reporters, and the envy of every other military organization in the States. In looking at the number of dead bodies scattered far and wide, I could not but meditate on the havoc which our dusty, ragged, and powder-stained Southerners had made in this, the finest regiment of the North!

From the uncertainty that prevailed regarding McClellan's force, position, and intentions, it was dangerous to push on the advance rapidly. Magruder therefore moved his division cautiously through the woods and along the wretched lanes, expecting to find the Federals drawn up in every open space we came across. A strong body of skirmishers, supported by a few pieces of artillery, followed the advance of the cavalry, who diligently reconnoitred every wood ere the main body followed, At a tortuous gait, regiment after regiment filed past Frazier's towards the south-east, in the direction of the river, halting incessantly, while artillery shelled the woods; feeling about in a wide expanse of timbered swamp for the ubiquitous McClellan and his "Grand Army of the Potomac." He could be found nowhere, and some began to imagine that he had effected an inglorious flight to James River, there to embark for parts unknown. The First North-Carolina cavalry — or rather what remained of that gallant regiment—was ordered to the front, and had lively recollections of the enemy's uncivil greeting at Frazier's Farm early on Sunday morning. They galloped forward gaily, however, at the bugle-call, and dashed off down the lane on a scout, north of where McClellan was supposed to be. All listened attentively for distant firing, and about one P.M., shots were rapidly exchanged to the south-east, towards the river, in the neighborhood of Carter's farm, about two miles distant. After a tedious advance of more than four hours, beating about through the timber, in this rugged, thickly-timbered swamp, the enemy were at last found, admirably posted in strong force!

The advance was now taken up with spirit; the men seemed delighted. It was thought that Holmes's division might still succeed in flanking the enemy near the river, and get in their rear. Jackson was on their left flank, and Longstreet close up on the right, Magruder being the centre; all our troops, consequently, were within a radius of ten miles, the wings gradually converging to a point. McClellan's only outlet was the river, where he had the advantage of his gunboats and transports. But it must be remembered that the ground towards the river was undulating, and rising far above the ordinary level in that vicinity, was admirable for defence. In fact, it was discovered that the enemy were strongly posted on Malvern Hill, (near the river;) and all approach, for more than a mile, being through open, undulating fields on Carter's farm, they had an unbroken view of our advance from the timber, and could sweep us at leisure with more than fifty pieces of different calibres! Woods to our rear, left, and right—open fields to the front gradually rising for half a mile; a plateau of six hundred yards still beyond; while farther still, commanding all approach, rose abruptly Malvern Hill, on and around which were massed their heaviest artillery.*

The reader may imagine our own situation compared with this admirably selected position, and the desperate work intrusted to us. It was McClellan's last stand, and there was every indication that he meant to defend it to the last extremity, as a means of protecting his further retreat to the river. The incessant cannonade from Curl's Neck, and the

---

* It has been said by Northern authorities that McClellan had more than one hundred pieces in position at this place, many of them being twenty-four-pound rifles.

untiring energy of the gunboats, rendered it impossible for Holmes to flank him, or get in the rear; while the absence of roads to our front, right, and left, prevented a vigorous advance in those quarters. Forming in the woods, however, our infantry advanced, and soon disposed of the Federal outposts, for they ran at the first fire, and many surrendered. While feeling our way in the timber, to the right and left of McClellan's formidable position, we were opposed by heavy bodies of infantry; but from their feeble style of fighting it was evident they were ordered to fall back gradually, so as to entice us into the open fields, where their artillery could play with effect. Our generals in front seeing the intention, halted their forces in the edge of the timber, and consulting with Magruder, explained the true posture of affairs. It was evident the enemy would not trust their infantry; and for us to succeed with them it was absolutely necessary for a heavy force of artillery to move up and cover any further advance.

It was now past four P.M., and if any thing was to be attempted the work must be quick and desperate! The artillery could *not* get up in time; hence, trusting to the impetuous valor of his troops, Magruder insisted upon charging the position, no matter what might be the cost! Cobb and others endeavored to explain, and invited Magruder to visit the scene! There was a run of more than six hundred yards up a rising ground, an unbroken flat beyond of several hundred yards, one hundred pieces of cannon behind breastworks, and heavy masses of infantry in support! Arguments were unavailing—Magruder was General, and ordered it—*he* was the only one responsible! Let the men advance and charge! Was he tipsy? I know not, though common report avows he was; and passing, I wondered whether he had returned to his old habits at such an important moment, to frustrate all our designs by passion and intoxication! Hundreds are willing to swear that he was unfit to command on that day, and complaints were afterwards made to the War Department regarding him. But to the battle.

Cobb was unwilling to slaughter his brigade, and told Magruder so, but added: "If you command me to go, I will charge until my last man falls!" He *was* commanded. Gathering his devoted Georgians and Louisianians around him, he explained the situation, and moved forward, with the promise of ample reenforcements. On the edge of the timber Cobb was exhausted, and gave over the command to Colonel Norman, of the Second Louisiana. Creeping through the woods as far as practicable, Norman deployed the brigade in open ground, and rushed up to the plateau at the "double-quick." Directly this gallant command arrived in full view, a flash ot light gleamed from the woods and hill in front, belching forth shell, canister, and grape in their midst; and the aim being accurate, scores of our men fell at every discharge. Heroically riding to the front, the intrepid Norman coolly gave commands in a clear, calm voice; his devoted companions closing up then shattered ranks, advanced with yells of defiance, and under the storm of fifty pieces, and thousands of rifles to their rear, young Norman advanced with colors flying to within a hundred yards of the guns, and there halted. With clothes all tattered, hatless, sabre in hand, this heroic Louisianian turned in his saddle, ordered his men to lie down, and anxiously looked back for the promised reenforcements. Woods to his rear, dark and silent, gave no sign of their approach; yet singly and alone, before heaven and earth, this man of steel held the ground, and though his command was momentarily wasting like snow, encouraged his veterans, re-formed the line, and yelled defiance at the masses of infantry who hovered near, but dared not approach. For more than twenty minutes Norman held his ground; but finding half the command lying dead, he gathered all that remained in compact order, and filed obliquely to the woods. But here he breathed his last. The Federals had sent through the timber a brigade to cut off his retreat. Our men, exasperated by their losses, gave a loud shout, and assailed them with such fury, that they broke and fled after a fight of ten minutes, leaving the remnant of this command to retire to the rear, to mourn the loss of hundreds, who, like Norman, fell, sabre in hand, with their face to the enemy.

Wright's brigade was also sent forward, but met with a similar fate. It seemed as if Magruder was intent on killing his men by detachments, for there seemed to be no settled plan of action; and instead of rapidly pushing forward reenforcements to succor those in front, the unfortunate commanders were compelled to stand before the enemy's pieces, without support, until decimated, and then retire as formerly. Several brigades at different times were hurled against this position, but with like success. Some advanced farther than others, and our dead were numerous under the cannon's mouth; but after running for a mile under a murderous fire, they lacked the strength to climb breastworks in the face or masses of the enemy. The Mississippi and some other brigades actually drove the enemy from the guns; but they were met by overwhelming numbers, who had rested all day in the shade, and had not been subjected to many hours' hard march- ing and fighting. To add to the horrors of the scene, and the immense slaughter in front of this tremendous battery, the gunboats increased the rapidity of their broadsides, and the immense missiles coursed through the air with great noise, tearing off the tree-tops and bursting with loud explosions.

It was now dark, and little could be done. We were gradually approaching McClellan's wings, and he considered it expedient to retire his infantry, leaving the work to be done by his artillery. By this time several of our pieces had been moved up to the front, and two companies of the Washington Artillery did great service in silencing some of the enemy's guns. Why those companies were not ordered up before, to cover our attack, may be explained, perhaps, by some future historian. All I know is, that curses were on every lip against Magruder, and from men whose position warrants me in thinking they had solid reasons for their angry vituperation. All I dare say now is, that I never heard a mortal man so despised and execrated among all classes of military men; and when the amount of carnage is considered, of which he was the occasion, it would seem that their violent language was excusable, for under those guns lay dead, that night, hundreds of the best and worthiest men the South ever produced — a bleeding, mangled monument, illustrative of the ignorance, stupidity, or drunkenness of one petted and flattered for talents he seldom exhibits.

As soon as darkness permitted, the enemy silently retreated from their position, and it was well they did so, for troops were gradually encircling, and would have captured them, ere the rising of the sun. Still eager for fight, our advance crept closer and closer, and during the night made a rush upon their infantry, and took the place, together with many prisoners, small arms, and several guns; but it must be admitted that the great mass of their forces had silently withdrawn into the swamp, none knew whither. Such a spectacle as the scene presented on this memorable hill none who saw it will ever forget. The dead, wounded, and dying of all regiments were scattered about in mangled heaps, for more than a mile, while around and underneath the guns, majors, captains, colonels, and dozens of our men were seen just as they had fallen, sabre in hand, and with face to the enemy! Many were headless — the swords of some broken; and leaning over one of the captured pieces was a young officer, who, I thought, was simply resting; on closer inspection I found him to be lifeless; he had died as he had stood, hatless, revolver and sword in hand! Truly, our loss at this place was horrible; the best brigades in the service — regiments which had acquired historic fame — were cut up unnecessarily, in the attempt to carry the place, unassisted by artillery.

Inside the battery sights as ghastly met the view. The few cannon which had been brought up towards the close of the day, did great execution among the masses drawn up here, and scores seemed to have fallen from the accuracy of our fire. A wounded Federal officer, whom I assisted, told me that all that was needed in our first assault was fresh troops to follow up the movement, for on more than one occasion the Federals rushed out from the batteries, and could not be induced to return. In several instances, indeed, our troops got in between the guns, and had cleared them, but the want of timely reenforcements defeated our plans. Several prisoners said it was downright madness in our generals to attack in the manner they did, and their gunners seemed to pity the immense sacrifice to which we had been exposed. Could not Lee have assumed command at this point when things were evidently going wrong? Undoubtedly; "but then," say some, "it would not have been 'in form' to take command from a major-general, and pretend to instruct him on the field." True, a general is supposed to know his business; but no sane person would argue that thousands of men must be sacrificed in his experiments if he has yet to learn the art of war. It is enough that men volunteer for the cause, and are willing to die, in the legitimate prosecution of warfare. I know of no rule that requires a commander-in-chief to remain quiet, merely from "professional delicacy," when subordinates are acting against the best counsel of those in front — contrary to the knowledge of men who have thoroughly reconnoitred the ground, and in defiance of all considerations arising from the strength of the enemy's position. If such is the result of that "professional delicacy" one commander bears another, the sooner it is abolished the better for thousands of brave patriots, who blindly believe that the talents of their commanders are commensurate with the position they hold.*

It is true, Malvern Hill was ours, but at a cost which the capture of that formidable position could never repay ; for I am certain thousands were unnecessarily slaughtered, and that had the advance been commanded by Longstreet, Jackson, or the Hills, not one half the carnage would have ensued. Although Magruder did eventually enter the work, it added nothing to his merit, but, if any thing, detracted from the little reputation he had gained at Bethel, at the expense of D. H. Hill. With such a magnificent command as was intrusted to him, Magruder might have rendered his name for ever illustrious; but from the moment that he commenced his advance

* It is much more pleasant to praise than to blame ; but truth and public opinion demand that I should speak of things as they really were ; and if my comments on Magruder's actions seem severe, I but simply reiterate, in a mild form, the sweeping denunciation his conduct met with at the hands of thousands who were present and in his command on that and other occasions. Subsequent to the "week's campaign," he was appointed chief in command of the Trans-Mississippi Department, comprising Missouri, Arkansas, Louisiana, (west of the river,) and Texas ; and was on his way thither, when an official telegram ordered him back to Richmond to answer a charge of drunkenness, etc., at Malvern Hill. The court-martial is said to have fully acquitted him, but his command was then and there circumscribed to that part of the Trans-Mississippi Department comprised in the State of Texas alone. Magruder soon began to show signs of activity and capacity in this distant station, and after a spirited action at Galveston, seized the place, took several hundred prisoners, and two or three vessels of war, including the Harriet Lane. Several Federal vessels escaped from the harbor while flying flags of truce ! The place was immediately fortified, and has not been recaptured. With the people of the South-West, Magruder is a great favorite.

down the railroad on Sunday afternoon until this miserable sacrifice of life at Malvern Hill, he did naught but fume, and fret, and quarrel with the best officers under him ; and his commands were sometimes so contradictory that those of his own staff could not comprehend or deliver them intelligibly to brigadiers or colonels. In a word, he acted as a man usually does when he is out of his proper sphere. As an engineer and artillerist there are few to surpass him, but intrust " planning " to him, and he fails. He can " execute " with vigor what Lee or Jackson are well fitted to plan, nothing more.

When it was discovered that McClellan had again retired, and was in full retreat, Lee instantly recommenced the advance, although it rained in floods. But the Federals seemed to have vanished once more in this densely-timbered swamp. The outposts saw no signs of them, and most of the day was lost before it was ascertained whither McClellan had fled. Towards night it was discovered he had conducted his whole force by a narrow road through a thick swampy wood, several miles in extent, and was safe under his gunboats at Harrison's Landing, having occupied the neighboring hills and strongly fortified them ! Our advance to his position could be made but by one road— that which he had traversed—and, as it was very narrow and swept by numerous artillery, pursuit was impossible. Some of our cavalry, who penetrated several miles through the swamp, captured a few prisoners in the bushes, and from them we learned the story of their last march and escape.

Malvern Hill was ordered to be defended to the last extremity, as that position alone insured the safety of the Federal army. Several parts of the hill were vacated, when our brigades impetuously advanced to the assault, but observing that single brigades were unsupported, the enemy returned. All were in breathless suspense ; for had we captured it early in the day, McClellan's army were in full view retiring rapidly towards the river, and could be shelled at discretion. When night fell, their retreat was taken up in earnest—our men were on three sides of them—and the greatest quietness prevailed, for it was thought the discharge of a single musket would have revealed their passage through the dense timber. Along this narrow road, then, the whole army had rapidly retired, and as the dead and wounded were an incumbrance at such a juncture, thousands were left behind to the mercy of the rebels! Wagons, stores, hospitals, guns—dismounted and not—were unheeded, and left in great number; while hundreds of foot-sore, lame, and exhausted men were picked up in every field. I myself saw not less than several squads of twenty or more coming to meet us, when our advance cavalry approached; while every house, barn, bush, or sheltering wood, contained hundreds of sick and wounded. The enemy's march through this narrow lane is represented to have been rapid—regiments mixed with regiments, men of all corps hurried along in great anxiety, ragged, weary, dirty, armed and unarmed, and perfectly dispirited. They were thoroughly beaten, and had the retreat lasted but a day or two longer, or had we overtaken and engaged them in any open space, they could not have stood an hour; in fact, they were so completely demoralized that all their anxiety was to reach the river, towards which they rushed in tremendous haste. Nor were hundreds satisfied when reaching the river; for, forgetful of discipline and all things else in a desire to remove far from danger, they seized the boats and hurried to the opposite banks, or to the various islands of the James. These latter were subsequently taken off by their own boats, but Confederate detachments on the south bank captured the former, who were immediately sent to the tobacco-warehouses of Richmond.

CHAPTER XXXVIII.

Recapitulation and "Official" Review of the "Week's Campaign"—Loss and Gain—Scenes and Incidents of the Struggle—The Federal Army Massed round the Heights of Berkeley—Night Attack by our Artillery, and Fearful Destruction—Subsequent Demonstration of McClellan—General Pope and other Northern Commanders rising in Favor.

WHEN it became known beyond all doubt that McClellan was safe, and strongly posted on the river bluffs at Berkeley, the pursuit was discontinued, his position being one that was peculiarly well adapted for defence. This had been proved during the Revolution of 1776, and in the year 1812, when British forces had occupied the same spot. Lee, therefore, did not seem at all inclined to push matters to an extremity, but disposed his divisions to prevent any advance of the enemy, and to precipitate an engagement should they endeavor to leave the position they had gained and attempt to retreat.

While our army under these circumstances was resting, to recover from its recent fatigue, business called me from camp to Richmond. I did not observe signs of any jubilation over our series of victories; business progressed as quietly as ever; there were neither speeches, dinners, balls, nor any demonstration remarkably indicative of joy or vanity. Every thing was quiet; people spoke of our successes as matters which had never been once doubted. "Southern men were sure to come off victorious if engaged with any thing like equal numbers," etc.; but all regretted the escape of McClellan. It was the darling desire of old gentlemen that "Mac" should be made prisoner and included in the long list of generals, hundreds of regimental officers, and over seven thousand privates then in custody. The churches, however, were well attended; prayers were offered up in thanksgiving for deliverance from danger, and to avert the further effusion of human blood; and to judge from the immense congregations that assembled for divine wor ship, it seemed that all were strongly impressed with sentiments of sincere thankfulness to God.

The various departments were as busy as usual, and particularly the War Office. It seemed certain, from the general activity, that Lee did not contemplate much idleness while summer lasted, and that active operations would recommence immediately the army had sufficiently recuperated, Where the next blow would be struck, none could imagine. Yet officers who knew, or thought they knew the secret, ominously winked and nodded, stroked their nose, and appeared very wise, or desired to be considered so. Hospitals were scattered over the entire town, and crowds of wounded men with bandaged heads or arms strolled about the streets in their patched and mud-colored clothes, while dandy clerks in departments donned fancy military gold-laced caps, elevated their eyebrows, and gazed about them with an air of infinite superiority, or, more properly speaking, of profound stupidity! Trains bound for the South conveyed hundreds of discharged and furloughed men, who, limping, bandaged, armless, or legless, seemed delighted at the idea of seeing their homes once again; while fond old couples looked with pride upon sons by their side on crutches, and never failed to answer inquiries, by telling in which battle they were wounded, and remarking upon their gallantry. In fact, every parent thought his son *the* hero of the campaign, and to hear patriotic old ladies talking of the war, one would be led to believe they would make excellent soldiers themselves.

As I have remarked on other occasions, there were no bounds to the volubility and enthusiasm of the ladies, young and old, and the appearance of a wounded man entering the cars was sure to bring many to their feet with a kind hand to assist them to the best seats. None were allowed to dress or pour water on wounds but the ladies, and they would hang around a poor ragged boy with as much tenderness and show him more kindness than if he were Emperor of all the Russias. The anxiety, care, kindness, and unceasing industry evinced by all classes of women for our wounded, in and out of hospital, far surpasses any conception that may be formed from words. Had our men been the sons, husbands, or brothers of those who interested themselves in their fate, they could not have received more kindness than they did from women of every rank and condition. Blankets were torn from their beds, flannel skirts converted into under-clothing, the finest of linen torn up for lint, wedding and other silk dresses cut up for flags, bandages, and rosettes; every thing, in fine, betrayed the unconquerable spirit that animated them, and when all else was given away, they had kind words or tears of sympathy by the bedsides of the suffering or dying!

It is almost superfluous to say that the anxiety of parents and others arriving in the city from distant parts was heart-rending. Some had been seeking sons or relatives for a week—hunting everywhere for the lost ones: some were found, but many, alas! slept upon the battle-fields; and to witness the affliction and tears of many as they searched hospital after hospital, was enough to move the heart of the most obdurate. Ministers and doctors were ever on the move, night and day; wagon-loads of captured ice were daily deposited at the hospitals; while the large amount of medicines, surgical instruments, bandages, stretchers, and ambulances, left behind by the Federals, greatly assisted the wants and comforts of our men. Lights burning all night in any dwelling was a sure sign of some wounded inmate; crape-streamers at doors, and a continual movement of hearses, told that scores were daily numbered with the dead. Long lines of open pits in suburban cemeteries were rapidly filling up, and the number of new-made graves spoke of hundreds of brave spirits slumbering beneath modest head-boards.

Strolling about one evening, after returning from a game at billiards, I heard a noise of laughter above me, proceeding from one of the rooms in the "Spottswood," and recognizing the voice of Dobbs, walked up and entered without knocking. There were at least ten persons crowded in one of the small rooms, all with their coats off, save the old Major; they were smoking, playing cards, and making much noise over some half-dozen bottles of Cognac. After much nodding and hand-shaking, I entered a quiet circle at the window, and, pipes being the order of the evening, my "sham" was soon glowing with a charge of "Billy Bowlegs' double extra," and the conversation became professional. Each had pet ideas regarding past events, and criticism ran wild and incoherent. One did not like *this* style of doing things, and another *that;* *this* general was unmercifully berated, and *that* one extravagantly praised; so that, attentive as I was, it was utterly impossible to arrive at any accurate sense of the prevailing opinion.

"I tell you," said Dobbs, after imbibing a large draught of brandy, and priming himself for a speech, "I tell you, gentlemen, that Lee's .plan surpasses any thing I have evei read in military history. Just look at the entire arrangement. When our main army fell back from Fredericksburgh, the Rappahannock, and Rapidan, and went to Yorktown to meet McClellan, Fredericksburgh was threatened by a large division under McDowell: Ewell was deputed to watch him, and did it well; but in the Valley there were not less than three army corps coming up to form a grand army to advance on Richmond from the west. Jackson was at Winchester with a small force, and was ordered to attack Shields, (Banks being sick,) so as to create a diversion in our favor. Although obliged to retire after the battle of Kearnstown, Jackson called on Ewell, and, receiving reenforcements from him, suddenly pounced down on Banks at Front Royal, and chased him to Washington, capturing immense quantities of baggage and thousands of prisoners. He retired again, and, recruited, rushed down the Valley, and instead of allowing Shields and Fremont to join McDowell, beat them both in detail, and obliged McDowell to fall back. Retreating again, Jackson begged for reenforcements, and they were sent. But while the Federal commanders were planning to entrap him, should he again go to the Valley, he made pretences of doing so, and by forced marches swooped down upon McClellan's right and rear, before the Federals in the Valley could recover from their astonishment and chagrin."

"True," said another, "it was a master-stroke of Lee; and when Branch at Brooke Bridge and Hill at Meadow Bridge assailed in front, the game was up with their right wing, for these, uncovering Mechanicsville Bridge, allowed Longstreet and D. H. Hill to cross likewise.

"The attack of Ambrose Hill was a spirited affair, and beautifully conducted.* Jackson was hovering in their

* Ambrose P. Hill is a Virginian; graduated at West-Point, and was brevet Second Lieutenant, First United States Artillery, first July, 1847, that being the time of his entering the service. We find him placed First Lieutenant, First Artillery, fourth September, 1851. He was among the first officers who left the old

rear,* and Branch fighting his way in our centre, so that before such a force they were *obliged* to fall back. Their defence of Mechanicsville, Ellison's Mills, and Beaver Dam Creek deserves credit, for had our men been less impetuous, we should have found every avenue to Gaines's Mills much more strongly fortified than we did. Think you the Federals dreamed of such a daring attack?"

"It would seem they had notions of moving, or their stores would not have been destroyed a week beforehand. Troops from all the States did well, but I think Louisiana, Mississippi, and Alabama lost more than any others up to Sunday night. The Texans at Gaines's Mill immortalized themselves; rushing across that wide expanse of open ground and capturing the guns surprised all.† General Lee is loud in praise of their

army and offered their services to the South, and was always looked upon as a "promising" officer; the part he has played in the present struggle for independence stamps him as a young man of real genius. He greatly distinguished himself at "Manassas," twenty-first July, "Mechanicsville," "Gaines's Mills," etc. He is now a Major-General.

* JACKSON DID IT.—"It is very easy, now that the affair is over, to perceive the cause of McClellan's recent reverse. At the last moment, when least expected, and equally to the surprise, we have no doubt, of President Lincoln, Secretary Stanton, and General McClellan himself, Stonewall Jackson rushed from the Valley of the Shenandoah, attacked our right wing, forced it back, and got in rear of our whole army, without weakening the rebel force massed in front of it by a single man. No general on earth could make head against such a *coup de guerre*. If McClellan had stood his ground and fought in such a position, nothing in the world could have prevented the utter annihilation of the army of the Potomac."—*New-York Paper.*

† A Texan soldier writes of this charge: "A splendid battery of thirteen guns, manned by regulars, was just beyond, belching forth destruction, and it seemed almost like certain death to venture upon the brow of the hill; but these were Texans. The most extraordinary fact about it was, that this terrible battle was being fought without any directions from officers on our side. We had lost all our field officers before we got to the first battery — the lieutenant-colonel mortally wounded, since dead; the major badly wounded, since dead; and many of the line officers killed or wounded. When I got to the top of that hill, I was almost completely exhausted, but as I got a breath, there I was, able and ready to go on when the word was given. The men had been firing from the brow of the hill, and had shot down many of the artillerymen and so many of their horses that they could not get their guns away. They stood to their guns well, only running when they could do nothing else. We pushed forward, and placed our colors upon the battery, but as the enemy were still firing upon us, we commenced firing in return. Pretty soon a strong force opened fire upon our left, and changing our front in that direction, we poured in a heavy fire, which soon brought them to taw, as the greater

gallantry. Hood, who commanded them, put himself at the head of his old regiment, and with a 'Come on, boys!' led them on right gallantly. He is now a 'full' general, I believe, and his skill and valor deserve it."

"I cannot comprehend," said another, "how it was that we lost so few, compared with the fearful carnage of the enemy."

"It would seem that 'quick' work suits us. Our lines were not so full as theirs, nor were reenforcements massed in our rear, and under fire, as with them. When the enemy fired it was wildly; our men were cooler, and understood the use of weapons better, so that their shots all told, and sometimes hit double, passing through and through, whenever we came in view of regiments drawn up behind each other; and if we *did* overshoot at any time, such shots told in the rear."

"I cannot see how our men could miss them, wedged as they were in a corner of the field when retreating by that single road; if more artillery had been present, the carnage among them would have been fearful. How did it happen that our pieces were not up sooner, Robins?" addressing an artillery officer.

"We *were* up in time, but not called upon. I think the artillery have reason to complain of you infantry, in taking up all the business, and not allowing us an opportunity. Did you ever hear what Featherstone said of us? At Beaver Dam Creek, there were twelve pieces playing against twice as many of the enemy, and Featherstone, commanding, anxiously watched us, to cover his infantry. We fired very accurately and deliberately, our shot and shell chipping their embrasures in beautiful style, and slicing off the parapets in large cakes, rapidly silencing their pieces. Featherstone was

part of two regiments threw down their arms, and ran to us, bringing their colors. Having delivered them over to another brigade, we pressed on in front, and drove the last Yankee from the field. As night was coming on, we were halted, and drawn up in line of battle. It was indeed a sad sight to look at the old regiment, a mere squad of noble men, gathered around their tattered colors. I could not realize that this little band of fifty or sixty men was the Fourth Texas. But it was even so. Out of five hundred and thirty men who went into the fight, there were two hundred and fifty-six killed, wounded, or missing; while many were completely broken down, and nearly every one was struck or grazed. We staid here all night without interruption, being heavily reenforced during the night."

25

in raptures, and exclaimed: 'By Jupiter, that beats all! Just look at our boys tumbling the breastworks about! Who would ever believe it of raw volunteers? Why, sir, the 'regulars' could not beat them! Gentlemen, I must confess, I entertained poor opinions of our artillery till now, and looked upon them as fit for little else but to waste ammunition, but the manner in which they fought and defeated Porter's 'regulars,' convinces me that we are a superior stock altogether.' Highly complimentary, wasn't it? The boys deserved such praise, for the constancy with which they served their pieces on all occasions was astonishing, particularly as two thirds of them were never under fire before. Had we remained stationary, our loss must have proved very heavy, for the enemy were very expert in getting the range. The first company that crossed at Meadow Bridge was fearfully cut up. When the pickets were driven from the bridge, our four pieces galloped across very gallantly, under a galling fire from great odds, and they held their ground nobly. Rushing up the road, they took up position on a knoll, and the rapidity with which those pieces were served astonished every one. By the way, you have observed Lee's system of 'reliefs' on the march, or in battle?"

"Yes, and an excellent one it is. It is neither right nor fair that one division or brigade be always kept in front; but when fatigued it should be relieved by another. Our numbers never permitted this system before, nor did it ever attract my attention until 'Seven Pines,' and there I could not but admire its utility. When a regiment had been some time under fire and was exhausted, another moved up, and maintained the vigor of attack, while the first remained at supporting distance as a reserve. The same rule was adopted with brigades, so that our advance never slackened its impetuosity. This was also practised at Gaines's Mills and elsewhere, when practicable, and with marked effect. The Federals seemed to follow the same plan, but where the multitude of their regiments came from, is a mystery—there seemed to be no end of them."

"To be candid," remarked one, very modestly, "I always entertained an idea, until this present war, that men were drawn out in a parallel line, and had to settle the business without shifting about so much as Lee seems to desire. A brigade or division is thrown forward, and after attacking until exhausted, another seems to take its place in some way incomprehensible to me; while the first is allowed to rest awhile, and than rushes forward again in some other direction, apparently as fresh as ever. Our brigade, I think, was moved about a dozen times at Gaines's Mills, but always had enough to do. It is impossible, however, for one in the ranks, or even a brigadier, to read the plans of a chief; all they know is their 'orders.' They are formed, and move forward or backward; fight, advance, fall back, advance again, and often find themselves at right angles with their first position. I suppose it is all right, and none of our business to inquire; but if fighting could be accomplished with fewer movements, it would please me infinitely more."

"That's the beauty of it!" said Dobbs, delighted. "That shows the brilliancy of a general's strategic genius. As you say, during the heat of battle, few except those in charge of the wings or reserves, can conceive any true notion of what is intended or transpiring. On the open plains of Europe, the field of action could be seen at a glance — but in such a varied country as ours, where most of the fighting is done in timber, it is impossible for any but a few to form an accurate notion of what is passing. I was talking with the aëronaut who ascended in our balloon during the week, and although several thousand feet above our battle-fields, and provided with powerful glasses, he was unable to ascertain any thing with precision. All he saw was smoking woods, the flash of guns, and columns of men hurrying to and fro, along dusty roads and lanes, for the clouds of smoke and dust enveloping the scene were so dense that all seemed wrapped in mystery. He plainly discerned McClellan's line of retreat, however, and made Lee acquainted with it; but when the Federals took to the swamps, and through the woods, all was obscurity again."

"Nevertheless, Federal balloonists have furnished their generals and journals with accurate maps of our position, but these were taken long before fighting commenced. But do you not think we might have done something on Saturday, and pushed the enemy more vigorously when on the north bank?"

"True, it seems that a whole day was lost, but then their fortified camps were in commanding positions, and I know not whether they *were* there on that day. I incline to the belief that they retreated on Friday night, and only maintained appearances during Saturday. It is certain that Magruder and Huger on the south bank were very slow, and were reprehensible for allowing so large a force to pass across their front, when pickets discovered their retreat on Saturday night."

"The enemy may boastingly talk of 'skedaddling,' but if the rear-guard did not hasten their movements down the railroad on Sunday afternoon, I'm no judge of running! It must have been a great mortification to the valiant Sickles to let all his beautiful silverware and private papers fall into our hands at 'Savage Station.'"

"Yes, and it must have delighted our railroad directors, when cavalry brought the news that they had left behind several magnificent locomotives just fresh from the maker's hands! When the railroad was cleared, a train was sent down, and two fine engines were discovered on the bridge with steam up, and the bridge on fire! They got the locomotives off, and the bridge was saved after some labor. Many cars were also found, up and down the track, all loaded, and apparently waiting for engines. Our advance had been too rapid, however, and the men were but too glad to escape with their lives."

"Poor old Casey got into disgrace again, I hear. He was in rear of their lines, and ordered to look after the hospitals and dépôts, but had not time to destroy them, so decamped, leaving many sick and wounded behind."

"But of all the fighting I think that at Frazier's Farm was the most desperate," said Dobbs, drinking again, and getting steam up.

"Oh! you simply think so, Major," said some one, laughing, "because hard marched and fatigued when you arrived there."

"*Think so?*" answered Dobbs indignantly. "But I *know so.* Just fancy, travelling over twenty-five miles along sandy, dusty roads, under a July sun, and coming up with the enemy about sundown, and they formed on a rising ground ready for business? Had I been Hill, I should have deferred matters until morning."

"Yes, and in the morning they would have vanished."

"Well, it was as well as it was," continued Dobbs. "We gave them a sound thrashing, but the villains fought obstinately enough, goodness knows! The position, as you know, was assailable only on one side, and as the road was an ascent, their artillery ploughed our advance unmercifully. The column was deployed without serious loss, however, but as we advanced through the timber the Federals met us at every turn, and for some time it was 'nip and tuck' with us, I can assure you. 'Forward' was the word continually ringing in our ears, and as we advanced up the 'rise' and through the woods towards their camps in the open fields, the enemy made several desperate attempts to turn our flanks, but without success. I never saw troops behave better than ours; nor did they yield an inch from any captured position, though assailed again and again by reenforcements. Those immediately in front, however, had much greater difficulty in advancing, for they were exposed to the full fire of batteries. How they escaped annihilation is a mystery. Wilcox, Featherstone, and Pryor did wonders, as usual, but their commands were sorely thinned by grape-shot, and many promising officers lost their lives there. The enemy's guns were not captured without a tremendous struggle; for since none of our pieces were on the ground, the fight on our side was maintained with infantry only. Advancing through those thick-growing pines was no joke for a corpulent fellow like me; and it required some squeezing occasionally, which was not very comfortable with the enemy in line before you, firing showers of shot. Thank goodness! I escaped with a single scratch, for which I cleaved the skull of the Yankee who gave it me."

"It would not have proved so desperate and unequal had Huger coöperated."

"Oh! yes, had he done so! but who ever expects fast movements from him? Had any of our divisions been within supporting distance we should have suffered less, but Magruder was at least five miles behind, and to attempt 'double-quick' movements along such roads, and through the timber at such a time of night, was impossible, for his men had been travelling all day also, and were perfectly exhausted. They did not arrive upon the ground until all was over; and had it not been for the in-

vincible spirit of Hill, the field and booty would never have
been ours.   When we had driven the enemy from the ground,
about eight P.M., after over two hours of severe fighting, all supposed the affair was over, but as we continued to advance, about
half-past nine P.M., such a terrific fire opened upon us that I
thought the world was coming to an end.   It was a fresh army
corps sent against us!   Such an apparition would have dis-
heartened any one but Hill.   He, seeing how matters stood, and
that they were determined to attempt a capture of the field and
spoils of war, gradually gave ground—no hurry, no confusion—
and as his men deployed, sent to the rear for succor.   That
was a trying moment, my boys!   Tired, perfectly exhausted,
and ready to faint from fatigue and long fighting, there we
were, a few shattered regiments of the advance, assailed at ten
P.M. by an entire corps!   On the enemy came, cheering, and making night hideous with their noises; they fired, but we lay low,
and, discovering their position, poured into them such accurate
volleys that they slackened pace.   Bidding us hold the ground
a little while, Hill went to the rear, but no reenforcements had
arrived; so, cheering on the remnants of some few brigades, he
moved them up at the 'double-quick,' and they advanced with
such loud shouts, and with so much apparent freshness, that the
enemy, imagining reenforcements had reached us, declined to
prolong the engagement, and left us masters of this second
field."

"Yes, it was a brilliant affair," said Robins.   "I was present,
but our guns could not be brought into position.   Considering
the strong position of the enemy and the failure of Huger to
arrive in time, it seems wonderful that Hill should have shown
so much hardihood in attacking, and displayed such brilliant
tact under adverse circumstances.   It is evident McClellan felt
sore about his defeat by a single weak division of ours, or he
would not have hurried forward fresh masses to recover the
ground.   I know not how many guns fell into our hands, but
counted six in one field, together with well-filled caissons, many
prisoners, and small arms.   It is a pity the advance did not
fall on Hill when we attacked Malvern Hill, for I am sure our
loss would not have proved so great."

"Yes," said Dobbs, "I am glad our brigade was not called

upon, for we were too much weakened to have accomplished much; but from general report I should judge it was a very much mismanaged affair. Those who *were* engaged are furious against Magruder, and it is currently said in camp that responsible men have reported him to head-quarters for drunkenness and total incapacity upon the field. I know not the truth or falsehood of the rumor, but it seems to be generally agreed that, although he commanded the finest troops in the service, he has accomplished less than any other general. The scene around Malvern Hill was awful. Battle-fields are sickening spectacles; but that one was terrible. All the woods for miles around are disfigured by the enemy's shot and shell; and as for iron bolts, thrown by the gunboats, I saw several to-day, each of them being about four inches in diameter and eighteen inches long. Those are fearful things to throw at the heads of respectable men of family like myself. If Yankee compliments are to be judged of by their length and weight, our enemies are the most villainously polite race of hypocrites on the globe; and glad am I we have solemnly foresworn for ever all fellowship or communion with them."

"I am sorry, Robins, the artillery had not fitting opportunities, for I am enthusiastic in their favor," said Frank, "and think them more than a match for the Federals at any time."

"Thanks for the compliment. I am glad we find favor in some quarters; for since the late fights every body has been cursing the artillery for not getting up in time to participate in the engagement, when in fact it was an impossibility."

"Of course it was," chimed in Dobbs. "No artillery in the world could pretend to keep pace with infantry over such a rough country. Why, sir, the roughest lanes in Europe far surpass our best roads here; for, ever since the war began, I have seen but one macadamized road in Virginia, and that was only thirty miles long; all the rest are common dirt or sand roads, over which it is almost impossible to travel. What artillery in the world could have advanced the morning after Malvern Hill? Rain poured in torrents, and cavalrymen could scarcely force their horses into a fast walk through the immense quantities of mud; as for the infantry, they manfully trudged along, knee-deep in mire. In Europe warfare is carried on differently. It usually happens there that the combatants meet in large plains, like Marengo, Austerlitz, Waterloo, and other places I have visited; and had it so chanced that *our* engagements were fought in such places, the war would have been long since decided. Our artillery are certainly not to blame for being behind time; the infantry marched too fast, and were hurried forward at the rate of thirty miles a day. Our youth seem predisposed in favor of artillery service; at one time nothing else was thought of in the whole South but artillery! artillery!"

"That spirit," said Robins, "was infused by the early exploits of the Washington Artillery Corps, Kemper's battery, and other organizations; and I must confess the efficiency of volunteers in that arm is surprising. Kemper's battery and the New-Orleans Artillery never fired other than blank cartridges before Bull Run and Manassas; yet such was their precision that the enemy frequently withdrew disabled and humbled—I mean the Federal 'regulars.' I cannot help thinking that the enthusiasm and 'pluck' of our boys have much to do with it. Being accustomed to arms from infancy, they are excellent judges of distance, and will travel all day to witness fine shooting. The first shots fired by Kemper at Bull Run completely smashed up Porter's artillery, and threw their reserves into utter confusion. Besides, those in artillery service are young, active, wiry fellows, and jump about the pieces with the suppleness of cats, dragging their guns about by hand as if they were playthings. It is my opinion that the artillery branch of our 'regular' service will surpass the world in efficiency."

"Did you observe how gaily Major Walton brought six of his pieces into action towards the close of Malvern Hill? The trumpets sounded, and off they went to the front as nimbly as if they had not marched many miles that day."

"Yes," said Robins. "I was then about a mile to the rear, and it being nearly dark, could not well distinguish the features of those about me. Standing against the side of a deserted farm-house, converted into a field hospital, I saw an oldish-looking man, dressed in a long overcoat and black felt hat drawn over his eyes, who was condoling with a grey-haired citizen about the loss of his son, but spoke in low tones; and I heard him say, with evident emotion: 'Yes, my friend, such is the fortune of this cruel, unnatural war, forced upon us by Northern fanatics; yet all will be brighter soon. Yes, yes, our poor, poor boys have suffered much within these few days, but, thank God! all is progressing favorably.' He was about to mount when I addressed him, and inquired if there was any news from the field? He answered politely that 'nothing new had transpired; we were progressing slowly!' It was President Davis! He had been on the field all day, and was ordered from the front by Lee; nor would the guards permit him, as a citizen, to cross the lines again without a 'pass!' It seems the President and two attendants had been close up to the front, and occupied an old deserted house, when Lee, being informed, requested him to go to the rear. He had not vacated the house more than five minutes ere four or five shells exploded and tore it down!

"One of the most gallant deeds I have heard was performed by a young Texan named Dickey at Gaines's Mills. When his brigade charged the batteries, they were met, among others, by two New-Jersey regiments. The shock did not last more than five minutes, for the Texans are remarkably good shots, so that after firing a volley they gallantly charged, and Dickey was fortunate enough to capture both standards! I saw them brought into Richmond by a cavalry escort, not less than two hundred prisoners following behind. It must have been a great mortification to them. That was 'On to Richmond' with a vengeance!"

"Wilcox, at Gaines's Mills," said another, "was in a terrible rage with his brigade, although as a temporary divisional general he commanded both Featherstone and Pryor. Finding that his men baulked a little at the brook, in face of obstruction and a heavy fire in front, he rushed forward, sword in hand, and threatened to cut off the head of the first Alabamian who hesitated to advance! All the generals were on foot, you know, so that it required much running about to keep the brigade in order; but, although Featherstone's men were supposed to be a reserve of the division in that action, they became so restive that he advanced up the centre, 'and arrived at the top of the hill sooner than the rest. Had he moved out of the woods alone his destruction was inevitable for the artillery of the enemy was numerous and powerful. It is said that the sight of Wilcox, Featherstone, Pryor, Whiting, Archer, Hood, and others advancing afoot, sword in hand, cheering on their commands through the woods and up the hill, was most inspiriting: the men cheered vociferously, and would have followed such commanders anywhere.

"'Come on, boys!' said little Whiting, who, though commanding a division, *would* lead his old brigade to the charge— 'Come on, boys!' said he in front, waving his cap and sword— 'quick, is the word! Here they are before us; you cannot miss them! Steady! Forward, guide centre, march!' and off they went up the hill, yelling and firing like madmen.*

"Ambrose Hill, at Mechanicsville, was ever in the front, regardless of danger, and, although his coat was torn in several places, miraculously escaped. I wish I could add the same of poor Featherstone, at Frazier's Farm, for he was desperately wounded towards the close of that fight; Colonel Taylor, of the Second Mississippi, was killed during the last volley at the same place. I single him out from among many other officers, for he was generally considered to be one of the most promising young men in the service. His praise was on every lip, and he must have risen rapidly: he was nephew to old Zachary Taylor, hero of the Mexican war, and President of the United States.

---

* Brigadier-General Daniel P. Whiting is a native of New-York, about fifty years of age, small in stature, thin, wiry, and active, an excellent officer in any department, and, though always in the infantry, proved himself an admirable engineer, by fortifying Harper's Ferry, in May, 1861. He entered the old service Second Lieutenant Second Infantry, July first, 1832; was Brevet Major April eighteenth, 1847; and full Major when hostilities commenced. He was assigned to Johnston's command in the Shenandoah Valley, May, 1861, as chief engineer there—Johnston on many occasions testifying to his merit and industry. In the absence of General Gustavus Smith, Whiting always commanded the division, and proved himself an officer of great ability at "Seven Pines," where he commanded the left attack. At the battle of "Gaines's Mills" he won immortal honor by the skilful manner of handling his division; and to cheer on the men sprang to the front on foot, cap in hand, fighting his way up-hill, through the timber, while his own brigade were cheering and making resistless charges. In fact, every brigadier did the same in that terrible conflict, while colonels acted as brigadiers, captains as colonels, and sergeants as captains. "Major" Whiting, as he is called, is much beloved by his men, and has always accomplished whatever he was ordered to do, which cannot be said of dozens of those who, without talent, have risen through social or political influence.

" Young Taylor was highly educated in military matters, and could do more with raw troops than any officer I ever knew. President Taylor's son is a brigadier, you know, and common report speaks of him as a highly scientific officer, and likely to eclipse his father's fame, should opportunities present themselves.

" There were several regiments of conscripts who participated in the late battles, and fought excellently ; in fact, I could not perceive any difference between them and the volunteers, for they never flinched, but carried every position assigned them. Conscripts or volunteers, native talent will be sure to come out in times like these—blood *will* tell. I saw a youth marching out of action with the remnants of a Federal flag wound round a wound in his arm. ' Where did you get it?' I inquired. ' I got *both* of them yonder—the wound and flag both. I shot down the color-bearer; but there was a big fight over it, and before I got clear some of our own men claimed it, and there was a general fight. Whether one of the Yanks shot me or not, I can't tell; but if the colonel hadn't come up and restored order, I should have been crushed to death, for there were at least half a dozen dead men on top of me; but having grasped the colors, they were torn from me, and this piece is all I've got. The rest is distributed among all the boys by this time. It wasn't good for much, so I bound up my arm with it! Darn 'em, I'm sorry I can't use this hand, or I'd go back, and make some of 'em howl, sure!' "

" A warlike friend of mine," said Dobbs, " who always had more to say about military matters than any half-dozen generals, was always talking of what *he* would do the first fight in which he participated. At Frazier's Farm, one of the first men I met walking to the rear was Robinson, with his hand bound up. ' Hallo! Rob,' said I; ' what's the matter? Hurt?' ' Hurt? I guess I am—*slightly!* I hadn't fairly got into it, Dobbs,' said he, ' 'fore some villain wounded me, and here am I laid up for a couple of months, and never had the pleasure of killing one of them yet!' While talking to Rob, I saw a youth binding up his leg behind a tree, fifty paces to the right of me, and had even spoken to him kindly, when a shot came, tore down the tree, and whiped his head off clean to the shoulders!

" The Yankees use their cavalry to force the infantry for-

ward, I understand, and it would seem that the number of
stragglers is very great with them; but in all my observations
during the week's campaign, I never counted more than two
dozen men straggling in *our* rear at any time; but owing to the incessant marching and consequent fatigue, I reasonably expected
to encounter many more. It seems a sense of honor animates
our troops, and they will not give up while strength lasts to
keep them going. I have frequently seen slightly wounded
men, just from the doctor's hands, moving to the front again;
and remember an instance of coolness in one middle-aged man
which I can never forget. While riding to the front I met an
Irishman of the Fourteenth Louisiana, retiring to the rear, his
rifle slung by his side, and a towel held to his face. 'Hurt,
comrade?' I inquired. 'Yes, sir,' was the answer, in a rich
brogue; 'the villains have hit me in the face,' said he, showing
his cheek half shot away; 'but if it didn't bleed so much I
should feel ashamed to go to the doctor's with such a bit of a
scratch, for our boys are whipping the devils in elegant style,
and I should like to be lending them a hand!' I told him to
bathe his face in the brook, over which our men had just clambered, and giving him about a pint of spirits from my canteen,
left him with his face well bandaged, sitting comfortably under
a tree, smoking his pipe; while, not more than half a mile in
front the battle raged with great fury, and shell fell thick and
fast in all directions.

"The greatest fortitude and patience were evinced by our
men under suffering, and I never saw but one instance where
any loudly complained. I have frequently seen men smoking
when under the surgeon's knife, and heard the wounded salute
each other wittily about their hurts. 'Hallo, colonel,' said one
fellow, lying on a door, going through the process of having
balls extracted, to his colonel, who was led forward for treatment; 'sorry to see you hurt, colonel—it will be a long time
ere either of us can dance in the Assembly Rooms, New.
Orleans, again.' 'Why, captain, is that you? you don't mean
to say they have "pinked" you at last, eh? The Yankees
seem to be distributing their favors impartially to-day. Cheer
up, old fellow, we are whipping them like the devil at all
points, so I hear. Come along, doc—my turn next!' 'Just
fill my pipe, doc,' another would say, 'before you commence

cutting, and if you've got such a thing handy as a drink of whiskey to give a fellow, it would considerably assist things, I think ; sharpen that knife a little, it looks blunt. There, now blaze away, and get through in the biggest hurry you can — let it be short and sweet,' etc."

"Well, now that all is over, what is your notion of the comparative loss, Major?" Frank inquired of Dobbs.

"From the amount of carnage * it would be difficult to form a correct opinion. I do not know the loss on the several fields, but learn that the Adjutant-General says our loss amounts to about fifteen thousand killed, wounded, and missing ; the number of the latter is comparatively small, so that we might say that in all the engagements of that eventful week we lost a grand total of fifteen thousand killed and wounded. Those figures are considered the maximum estimate."

"As to the number of guns and small arms captured, it would be difficult to say," remarked Robins, being referred to on that point. "From the Brooke Turnpike to Meadow Bridge I saw one ; from the last-named place to and including Mechanicsville, I counted six—not reckoning siege-pieces taken in reverse ; at Ellison's Mills, Beaver Dam Creek, and Gaines's Mills, I saw twenty ; at Frazier's Farm half-a-dozen, and at Malvern Hill as many more. Lee estimates the captured field-guns at forty or more, not including many siege-pieces, several dozen caissons and ammunition wagons, together with thirty thousand stand of arms, fit for use, and half-a-dozen or more stand of colors. There was a very large banner captured by Major Bloomfield, of Magruder's staff, when his division pushed down the railroad on Sunday afternoon. Prisoners state that this memorable flag was made by ladies in New-England, and given to McClellan, to be raised.

---

* From a Norfolk paper of a recent date we learn that " since the battles near Richmond, certain Irishmen at Old Point have hauled up in their seines large numbers of legs and arms which had been amputated from the wounded received at the fortress, and thrown to feed the sharks in the Roads. What will the Yankee nation say of the disposition made by their surgeons of the dismembered limbs of the army of the Potomac? They will anxiously inquire whether McClellan indeed retains so little of Virginia soil as not to afford him decent burial-place for the mangled limbs of his followers."

on the dome of the Capitol when the Federal forces entered Richmond!"

"As for their dead," a competent authority remarks, "from personal inspection of the various fields, I should judge they lost three times as many as ourselves, nor shall I be far wrong in estimating their casualties at forty thousand killed and wounded, not including more than seven thousand rank and file, a long list of officers, and a dozen generals, now prisoners in our tobacco warehouses. I see it stated in Northern journals that it is supposed McClellan has not more than sixty-five thousand effective men, at Berkley, out of a force of over one hundred and ten thousand with which he commenced the week's campaign."

"In round numbers, then," said one, "it can be stated that our losses may be put at no higher figure than fifteen thousand killed, wounded, and prisoners, without loss in generals; and that the loss of the enemy is not less than forty-seven thousand killed, wounded, and prisoners, besides several general officers killed and prisoners. In addition they have lost forty field-pieces, six or more siege-pieces, thirty thousand stand of improved small-arms, half-a-dozen flags, drums, full sets of brass instruments, thousands of tons of stores and ammunition; hundreds of wagons, caissons, horses, mules, tents; several fine locomotives, carriages, and freight cars; immense supplies of medicines, clothing, and shoes; important private and public papers, harness, fodder, and a thousand other things too numerous to mention."

"All these things we *know*," added Dobbs, "from ocular proof! How much more fell into our hands can only be learned from Stuart and other cavalry leaders, who have been scouring the whole country for weeks, and adding to the list every day. But what were the total of both armies prior to the week's operations — can any one tell?"

"*I* may form a correct idea," said Frank. "During the battle of Gaines's Mills, I was sent across the Chickahominy to Magruder's quarters at Garnett's Farm — almost in a direct line with the battle-field. President Davis, and many others, sat on the portico, observing the progress of the fight through their field-glasses, at a distance of not more than two miles in a direct line. Some one remarked to Magruder that Lee was pushing the enemy closely on the north bank, and that night would close upon another great victory. 'Yes,' Magruder answered, in his usual lisp, 'they ought to accomplish something, since they have Jackson, Longstreet, the Hills, Whiting, and others, over there.' I heard President Davis remark, subsequently, to a senator, that our force *then* over the river was fifty thousand men. Our force on the south bank, at that moment, did not muster more than fifty thousand, so that our whole effective strength did not reach to *more* than one hundred thousand fighting men.* From observations I heard dropped by those high in command, it was generally believed, from the large number of Valley troops found with him, that McClellan's whole effective force amounted to *more* than one hundred and ten thousand men, but at a rough guess it was that number, at the *lowest* estimate!"

"Well," said Dobbs, seizing the bottle, and half filling a tumbler, "the best and most accurate total is, that we have thoroughly whipped and routed them! So 'here's to Lee and our gallant boys!'"

The toast was responded to enthusiastically, and not until late in the night did the speech-making, patriotic, and song-singing company depart, leaving empty bottles, pipes, cigars, chairs, and tables strewn around the room in artistic confusion, besides several of the "glorious" company stretched at full length on the beds and floor!

The Northern army, swept from our front, had massed round the heights of Berkeley, strongly fortified and reenforced, while a very large fleet of transports and gunboats was but a few hundred yards distant in the river, unloading supplies, and protecting the position from any sudden attack by the Confederates. The rebels, in the form of a semicircle, were intently watching and preparing for the further movements of McClellan, certain that should he dare come forth, the remains of his once proud and numerous army would be annihilated. McClellan, however, was far too weak and wise to attempt any advance, and retreat he dared not; had he stirred from his position to fall back down the peninsula, he would most surely

---

* I have since learned that this estimate of the Confederate force is incorrect—it did not muster ninety thousand effective men.

have been overtaken and routed, but by remaining where he then was, the fleet was his protection and main hope. All this time the Federals under Pope were concentrating round Fredericksburgh, and preparing to advance from the north and east, in which case McClellan, being reenforced, was, if possible, to coöperate on the peninsula. Pope took command of his army with a grand flourish of trumpets, and his bombastic promises highly delighted Northern leaders and newspaper writers, who, as usual, endeavored to hide McClellan's inglorious defeats by claiming them as victories. They argued that, although the latter had now but seventy thousand out of more than one hundred and twenty thousand men, " he was considerably nearer Richmond than ever," and that " his change of base would culminate in the speedy reduction of the rebel capital!"

From early indications, Lee was satisfied that McClellan would not again operate on the peninsula, but had concluded to transport most of his forces to the Rappahannock, and form a junction with Pope. For this purpose, although maintaining daily picket-fights with our forces, immense numbers of transports assembled in the James River, and it was determined to try our rifled artillery upon them at some unsuspected moment. As a division of our troops, well concealed, were on the south side of the James, General Pendleton was ordered there with a hundred guns, and he concealed his movements under cover of thick timber. Every thing being prepared and his own position admirably screened, Pendleton gave the signal, and all our guns opened with a deafening roar, shortly after midnight. Every shot told with fearful effect, for the guns had been sighted at sunset, and after a few discharges the vessels were rocking, and rolling, and crashing beneath our weight of metal, while to swell the uproar the gunboats instantly extinguished their lights, and commenced shelling us furiously. The enemy's missiles, however, passed overhead without disabling one of our guns, or killing more than three men in Dabney's heavy battery, and wounding some half-dozen others. The loss among the shipping, on the other hand, was fearful, for as their transports numbered many score, and were all clustered together round Harrison's Landing, the crash of timber, the shrieks, the mingling of voices, and the general commotion were fearful.

But our artillery did not pay exclusive attention to the vessels, for as the camps and fires of McClellan's army were clearly in view on the opposite hills, and not more than half a mile distant, showers of shell were thrown amongst them. Very soon barns and outhouses were in flames; the greatest confusion was apparent among the troops, soldiers in all sorts of attire rushing wildly to and fro. At length morning dawned, and where shipping had been in unsuspecting quiet the night before, nothing was now to be seen but floating wrecks or masts above water, stores, timber, bales, boxes, and boats thrown upon the beach; as for the enemy, not a tent or soldier could be seen for miles on their old camping-grounds; all had disappeared as if by magic. The destruction visible on every hand verified the fearful havoc which the night attack of Pendleton's artillery corps had occasioned among the dispirited but snugly provided-for enemy of the day before. The attack was so unexpected and violent that the enemy were paralyzed in the dead of night, and although neither their press nor generals ever mentioned the circumstance, except in ambiguous terms, we had other evidence that the disaster was appreciated by those who were the witnesses and sufferers by it. Prisoners of the better class subsequently confirmed our convictions that the loss was so great, and followed so quickly after their disastrous handling in the "Week's Campaign," that they *dared* not inform the North of the destruction of transports and supplies, or of the sudden change of camps during that fearful cannonade.

Some of Cobb's legion on picket-duty next day picked up many stragglers, who naïvely said that "the assault was so sudden, fearful, and accompanied with such havoc and disorder, it seemed as if the Last Day had arrived;" for regiments were hurriedly formed and marched away in the darkness, many having no other covering but their drawers. Many thought the occasion presented a fine opportunity for a night attack on the land side, but McClellan's favorite style of planting cannon on high grounds and throwing up strong intrenchments, had taught our men much respect for that branch of the service, although for the infantry they entertained an habitual and pro-

26

found contempt, and were as ready to attack them by night as by day.

A few days subsequent to this success, McClellan made demonstrations as if intending to cross part of his force from Berkeley and operate on the south side of the James River. Our infantry were withdrawn a few miles inland to Petersburgh, to watch this new combination. It was known that heavy reenforcements had reached McClellan, and he seemed inclined to advance up both banks and attempt to destroy our water-batteries at Fort Darling, so as to allow the gunboats to proceed up the river to Richmond. He was closely watched by Lee, who had also been intently studying the programme of General Pope, now industriously engaged in gathering a large army north of the Rappahannock at Culpeper, with a strong advance-guard south of it near Gordonsville. It was well known to us that great expectations were entertained of Pope's movement towards Richmond, and that he had made extravagant boasts of his intentions to turn the tide of fortune, and sack Richmond in an incredibly brief time.

But as this new army was preparing to move round our left, while watching McClellan with our centre and right more than a hundred miles away from it, divisions and bickerings seemed to exist in those two grand wings of the Federal army. McClellan, thoroughly defeated in his own attempt, looked upon Pope as an upstart and braggadocio, who, by dint of trickery and politics, had become chief favorite of the Cabinet, from which he could obtain any amount of support and unlimited supplies, which had been denied to the late Grand Army of the Potomac. More than this, it was known that one or more generals of division (General Kearny in evidence) had asked relief from duty under McClellan, looking upon him as an arrant humbug, and had been assigned to Pope's army. General McDowell also—who for many months before had been stationed at Fredericksburgh, and was promised chief command of this movement when joined by Banks, Blenker, Milroy, Shields, and Fremont from the Shenandoah Valley and Western Virginia, but whose hopes had been destroyed by the rapid marches and victories of Jackson over those generals at various places—now felt extremely humiliated to find his plans and chief command intrusted to one incompetent, and himself rated as a third-class subordinate in the same enterprise; General N. P. Banks, of Massachusetts, being second to Pope. Politics had much to do with these appointments. McClellan was a Democrat, and though opposed to abolitionism, never allowed party feeling to influence him, always taxing his capacity to the utmost to gain success. He had been defeated many times, and still was looked upon as an able man, particularly in the South, where military critics reviewed his course impartially, and awarded that praise which ability and bravery deserved. Pope and Banks were both uncompromising negro-worshippers, and as military men were laughed at by the whole South. McDowell, also, was known to be a Democrat, and, though too good a soldier to allow politics to interfere with duty, was discarded, and assigned an unimportant command, while striplings of the East, from political influence, were placed above him. All these things were fully known to us, and no movement occurred in either army of which we were not cognizant. Our lines before the enemy were so well kept that few were aware of any movement preparing; but as the foe were becoming very active on the line of the Rappahannock, and daily glorifying themselves in the newspapers about some trifling cavalry skirmish with our scouts, it was evident their advance under Banks was about to move into an eligible position. As soon as this was ascertained, his old friend, the inevitable "Stonewall," received marching orders with his division to proceed from the main army and creep upon him, which he did in his usual brilliant style, and with his wonted success.

CHAPTER XXXIX.

Movements of Beauregard's Army in Mississippi, after the Battle of Shiloh—Our Defences at Corinth—General Halleck takes Command of the combined Armies of Buell and Grant, and follows on to Corinth—Both Armies intrench—Magnitude of the Federal Works—Beauregard suddenly retreats to Tullahoma—Policy of his Retreat—The Federals do not follow—Part of our Force detached from Beauregard, and, under command of Van Dorn, sent to defend Vicksburgh against the Fleet of Commodore Farragut advancing up from the Gulf, and Commodore Foote's Squadron of Gunboats coming down the River from St. Louis—Building of the Rebel Ram Arkansas—She forces the Mouth of the Yazoo River, and runs the Gauntlet of the Fleet—Night Bombardment of Vicksburgh—Flight of the Federals—Capture of a Federal Despatch Boat.

"DEAR FRIEND: My last letter contained details of the battle of Shiloh on the first and second day; of the first day's victory, of Albert Sydney Johnston's death; and of our reverse and retreat on the second day, before the combined armies of Buell and Grant. I also informed you that the retreat was covered by General Breckinridge, with his Kentuckians, and of the admirable manner in which he performed that difficult task. 'General,' said Beauregard, riding up with his staff; 'we must retreat; we cannot maintain an unequal contest against such odds of fresh troops. The command of the rear-guard is given to you. This retreat must not be a rout—if it costs your last man, it must not be so!' The army was withdrawn from the field as if in review, and Breckinridge covered the retreat so skilfully that the enemy halted, and did not pursue us more than a mile from the field. This was partly owing to their own exhausted condition; for next day the pursuit was taken up by General Pope, who captured several hundred of our sick and wounded in the timber. Many, doubtless, were like those who lagged behind in your retreat from Yorktown—men who lacked patriotism, who had enlisted from disaffected or unsound districts, had become lukewarm, and, for the sake of peace and comfort, willingly became prisoners to the numerous and well-conditioned forces of the enemy.

"When we reached Corinth I was glad to hear that Price, with a division of Missourians, had crossed the Mississippi, and formed a junction with Van Dorn and a few Arkansians, the trans-Mississippi campaign being considered closed for some time. Within a few days, we learned that the tremendous forces of Grant and Buell, combined under command of Halleck, were slowly advancing. It was reported that they swarmed over the country like locusts, eating or destroying every thing, carrying off property, capturing negroes, and impressing them into service.* Driving in our pickets, they

---

* As a specimen of the behavior of Federal troops in the West and South, I subjoin the following from their own organs: The *Louisville* (Kentucky) *Democrat*, which for safety was printed over the Ohio River at New-Albany, thus speaks of their soldiery in Athens, Alabama: "General Turchin said to his soldiers that he would shut his eyes for two hours, and let them loose upon the town and citizens of Athens—the very same citizens who, when all the rest of the State was disloyal, nailed the national colors to the highest pinnacle of their court-house cupola. These citizens, to a wonderful degree true to their allegiance, had their houses and stores broken open, and robbed of every thing valuable; and, what was too unwieldy to be transported easily, was broken or ruined. Safes were forced open, and rifled of thousands of dollars; *wives and mothers were insulted, and husbands and fathers arrested if they dared to murmur ;* horses and negroes taken in large numbers; ladies were robbed of all their wearing apparel, except what they had on; in fine, *every outrage was committed, and every excess indulged in that was ever heard of by the most savage and brutal soldiery towards a defenceless and alarmed population.* All this was done by those who pretend to represent the United States Government. . . . I know similar acts disgraced the same brigade when we occupied Bowling Green, (Kentucky,) but the matter was hushed up to save the credit of our army, hoping it would never occur again."

The *St. Louis* (Missouri) *Republican*, a Federal journal, and the most responsible organ in the West, says: "In Monroe County, Missouri, near the Salt River railway bridge, as Mr. Lasley and family were returning from church, together with a party of young ladies and gentlemen, who were visiting them at their country-house, they found their dwelling and grounds occupied by Federal troops, who had been stationed at the bridge. Suspecting no harm, though finding the grounds guarded, they advanced towards their residence, when Mr. Lasley was ordered to get down and go to Palmyra. He replied, that they must permit him to enter the house, and get a thicker coat, as he would be absent all night. This was not allowed; but they placed him and James Price (young son of a poor widow) and young Ridgeway (only son of aged parents) in front of the Federal lines. They were then insulted grossly by the officer commanding, without explanation of any kind; and Mrs. Lasley, thinking they were going to be shot, rushed towards her husband; but Mr. Lasley and young Price fell dead at the one moment, and from the same volley. Young Ridgeway ran to the woods, but was pursued and shot. Mr. Lasley and young Ridgeway had both taken the oath of allegiance, and were under heavy

had occupied the northern end of the New-Orleans and Memphis Railroad; they had also seized Memphis, sunk our little improvised fleet of gunboats there, after a noble fight, in which we inflicted considerable loss; had pushed along the Charleston and Mississippi Railroad, the west end of which they occupied; and had camped about three miles from Corinth.

"This was a startling position for us truly! Our main railroad communication with Richmond, *via* Chattanooga, in the enemy's possession, and we obliged to travel many hundred miles round by way of Mobile, Alabama, and Georgia, to keep the communication open! As there are but two lines of railroad, both had been taxed to the utmost before this disaster. What could we do with but one, while the enemy had several outlets by land and river communication as well for advance as supplies? To add to our misfortunes, Corinth was a wretched site for a camp, utterly destitute of water, good or bad, and what little could be obtained was scooped up from the sand, or from pools fed by occasional rains. You are acquainted with the place, having camped here before going to Virginia; and you know, although there were at that time not more than ten thousand men here, the water was so bad that many gave ten cents a gallon for such as they could get from an indifferent well at the hotel. Except to keep open the railroad traffic with the South, Beauregard would not have held the place five minutes, particularly as out of thirty-five thousand men present, the heat, insufficient and bad food, wretched water, and other causes, had reduced our effective strength to about twenty-five thousand.

"To these disagreeable circumstances add the fact that Halleck did not seem inclined to fight us in our breastworks, but occupied ground north of the town, which, you know, is higher than our side, and, intrenching himself there, depended on time and patience to work up till within shelling distance, and then destroy us at leisure. Notwithstanding our small force and

bonds. Before this crime was committed the soldiery had taken possession of Mr. Lasley's house, and helped themselves to every thing they needed, had forced the old cook to prepare dinner for them, and destroyed many articles of furniture, etc." These are but mild instances of what the Federal soldiery have done, in various places, to harmless citizens.

the tremendous odds against us, Beauregard put a bold face upon matters; frequently marched out and offered battle, but, to our surprise, found the enemy unwilling to leave their intrenchments, which grew larger and more numerous every day. Halleck's losses, however, must have been truly appalling; for if our own troops were discouraged, though born on the soil and accustomed to the heats, rains, sudden changes, and abominable water, what must be said of men suffering from similar causes, who were never South before in their lives, and who had been accustomed to every necessary in the field?

"As long as Halleck held the railroad in our front and another on our left flank, he seemed sufficiently contented to advance slowly upon us, and having more or less completed a vast line of elaborate breastworks, began to manœuvre on our right, so as to gain possession of the east branch of the Mobile and Columbus road; thus leaving Beauregard in possession of but one line to the South, namely, the south branch of the New-Orleans and Memphis Railroad. This intention was early perceived by Beauregard, who moved counter to the design, without weakening Corinth itself.

"The labor and pertinacity of Halleck were wonderful. Having to make roads as he advanced into the interior, he employed large bodies of men, and when trenches were opened before Corinth, his army had completed several fine military roads from the Tennessee River to his immediate front. By these roads ponderous guns and immense trains of supplies were drawn from his base of operations on that river, so that for a distance of thirty miles or more, ox, horse, and mule teams were unceasingly moving by night and day, to facilitate the construction of his works. Sickness, however, greatly weakened his forces, and chills, fevers, chronic disorders, and agues, filled the hospitals. Still, his sanitary system was much superior to ours; scores of deep wells were bored, and an ample supply of water obtained for his men, while we in Corinth were almost decimated for the want of a sufficient quantity; and the surrounding country was filled by our sick men, too weak to stand, reduced to skeletons from heat and exposure.

"It soon became obvious that if Halleck would not advance from his works, we should either be compelled to retreat at no distant day, or be massacred at discretion by the enemy's guns, which were daily advanced nearer and nearer with apparent impunity. The Federals were sorely afraid we would retreat, as in that case their mammoth trenches and laboriously constructed roads would but ill repay them for their patience and long-suffering. This affliction, however, we could not spare them. Immense roads, as I have said, had been dug and levelled through miles of timber, unheard-of supplies of shot, shell, and mammoth mortar batteries had been brought to the front with infinite labor, and much sacrifice of life and money, when early one morning our whole army quietly decamped towards Tullahoma, and ere the mists had risen were beyond sight or hearing!

"A few regiments were thrown out to our front as usual, and maintained picket-firing, but were much surprised to receive orders to fall back; they could not believe the army had left, for the movement had taken place so quietly, orderly, and unexpectedly, that it required ocular proof to convince them of the fact! When the pickets retired from the front, the enemy quickly perceived it, and, though much astonished, prepared to pursue. Mortified at the failure of their designs, they followed our trail vigorously, and, owing to some miscarriage of orders, two trains of miscellaneous but not valuable baggage fell into their hands, together with several hundred sick, and a few old arms. I cannot say with absolute certainty, but believe we did not lose a single gun, caisson, or a pound of ammunition; to account for which it is necessary to add that Beauregard had been quietly withdrawing from Corinth for a space of three weeks, but so strictly had all orders been fulfilled, and so secretly, that three fourths of the army were ignorant of the fact, and would not believe it! It was true, nevertheless, and had it not been for the accidental capture of the two small baggage-trains, through wilful carelessness, this celebrated retreat would perhaps stand unrivalled in the history of warfare, as being the most secret, successful, and disastrous blow which a feeble army ever dealt to an all-powerful and confident enemy.

"Your description of Johnston's retreat from Manassas leads me to believe that Beauregard was desirous of emulating your commander; the result at any rate does him infinite credit. Halleck had stored his camps with immense supplies; he had destroyed hundreds of horses, wagons, mules, and carts, in the work of transportation; had prepared for a bombardment of an indefinite period; built magazines and barracks, repaired rail roads, and erected bridges, *thus occupying the whole spring in preparation;* and now in one moment all these plans were thwarted, and the hot season too far advanced for his troops to move a mile farther into the interior! The disappointment was equal to the loss of a battle, if not worse. As for ourselves, save a few hundred sick, and the baggage-trains already mentioned, together with two old locomotives, we lost scarcely any thing worth mentioning, and arrived at Tullahoma without adventures of any kind, save flying rumors from the rear, where General Pope was following us up, shelling the woods furiously on every hand, but never approaching within gunshot of our rear-guard. The distance was twenty miles south of Corinth, and the place selected for our stand an excellent one to protect the south branches of the Mobile and New-Orleans railroads. The season, as I have said, made it impossible for the enemy to follow, (it was the month of June,) so, finding a supply of good water, and eligible sites for fortifications, we settled down comfortably, and had no fear of consequences.

"You may imagine Halleck's chagrin on discovering our retreat! as might be expected, the whole North was railing at us for running away, calling us 'cowards,' for not remaining to be shelled out at discretion! Much comment, too, has been made in our army regarding this movement; it took the Confederacy by surprise; opinions differ materially, and it is said that the War Office blames Beauregard for allowing himself to be driven to any such necessity. I doubt this report, but let us reason the matter a little, though I am not aware of the opinions formed by military critics in Virginia regarding it. 'First. Why did B. fall back upon Corinth and fortify it, after the defeat at Shiloh? To protect communication by the two main roads intersecting there.' 'Second. Was that object accomplished, or could he have done so by remaining there? No; the fall of Memphis gave all the roads north of Corinth to the enemy; they approached and threatened B.'s left along the western branch of the Mobile and Columbus road, which was unavoidable, and were manœuvring on his right to gain the eastern sec-

tion; Corinth was indefensible, and by falling back he protected the southern branches of both roads, had a better position to
fortify, and the health of his troops secured.' 'Third. But why
fortify and decimate his troops by remaining there, when its in-
defensibility was 'seen at a glance? To hold their large unacclimated army in check, decimate them in a much greater ratio
than his own, compel them to waste their only available season
fruitlessly, and gain the objects of a campaign, without shedding
blood!' 'Fourth. But did B. prove himself a general in allowing Halleck to approach by parallels, when he could have prevented it by counter-works? No, if Halleck had gained the
object of these works; yes, because he intended to leave, and
did leave them, ere the bombardment opened!' 'Fifth. What
then did B. gain by holding and in finally leaving Corinth?
He gained time; held the enemy in check without a battle—
the result being as valuable as if gained at the price of blood—
and by retreating at the time he did, out-generalled the enemy,
rendered them powerless to move, and saved Mississippi from
the inroad of a large army, which would have followed him into
the interior at an earlier season of the year, but was now unable to do so from weakened forces and the great heats.' 'Did
not B.'s army suffer extremely, and what was the ratio between
friend and foe from the same causes? The army suffered extremely from sickness, but not mortality; while, from being
unacclimated, the reverse was the case with the enemy—the
ratio between us in mortality was as seven to one! The figures
are from the acknowledged returns of both generals. Our extraordinary expense in holding Corinth during the spring was
but trifling; Halleck's expenditure was enormous in amount.'

"But to return to my narrative :

"We had scarcely arrived at Tullahoma ere it was known
that Farragut's fleet from New-Orleans, and Foote's from the
Upper Mississippi, were approaching, to unite against the batteries at Vicksburgh—the only town which prevented the free
navigation of the river by the enemy. As it was thought that
a land force would coöperate with the gunboats, our brigade
was sent to assist in the defence of the stronghold. Van Dorn
was appointed to command the post, and did every thing in his
power to place the city in a good posture for defence.

" Vicksburgh, situated on the east bank of the river, did good service as a dépôt and rendezvous for the trans-Mississippi States during the war, being the only safe crossing-place for us. Thousands of men, supplies, and *matériel* were continually passing to and fro—much of our provisions for the armies in the East and West being derived from Texas, parts of Louisiana, and Arkansas. In short, could the enemy silence our batteries and seize the town, all the agricultural products of the Northern and Western States would pass down unmolested to the Gulf ; the enemy would gain free access to the whole river front, supply themselves abundantly with cotton, sugar, molasses, and other products, disjoin the east and west Mississippi States, and, having us fairly on the flanks, could operate with impunity upon numberless points, divide our forces, and perhaps subjugate us piecemeal. The east bank of the river, for several miles above Vicksburgh, gradually rises higher than the common level, so that immediately above the city there are high bluffs, which command the river north and south, cover the town, and can sweep the peninsula across the stream, formed as it is by windings of the river, and subject to overflows. The Mississippi, above Vicksburgh, runs west to east, and, suddenly bending, runs north and south ; so that the point of this peninsula came immediately under our guns at the bluffs, and few boats could pass or repass without receiving damage, since the stream at that point was not half a mile across, and the navigable channel immediately under our batteries ! As will be seen at a glance, Vicksburgh was an all-important point to the enemy, who, apart from military ends, desired free navigation for their commerce ; it was a vital position to us for the same reasons, independent of the fact that its occupation would end our campaigns west of the river, throw those States into the hands of the enemy, and cut us off from regular and large receipts of commissary stores.

" As the enemy had swept every thing before them on the river north and south of Vicksburgh, it was considered we could make but a feeble resistance. The country around was only a cotton district, short of agricultural supplies, and connected with the interior and main army at Tullahoma by a single track of railroad, much overworked and unsound. As June advanced, and the rivers began to rise, the smoke of nu-

merous gunboats above and below the city proved that the
enemy were busy reconnoitring, and slowly approaching their
object.   Foundries and workshops were kept busy night and
day; timber was hewn on every side for breastworks, magazines, and hospitals; and, within a few days, formidable earthworks and rifle-pits were dug on every hand, the river-bank
being lined with marksmen to sweep the decks should an enemy appear.   The streets running parallel with, and at right
angles to, the stream, were cleared of all combustible material,
and orders were given for women and children to leave immediately.   The former, for the most part, refused to go; many
dug holes in the ground, and made them bomb-proof and comfortable, so that, if forced by the gunboats, they could seek
refuge therein.   The whole town was burning with patriotism,
and women were more fierce, if possible, than the men.

"All was prepared for the expected bombardment, yet business went on as before, to some extent, and there was nothing
of that flurry and excitement visible among the people which
thoughts of a cannonade might naturally create.   Batteries on
the bluff were manned night and day, but so concealed, it was
impossible to discover the position or number of pieces.   In
truth, we had not more than twenty guns, and our artillerists
were mere novices.   They were eager for the 'fun,' however,
and were ably supported by some splendid troops from Louisiana, Kentucky, and Mississippi, who would 'rather fight than
eat.'   The women seemed to have changed their feminine na-
tures; they wished every building srushed to powder rather
than give up; and if any of the Northern soldiery could have
seen them, young and old, arming for the worst, and bent on
mischief, it would not have given them a very pleasing idea of
the reception prepared for a Federal landing!   Every thing ingenuity could devise was resorted to by chivalric dames to facilitate military preparations — expense, loss, fatigue, and danger
were despised, and all were in rivalry to make sacrifices for the
common cause, and even stripped sheets and blankets from
beds for the use of the sick.   More than this: it was announced
that the commandant of the town needed flannel for ammunition, and none could be obtained; in less than an hour several

hundred flannel petticoats were sent to him with compliments of the late wearers! Could women do more?

"I was on picket duty one morning at the river bank, south of the town, when a gunboat was seen coming up round the bend, with a white flag flying, and much speculation ensued as to the cause. A boat soon landed at the wharf, and communicated with the commandant, asking for the surrender of Vicksburgh, in the name of Commodore Farragut, United States Navy. The answer was instant, 'Mississippians never surrender!' and the gunboat departed. All now knew what was in store, and began cleaning arms, preparing for the combined attack of both fleets, which none could doubt would attempt to unite and destroy us. The following day, from bluffs above town and on high grounds at the mouth of the Yazoo, a few miles above Vicksburgh, we could plainly see Foote's fleet of gunboats, rams, and transports steaming down towards us, and at evening descried the smoke ascending from their funnels, while anchoring west of the peninsula before described. From the winding of the river, this peninsula faces — or, as sailors would say, 'lies broadside to' — Vicksburgh, being about half a mile across; so that were it not for timber, a vessel would be in sight for twenty miles or more, ere rounding the point, and passing under the bluffs.

"A day or two after an answer had been returned to Farragut, one of his iron-clads was signalled from below; and soon after appearing round the southern bend, put on steam, and advanced rapidly and boldly towards us, evidently bent on running the gauntlet of our guns, and joining Foote's fleet, snugly anchored west of the peninsula, and screened from view by the woods. Coming within distance, it was perceived she carried numerous and heavy guns, was shot proof, and had no one visible on deck! When nearing town, under full head of steam, some of her ports opened, and heads thrust out, shouted to pickets on the bank, 'O, you God d—d sons of ——!' and a torrent of such like compliments. They were instantly answered by a volley of small-arms, and quickly dropped the port-screens. When abreast of the city, and steaming boldly to round the point, three or four of our guns opened fire with round-shot, which plunged about the gunboat, spurting up jets and columns of water around her. Still pushing forward, her helm answered readily, and when rounding the point and abreast of the bluffs, a quick succession of bright flashes glanced from her dark sides, and, amid deafening roars, the ground was ploughed up in all directions round our guns, while quick answers from our side made the water spout around her, as if a thousand whales were blowing. Thus it continued for some time, without intermission — the gunboat throwing eleven-inch shell, and our batteries vomiting round-shot. Though not disabled, it was clear the boat had been repeatedly struck; yet when rounding the point and getting out of danger, she gallantly presented her port-guns to the batteries, and, giving a parting broadside, was soon hid from view by the trees, and safely anchored with Foote's flotilla.

"It was now apparent that we could do but little with the enemy's iron-clads, for our shot glanced from their sides in showers of sparks, and damaged them but slightly : so that it was deemed necessary to erect a strong battery south of the town for the better reception of other visitors. They were not long in coming, for being informed of the inefficiency or insufficiency of our batteries, several others ran past, inflicting no injury, but in many cases receiving much. The two fleets having now formed a junction, prepared to bombard the town, and by way of preliminary, to get the range, sent several dozen eleven-inch shell across the peninsula, which, save a horrible screaming noise, did little harm, more than throw up tremendous clouds of dust and sand wherever they chanced to fall. The transports of the enemy now began to assemble rapidly, until a truly formidable fleet was gathered, and all imagined them heavily freighted with troops destined to coöperate on land. Had the peninsula been less thickly timbered, our batteries could have played sad havoc among them, for the distance was not more than a mile in a direct line, yet every shell thrown by us was waste of ammunition, since the vessels were so close in shore, that it required more skill than our gunners possessed to clear the woods with nicety and drop shell among them, drawn up as they were in single line, broadside to the beach.

"But while the enemy at early dawn or in the cool of

evening, and even long after starlight, were amusing themselves with cannonading, Commodore Lynch and a few young naval officers were up the Yazoo River, preparing a little surprise for them. Having blockaded the passage to the enemy with immense rafts, cut in, and floated down from, extensive forests in that vast region of swamps, they commenced building a huge rough iron-clad, called the Arkansas, which was destined to sally out and drive off the enemy. The Federal commodores were fully aware of our activity up that river, and correctly informed by negroes of all our doings with the ships and craft which had taken refuge there. The Star of the West, which attempted to reenforce Fort Sumter at the beginning of the war, had been captured by us off the Gulf Coast, and taken into New-Orleans; but when Farragut took that city, this, with some three or four other sea-vessels, and a fleet of magnificent Southern steamboats, steamed up the Mississippi, and had run far up the Yazoo River, and were then under the orders of Commodore Lynch. The enemy had detached three of their finest gunboats from the fleet at Milliken's Bend, to watch the mouth of the Yazoo; and to be ready for any emergency, they kept up steam night and day. So much for the Yazoo at present, but I shall have more to tell you by and by.

"The Federal fleet maintained a hot and vigorous cannonade upon the city at all hours, save during the intense heat of midday. Their troops were landed from transports, but never came within view. From scouts, who volunteered as spies, we ascertained that they had seized hundreds of negroes in that part of Louisiana, and were actually digging a canal from Milliken's Bend across the peninsula, which, it was hoped, would divert the waters of the river from its proper bed, and leave Vicksburgh high and dry as an inland city! The idea was a bold one, and originated with General Pope, who, not able to pass 'Island No. 10' some months before, dug a canal across a small peninsula near New-Madrid, in Missouri, and got safely in the rear of the island, and captured it. The present undertaking, however, did not promise like results; for the stream was strong, and would not be diverted. Hundreds of men, both whites and blacks, sank and died under the labor of cutting this canal, before the attempt was discontinued.

"And still the bombardment progressed. Thousands of shell, round shot, and other missiles were hurled at our devoted city; but, strange to say, except in some half-dozen instances, I know not one house which was more than slightly injured. The enemy, on the other hand, suffered much from their very inaction. The heats of July and the fever of August told fearfully upon their unacclimated troops, cooped up in their ships amid smoke and heat, and the deathly night-vapors of the land and water. Though suffering extremely in every way, they were farther from realizing their hopes than ever. It was computed they had at anchor more than twenty gunboats playing on the city, together with a land force of several thousand men, and scores of transports and flats. Ordnance officers affirmed that they had fired more than twelve thousand eleven-inch and other shells during the month, without counting rockets, round shot, and iron bolts. For a few days they were inactive, but did not prepare to depart. They had abandoned the canal project after digging more than a mile, and negroes informed us that their wheelbarrows and tools were scattered around the peninsula, where every house was converted into an hospital. The commodores were nonplussed; and as their large fleets lay at anchor on the rippleless copper-colored river, with a cloudless sky, under the scorching sun of August, without the echo of a voice, without the motion of a leaf, or the flapping of ensigns from a breath of air, the cries of sand-cranes flying to and fro reminded one of some river of death, with hospitals for ships and spectres for crews.

"But while the enemy were thus inactive, Commodore Lynch was hard at work night and day, ably assisted by young officers and citizens, fitting out the ram Arkansas in the Yazoo River. The name of this stream literally means 'River of Death,' so called by the Indians (Choctaws) from the fevers, chills, and agues, which it caused in ancient times. In a direct line north from Vicksburgh, it is not more than twelve miles distant; so that it formed an admirable protection to our right flank, and in case of attack, Haynes's Bluff, some miles from the mouth, was well fortified and mounted, while yet farther above was moored an enormous raft made of huge rough logs, and so constructed that it could be opened from above, but not below. A few miles still beyond (near Yazoo City) Commodore Lynch had improvised a ship-yard, and was busy in reconstructing various boats for river service. You smile, perhaps, but let me explain, and your sarcasm may change into admiration for the indefatigable industry of those engaged there.

"In the first place, although several small steam sea-vessels, and a magnificent fleet of river passenger and freight boats had escaped from New-Orleans, and were far inland, up the Yazoo, they were not safe. Naval officers knew the enemy would soon visit the mouth of the river, and accordingly they lost no time in building a raft to retard their progress, and put bounds to Federal curiosity. Many old rafts of huge cypress logs found moored in the Yazoo and its tributaries were floated down; woodmen were busy in the timber at various places, cutting down immense trees, the sound of whose fall, crashing in the forest, was like distant thunder, so that in less than a week a raft was formed in two parts, which, when made fast, would stand 'butting' from all the 'rams' in Lincolndom. Nor could the enemy fire it, for the timber was so green, or so perfectly saturated from months and years of exposure in the water, it might well defy all the turpentine North-Carolina could produce in a century to kindle a single stick of it. This necessary work having been speedily and well accomplished, Lynch and his officers razed one of the vessels, and began the formation of the ungainly Arkansas. Carpenters, wood-choppers, sawyers, blacksmiths, voluntarily gave a hand to expedite proceedings, an old engine was placed in her, and the work of plating commenced. But how were they to get a sufficient supply of plates, bolts, screws, and machinery, remote as they were from every source of supply, in an out-of-the-way river, far from Vicksburgh, thirty miles from the nearest railroad station, and close to a very small town, devoid of every thing but cotton and pretty women? It would puzzle me to tell how, but by superhuman exertions many things were procured, the vessel was completed, four large guns were placed aboard, and sufficient ammunition; and, lastly, plenty of volunteers were not wanting to man her, particularly as it was certain she would have terrible fighting to do ere reaching Vicksburgh, the point of destination.

"When finished and ready for service, I visited her, and

27

seeing how much indifferent material had been used in the construction, concluded that she would be sent to the bottom in less than no time, when opposed to the magnificent rams and iron-clads watching for her at the mouth of the Yazoo, or drawn up in parallel lines to receive her when passing the channel of the great river. She was large, rough, strong, and ungainly—vulnerable in many places, and the top imperfectly covered; so that should a stray shell drop through the roof, her destruction was almost certain, as the magazine was somewhat exposed. Many were desirous of commanding, as it was hoped she might eclipse the doings of the old Merrimac in Hampton Roads, which sank two large frigates and damaged the Monitor; but, after a little reflection, Commodore Lynch gave her in charge of a Mississippian, late of the old naval service, whose name was Brown. This officer grumbled much at the deficiencies apparent in the craft, and particularly at the engines, which were old and of doubtful capacity.

"'Do you refuse to command, sir?' asked the little Commodore; 'if there is any thing you object to in her, state it, and I will go myself—either you or I must command!'

"'I do not object, sir,' was the quick reply. 'If you take command, I only ask to be captain of a gun—for I'm bound to go in her, in one capacity or other.'

"'Very well, sir,' said the Commodore, going ashore in his quiet, meek manner; 'make things ship-shape immediately, and wait for orders.'

"Things were soon prepared, and orders received. It was deemed advisable to keep the hour of her departure a secret, yet it became known in some way to the enemy at the mouth, who steamed off and on all the time. At night the raft was unexpectedly opened by a few midshipmen, and the Arkansas slowly and noiselessly floated several miles down the stream, and was perfectly lost in the dense fogs which fall at evening. Next morning, at daylight, steam was raised, and by keeping close to the heavily timbered banks, she cautiously proceeded; and, as the fog lifted, espied three of the enemy's finest gunboats and rams in the river, near the mouth. Two of them backed down into the Mississippi, while the largest opened fire immediately and very briskly. The Arkansas was moving but slowly on account of her defective engines, but fired deliberately and with telling effect, crippling the enemy at the first broadside, who ran their magnificent craft upon the bank, and struck colors at the moment our boat was passing. Captain Brown, finding his engines to be useless, depended solely upon the stream, and could not stop to take the splendid prize, for he knew many boats would soon appear to oppose his exit from the mouth of the Yazoo; so, although using more steam than could be generated, he boldly pushed into the Mississippi, rapidly firing at the two gunboats retreating before him.

"At this point of the action we could discern all that transpired from our batteries on the bluffs. As soon as the Arkansas rounded from the Yazoo, the whole Federal fleet hoisted anchor, and formed in two lines—one each side of the channel! Frigates, rams, 'gunboats — all were ready to annihilate that iron-clad mass of timber slowly floating towards them. Presently an iron-clad left her position, and boldly steaming up between the lines of dark hulls, opened fire at a considerable distance. The Arkansas was silent, and nothing was seen but a rush of steam as the monster slowly entered the channel, which seemed to please her single enemy, who steamed up nearer and fired again. In an instant the bow gun of the rebel replied, smashed the boiler and machinery of the enemy—men jumped overboard, and the vessel sank immediately! This exasperated the fleet, which now opened with a terrific roar from both squadrons, until the side of the Arkansas looked like a mass of sparks floating between parallel lines of curling smoke. Few dared approach, however, and those who dared to do so received such a fearful handling that they immediately put back, and were content to fire at a distance. To us on the bluff, spectators of the scene, the slowness of the Arkansas was unaccountable, for she seemed encircled with fire and doomed to destruction ere emerging from the ordeal. ' What's the matter with her?' 'Why don't she clap on steam and rush through them?' 'They'll sink her in three minutes!' were the remarks of all. Yet onward she came, slowly picking her way, the enemy believing she was only enticing them in her path by apparent slowness! This was not the case, however; her engines were worthless, and audacity alone was car-

rying her through. Still fighting at long range, the Federal
fleet slowly followed, and the nearer she approached the bluff
the quicker the Arkansas fought, until finding her safely under our guns, the enemy gave up the chase, and amid our
cheers on the bluff and a salvo of guns, the Arkansas slowly
turned the Point and was moored before the city!

"From the commotion visible among the enemy's vessels of
all classes, the activity of small boats passing to and fro, and
the succession of signals exchanged between commanders, it
was evident that many of them were badly crippled, for several
were towed to the banks, and run upon the sand. One vessel
had sunk, several were towed away, while the vigorous working of pumps among them testified that shots had penetrated in
different quarters, and that they felt infinite relief in the escape
of the Arkansas. Various fragments of wreck soon floated
down from the scene of conflict, which proved that chance shot
had visited more than one unlucky transport; while with glasses we could perceive two powerful gunboats at the mouth of
the Yazoo, which, like ants, were dragging their crippled companion out of further danger.

"It was vexatious to think that all the spoil was escaping us,
and we felt particularly annoyed that the gunboat which had
struck her colors to the Arkansas in the Yazoo should thus
easily escape, for it was the finest in the fleet. It could not be
helped, however, and when the truth became known, regarding the utter failure of our engines, and the danger to
which the Arkansas had been exposed during her passage, we
could only feel surprise that she had done so well and inflicted
so much loss upon the enemy; had the fleets known the true
cause of her slow progress, not a fragment of her would ever
have floated down so majestically and triumphantly.

"Towards evening, many of the enemy's transports moved
up the river, and preparations were made on board the gunboats which seemed to indicate that powder and ball were intended for us in earnest. As night closed in, none expected an
engagement of any kind, but alarm-guns warned the garrison
to be on the alert, when, sooner than expected, several vessels
appeared before our upper batteries, and the engagement opened with great fury. While the bluff batteries were contending

with most of the fleet, several of Farragut's squadron ran past, and opened with an awful roar upon the Arkansas, lying broadside to shore ; while several boats from below engaged our guns south of the town. Although the night was quite dark, so frequent and rapid were the flashes of the guns on both sides that every thing was distinctly visible. The noise was astounding. The bluff batteries above, and south batteries below, the town, seemed all on fire, while the Arkansas, engaged with several heavy gunboats and frigates, was rocking from the immense weight of metal hurled at her every moment ; but as she was bound fast to shore, and the enemy could not remain stationary in the stream, their vessels slowly drifted past towards the lower batteries.

"For a long time this unearthly noise was maintained on both sides, and it was once supposed that Farragut's boats would grapple with the Arkansas and take her; but such was her steady and destructive fire, that they slunk off in the darkness to longer distance, and never seemed inclined to try it again. The woods facing Vicksburgh were literally blown down by chance shots from our side, while the river was all afoam with hundreds of water-columns rising and falling every minute from the same cause. It is more than probable that if our batteries had not concentrated their fire upon the enemy engaged with our solitary iron-clad, it would have fallen into their hands ; but such a shower of shot and shell assailed them from three points, and so incessant was the storm of small-shot poured into their ports and decks, that it was impossible for a human being to appear without instant loss of life. After a fierce and obstinate engagement, the enemy's boats escaped down the river in a crippled condition, while the upper fleet moved up-stream with great expedition amid the prolonged and enthusiastic cheering of our garrison and citizens, who lined the works, making night hideous with their wild and defiant shrieks.

"Thus ended the first bombardment of Vicksburgh. I am sorry to say that not less than four or five of our men were killed and some half-dozen wounded on board the gallant iron-clad, most of them receiving injuries in the night attack of the enemy's gunboats. Beyond these casualties I hear of none whatever throughout the garrison. All are in the highest spirits, and desirous of meeting the enemy again at any time and in any number. Yours always,   * * *

" P. S.—I open this to say that our cavalry and a light battery far up the river have succeeded in capturing the Federal despatch-boat, and destroyed it, after securing all the letters and despatches of the fleet. I glean this from head-quarters; the telegram came an hour ago. Van Dorn says the enemy admit a great loss among them from various causes, and are afraid the Arkansas may run down to New-Orleans and play havoc among them there! Four gunboats are disabled, two sunk, and several others require expensive repairs. More anon."

CHAPTER XL.

DESPITE the manœuvring of McClellan's forces south of the James River, and the threatened advance of Burnside from Suffolk and Norfolk, as if to form a junction and coöperate with him, the true state of the case was soon perceived by our corps of observation at Petersburgh. Either indecision prevailed in the councils of the two generals, or all their movements near the seaboard were intended to hold us in check upon the James, while the large forces of Pope, on the Rappahannock and Rapidan, should obtain eligible positions, and perhaps advance so far as to be beyond our power to arrest them. It is possible that conflicting opinions existed between McClellan and Burnside, as was also known to be the case between the first-named and Pope. Burnside was ambitious—he was considered "a successful man," from his capture of Roanoke Island, and "full of promise;" McClellan had yet to win his spurs, and was now bullied by a brutal press for being unsuccessful. Burnside was politically allied to the Government; McClellan was not. Burnside was desirous of superseding McClellan in command of the "Grand Army," or what remained of it, while the latter was actuated by pure military feeling, and perhaps scarcely cared *who* commanded, if only success could be insured. Thus, although it seemed probable at one time that a junction of their forces might ensue, McClellan's desires were thwarted, and Burnside was ordered round to reenforce Pope.

Finding that the expected reenforcement of Burnside was hopeless, McClellan withdrew his troops from the south side, and quietly prepared to leave the peninsula, which he now considered untenable. But before this final movement of the much-abused McClellan took place, General Lee perceived the scene of action was rapidly changing from the James to the Rappahannock, and that every available man at the North was being despatched with all haste to Pope. Banks, with a strong corps of New-England troops, was stationed within a short distance of Culpeper Court-House, while strong detachments of cavalry and artillery had penetrated even so far southward as Gordonsville, but did not retain possession of that all-important point. They were merely feeling the way to its ultimate occupation. This was perfectly known to us and the value of Gordonsville fully appreciated; for the only two routes to Richmond and the South united there, and, if once strongly garrisoned by the enemy, they would circumscribe all our operations, and cause the fall of Richmond without the absolute necessity of losing a man.

Secrecy has been the characteristic of all our movements; civilians are seldom allowed admission to our camps under any pretence ; strong guards always encircle our lines, so that it is almost an impossibility to gain entrance. Thus, until the latest moment, none know the destination of troops, or the object in view, and even then brigadiers are frequently no better informed than the humblest patriot in the ranks. If this is true of movements generally, it is peculiarly so in regard to the rapid marches of " Stonewall ;" for a person might as reasonably " whistle jigs to a mile-stone " as attempt to gleam information from the sharp-eyed, tart, sarcastic, crabbed-spoken Jackson. When his corps received orders to move, some imagined merely " a change of camps," or some such indifferent movement; yet when Richmond was left far to the south, and the column proceeded rapidly in a north-western direction, many old campaigners began to whistle ominously, and with a mysterious wink in the direction of the Shenandoah Valley, would sarcastically observe, " Lee's short of rations again! Jackson's detailed to go to the commissary !" in allusion to the immense supplies more than once captured by Jackson from the unfortunate Banks.

While our columns were toiling along the dusty roads, in a

westward course, cavalry had been pushed ahead several days before, and were scouring the country in all directions southwest, driving small detachments of the enemy before them. No action or combat of importance, however, had occurred save in the neighborhood of Gordonsville, where a sharp cavalry encounter took place, with loss on both sides; yet the enemy rapidly fell back towards the Rapidan, and seemed disinclined to operate in the fine open country south of it. This was generalship. They knew not what force was approaching; by crossing the stream and destroying the bridges, a deep unfordable river was left in our front, which would occasion much delay; and as Culpeper was as a pivot-point by which the enemy could keep open the communication with their main army under Pope, approaching east by north; with Miles advancing from the west through the Valley with a heavy force, and with Washington nearly due north; Banks had massed his troops in a wooded plain near Cedar Mountain. Pope was not more than thirty miles to his left, with large masses advancing; while Miles, with fourteen thousand of all arms, was midway up the Valley, distant some forty or more miles to his right. The passage of the Rapidan, it was well known, would be hotly disputed, and particularly at the railroad-bridge, for all the best roads to Culpeper cross and recross in the neighborhood. When, therefore, our advance appeared on the south bank, fierce and heavy cannonading ensued, which lasted several hours, and was so obstinately maintained on our part as to attract the attention of Banks himself, inland and farther up the stream.

It was confidently expected we should cross at this point, but Jackson had made other arrangements, and unexpectedly crossed over much higher up, north-westward, without the loss of a man. Our movements were evidently too rapid for Banks; indeed, no possible despatch could save him, for if we were so inclined, it was in our power to force a general engagement before any of the other divisions could arrive to his succor.

Once across the river, our order of march was changed; so that at any given moment the columns could deploy and not be subjected to confusion or surprise. With strong detachments of cavalry to the front, fanned out in skirmishing order, the enemy's movements were closely watched; light-armed, well-tried infantry followed at intervals, supported by light and active batteries, and, last of all, the main army which, in separate columns, pushed along roads and through the fields with elastic step, expecting every moment to be thrown into line.

While standing on a hill which overlooks the railroad-bridge, the panorama of this beautiful grass country was presented to my view in a charming prospect. At my feet ran the Rapidan, flowing north-eastwardly, and debouching in the Rappahannock many miles away. All the landscape, north and east, was an undulating plain, plentifully timbered at intervals, while to the north-west and west rose parallel chains of hills and mountains, which, farther inland, inclose the beautiful Valley of the Shenandoah. In the gorgeous sunset of an Indian summer, with its varied tints of blue, gold, purple, and orange, the face of the country was one indescribable vista of sunlight and shade. In the distance various streams pursued their devious course, now lost in the forest, now sparkling in the open—only the pen or pencil of one inspired could give the faintest conception of this verdant, fruitful, and delightful region. Far away in the distance, white and red brick houses dotted the undulating farms; yet not a sign of life was discernible, no flocks, no cattle, no horses; the country was deserted—the young in the army, the old ruthlessly driven from their homesteads.

When the sun was sinking, distant reports of musketry, far in advance, informed us that our vanguard were already skirmishing with the enemy, and driving in their outposts. Most of the firing seemed to be in the direction of Cedar Run, or Cedar Mountain, about seven miles from Culpeper, where the enemy were drawn up in order of battle, with an effective strength of more than thirty thousand men, well supplied with artillery. The day was too far advanced for an engagement and as their precise position could not be ascertained, Jackson was busily engaged along our lines, making every disposition for the morrow.

From dusty and weary scouts who arrived during night, we ascertained something regarding the true position of Banks's army. A few of these adventurous spirits had been prowling

about the enemy's encampments in different parts of the
country, and had discovered the following facts: One of the
enemy's army corps, under Sigel, was on their right among the
hills at Sperryville, watching the roads and all direct communication with their rear at Mount Washington, Warrenton, and
Manassas Junction; a heavy force was stationed on Pope's left,
at or near Waterloo on the Rappahannock, while somewhat to
the rear of Banks and Pope was McDowell's corps. It was
concluded with reason that these various bodies would be unable to appear upon the field to assist Banks, should Jackson
force him to engage on the 'following day, (Saturday, August
ninth.)

During the night, pickets, in our extreme front, were popping
away at each other occasionally, and early in the morning our
advance was resumed, cautiously and slowly. As the country
was admirably adapted for concealment, our strength and position were never truly ascertained by the enemy's cavalry outposts, so that although our cavalry on the right were enjoying
a merry time with those of Pope, our artillery gradually approached Cedar Mountain, and took up a strong position on the
north side of it, unknown to the enemy. As this mountain-side
commanded the sloping corn-fields and woods, stretching away
at its base and sweeping the Federal advance, Jackson ordered
to advance large bodies of skirmishers in order to draw the enemy forward.

Desultory picket-firing occupied most of the morning; and
when noon had passed, many imagined that old "Stonewall"
would defer an attack till the morrow; but those who had served
with him, knowing well his mode of warfare, laughed at the idea.
"Jackson is too wise to defer an engagement," said they; "and
is fully aware that, by to-morrow, Sigel and others will be up
within supporting distance and may overwhelm him. Besides,
when our general commences late in the day, he can soon beat
his enemy if both are equal in force; but if he gets badly
handled, he can still fight on until dark, and if need be, receive
reenforcements or retreat during night." Such in truth had
been Jackson's method in many engagements; for, nearly always outnumbered, he had either vanquished the enemy before
nightfall after a few hours' engagement, or had securely retreated after severely punishing them. So on this occasion, when

skirmishing became more brisk during the afternoon, and our advance posts gradually fell back towards the mountain, it was evident that Banks was determined to push us hard, and begin the engagement. This exactly suited Jackson, who had posted a heavy force of artillery on the hill-side, which at a given signal would open upon the enemy's flanks and finish the work.

It was now about five o'clock in the evening, the infantry fire had become more regular and sustained; regiments could be plainly seen advancing or retreating through the fields, but what precise order of battle was maintained upon our side could not be well ascertained on account of the broken character of the country. Clearly, Banks was ignorant of the existence of a flanking force ready to assail him from the hill, or he would not have advanced his infantry so close under it. His immediate object was to capture or displace some few pieces of artillery which, posted in the edge of a wood, caused much destruction among his advancing columns, which pieces also he foolishly imagined were unsupported. The infantry thus far had been hotly engaged on both sides, and it rather appeared as if ours were falling back. But this was a *ruse*.

Gathering together several brigades in which he had most confidence, Banks ordered them to charge the guns before mentioned, and Crawford's brigade gallantly rushed forward in fulfilment of the order. Our gunners seeing the intended movement, slackened fire, and reserved their strength until the proper moment; while several regiments of infantry, in support, cocked their rifles and lay on their faces concealed in the timber. As soon as the attacking column had emerged into open ground and deployed, advancing with shouts to the charge, grape, canister, and shell assailed them from several pieces, and broke them in a moment.

Banks was angry, and determined to force our position. Other brigades were quickly brought to the front and advanced over the dead bodies of their comrades, our gunners watching their approach, and at the right moment discharging their pieces with such accuracy that the attacking force seemed literally to melt away. Then our infantry suddenly rose from their ambush, and giving a withering volley at short distance, yelled and charged. Broken and demoralized as they undoubtedly were after this short but bloody engagement, it required but little more effort to rout the enemy's right wing. This was accomplished by suddenly throwing forward our left, which threw the enemy into such confusion that one whole brigade, under General Prince, was reduced to a crowd of fugitives, running they knew not whither.

The attack of Banks had evidently failed, his centre and left were irreparably broken; while, to add to his confusion and dismay, our cannon on the hill-side, immediately commanding the field, opened rapidly upon his broken forces, as they retreated in the wildest confusion from the scene. The advance was now taken up, and we drove the remnants of their army before us a considerable distance; but they retired so rapidly that was impossible to overtake them. From causes, then unknown to me, we were suddenly halted, and took up positions originally occupied when the action opened two hours before. Finding us disinclined to pursue, Banks halted his men also, not far from the battle-field, and the smoke of their camp-fires was soon seen ascending over the trees.

While our weary soldiers were seeking rest after this brief but bloody battle, parties of horsemen moved from point to point, apparently to guard against any attempt on the part of the enemy to occupy the battle-field and despoil it of our valuable booty. This was our first surmise; but when it was ascertained that squadrons of Stuart's cavalry were also in motion, it was certain that some dashing achievement was in contemplation. It was like watching a succession of scenes on the stage. As the evening grew dark a party of horsemen appeared on the field as if to take notes; several of them dismounted, and appeared to be conversing angrily and gesticulating wildly, when suddenly a party of our men dashed from the thicket and madly spurred towards them. The enemy were annoyed, but evidently were not to be surprised, for, the distance being considerable, they hastily remounted and galloped off. Our troopers boldly plunged forward after them, and frequent shots were heard in the direction they had taken. After some time our men returned with a few prisoners, who informed us that the Federal horsemen pursued were none other than General Pope and other officers of distinction, who, it seems, had the impudence to ride upon the ground in order to make it appear that the field was theirs!

Every one thought it a pity that Pope had not been captured; our men heartily hated him for his ruthless cruelty* to the inhabitants of the country, and his extraordinary amount of vanity and bombast. It was ascertained from these prisoners, also, that General McDowell's forces had arrived, and that Sigel was rapidly approaching, so that by the morrow there would be two full corps before us, irrespective of Banks, who was still in front. It was well, therefore, that Jackson had not pushed forward too far, or it must have precipitated an engagement on the morrow, in which he could not reasonably have expected to be successful. The commands of McDowell, Sigel, and Banks, amounted originally to sixty thousand men, with a heavy force of artillery; while the most that Jackson could muster numbered from twenty thousand to twenty-five thousand. Posted as we were, our position could have made a

---

* I think it unnecessary to dwell at length upon the brutality practised by Pope's troops upon the poor people of Virginia, but annex one instance as an example of their ruffianism and cowardice. The facts are derived from a private and confidential letter:

"Federal atrocities in Virginia far outstrip all tales of fiction. Rape, arson, and theft seem to be the constant attendants of an army professing to fight for the Union. A recital of the horrible murders that mark its bloody attack, one might suppose, would appal the doomed of Hades. Mrs. Fitzhugh, of Ravensworth — mother of the late Andrew Fitzhugh, of the Navy — a lady of distinguished position, and one singularly embodying the graces and virtues of her sex, was brutally murdered in front of her house. Ravensworth, the family-seat of the Fitzhughs, you know, is one of the oldest estates in Virginia; it has been in the family since the reign of Charles the Second, from whom it was received as a grant, and has ever been noted as a place where a profuse hospitality was dispensed by as gentle and refined a people as live.

"The old lady, who was over eighty years of age, infirm and blind, leaning on the arm of her maid, was taking a little exercise in front of her mansion, when the girl suddenly cried out, 'O mistress! there come the Yankees!' and in terror ran to the house. Mrs. Fitzhugh called out to her, 'Don't leave me alone with these vile Yankees!' when one of them approached, and, with the butt of his gun, killed her! Shortly after, two of her daughters, who had been visiting a neighbor, returned. One of them was seized and sent to Washington a prisoner — the other, so appalled at seeing her mother weltering in blood, became speechless! The latter was left by the soldiers, who, on retiring, laughingly remarked: 'Well, you can now bury the old hag — God b—t her!'" Instances like this could be multiplied, but their recital is too revolting. Indeed, none would ever credit the atrocities of Pope's army were they not upon the spot and eye-witness to them.

strong defence, if attacked in force by Pope on the morrow; but of this there were no indications.

Perceiving that his old friend Banks was unwilling to leave the vicinity of the battle-field, and positive that he would, as usual, claim it as his own, Jackson determined to put the disputed question beyond all doubt by forcing him, in a rough sort of way, to change his camps at an inconvenient and uncomfortable time. About midnight, therefore, while the beaten and prostrate enemy were fast asleep round their smouldering camp-fires, our artillery on the hill-side suddenly opened, and, with a deafening roar, threw shot and shell among them with great rapidity and precision. In truth, it was a pretty sight to see this dark hill-side, in bold relief against a pale blue sky, suddenly illuminated by a semi-circular sheet of flame, hurling death and destruction upon the numberless flickering camp-fires that dotted the plain. It was sad, at the same time, to reflect upon the fate of men thus aroused from sleep to be hurried into eternity. Such, however, are the stern necessities of war.

The noise and confusion among the awakened slumberers were indescribable, and pickets at the outposts informed us that they could distinctly hear field-officers shouting and galloping about in the darkness, vainly endeavoring to rally their commands. Wagons and guns, infantry and cavalry, were suddenly put in motion, and the receding noise did not subside for several hours. The loss to the enemy by this unexpected cannonade must have been great, yet, whatever it might have been, their generals never openly confessed to it. All that we could subsequently gather amounted to this — that large masses of men were so panic-stricken, that, with or without officers, they rushed to the rear, and did not stop running until they reached Culpeper.

While all had reason enough to rejoice in the signal discomfiture of a foe who had been laying waste the land with fire and sword, many mourned the untimely end of Brigadier-General Winder, who had fallen during the day while gallantly leading his command into action upon the enemy's flank. The event was particularly memorable ; and the more to be lamented from the fact that it occurred while extricating the original "Stonewall brigade" from an awkward position to which it had been forced by the superior numbers of the enemy. Our men, however, had amply revenged his fall. General Prince, together with thirty commissioned officers, and upwards of three hundred other prisoners, had been marched to the rear and sent to Richmond. The officers, indeed, were handcuffed and treated in the exact manner prescribed for the rebels by Pope and his inhuman subordinates, who had been ruling with a rod of iron among a peaceable and inoffensive rural population. The number of arms found upon the field I never ascertained, but knew that the booty was considerable.

All expected that hostilities would recommence on the morrow, but from ignorance of our true position and strength, Pope deferred all operations for that day. The enemy, however, were so anxious that the field should be regarded as their own, that when our burying parties were set to work they made a pretence of performing the same duty. They did not, however, confine themselves to the removal of the dead, but began to gather up the scattered arms, leaving the dead to our charge. Perceiving this, our artillery opened with such effect as to completely disperse them. Next day, however, Jackson sent forward a flag of truce, giving Banks permission to bury his dead, which was readily accepted; provision was of course taken to prevent the Yankees from prying too closely into our position and number. During the truce many officers of both armies met and conversed upon the field, and all seemed animated with the best of feeling. General Stuart was among the first to mount his horse to trot over the field; and while engaged in conversation, up rode his old companion in arms, Brigadier-General Hartsuff, of the Federal cavalry, and politely saluting him, jocularly remarked: "Hallo! Stuart, my boy, how goes it? who'd a thought of such changes within so short a time? I was over you once, you know; now you're a full major-general, and I but a simple brigadier."

It cannot be denied that much bravery had been displayed by both armies in this brief encounter, and the brigades led forward against our batteries behaved wonderfully well. This did not surprise us when we learned that they were for the most part composed of New-York and Pennsylvania troops. Many of our own officers, indeed, had shown unexampled pluck and endurance; one instance of which particularly struck me. A major in command of his regiment (the colonel being disabled) had led it into a rather "hot" place, and was obliged to retire, with part of his nose shot off, his left arm shot through and through, the toe of his boot shot away, and he had a flesh wound in his thigh. Having had his nose bandaged and his arm put in a sling, while the regiment was re-forming, he mounted his horse again and shouted out, "Come on, boys, forward! we'll pay 'em off for that last trick of theirs;" and pushed forward into battle again. I was also informed of a brave colonel, who, being shot, had fallen from his horse and injured himself much internally. His sole thought, however, was of his regiment, and though unable to ride, begged two men on foot to support him in the rear, so that he might superintend the movements of his men, just as the enemy were in full flight from the field.

Jackson's inactivity surprised all who knew him. None could imagine why he remained so long before a powerful enemy, and made no movements of any kind. It seemed, however, that he was waiting for some demonstration from the foe, and this not being vouchsafed, he was content to fall back again at his leisure over the Rapidan, and there await the main army, which all knew was now rapidly marching from Richmond to coöperate with him. McClellan, we were informed, had effected his 'escape from Harrison's Landing, and was doubtless transporting his troops to Washington. It was possibly Lee's plan to overwhelm Pope and his "Army of Virginia" ere the remains of McClellan's "Army of the Potomac" could come to his assistance. This, however, was only the gossiping surmise of subordinate officers, for generals of divisions never opened their lips, nor even deigned to smile. It seemed to be the ambition of those mysterious individuals, now in particular, to exhibit a cold and reserved demeanor; to be active, and at the same time solemn in their deportment.

28

CHAPTER XLI.

August twelfth to thirty-first.—Pope, still in force, watches Jackson on the Rapidan—
The rapid Concentration of Confederate Forces there—Retreat of Pope to the Rappahannock, who establishes his Head-quarters at Catlett's Station—Stuart makes an effort to capture that General, but arriving too late, seizes all his Wearing Apparel, Books, Papers, Plans, Private and Official Correspondence—Successful Flank Movement of Jackson round Pope's Right and Rear—He captures and destroys immense Stores at Manassas Junction, and disperses a Brigade sent from Alexandria to protect them—Sudden Retreat of Pope's Army towards Manassas—Engages Jackson with superior Forces, but without Results—Advance of Longstreet through Thoroughfare Gap, who soundly thrashes General Reno, stationed there to dispute the Passage—Longstreet forms a Junction with Jackson on the latter's Right—Arrival of General Lee—Heavy Reenforcements pour into Pope's Army— Second Battle of Manassas—Rout of the Enemy—Scenes on the Battle-field.

WE had not remained many days south of the Rapidan before we received large reenforcements, and the activity of couriers and quartermasters betokened an early movement. Many of our scouts had been out several days, but we could glean little from them except that Pope was still in front, and that firing was of daily occurrence across the river. On the sixteenth we learned that a change of position had taken place among the enemy, and that Sigel's corps was acting in our immediate front: next day it was ascertained that their whole army was moving, but very slowly.

Although opposed by powerful artillery, a part of our infantry crossed the river and took up the pursuit; Stuart's cavalry and flying artillery, as usual, being the first to exchange shots with Sigel's rear-guard, causing it much damage. From the eighteenth to the twentieth heavy firing was maintained almost without intermission. Yet so well did Sigel handle his men, that they were able to cross the Rappahannock on the twentieth, almost without loss. Not only so, but they defied our attempts to cross in pursuit; indeed, such was the strength of their artillery, it would have been madness to hazard such an undertaking.

Demonstrations were made at various fords, but as the river was broad, and we had no pontoons, it was easy for Pope to hold us in check.

Detachments of cavalry, however, passed the river daily, and made spirited dashes among the enemy, frequently capturing both prisoners and stores. On one occasion Stuart personally led a few squadrons, and making a sudden rush upon Pope's head-quarters, (situated at Catlett's Railway Station,) nearly succeeded in capturing that pompous commander, who was warned of his danger by some traitor, and barely escaped for the second time. Four companies of rifles were stationed near the house, but at the first volley from our men they ran to the woods, leaving the house and all its treasures an easy prey. The cavalry were much incensed at losing Pope; and, dividing into small parties, galloped down every road with the hope of overtaking him, while others remained behind to secure the spoil.

Among the articles found by our troopers were Pope's public and private papers, including plans, maps, estimates, and returns of forces, promises of reenforcements, with statements of their strength, the possible time and place of junction, and the amount of stores at various dépôts. Much clothing was found, including new full-dress suits for General Pope and his staff, also a quantity of private baggage, wines, and liquors. Doubtless it was dangerous work for those gallant troopers to penetrate so far within the enemy's lines, yet such was the antipathy and disgust felt by all for the vain-glorious and silly man commanding the enemy, that they would willingly have undertaken any enterprise which promised his capture.

While General Lee was making the demonstrations to which I have alluded at various points of the river, Jackson's forces, some twenty-five thousand strong, left the main body on the twenty-fifth and proceeded towards the head-waters of the Rappahannock. As usual, he was unencumbered with baggage or other impediments to a rapid march through the mountains, save a sufficient quantity of spare ammunition and the necessary guns. Passing through the delightful region of Mount Washington, he pushed forward rapidly towards Salem, and turning the head of his column, proceeded eastward parallel with the Manassas Gap Railroad, until he reached the village of Gainesville. All this section of country was minutely known to every soldier in his command, and when the head of the column was filed to the right at Salem, no one doubted but that the true object of the expedition was to get in the rear of Pope's army, and destroy his communications and stores. Yet it must be confessed that many complained of the supposed imprudence, if not madness, of the adventure. "Look facts fully in the face," said one; "here we are marching in the rear of an enemy more powerful than ourselves, far from all supports, liable to be broken up by superior numbers from Washington on the one hand, or to be literally annihilated should Pope face about and coöperate."

"'Tis just like him," said another; "no one can imagine what he's about; it was always so in the Valley and elsewhere—plenty of marching and fighting, and mighty little to eat, except what we chanced to capture."

"As to rations," said a third, "I know not what we shall do; we are on half allowance now, and to-morrow we shall have to fast and fight as usual. I heard that the Commissary General spoke to Jackson upon this point, but he simply answered: 'Don't trouble yourself; the enemy have a super-abundance—their dépôts are not far in advance!'"

That this was possibly true, all would admit; yet the more prudent looked upon the expedition as "rash," while they stoically observed: "If Jackson isn't afraid of *his* carcase surely *we* need not be so particular!" The event justified their confidence, for upon the arrival of our troopers at Bristow, the first railroad station connecting with Pope's rear, large quantities of stores were discovered. The guards at the station decamped expeditiously upon the first appearance of our advance squadron, and, running towards Manassas, spread the alarm. The commandant of that post could not or would not believe the story; he imagined it to be simply a small marauding party approaching, yet telegraphed the rumor to Pope and to the commandant of Alexandria.

The station-master at Manassas was very much mistaken, for our forces suddenly surrounding the Junction, captured every thing without a blow. A brigade, we were informed, was approaching from Alexandria, but it was surprised by an ambush and dispersed, the commander being killed. The amount of stores that here fell into our hands was astonishing. Among the more important items were nine cannons; seven trains heavily laden with stores; ten first-class locomotives; fifty thousand pounds of bacon; one thousand barrels of beef; two thousand barrels of pork; five thousand barrels of superfine flour; vast quantities of hay, oats, and corn; thirty thousand ready-made loaves; and an immense amount of hard bread, ammunition, etc. The telegraph-office was found intact, and the advance had not been many minutes at the station ere the operator was compelled to transmit a message to Alexandria, calling for an immediate supply of artillery and wagon-harness, together with many other things of which we stood greatly in need. Thanks to the business-like despatch of those at Alexandria, a train soon appeared bringing the supplies; the distance was not great, and to insure its safety, no sooner had it crossed Bull Run Bridge than the rails were torn up, so that it was impossible to return again, even had the engineer discovered the trick. Of eatables and drinkables there was no end; clothes, arms, military and sutler's stores, powder, shot, shell, cartridges—every thing, in fine, was found here which a needy, ragged, hungry, and travel-stained army might desire, either as necessities or superfluities. In truth, our hungry troops had a perfect feast, and what could not be of use was immediately destroyed. Many hours had not elapsed since our arrival ere the station, locomotives, out-houses, store-houses, and superfluous stores were in a blaze, sending forth vast columns of smoke, which must have been discernible over an area of many miles.

But this sort of thing could not be done with impunity. When couriers, hot and dusty, galloped up to head-quarters at the Junction, and reported firing in the direction of Bristow, it was evident that the truth had now become fully known to Pope, and that, having hurriedly broken up encampments around Warrenton, he was swooping down upon us with his whole force! This news was matter for serious consideration; and many said: "Suppose they drop upon us on the other side from Alexandria? if so, we are gone chickens, and old 'Stonewall' is played out!"

Jackson, however, had not been neglectful of chance combinations when revolving his plan, and knew upon what amount of coöperation he could himself rely. Yet upon the first news of Pope's advance, he drew his corps together, and did not seem to heed the heavy skirmishing and occasional cannonading going on with his rear-guard and the enemy's advance. Although fully aware of the immense odds approaching against him, he seemed determined to hold them in check, and was bold enough to place his corps in a naturally strong position which was parallel with the enemy's line of retreat along the roads to Centreville, his right being stretched in the direction of Thoroughfare Gap to keep open communication with the main army, which we surmised was not more than two marches behind.

Meantime, facts became known which made those in the secret look gloomy enough on the evening of the twenty-seventh. An inevitable fight on the morrow began to be mysteriously spoken of around the camp-fires. The enemy were massing in our front. "If we are not soundly whipped," said one, "it is a mercy of Providence." "True," said another, "we are over-matched, yet our position is a strong one, and if there was any positive prospect of being thrashed, Jackson is the last man in the world to be caught in such a trap." "Yet 'trap' it seems to be," observed one, very emphatically; "we are outnumbered three to one in front: reports have come in of troops on the move from Alexandria and Washington." "Yes, but then our army is advancing from Thoroughfare Gap." "*Are* they? not at all! the Federals are strongly posted there, and hold it with many cannon!" This announcement elicited a long whistle from many, while others buried their chagrin in cups of coffee and smoked in silence. "Who told you?" one ventured to ask. "Wilkinson; he was sent off with orders, and could not get through—an entire division holds the place!" "Well, say no more about it," said a fat old major of foot; "any thing for a change. I'd rather fight any time than be eternally marching; I suppose Jackson knows more about these things than we do—at all events, he puts a bold face upon matters, and instead of running away as a *scarey* general would, he plants himself firmly along their line of march and defies them! 'Tis evidently a fight or a foot-race with somebody, so throw a few sticks on the fire, Captain, and let's take a nap—some of us may be hit or cut before to-morrow evening!"

Word was brought during the night that the enemy were moving across our front, but massing on our right; so that when picket-firing began at dawn in the latter direction, the enemy's plans were very clearly developed—they desired to cut us off from communication with troops rumored to be marching to our relief. Ambrose Hill, however, who was said to be in command of our right, handled his men with more than usual ability, and prevented this design being executed. Prisoners captured informed us of the commands they severally belonged to; from whom it appeared that Heintzelman was moving against our left under Ewell near Centreville; Sigel was operating against the centre under Jackson; and Porter, with his regulars and powerful artillery, was opposed to Hill, McDowell being in reserve. Banks was not mentioned, and his position was unknown. This news confirmed our former suspicions that McClellan was reenforcing Pope as rapidly as possible, his various corps being despatched from Alexandria as speedily as they arrived there!

Firing now became regular with the infantry, and booming of cannon resounded among the hills with a long rolling sound like the echo of thunder. Light lines of smoke ascending over the landscape, and the long crackling sound of rifles as regiments delivered volleys, made the whole scene exciting and sublime. Long black lines of men advancing in columns, or wheeling when deployed, moving in all directions across the light green landscape, the explosion of shell among them causing death and disorder; the hurried motion of field officers, and furious galloping of orderlies and couriers; the meeting of regiments, their mutual volleys, and advance or retreat, with active batteries rushing here and there, unlimbering and firing, or limbering and hurriedly retiring—these were the constant sights presented by the enemy and ourselves in the vain endeavors of the former to turn our flanks. Loud above the general din was heard the roar of the regular cannonade maintained by both sides, as shell screamed through the air on their mission of death, and, tearing through the trees, exploded with an awful crash.

Hour after hour was this fearful and unequal contest continued. Again and again would the enemy pause and re-form; attack succeeded attack, and charge followed upon charge. Each time the foe seemed to throw himself upon us with redoubled fury, each time to be baffled, dispirited, and broken, until it seemed impossible that even Jackson himself could withstand the repeated shocks The greatest efforts of the enemy seemed to be concentrated against our right, under the immediate command of Jackson, as if it were the desire of Pope to crush or isolate him before the possible arrival of Longstreet and Lee. Whatever the object in view, Pope signally failed in turning the right, and although we slowly and cautiously gave ground, and punished his ill-timed advances with immense slaughter, night was gradually approaching, and couriers from Longstreet brought the joyful news that he had successfully beaten the enemy at Thoroughfare Gap,* and would form a junction with us in a few hours.

Although still hard pressed by the heavy forces of the enemy, and obliged to give ground from physical weakness alone, this news was passed from brigade to brigade, and from regiment to regiment, with such rapidity that, although completely exhausted, they rent the air with such an outburst of enthusiasm as to drown almost the fearful din of battle. Until night did this unequal contest last; but although we were forced to fall back some distance, this was effected with so much order and precision, that the movement appeared like a grand review. When the sun sank upon the scene, all was over; the enemy did not dare to pursue. Longstreet's .approach was perhaps known to them, and they were unwilling to encounter our combined forces without receiving reenforcements, or making proper dispositions for that eventuality.

The position assumed by Jackson at sunset was, if possible, stronger than that previously held. Feeling positive that no new attack was contemplated, and that Longstreet had formed

---

* This was subsequently verified. We learned from some of General Reno's forces, after the second battle of Bull Run, that they were the troops intrusted with the defence of Thoroughfare Gap, but being hard pushed by the Confederates, had retired upon General Porter's corps, with which they had subsequently acted· Hooker was also with Pope.

on our right wing, our men stacked arms, pickets were thrown out in front, some few fires were lit, and our wearied men betook themselves to sleep. Having several friends acting under Longstreet, I rode over to his position, and after much annoyance at the challenges of numerous sentinels, posted in out-of-the-way places, and many mistakes in picking my way in the dark, at last found the regiments and the individuals I desired to see.

Chatting round the camp-fire, of that day's events, I ascertained that the enemy might have made a stout resistance at Thoroughfare Gap, but fled at the first fire. Longstreet's forces had travelled rapidly towards us; for the firing being audible, they were naturally impatient to rush to our assistance. On approaching the Gap no enemy was visible, but as the Seventh and Eighth Georgia were pushing forward in advance, the enemy suddenly opened several field-pieces, and commenced to sweep the road. "Oh! they are there, are they?" said Longstreet, laughing. "Well, we'll soon dislodge them, boys," and immediately ordered up several pieces of artillery, which, galloping forward, opened upon the enemy so furiously and with such accuracy, as to shelter our infantry and clear the summit of the road. This was quickly accomplished, but our artillery were not content—they rushed up the rise and began to shell the foe, who hastily retreated into open grounds beyond. Their infantry then finding themselves unsupported, fell back in disorder.

The arrival of Longstreet was hailed with loud applause, not unmingled with regret that Lee was still absent, it being certain that hostilities would recommence on the morrow. In what direction the blow might fall was uncertain; but the best disposition was made to meet it when our reenforcements took up a position which threatened the enemy's flank. Signal-rockets were continually ascending along the Federal front, and from the number of camp-fires, and the amount of noise within their lines, it was shrewdly conjectured that heavy forces were arriving and taking up positions during the night. The incessant passing and re-passing of pickets, in addition to other noises, effectually banished sleep. Exhausted, sick, hungry, and annoyed, I rolled about, until a sergeant slapped me upon the back, when I jumped to my feet, and proceeding to a cottage near by, found several secretaries hard at work, and was ordered off on business many miles to the rear.

Shaking myself together, so to speak, I rinsed my face and hands, watered my horse in a brook, and quickly saddled; strapped on a small bundle of fodder, in case of need, buttoned my old overcoat to the throat, lit my pipe, and slowly picked my way through long lines of recumbent troops, until I was far to the rear, journeying alone over a deserted country, without guide or compass, save the dark and rugged outline of distant mountains, or the bright constellations studding a light blue sky.

As I slowly trotted forward along the well-beaten road, I occasionally came upon some small party of fatigued and exhausteds tragglers, who, to the number of four or half-a-dozen, had lit fires, and were for the most part asleep; yet, as soon as my horse's hoofs were heard approaching, some one of the group would jump to his feet and "halt" me. I did not wonder at the stragglers I thus met, for their marches had been long and rapid, and were their numbers greater I could have excused it, for ill-fed, wretchedly clothed and shod as they generally were, they must have been made of steel to withstand the hardships and privations of the past few days. Even I, who was in the saddle on a march, was perfectly exhausted, and for humanity's sake would not force my poor horse to more than a trot, except necessity compelled it. Yet such was the pride of these poor weary fellows, that to my cheerful remarks they would always answer: "We didn't fall out o' ranks scared of the Yanks, lieutenant, but our feet are all in blisters and cut with hard marching—we'll soon catch up with the boys to-morrow!"

As I progressed still farther on my journey, the large number of smouldering camp-fires dotted right and left of the main road, told me I had fallen in with whole brigades marching to the front; and the number of "halts" to which I was subjected by the guards, and the numerous questions put to me by half-sleepy and yawning "officers of the guard," were, to one in my position, vexatious in the extreme. Sometimes the cracking of whips and loud oaths of teamsters told me of wagon-trains fast in the ruts or mire; occasionally I passed a battery unable to move farther from the exhaustion of the animals, while artillerymen at the heads of sweating, snorting, and foaming horses, or at the wheels, greasing the axles, or pulling with ropes, evinced the anxiety which possessed all to be pushing to the front. Here and there camp utensils, blankets, and knapsacks, had been thrown upon the road side to lighten the wagons, more than one of which vehicles was upset by the road-side, and the horses, tethered or hobbled, were enjoying themselves in the high grass. Quartermasters, commissaries, and wagon-masters would occasionally pass at a swinging gallop, searching for stray teams or superintending occasional mishaps, fretting and swearing as those important officials are often wont to do. All the roads were well watched, however, and occasional bonfires on the hills told me that the signal-corps was wide awake, for occasionally their burning brands were rapidly at work, repeating or transmitting telegrams from point to point.

A few hours' ride brought me to my destination soon after sunrise, and having despatched my business, all I could do was to wait for further orders. My horse having been first cared for, I hung my saddle in a tree, near the door of a small cottage to which I had been directed, threw myself full length upon a bench, and was soon fast asleep.

I know not how long I had slept, but was awakened by voices at the door: "Lord a mercy, what a noise them cannons do make to be sure—they're fightin' agin at Manassas, *I* know. Just listen!" said an old housewife. I started up and stepped to the door; the loud and regular discharge of ordnance fully told me that some part of our lines was being furiously attacked. The heavy "thuds" which occasionally caught the ear were undoubtedly from howitzers, while the sharp, ringing sounds which could be occasionally heard, indicated rifled ordnance. An action of some sort was certainly going on, and I felt uneasy at my own inactivity. "Don't be impatient, my boy," said an old officer; "you are as much on duty here as elsewhere—besides, I don't think it is a general action, for I understand Lee has not passed here many hours, and he would surely be on hand if aught of that kind was anticipated. They are making a devil of a smoke, though," continued the Major as he mounted a hill close by to observe. "Here, take the glass and look for yourself—it doesn't seem to be much more than ten miles in a direct line."

I took the glass and distinctly observed light clouds of white smoke wafting over trees in the eastern landscape, but at that distance nothing definite could be made out. "Oh! don't trouble yourself," said the major; "I'm sure you're no field-marshal — Lee, Longstreet, and Jackson can get along pretty well without you for a few hours. As to the boys, they can take care of themselves at any time—so let your horse alone, and sit down; I think I've got a few cigars and a drop of good Bourbon somewhere—there, drink away, and smoke till you're tired—they cost me nothing, I got them from Dan Sickles's stores, which our boys captured at Savage Station." I tried the articles and found them to be good.

"Dan seems to be no bad judge of whiskey and cigars, does he? but, Lord! how mad he must have been to lose all his plate, private papers, and fine clothes, at Savage's, eh?" and as the Major's nose became redder at every additional glass, he took an extra bumper to raise steam, threw his heels upon the writing-table, and launched forth into a very long-winded story of his personal prowess, until I began mentally to inquire "where he generally buried his dead."

Although in appearance very friendly to the Major, I could not but loathe him in my very heart, for he was one of a class of brigade and divisional quartermasters who were the greatest hypocrites and rogues left unhung. He seemed to be totally absorbed in self; his personal baggage was large and miscellaneous; beds, bedsteads, chairs, tables, a full and large equipment of mess furniture, washing apparatus, and I know not what besides; the traps of his clerks and assistants demanded far more transportation than was allowed even to two full companies of foot; upon a march it is pretty certain the poor privates could not find room for the stowage of a coffee-pot or frying-pan, while his own wagons had the finest horses, and were always in front. If any of the wagons required an additional horse or two to pull up a hill, he would always order them to be "lightened," so that many a poor lad's extra wearing apparel was thrown upon the roadside, together with pots and pans without number, and to all remonstrances he would gruffly answer, "Wagon-master, push ahead," not caring a jot if the whole regiment or brigade had not a single pot in which to cook their rations.

Like others of his stamp, the Major found time to speculate in horses or mules, and as such things could not be done without "go-betweens," there were understrappers in his department, who realized hundreds of dollars per month, through such purchases. He would keep in hand for months at a time, thousands, I might say hundreds of thousands of dollars, which should have been paid away to the troops, and if spoken to he would answer: "Pay? oh! certainly, I'd have paid the men long ago, but the pay-rolls were incorrect, and I had to return them to be re-written." Many of our brigade quartermasters, particularly if on detached service, were of this worthless character—in truth many were an encumbrance to the army; and had fiery Longstreet or Jackson hung a few of them as Napoleon is said to have done on more than one occasion, the whole army would have been the better for it.

The firing towards Manassas continued throughout the day, but it was not till sunset that I received orders to return to the army. Glad enough I had mounted and faced "homewards" again; I started towards Manassas at a rattling pace, feeling certain if Lee arrived there would be "lively times" in the morning. I had not proceeded many miles along my circuitous route, ere I fell in with cavalry patrols and pickets, who were extremely vigilant; and although custom has made me sharp-sighted at night, I confess they frequently halted me ere I had the slightest notion of being within many miles of their vicinity. To add to my misery and delay, I had not the "countersign," and was marched off to the nearest guard-post to account for myself.

"Can't help it, comrade," said the cavalry-man: "I believe your words, and think I have frequently seen you before; but orders are orders, you know, and we must obey." I was handed over to the next picket, and so on, until I reached the central picket station, where the captain commanding examined me rigorously, and upon presenting papers of identity, he politely gave me the countersign, saying: "It was well, perhaps, you fell in with our men, for the road you were taking must have led you nearer the present lines of the enemy than you care about finding yourself, I know: the countersign I have given you is good among the outer pickets; when you reach the infantry, be careful how you act, for they have another one, and are particularly wakeful to-night, and thick as flies!"

Acting upon this advice, I plunged forward boldly, and was in high spirits, singing right heartily, for our numerous encampments were visible for many miles around. "Halt! halt!" was the challenge suddenly given by half-a-dozen; and from their guns levelled at me, I saw there was no fun about them. "Who goes there?" "Officer without the countersign!" "Advance, officer!" and I did so very meekly, for could they have seen me even wink improperly, I should have been instantly riddled with half-a-dozen shots. I here went through the operation of being handed over from one to another, until fairly out of patience. The corporal of the guard would do no more than hand me to the sergeant, the latter to the lieutenant of the guard; the last to the officer of the night, and he to the officer of the day; so that, from being handed from one to another, it got rumored abroad among some idle soldiers that I was a "spy," and soon there was a large crowd at my heels, bestowing upon me all manner of uncomplimentary epithets. The rumor spread among the regiments through which I was then passing; and while in the tent of the officer of the day making explanations, I heard one loquacious gentleman, who was peeping through a rent in the tent, exclaim: "The captain's got him—he's a spy, and they've got the papers on him! I hope they'll detail me as one of the firing party; won't I let him have it good!"

After a few moments of explanation, I remounted again; and my sudden transformation into a good and true Southerner seemed to have caused infinite disgust to many, but particularly to the ragged gentleman who was so anxious to make one of the "firing party." *

* The feverishness of our men regarding "spies" during these eventful days, was highly excited by the following incident: While Longstreet's corps was hurrying forward to Jackson's relief on the twenty-eighth, several brigades in advance on dif-

I had yet a long and weary journey before me, through miles of camps; and as I picked my way through long lines of stacked arms, glistening in the fire-light, I could not but smile at the stoical indifference evinced by nine tenths of the men for the dreadful work in store for them on the morrow. Some were oiling the locks of their guns; others, in shirt-sleeves, were ramming with wipers to cleanse the barrels of their pieces. Hats, caps, coats, stockings, accoutrements, and the like, were suspended from branches overhead, while orderly sergeants were busy with ammunition-boxes, issuing extra rounds. Some were asleep near the fire, others frying bacon or making coffee; while round such a fortunate youth were sure to be some half-dozen epicures shouting out, "I'll take the grounds after you!" "After you," said one. "Next after you," shouted another; so that it seemed the coffee-grounds had to do service half-a-dozen times round. I passed through several artillery camps— the ringing or clanking of chains, and the disposition of harness for instant use, proved the instinct which all felt regarding the event of the next day.

All this I observed on the extreme wing of our army; but when I proceeded farther, I saw long lines of wounded being conveyed away, and afterwards counted hundreds of dead. There had been a desperate fight, I was told, principally in Longstreet's wing, and rumor said he had been obliged to give ground. I could learn nothing definite regarding the engagement; but the cavalry captain's remark to me, that "I was on

---

ferent roads were observed to halt, thereby stopping all further progress of the corps. Very angry at this, Longstreet trotted to the front, and was informed that a courier had brought orders from General Lee to that effect ! "From General Lee ?" said he, his eyes glowing with rage. "Where *is* that courier?" he asked. "There he goes now, General, galloping down the road." "Keep your eyes on him, overtake him, and bring him here." This was soon accomplished. "By whose orders did you halt my brigade ?" asked a brigadier. "As I have already told you— by General Lee's ! I have orders for Longstreet, and must be off to the rear !" "Here is Longstreet," said that General, moving forward. "Where are your orders !" The spy was caught ! He turned red and pale, his lip quivered—he was self-condemned. "Give this man ten minutes, and hang him ! Let the columns push forward immediately." In fifteen minutes the spy was lifeless, hanging from a tree by the roadside ; but before death, confessed that although a Virginian and a Confederate soldier, he had been in communication with the enemy over ten months, and was then acting for General Pope.

the road to the enemy's lines," seemed to indicate that Long-street had been obliged to fall back some distance. The fight-ing was represented to me as having been awful: the enemy had been reenforced by nearly all of McClellan's Peninsula force, and suddenly hurled against our right. No loss, in can-non or general officers, was reported; but it was said that, act-ing strictly on the defensive, we had inflicted terrible punish-ment upon them with our artillery as they advanced in masses against us. The position occupied by both was almost identical with the ground in the first Battle of Manassas, except that we were on the north and they on the south side of the Run.

Very little notice seems to have been taken of this engage-ment in official circles. I learned, however, that the true ob-ject of the Federal attack was to extricate their left somewhat, and to push their right into Centreville, so as to keep open com-munication with Washington and Alexandria for the receipt of reenforcements and supplies; of which they stood greatly in need, since Jackson's visit to the Junction on the twenty-sev-enth. Reconnoitring parties were sent out during the night, who reported that the enemy had drawn in their left wing con-siderably, thus shortening, but perhaps strengthening, their line. Be that as it may, preparations were busily going on among us to open the battle on the morrow; and the determination of all seemed to be to push Pope harder on this occasion than ever before, and to give him a clear, unclouded view of men whose faces he pretended never to have seen.

Couriers, orderlies, and colonels were moving about all night; and although the army seemed to rest in peace, one half the men were wide awake, revolving the chances of the morrow and wishing the affair were over. Part of Longstreet's corps was on the move early in the morning, and seemed to be cau-tiously taking up positions nearer the enemy's left. As this movement was continued, sharp skirmishing occurred in his immediate front, and soon after extended rapidly along the whole line. Nothing of moment occurred, however, between the two armies for many hours in the morning; indeed, it was past noon when the action really commenced.

The advance of our right seemed greatly to annoy the en-emy's left, which it evidently outflanked, and they determined to open upon us suddenly, and with great fury, hoping to annihilate it before the arrival of reenforcements. Contrary to custom, therefore, the enemy did not cover their advance with skirmishers, but came forward in regular battle line, and would have taken our sharpshooters by surprise; but the latter had been in service too long to be imposed upon by any such Yankee notion, and, instantly retreating, gave the alarm that the enemy were approaching in serried lines, one being within easy supporting distance behind the other. " So *they* are the attacking party, are they?" said an old brigadier as he sat upon his horse smoking a cigar. "Forward, boys! we also are advancing, so there must be music of some sort shortly."

He had proceeded but a few hundred yards through the fields and woods, when the enemy's approaching line was revealed by the glitter of their bayonets. A volley was fired and returned; then our men moved forward again, and continued this mode of proceeding throughout the engagement: but every time the enemy gave ground, our active batteries would gallop to the front and give them such a vigorous shelling, as completely broke the order of their retrograde movement. From such information as I could glean, while passing from point to point, it appeared that our advance was almost in the form of two sides of a square, the enemy's left being the particular object of our main attack.

The general advance was a beautiful sight. As far as the eye could range, two parallel lines of glittering bayonets were flashing in the sun; now the Federal lines halted suddenly, a gleam of sunlight told that their rifles had been brought to the "ready," and a moment had not elapsed ere a long flash was seen, light curls of smoke arose, and the rattling echo of their volleys was carried on the wind. A yell arose, and was borne from wing to wing with the quickness of light, when quickly a rapid irregular fire was returned, and the clatter continued as fast as our men could load. Onward they went—now the long line could be observed passing through open fields, skirmishers in front popping away at the retiring foe. The line again would disappear in the woods. A brief pause would ensue, followed by the clatter of our artillery riding to the front, and

29

the awful roar of the guns.   Then, again, a shout, telling that our men had resumed the advance.

Cannonading was terrific along our whole front, but on the right Fitz-John Porter's and Longstreet's artillery literally shook the earth.   Their left giving way, a sudden attack was made on their centre, commanded by McDowell and Sigel.   The assault was neither long nor doubtful, for the enemy retired at the first volley, and such was their evident confusion, that it at one time seemed as if their whole army was giving way to panic; yet, through the exertions of Sigel, the gap in their centre was quickly filled up, and the fight maintained there with obstinacy and generalship.   An attempt made to turn our left signally failed.   The flanking force was soon discovered approaching, and allowed to come within a reasonable distance, when a powerful artillery force opened at the head of the column, and literally smashed it.   Thus, on the right and centre, our forces were rapidly dispossessing the enemy of his position, and no one doubted the issue of the conflict.   Along the whole line, clouds of dust and smoke, the booming of artillery and rattle of small arms, told of the unflinching courage and pertinacity of our men;   while long lines of ambulances and stretchers, proceeding to the rear, fully proved that although victory was evidently ours, we had dearly paid for it.   Fiery Longstreet, with his impatient and gallant corps, was rapidly pushing our right, while shot and shell ploughed the ground in all directions around him.   Lee in the centre, calm and collected, moved from point to point among his troops, smiling good-humoredly with the consciousness that he was gradually pressing hard on the masses of the foe; while old "Stonewall," as usual, was in a very tempest of shot and shell, and smoke and dust, holding on like grim death to his position on our left, and punishing the enemy frightfully with his well-disposed artillery.   Thus, in truth, all our generals were hotly engaged at different points of the line.   The impetuous Ambrose Hill was with Ewell and others under Jackson, and had enough to do to keep time with the rapid movements of their chief.   The satirical, stoical D. H. Hill was there, cold as ice, and firm as a rock.   Evans, Stuart, McLaws, Maxey Gregg, Jenkins, Barksdale, Whiting, Archer, Pickett, Field, Walton, Pendleton, and a host of other historical heroes, were in command to-day, and each seemed to rival the other in prudence and valor; while Hood and his Texans far outshone all their previous deeds by their present acts of daring.

Over all the field the battle was going favorably for us, and no complaint was uttered on any hand—all seemed to desire to get as close to Pope as possible, and to show their powder-blackened faces to him. I believe there was not a single man in the whole army but would have swam through rivers of blood to have caught that mendacious hero alive; not all the wealth of Peru would have been half so acceptable to our enraged men as the capture of that vain and pompous leader, whose rule in Virginia had been marked with such wanton waste of property, such tyranny over the inhabitants, and so many instances of petty revenge. Such a fortune, however, did not fall to our lot, for John Pope, the self-created hero, took great pains to keep from the front, and never allowed himself to ride within two miles of the actual battle. Several of the Federal generals, however, chiefly brigadiers, boldly rode to the front, and cheered on their men. Sickles and Meagher were singled out and disabled.* Wherever I rode along our extended and ever-changing front, prisoners of all grades, cannon, flags, and other trophies were passing to the rear; while every patch of timber was converted into a temporary hospital, where surgeons in blood-stained garments were busily plying the knife. Moans, groans, and death-cries arose on every hand, mingling with the distant roar and rush of battle; while the wounded, both friend and foe, forgetful of all enmity, dragged themselves to the same spring to quench their thirst. Headless or limbless bodies were seen at every turn; stray shot and shell from the enemy ploughed up the ground, or exploded among the wounded; while riderless horses, foaming and frightened, rushed to and fro, in all directions, or limped and tottered till they fell. Still "Onward!" was the word from all. Ammunition wagons slowly followed the line of battle, while in wood and field, across creeks and brooks, the roar of battle

---

* Among hundreds of line officers who fell was Colonel Fletcher Webster, Twelfth Massachusetts Volunteers, eldest and sole surviving son of the great American orator and statesman, Hon. Daniel Webster, of Massachusetts.

continued, and long lines of smoke curling over tree-tops were wafted away westward by the rising breeze of evening.

This was a terrible battle, truly — prisoners confessed that our artillery fire on their left and right had been truly appalling. From a comparison of names and positions we learned that, independent of Pope's own force, all, or nearly all, of McClellan's army had arrived in time to participate in the engagement, and that the severest fighting had been done by them. They had been force-marched, they said, to get up in time, and though exhausted, were thrust into the most dangerous positions, and oftentimes left without supports. The loss among their field officers had been great, and whole brigades were so loth to engage, that they broke up on the instant of confronting us. McClellan's men, we were told, were heartily sick of the war — all their hopes and ambition had been completely broken in the campaign before Richmond, and they possessed little heart to engage us again so soon, particularly under the leadership of such a "granny" as Pope. "In fact," said an officer to me, "this Manassas No. 2 bids fair to rival No. 1—the ground seems fatal to us—we have been led out by John Pope to-day for wholesale slaughter; unless McClellan comes to its instant relief with some additional corps, you may rely upon it, our retreat will turn into a perfect rout."

Having orders to proceed from the centre to our right, I had to cross the Bull Run, and such a sight I never wish to witness again. The wounded and dying of both armies lined the banks in all manner of attitudes. Some, in the endeavor to drink, had tumbled in, and from weakness unable to extricate themselves, had been drowned; others in the water, clung to branches, and thus sustained themselves, but often let go their hold and disappeared. All the meadows were trodden down, and were brown, wet, and bloody, hundreds of bodies had been ridden over and crushed by artillery or cavalry, so that the remains of poor humanity were scattered and crushed in the most revolting manner. This was no time to philosophize, however; the battle still went on, and as I followed the line pursued by Longstreet, carnage and sickening sights met me at every turn. Now I came upon a spot where artillery had been hotly contending — the trees around were broken, riddled, or blown down, caissons were upset, dead horses in scores lay scattered about, while the grass and sand were purpled with blood. Fences were gone, houses knocked into splinters or undistinguishable heaps of brick—small arms, cannon, and long lines of dead were on every hand, and yet the fight continued in the direction of Centreville very warmly. The enemy were simply fighting to secure their retreat, so that at evening when the firing slackened, and we had driven them a great distance, I was glad to think the battle was drawing to a close for that day. It seemed to me, however, that the enemy's new position on Centreville Heights was a formidable one, and I was not at all pleased to see indications of their camping or staying there.

Except a few occasional shot and shell, the battle was over—the enemy were driven from all their positions, and our whole army was completely exhausted with their labors of the past few days. Of the numbers lost by us I could not form an estimate; we had suffered severely, it is true, but the punishment inflicted on the enemy was really awful. Our captures in prisoners had been very considerable, and great numbers were paroled and sent forward to the enemy's lines in the Valley or to Harper's Ferry. Pope had been unmercifully thrashed by Lee in this memorable battle, and every Southerner rejoiced, but was heartily amazed that the immortal John had not shown his face during the day, where thousands were on the lookout for him.

Much ammunition and many stores fell into our hands. This was grateful news to the men, for we needed both very much, and our transportation trains were inadequate to the duty of regularly supplying us. Jackson was vexed that so much of the enemy's baggage had escaped, and the battle had not been over many hours ere he was preparing to sally forth and get on their flanks, with a view to further captures; for myself, I could not help thinking that Manassas was glory enough for one day, and felt heartily glad I was not one in his marching division. Truly, Jackson was the most restless leader the world ever saw, and he seemed to have very little consideration for the bones and sinews of his men, so that, when remonstrated with, he simply answered: "The men like it—we shall find plenty of provisions on the route, if the enemy have any."

CHAPTER XLII.

I WAS so much fatigued when the engagement closed that I would fain have gathered a few sticks and bivouacked where sunset found me, but falling in with a cavalry party detailed to watch the enemy during night, we rode over a large part of the battle-field, and pickets being posted, the "reliefs" luckily found a few tents standing, left like thousands of other things in the hurry of retreat, and we camped there. Barrels of cracker-bread, some excellent corned beef, and half a sack of ground coffee were also discovered in beating about through the timber, so that fires being lighted, we unslung our mess traps, and were soon engaged in ravenously devouring our highly prized supper. The coffee proved a great luxury to the whole party, few of whom had tasted this beverage since the capture of stores before Richmond in June. Had the oldest and best of wines been offered in exchange, I doubt if any would have parted with their steaming cups of Rio.

We formed several groups round as many fires, lighted near the tents, and with the all-consoling pipe, soon found our-selves launching forth into the merits and ups and downs of Pope's eventful campaign. Some troopers of the party, how-ever, had made a discovery of something stronger than coffee, and having found a violin among the deserted effects of the departed Yankees, were dancing to a lively tune. With long, uncut beards, whiskers, and moustaches, heavy riding-boots, and sabres, and attired with Yankee light-blue overcoats, our troopers capered about with all the elegance of young bears. It was impossible to blame them for their gaiety; they had been fearfully overworked, and although sent out again on outpost duty, were sufficiently far from the front to attract attention. Our bivouac had evidently been a general quartermaster's camp; we found so many things belonging to such a department, as put the matter beyond doubt. In the largest of the tents were his desks, stools, tables, and bed — in others were provisions of various sorts, as if some commissary also had been in company, while much hay, straw, and corn, proved very acceptable to our half-starved animals. We could plainly discern the enemy's camp-fires on Centreville Heights, and rockets were frequently bursting in the air, conveying intelligence from point to point. The greatest number of troops seemed to be stationed farther up the roads towards Fairfax, judging from the large luminous bodies of clouds hanging in that direction.

Except the snorting of horses, nothing was heard during the night—the first relief fell in about midnight, and trotted off in the darkness—the old guard returned and brought no news. How long I remained half dozing or sound asleep, I know not, but as my boots became very hot from being near the fire, I awoke in a bad temper, and found not less than half-a-dozen Federal prisoners sitting on logs round the fire, who were talking in subdued tones. They were infantry men — two were officers, and at a short distance I could perceive one of our over-coated and heavy-heeled cavalry men standing guard with his carbine cocked.

The prisoners had been captured near the banks of Bull Run, secreted in the bushes, and had surrendered without resistance. They were dusty, ragged, hungry, and haggard, or their looks very much belied them; so that finding I could not sleep, I sat up by the fire, lit my pipe, and began conversing with the officer commanding our party, who was still awake. After a few hints, he understood me, and invited the officers to a drink of liquor, and laid our crackers and coffee before them, so that many minutes had not elapsed ere the whole Federal party were busily engaged cooking, and seemed very grateful for our considerate behavior. " Men must eat, you know," said the commandant, sucking his pipe, "whether friend or foe — pitch into the grub, fellows," said he, " you'll have a long march to-morrow." ' Some of the men cooked for the two officers, who, after eating, played with empty pipes—a hint which was quickly perceived. I gave them a little tobacco, and the privates being allotted a tent, bundled in among the straw, and were happier than if sleeping in the St. Nicholas Hotel. The commandant and myself were soon engaged in conversation with the two officers, whose eyes we kept from closing by giving occasional draughts of whiskey, a process they did not seem averse to, for one of them, a red-nosed lieutenant, seemed such an adept in emptying a small half-pint cup, that I would wager he could account for a dozen at any time, and never even cough or wink. We did not try the experiment with him, however, but adroitly managed to keep the stone jar on our side of the fire, without wounding his sensitiveness.

" Ah! you always manage to out-manœuvre 'us," said one. "Had it not been for Cedar Run, this present disaster would not have befallen us. How so? That is very plain; for if Pope had been able to maintain his position south of the Rappahannock, all McClellan's and Burnside's forces would have reenforced him at Fredericksburgh; instead of that, our men were ordered to Aquia Creek. It was thought we could hold the north bank of the Rappahannock for some short time; but when Pope was forced back on Manassas by Jackson's flank movement, the point of debarkation was again changed to Alexandria—a considerable distance in our rear. Thus your General Lee seemed to understand the anxiety of Pope to be reenforced, and, by rapid movements, prevented the mass of those troops arriving until too late."

" Well, those which *did* arrive did not do much, I think. Prisoners from McClellan's men say that the whole army was disaffected, and that general officers made no bones about calling Pope a fool publicly."

"True, those troops of McClellan, which arrived on the twenty-eighth and twenty-ninth did not *do* much, as you say, but I can assure you they *suffered* much—yes, horribly—and more's the pity that such willing men should have been sent to wholesale slaughter under the orders of such a cabbage-head as Pope. Parts of Burnside's and Hunter's troops which had been long in the field and had been hurried on to Pope, were expected to work wonders, but, upon the proof, broke into disorder. Besides, we had no regular supplies. Your generals had appropriated or destroyed the dépôts at Manassas; the railroad to our rear also had been destroyed in part by your cavalry, so that, you may scarcely believe it, we have been living for the past week very irregularly and precariously, while, worse than all, our ammunition was scant, and there seemed to to be no fixed arrangements for supplying us with any thing from Alexandria or Washington. I am heartily sick of the business."

"Yes," chimed in Rednose, "I wish I was strolling up Broadway to-night," —"into some bar-room," he might have added, for, from a sidelong glance cast at our precious stone jar, he evidently wanted "a whet," sugar or no sugar.

In answer to inquiries, the first speaker continued: "I always heard that Cedar Run had cost Banks upwards of three thousand men, killed, wounded, and prisoners, and ·during the last three fights, I should judge we could not have lost less than fourteen thousand more.* I did not hear that we had lost thirty pieces of artillery, but your statement is doubtless correct, for I know we must have suffered fearfully, judging from the hurry and confusion of retreat. Your pickets informed me, that all the roads are literally blocked up with wagons, caissons, and cannon. I do not doubt it, for it is no use disguising the fact that we were completely routed. Your attack upon our left was a fierce affair, and Porter suffered terribly. Had your assault upon our centre succeeded as well,

---

* General Pope admitted, unofficially, that his losses during the twenty-eighth, twenty-ninth, and thirtieth amounted to over seventeen thousand killed, wounded, and prisoners, but the authorities at Washington contradicted the report, and said the total would not be more than eight thousand, as many stragglers were returning to the ranks again. Pope certainly had better opportunities of knowing the truth than General Halleck, for when General Sumner and others joined him near Centreville with twenty thousand men, Pope said they had arrived too late, and would barely fill up the loss sustained by him during the week. It will not be possible to know the whole truth till all is over, for the North always misrepresents matters.

we should never have reached Centreville alive. Sigel behaved like a hero there, and so did McDowell; had they not rushed into the wide gap with fresh troops and stubbornly defended it, our whole army would have been divided and slaughtered piecemeal.

"It is true, as you have been told, that we never had confidence in Pope; we all felt that he was perfectly bewildered during the week, galloping from this place to that, giving orders one minute and countermanding them another. We did as directed, however, and here we are, prisoners, but might have fallen into worse hands, judging from your hospitality and kindness." We explained that several thousand (six thousand) prisoners had been captured during the past few days, and were paroled as far as convenience would permit, which news surprised them; but the bare idea of a parole, and the possible chance of strolling up Broadway ere many days, had a visible effect upon Mr. Rednose, who unceremoniously seized our jar, and helped himself to a very considerable suck therefrom.

As conversation continued, we ascertained from the Federal captain who had been speaking, that he was employed on the staff during the day, and had traversed the greater part of the field, so that his remarks were not all hearsay. He described the loss of the enemy as being truly considerable, and did not deny that their line officers had suffered much. Banks had not participated in the engagement, and it was generally supposed he had been cut off by our forces.* The various brooks and streams were represented as quite discolored, and contained many bodies of friend and foe—temporary and other bridges were broken at different places, and cannons, wagons, and horses were not unfrequently seen partly submerged.

Nothing in the world could have induced me to travel over that blood-stained plain—one battle-field is much like another, and I had seen so many, that few things novel would have repaid me for the labor, had I been so inclined. Nothing but revolting, sickening sights could be met with; and save the lights of burying parties, and ambulance trains slowly moving

---

* This was incorrect, for he joined Pope on the march from Centreville, but lost much of his baggage, as usual.

to and fro in all directions, little was there to tempt me from my couch of straw. What might transpire on the morrow none could-imagine, but reports were confirmed that Jackson was busily engaged in provisioning his corps from captured stores, and no one doubted that he would soon be in motion. The probable object of his anticipated movement I have alluded to at the end of the preceding chapter.*

Long before daylight on the morrow, (August thirty-first,) our videttes were relieved, and others fully rested took their place. Few things of value were left for them; our troopers during the night had ransacked the woods, and appropriated every thing which could be of use or ornament. Coffee, cracker-bread, sugar, and shoes, were in most demand, while

---

* A Southern gentleman thus writes of Jackson, whom about this period he saw for the first time: "There you see self-command, perseverance, indomitable will, that seems neither to know nor think of any earthly obstacle, and all this without the least admixture of vanity, assumption, pride, foolhardiness, or any thing of the disposition to exert its pretensions, but from the quiet sense of the conviction of his relative position, which sets the vexed question of self-importance at rest; a peculiarity, I would remark, of great minds. His face also expresses courage in the highest degree, and his phrenological development indicates a vast amount of energy and activity. His forehead is broad and prominent, the occipital and sincipital regions are both large and well-balanced; eyes expressing a singular union of mildness, energy, and concentration; cheek and nose both long and well formed. His dress is a common gray suit of faded cassimere, coat, pants and hat—the coat slightly braided on the sleeve, just enough to be perceptible, the collar displaying the mark of major-general. Of his gait it is sufficient to say, that he just goes along; not a particle of the strut, the military swagger, or 'turkey-gobbler' parade, so common among officers of small rank and smaller minds. It would be a profitable study for some of our military swells to devote one hour each day to the contemplation of the 'magnificent plainness' of old Stonewall. To military fame, which they can never hope to attain, he unites the simplicity of a child, the straightforwardness of a Western farmer. There may be those who would be less struck with his appearance as thus accoutred, than if bedizened with lace and holding the reins of a magnificent barb caparisoned and harnessed for glorious war; but to one who had seen him as I had, at Coal Harbor and Malvern Hills, in the rain of shell and the blaze of the dead lights of the battle-field, when nothing less than a mountain would serve as a breastwork against the enormous shells, and iron bolts twenty inches long, which showered and shrieked through the sickly air, General Jackson in tatters would be the same as General Jackson in gilded uniform. Last Sunday he was dressed in his old faded uniform as usual, and bestrode as common a horse as one could find in a summer's day. In my view he is without peer—he is a nonpareil. He has enough energy to supply a whole manufacturing district, and enough genius to stock two or three military schools like West-Point."

others found overcoats, new saddles, and harness, canteens, and illustrated newspapers; so that when the old guard fell in and trotted back to camp, with large bundles of hay and bags of corn strapped on behind them, few regretted having been sent to the front during night. From the loud conversation and laughter continually going on in their ranks, I had a shrewd suspicion that *another* barrel had been discovered somewhere in the woods; but while taking frequent sucks from their canteens, they winked knowingly at one another, and "never let on" to the commanding officer.

As I approached head-quarters through the numerous infantry camps the men were busy cleaning their arms, and ammunition was being distributed. "I wish the commissary would come along," said one hungry-looking fellow, "for we've been fed on nothing else but cartridges for the past week!" All was bustle and preparation; but the transportation trains, artillery horses, and the ambulance corps looked so jaded and worn, that I could not help thinking our army was too much prostrated to commence the line of march on that day. In truth, every one was fatigued, and had been fearfully overworked. As to our cattle — the chief machinery of an army — they seemed more dead than alive, and were as bony as Rosinante, nor could all the coaxing in the world, or an abundance of captured hay and corn, tempt them from hanging their heads dejectedly or lying immovable upon the ground. Our mules, even—those animals which stand up under all fatigue like things of steel—were spiritless, and their raw sides told plainly of the fearful labor and forced marches to which they had been subjected. Men and animals seemed inclined for sleep; and I noticed more than one youngster, with a bandaged head or limb, moaning in his sleep; fatigue had numbed the sense of pain. They were too proud to leave ranks for a flesh wound; and there many of these heroic boys lay fast asleep against the trees, with half a blanket thrown round them, their toes protruding from their boots, their garments in rags, and their faces blackened with powder.

"Surely we can't move to-day," I remarked to an aide I met, who, rein in hand, was leading his animal to a brook.

"I hope not," was the reply. "If we do, *I* shan't; in fact,

I *can't!* I've been out half the night, and am more dead than alive; in fact, I will shun head-quarters till perfectly rested; for if I go there, I shall be surely accommodated with another night ride of thirty miles. I was bogged and bothered last night, and came within an ace of being taken, for the enemy's camps were not more than half a mile from me, and no fires burning. They are moving—I suppose you have heard it?— and Jackson is moving also. He started out early this morning, through the hills on our left; and report says he'll fall upon their flanks near Fairfax or Fall's Church. Lee, at the same time, will push the rear — mind if he don't; and then there'll be another big fight, sure, and a few more thousands of us will be tumbled over."

The information was correct. Jackson, with scarcely any thing to encumber him but ammunition, was off on a forced march; but his wagons (nearly all empty) were to start towards Leesburgh, and be there within three days. What did this mean? The movement of our trains was always an unerring thermometer of coming events; but why send them into Loudon, when the enemy are in force round Winchester, but thirty miles from Leesburgh? Such were my thoughts, and I felt nonplussed.

"Hold on awhile," whispered a friend, "there's a heavy cavalry force sent into the Valley, which will soon dislodge them, and send them into Harper's Ferry, howling. Who knows, but we may go into Maryland ere many days?" continued my friend, slapping me on the back in triumph.

"Who knows, indeed?" I thought, and smoked in silence. I felt annoyed to think that camp rumors regarding an invasion of Maryland might prove true. The people of that State had done but little for us, and were playing fast and loose with both parties, and as a State it was unworthy of our assistance. It could not be denied that we were far from being in a fit condition to meet the fierce tide of opposition which would surely roll against us; for my knowledge of Northern craft and hypocrisy convinced me that the enemy had a large force scattered through the States, which would be rapidly concentrated around Washington by land and water, against which a tired, hungry, shoeless, and jaded army of seventy-five thousand men could effect but little. When we suddenly broke up camps round Richmond to pounce upon Pope, our whole available force did not muster more than eighty-five thousand; and allowing for losses at Cedar Run, and the three days' engagements on the plains of Manassas, ten thousand may be safely deducted from that total, if not more. A strong, unconquerable will was the sole motive power which had hitherto kept our army moving, but how long even *that* would respond to the many trials, privations, and battles yet in store, was a question of anxiety to me; for if our men were made of oak or steel, they could not have been more severely and fiercely tried than they had been during June, July, and August. "Our Generals know best," I thought, in conclusion, and, with that conviction, said nothing.

Next day (September first) it was understood that Jackson was fully in position on the left flank of the retreating enemy, and Lee began his advance upon Centreville. Little opposition was met with, and we followed on as rapidly as prudence and caution would permit. Pope's army was evidently in a state verging on open panic, so that when our advance guards assailed their rear on various roads, they broke into confusion, leaving much of their baggage in our hands. The succession of combats that ensued at various times during the day and the morning following were not of great importance, yet many fresh troops which acted as their rear-guard suffered considerably; two leading generals, and many other officers of note, being killed, while vainly endeavoring to rally their panic-stricken troops.*

Fast as they retreated towards Arlington and Alexandria, they

---

* The enemy's loss in these skirmishes has been estimated at more than ten hundred killed and wounded. Among many officers who fell were Generals Stevens and Kearny. The latter met his death in a singular manner. The Federal cavalry finding Jackson close upon their flank, and Lee in hot pursuit at the rear, in the neighborhood of Fairfax Court-House, beat a hasty retreat, and infantry becoming alarmed, abandoned every thing, and ran also. Stevens and Kearny immediately faced about with their divisions; and while the latter was out reconnoitring, he suddenly came upon one of our Georgia regiments. Perceiving danger, he shouted, "Don't fire—I'm a friend!" but instantly wheeled his horse round, and, lying flat down upon the animal, had fairly escaped many bullets, when one struck him at the bottom of the spine, and, ranging upwards, killed him almost instantly.

did not effect their inglorious flight within those mighty strong-holds without much annoyance and loss from our active cavalry, who hung in clouds upon their rear, pistolling and sabring with but little opposition. All the roads, indeed, gave endless tokens of the many combats which had ensued, for dead, wounded, baggage, and prisoners were numerous. It was never expected by the humblest drummer in our ranks that Lee would attempt any assault upon Arlington Heights or the intrenched camps extending for miles round Alexandria. Lee's estate was on the Heights, and no one knew better than he the almost impregnable nature of the many fortifications thrown up there in the fall of the previous year. Operations were contemplated in another direction. Jackson was proceeding towards Leesburgh by the Drainsville (or river) road, while many troops were marching parallel to him on the Gum Spring road, so that the Upper Potomac was evidently intended to be our next field of operations.

In following the general line of march, which was now well beaten by the passage of troops, I frequently fell in with an old acquaintance; and the scenes through which we passed were familiarly known to me. I have before remarked on the great fertility of the fields of Loudon and adjacent counties compared with the plains of Manassas and parts of Fauquier County, through which we had but recently marched. I was informed, indeed, that the old farmers had been advised by Confederate officers to stay at home and cultivate their fields, even when we had retreated thence seventeen months before; so that well-stocked barn-yards and abundant crops of every sort of grain were now awaiting our long lines of empty wagons which accompanied us. The behavior of Federals to the inhabitants had been cruel and exacting; but not dreaming of our ever visiting those parts again, they never imagined these accumulated crops would by any chance fall into our hands. Their calculations were incorrect, and our advance was pursued so rapidly that we gave no opportunity for their removal or destruction.

Our march was greeted everywhere with loud demonstrations of joy; and when it became known that our destination was Maryland, enthusiasm ran wild. Old and young, white and black, thronged the roadsides with banners and waving handkerchiefs. Gray-haired fathers and half-frantic mothers sought sons and relatives in the various regiments which continually passed along the hot and dusty roads. Everywhere it seemed a holiday. The mere fact that the enemy had been repeatedly whipped, filled every one with so much joy, that women young and old wept freely, while old men waved their hats and tossed them in the air with delight. Tables were spread for us by the roadside, and superintended by some bright-eyed girl, while darkies grinned, and laughed, and skipped about with all the grimaces and antics of young monkeys. Nods of recognition were frequent along the Gum Spring road, for our brigade had been stationed many months in Loudon; and as we approached Leesburgh, I was met by farmer Wilkins, who, in a white felt hat, blue homespun coat, and yellow leather riding-breeches, fell into line, and almost squeezed my fingers off in his warmth and excitement. From him I learned some particulars regarding Yankee rule on the Upper Potomac since our departure, and the recital affected the old man even to tears—"Not that I weep for the loss of my sons," said he; "but I *do* cry because I am not young enough to bear arms against the cursed wretches who have been quartered among us so long."

It grieves me to omit the many instances of petty despotism in Leesburgh which my friend related to me; but a single example must suffice. I must premise that the first act of Geary's men had been to sack the shop of Dr. Motts, an apothecary, and gut the building. Geary himself took up his quarters in Motts's residence, to the great discomfort and annoyance of madame and the children—the doctor being with us in the army. From this residence Geary issued various rhapsodical orders, and strutted about with a clanking sabre like a modern Alexander, before whom all the rustic population were expected to bow down.

Dr. Janney, an old gentleman of sixty years, was summoned before him. "You were President of the State Convention which decided upon secession, Mr. Janney?" "I feel proud to own it," was the calm reply. "I want accommodation in your house, sir, for several officers. I hear you refuse." "I have no accommodation in the house, sir, for more than my family. I *can not* accommodate your men, and *would* not if I could." Despite his years, his tottering gait and infirmities, he was immediately sent to Washington, and incarcerated in a loathsome prison. He was desired to take the oath of allegiance as the price of his release, but the brave old man smiled, and replied with scorn: "Never, while there is breath in my body!"

My old friend finished his narrative by telling me that the enemy had, during our absence, erected several pontoon-bridges over the river, at various points; and although some of them required repairs, he was certain we could avail ourselves of them, and soon render them practicable for crossing into Maryland. The river was low, however; and even should the temporary bridges prove worthless, there were several fords by which we could cross, and establish ourselves in the rear of the many Federal fortifications which in times past had frowned so ominously on our small force under Evans.

We were now approaching Leesburgh. The town lay at the foot of the hills over which we were then crossing, and the loud roar of voices, and waving of banners, told me that the head of our column was entering the place amid the wildest demonstrations of its inhabitants. Bands played, colors waved, men shouted, women wept, and all was a scene of dust, confusion, and noise. "Dixie," "Maryland," the "Bonnie Blue Flag," and the "Marseillaise," were drowned in the tumult of voices, bumping of wagons, jingling of artillery, and the heavy tramp of infantry. Vainly did ambitious musicians blow till red or black in the face; the mouths of commanders were seen to move, and gestures followed, but no sounds of command were audible; yells, cheers, shouts, laughter, and rapid high-toned greetings were heard on every hand, until I began to think we were marching into Bedlam. Bread, cheese, butter, eggs, meats, fruits—every thing eatable was strewn on the sidewalks; while loaves of bread were flying through the air in all directions, which were quickly caught and stuck on the men's bayonets. The bayonet, indeed, was particularly useful in this respect, and I could not help noticing that many had new shoes, loaves of bread, chunks of pork and fresh meat, dangling thus from bayonet-points; while cups of tea, coffee, soup, and the like

30

were freely handed to our thirsty fellows, who hastily drank and joined ranks again.

Our officers kept moving, however, and no halt was sounded until we were a considerable distance beyond town, and strict guards were placed to prevent stragglers from going to or staying there. I learned that Jackson's corps had travelled by the Drainsville road, passed over Goose Creek, two miles east of and below Leesburgh, had rapidly pushed ahead to Point of Rocks, where he crossed, broke up the Baltimore and Ohio Railroad there, thus isolating Harper's Ferry from all telegraphic and other connection with Washington, and was still pushing forward towards Frederick, the State capital of Maryland. Such rapid marching seems incredible with defective transportation and worn-out troops. It must be confessed, however, that no part of our army was troubled with loaded trains, for, except extra ammunition, all the wagons were empty!

Parties of our cavalry swam their horses at Edwards's Ferry, and having scoured the country far and wide, even to within a short distance of Washington, (thirty miles off,) returned with information to the effect that no enemy was visible—all their numerous earthworks were tenantless, and no opposition need be expected to our crossing. Among other points, it was ascertained that White's Ford, Coon's Ford, Ball's Bluff, and other places could be well crossed by infantry and cavalry, and, if repaired, the enemy's old pontoons would prove safe enough for artillery and other trains. These places were selected, and the work of crossing immediately began. Cavalry with light artillery landed first; and at different places infantry were pouring across, the water in many parts of the shoals not being more than two or three feet deep. It was a refreshing amusement on a warm day, and our dusty infantry seemed to enter into the spirit of the thing with right good will. Accidents would sometimes occur, and many a field officer, from indiscretion or bravado, deviated from the prescribed route, and suddenly found himself, horse and all, floundering about in deep water, amid the derisive groans and jeers of his troops; while an odd Dutchman or two were observed standing on the banks, bewailing the loss of their drums, as the huge instruments floated and rolled down stream towards Washington.

Considering all things, our passage of the Potomac was a decided success, and no sooner accomplished than instant dispositions were made for moving on towards Frederick, and forming line with Jackson, already in battle array there. Bands played " My Maryland," until the sound was oppressive; for I did not believe at the time that our occupation of any portion of the State would be of great duration. We had not been long upon the march, however, ere cavalry men and quartermasters rode a considerable distance into the interior, and were soon actively engaged in buying up whatever stores could be or service to us, so that we had not progressed far 'ere many things were delivered out in rations, which had been unknown to the majority of us for many months. It was evident that chiefs of the quartermaster's and commissary departments had received full and final instructions, and were obeying them with alacrity, and to the letter. No violence or incivility was shown on our part, our agents were received with much urbanity, and all transactions were satisfactorily arranged with Confederate scrip or Federal paper. The few inhabitants we met betrayed evident pleasure at our arrival, but were extremely cautious and circumspect in showing it. They would look on and smile as we passed, but seemed much constrained in manner, as if feeling certain that Union men were in their midst quietly taking note of all actions or expressions, and ready to divulge names at fitting opportunities. Some few young men openly avowed their Southern feeling, and joined us, but the greater number stood aloof as if thinking, " I should much like to assist you if I dare; but how long will they remain ? I am between two fires ; I must sacrifice principle and secure my home. Let them fight it out; for Maryland will go with the strongest." Women were more ardent in their expressions than men; and while I cannot but despise the thousands standing with hands in pockets idly looking on, while Southern States were fighting their battles, I must admire the beauty, kindness, and whole-souled fervor of Maryland women, who, in thousands of ways, evinced their loyalty and love for our cause.

But while various divisions of our army were taking up positions between Frederick and the river, movements were transpiring in other directions. It was said that a heavy force under Johnston was between Fairfax and Centreville, watching the enemy's movement round Arlington Heights and Alexandria; and that, should they think proper to sally forth from those strongholds, and make a rush for Richmond by the Manassas route, while Lee was far away, their progress would be stopped at Centreville by heavy earthworks and batteries, which had been hurriedly thrown up there for that purpose. The report was plausible, and the necessity for such precautions admitted by all, but whether any such force or fortifications existed in *fact* I have never been able to learn with certainty.

Cavalry were reported advancing rapidly upon Winchester, and accounts came in of several severe skirmishes with the Federals under White, who was said to be falling back upon Harper's Ferry, where General Miles commanded with thirteen thousand men and fifty guns. I also heard that some of our forces had branched off from Leesburgh, and were marching towards the village of Berlin, situated but a few miles from, and in the rear of, the Maryland Heights, commanding Harper's Ferry from the north bank of the Potomac; while others were said to be secretly moving towards the Loudon Heights, which could command part of Harper's Ferry, Bolivar, Bolivar Heights, and a large area of the Shenandoah Valley from the south side of the Potomac. This information was given with much secrecy; but I could scarcely credit the idea that Miles and White were such blockheads as not to be aware of the fact that forces were thus secretly massing in different directions, and only waiting for final orders to encircle them. From their actions one would be led to suppose Federal commanders were asleep, or that they thought all Confederate attacks would come from the direction of Winchester, where much of our cavalry was stationed, foraging and the like. Suffice it to say, that many of our troops must have been elsewhere than in line be-tween the Potomac and Frederick, for, except Jackson's corps, I saw few others there.

We had now been in Maryland some time, and were drawn up in line-of-battle night and day, yet no enemy appeared. A full week had elapsed since we fired our last shot at the Federal rear-guard near Fairfax; and, although in the enemy's country, accumulating and transporting into Virginia vast quantities of supplies, no signs were visible of the Federals' approach, and the usual greeting among us was the stereotyped expression used by McClellan during the winter months of '61 and the early part of '62, namely: "All quiet on the Upper Potomac to-night!"

Our various departments were extremely busy, and from their energy and industry were evidently making the most of their time. New wagons and teams were being bought in all directions; our cavalry had been scouring the whole country far and wide to our rear, having penetrated to Chambersburgh and other towns of Pennsylvania; and as they sent to our lines all that they purchased or appropriated, vast quantities of all things were being transported to the river and sent across into Virginia. In fact, wagon-trains were unceasingly moving, with captured or purchased supplies, from the first moment we put foot on Maryland soil.

General Lee had issued a stirring Address to the Marylanders, and it was hoped that it might have some effect upon the sluggish population of that State, who sighed over their wrongs, but sat and apathetically gazed while others achieved her independence. Few responded to the call — all were calculating chances dimly foreshadowed in their future; and it may be that thousands in distant parts of the State, and particularly in Baltimore, would have willingly rushed to meet us, but the Federal system of espionage was so scientifically arranged that a cat could not mew in Baltimore without the fact being instantly recorded in full at the provost-marshal's office.

From reports daily reaching us, previous rumors were confirmed, that Pope, having resigned, had been sent to quell Indian uprisings in Minnesota Territory, and that McClellan was once again in power. It was also known that heavy forces from all parts of the States were rapidly arriving at Washington; and that his army, thus hurriedly formed from the remnants of every command in the service, far outnumbered ours, and indications were given that an onward movement would soon commence. Our generals had important work to accomplish, however, before McClellan could possibly arrive; hence it did not at all surprise us to learn that Jackson, as usual, was about to take the initiative.* On the tenth, reports came in that the

---

* Jackson was the observed of all observers during our stay in Maryland, and hundreds travelled many score miles to see the great original "Stonewall," against

Federal cavalry advance-guard had already reached the Monocacy river, a few miles fronting our line above and below Fredericksburgh, and that heavy skirmishing had occurred there. This was positive proof that McClellan was advancing, and far more rapidly than we had expected.

On the eleventh, our line from Frederick to the Potomac was suddenly broken up, and Jackson's corps proceeded very rapidly towards Hagerstown, as if intending to penetrate into Pennsylvania. Ambrose Hill moved his division towards Jefferson, as if going in the direction of Harper's Ferry. The whole army, indeed, was leaving the open country, and taking up positions on the west side of the South Mountain, which, extending in a long chain, presented a natural barrier to McClellan's further advance. Up to the present time, he had enjoyed the advantage of but one good road from Washington to Frederick, and beyond the latter place, if he should be tempted to push on so far, he would find none but the ordinary dirt roads. Nay, worse than this: should he attempt to pursue our supposed retreating army, he must of necessity pass the mountain chain through several gaps—one being at Boonesborough; one southward of the latter place, called Turner's Gap, on the Middleton road; another, more southwardly still, called Crampton's Gap, on the Burkittsville road; and one near the Potomac, on the direct route from Petersville to Harper's Ferry. To delay McClellan's movements through these mountain passes, D. H. Hill had thrown his own division and a few other troops into these gaps; Hood, with his brave Texans and others, held Boonesborough; Hill himself was at Turner's Gap, on the Federal main line of advance; and the other generals at the points lower down towards the river. All these passes had been forti-

which Federal generals had so often broken their heads. Crowds were continually hanging round his head-quarters, and peeping through the windows, as if anxious to catch him at his "incantations," for many believed he was in league with the Old Boy and had constant intercourse with him. Others, again, actually thought that he was continually praying, and imagined that angelic spirits were his companions and counsellors; and it was not until the great man had mounted his old horse, and frequently aired himself in the streets, that many began to think him less than supernatural. His shabby attire and unpretending deportment quite disappointed the many who expected to see a great display of gold lace and feathers; and when he ordered his guards to clear his quarters of idle crowds, many went away muttering: "Oh! he's no great shakes after all!"

fied by Hill, who on the twelfth had all things in readiness to fiercely dispute all attempts at assault. It was not expected that he could hold the vast numbers of the enemy at bay for an indefinite time; but all who knew D. H. Hill and Hood were conscious that the enemy would have hot work before dislodging them, and must lose much time in doing so.. This, in fact, was all that Lee originally intended, as the events that now rapidly succeeded each other fully demonstrated.

Reports having reached him on the eleventh, while on the banks of the Monocacy, that Miles and White were strongly fortified at Harper's Ferry, and that the Confederates had made no demonstrations in that direction, McClellan imagined that those generals were able to withstand a siege of many weeks, if so compelled, and that little danger was to be apprehended from any rebel diversion in that direction. The strong positions occupied by D. H. Hill in the South Mountain passes appeared so formidable, and the small force was so well and so ostentatiously displayed, that McClellan imagined the mountain barrier to be garrisoned and supported by the whole Confederate army, so that much valuable time was consumed by him in preparing to dislodge it. From the eleventh to the thirteenth, little or nothing was attempted by him, save frequent reconnoissances; and although the roads from the Monocacy to Frederick* and the

---

* Some very amusing scenes occurred in Frederick during our retreat from that place. On the morning of the twelfth few troops were there save two or three squadrons of Stuart's cavalry. Burnside's forces were rapidly advancing upon the town, and his cavalry were not more than two miles distant. Leave-takings were going on, and patriotic young Marylanders, who had joined our army, were on doorsteps, talking to or kissing their sweethearts, desirous of remaining until the last moment. A great noise and much dust visible at the east end of the town told of the Federal advance, and all our young love-sick soldiers immediately mounted and left the place. Within a few moments, up rode a few squadrons of Federal cavalry, commanded by a Dutch major with immense moustache. Halting before the city hall, with a great fuss and show, he exclaimed: "Vere ish de Got tam repels? Vere ish de Got fur tam Stuart — vere ish he mit his cavalrie? Let me shee him, unt I show him some tings!" A lady present told him that a few of Fitz-Hugh Lee's cavalry had just left. "Goot! young voomans," said Meinheer, and immediately started in pursuit, saying, "Ve show de repels some tings." The major and his command had fairly got into the main street, when a few squadrons of Confederate cavalry met them, and both parties rushed together in strife, and, within a few moments afterwards, the Federals retreated, amid the hoots and groans of those at the windows. The Dutch major was, shortly afterwards, pulled out of a cottage, and with a table-cloth wound round a slight wound in his head, was sent to our rear.

South Mountain were open to him, his advance was slow and tedious; while, on the other hand, Confederate generals were unusually active, and preparing to capture the Ferry, together with the garrison and its numerous supplies. The position of D. H. Hill in the mountains had been designed for no other purpose than to occupy the roads and delay McClellan until Miles and White had surrendered.

While the shrewd and calculating Hill was deceiving McClellan's advance, Jackson and others were busily availing themselves of the precious time thus gained to achieve success at the Ferry. Having started from Frederick on the eleventh, Jackson rapidly pushed ahead on the Hagerstown road, as if intending to occupy that place, but immediately branched off to the left towards the Potomac, and crossed it the same night at Williamsport. No opposition was met with, and the column still proceeded onwards, our cavalry advance having a few hours before handsomely driven Colonel White and the Federal cavalry from Martinsburgh, where many useful stores were discovered and appropriated. Still moving forward, Jackson pursued the Shepherdstown road, and arrived within sight of Bolivar on the afternoon of the twelfth. The range of hills in Bolivar was occupied by the enemy, and extensive earthworks had been dug to defend them. It was evident at a glance that while the enemy held the formidable positions of the Maryland and Loudon Heights, frowning as they were with cannon, and fully commanding the Bolivar Heights and the whole country for many miles round, that any attack upon Bolivar and its surroundings would be mere waste of life and powder. So that having opened a furious cannonade on the latter place to attract attention and detain the main body of the enemy on the Virginia side of the river, Jackson was relying upon the attack which other parts of our force was hourly expected to make from the rear of the Maryland Heights. It was known that nearly every gun on those heights pointed up the Shenandoah Valley, and little harm was expected from them when taken in reverse.

On Friday, simultaneously with Jackson's appearance before Bolivar, west of the Potomac, a large infantry force of ours made its appearance at Solomon's Gap, and was three miles away eastward on the Heights, gradually approaching the highest point of the mountain-chain, which overlooks Harper's Ferry at the river. A close inspection of the ground satisfied us that our attack in that direction would be "up-hill" work; the top of the heights having been cleared of superfluous timber, it was seen that the enemy had erected barricades of wood, from behind which light artillery could play upon our advance. The position was truly formidable, and, if provisioned and garrisoned properly, was capable of holding out for any length of time.

Towards sunset, our men had gradually worked their way within a few hundred yards of the enemy's main position, and skirmishing became exceedingly brisk and lively. During the entire afternoon, we could plainly hear and sometimes see Jackson's artillery shelling the enemy in and around Bolivar; and when darkness came on, we all felt certain that the next day would find us masters of the position, from which we could shell the enemy out from the Bolivar Heights across the river, and thus fully invest the place.

Next morning at sunrise we opened fire, and a fierce struggle of infantry commenced for the possession of the Maryland Heights, while, at the same time, Jackson was gradually pushing the enemy in all directions from his front. Towards noon, after repeated efforts, and in the face of artillery which had been turned on us, our men rushed over the barricades and successively took several very strong positions, from which determined men should not have been so easily repulsed. Making one final charge, the heights were cleared, and the enemy driven in great confusion down the opposite side. Three shells thrown towards Bolivar Heights, and the loud yells of our men, telegraphed our success to Jackson, who now attacked the enemy from every side. His advance, the smoke of which was seen about one mile away in the Valley, was slow and all "up-hill," yet he was gradually forcing the enemy from their strong positions; but was unwilling apparently to sacrifice many men in the accomplishment of his purpose by an assault in force, rightly concluding that their position would prove untenable after our possession of the Maryland Heights.

At the close of the second day's operations, Jackson had turned the enemy's left on the Bolivar Heights; our troops were in full possession of the Maryland Heights; and all were busily engaged in placing cannon in position for the morrow's work. The whole scene below us was animating. The long lines of Federal brigades on the hill-sides and in the valley were all turned towards Jackson in the west; smoke of the batteries curled away from the woods, while on every hand we could perceive our forces taking up positions from which a perfect shower of shot could be thrown upon the gradually contracting lines of the enemy. Troops and artillery were already on the Loudon Heights to our left, batteries swept the Charleston, Shepherdstown, and Sandy Hook roads; and all that the Federals did was to protect or destroy the several bridges by which our forces on the east could communicate with Jackson on the west side of the stream. In short, the enemy's fate was sealed; they could not live long under our concentrated fire from various directions, and they must soon surrender. Yet they were evidently fighting against time, and seemed determined to stand and be slaughtered rather than capitulate; for the fact was possibly known to them as to us, that McClellan was not twenty miles distant, with an overwhelming force; and should D. H. Hill in the mountain-chain give way, and fail to hold him in check, nothing could prevent the place from being speedily relieved.

Next morning, all was silent, and the enemy perhaps imagined that circumstances had forced us to abandon the siege. Great activity was observed among them, as we could plainly perceive from the Maryland and Loudon Heights, thousands of feet above the scene. Immediately after noon, Jackson's attack was recommenced with great fury; while, to add to the enemy's dismay, batteries on the Loudon and Maryland Heights, and from every hill in our possession, were pouring shot and shell upon their masses below, so that they knew not where to look for shelter, and were moving about in all directions. The people in Harper's Ferry itself were running to and fro like madmen, vainly endeavoring to escape the shells that were bursting in and around the place. Officers on horseback were galloping furiously through the streets; infantry endeavored to screen themselves as best they could behind houses, rocks, earthworks, and the like; while the long line of smoke around Bolivar Heights told of Jackson's steady advance upon those positions. At sunset, the Federals were pushed into the valley, and seemed huddled together in a small space awaiting slaughter. Had daylight lasted a little longer, or the attack commenced sooner, the work would have ended on Sunday, the fourteenth.

At nightfall, all was bustle in throwing up works still nearer the enemy, and additional guns were planted in all directions, for it was evident that our officers were pushed for time, and seemed determined to bring matters to a climax early on the morrow. When morning dawned, the bombardment was recommenced, our batteries vomited fire and smoke from every point of the compass, while the echo of so many pieces among the mountains not only made it impossible to hear ordinary sounds, but it seemed that the very hills trembled to their foundations. At length white flags began to appear at various points along the enemy's lines, and the firing gradually ceased. I saw a party of horsemen ride towards Jackson's position on Bolivar Heights, and, after some short time, our signal corps telegraphed that the enemy had unconditionally surrendered.

This fact was soon known throughout our whole force, and loud, long yells rent the sky; from hill and plain the roar of voices could be heard in all directions, but those who understood the true position of affairs were loth to cheer or give way to any extravagant demonstrations of joy; for on the previous day many of us had heard heavy cannonading going on eastward, and couriers, hot, dusty, and jaded, brought word that a fierce engagement had taken place at the several passes in the South Mountains. It was understood that D. H. Hill had been particularly pressed at Turner's Gap, and was forced to relinquish his position at nightfall, after having sustained severe loss, and inflicted much punishment upon the enemy. No one doubted that Hill had fought heroically; but from the moment that Hooker and Reno's corps attacked him at three P.M. the previous day, it was evident he was greatly outnumbered, and unable to extend his line of defence over many points of the mountain, which commanded and overlooked the Gap. Hood, who had been fighting higher up the mountain-chain, and defending the pass at Boonesborough, rapidly gathered his men and marched to Hill's relief; and it was doubtless the headlong, reckless valor of these reenforcements which saved Hill from total discomfiture. The loss on either side at Boonesborough, Turner's Gap, and Crampton Gap—the latter being forced by Franklin's corps on the same day—was severe for the time all were engaged; and if twenty-five hundred killed, wounded, and prisoners is put down for our casualties, I am sure it will not more than cover the total. Of the enemy's loss we had no positive information, but as they were the assailants, it was possibly much greater.*

Hill's obstinate defence of the mountain-passes had, however, delayed McClellan from marching directly to the relief of Harper's Ferry; and thus gained a day's time for Jackson, who, as we have seen, was on the eve of accomplishing the conquest of Harper's Ferry on the fourteenth. Yet Jackson was in a critical position; he was fully aware that McClellan was now west of the South Mountains, and pushing after Longstreet and Hill in the direction of Sharpsburgh. Time was more precious then than ever; hence it was that Jackson opened his bombardment on the fifteenth so early in the morning. Our various army corps and divisions were very much scattered, and as the enemy were rapidly following Lee, the greatest expedition was necessary to form a junction with him before any heavy engagement could take place.

When Miles, therefore, after a council of war, had run up white flags† in different parts of his lines, and the capitula-

* Brigadier-General Garland was the only officer of note among the Confederates who fell at South Mountain. McClellan admitted the Federal loss to be some twenty-five hundred killed and wounded. Major-General Reno was killed there just as the action closed.

† The moment white flags were raised in token of surrender, General Miles was struck by a cannon-shot, and his thigh was torn away. "O my God! I am killed!" he exclaimed, and fell from his horse. His death was purely accidental; for the smoke of batteries and the haze of morning prevented our gunners from detecting truce-flags then flying. Among the twelve thousand troops and over three hundred commissioned officers captured, I noticed many of the following regiments, namely: Eighty-seventh, Thirty-second, Third, and Sixtieth Ohio Infantry; the Twelfth, One Hundred and Twenty-sixth, One Hundred and Eleventh, Thirty-ninth, One Hundred and Fifteenth, and One Hundred and Thirty-fifth New-York Infantry; First and Third Maryland Home Brigade, (infantry;) Sixty-fifth Illinois, Ninth Vermont, Fifteenth Indiana. Several New-York, Ohio, and Indiana batteries were attached to these various regiments. Of artillery, over fifty pieces fell into our hands, and, among them, twelve three-inch rifled guns; six of James's steel guns, rifled; six twenty-four-pound howitzers; four twenty-pound Parrott guns, rifled; six twelve-pound guns, rifled; four twelve-pound howitzers; two ten-inch Dahlgren

tion was officially announced, the enemy were ordered to march
into the village of Bolivar and stack arms, which they did with
much apparent reluctance. There were no signs of insubordina-
tion or mutiny — all passed off very quietly and orderly ; and
as they filed past in fours, and took up the line of march eastward towards the Ferry, to commence their journey to Washington, many began to laugh and smoke good-humoredly, jocularly observing that they " hoped it would be a long time ere
their parole would be broken by any exchange." The sudden
change in the position of affairs within so few hours made us
languid and sleepy ; where all had been life and bustle, noise
and carnage, but three hours before, was now all quietness and
peace.* The enemy were busy in packing knapsacks and haversacks ; regiments marching by with arms, returned in a few
moments without them ; wagons of every description, cannon
of every calibre, officers of every grade, and troops from every
State, were passing and repassing towards our headquarters,
and within a few hours all had filed past on parole. Then,
many of our troops began to move up the Potomac towards
Williamsport to join Lee, and participate in the great engagement which was expected to take place between the two
armies.

guns ; one fifty-pound Parrott gun, rifled ; six six-pound guns, rifled ; and several
of "Fremont's" guns, namely, mountain howitzers. Most of these guns were of
superb manufacture. In addition to these were several captured on the Maryland
Heights, namely: two one hundred and twenty-six-pound rifled guns ; one ninety-
six-pound rifled gun ; and four brass Napoleons, rifled. The commissariat was
found to have more than sufficient rations for two weeks for fourteen thousand
men, besides large quantities of forage, hay, straw, corn, meal, etc. Their wagon-
train consisted of over two hundred wagons, with excellent teams and harness.
The number of arms taken was over twelve thousand, with complete equipments
for twice that number of men. Of ammunition, medicine, and general stores, we
secured large quantities. Several regimental flags were discovered among our
spoils ; but the enemy made away with many, to prevent them falling into our
hands. The casualties on our part were not numerous ; the enemy suffered considerably from our concentrated fire.

* An unfortunate Yankee letter-writer, who was among the prisoners, saw Jackson for a moment, and thus describes him : "Old Stonewall, after riding along the
river-bank, returned to Bolivar Heights, the observed of all observers. He was
dressed in the coarsest kind of homespun, seedy and dirty at that ; wore an old hat
which any Northern beggar would consider an insult to have offered him ; and in
his general appearance was in no respect to be distinguished from the mongrel
bare-footed crew who followed his fortunes. I had heard much of the decayed
appearance of the rebel soldiers, but such a looking crowd! Ireland in her worst
straits could present no parallel ; and yet they glory in their shame !"

CHAPTER XLIII.

McClellan's unaccountable Inaction—Activity of Lee and Jackson—Engagements at the South Mountain—Approach of the Federals to Sharpsburgh—Battle of Antietam, or Sharpsburgh, September seventeenth—An Indecisive Engagement—Retreat of the Southern Army into Virginia—Jackson guards the Rear, and Repulse of the enemy's Advance-Guard, etc.

FROM a general review of our operations between the time of Jackson's departure from Frederick on the eleventh and the surrender of Harper's Ferry on the fifteenth, and from an estimate of the forces and the distance of the two armies operating within so few miles of each other during that time, McClellan's tardiness of action, in the face of Jackson's small force and activity, seemed to me inexplicable. The advance posts of the Federal cavalry exchanged shots with ours on the banks of the Monocacy on the eleventh, and at that time the true state of affairs must have been known to Federal commanders, for Union sympathizers were numerous, and many escaped through our lines who could have given every information. On the twelfth, when Jackson had crossed into Virginia, and appeared before the enemy, strongly posted on the Bolivar Heights, numerous cavalry men had left Miles's command, who, doubtless, did fully inform McClellan of the contemplated investment of Harper's Ferry. Under these circumstances, his divergence from the true route to the Ferry by Petersville and Crampton's Gap, to attack Hill in the strong positions of Boonesborough and Turner's Gap, was unaccountable, unless, indeed, he was misled by fabulous rumors regarding our strength and resources at the former place.

Had McClellan acted with energy, and taken the river road to Harper's Ferry, there was nothing to prevent him from raising the siege; and by passing over into Virginia, he would have completely cut off our retreat by the several fords above. It is true that such a movement would have left Maryland unprotected, and Lee might have marched on to Washington without serious resistance, and this may be the true reason for McClellan's movements. He could have had no doubt that Lee would have willingly availed himself of such a chance, and, having a shorter route to travel, he might have outmarched him, and taken Washington, perhaps, ere the Federal commander could have traversed the south bank, and arrived at the Chain, or Long Bridges, to cross over and oppose him. Nevertheless, when he heard of the investment on the twelfth, he might certainly have relieved the place from the Maryland side, at least; or, by suddenly and rapidly marching on Lee and Longstreet, have forced an engagement, and possibly defeated both those generals before Jackson, Ambrose Hill, and McLaws could have reenforced them. The truth is, McClellan was too slow and ·cautious—he was not equal to the occasion; and while revolving the chances before him, Miles surrendered, and part of our force had crossed into Maryland again, and was quietly waiting in Lee's lines for the Federal advance.

When Lee was made aware of D. H. Hill's retreat from the various gaps in the South Mountain, and that McClellan's army was pouring through them, he became fully convinced that the Federal commanders were determined to provoke a general engagement before Jackson and others could come to his relief. On the evening of the fifteenth, therefore, when fully assured of the fall of Harper's Ferry, he withdrew his forces (fifty thousand strong) towards Sharpsburgh, and crossing Antietam River, arranged his line of battle on the west bank, and seemed determined to hold the position until the arrival of his whole force. On that same day, McClellan's army, some ninety-five thousand strong, with three hundred pieces of artillery, were at Reedysville, but a few miles east of the river, and was reported to be slowly approaching.

The Antietam River strikes the Potomac almost at right angles, and is spanned by three bridges; the centre one being on the direct road to Sharpsburgh, not more than three quarters of a mile beyond; the second was about two miles lower down, and commanded a road which swept towards the Potomac; and the third was at least two miles above the central one, and conducted a road which led direct to Hagerstown. Beyond this upper bridge the stream is fordable in many places. The river runs through a small valley, and parallel with it the land gradually rises, but on the west bank is far more hilly and broken than on the east; while at the bridge leading direct to Sharpsburgh, and at the lower one, all approach is commanded by bluffs or hillocks, so that a defending force could be well screened behind them, and any troops attacking be exposed to great loss in attempting to force a passage. At the upper parts of our line, which was formed on or behind this series of undulations, the stream stretched away to the east, so that an enemy could easily ford the river above us, and operate on our left flank.

Our forces were so disposed as to command all approach to the bridges over the Antietam; Longstreet commanding the right, Lee the centre, and D. H. Hill the left; but our line appeared so weak, scattered as it was over more than four miles, that it seemed almost impossible it could withstand a numerous enemy energetically assailing it. On the fifteenth, our cavalry were busy annoying the enemy's advance, and conducting long trains within the lines, which were immediately sent forward into Virginia. Meanwhile the long line of dust rising over the landscape in various directions, and the appearance of white canvas-covered wagons slowly moving over the light green fields, or disappearing in, and emerging from, the woods, gave every evidence that an immense force was cautiously approaching to the attack. Our main army was in perplexed thought regarding Jackson's movements, and felt extremely anxious for his speedy junction. Strong picket-guards were thrown out; light artillery, with heavy infantry supports, were within short distance of the bridges; and active squads of cavalry were continually moving from point to point along our whole front.

On the sixteenth, when the mists of morning had risen from the landscape, the smoke of camp-fires extending east of the river told us that the enemy had placed their troops in position parallel to ours; but, from the quantity of smoke ascending, we judged that their centre and right centre were much more heavily guarded than any other portion of their lines. Severe skirmishing took place with bodies of troops along both banks of the river, and, as would appear, with some effect on our side, for the enemy seemed to desist, and never endeavored to make any decided advance in their centre or left. It would appear that McClellan was as totally unaware of our position as of our strength, for he instantly opened a furious cannonade along our whole front, and on his left (commanded by Burnside) the storm of shot and shell was so fierce and incessant that numerous missiles passed harmlessly over our heads, and fell within the village or town of Sharpsburgh, causing much destruction of property. Perhaps it was the desire of McClellan to ascertain our force and true position, but in this he was grievously deceived, for, except a few field-batteries which here and there replied to his vindictive cannonade, no display of force was made on our side. We bided our time patiently, feeling assured that Lee had successfully deceived them as to our position and force, and that their main attack would be delayed until the arrival of Jackson and others should reenforce and equalize the strength of our lines.

Soon after noon, while the rival batteries were contending at the centre and lower bridges, and other parts of the line, the appearance of heavy forces approaching to and threatening our left, gave positive assurance that the enemy were about to commence operations by out-flanking and attacking us in the weakest part of our position. Hood and other stubborn leaders held this ground, and the fight soon became animated and determined. The enemy, in strong force, had appeared at the upper bridge and fords above about three o'clock P.M., and forced a passage; but, although our defence of those positions, from paucity of forces, was somewhat feeble, the Federals suffered extremely ere gaining a positive footing west of the stream. As their advance for the most part was through open fields, and over very gently-rising grounds, the sweep of our artillery, and accurate aim of the best sharpshooters in the world, (Texans,) told with disastrous effect upon their heavy columns. Confusion was frequent among their ranks, and it required the utmost efforts of the officers, aided by their personal example, to induce the troops to keep ranks and advance upon us. Field-officers rode to the front with a great show of gallantry; but it was not until fully satisfied of our weakness that they moved forward with any spirit of determination.

To us it was matter of surprise that the few troops protecting our left should have made such a determined resistance,

31

and have held so long the large forces of the enemy in check. Nor did the news of their withdrawal from the disputed position cause any annoyance, for we were well aware that the gently-rising ground extending to the dense woods beyond was still held by them, and that it commanded all approach in that direction. The enemy, indeed, seemed well contented to remain in the captured belt of timber, and did not dare to occupy the open grounds and fields of still standing corn which intervened between their own position and ours. Yet, from the multitude of fresh troops pouring upon the scene, and taking up positions to our front and left, it was immediately perceived that their real object was to turn it, and threaten our retreat to the Potomac. Their numbers were so great that many of us felt uneasy for the morrow, and their pickets in many places were uncomfortably near to ours. How long Jackson would be absent none could conjecture, and great uneasiness was manifested by many high in command.

It is possible, however, that the enemy's early discovery of our weakness on the left saved us from disaster, for they instantly began to mass most of their troops in that direction, thus forewarning Lee where to send all available reenforcements that might arrive during the night or on the morrow. No demonstration of a serious character had been made on our centre or right during the day, and it was reasonable to suppose that the heavy concentration of troops against our left was more than a feint; for, should the impending action be severely pressed on the next day, the distance was too great for these masses to be countermarched against any other parts of our line. Our outposts were unusually vigilant and active during night, and kept head-quarters fully informed of all that transpired. The enemy had gained ground in no direction save the left, and our new position there was considered preferable to the first, from which we had been driven during the afternoon, for the corn-fields were excellent shelter, the fences good concealment and protection against infantry, while to the rear of these the ground gradually rose to thick woods, in which were planted several excellent batteries.

While seated round camp-fires, and chatting during the silence of night, faint sounds of cheering in our rear, the gradually increasing noise caused by the arrival of mounted men, the sounds of artillery bugles, and the perceptible tramp of heavy colums, gave pleasing indications of the approach of reenforcements.   The arrival of couriers and the jingle of artillery soon dispelled any doubt that existed about the character of the new arrivals; it was the victorious Jackson advancing from Harper's Ferry, and his columns came in with such order, and made such a rustle among the deep deposit of leaves, that it seemed to doubly magnify their numbers and strength.   They swiftly passed through the woods and took position on the left. which movement occasioned many changes, so that regiments and batteries were continually passing to and fro.   Faint cheering was occasionally heard within the enemy's lines during the night, and the shouts of the drivers proved that their artillery was in motion.   On our right and centre, all was remarkably quiet; but on our left frequent picket-firing aroused the advanced posts, for the sentinels of both armies were extremely close, and ours, concealed in fields of standing corn, occupied all our front down to the fence, where a small space of open fields intervened between our position and that of the Federal army.

As morning approached, many of our men sallied forth beyond the standing corn, to despoil the Federal dead; and this being perceived, brought out the enemy's pickets, who opened a brisk and lively fire.   It must be confessed the audacity of our men in this proceeding was beyond all precedent; for, in the woods immediately beyond, the enemy were in imposing force, and certainly flushed with their success of the previous evening.

A constant picket-firing on our left gave warning that the action would soon open, our troops rose long before day, and the most provident cooked themselves breakfast, and, smoking their pipes, sat in groups, chatting sociably, not knowing at what moment all would be summoned to "fall in."   Soon simple picket-firing was succeeded by the roar of musketry; whole volleys occasionally broke upon the ear at different points of the line, which, together with the occasional roar of howitzers and rifled pieces, was more than enough to rouse the entire army.   Commanders were busily engaged, and rode from place to place, with a business-like air; no hurry or confusion was visible; all seemed to look upon the matter with indifference and cheerfulness. Most of our troops had smelt powder long before, and they simply said, "Another day's work is before us," and tightly buckled their straps and belts, as if bound for a march, or a long fatiguing drill.

Fighting on our left now commenced in earnest; troops which had been prowling about fields fronting the standing corn were seen to hasten their movements, and on came the Yankee line of battle in good order. Observing our clouds of skirmishers rapidly withdrawing from their front, and disappearing in the corn-fields, they gave loud cheers, and thought that little resistance would be offered until they had arrived at the top of the hill, or had found shelter in the woods. Their mistake was a grievous one. As the Federal line of battle reached the fence, up rose our men from their concealment among the corn, and delivered successive volleys right in the faces of their foes, who, surprised and staggering with loss, retreated back over the open ground, and were cut up fearfully by our batteries, which now opened with rapidity from our rear. So accurate was the fire that whole files of Federal soldiers lay dead, parallel with the fence.

Hundreds of shell from the enemy now dropped in all directions, making our position in the standing corn very unpleasant; and although we disputed their advance stubbornly, they gradually forced us back, until they penetrated into the corn-fields, which their heavy line of battle bent and broke, as they came sweeping onward with loud cheers. Supposing us to be beaten at this point, their commander lost no time, but seemed determined to push forward rapidly and smash our left wing. As brigade after brigade rushed gallantly forward, they were subjected to a continuous and galling fire; but no token was given of our strength in the dense timber, to which our men now fell rapidly back, in skirmishing order. When the enemy had traversed the corn-fields, and reached the summit of the "rise," the ground slightly "dipped" towards the fence and road, so that our commanders in the woods had full view of the Federal force as it advanced. Every fence and every tree was made available by our sharpshooters, who constantly poured into their heavy masses a galling fire. Still onwards they came impetuously, and, from their hurried movements, were apparently breathless. Down went every fence in their path, as they rapidly crossed the road towards the woods, and lustily they cheered, as the last of our skirmishers disappeared from their front, and were lost in the dark, thick timber.

All was silence within our lines; regiments were lying flat on their faces with rifles cocked, and cautiously peered at the enemy as they came rushing into the woods in great masses, and with much noise. Suddenly, up rose Jackson's line of battle, the enemy halted, a moment of awful silence ensued, no man stirred, and then deafening, quick, accurate, and numerous volleys broke from our lines. The enemy were too thick to be missed; and, amid frightful loss and confusion, they broke and rushed forth from the woods, trembling like beings who had seen some dreadful apparition.

Soon as these fugitive masses had gained open ground, our batteries in rapid succession broke loose, belching forth grape and canister in such profusion that the infernal storm could be heard raining upon them with a hissing noise, and it literally ploughed furrows in the dark, confused masses, so that daylight could be seen through them at every discharge. Round shot bounded and bounced, and shells, after whizzing over head dropped with loud explosions in the dark groups rushing through the corn-fields and dotting the landscape. The carnage was frightful. Through these fields the enemy (exulting in their success of the previous day) had come cheering in dense lines but a few moments before; they had swept from their front every man opposed to them, and had entered the woods with deafening shouts. They had not been lost to view many minutes ere they rushed back in confused, bleeding, staggering masses of human beings, without order, without officers, pursued by our lines of battle; rapidly our brave fellows pushed over the well-fought fields, and, amid showers of shell, kept close to the fleeing foe, and incessantly poured into their shattered ranks murderous volleys, which whistled through the corn, and peopled every acre with scores of dead.

Field officers of the enemy gallantly rode to the front, and endeavored to rally their brigades. Reenforcements were seen approaching to their relief through open fields beyond; but onward pressed our victorious men, and did not halt until the foe was safely screened in their original position of the morning.*

Fighting on the left had now lasted several hours—our men were thoroughly exhausted, and unable to advance farther upon the enemy. In truth, it would not have been wise to do so; for our present position for defence was preferable ground to any we could win. Cannonading now opened with great fury on both sides; and it was soon ascertained that the foe was largely reenforced, and beginning another advance.† This they did in gallant style; but were met again by such a determined, withering fire, and their loss was so great, that no impression could be made upon our position; not only were they loth to follow us into the woods, but they were quickly beaten and demoralized in open ground. Constant volleys were now exchanged by both sides; and, as reenforcements arrived for Jackson, they were immediately thrown in front to withstand the third attack,‡ then organizing along the enemy's right, which was to be composed of all the commands there present.

The new line of the enemy seemed to be of immense strength; but as they came fully into view our artillery opened upon them with such rapidity and accuracy that great confusion and disorder began to reign ere they came sufficiently close to exchange shots with our infantry. Long and constant volleys resounded along our whole wing; both combatants were stationary; sometimes we slightly gave ground, and again recovered it, until at last our fire began to tell among the enemy; and it seemed that little was now required to drive them completely from the field. While indecision seemed to reign among Federal commanders, ours were unanimous for an advance; and, when the order was received, loud cheers and yells burst forth from all our troops, and the cannonade re-opened with redoubled fury. The onset was furious, nothing seemed to withstand the impetuosity of our men; the enemy gradually withdrew from the open grounds in much confusion. Fresh divisions§ were hurried to the front to check our advance.

---

* This first attack had been opened on our left by Hooker's corps.

† The second advance was made by Sumner's corps.

‡ This was made by Mansfield's corps.

§ Sedgwick's corps.

The meeting was terrible, but the shock of short duration: beaten again and again, they were at last driven beyond the position originally occupied, when Hooker's attack began the previous afternoon.

Through woods and copse, across corn-fields and ploughed fields, grassy slopes and meadows, over gullies, ditches, brooks, and fences, the combatants in this wing had contended since early morning, and their lines had advanced or retreated again and again, until it seemed that every acre of the landscape was strewn with dead. Tokens of carnage were visible on every hand; the woods were torn and shattered; the corn and grass were trodden under foot; outhouses and farmhouses were heaps of blazing ruins; while for miles, long lines of smoke ascended over the fertile valley, and numerous batteries uninterruptedly belched forth showers of shot and shell. Still the contending lines swayed and advanced, or broke and retreated, so that, to civilized beings, it seemed like some ghastly panorama of things transpiring in a nether world.

Jackson's impetuous advance at length halted. His men had far surpassed their olden fame; but it soon became apparent that weakness was enfeebling our efforts, and that without re-enforcements we could not maintain the conquered ground, should any fresh body of the enemy assail us. Indications were not wanting to prove the enemy's activity, and the signal corps soon gave warning that fresh and heavy masses were concentrating and forming, to make a final effort to dislodge us from our advanced position. Soon the enemy appeared to our front again, and advanced with a steadiness which plainly indi-cated they had never yet pulled trigger during the day. The meeting was fierce, vindictive, and bitter; volleys were given and returned incessantly, their artillery slowly moved up to the front, and our line began to fall back with regularity and coolness. We would again retrace our steps, and invite them into the woods, where their first attacking corps had so sudden-ly melted away. Slowly we fell back, and still more cautiously did the enemy pursue. For some time the fight was maintained by us in open ground, and our superior fire inflicted great loss among them. Through the corn-fields once more we enticed the enemy onward, and boldly they advanced to try there again the fortune of war. Once within the timber our generals quickly prepared for their coming, and fell back some distance.

Forward still the enemy came over the numerous dead of their own army; but, ere they entered the woods, they opened a long and fierce cannonade, throwing hundreds of shell and round shot on those spots which we were supposed to occupy. Our men, however, having re-formed much farther back than at first, these missiles fell short; not a man of our line was touched, but all lay quietly on their faces until daylight was shut out from our front by the dark massive lines of the enemy, who, slowly approaching, made the woods echo with their cheers. Cautiously they advanced, and single shots of sharp-shooters resounded through the forest, as of solitary hunters in search of game. Moving forward up a gentle rise, their long lines came full in few, and instantly our artillery and infantry opened upon them with a deafening roar. Branches and leaves showered down on friend and foe alike; trees cracked, and bowed or toppled over, and fell with a crash among the enemy in low ground, and still volleys upon volleys whistled through the cover, until it seemed as if the clouds had opened and rained down showers of bullets. The smoke, confusion, dust, and noise were indescribable; and how long the fierce conflict lasted I knew not, but it seemed to me an age.

Bravely had the enemy assailed us, and gallantly were they repulsed. Jackson could not be moved, but held his ground; and, taking advantage of apparent indecision and mystification, gave the word to advance, and this, the fifth corps sent against him, was hurled bleeding, staggering, and defeated from his front, and retreated from the timber with great loss.

But Jackson was too weak to attempt another advance, and was content to hold the enemy in check until positive information could be ascertained of McClellan's operations on other parts of our lines.

It was now past noon. The conflict had raged with varying fortune on our left, but from the general line of fire visible over the landscape, it was evident we had not lost ground, and could not be dislodged from the position our leaders had select-ed. At the centre, heavy cannonading was going on, which in many instances was disastrous to our wounded, for the enemy's missiles flying high, coursed over our line, and fell in the village of Sharpsburgh, or caused much distress to our ambulance trains. Groups of officers towards the left had been for several hours anxiously watching the development of the Federal attack, but now that the heaviest firing had ceased, and the action seemed to dwindle down into a cannonade, they returned to the centre and right, apparently well pleased with the aspect of affairs, and judged that McClellan would next attempt to feel or force our other wing. Every hillock commanding a view of the battle-field was dotted with mounted officers, who smiled as they looked to the left, and said: "Jackson bravely maintains the ground. They cannot force him from his position: he holds on to it like grim death!" "Yes," said another, sitting sideways in his saddle, and smoking a cigar, "and here are we doing nothing. By Jove, the cannonade is becoming heavy on the right! See their troops yonder moving forward! *Our* turn comes next. Gentlemen, every man to his post!" and the group of officers broke up as each galloped off to his command.

For miles over these beautiful fields the smoke of battle curled away in snow-white clouds. The roar of artillery was regular and slow, while the patter of distant musketry, and the sharp, ringing, crackling noise of rifle volleys kept every sense alive to the dreadful work transpiring on all sides. Patches of wood up and down the lines were filled with smoke; bright flashes from hill and hollow shot forth in all directions; lines were seen to form and advance, others to waver and break; banners rose and fell; the bright flash of bayonets and the stream of fire all too plainly told of deathly strife on every acre of the scene.

It was now near four o'clock, and all felt anxious for the end to come. The better informed felt certain that another attack was intended, but whether McClellan would hurl his hosts at our centre or right none could tell. The doubt was soon set at rest. Heavy infantry firing burst forth towards the lower bridge, upon which several of our batteries in cannonading position opened with great energy and fury. The enemy's artillery replied, and the firing became general. Gradually falling back, our infantry moved through the open fields, delivering volleys as they retreated, and enticed the enemy up the rising ground, on top of which our artillery was posted. Fast as they crossed the bridge, shot and shell assailed them, until it seemed as if the passage was literally blocked up with heaps of dead. Our round shot, striking the heavy stonework of the bridge, knocked out fragments in all directions, while shells fell thick and fast, exploding among their advancing columns.

Gradually retiring, our infantry re-formed in woods to the rear of artillery, and seemed desirous of enticing the enemy still onwards. Forward they came, and gallantly; their force was very great, and it suffered much from our active batteries, which limbered and retired towards the woods, but ever maintained a fierce fire upon the heads of their columns. As soon, however, as the enemy had ascended the "rise" from the bridge, and come within full view of our force drawn up near the woods, incessant volleys assailed their line of battle, and it began to melt away. The storm of shot and shell which met the Federal advance was awful. Every imaginable spot was alive and swarming with combatants. Reenforcements had arrived, and rushed into the fray with loud cheers, so that the dark woods seemed filled with men where none had been before. The Federal advance was arrested; their leading regiments had been literally blown to pieces, and although succor was momentarily arriving, it only served to fill up the fearful gaps everywhere visible in their line. For some short time the battle raged with great fury, and although hard pressed, the enemy would not yield his ground; but when our artillery had opened at shorter distance, and our infantry advanced to closer quarters, their line began to fall back, and our men followed over heaps of lifeless and mangled carcases.

But while this deafening cannonade continued on our right, and the enemy were being slowly driven back to the bridge, we could distinctly hear heavy artillery practice to our left, which informed us that the attack had been renewed in that quarter, and that Jackson was, as usual, full of business. The whole line of battle seemed to have gained new life and animation, and both sides were fighting earnestly and with vigor. The engagement could not last long, for the sun was fast sinking, and if the enemy meant to achieve something great, it was time for McClellan to have commenced. Nothing of moment occurred at our centre; both wings were seriously engaged, Jackson on the left was immovable, and Longstreet on our right was gradually driving the enemy towards the bridge. The carnage here was frightful, and as our shot and shell plunged into their retreating ranks, the whole vicinity of the bridge seemed strewn with bodies, horses, wagons, and artillery.

Both attacks of the enemy upon our wings had failed, and they had been repulsed with fearful slaughter. Franklin, Sumner, Hooker, Mansfield, and other corps commanders on their right, had been fought to a stand-still. They were exhausted and powerless. Burnside, on their left, had been fearfully handled by Longstreet, and was driven in confusion upon the bridge, which he held with a few cannon, and suffered every moment from our batteries on rising ground. We did not desire the bridge, or it might have been held from the beginning, and, save a desultory cannonade, the enemy were now inactive and exhausted. When the sun sank all felt infinite relief from the fatigue and dangers of the day, and although it could not be said we had gained a battle, we certainly could boast of having defeated our enemy's plan throughout the entire day, and though inferior in force, had frequently hurled them back upon their original position with frightful loss.

Every one imagined that the struggle would be resumed on the morrow, and our lines sank to rest upon the ground, with the dead and dying around them. Many of the men prowled about, picking up various articles from the Federal dead, while burying parties were hard at work, and ambulances engaged in removing the wounded. Sharpsburgh itself was one entire hospital, and the inhabitants assisted our wounded with much tenderness and care. Every house and every cottage had some afflicted tenant; but all our men bore up under their sufferings with that unflinching fortitude which has ever characterized them throughout the war.

The night passed wearily by. Camp-fires burned brightly, but quietness reigned throughout the lines undisturbed by any demonstration of the enemy. Friends met friends around the fires, and spoke of dangers past. This officer was reported dead and that one wounded; one had lost his leg, another his arm; Colonel Smith had been blown to pieces, and General Jones desperately hurt; shells had exploded in the midst of a general's staff and disabled every man; hats and coats had been perforated, and no one could move twenty paces without seeing many with heads or arms bandaged, or, pipe in mouth, limping to the rear. In one place, a youth was lying near a camp-fire dying, the embers lighting up his pallid features as he opened his eyes and kissed a brother kneeling by his side. Now, I met half a dozen stalwart men, bearing their wounded and moaning colonel to an ambulance. Again, I passed a group of busy surgeons, cutting and probing their dumb patients; now couriers and orderlies dashed furiously by; a general and his staff slowly trotted off in one direction, regiments and batteries passed on in another. All the horrible sights of a battle-field were frequent and hear-trending, while groans reached the ear from every barn and every house, and through the whole length and breadth of the woods. Preparations were still going on for a renewal of the conflict on the morrow, should the enemy force it; but in my inmost heart I hoped and prayed that Providence might postpone it, for our own men were thoroughly exhausted with long marches and hard fighting, and lay upon the ground in battle-line as helpless and quiet as children.

The morning broke, and all was bustle and preparation, but the enemy moved not. Smoke from camp-fires slowly ascended in all directions, and their ambulances, like ours, were creeping over the scene in sad procession. Still we knew not at what moment the dark masses of the foe might again appear; it was cause for rejoicing when it was whispered that preparations were already progressing for our retreat, and that all the wagons had gone up the river towards Williamsport.

The next day passed without any thing of moment transpiring, and during the night the bulk of our troops began to retreat, but with great coolness and order. Jackson was intrusted with the rear-guard, and next morning (nineteenth) the last of our regiments withdrew from the scene without hindrance or molestation. Some cavalry encounters occurred, it is true, but not of such importance as to retard our movements; and save a few shots occasionally exchanged with our rear-guard, nothing indicated that the enemy were in such "hot" pursuit as their official telegrams subsequently stated. The retreat was slow, orderly, and unmolested. Jackson conducted it; and his dispositions were so skilfully made that they fairly defied any effort the enemy might make to inflict loss or make captures. It cannot be denied that large numbers of dead and wounded were left behind to the tender mercies of the foe, but all who could be removed were carefully provided for, and safely conveyed into Virginia. Save some half-dozen disabled cannon or caissons, and a few arms, little was left in the enemy's hands of which they could truthfully boast.*

Jackson managed the retreat so skilfully that the enemy were completely unaware of the destination of our forces. Save a

---

* Being on the defensive, our loss was much less than that of the enemy, who, in attacking, advanced over open ground, and were much exposed to our accurate fire. From the best sources of information, I learn that our killed and wounded amounted to eight thousand, exclusive of a few prisoners; one thousand of our wounded were left behind, and a convention entered into for the burial of the dead. It has been stated by Northern journals that we lost thirty thousand in all, but this is pure fiction. Among our losses in this engagement were General Stark and Brigadier-General Branch killed; Brigadier-Generals Anderson, Wright, Lawton, Armsted, Ripley, Ransom, and Jones, wounded. I learn that during the thirty hours, or more, which intervened between the engagement and our retreat, little was left upon the battle-field in cannon or arms, but every thing worth attention was carried off. Although the enemy claim to have captured thousands of arms and dozens of cannon, I need not add that this, for the most part, was all imagination.

McClellan's loss has been placed at twelve thousand killed, wounded, and missing; and I think the estimate below reality. Among his killed were Generals Mansfield, Richardson, Hartsuff, and others; and among a fearful list of generals wounded were Sumner, Hooker, Meagher, Duryea, Max Weber, Dana, Sedgwick, French, Ricketts, Rodman, and others.

It is almost unnecessary for me to say that McClellan claimed this battle as "a great victory" for the Union cause, but did not do so until fully assured of our retreat into Virginia. Why his boastful despatch to Washington was not penned before our retreat from Sharpsburgh is evidence sufficient to show that he still feared, and would not shout "until he was out of the woods." In truth, the Northern press acknowledged that with an inferior force we had thrashed them to a stand-still; so much so, that McClellan could only muster two regiments of infantry with two guns to follow in pursuit, and was not aware of our departure until many hours after we retreated. It was called an "indecisive battle" by McClellan's warmest partisans, and many said "it required another engagement to decide Federal superiority."

few shots enchanged on either side, nothing of moment occurred; and our whole army was established on the south bank ere the Federals had positive knowledge of the movement.* On the twentieth, however, their army began to move — Fitz-John Porter taking the advance, who judged, from the extremely quiet look of all things on the Virginia shore, that we were far inland. Barnes's brigade of Pennsylvanians, supported by one of "regulars," under chief command of General Sykes, moved towards the river, and forded the stream at Boteler's Mills. Heavy guns were planted on the Maryland shore to cover their crossing.

Jackson had felt certain that the enemy would attempt to pursue, and he made no display of force likely to intimidate them. The passage of the river was undisputed, except by a few small field-pieces; and when they had landed in Virginia, our gunners took flight in apparent trepidation. The enemy quickly perceived this movement, and imagining that our forces were demoralized, they rushed forward with much cheering. The division of Ambrose Hill, however, was cleverly concealed from view; and when the enemy had advanced sufficiently far, several of our batteries opened upon them, and Hill's troops attacking in front and flank, unceremoniously began the work of slaughter. Their surprise, confusion, and loss were so great, and effected so quickly, that they rushed back towards the river in great haste; but such was the impatience and ardor of our men, that scarcely one of the Pennsylvania brigade escaped death or capture. The stream was literally blocked up with dead, and although the enemy maintained a heavy cannonade upon us, it could not restrain the impetuosity and rapidity of our attack.

Leaving heaps of slain behind, and unheeding the constant cannonade maintained from Maryland, our forces withdrew to-

* When McClellan heard of our backward movement on the nineteenth, he tele-graphed to Washington: "I do not know if the enemy is falling back to an interior position, or re-crossing the river. We may safely claim the victory as ours." He did not assert this until more than thirty hours had elapsed subsequent to the en-gagement at Sharpsburgh! Some few hours after the above telegram, he consoled the authorities at Washington by saying: "Our victory is complete! The enemy is driven (?) back into Virginia. Maryland and Pennsylvania are now safe!" Again he added; "The Confederates succeeded in crossing the Potomac on Friday morning with all their transports and wounded, except some three hundred of the latter!"

wards the Opequan, and drew up in line of battle on the west side of it, our left extending to Williamsport and the Potomac. Although we were in battle array many days in anxious expectation, the Federals remained quiet in Maryland, and made no attempts to disturb us. A large mass of our troops had gone up the Valley towards Winchester, and halted there, and by degrees the whole army followed in the same direction, carefully carting and conveying away every-thing that could be of use; so that large part of the harvests recently gathered fell into the hands of our commissaries and quartermasters, thus leaving the whole country once again barren of supplies for any pursuing force.

The only episode which enlivened our monotonous inactivity was a cavalry engagement (October second) between a small detachment of Stuart's command and a heavy force under Pleasanton. The enemy were very desirous of ascertaining our whereabouts and strength; and for this purpose a considerable number of cavalry and twelve pieces of artillery crossed the stream near Shepherdstown, and advanced up towards our lines. They were met by Fitz-Hugh Lee, and sharp fighting ensued; but the latter, being overpowered, bravely maintained the combat, and sent for reenforcements. Stuart was immediately in the saddle, and swooping down upon Pleasanton, with a fresh force, drove that commander from the field, and pursued him to within a short distance of Shepherdstown, where a large force of the enemy were then stationed. This cavalry encounter was a smart affair, and conducted by both leaders with marked ability. Had not darkness ensued, our captures would have proved considerable, as the Federals were completely routed, and their rear-guard dispersed in much confusion long ere they reached Shepherdstown.

Northern newspapers made such boast regarding the battle of Sharpsburgh and of the "rebel rout," that their fervid imaginings caused much amusement and ridicule among our men, who by long experience had become accustomed to the falsity of their official statements; so that when we daily read their loud bellowings and ecstatic glorifications about "thirty thousand rebels killed and wounded, thousands of prisoners, and immense spoil," etc., we could but smile, and despise their mendacity even more than ever.* "Every rebel had been driven from Maryland and Pennsylvania," we were informed, and "our hosts lay trembling at their feet," whenever McClellan should give the order to march; yet while their faces were radiant with joy, and stump orators expanded their jaws in rhapsódical orations of self-laudation, the whole country was suddenly awe-struck at the audacity of Stuart.

Selecting twelve hundred from the best mounted men of his division, (October tenth,) Stuart crossed the Potomac, and without hindrance made a bold push for Pennsylvania, in McClellan's rear. In truth, he had been engaged in appropriating or destroying vast amounts of Federal property for over twenty-four hours ere the foe believed the report to be more than rumor; and then McClellan coolly informed the nation that it "need not be alarmed, his whole cavalry force was on the move in pursuit;" that "Stuart and his command would be killed or captured within a few hours, for it was impossible to escape through the trap prepared for them." Stuart's movements were rapid, indeed, and the amount of army stores destroyed on his route was very great. At Chambersburgh were large dépôts of clothing, shoes, blankets, harness, and many horses, brought by railway for McClellan's army, and of which it stood greatly in need. All needful supplies were taken by our men, and the rest destroyed.

The consternation among the inhabitants of the several towns and villages in Stuart's route was laughable indeed: all military men were paroled; all horses and mules were seized for our service, but no injury done or appropriation made of any other species of private property. Pompous mayors of towns, with goose-like processions of sleek aldermen, or bilberry-nosed politicians of snug little villages, who shortly before had astonished the ears of groundlings with spasmodic bursts of patriotic eloquence, now meekly came forth to meet Stuart's troopers, with

* McClellan says in his official despatch: "We lost two thousand and ten killed, nine thousand four hundred and sixteen wounded, and ten hundred and forty-three missing. In killed, wounded, and prisoners, it may be safely estimated that the enemy lost thirty thousand of their best troops." This, of course, is erroneous; but a general who cannot positively state whether he is victorious or defeated until his enemy has retreated some fifty hours subsequent to an engagement, may be "safely" allowed a broad margin for his fevered and excited imagination.

ludicrous gait and manner. It was certain, however, that McClellan and his whole army were on the alert; and as the telegraph had informed him of our route and strength, none doubted that the enemy would make strenuous exertions to watch the roads and guard every ford between Washington and Shepherdstown. When Stuart had proceeded as far Gettysburgh, some imagined he would return; but crossing the Monocacy, he rapidly pushed down its east bank, and, during night, successfully passed large detachments of troops on McClellan's left wing.

Every highway and by-path in this part of Maryland was minutely known to Stuart, who now stole through the country around Poolesville, and directed his course towards Edwards's Ferry, a few miles from Leesburgh. To screen the true number of his force, and distract the enemy's attention, his command was divided into several parties, which sought the river at various points and crossed by different fords. The Federal plans became confused from various conflicting statements brought by their scouts and spies, so that ere they had determined upon any settled plan of action, Stuart had crossed the Potomac with his booty, and without the loss of a man, at the same time bringing away more than six hundred mules and horses, laden with all manner of supplies. It might be said with truth that he had fully remounted his whole command while on the raid, besides the six hundred animals heavily burdened with clothing, arms, and except a few shots exchanged with the disappointed enemy, who arrived at the river's edge in time to witness our triumphant crossing, this, the second of Stuart's grand tours of inspection round McClellan's lines, was effected without the expenditure of powder, and left their whole army in senseless astonishment at the audacity and success of our dashing troopers. For nearly three days they had been burning and seizing without let or hindrance, and had travelled more than a hundred miles around the enemy, baffling telegrams, plans, scouts, spies, generals, and thousands of travel-stained and jaded cavalry.

32

CHAPTER XLIV.

McClellan again invades Virginia—Sigel is pushed forward from Washington, and takes Position at Manassas—The Federal main Army moves East of the Blue Ridge, and has Head-quarters at Warrenton—Lee marches in a parallel Line through the Shenandoah Valley—Surprise and Flight of Sigel upon the Appearance of Confederate Cavalry—Change of Federal Commanders—Rapid March of the Federals to the Rappahannock—Battle of Fredericksburgh, December thirteenth.

How long McClellan would remain motionless in Maryland, or what caused his inaction, were to the many an insoluble problem. Although the daily demand of the Northern journals was for an immediate "on to Richmond" movement, the enemy seemed to be exceedingly loth to place foot again on Virginian soil. The Southern army was represented to be greatly demoralized by the "splendid and glorious" victory of Antietam; nevertheless, the Northern leaders in the field betrayed the greatest caution, and endeavored to surprise General Lee by every artifice which cunning could suggest. Southern generals, however, could not be hoodwinked; their eyes and ears were open to every movement; and they were accurately informed of all that transpired within McClellan's camp. How this information was obtained, or by whom, must ever remain profound mysteries to me; yet I confess the daily programme of Federal movements was as freely discussed by groups of officers at camp-fires round Winchester as they could have been in the large invading army of Maryland.

Winchester was our pivot-point — whether for offensive or defensive operations — in the Valley; and had the enemy advanced up the Shenandoah, I see nothing in the world which could have prevented us from defeating them either *en masse* or in detail; for the ground from Bunker Hill, near Charlestown, to and beyond Winchester and Strasburgh, was admirably adapted for defence. At the latter place, Lee could have assumed a position which, fortified as he alone knows how, might have defied the best and most numerous armies in the world. McClellan was shrewd, and fully alive to the difficulties of that route; he had no supplies at hand in such a region, and could not be regularly served by his trains over a deserted and mountainous country. More than this, the possession of Winchester gave opportunities for Lee to pass between him and Washington.

Having again fortified Harper's Ferry, the Federal army poured into Virginia, and took up their line of march east of the Blue Ridge; thus always presenting front to Lee, who in a parallel line slowly proceeded up the Valley, carefully watching any weakness in their front through which he could break and disjoint it. Both generals were looking into each other's eyes; but McClellan might have gazed for ever, and never divined any thing flitting across the mind of the calm-faced, smiling, modest, and unpretending visage of Lee. His face was a blank—all pallor and thought; but not a wrinkle, flush, twitch, or motion of the eye, gave the remotest idea of his thoughts and intentions. He passed from point to point without ostentation or show; his movements were quiet, undemonstrative, and calm; whether commanding generals or listening to couriers, he was the same as he had ever been — an impenetrable block of marble.

McClellan's movements seemed to indicate that indecision ruled in his councils. Sometimes there were tokens of an advance; then again a few days would suffice to dispel such conjectures, and warrant ideas of his speedy retreat; thus it was not until his head-quarters had been fully established at Warrenton, that we became sanguine and positive of his timidity. The Federal army was much larger than ours, and furnished with supplies beyond any thing hitherto imagined in warfare; nor had its chief commenced his march, despite the blusterings and anathemas of quill-valiant editors, until fully and superabundantly reenforced and equipped.

Some time before his own advance, McClellan had pushed Sigel forward from Washington to Manassas Junction, with a reported force of thirty thousand men, but these were said to be levies and unreliable. Railroad communication was once again perfected from Alexandria to Warrenton, and it soon became palpable that, as the main army was massed round the latter place, we might look to that point for indications of future movements. Whatever the intentions of Federal generals in their choice of routes, it was evident that the main object in view was the surprise and capture of Richmond by every possible means; but it was also clear that to accomplish this the enemy must cross the Rappahannock at *some* point, so that our generals in the Valley held their troops well together for instant movement, nor was there any thing neglected in our arrangements which could in any manner facilitate the rapid concentration of forces at various points.

Longstreet's corps was clustered at the mouth of the Valley, ready to take position at any point behind the Rappahannock. Daily drill was incessant and severe, discipline was at its highest pitch, and reviews were not unfrequent among the various. brigades and divisions. At no period of the war were we more confident and gay; extensive appropriations and purchases during our brief sojourn in Maryland and on the Pennsylvania border, had replenished our stores to such a degree, and Government had been so active meanwhile, in manufacturing uniforms and the like, that we scarcely knew ourselves; we were now so good-looking and comfortable, that we smiled to think how many of our former friends would mistake us for gentlemen! Slowly our army crept up to the mouth of the Valley, and equally slowly were McClellan's forces gathered around him at Warrenton.

September and October had passed without any demonstration of moment from the enemy, and now cold, bleak November whistled over the fields and mountains of Virginia. The army began to imagine that winter-quarters were intended, but from the temper of the Northern journals received in camp, it was plain that movements of some kind would be forced upon McClellan. About the tenth of November, unusual activity among the enemy occasioned more than ordinary vigilance with our outposts, and, to the astonishment of every one, a Federal deserter informed our guard of McClellan's dismissal, and of the appointment of Burnside as chief in command, adding, that their forces were almost upon the point of open mutiny in consequence.

Although this was fresh news to us, our generals smiled, having evidently known the fact long before our advanced posts. They well understood that McClellan had been superseded through political jealousy, on the plea of apparent inaction, and, consequently, that the new commander would be expected to march against us forthwith, to satisfy the universal clamor of the North, even should their army and journals reap naught but defeat and disgrace from such a movement. But even *that* was something! it was food for "sensation;" illustrated journals could luxuriate in bloodthirsty wood-cuts, to please the million; other favorites would be forthwith installed in place; and an endless batch of fresh commissions and army contracts be issued for the delectation and emolument of office-holders or political partisans. All this was something, and fully appreciated by our commanders, who complacently smoked, and tightened the reins of discipline among us even more than ever.

On the thirteenth there was proof positive that grand movements were transpiring within the enemy's lines, and it became generally known that Burnside was breaking up camps, and proceeding to the lower Rappahannock. Many argued that such a change of base was commendable in the Federal chief; for his dépôts, at Acquia Creek, could be supplied by transports, and stores conveyed inland by railway running from that point to Fredericksburgh. Whether he wished to force a passage over the river at Fredericksburgh, or merely intended to prepare for winter-quarters, were matters of some speculation.

Burnside's movements, however, were no secret to our leaders; for Longstreet's corps immediately marched to Fredericksburgh, and arrived there before any large body of the enemy had appeared. It is true that the Stafford Heights, on the north bank of the river, were held by a Federal detachment many days ere the approach of their main army, but they had never attempted to cross over into the town. Picket-firing was constant along the river; but despite all this waste of powder, there were many who sincerely believed that Burnside had no serious intention of attacking, regarding this movement as a harmless display of force to divert our attention from his real designs. On the seventeenth, however, all surmise was banished from our minds. General Sumner appeared before the place, and demanded its immediate surrender. The Mayor politely refused to recognize such a demand; and the town being filled with our troops, the municipal authorities were extremely valiant on the occasion, and apostrophized Jupiter and all the gods in fine style. Women and children, for the most part, were conveyed from town, and active preparations set on foot for fiercely disputing the passage of the river, by the construction of field-works on the hills and bluffs which ran parallel with the stream south of the city. All was done in secrecy, however; and, from the apparent quietness of our lines, the enemy were unable to form any conjectures of our position and force.

The left wing under Jackson had not arrived, though it was rapidly pushing towards us; yet ascertaining that Sigel still held his corps at Manassas, and had not moved nearer to Burnside, Jackson sent a strong force of cavalry to reconnoitre, and their appearance filled the enemy with so much dismay that they instantly broke up camps and fled in disorder to Washington. It was supposed that this cavalry detachment was Jackson's advance-guard, and that we were endeavoring to get between them and the capital, as of old. Whatever their ideas, the retreat was a most hurried and disgraceful affair; whole regiments threw down their arms and rushed towards Alexandria post haste, shouting: "Jackson is coming! he is again in our rear!—Old Stonewall, with one hundred thousand men, is marching on Washington!"

On the twenty-first, Burnside personally demanded a surrender of the town, and threatened to bombard it in case of refusal. The threat was treated with the contempt it deserved, and every non-combatant was ordered from the place. It was now daily expected that the enemy would make some desperate attempt at crossing in face of all opposition; yet day followed day until November had passed, and still no signs of Federal movements.

Our position at Fredericksburgh was admirably chosen. We were posted on a range of hills which more or less extended from a bend of the river on our left to some six miles, and across the Massaponax River, which ran at right angles with the Rappahannock, and formed the right of our lines. In truth, it might be said that the landscape from these hills to the river was like an amphitheatre; the intrenched Confederates having all the boxes, the stage being the valley in which is placed the red-brick town of Fredericksburgh. The Rappa- hannock is seen to run above and below the place; and, except a few houses scattered here and there over the scene, there is nothing to relieve the eye from the bleak, dry, cold, frosty, and windy aspect of the whole. All the woods are leafless, and the cold dry branches rattle in the piercing winds like skeletons in chains. Few fires are seen to burn in Fredericksburgh, and smoke ascends but seldom. Our men are quartered in deserted houses, and keep vigilant guard along the river-bank, both night and day; and, although piercing winds and sleet and rain, prevail, the active picket walks his post, and none can move without being sharply challenged. The men have dug pits along the river to conceal themselves under fire and for shelter. The enemy have done the same; and it is so cold and dreary that none can imagine any general would have the heart to move troops in weather like this, when guards have fre- quently have been found frozen and dead at their post.

The enemy's position and strength are also concealed; and they likewise can look down into the town from the Stafford Heights, and could destroy it in ten minutes with the formida- ble array of guns and batteries which overlook and are pointed at it. During cold, frosty nights, we can hear their trains run- ning from Acquia Creek, and they can hear ours also; for guns of heavy calibre and all munitions of war are being rapidly brought to the front from Richmond; and every hill command- ing a view of the valley at our feet is swept by cannon, but so concealed by undergrowth, woods, or undulations, that the enemy cannot detect them.

The hills to our extreme left, near a bend of the river, are crowned by the residence of Dr. Taylor; to the right of these a road runs from Fredericksburgh to the Wilderness and Chan- cellorsville; to the right of this road rise Stansbury Hill and several others; to the right of these runs a plank road leading from the centre of the town through our left centre; to the right of this is the enceinte called Marye's Hill. Hazel Creek runs between this latter position and Lee's Hill, which, from its altitude, was selected for head-quarters.

The Richmond railway divided our left under Longstreet from our right under Jackson, the latter being strongly posted on a series of hills and well fortified; the extreme right and right flank being in charge of Stuart. The force of Longstreet on the left included the divisions of Ransom, McLaws, and Picket, Anderson being on Marye's Hill; Cobb being posted behind a strong stone wall at the right base of the latter, commanding all approach up the open lands of the Hazel Creek, while Hood and others filled up the space to the railroad where our right commenced under Ambrose Hill, Early, and others, up to Stuart, who, with his mounted division, light artillery, and infantry, held the extreme right and right flank. D. H. Hill was held in reserve. Heavy batteries protected our extremes, right and left. The Washington artillery corps was detailed for special duty at Marye's and Lee's Hills, and Colonel Walker was posted on our right.

The distance of the enceinte from town was not more than four or five hundred yards. Other places on the right and left of our lines were a considerable distance from it and the river; but in the more exposed positions nearest town, long lines of breastworks had been dug, behind which our men could be admirably posted when necessity demanded it. In truth, the position, though naturally strong, had been carefully improved by our indefatigable engineers, and batteries were numerous at all points; so that, with our army of eighty thousand, we could complacently remain undemonstrative until the enemy should foolishly advance. Pickets from various brigades were scattered up and down the river, Barksdale's Mississippi troops occupying the town. Cavalry patrols were frequent at all points of the river, closely watching the enemy, who, down the stream at Hamilton's crossing, were particularly busy, as if preparing to force a passage. From the latter point, a road leads round to the rear of our right, and others running south of the town passed through its centre; so that much attention was paid to the enemy's manœuvres, for the threatened attack in this quarter was the most practicable and scientific they could have selected.

Notwithstanding frequent demonstrations it was evident the enemy were disinclined to move; a tardiness which very much surprised us, as Burnside's sudden and rapid change of base from Warrenton had led many to believe that his movements generally would be expeditious. As this state of inaction was distasteful to our leaders, and particularly so to Stuart and his restless brigadiers, cavalry frequently crossed the river, and made annoying incursions upon the Federal rear, and effected all manner of captures without hindrance from the enemy. On the twenty-eighth of November cavalry crossed by one of the upper fords and captured several squadrons of Pennsylvania horse on duty at the outposts, and did not lose a man; for the foe meekly surrendered without making the shadow of resistance. Fitz-Hugh Lee and Hampton also frequently distinguished themselves; and, operating on the enemy's line of supply, dashed into Dumfries and other places, dispersing the guards, and making a clean sweep of every thing; so that, from our constant boldness, the enemy were bewildered, and knew not on which flank to look for Stuart's ubiquitous troopers; for they were successively here, there, and everywhere, burning, capturing, annoying, or fighting, and, by their activity and nerve, seemed to magnify their numbers tenfold.

The first week in cold, bleak December had passed over our cheerless lines, and every expedient was resorted to by our troops to keep themselves warm. Wood was scarce to the front in many places, and our men on duty could be seen blowing their fingers and holding conversation with Federal guards;* but, on the ninth and tenth, unusual activity seemed

---

* Amusing conversations frequently occurred between outposts on the river banks:

"How are you, rebels?" asked a Yankee, one cold morning, blowing his fingers. "Oh! not very good to-day," was the reply. "We have suffered an awful loss! Jackson has resigned!"

"Jackson resigned!" was the astonished exclamation in rejoinder. "Why, how was that?" asked the Federals, who greatly feared the very name of old Stonewall.

"Oh! he resigned because they removed his commissary-general, and he wouldn't stand it."

"His commissary-general, eh? Then who was he?" they inquired in much surprise.

"Banks!" was the significant reply.

The sarcasm was well applied, and so acutely felt by the enemy, that they immediately opened fire from pure vexation.

to prevail on the Stafford Heights, and outposts brought in word that during the night heavy wagon-trains could be heard moving, and the noise and cursing of teamsters whipping their horses, mules, and oxen, were very frequent immediately opposite the town. This was explained when, on the eleventh, as soon as the fog lifted, our men in town espied large numbers of the enemy engaged in constructing pontoon bridges, and immediately opened upon them a galling and destructive fire. From their screened position, it was impossible to touch our men with gun-shot or rifle, for they were scattered in all directions, in houses, barns, and every imaginable place where shelter could be obtained. The incessant fusilade so annoyed the enemy as to cause the total suspension of their bridge-building; and, at last, several field-pieces were brought to bear upon us for some time, and our sharpshooters desisted.

Taking advantage of this, bridge-building was commenced again, and swarms of the enemy could be seen like magnified ants moving to and fro with beams and boats, and a thousand etceteras required in their unpleasant undertaking. Our sharpshooters recommenced their fire, and the enemy retired. Vexed and annoyed at our impudence and pertinacity, they pointed more than a hundred guns at the town, and commenced an earth-shaking cannonade; the smoke and flame from their pieces on the Stafford Heights were so great that it seemed as if the earth was vomiting forth sulphurous lava. Houses fell, timbers crashed, dust rose, flames ascended, and, from our position as spectators in the boxes of this amphitheatre, it seemed as if we were innocently gazing at some noisy and smoky episode of Napoleon's wars, as often represented on the French stage. The whole town seemed alive; one ran here, another there. Unlucky citizens, who remained too long, or had screened themselves in hopes of the enemy's speedy arrival, now came forth from their hiding-places, and not a few Dutch Jews were observed panting under heavy loads of tobacco, which they had secreted. Shells of every size and form were screaming and whizzing through the air, and their explosion was always attended by a sudden uprising of beams, dust, doors, chairs, bedsteads, and the like, until at last the place looked like a vast broker's shop, filled with odds and ends of things indescribable.

How our valiant pickets fared during this terrific visitation, I know not; they scorned to retreat, and still maintained an accurate fire. It was not until a large Federal infantry force had crossed above and below town that they withdrew from their covert of smoking and burning ruins.

Lee seemed perfectly satisfied with the aspect of affairs. Burnside was constructing several bridges under cover of the town, in which they hoped to conceal any force that crossed. Franklin on their left was similarly engaged near the mouth of the Massaponax; and Sumner was above town near Falmouth, busy in the same occupation. We could not successfully prevent the construction of these bridges—those at Fredericks-burgh itself were the most numerous and important, but perfectly hidden from our view by the town; and it is possible, judging from his inactivity, that Lee was not desirous of molesting their labors, but too happy indeed to see them perfectly unconscious of the coming storm.

During the eleventh and twelfth the enemy were rapidly crossing at the various bridges; and we could see them marshalling their hosts in the valley. Franklin's wing had first crossed, and proceeded to form line parallel with the stream; his left in full force close to the Massaponax, and his right beyond Deep Run Brook. Beyond this point to and in front of the town, no troops appeared in numbers. The Federal right, under Sumner, had crossed at and above the town by several bridges, and its left rested close to the city; so that the entire left and right of the Federal army were plainly in view, in columns or deployed; but in the centre, opposite to our enceinte of Marye's Hill, no troops appeared, though it was evident that Fredericksburgh literally swarmed with them; and that a few well-directed shells could have caused the instant and noisy upheaving of the whole living, motionless mass concealed there. Federal dispositions continued without hindrance on our part. Our front was very quiet and unpretending, and, as we peered over breastworks or peeped from long lines of rifle pits at the dark lines wheeling and marching in open ground, we could not but confess that their generals should be capable of accomplishing something astonishing with such a host as that, supported and covered as it was by numberless batteries on the hills and bluffs behind.

Strict and vigilant guards were numerously posted at all points down in the valley during night, and they occasionally heard the Federal countersigns exchanged; but the greatest secrecy marked the conduct of our cavalry at the mouth of the Massaponax, for it was uncertain what Franklin might attempt under cover of the night, as his force was apparently very large, and so stationed as to be able to take up the line of march to our right rear, should it have been determined to open the engagement in that manner.

The morning of December thirteenth dawned, and all was feverish expectation. Noises from the valley and loud-toned commands told of Federal leaders marching and counter-marching in the fog and mists. None now doubted the certainty of battle, but prepared for it with calmness and determination. The rattle of picket-firing on our right gave tokens of the prelude, and all desired that the sun would lift the foggy veil from the valley. Between nine and ten o'clock the view was clear, and there stood our enemies, right, left, and centre, just upon the point of moving. Couriers, generals, and aides were prancing and dashing about in the valley, and as our mounted men raced to and fro in hot haste to our rear, they would turn a hasty glance at the imposing scene below and hurry onwards. The report of artillery on our right, and the rattle of rifles, told of an engagement which increased in intensity every moment. Batteries on Stafford Heights opened on our left and centre, and numerous shells were screaming and bursting in all directions around the base of Marye's and Lee's Hills. Our guns replied coolly and deliberately, and hostile shot and shell coursed to and fro overhead, throwing up columns and clouds of dust wherever they fell. The Federal right, under Sumner, was the especial and favorite object of all our cannoniers, and (as an artillery officer coolly observed) our shell fell and burst "beautifully" among their closely-packed brigades. I have heard of and seen "daylight" let though an approaching column, but never, until at Fredericksburgh, did I see complete "lanes" ploughed out of human bodies.

It was now near noon, and the crash of musketry to our right told that Jackson and his wing were fully engaged, and, as usual, repulsing the enemy at every point; but the threatening aspect of the foe at our centre and left drew the attention of all to those quarters.

The cannonade from Stafford Heights had now increased to such a pitch of fury that none doubted its object. Their attacking columns began to move, and moments seemed like ages of suspense. Our fire had been feeble, but now that their masses came forward—one immediately in front, and one on each flank of Marye's Hill—our infantry suddenly rose and poured such rapid volleys into them that the advance was impeded by their own dead. As for our cannon, I can only say that they *could not miss the enemy*, whose fearful and swift destruction was appalling to see. Unheeding the cannonade from across the river, the Washington artillery corps paid exclusive attention to infantry before them, and shells dropped among their masses, making fearful rents at every discharge. The crackling of bursting shells and sharp ring of the rifle were incessant—a flank fire assailed them from our extreme left, so that regiments never advanced farther than to the base of our position; and as they halted, and staggered or swayed, and broke, our men, from breastworks and rifle-pits, and from every imaginable place, were pouring into their bleeding masses showers of small shot.

Again and again were the enemy re-formed, and advance succeeded advance as fresh regiments rushed over heaps of slain, to be themselves torn in an instant into mangled and bleeding shreds. The position was unassailable—a sheet of flame streamed across our whole front, and destroyed every thing mortal that approached it. Some of the Federal regiments marched farther than others, and even ascended the "rise," but here infantry uprose and checked them, and again would the enemy pause, feebly struggle, and reel back into the valley exhausted and bleeding. The sight was horrible. It was not a scientific battle, but a wholesale slaughter of human beings for the caprice of one man, who, two miles across the river, sat upon the heights, glass in hand, complacently viewing the awful panorama below.*

---

* Northern accounts stated that Burnside sat on the heights round the "Phillips House," and attentively scanned the whole field with a "strong glass." They also added, judging from the fearful slaughter, that the "strong glass" alluded to was "possibly one of double extra whisky!"

But if the enemy had mercilessly sacrificed life in their insane attempt to storm Marye's Hill, they had been extremely busy, likewise, before other parts of our position. It was conceived possible to flank the enceinte by moving up the open grounds of the Hazel Creek, and sever our right and left. A large body was soon espied moving up to the stone wall which protected that position, and were unmolested in their advance, for Cobb carefully screened his men, and although the Federal batteries covered this movement, their shot and shell did trifling damage; nor did our pieces on Marye's Hill, Lee's Hill, or Hill's position south of the railroad, give any token of resistance. The Federal advance, therefore, was quickly accomplished; but when the enemy came sufficiently near, our troops rose up from their ambuscade, and batteries acting in concert, poured such terrific volleys upon them from front and flanks that they retreated in amazement and confusion. Like the attacks on our left, on Marye's Hill, and elsewhere, they repeatedly re-formed and attempted other advances; but the delivery of our rifle and artillery fire was so cool, regular, and destructive, that they gave up the assault in despair. Nothing could surpass the consummate steadiness of our troops in face of these successive attacks. Not more than one third were in actual line of battle, for the rest were drawn up to the rear, ready to be sent in any direction required; but what few were in front looked upon the affair as virtually settled, and went to work as indifferently as butchers engaged for a busy day's work in the shambles. Ambrose Hill's position was also assaulted early in the day, and report said that some of his young troops had given way; but the gap thus occasioned in his line was soon filled up. The enemy, who had obtained a footing in woods to his front, were driven thence with such fury that the entire Federal line from left to right was forced into the valley; and Stuart's, Walker's, and Walton's batteries pelted them with shot and shell from front and flanks without mercy.

The battle thus far had prospered with us; the enemy had frequently paused and then attacked again, but the mounds of dead on every hill-side, and numerous black and motionless spots which dotted all our front, even to the streets of Fredericksburgh, gave sickening evidence of their fearful loss and blind insanity. It was now far past noon, and the sun was fast sinking in the west; our generals were restless and active as ever ; cannon still belched forth from either side, but from the long pause and re-formation going on among the dark lines below, it was conjectured they would not desist from their mad project until another grand assault had been attempted. Their force was still formidable in appearance, but evidently dispirited, and the continual and rapid movements of mounted officers in all directions, gave evidence of their industry and anxiety to restore discipline, confidence, and courage.

Long lines of stretcher-bearers, thus early in the day, were slowly winding in sorrowful procession in all directions, while a multitude of ambulances, with yellow flags flying, could be discerned winding over the hills beyond the river. The town seemed crowded with troops, for we could occasionally catch glimpses of them as their bayonets flashed in the many streets, and from church-steeples, house-tops, and on the Stafford Heights, their signal corps was busy in telegraphing orders from point to point. Lee, Longstreet, and Jackson, had been in frequent conference during the day ; but the illustrious heroes appeared so calm, indifferent, and smiling, that as they slowly walked their horses from point to point, receiving messages or giving orders, it was clear they were confident of a successful issue to our laborious day's work of slaughter.

When the first gun had opened in the morning, Lee slowly trotted along our whole front, and took up his position on the extreme right of our lines, where Stuart and his horse artillery were making sad havoc with Franklin's left flank. It was imagined by all that the enemy would deliver a grand assault upon Jackson's position, and endeavor to penetrate or sever it along the roads which lead around and through it at several points ; but when Lee observed the feebleness of their attack in that quarter, and how easily they were driven pell-mell into the valley again, he retraced his steps and took his stand in full view of Marye's Hill. On Lee's Hill were several very large guns, recently made at Richmond, which maintained a furious roar all day, and seemed to be a favorite mark for the foe, who, from their elevation on Stafford Heights, threw over hundreds of complimentary shell, but without doing more damage than blowing up vast heaps of earth. It cannot be denied, however, that Federal artillerists maintained an accurate and steady fire upon our whole front, but the troops exposed were so few that little damage was done to life or limb. *Their* pieces were directed at a few sharpshooters behind earth embankments, *ours* were pointed at dense masses of men; hence it was that not one out of ten shells ever inflicted damage upon us; but every fragment of our grape made a rent in their attacking columns, and left its monument of bleeding carcasses.

"Their practice is good," said a distinguished artillery officer, viewing shells fall and explode a few feet below him round the base of Marye's Hill, and among our line of busy sharpshooters.

"Yes, it is excellent," was the rejoinder from an old brigadier, who, with slouched felt hat and cigar, was gazing on the scene below with much interest. "It is well, colonel," he added, "that Lee has kept two thirds of his troops from the front, or we should lose considerably. How many pieces have they, think you, on the heights?"

"I have been narrowly scrutinizing their force all day, General, and imagine they have considerably more than one hundred thousand men before us, and over three hundred guns. I should judge that one hundred of the latter are on the heights, and certainly many of them are of heavy calibre."

One or two shells thrown with great rapidity and precision fell within a few feet of these officers, who took the hint and moved away. I learned that the infantry attack on Hill's and Cobb's positions had been very severe, and was desperately maintained by both sides for some time, but except the fall of General Maxey Gregg,[*] who was shot in the side and spine while leading on his brave South-Carolinians, I had not heard of any casualties among our officers. In truth, our loss along the whole line was remarkably small, and amazed many who

---

[*] This officer, when wounded, said: "Tell the Governor (of his native State) if I am to die this time, I cheerfully yield my life for the independence of South-Carolina!"

could not conceive it possible that so many shot and shell had been hurled at us, and with such little effect.

The troops we had seen all day in the town now advanced into the valley and deployed. Every preparation was seemingly perfected for a general and final advance. Skirmishers fell back and rallied on their regiments; artillery opened again upon their columns from every direction, and numerous well-served Federal batteries returned our fire with a deafening roar. Dust and shells were flying in all directions, but on came that glittering mass of bayonets, extending for miles in front, and again they assailed our position with spirit and determination; but melting ranks and confusion, indecision, and exhaustion, were more than men could bear, and again they slowly retired to the river's edge, broken, dispirited, and beaten.

This seemed to be their last attempt, and, except a continual cannonade, all operations ceased. The sun had dipped beyond the hills, and a thick white vapory fog slowly fell along the whole river, screening their force and movements from view; but to guard against all surprise, pickets and sharpshooters were thickly posted in the valley, which now became more cloudy and obscure, so that, except to the immediate front of Marye's Hill, no movement of the enemy could be well discovered. Trickery was expected, and strict guard maintained at all points. Since the artillery ceased, nothing could be heard except the groans of unhappy, mangled, wounded, and dying thousands, who lay in unsightly groups all around our various positions and at the base of the hills. An alarm was soon given of the enemy's approach, and our whole line was again on the alert, when rapid firing broke out at the right base of Marye's Hill, which Cobb had so well defended from behind the stone fence. It appeared that a heavy body of the enemy had quietly ascended up the banks of the Hazel under cover of the evening, and thought to seize that position, thus getting into the rear of Marye's Hill; but they were received so coolly, and with such a destructive fire, that they retreated with the utmost expedition and in the greatest confusion.

Thus the slaughter at Fredericksburgh closed. Sumner, Hooker, Wilcox, Meagher, French, and a host of other leaders, had been routed on our centre and left — Franklin, Meade,

33

Jackson, Bayard, and Stoneman, had met with a fearful repulse on the right; for miles their dead and wounded lined the front of our works, and were scattered up and down the valley in great profusion; but even nature seemed shocked at such frightful carnage, and mercifully threw a veil of fog and darkness over the crimsoned valley.

Cold and bitter as was that bleak December night—cheerless and sad to thousands in the valley, whose oozing wounds were frosted and frozen — few went forth to assist them, save from our own lines; and there those frightful masses lay huddled together, the dying with the dead; some jerking in the last throes of death, others gasping for water, writhing with agony, laughing deliriously, cursing demonically in all the tongues of Europe. Save for the quick, sharp challenge of vigilant pickets posted in the valley, the lightsome footfalls of relief guards, gliding like shadows through the mists in their journeys to the front, the moans ascending on every hand, and the click of spades in the hands of those strengthening breastworks, all had subsided into a death-like calm. None unaccustomed to war would imagine that so many thousands of men were grouped closely together in the valley or on the hills ready to renew the awful scenes just enacted. Exhausted and unstrung, our men were fast asleep, and many of them far to the front among the dead and dying; yet let me not deny that, wearied though we were, the distant moan or faltering supplication often caused us to rise and give relief to some expiring enemy. Most of our own men had been cared for, and taken to the rear, but heaps upon heaps of the foe were scattered in every direction, and one could not move a dozen yards without stumbling against some voiceless, inanimate carcase, or slipping in pools of blood or scattered entrails.

Such is war—"glorious" war—glorious indeed when troops had fought as ours had done for liberty and birthright, but in every other sense the most horrible and lamentable curse that God could permit his people to inflict on each other!

Morning dawned, the mists arose, and still the enemy were there. No token gave indications of a further advance. The whole day passed without a movement of any kind, and no disposition seemed to be made for the care of the enemy's dead or wounded. In pure compassion for the heart-rending spectacle before us, many of the sufferers were collected and attended to by our surgeons, but as none knew at what moment hostilities might again re-commence, we could not enter heartily into the work of charity. Many of our men were never allowed to be exposed in front, and the few on duty there were for the most part employed in repairing old or building new breastworks. Next day passed as the former one, and still no signs of the enemy's coming. Their lines were apparently in excellent order, and the Stafford Heights frowned ominously with additional batteries; so that had we advanced into the valley, a fearful cannonade would have assailed us. In the evening, we all imagined that the morning would surely usher in a decisive engagement, whether offensive or defensive on our part; but during night a fearful storm arose, so that we could neither hear nor see our own patrols, and as morning advanced, and the valley cleared, we discovered that the whole Federal army had escaped under cover of night, and were safely on the north bank again.

When the enemy's retreat became known to our army, loud yells rent the sky, and must have been plainly audible to Burnside's forces across the river; but whether these were indicative of rage or pleasure at the retreat I cannot imagine, but fancy they arose from a commixture of both those feelings. It soon became known that a convention had been entered into for the burial of dead, and the valley swarmed with our troops, who were speedily engaged in the work of interment; but when I visited the town, and beheld the sad havoc done there by the Vandals, I almost felt sorry to think I had ever given a cup of water to their wounded and dying. Every house was gutted and robbed; furniture, bedding, and household goods of every kind were maliciously broken and scattered through the streets; doors, windows, banks, churches, school-houses, all were destroyed or despoiled, while in every dwelling, amid pools of blood, were laid their dead and dying, whose pallid faces, staring eyes, gaping wounds, and frigid limbs, twisted into frightful distortions, met the Southern soldier at every turn in this once pleasant and hospitable town, so wilfully destroyed. The bombardment had done great mischief; houses were tottering to their foundations, and everywhere gave proof of the passage

of shell and bullet among smouldering ruins; but it remained
for these valiant invaders to give a finishing touch to their bar-
barism by despoiling and desecrating churches, accumulating
filth in the holiest of places, wantonly destroying all that came
to hand, and then leaving their dead and wounded to the care
of those whose residence or property it had once been.

I have read of Goths and Vandals, of Huns and Danes, but
never could I have conceived of a boastful enemy, laying claims
to the highest civilization, capable of exhibiting such low caste
on the battle-field, or so much petty malice among an unoffending people, as these same hordes of hypocritical Yankees,
whom it has been my fortune to meet in a short but exciting
military career from Bull Run to Fredericksburgh.*

---

* The Confederate force at Fredericksburgh has been estimated at eighty thousand, with three hundred guns, of all calibres.   Our total casualties amounted to
two thousand or twenty-five hundred.   Among the killed were General Maxey
Gregg, of South-Carolina; and among the wounded, Generals Hood, Cobb, and
Jenkins.

Burnside's forces, according to Washington reports, amounted to one hundred
and forty thousand or one hundred and fifty thousand men, with three hundred
guns.   It was paraded at the North, before the slaughter, that Burnside commanded
the finest army ever raised, and that it included all the "regulars" and "veterans"
of the service, who had been expressly gathered in order to insure success.   Their
total loss in killed, wounded, and missing, has been placed at from fifteen thousand
to twenty thousand by Northern journals of respectability.   Among their killed
were General Bayard, chief of cavalry, and General Jackson.   Among the wounded,
General Stoneman, General Vinton, General Gibbons, General Caldwell, General
Meagher, General Kimball, and others.   This defeat and slaughter sent such a
thrill of horror through all classes at the North, that official inquiry was demanded,
when it appeared that General Sumner, of the right wing, General Franklin, of the
left, and General Hooker, of the centre, had decided against the movement in a
council of war, but that Burnside did not heed their advice, but resolved on crossing; thinking that through feints made lower down the river he had deceived Lee
as to his true designs, and that troops being sent in that direction, the Confederate
left and centre would be weak to any large assaulting force.   The committee of inquiry sent from Washington greatly underrated the Federal losses.   They say in
their report that "they are well pleased with what they saw, and regard the result
as infinitely less serious than was previously apprehended.   It appears now that the
total casualties will hardly exceed ten thousand.   Of these about one thousand
were killed; some seventeen hundred were so badly wounded that two thirds of
them will die of their wounds, and the rest will be permanently disabled.   Of the
others, the wounds are more or less serious; but a majority are expected to recover
and be again fit for duty.   It has been ascertained that about eighty-one per cent
of the wounds were occasioned by Minié balls, fifteen and a half per cent by shells,
and three and a half per cent by round shot."   Such was the destruction of hu-

man life that Federal accounts mention whole divisions which could muster but a few hundreds after the battle. Some regiments were decimated, and others had not more than a company left to answer roll-call! Although they had fitting opportunities to bury part of their dead subsequent to the battle, that unpleasant office was left to us, for the most part; and to deceive us as to their retreat, they propped up dead bodies to counterfeit sentinels, in many places, with placards fastened to them, ridiculing and cursing the "rebels" who buried them. This was very decent and valiant conduct certainly, and is worthy of record.

Library of Congress Cataloguing in Publication Data

English combatant.
Battle-fields of the South.
(Collector's library of the Civil War)
Reprint. Originally published: New York: J. Bradburn, 1864.
1. United States—History—Civil War, 1861-1865—Campaigns.
2. United States—History—Civil War, 1861-1865—Personal narratives, Confederate.
3. United States—History-Civil War, 1861-1865—Participation, British.
I. Title.
E470.2.E53 1984   973.7'3   83-17900
ISBN 0-8094-4392-9 (library)
ISBN 0-8094-4391-0 (retail)

Printed in the United States of America